Illinois Motions In Limine

by Scott D. Lane, Esq.
Stephanie Hoit Lee, Esq.
David N. Finley, Esq.

WEST®
A Thomson Reuters business

For Customer Assistance Call 1-800-328-4880

Mat #40732860

ISBN 978-0-314-91814-7

ABOUT THE AUTHORS

Scott D. Lane, Esq.

Scott D. Lane, Esq., is a partner in the Chicago office of Lane & Lane, LLC, a firm which specializes in medical malpractice and professional negligence, motor vehicle accidents, premises and product liability, and related areas involving serious personal injury and wrongful death. Prior to his association with Lane & Lane, LLC, Mr. Lane was a Cook County Assistant State's Attorney. He frequently lectures at bar association seminars on topics pertaining to civil litigation and is codirector and a faculty member of the Illinois State Bar Association Trial Techniques Institute. He is an instructor at the Loyola University of Chicago School of Law and has coached the Loyola Trial Team. He is a contributing editor to Lane's Goldstein Trial Techniques and Lane Medical Litigation Guide and has authored numerous published articles and chapters on trial practice. Mr. Lane is an active member of the Chicago Bar Assoc., Decalogue Society of Lawyers, Illinois State Bar Assoc., American Bar Assoc., Illinois Trial Lawyers Assoc., the American Association for Justice (formerly known as "ATLA"), the American College of Legal Medicine, and the International Society of Primerus. He has been named one of Illinois' "Super Lawyers" by Chicago Magazine and was selected as one of Illinois' "40 Attorneys Under 40 to Watch" in 2002. He received his Bachelor of Arts degree, Cum Laude, from Southern Methodist University and is a 1988 graduate of Loyola University of Chicago School of Law, where he was a member of the Law Review and the Trial Team.

Stephanie Hoit Lee, Esq.

Stephanie Hoit Lee has a solo practice specializing in appellate and motion research, brief writing, and appellate oral argument in complex cases. She is a member of the Illinois State Bar Association and is admitted to practice in the 7th Circuit Court of Appeals and the Northern District Court of Illinois. Prior to her solo practice, Ms. Lee worked for the McHenry County State's Attorney's Office, the Cook County Public Guardian's Office, the Hennepin County Attorney's office, the Legal Aid Society of Minneapolis and several private firms.

She received her Bachelor of Arts, with Honors, from the University of Wisconsin-Madison, and is a 1993 graduate, Cum Laude, of the University of Minnesota Law School.

She has written more than 100 briefs for the State's Attorneys Appellate Prosecutor's office and has performed contract work for a variety of attorneys in private practice. She is co-author of *Federal Motions in Limine, Federal Summary Judgment and Related Termination Motions,* and *Illinois Motions in Limine*. She has published several journal articles and is an update contributor to *Lane's Goldstein Trial Techniques* and *Lane Medical Litigation Guide.*

David N. Finley, Esq.

David N. Finley, Esq., has nearly 20 years of combined experience in litigation and legal publishing. He has conducted extensive legal research in State and Federal courts, and has worked up a number of cases for trial and arbitration. He is the creator and co-author of *Federal Motions in Limine* and *Federal Summary Judgment* and *Related Termination Motions* as well as nearly two dozen additional state versions of the in limine motion line. He is the creator and former Editor-in-Chief of the national voir dire newsletter, *The Jury Expert.* He graduated from Hastings College of the Law and has taught Legal Research and Writing at Chapman University School of Law.

Additional Contributors

The publisher acknowledges and thanks the following attorney advisors for their assistance:

Alisa Arnoff, John W. Bell, Mark Brown, Mary Ellen Cagney, Timothy J. Cavanaugh, Barry Chafetz, Michael W. Clancy, Gregory D. Conforti, Joseph R. Curcio, Charles Delano, Thomas A. Demetrio, J. Timothy Eaton, Guy Delson Geleerd, Jr., Morris Lane Harvey, R. Michael Henderson, Michael F. Henrick, Eugene K. Hollander, Blake Horwitz, Peter D. Hoste, Brian J. Hunt, Matthew L. Johnson, William V. Johnson, Mark Karno, Timothy W. Kelly, Shawn S. Kasserman, Paul R. Kesselman, Daniel S. Kirshner, Daniel M. Kotin, Terrence J. Lavin, Tom Leahy, George Leynaud, Stephen I. Lane, Robert A. Loeb, John Loevy, Michael G. Mahoney, Michael Marovich, Monica E. McFadden, Robert R. McNamara, Robert J. Napleton, Jan H. Ohlander, John J. Perconti, Darcy Proctor, Charles P. Rantis, George Ripplinger, Abbey Romanek, Mark Rouleau, Patrick A. Salvi, Michael P. Schostok, Scott C. Sands, Gregory E. Schiller, Peter Segal, Mathew B. Smith, James J. Stamos, Timothy Touhy, Craig A. Tomassi, James B. Zouras.

HOW TO USE THIS BOOK

1. Overview

ILLINOIS MOTIONS IN LIMINE is designed to help you quickly find authorities for a number of key *in limine* motions. The text contains important trial motions for general use in civil and criminal cases with citations from the applicable state and federal court jurisdictions.

We welcome your feedback and/or contributions regarding other possible motions, motion issues or any additional matter.

2. Quick-Research Format

ILLINOIS MOTIONS IN LIMINE is organized in a unique "quick-research" format that allows you to zero in on key authorities and suggested motion text while in your office or in court. Other than the first chapter, which provides an overview of *in limine* law, every chapter contains the following quick-research format:

1. Suggested Motion Text
2. Motion Summary
3. Supporting Authorities
4. Opposition Authorities
5. Sample Motions

Note that this text contains a useful compendium of citations and samples on a number of commonly filed motions *in limine*. The authors have attempted to include key citations to support each motion and provide a starting point for further research. If you do not find support for your motion in this book, check other known evidence resources. Once you have found a helpful case, read it in full to be sure that the point is applicable to your facts and cite check it to ensure that it is still good law.

Readers should also note that this text is designed to answer *specific* questions, and thus it is often not necessary to read the full text to find relevant authorities for your briefs. In following with this format, the authors have repeated key citations in various chapters or within existing chapters to allow for easy compilation of necessary citations, without referring to prior or subsequent areas of the text. Cross-references are also provided to help locate related citations.

While the authors have attempted to include many essential motions, not every *possible* motion, fact pattern or motion issue can be covered in this text. Readers should also note that the citations represent the law as it existed at the time the text was submitted for publication and that the law may have changed in certain areas prior to or subsequent to the final release date. Again, all citations in this text should be cite checked to ensure continued validity before use in briefs or other legal documents.

We invite all attorneys to submit sample motions in limine for possible inclusion in the next edition of this book. When motions are selected for publication, the attorneys who drafted them are named in the book as the authors of those motions. Please redact any information that you do not want published prior to submitting a motion. Please note that we cannot guarantee publication of the motions and by submitting motions for consideration, you waive any copyright claim to the motion(s) submitted. Please send your samples to lee@lawshl.com.

WESTLAW ELECTRONIC RESEARCH GUIDE

Westlaw—Expanding the Reach of Your Library

Westlaw is West's online legal research service. With Westlaw, you experience the same quality and integrity that you have come to expect from West books, plus quick, easy access to West's vast collection of statutes, case law materials, public records, and other legal resources, in addition to current news articles and business information. For the most current and comprehensive legal research, combine the strengths of West books and Westlaw.

When you research with westlaw.com you get the convenience of the Internet combined with comprehensive and accurate Westlaw content, including exclusive editorial enhancements, plus features found only in westlaw.com such as ResultsPlus™ or StatutesPlus™.

Accessing Databases Using the Westlaw Directory

The Westlaw Directory lists all databases on Westlaw and contains links to detailed information relating to the content of each database. Click Directory on the westlaw.com toolbar. There are several ways to access a database even when you don't know the database identifier. Browse a directory view. Scan the directory. Type all or part of a database name in the Search these Databases box. The Find a Database Wizard can help you select relevant databases for your search. You can access up to ten databases at one time for user-defined multibase searching.

Retrieving a Specific Document

To retrieve a specific document by citation or title on westlaw.com click **Find** on the toolbar to display the Find a Document page. If you are unsure of the correct citation format, type the publication abbreviation, e.g., **xx st** (where xx is a state's two-letter postal abbreviation), in the Enter Citation box and click **Go** to display a fill-in-the-blank template. To retrieve a specific case when you know one or more parties' names, click **Find by Title**.

KeyCite®

KeyCite, the citation research service on Westlaw, makes it easy to trace the history of your case, statute, administrative decision or regulation to determine if there are recent updates, and to find other documents that cite your document. KeyCite will also find pending legislation relating to federal or state statutes. Access the powerful features of KeyCite from the westlaw.com toolbar, the **Links** tab, or KeyCite flags in a document display. KeyCite's red and yellow warning flags tell you at a glance whether your document has negative history. Depth-of-treatment stars help you focus on the most important citing references. KeyCite Alert allows you to monitor the status of your case, statute or rule, and automatically sends you updates at the frequency you specify.

ResultsPlus™

ResultsPlus is a Westlaw technology that automatically suggests additional information related to your search. The suggested materials are accessible by a set of links that appear to the right of your westlaw.com search results:

- Go directly to relevant ALR® articles and Am Jur® annotations.
- Find on-point resources by key number.
- See information from related treatises and law reviews.

StatutesPlus™

When you access a statutes database in westlaw.com you are brought to a powerful Search Center which collects, on one toolbar, the tools that are most useful for fast, efficient retrieval of statutes documents:

- Have a few key terms? Click **Index**.
- Know the common name? Click **Popular Name Table**.
- Familiar with the subject matter? Click **Table of Contents**.
- Have a citation or section number? Click **Find by Citation**.

- Or, simply search with **Natural Language** or **Terms and Connectors**.

When you access a statutes section, click on the **Links** tab for all relevant links for the current document that will also include a KeyCite section with a description of the KeyCite status flag. Depending on your document, links may also include administrative, bill text, and other sources that were previously only available by accessing and searching other databases.

Additional Information

Westlaw is available on the Web at www.westlaw.com.

For search assistance, call the West Reference Attorneys at 1-800-REF-ATTY (1-800-733-2889).

For technical assistance, call West Customer Technical Support at 1-800-WESTLAW (1-800-937-8529).

Summary of Contents

Table of Contents

CHAPTER 1. MOTION IN LIMINE LAW

I. OVERVIEW

A. IN LIMINE LAW AND PROCEDURE

B. DRAFTING SUGGESTIONS

II. SAMPLES

CHAPTER 2. PREJUDICIAL EVIDENCE

I. MOTION AUTHORITIES

A. MOTION TO EXCLUDE PREJUDICIAL EVIDENCE, GENERALLY

B. MOTION TO EXCLUDE EVIDENCE THAT WILL WASTE TIME

C. MOTION TO EXCLUDE CONFUSING OR MISLEADING EVIDENCE

D. MOTION TO EXCLUDE EVIDENCE USED TO CREATE AN EMOTIONAL BIAS

E. MOTION TO EXCLUDE OR LIMIT CUMULATIVE EVIDENCE

II. SAMPLE MOTIONS

CHAPTER 3. IRRELEVANT EVIDENCE

I. MOTION AUTHORITIES

A. MOTION TO EXCLUDE IRRELEVANT EVIDENCE

B. MOTION TO EXCLUDE EVIDENCE OF MATTERS NOT IN CONTROVERSY

II. SAMPLE MOTIONS

CHAPTER 4. WRITINGS & PHYSICAL EVIDENCE

I. MOTION AUTHORITIES

A. MOTION TO EXCLUDE EVIDENCE LACKING FOUNDATION

B. MOTION TO EXCLUDE WRITINGS, GENERALLY

C. MOTION TO EXCLUDE GRUESOME OR INFLAMMATORY PHOTOGRAPHS

D. MOTION TO EXCLUDE PREJUDICIAL FILM OR VIDEOTAPES

E. MOTION TO EXCLUDE PUBLISHED ARTICLES AND TEXTS

F. MOTION TO EXCLUDE POLICE REPORTS AND OTHER TYPES OF ACCIDENT REPORTS

G. MOTION TO EXCLUDE LETTERS

H. MOTION TO EXCLUDE MAPS, MODELS & CHARTS

I. MOTION TO EXCLUDE IMPROPER MEDICAL RECORDS, REPORTS OR BILLS

II. SAMPLE MOTIONS

CHAPTER 5. TESTS & RELATED SCIENTIFIC EVIDENCE

I. MOTION AUTHORITIES

A. MOTION TO EXCLUDE TESTS, EXPERIMENTS AND RELATED TESTIMONY AND EVIDENCE

B. MOTION TO EXCLUDE "JUNK SCIENCE" AND RELATED EVIDENCE

II. SAMPLE MOTIONS

CHAPTER 6. DISCOVERY MOTIONS

I. MOTION AUTHORITIES

A. MOTION FOR EVIDENTIARY SANCTIONS

B. MOTION TO EXCLUDE EVIDENCE OF CLAIMS DENIED DURING DISCOVERY

C. MOTIONS REGARDING EXPERT DISCLOSURES AND EXPERT DEPOSITIONS

D. MOTION TO EXCLUDE STATUTORILY PRIVILEGED INFORMATION

C. MOTION TO EXCLUDE CHARACTER EVIDENCE USED TO PROVE CONDUCT

D. MOTION TO EXCLUDE EVIDENCE OF PRIOR FELONY CONVICTION

II. SAMPLE MOTIONS

CHAPTER 8. WITNESS EVIDENCE

I. MOTION AUTHORITIES

A. MOTION TO EXCLUDE IMPROPER OPINIONS

E. MOTION TO EXCLUDE TESTIMONY OF JUDGE, ARBITRATOR, MEDIATOR OR JUROR

F. MOTION TO EXCLUDE WITNESS FROM COURTROOM PRIOR TO TESTIFYING

G. MOTION TO EXCLUDE COMMENT ON EXERCISE OF PRIVILEGE (NOT TO TESTIFY)

H. MOTION TO EXCLUDE EVIDENCE OF NON-CALLED WITNESSES

B. MOTION TO EXCLUDE IMPROPER ARGUMENTS OR COMMENTS IN OPENING STATEMENT

C. MOTION TO BAR PREMATURE REBUTTAL TO AFFIRMATIVE DEFENSES

D. MOTION RE REFERENCE TO LOST OR DESTROYED EVIDENCE

II. SAMPLE MOTIONS

CHAPTER 10. PERSONAL INJURY MOTIONS

I. MOTION AUTHORITIES

A. MOTION TO EXCLUDE EVIDENCE OF COLLATERAL SOURCE PAYMENTS

B. MOTION TO EXCLUDE EVIDENCE OF INSURANCE

C. MOTION TO EXCLUDE SETTLEMENT EVIDENCE

D. MOTION TO EXCLUDE EVIDENCE OF OTHER ACCIDENTS

G. MOTION TO EXCLUDE EVIDENCE OF DRIVER'S LICENSE SUSPENSION

H. MOTION TO EXCLUDE EVIDENCE OF FAILURE TO WEAR SEAT BELT

I. MOTION TO EXCLUDE EVIDENCE OF ALCOHOL CONSUMPTION

J. MOTION TO EXCLUDE EVIDENCE OF PRIOR D.U.I.

K. MOTION TO EXCLUDE EVIDENCE OF PARTY'S HEALTH OR INJURIES WHERE NOT AT ISSUE

L. MOTION TO EXCLUDE ACCIDENT RECONSTRUCTION AND BIOMECHANICAL EVIDENCE

M. MOTION TO EXCLUDE EVIDENCE OF PARTY'S FINANCIAL STATUS

N. MOTION TO EXCLUDE TAX EVIDENCE

O. MOTION TO EXCLUDE LIABILITY EVIDENCE WHERE LIABILITY NOT AT ISSUE

II. SAMPLE MOTIONS

APPENDIX

Chapter 1

Motion in Limine Law

I. OVERVIEW

A. IN LIMINE LAW AND PROCEDURE

B. DRAFTING SUGGESTIONS

II. SAMPLES

KeyCite®: Cases and other legal materials listed in KeyCite Scope can be researched through the KeyCite service on Westlaw®. Use KeyCite to check citations for form, parallel references, prior and later history, and comprehensive citator information, including citations to other decisions and secondary materials.

I. OVERVIEW

A. IN LIMINE LAW AND PROCEDURE

§ 1:1 Description and purposes of motion

A motion in limine is a motion generally used to preclude prejudicial or objectionable evidence before it is presented to the jury. *Lundell v. Citrano*, 129 Ill. App. 3d 390, 395–96, 84 Ill. Dec. 581, 472 N.E.2d 541 (1st Dist. 1984); *Department of Public Works and Bldgs. v. Roehrig*, 45 Ill. App. 3d 189, 194–95, 3 Ill. Dec. 893, 359 N.E.2d 752 (5th Dist. 1976). The motion may also be used to admit evidence. See § 1:3, Typical use of motion, infra.

The primary advantage of the motion is to avoid the futile attempt of trying to undo the harm done where jurors have been exposed to damaging evidence, even where stricken by the court. *Lundell v. Citrano*, 129 Ill. App. 3d 390, 395–96, 84 Ill. Dec. 581, 472 N.E.2d 541 (1st Dist. 1984); and *Department of Public Works and Bldgs. v. Roehrig*, 45 Ill. App. 3d 189, 194–95, 3 Ill. Dec. 893, 359 N.E.2d 752 (5th Dist. 1976).

Motions in limine serve other purposes as well, such as: permitting more careful consideration of evidentiary issues than would take place during the heat of battle during trial; minimizing side-bar conferences and disruptions during trial; and, by resolving potentially critical issues at the outset, enhancing the efficiency of trials and promotion of settlements. See *Cook v. Gould*, 109 Ill. App. 3d 311, 315, 64 Ill. Dec. 896, 440 N.E.2d 448 (3d Dist. 1982); and *Department of Public Works and Bldgs. v. Roehrig*, 45 Ill. App. 3d 189, 194–95, 3 Ill. Dec. 893, 359 N.E.2d 752 (5th Dist. 1976).

Tip: Counsel should file as many motions in limine as necessary to exclude potentially damaging prejudicial evidence, rather than waiting and objecting at the time of trial. The following points address why this is important:

(1) It is difficult to "unring the bell". In other words it is difficult to undue the harm after the jury has heard the damaging evidence.

(2) If counsel forgoes a motion in limine and simply objects during trial in the presence of the jury, the objection and the court's instruction to disregard the inappropriate evidence will only serve to *highlight* the inadmissible and prejudicial evidence.
(3) Juries do not like objections because it appears as if the objecting attorney is trying to hide something.
(4) Motions in limine educate the moving party before trial regarding how the court will rule on the motion. Rulings on a motion in limine are interlocutory and can be modified at any time. Therefore, an adverse pretrial ruling will allow the movant an opportunity to persuade the court to change its ruling prior to the time the evidence becomes an issue in the case. Additionally, the filing of a motion in limine (even where eventually denied) allows the movant an opportunity to learn how the opposition intends to use the evidence.
(5) Motions in limine streamline the case, shorten the trial and reduce costs.

§ 1:2 Authority for motion

While not expressly authorized by statute, motions in limine are commonly used trial tools that are entertained and granted within the trial court's inherent powers. *Swick v. Liautaud*, 169 Ill. 2d 504, 520–21, 215 Ill. Dec. 98, 662 N.E.2d 1238 (1996); *People v. Watkins*, 220 Ill. App. 3d 201, 163 Ill. Dec. 194, 581 N.E.2d 145 (1st Dist. 1991); *Cochran v. Great Atlantic & Pacific Tea Co., Inc.*, 203 Ill. App. 3d 935, 938, 148 Ill. Dec. 923, 561 N.E.2d 229 (5th Dist. 1990); and *Department of Public Works and Bldgs. v. Roehrig*, 45 Ill. App. 3d 189, 194–95, 3 Ill. Dec. 893, 359 N.E.2d 752 (5th Dist. 1976).

The following rules and cases may provide support for many in limine motions:

> As noted above, it has been held that motions in limine are properly considered through the trial judge's inherent powers to admit or exclude evidence. It has also been held that a party can raise a *Frye* objection to scientific evidence through a motion in limine.

Agnew v. Shaw, 355 Ill.App.3d 981, 990–91 (1st Dist. 2005).

For further citations related to scientific evidence and Frye analyses, see Chapter 5, Tests & Related Scientific Evidence, infra.

Federal Rule of Evidence 403 states:

> Although relevant, evidence may be excluded if its probative value is substantially outweighed by the danger of unfair prejudice, confusion of the issues, or misleading the jury, or by considerations of undue delay, waste of time, or needless presentation of cumulative evidence.

It must be noted that this Rule has not been codified in Illinois. However, Illinois cases have stated that Illinois has a common-law rule that is comparable to Federal Rule of Evidence 403. See *People v. Walker*, 335 Ill. App. 3d 102, 112, 268 Ill. Dec. 654, 779 N.E.2d 268 (2d Dist. 2002), as modified on denial of reh'g, (Oct. 24, 2002) and judgment aff'd, 211 Ill. 2d 317, 285 Ill. Dec. 519, 812 N.E.2d 339 (2004); and *People v. Peete*, 318 Ill. App. 3d 961, 966–67, 252 Ill. Dec. 821, 743 N.E.2d 689 (4th Dist. 2001). Therefore, it is arguable that Federal Rule of Evidence 403 can be considered as persuasive authority in Illinois. For expanded citations, see § 2:1 to § 2:4, infra.

Illinois also provides for the exclusion of relevant evidence where the probative value is substantially outweighed by the danger of undue prejudice, issue confusion, misleading the jury, or undue consumption of time. See *People v. Walker*, 335 Ill. App. 3d 102, 112–13, 268 Ill. Dec. 654, 779 N.E.2d 268 (2d Dist. 2002), as modified on denial of reh'g, (Oct. 24, 2002) and judgment aff'd, 211 Ill. 2d 317, 285 Ill. Dec. 519, 812 N.E.2d 339 (2004); *People v. Peete*, 318 Ill. App. 3d 961, 967–68, 252 Ill. Dec. 821, 743 N.E.2d 689 (4th Dist. 2001); *Gossard v. Kalra*, 291 Ill. App. 3d 180, 182, 225 Ill. Dec. 725, 684 N.E.2d 410 (4th Dist. 1997); and *Rusher v. Smith*, 70 Ill. App. 3d 889, 894, 26 Ill. Dec. 905, 388 N.E.2d 906 (5th Dist. 1979).

Illinois law also provides for the exclusion of irrelevant evidence. See *Preston ex rel. Preston v. Simmons*, 321 Ill. App. 3d 789, 803, 254 Ill. Dec. 647, 747 N.E.2d 1059 (1st Dist. 2001) (trial judge should not permit such wide latitude on cross-examination that it undermines the rule that only relevant evidence is admissible); and *Carillo v. Ford Motor Co.*, 325 Ill. App. 3d 955, 968, 259 Ill. Dec. 619, 759 N.E.2d 99 (1st Dist. 2001) (proper to exclude evidence that is irrelevant to the issues being tried).

Federal Rule of Evidence 401 defines relevancy as,

> evidence having any tendency to make the existence of any fact that is of consequence to the determination of the action more probable or less probable than it would be without the evidence.

Illinois has adopted this definition of relevancy through case law. *Spencer v. Wandolowski*, 264 Ill. App. 3d 611, 617, 201 Ill.

Dec. 422, 636 N.E.2d 854 (1st Dist. 1994); and *People v. Monroe*, 66 Ill. 2d 317, 321–22, 5 Ill. Dec. 824, 362 N.E.2d 295 (1977).

Federal Rule of Evidence 103(c) provides:

> Hearing of Jury.—In jury cases, proceedings shall be conducted, to the extent practicable, so as to prevent inadmissible evidence from being suggested to the jury by any means, such as making statements or offers of proof or asking questions in the hearing of the jury.

Although this rule has not been specifically codified in Illinois, Illinois has adopted other Federal Rules of Evidence through case law. See e.g. *People v. Monroe*, 66 Ill. 2d 317, 321–22, 5 Ill. Dec. 824, 362 N.E.2d 295 (1977); and *Spencer v. Wandolowski*, 264 Ill. App. 3d 611, 617, 201 Ill. Dec. 422, 636 N.E.2d 854 (1st Dist. 1994) (adopting Federal Rule of Evidence 401). Therefore, cites to the Federal Rules of Evidence can often be cited as persuasive authority in Illinois. See also *Beasley v. Huffman Mfg. Co.*, 97 Ill. App. 3d 1, 5, 52 Ill. Dec. 560, 422 N.E.2d 241 (3d Dist. 1981) (purpose of a motion in limine is to prevent prejudice by determining admissibility issues outside of the jury's presence before the jury is exposed to the evidence); *People v. Graves*, 74 Ill. 2d 279, 279–83, 24 Ill. Dec. 153, 384 N.E.2d 1311 (1979) (contempt order against attorney was proper for mentioning an issue in front of the jury after being ordered at a side-bar conference not to do so); *Department of Public Works and Bldgs. v. Roehrig*, 45 Ill. App. 3d 189, 194–95, 3 Ill. Dec. 893, 359 N.E.2d 752 (5th Dist. 1976) (purpose of motion in limine is to prevent inadmissible evidence from being suggested to the jury) and *Maxwell v. Habel*, 92 Ill. App. 510, 1900 WL 3466 (1st Dist. 1900) (if trial judge is concerned that an offer of proof might prejudice the jury, the offer can be made outside the presence of the jury).

Illinois Supreme Court Rule 218 states:

> Pretrial Procedure.
>
> (a) Initial Case Management Conference. Except as provided by local circuit court rule, which on petition of the chief judge of the circuit has been approved by the Supreme Court, the court shall hold a case management conference within 35 days after the parties are at issue and in no event more than 182 days following the filing of the complaint. At the conference counsel familiar with the case and authorized to act shall appear and *the following shall be considered*:
>
> (1) the nature, issues, and complexity of the case;
>
> (2) the simplification of the issues;
>
> (3) amendments to the pleadings;

(4) the possibility of obtaining admissions of fact and of documents which will avoid unnecessary proof;

(5) limitations on discovery including:

(i) the number and duration of depositions which may be taken;

(ii) the area of expertise and the number of expert witnesses who may be called; and

(iii) deadlines for the disclosure of witnesses and the completion of written discovery and depositions;

(6) the possibility of settlement and scheduling of a settlement conference;

(7) the advisability of alternative dispute resolution;

(8) the date on which the case should be ready for trial;

(9) the advisability of holding subsequent case management conferences; and

(10) any other matters which may aid in the disposition of the action.

(b) Subsequent Case Management Conferences. At the initial and any subsequent case management conference, the court shall set a date for a subsequent management conference or a trial date.

(c) Order. At the case management conference, the court shall make an order which recites any action taken by the court, the agreements made by the parties as to any of the matters considered, and which specifies as the issues for trial those not disposed of at the conference. The order controls the subsequent course of the action unless modified. All dates set for the disclosure of witnesses, including rebuttal witnesses, and the completion of discovery shall be chosen to ensure that discovery will be completed not later than 60 days before the date on which the trial court reasonably anticipates that trial will commence, unless otherwise agreed by the parties. This rule is to be liberally construed to do substantial justice between and among the parties.

(d) Calendar. The court shall establish a pretrial calendar on which actions shall be placed for consideration, as above provided, either by the court on its own motion or on the motion of any party. (Emphasis added.)

§ 1:3 Typical use of motion

A typical in limine order excludes the challenged evidence, as is discussed in the prior sections. *Department of Public Works and Bldgs. v. Roehrig*, 45 Ill. App. 3d 189, 194–95, 3 Ill. Dec. 893, 359 N.E.2d 752 (5th Dist. 1976).

Motions in limine may also be used to admit evidence. *People v. Drum*, 321 Ill. App. 3d 1005, 254 Ill. Dec. 898, 748 N.E.2d 344 (4th Dist. 2001). A motion in limine to admit evidence will have the benefit of further streamlining issues, and will often lead to stipulations. Further, the motion will educate the moving party regarding how the opponent will attack the evidence and how the judge will rule on the admissibility of the evidence, which will likely assist the moving party in determining what foundation will be needed to satisfy the judge.

An in limine order may also direct counsel, parties and witnesses not to refer to the excluded matters during trial. *Cook v. Gould*, 109 Ill. App. 3d 311, 315, 64 Ill. Dec. 896, 440 N.E.2d 448 (3d Dist. 1982); and *Department of Public Works and Bldgs. v. Roehrig*, 45 Ill. App. 3d 189, 194–95, 3 Ill. Dec. 893, 359 N.E.2d 752 (5th Dist. 1976). Violating an order restricting the mention of evidence can result in a finding of contempt and/or a mistrial. *People v. Graves*, 74 Ill. 2d 279, 279–83, 24 Ill. Dec. 153, 384 N.E.2d 1311 (1979).

See also *Cunningham v. Millers General Ins. Co.*, 227 Ill. App. 3d 201, 205, 169 Ill. Dec. 200, 591 N.E.2d 80 (4th Dist. 1992) (if evidence could be prejudicial, it might be prudent to grant a motion in limine until a clear basis for the admission of the evidence appears).

§ 1:4 Typical use of motion—Limitations on use

Chubb/Home Ins. Companies v. Outboard Marine Corp., 238 Ill. App. 3d 558, 567–68, 179 Ill. Dec. 591, 606 N.E.2d 423 (1st Dist. 1992) (orders regarding motions in limine are subject to review by the trial judge throughout the proceedings).

Lundell v. Citrano, 129 Ill. App. 3d 390, 395–96, 84 Ill. Dec. 581, 472 N.E.2d 541 (1st Dist. 1984) (it is improper to use a motion in limine to prevent the opposing party from introducing relevant and admissible evidence).

Reidelberger v. Highland Body Shop, Inc., 83 Ill. 2d 545, 549–58, 48 Ill. Dec. 237, 416 N.E.2d 268 (1981) (trial court abused its discretion by granting a new trial for the opposing party's alleged violation of an unclear in limine order).

Reidelberger v. Highland Body Shop, Inc., 83 Ill. 2d 545, 549–58, 48 Ill. Dec. 237, 416 N.E.2d 268 (1981) (a trial judge should not enter an in limine order that is too complicated for the parties to clearly understand what is precluded).

Bell v. City of Joliet, 83 Ill. App. 3d 103, 104–05, 38 Ill. Dec. 509, 403 N.E.2d 740 (3d Dist. 1980) (a motion in limine should not be granted when the rules of evidence do not require that the matter at issue be excluded from the trial).

Bradley v. Caterpillar Tractor Co., 75 Ill. App. 3d 890, 899–900, 31 Ill. Dec. 623, 394 N.E.2d 825 (5th Dist. 1979) (a motion in limine is a useful tool but care must be exercised to avoid indiscriminate application).

326, 738 N.E.2d 542 (1st Dist. 2000). Of course, in some circumstances, the court may sanction counsel or a party where the violation of an order in limine is blatant or intentional.

§ 1:9 Typical use of motion—Preservation of objections—Must object at trial—Civil cases

In the event a motion to exclude evidence is denied prior to trial, the opponent of the evidence must object at the time the evidence is offered at trial to preserve the error for appeal. Additionally, the error must be included in the party's post-trial motion. If a motion in limine to admit evidence is denied, a party must make a sufficient offer of proof to preserve the error for appellate purposes. *Schuler v. Mid-Central Cardiology*, 313 Ill. App. 3d 326, 333–34, 246 Ill. Dec. 163, 729 N.E.2d 536 (4th Dist. 2000) (if a motion is in limine is denied, the party that brought the motion must object when the evidence is presented at trial or the issue is waived for appeal).

Wheeler-Dealer, Ltd. v. Christ, 379 Ill. App. 3d 864, 319 Ill. Dec. 79, 885 N.E.2d 350, 355–56 (1st Dist. 2008) (in order to preserve its objection, a party was required to renew its objection to parol evidence when the evidence was offered at trial, even though the party objected to the evidence prior to trial).

Sobczak v. General Motors Corp., 373 Ill. App. 3d 910, 925–26, 312 Ill. Dec. 682, 871 N.E.2d 82 (1st Dist. 2007), appeal denied, 226 Ill. 2d 609, 316 Ill. Dec. 551, 879 N.E.2d 939 (2007) (the plaintiff waived his objection to the opposing party's statement in opening remarks regarding the number of alcoholic drinks the plaintiff consumed before the incident in question, by failing to object at trial).

In re Marriage of Saheb and Khazal, 377 Ill. App. 3d 615, 626–27, 316 Ill. Dec. 801, 880 N.E.2d 537 (1st Dist. 2007) (party waived any objection to the fact that a guardian ad litem provided an oral instead of the required written report, by failing to object at trial).

Addis v. Exelon Generation Co., L.L.C., 378 Ill. App. 3d 781, 794–95, 316 Ill. Dec. 949, 880 N.E.2d 685 (1st Dist. 2007), appeal denied, 228 Ill. 2d 529, 321 Ill. Dec. 554, 889 N.E.2d 1114 (2008) (party waived any objection to alleged improper comments and evidence by failing to object at trial).

Chicago Exhibitors Corp. v. Jeepers! of Illinois, Inc., 376 Ill. App. 3d 599, 609–610, 315 Ill. Dec. 129, 876 N.E.2d 129 (1st Dist. 2007) (party waived certain affirmative defenses by failing to raise them in the trial court).

Brdar v. Cottrell, Inc., 372 Ill. App. 3d 690, 702, 311 Ill. Dec.

99, 867 N.E.2d 1085 (5th Dist. 2007), appeal denied, 224 Ill. 2d 572, 312 Ill. Dec. 654, 871 N.E.2d 54 (2007) (party waived objections to certain testimony by failing to renew a pretrial objection at the trial and by failing to raise the specific grounds for the objections that were later raised on appeal).

Lopez v. Northwestern Memorial Hosp., 375 Ill. App. 3d 637, 647–48, 313 Ill. Dec. 796, 873 N.E.2d 420 (1st Dist. 2007) (party waived certain objections by failing to raise them in a post-trial motion).

Jones v. Rallos, 373 Ill. App. 3d 439, 311 Ill. Dec. 450, 869 N.E.2d 124 (1st Dist. 2006) (by failing to address the issue again during the trial, the defendant waived her claim that certain evidence was improperly barred as a result of the plaintiff's motion in limine), judgment vacated, *Jones v. Rallos*, 225 Ill. 2d 636, 314 Ill. Dec. 13, 873 N.E.2d 943 (2007) ("The appellate court is directed to reconsider its judgment, with additional analysis of whether any error in the trial court's decision to permit plaintiff-appellee to elicit evidence of defendant-appellant's failure to pass board-certification examinations constitutes no more than harmless, non-reversible error.").

Spurgeon v. Mruz, 358 Ill. App. 3d 358, 295 Ill. Dec. 170, 832 N.E.2d 321, 322–23 (1st Dist. 2005) (party waived consideration of his motion to bar the opposing party's expert for a discovery violation, when the party failed to renew the objection during trial at the time the testimony was offered).

Sullivan-Coughlin v. Palos Country Club, Inc., 349 Ill. App. 3d 553, 285 Ill. Dec. 676, 812 N.E.2d 496 (1st Dist. 2004) (party waived the issue of whether blood-alcohol evidence should have been admitted, by failing to raise the issue again at trial or to make an offer of proof, after the trial judge had granted the opposing party's motion in limine to exclude the evidence).

York v. El-Ganzouri, 353 Ill. App. 3d 1, 10, 288 Ill. Dec. 529, 817 N.E.2d 1179 (1st Dist. 2004), judgment aff'd, 222 Ill. 2d 147, 305 Ill. Dec. 43, 854 N.E.2d 635 (2006) (a motion in limine, without a trial objection, is generally insufficient to preserve the alleged error for appeal).

Chubb/Home Ins. Companies v. Outboard Marine Corp., 238 Ill. App. 3d 558, 567–68, 179 Ill. Dec. 591, 606 N.E.2d 423 (1st Dist. 1992) (if a motion is in limine is denied, the party that brought the motion must object when the evidence is presented at trial or the issue is waived for appeal).

Beasley v. Huffman Mfg. Co., 97 Ill. App. 3d 1, 5-6, 52 Ill. Dec. 560, 422 N.E.2d 241 (3d Dist. 1981) (if a motion is in limine is denied, the party that brought the motion must object when the evidence is presented at trial or the issue is waived for appeal).

Bell v. City of Joliet, 83 Ill. App. 3d 103, 104–05, 38 Ill. Dec. 509, 403 N.E.2d 740 (3d Dist. 1980) (if the rules of evidence require that the matter at issue be excluded, the trial judge has the discretion to either grant a motion in limine and order it excluded prior to trial or deny the motion in limine and allow the party to object to the matter at trial).

§ 1:10 Typical use of motion—Preservation of objections—Must object at trial—Civil cases—Preservation of objections—Distinguish criminal cases

People v. Whirl, 351 Ill. App. 3d 464, 466, 286 Ill. Dec. 646, 814 N.E.2d 872 (2d Dist. 2004) (a motion in limine, in addition to raising the disputed issue in a post-trial motion, is sufficient to preserve the alleged error for appeal, even without a trial objection).

People v. Barajas, 322 Ill. App. 3d 541, 552–53, 255 Ill. Dec. 565, 749 N.E.2d 1047 (1st Dist. 2001) (a motion in limine or a trial objection, in addition to including the issue in a post-trial motion, is sufficient to preserve the issue for review)

People v. Hudson, 157 Ill. 2d 401, 434–35, 193 Ill. Dec. 128, 626 N.E.2d 161 (1993) (a motion in limine preserved an issue for appeal, when the issue was also included in a post trial motion).

§ 1:11 Typical use of motion—Preservation of objections—Must object at trial—Civil cases—How to preserve error

An order in limine is an interlocutory order and always remains subject to reconsideration by the court during trial. *Jones v. Chicago Osteopathic Hosp.*, 316 Ill. App. 3d 1121, 250 Ill. Dec. 326, 738 N.E.2d 542 (1st Dist. 2000); *Schuler v. Mid-Central Cardiology*, 313 Ill. App. 3d 326, 246 Ill. Dec. 163, 729 N.E.2d 536 (4th Dist. 2000). Therefore, in civil cases, whether a motion in limine is granted or denied, the motion itself does not preserve the issue for appeal. *Jones v. Chicago Osteopathic Hosp.*, 316 Ill. App. 3d 1121, 250 Ill. Dec. 326, 738 N.E.2d 542 (1st Dist. 2000). When a motion in limine to exclude evidence is denied, in civil cases a contemporaneous objection to the evidence at the time it is offered is required to preserve the issue for appeal. *Simmons v. Garces*, 198 Ill. 2d 541, 261 Ill. Dec. 471, 763 N.E.2d 720 (2002); *Jones v. Chicago Osteopathic*

Hosp., 316 Ill. App. 3d 1121, 250 Ill. Dec. 326, 738 N.E.2d 542 (1st Dist. 2000). The party must also include the alleged error in the party's post-trial motion or any claim of error is waived on appeal. *National Blvd. Bank v. Georgetown Life Ins. Co.*, 129 Ill. App. 3d 73, 84 Ill. Dec. 330, 472 N.E.2d 80 (1st Dist. 1984). A new-trial motion, in addition to the motion in limine or the trial objection, is crucial to preserving any claim of error in a criminal case. See *People v. Boclair*, 129 Ill. 2d 458, 476, 136 Ill. Dec. 29, 544 N.E.2d 715 (1989); *Lopez v. Northwestern Memorial Hosp.*, 375 Ill. App. 3d 637, 647–48, 313 Ill. Dec. 796, 873 N.E.2d 420 (1st Dist. 2007) (party waived certain objections by failing to raise them in a post-trial motion).

In an event a motion in limine to exclude evidence is granted or a motion to admit evidence is denied (i.e. the evidence is excluded), to preserve the error in the exclusion of evidence for appellate purposes, the proponent of the evidence must make an adequate offer of proof in the trial court. An adequate offer of proof requires the party to inform the trial court, with particularity, of the substance of the witness's anticipated answer. An offer of proof that merely summarizes the witness's testimony in a conclusionary manner is inadequate. *Snelson v. Kamm*, 204 Ill. 2d 1, 272 Ill. Dec. 610, 787 N.E.2d 796 (2003). The failure to provide the trial court with a formal offer of proof results in waiver of the issue on appeal. The purpose of the offer of proof is to inform the trial court, opposing counsel, and the appellate court of the nature and substance of the evidence sought to be introduced. *Dillon v. Evanston Hosp.*, 199 Ill. 2d 483, 264 Ill. Dec. 653, 771 N.E.2d 357 (2002). Again, to preserve the error for appeal, the party must also raise the error in a post-trial motion. *National Blvd. Bank v. Georgetown Life Ins. Co.*, 129 Ill. App. 3d 73, 84 Ill. Dec. 330, 472 N.E.2d 80 (1st Dist. 1984).

§ 1:12 Typical use of motion—Preservation of objections—Must object at trial—Civil cases—Appellate review

The appellate court will not disturb the trial court's ruling on a motion in limine absent a clear abuse of discretion. *Hallowell v. University of Chicago Hosp.*, 334 Ill. App. 3d 206, 267 Ill. Dec. 632, 777 N.E.2d 435 (1st Dist. 2002). A trial court's improper ruling on a motion in limine will constitute reversible error only when the ruling is prejudicial to the outcome of the trial. *Jones v. Chicago Osteopathic Hosp.*, 316 Ill. App. 3d 1121, 250 Ill. Dec. 326, 738 N.E.2d 542 (1st Dist. 2000).

Counsel should keep in mind that the specific grounds for

exclusion must be raised at the trial level or the issue will generally be considered waived on appeal. See *In re Detention of Sveda*, 354 Ill. App. 3d 373, 376–77, 289 Ill. Dec. 912, 820 N.E.2d 987 (1st Dist. 2004) (party waived appellate review of the claim that the trial judge should not have admitted scientific evidence without a *Frye* hearing, because, although the party filed a motion in limine to exclude the evidence, the party did not raise that specific claim as a grounds for exclusion).

See also *Lopez v. Northwestern Memorial Hosp.*, 375 Ill. App. 3d 637, 648, 313 Ill. Dec. 796, 873 N.E.2d 420 (1st Dist. 2007) (party waived any alleged violation of an in limine by failing to include the written in limine order in the record on appeal).

§ 1:13 Timing of motion

Motions in limine are typically brought at the beginning of trial, but may also be brought during trial. *Neal v. Nimmagadda*, 279 Ill. App. 3d 834, 845–46, 216 Ill. Dec. 364, 665 N.E.2d 424 (1st Dist. 1996). Circumstances change during the course of trial and so does the status of evidence, making the use of a motion in limine during trial appropriate and effective. See § 1:16, Procedural requirements—Local rules, regarding possible additional timing restrictions.

See also *Chubb/Home Ins. Companies v. Outboard Marine Corp.*, 238 Ill. App. 3d 558, 567–68, 179 Ill. Dec. 591, 606 N.E.2d 423 (1st Dist. 1992) (orders regarding motions in limine are subject to review by the trial judge throughout the proceedings).

See also *Somers v. Quinn*, 373 Ill. App. 3d 87, 98-99, 310 Ill. Dec. 848, 867 N.E.2d 539 (2d Dist. 2007) (objection to an untimely motion in limine was waived by failing to raise the objection at the time of the motion).

§ 1:14 Scope of motion

The scope of a motion in limine is any kind of evidence that could be objected to at trial, as irrelevant or unduly prejudicial. *Department of Public Works and Bldgs. v. Roehrig*, 45 Ill. App. 3d 189, 194–95, 3 Ill. Dec. 893, 359 N.E.2d 752 (5th Dist. 1976).

Sometimes a proper motion can bar an entire theory or even dispose of the entire case. See e.g. *Paquet v. Steiner*, 239 Ill. App. 3d 866, 867–71, 180 Ill. Dec. 546, 607 N.E.2d 615 (2d Dist. 1993) (trial judge properly excluded expert testimony and then granted summary judgment based upon the lack of expert testimony, when no expert was disclosed in a timely fashion and there was no justifiable reason for the delay in disclosure); and *Golembiewski v. Hallberg Ins. Agency, Inc.*, 262 Ill. App. 3d 1082, 1086–87, 200 Ill. Dec. 113, 635 N.E.2d 452 (1st Dist. 1994) (trial judge properly precluded the testimony of the defendant's president, precluded the defendant from offering a defense and ordered the defendant's attorney to pay the plaintiff's attorney's fees when the defendant's counsel improperly interfered with the ability of the plaintiff to conduct a full deposition of the defendant's president).

See also *Cunningham v. Millers General Ins. Co.*, 227 Ill. App. 3d 201, 205, 169 Ill. Dec. 200, 591 N.E.2d 80 (4th Dist. 1992) (if evidence could be prejudicial, it might be prudent to grant a motion in limine until a clear basis for the admission of the evidence appears).

But see *Bradley v. Caterpillar Tractor Co.*, 75 Ill. App. 3d 890, 899–900, 31 Ill. Dec. 623, 394 N.E.2d 825 (5th Dist. 1979) (a trial judge should not enter an in limine order that is so broad that it precludes a party's entire case).

§ 1:15 Procedural requirements—Oral motions

Case law demonstrates that courts sometimes grant oral motions in limine. See e.g. *People v. Love*, 327 Ill. App. 3d 313, 321–22, 261 Ill. Dec. 580, 763 N.E.2d 829 (4th Dist. 2002); and *Kapsouris v. Rivera*, 319 Ill. App. 3d 844, 847, 254 Ill. Dec. 387, 747 N.E.2d 427 (2d Dist. 2001). However, the better practice is to put the motion and proposed order in writing. See *Crawford County State Bank v. Grady*, 161 Ill. App. 3d 332, 341, 112 Ill. Dec. 869, 514 N.E.2d 532 (4th Dist. 1987) ("Oral in limine motions and orders provide fertile ground for confusion and misunderstanding during trial"); *Lundell v. Citrano*, 129 Ill. App. 3d 390, 395–96, 84 Ill. Dec. 581, 472 N.E.2d 541 (1st Dist. 1984) (motions in limine should be written and should include a clearly drafted proposed order); *Lockett v. Bi-State Transit Authority*, 94 Ill. 2d 66, 76-77, 67 Ill. Dec. 830, 445 N.E.2d 310 (1983) (oral motion and order in limine were not sufficiently clear to allow a violation of the order to form the basis for reversal); *Compton v. Ubilluz*, 353 Ill. App. 3d 863, 289 Ill. Dec. 271, 819 N.E.2d 767 (2d Dist. 2004) (appellate court was unable to review an issue because there was no clear written motion in limine or order in limine and therefore, the record was incomplete).

See also *Lopez v. Northwestern Memorial Hosp.*, 375 Ill. App. 3d 637, 648, 313 Ill. Dec. 796, 873 N.E.2d 420 (1st Dist. 2007) (party waived any alleged violation of an in limine by failing to include the written in limine order in the record on appeal).

§ 1:16 Procedural requirements—Local rules

In addition, some local jurisdictions may impose additional procedural requirements under the authority of Illinois Supreme Court Rule 218.

Illinois Supreme Court Rule 218 states:

Pretrial Procedure.

(a) Initial Case Management Conference. *Except as provided by local circuit court rule*, which on petition of the chief judge of the circuit has been approved by the Supreme Court, the court shall hold a case management conference within 35 days after the parties are at issue and in no event more than 182 days following the filing of the complaint. At the conference counsel familiar with the case and authorized to act shall appear and the following shall be considered:

(1) the nature, issues, and complexity of the case;

(2) the simplification of the issues;

(3) amendments to the pleadings;

(4) the possibility of obtaining admissions of fact and of documents which will avoid unnecessary proof;

(5) limitations on discovery including:

(i) the number and duration of depositions which may be taken;

(ii) the area of expertise and the number of expert witnesses who may be called; and

(iii) deadlines for the disclosure of witnesses and the completion of written discovery and depositions;

(6) the possibility of settlement and scheduling of a settlement conference;

(7) the advisability of alternative dispute resolution;

(8) the date on which the case should be ready for trial;

(9) the advisability of holding subsequent case management conferences; and

(10) any other matters which may aid in the disposition of the action.

(b) Subsequent Case Management Conferences. At the initial and any subsequent case management conference, the court shall set a date for a subsequent management conference or a trial date.

(c) Order. At the case management conference, the court shall make an order which recites any action taken by the court, the agreements made by the parties as to any of the matters considered, and which specifies as the issues for trial those not disposed of at the conference. The order controls the subsequent course of the action unless modified. All dates set for the disclosure of witnesses, including rebuttal witnesses, and the completion of discovery shall be chosen to ensure that discovery will be completed not later than 60 days before the date on which the trial court reasonably anticipates that trial will commence, unless otherwise agreed by the parties. This rule is to be liberally construed to do substantial justice between and among the parties.

(d) Calendar. The court shall establish a pretrial calendar on which actions shall be placed for consideration, as above provided, either by the court on its own motion or on the motion of any party. (Emphasis added.)

Many local jurisdictions have adopted cut-off dates and procedural requirements based upon Illinois Supreme Court Rule 218. See e.g. the Fourteenth Judicial Circuit Rule 6.9, which provides:

> *All motions in limine shall be filed with the Court four days prior to the pre-trial conference*, with copies served upon opposing counsel or to any party not represented by an attorney not later than seven days prior to the final pre-trial conference. (Emphasis added.)

Thus, it is extremely important to consult the local rules of the jurisdiction in which the matter is pending.

§ 1:17 Procedural requirements—Local rules—Caution regarding local rules

Counsel should be aware of local rules that may impose stricter notice and filing requirements. Local rules may also impose significant procedural restrictions that can create additional traps for the unwary. To avoid any pre-trial surprises, check your jurisdiction's local rules early in your case and be sure follow all procedural requirements and mark your calendar accordingly.

For example:

The Fourteenth Judicial Circuit has Rule 6.9, which provides:

> *All motions in limine shall be filed with the Court four days prior to the pre-trial conference*, with copies served upon opposing counsel or to any party not represented by an attorney not later than seven days prior to the final pre-trial conference. (Emphasis added.)

The Eighteenth Judicial Circuit has a required pretrial form that states:

> LITIGATION CONFERENCE ORDER
>
> Pursuant to Illinois Supreme Court Rule 218:
>
> The above cause is set for trial on ________ at ________ in courtroom ________. A final litigation Pretrial Conference will be held in the chambers of Judge ________ on ________ at ________. Counsel who will try the case shall appear.

Pretrial Materials. On or before ______ counsel for the parties shall furnish to the Judge's secretary the following materials:

(1) *Stipulation of Uncontested Facts.* A comprehensible written stipulation of uncontested facts to become a part of the evidentiary record in the case and which, in jury trials, shall be read to the jury by the Court. Counsel for plaintiff has the responsibility to prepare the draft of a proposed stipulation which speaks to the complaint; counsel for counter, cross or third party complainants has a like responsibility in respect to stipulations which speak to those causes of action. Counsel for any defendant or counter-defendant which has raised an affirmative defense has a like responsibility to prepare a stipulation of uncontested facts.

(2) *Agreed Statement of Contested Fact Issues.* An agreed statement signed by counsel for all parties of the nature of the case and the contested fact issues. In jury trials the statement may be read to the jury panel by the Court during voir dire and may be referred to by the parties and the Court at any appropriate time during the trial. The responsibilities of counsel are as stated in paragraph (1) above.

(3) *List of Witnesses, Exhibits and Depositions.* A statement from each party, signed by each party's respective counsel, containing:

(a) The names of all witnesses who may be called by that party and a very brief statement of the witness's anticipated testimony. The parties are directed to stipulate to the qualification of expert witnesses. If any party disputes the qualifications of an expert, the factual and legal basis for that objection shall be set forth in this statement;

(b) A list describing all exhibits which may be offered by each party with copies of documentary exhibits pre-marked and attached thereto. All exhibits shall be marked for identification prior to trial, and photocopies of all documentary exhibits so premarked shall be attached to this statement.

At trial, counsel will be expected to have a copy of each exhibit for the Court, opposing counsel, and the court reporter. The parties are directed to stipulate to the authenticity of exhibits. The issue of authenticity for an exhibit shall be deemed waived, unless counsel indicates in this statement an exhibit to which the authenticity has not been stipulated and why;

(c) A designation of all evidence deposition testimony which will be offered substantively by each party. Transcripts of depositions which the parties intend to introduce into evidence or read must accompany the statement. Likewise, any videotaped evidence deposition which any party intends to offer as substantive evidence must be provided with the statement.

Unlisted witnesses, exhibits and undesignated deposition testimony may not be called or offered at the trial, except for purposes of impeachment. The examination of witnesses or offer of exhibits will not be interrupted during the trial to afford opposing counsel an opportunity to inspect a listed, pre- marked exhibit.

(4) *Contested Issues of Law.* Counsel for each party shall file a statement designating the contested issues of law. This statement shall, in a very succinct fashion, refer to stipulated or contested fact issues when necessary. Counsel for each party shall cite each case which they rely upon to support their respective positions. Legible copies of all such cases shall be attached to this statement.

(5) *Estimated Length of Trial.* Counsel for each party shall estimate the total time required to complete the trial.

(6) *Trial Briefs.* Each party shall file a trial brief. The purpose of a trial brief is full and complete disclosure of a party's theory of the case. The trial brief shall include a statement of the nature of the case; a full and complete statement of the facts the party expects the evidence will establish; the party's theory of liability or defense based on those facts, together with authorities in support thereof; the party's theory of damages or other relief in the event liability is established, together with authorities in support thereof; the party's theory of any anticipated motion for directed verdict, together with authorities in support thereof; in jury cases, the party's authorities in support of particular requested jury instructions.

(7) *Voir Dire Examination.* In jury trials, each party shall submit in writing proposed questions unique to this case for use by the Court in its interrogation of prospective jurors.

(8) Motions In Limine. All motions in limine shall be in writing and submitted by the party tendering them. Any motion in limine not presented pursuant to this schedule will be deemed waived, except where the grounds arise or become apparent during the course of the trial.

(9) *Proposed Findings of Fact and Conclusions of Law.* Counsel for each party shall prepare proposed findings of fact and conclusions of law which he or she believes should be accepted by the Court after hearing the evidence.

(10) *Proposed Jury Instructions.* In jury trials, each party shall submit the original and two (2) copies of proposed jury instructions on: (a) issues made by the pleadings, I.P.I. 21.00, et seq.; (b) burden of proof—res ipsa loquitur, I.P.I. 22.00, et seq.; and (c) damages, I.P.I. 30.00, et seq. The copies shall identify the tendering party and the authority for the instruction. The originals shall be unmarked in a form suitable for submission to the jury. (Emphasis added.)

B. DRAFTING SUGGESTIONS

§ 1:18 Overview

Unlike pretrial motions, which are typically filed and argued one at a time, motions in limine usually come in bunches. It is not unusual for a trial judge to be presented with literally dozens of in limine motions—for each party—in a single case. Thus, it is not difficult to imagine the court's disdain for poorly drafted, overly verbose, or needlessly filed motions. It is also not difficult to understand why attorneys often face such an uphill battle in getting motions in limine granted.

Motions in limine should be in writing and filed with the Court. At the time the motions are heard, a court reporter should be present to preserve the record. The motion itself should contain sufficient facts to educate the judge so that he or she can understand the issues involved and place the evidence in its proper context. Each motion should be written in a clear and concise manner. The case law cited and relied upon should be on point and as current as possible. There are no specific rules as to the format of the motions themselves. Some counsel like to prepare one document that contains several motions in limine. Other attorneys prefer to prepare each motion as a separate document. Many attorneys use a combination of these approaches; for example, the basic motions are included in one document, while each of the more complex and/or longer motions are drafted as separate motions. Counsel should use the approach that works best for him or her. To avoid any confusion and to preserve the record, immediately after the motions are ruled upon, an order with respect to the motions should be drafted and entered by the court.

The following suggestions should enhance your chances of success.

§ 1:19 Overview—Be clear

Compton v. Ubilluz, 353 Ill. App. 3d 863, 289 Ill. Dec. 271, 819 N.E.2d 767 (2d Dist. 2004) (appellate court was unable to review an issue because there was no clear written motion in limine or order in limine and therefore, the record was incomplete).

Lockett v. Bi-State Transit Authority, 94 Ill. 2d 66, 76-77, 67 Ill. Dec. 830, 445 N.E.2d 310 (1983) (oral motion and order in limine were not sufficiently clear to allow a violation of the order to form the basis for reversal).

Reidelberger v. Highland Body Shop, Inc., 83 Ill. 2d 545, 549–58, 48 Ill. Dec. 237, 416 N.E.2d 268 (1981) (trial court abused its discretion by granting a new trial for the opposing party's alleged violation of an unclear in limine order).

Reidelberger v. Highland Body Shop, Inc., 83 Ill. 2d 545, 549–58, 48 Ill. Dec. 237, 416 N.E.2d 268 (1981) (a trial judge should not enter an in limine order that is too complicated for the parties to clearly understand what is precluded).

Bradley v. Caterpillar Tractor Co., 75 Ill. App. 3d 890,

899–900, 31 Ill. Dec. 623, 394 N.E.2d 825 (5th Dist. 1979) (a trial judge should not enter an in limine order that is too complicated for the parties to clearly understand what is precluded).

◆ **Note:** If your motion will require the court to speculate, your chances of success are slim. Instead, a better strategy may be to preserve your motion until you anticipate that the evidence will be proffered or other preliminary facts emerge that will give the court a factual basis to make its ruling. See *Chubb/Home Ins. Companies v. Outboard Marine Corp.*, 238 Ill. App. 3d 558, 567–68, 179 Ill. Dec. 591, 606 N.E.2d 423 (1st Dist. 1992) (orders regarding motions in limine are subject to review by the trial judge throughout the proceedings); and *Bell v. City of Joliet*, 83 Ill. App. 3d 103, 104–05, 38 Ill. Dec. 509, 403 N.E.2d 740 (3d Dist. 1980) (if the rules of evidence require that the matter at issue be excluded, the trial judge has the discretion to either grant a motion in limine and order it excluded prior to trial or deny the motion in limine and allow the party to object to the matter at trial); but see *Cunningham v. Millers General Ins. Co.*, 227 Ill. App. 3d 201, 205, 169 Ill. Dec. 200, 591 N.E.2d 80 (4th Dist. 1992) (if evidence could be prejudicial, it might be prudent to grant a motion in limine until a clear basis for the admission of the evidence appears).

§ 1:20 Overview—Be succinct

As with all motion writing, less is often more. If the court is familiar with the general facts of the case, there is no need to recite a lengthy restatement of the case history. Instead, a few introductory paragraphs advising the court of the pertinent facts relating to the motion issue is usually sufficient. Regarding the general authority for a motion in limine, a brief citation to a key case such as *Department of Public Works and Bldgs. v. Roehrig*, 45 Ill. App. 3d 189, 194–95, 3 Ill. Dec. 893, 359 N.E.2d 752 (5th Dist. 1976) will suffice.

If you have a specific citation supporting your argument, cite it early and then spend the balance of the motion explaining, as succinctly as possible, why the facts in your case support the requested exclusion or other in limine ruling.

Lundell v. Citrano, 129 Ill. App. 3d 390, 395–96, 84 Ill. Dec. 581, 472 N.E.2d 541 (1st Dist. 1984) (motions in limine should be written and should include a clearly drafted proposed order).

Bradley v. Caterpillar Tractor Co., 75 Ill. App. 3d 890, 899–900, 31 Ill. Dec. 623, 394 N.E.2d 825 (5th Dist. 1979) (a trial judge should not enter an in limine order that is so unduly broad that it precludes a party's entire case).

But see *Fakhoury v. Vapor Corp.*, 218 Ill. App. 3d 20, 23-24, 160 Ill. Dec. 942, 578 N.E.2d 121 (1st Dist. 1991) (a party who received the requested relief from a motion in limine cannot later argue that the motion was intended to pray for broader relief than was actually clearly requested).

§ 1:21 Overview—Have a legal basis for exclusion

Bell v. City of Joliet, 83 Ill. App. 3d 103, 104–05, 38 Ill. Dec. 509, 403 N.E.2d 740 (3d Dist. 1980) (a motion in limine should not be granted when the rules of evidence do not require that the matter at issue be excluded from the trial).

§ 1:22 Overview—Include all possible grounds for exclusion

Counsel should keep in mind that the specific grounds for exclusion must be raised at the trial level or the issue will generally be considered waived on appeal. See, e.g., *In re Detention of Sveda*, 354 Ill. App. 3d 373, 376–77, 289 Ill. Dec. 912, 820 N.E.2d 987 (1st Dist. 2004) (party waived appellate review of the claim that the trial judge should not have admitted scientific evidence without a *Frye* hearing, because although the party filed a motion in limine to exclude the evidence, the party did not raise that specific claim as a grounds for exclusion).

II. SAMPLES

◆ **Important Note:** The samples on the following pages, and at the end of each printed chapter, illustrate how the authorities cited in this text can be used to support an argument in your in limine motion briefs. The motions are examples only, and should not be reproduced verbatim for filing. The facts, parties and witnesses are fictional. The format does not necessarily comply with state or local rules. For space purposes, captions, exhibits and declarations are not included. Regarding general motion format requirements, see Illinois Supreme Court Rule 131. Also, be sure to review any local rules for the court where the motion will be filed.

Other than the samples in Chapter 1, which are included for general illustrative purposes, the samples provided throughout the balance of this text relate specifically to the subjects covered in the chapter where located.

§ 1:23 Sample in limine brief

TO: ALL PARTIES AND THEIR RESPECTIVE ATTORNEYS OF RECORD:

PLEASE TAKE NOTICE THAT plaintiff hereby moves this Court for an order excluding any and all evidence, references to evidence, testimony or argument relating to a prior automobile accident that occurred on or about March 1, 1997, and any injury to plaintiff arising from that accident.

This motion is based upon the grounds that any injuries to plaintiff arising from the prior accident are unrelated to the injuries for which plaintiff is seeking reimbursement in this case, and are therefore irrelevant. Allowing the evidence in this case would prejudice the plaintiff and cause jury confusion.

This motion is made under the provisions of Illinois case law, and is based on the supporting Memorandum of Points and Authorities, the pleadings and papers on file in this action, and upon such of the argument and evidence as may be presented prior to or at the hearing of this matter.

Dated: *[date]*

MEMORANDUM OF POINTS AND AUTHORITIES

1.
PRELIMINARY STATEMENT

This action arises from a rear-end accident that occurred on September 18, 1998, whereby the plaintiff incurred severe neck and back injuries, property damage and lost wages.

During discovery, defendant submitted several custom interrogatories regarding a prior unrelated automobile accident, which occurred on March 1, 1997. In that accident, the plaintiff broke his jaw when his face struck the steering wheel of his vehicle. Plaintiff has been completely forthcoming regarding this accident, while preserving multiple objections based on relevance and prejudice. A copy of plaintiff's Response to Defendant's Interrogatories is attached hereto as Exhibit "A."

The prior accident occurred more than 16 months before the accident in the present case. At the time of the subject accident, plaintiff's jaw was more than 95% healed, according to his prior treating physician, Dr. Mandible. Plaintiff is making no claim for the jaw injuries in this action. A copy of Dr. Mandible's Final Report is attached hereto as Exhibit "B."

Plaintiff's current treating physician, Dr. Cervical, examined the plaintiff on September 19, 1998—one day after the subject accident—and examined plaintiff's jaw. (Plaintiff identified the jaw injury on a New Patient Questionnaire prior to being examined by Dr. Cervical.) At that time, Dr. Cervical noted that the jaw appeared to be "completely healed" and noted that the plaintiff had no complaints of jaw pain. A copy of Dr. Cervical's medical report dated September 19, 1998, is attached hereto as Exhibit "C."

By this motion, plaintiff seeks an order precluding the introduction of any evidence, or mention of evidence, pertaining to plaintiff's prior accident or any injuries arising from the accident. The motion is based upon the grounds that the injury is unrelated to any claim in this case, and is therefore irrelevant and will unfairly prejudice the plaintiff and confuse the jury.

2.
THIS COURT MAY EXCLUDE PREJUDICIAL EVIDENCE IN ADVANCE OF TRIAL BY WAY OF AN IN LIMINE MOTION

This Court has the inherent power to grant a motion in limine to exclude any kind of evidence that could be objected to at trial, either as irrelevant or because it is more prejudicial than probative. *Swick v. Liautaud*, 169 Ill. 2d 504, 520–21, 215 Ill. Dec. 98, 662 N.E.2d 1238 (1996); *People v. Watkins*, 220 Ill. App. 3d 201, 163 Ill. Dec. 194, 581 N.E.2d 145 (1st Dist. 1991); *Cochran v. Great Atlantic & Pacific Tea Co., Inc.*, 203 Ill. App. 3d 935, 938, 148 Ill. Dec. 923, 561 N.E.2d 229 (5th Dist. 1990); and *Department of Public Works and Bldgs. v. Roehrig*, 45 Ill. App. 3d 189, 194–95, 3 Ill. Dec. 893, 359 N.E.2d 752 (5th Dist. 1976).

The law is clear that this Court has the authority to exclude evidence where there is a substantial danger that the probative value will be outweighed by the danger of undue prejudice. Federal Rule of Evidence 403 states:

> Although relevant, evidence may be excluded if its probative value is substantially outweighed by the danger of unfair prejudice, confusion of the issues, or misleading the jury, or by considerations of undue delay, waste of time, or needless presentation of cumulative evidence.

Although this rule has not been specifically codified in Illinois, case law has stated that Illinois has a common-law rule that is comparable to Federal Rule of Evidence 403. See *People v. Peete*, 318 Ill. App. 3d 961, 966–67, 252 Ill. Dec. 821, 743 N.E.2d 689 (4th Dist. 2001); *People v. Walker*, 335 Ill. App. 3d 102, 112, 268 Ill. Dec. 654, 779 N.E.2d 268 (2d Dist. 2002), as modified on denial of reh'g, (Oct. 24, 2002) and judgment aff'd, 211 Ill. 2d 317, 285 Ill. Dec. 519, 812 N.E.2d 339 (2004).

In addition, Illinois cases have specifically held that evidence should be excluded when the prejudicial impact of the evidence outweighs its probative value. *Department of Public Works and Bldgs. v. Roehrig*, 45 Ill. App. 3d 189, 196, 3 Ill. Dec. 893, 359 N.E.2d 752 (5th Dist. 1976) (exclusion of evidence of prior condemnations in a condemnation case because the prejudicial impact outweighs the probative value of it); *People v. Holman*, 257 Ill. App. 3d 1031, 1033–34, 196 Ill. Dec. 457, 630 N.E.2d 154 (2d Dist. 1994) (evidence is admissible if it is relevant and if the prejudicial impact does not substantially outweigh the probative value of it) and *Hulsebus v. Russian*, 118 Ill. App. 2d 174, 180–81, 254 N.E.2d 184 (2d Dist. 1969) (trial judge had discretion to exclude a gruesome photograph of the plaintiff during surgery because other evidence established the extent of the injury and because the photograph was likely to inflame and prejudice the jury). In the instant matter there is a strong probability that the admission of the plaintiff's past injuries will create a substantial danger of undue prejudice. Therefore, the authorities described above justify the preclusion of the requested evidence in this case.

Furthermore, this Court has authority to hear and determine the question of the admissibility of evidence outside the presence or hearing of the jury. See *Beasley v. Huffman Mfg. Co.*, 97 Ill. App. 3d 1, 5, 52 Ill. Dec. 560, 422 N.E.2d 241 (3d Dist. 1981) (purpose of a motion in limine is to prevent prejudice by determining admissibility issues outside of the jury's presence before the jury is exposed to the evidence); *People v. Graves*, 74 Ill. 2d 279, 279–83, 24 Ill. Dec. 153, 384 N.E.2d 1311 (1979) (contempt order against attorney was proper for mentioning an issue in front of the jury after being ordered at a side-bar conference not to do so); *Department of Public Works and Bldgs. v. Roehrig*, 45 Ill. App. 3d 189, 194–95, 3 Ill. Dec. 893, 359 N.E.2d 752 (5th Dist. 1976) (purpose of motion in limine is to prevent inadmissible evidence from being suggested to the jury) and *Maxwell v. Habel*, 92 Ill. App. 510, 1900 WL 3466 (1st Dist. 1900) (if trial judge is concerned that an offer of proof might prejudice the jury, the offer can be made outside the presence of the jury). See also Federal Rule of evidence 103(c) which provides:

> Hearing of Jury.—In jury cases, proceedings shall be conducted, to the extent practicable, so as to prevent inadmissible evidence from being suggested to the jury by any means, such as making statements or offers of proof or asking questions in the hearing of the jury.

Although this rule has not been specifically codified in Illinois, Illinois has adopted other Federal Rules of Evidence through case law. See e.g. *People v. Monroe*, 66 Ill. 2d 317, 321–22, 5 Ill. Dec. 824, 362 N.E.2d 295 (1977); and *Spencer v. Wandolowski*, 264 Ill. App. 3d 611, 617, 201 Ill. Dec. 422, 636 N.E.2d 854 (1st Dist. 1994) (adopting Federal Rule of Evidence 401).

3.
ANY REFERENCES TO PLAINTIFF'S PRIOR INJURIES ARE IRRELEVANT AND SHOULD BE EXCLUDED

This Court has authority to exclude irrelevant evidence. Federal Rule of Evidence 401 defines relevancy as,

> evidence having any tendency to make the existence of any fact that is of consequence to the determination of the action more probable or less probable than it would be without the evidence.

Illinois has adopted this definition of relevancy through case law. *People v. Monroe*, 66 Ill. 2d 317, 321–22, 5 Ill. Dec. 824, 362 N.E.2d 295 (1977); *Spencer v. Wandolowski*, 264 Ill. App. 3d 611, 617, 201 Ill. Dec. 422, 636 N.E.2d 854 (1st Dist. 1994).

Illinois case law provides that evidence may be properly excluded where it is not relevant to matters at issue. See *Preston ex rel. Preston v. Simmons*, 321 Ill. App. 3d 789, 803, 254 Ill. Dec. 647, 747 N.E.2d 1059 (1st Dist. 2001) (trial judge should not permit such wide latitude on cross-examination that it undermines the rule that only relevant evidence is admissible); *Vojas v. K mart Corp.*, 312 Ill. App. 3d 544, 552, 245 Ill. Dec. 144, 727 N.E.2d 397 (5th Dist. 2000) (the burden of establishing relevance is on the party offering the evidence); *Cochran v. Great Atlantic & Pacific Tea Co., Inc.*, 203 Ill. App. 3d 935, 937–38, 148 Ill. Dec. 923, 561 N.E.2d 229 (5th Dist. 1990) (trial judge has inherent power to exclude irrelevant evidence); *Pagel v. Yates*, 128 Ill. App. 3d 897, 903, 84 Ill. Dec. 180, 471 N.E.2d 946 (4th Dist. 1984) (exclusion of irrelevant and confusing document); and *Benson v. Bradford Mut. Fire Ins. Corp.*, 121 Ill. App. 3d 500, 510, 76 Ill. Dec. 774, 459 N.E.2d 689, 47 A.L.R. 4th 759 (2d Dist. 1984) (trial judge had discretion to exclude irrelevant witness testimony).

In the present case, plaintiff is making no claim for injuries relating to his jaw. The pertinent medical records clearly show that the prior jaw injury is in no way similar to plaintiff's neck and back injuries in this case. See Exhibits "B" and "C."

The Court should therefore exclude any and all evidence, including any mention of evidence, relating to the March 1, 1997, accident or any injuries arising from that accident.

4. EVIDENCE OF PLAINTIFF'S PRIOR ACCIDENT AND INJURIES SHOULD BE EXCLUDED TO AVOID PREJUDICIAL JURY CONFUSION

As noted above, Federal Rule of Evidence 403 states: "Although relevant, evidence may be excluded if its probative value is substantially outweighed by the danger of unfair prejudice, *confusion of the issues, or misleading the jury*, or by considerations of undue delay, waste of time, or needless presentation of cumulative evidence." (Emphasis added.) Illinois cases have stated that Illinois has a common-law rule that is comparable to Federal Rule of Evidence 403. See *People v. Walker*, 335 Ill. App. 3d 102, 112, 268 Ill. Dec. 654, 779 N.E.2d 268 (2d Dist. 2002), as modified on denial of reh'g, (Oct. 24, 2002) and judgment aff'd, 211 Ill. 2d 317, 285 Ill. Dec. 519, 812 N.E.2d 339 (2004); and *People v. Peete*, 318 Ill. App. 3d 961, 966–67, 252 Ill. Dec. 821, 743 N.E.2d 689 (4th Dist. 2001).

In addition, Illinois case law has specifically held that the Court may exclude unreliable or potentially confusing evidence. See *Bachman v. General Motors Corp.*, 332 Ill. App. 3d 760, 785–88, 267 Ill. Dec. 125, 776 N.E.2d 262 (4th Dist. 2002) (exclusion of prior occurrence evidence because the admission of it would confuse and mislead the jury); *Hulman v. Evanston Hosp. Corp.*, 259 Ill. App. 3d 133, 147–49, 197 Ill. Dec. 319, 631 N.E.2d 322 (1st Dist. 1994) (exclusion of hospital pamphlet because there was already testimony about it and because it included irrelevant material that might confuse the jury); and *Congregation of the Passion, Holy Cross Province v. Touche Ross & Co.*, 224 Ill. App. 3d 559, 578–79, 166 Ill. Dec. 642, 586 N.E.2d 600 (1st Dist. 1991), judgment aff'd, 159 Ill. 2d 137, 201 Ill. Dec. 71, 636 N.E.2d 503 (1994) (proper to exclude relevant evidence to prevent jury confusion).

In the present case, there is a substantial danger that jurors might believe that the plaintiff's prior jaw injury somehow relates to his current neck or back injuries. As is shown in Dr. Mandible's Final Report (Exhibit "B") and Dr. Cervical's Report (Exhibit "C"), the two injuries are unrelated. Any evidence of the prior injury will only serve to confuse the jury and unfairly prejudice the plaintiff.

The Court should therefore exclude any and all evidence, including any mention of evidence, relating to the March 1, 1997, accident or any injuries arising from that accident.

5.
EVIDENCE OF PHYSICAL CONDITIONS THAT ARE NOT AT ISSUE ARE PROPERLY EXCLUDED

In *Cancio v. White*, 297 Ill. App. 3d 422, 428–30, 232 Ill. Dec. 7, 697 N.E.2d 749 (1st Dist. 1998), it was error to allow evidence of plaintiff's pre-existing arthritis when there was no clear proof of a direct link to the injury that was at issue in the case.

In *Vojas v. K mart Corp.*, 312 Ill. App. 3d 544, 551–53, 245 Ill. Dec. 144, 727 N.E.2d 397 (5th Dist. 2000), the court held that the party offering the evidence of a prior injury must prove that it is relevant to the current injury.

In addition, in the case of *Obszanski v. Foster Wheeler Const., Inc.*, 328 Ill. App. 3d 550, 558–60, 262 Ill. Dec. 585, 765 N.E.2d 1193 (1st Dist. 2002), the court ruled that the defendant should not have been permitted to introduce evidence of the plaintiff's subsequent injury unless the defendant could establish that the new injury was the cause of the plaintiff's current distress.

Based on the foregoing authorities, this Court should exclude any references to physical injuries or ailments that are not at issue in this cause.

6.
CONCLUSION

Based on the foregoing, the plaintiff respectfully requests that this Court exclude any testimony or documentary evidence, or mention of any evidence, regarding the accident dated March 1, 1997, or any injuries arising from that accident.

Dated: *[date]*

By: ________________
[name of counsel]
Attorneys for PLAINTIFF,
[name of plaintiff]

§ 1:24 Sample in limine order

ORDER

GOOD CAUSE APPEARING, IT IS HEREBY ORDERED that *[insert requested evidentiary ruling, e.g., defendants shall not present any testimony or evidence and shall not argue or re-*

fer to the plaintiff's prior accident of March 1, 1997, or any injuries arising from that accident.]

IT IS HEREBY FURTHER ORDERED that defendants, defendants' counsel and defendants' witnesses shall:

1. Not mention, refer to, or attempt to convey to the jury in any manner, either directly or indirectly, any of the facts mentioned in this Motion, without first obtaining permission of the Court, outside the presence and hearing of the jury; and
2. Not make any reference to the fact that this motion has been filed; and
3. Warn and caution each of defendants' witnesses to strictly follow the same instructions.

Dated: *[date]*

____

JUDGE OF THE SUPERIOR COURT

Chapter 2

Prejudicial Evidence

I. MOTION AUTHORITIES

A. MOTION TO EXCLUDE PREJUDICIAL EVIDENCE, GENERALLY

B. MOTION TO EXCLUDE EVIDENCE THAT WILL WASTE TIME

C. MOTION TO EXCLUDE CONFUSING OR MISLEADING EVIDENCE

D. MOTION TO EXCLUDE EVIDENCE USED TO CREATE AN EMOTIONAL BIAS

E. MOTION TO EXCLUDE OR LIMIT CUMULATIVE EVIDENCE

II. SAMPLE MOTIONS

I. MOTION AUTHORITIES

A. MOTION TO EXCLUDE PREJUDICIAL EVIDENCE, GENERALLY

All "good" evidence that supports the proponent's position will naturally be "prejudicial" to the opponent. The issue for the court to decide is whether any *undue* prejudice outweighs the probative value of the evidence. Where the undue prejudice outweighs the probative value, the evidence should be excluded.

§ 2:1 Suggested motion text

[Name of moving party] hereby moves this Court for an order excluding any and all evidence, references to evidence, testimony or argument relating to *[describe prejudicial evidence]*. The motion is based upon the ground that the probative value of the evidence is substantially outweighed by the danger of undue prejudice to *[name of moving party]*.

§ 2:2 Motion summary

This motion is used to exclude prejudicial evidence. The motion is primarily based upon the balancing test that has been established through Illinois case law. Such case law provides the key source for excluding evidence that will result in an undue consumption of time or will create a substantial danger of undue prejudice, confusion of issues or misleading of the jury. In general, even relevant evidence may be excluded if the probative value is substantially outweighed by the risk of undue prejudice. See *People v. Walker*, 335 Ill. App. 3d 102, 112–13, 268 Ill. Dec. 654, 779 N.E.2d 268 (2d Dist. 2002), as modified on denial of reh'g, (Oct. 24, 2002) and judgment aff'd, 211 Ill. 2d 317, 285 Ill. Dec. 519, 812 N.E.2d 339 (2004); *People v. Peete*, 318 Ill. App. 3d 961, 967–68, 252 Ill. Dec. 821, 743 N.E.2d 689 (4th Dist. 2001); *Gossard v. Kalra*, 291 Ill. App. 3d 180, 182, 225 Ill. Dec. 725, 684 N.E.2d 410 (4th Dist. 1997); and *Rusher v. Smith*, 70 Ill. App. 3d 889, 894, 26 Ill. Dec. 905, 388 N.E.2d 906 (5th Dist. 1979).

◆ **Note From the Editor:** The cases cited in this section support the general proposition that prejudicial evidence may be excluded through a balancing test. Because of the importance of this concept, you will find these cases cited throughout the balance of this text, in addition to more specific case authorities supporting your point. While this format might appear repetitive when chapters are read sequentially, we have chosen to include multiple references to certain key concepts and cases in every chapter as a reminder that they should be discussed *in addition to* whatever other authorities may support your motion. Note that we have also followed a similar format for the citations relating to irrelevant evidence (see Chapter 3, Irrelevant Evidence).

§ 2:3 Supporting authorities—Exclusion of prejudicial evidence

Federal Rule of Evidence 403 states:

> Although relevant, evidence may be excluded if its probative value is substantially outweighed by the danger of unfair prejudice, confusion of the issues, or misleading the jury, or by considerations of undue delay, waste of time, or needless presentation of cumulative evidence.

It must be noted that this Rule has not been codified in Illinois. However, Illinois cases have stated that Illinois has a common-law rule that is comparable to Federal Rule of Evidence 403. See *People v. Walker*, 335 Ill. App. 3d 102, 112, 268 Ill. Dec. 654, 779 N.E.2d 268 (2d Dist. 2002), as modified on denial of reh'g, (Oct. 24, 2002) and judgment aff'd, 211 Ill. 2d 317, 285 Ill. Dec. 519, 812 N.E.2d 339 (2004); and *People v. Peete*, 318 Ill. App. 3d 961, 966–67, 252 Ill. Dec. 821, 743 N.E.2d 689 (4th Dist. 2001). Therefore, it is arguable that Federal Rule of Evidence 403 can be considered as persuasive authority in Illinois.

Donnellan v. First Student, Inc, 383 Ill.App.3d 1040, 1053–56, 891 N.E.2d 463 (1st Dist. 2008) (a surveillance video was properly excluded as unfairly prejudicial and confusing).

Boren v. BOC Group, Inc., 385 Ill.App.3d 248, 256–58, 895 N.E.2d 53 (5th Dist. 2008) (counsel's remarks describing lawsuits like the plaintiff's as a "cottage industry" were inflammatory and prejudicial and caused grounds for granting a new trial).

LaSalle Bank N.A. v. C/HCA Development Corp., 384 Ill.App.3d 806, 820–23, 893 N.E.2d 949 (1st Dist. 2008) (trial court had discretion to determine that evidence that a defendant doctor had a general financial incentive to avoid making referrals to specialists was unfairly prejudicial in this case because the defendant doctor had actually made referrals to specialists in other instances).

Downey v. Dunnington, 384 Ill.App.3d 350, 387–89, 895 N.E.2d 271 (4th Dist. 2008) (evidence that the defendant's father was a minister was irrelevant and prejudicial and should not have been admitted but the error was harmless).

Dukes v. Pneumo Abex Corp., 386 Ill.App.3d 425, 438–39, 900 N.E.2d 1128 (4th Dist. 2008) (a letter written by a now deceased employee of a party, on a subject outside of the scope of the individual's employment responsibilities, was inflammatory and prejudicial and should not have been considered as an admission of a party).

Boren v. BOC Group, Inc., 385 Ill.App.3d 248, 254–57, 895 N.E.2d 53 (5th Dist. 2008) (photograph of a billboard advertisement which was offered to suggest that cases like the plaintiff's case were solicited and created by lawyers was irrelevant, prejudicial, misleading and confusing and caused grounds for granting a new trial).

Aguirre v. City of Chicago, 382 Ill. App. 3d 89, 320 Ill. Dec. 512, 887 N.E.2d 656 (1st Dist. 2008) (polygraph evidence was excluded as more prejudicial than probative and as confusing to the jury).

Yoder v. Ferguson, 381 Ill. App. 3d 353, 319 Ill. Dec. 380, 885

N.E.2d 1060 (1st Dist. 2008), appeal pending, (Sept. 1, 2008) (trial court had discretion to exclude evidence of a derogatory term from a statement because the prejudicial impact of it outweighed its probative value).

Werner v. Nebal, 377 Ill. App. 3d 447, 454–56, 316 Ill. Dec. 89, 878 N.E.2d 811 (1st Dist. 2007) (trial court properly excluded evidence regarding child support arrearages and threatening statements, as more prejudicial than probative).

People v. Evans, 373 Ill. App. 3d 948, 960–61, 311 Ill. Dec. 907, 869 N.E.2d 920 (1st Dist. 2007), appeal denied, 225 Ill. 2d 648, 314 Ill. Dec. 830, 875 N.E.2d 1117 (2007) (evidence of weapons, other than the murder weapon, should not have been admitted) (harmless error).

People v. Robinson, 368 Ill. App. 3d 963, 974-75, 307 Ill. Dec. 232, 859 N.E.2d 232 (1st Dist. 2006), appeal denied, 223 Ill. 2d 670, 310 Ill. Dec. 255, 865 N.E.2d 975 (2007) (in an aggravated DUI case, evidence of the defendant's two prior DUIs was unfairly prejudicial and should not have been admitted).

Spyrka v. County of Cook, 366 Ill. App. 3d 156, 165-69, 303 Ill. Dec. 613, 851 N.E.2d 800 (1st Dist. 2006) (video animation should not have been admitted because it was not used as a demonstrative aid to help the jury understand the testimony but rather was prejudicial and confusing to the jury when it appeared to re-enact the actual incident).

People v. Calderon, 369 Ill. App. 3d 221, 228-29, 307 Ill. Dec. 486, 859 N.E.2d 1163 (2d Dist. 2006) (trial court did not abuse its discretion by allowing a witness to be impeached with evidence of his most recent felony conviction and by excluding evidence of his two other felony convictions as more prejudicial than probative).

Thornton v. Garcini, 364 Ill. App. 3d 612, 617–18, 301 Ill. Dec. 386, 846 N.E.2d 989 (3d Dist. 2006) (when prejudicial newspaper articles, which favored one party over the other, had been seen by some of the jurors, the trial court erred by failing to grant a mistrial).

People v. Boand, 362 Ill. App. 3d 106, 124–26, 297 Ill. Dec. 880, 838 N.E.2d 367 (2d Dist. 2005) (the trial court erred by admitting evidence of certain uncharged sex offenses in a trial for drug-induced homicide and involuntary manslaughter, where the evidence was irrelevant and prejudicial).

Nelson v. Upadhyaya, 361 Ill. App. 3d 415, 422–23, 297 Ill. Dec. 53, 836 N.E.2d 784 (1st Dist. 2005) (trial court erred by admitting articles regarding the proper standard of care that were published after the incident in question where the articles were irrelevant and prejudicial when they were offered to suggest the standard of care at the time of the incident).

People v. Bohn, 362 Ill. App. 3d 485, 486–91, 298 Ill. Dec. 649, 840 N.E.2d 762 (2d Dist. 2005) (the trial court did not abuse its discretion by excluding evidence that a witness was arrested for allegedly possessing the same drugs that the defendant was accused of possessing; evidence was irrelevant, prejudicial and confusing).

Hubbert v. Dell Corp., 359 Ill. App. 3d 976, 985, 296 Ill. Dec. 258, 835 N.E.2d 113, 61 U.C.C. Rep. Serv. 2d 114 (5th Dist. 2005) (the trial court erred by admitting a deposition from another case, where the party against whom the deposition was admitted had not been present at the deposition and did not have the opportunity to cross-examine the deponent).

Krklus v. Stanley, 359 Ill. App. 3d 471, 295 Ill. Dec. 746, 833 N.E.2d 952, 965–66 (1st Dist. 2005) (suggestion that a party had fabricated evidence as a cover-up attempt was properly excluded as speculative and as more prejudicial than probative).

People v. Whirl, 351 Ill. App. 3d 464, 466–67, 286 Ill. Dec. 646, 814 N.E.2d 872 (2d Dist. 2004) (trial court failed to properly balance the prejudicial impact of prior convictions for similar offenses against the probative value of the convictions; trial judge erred by admitting impeachment evidence of multiple prior convictions).

Montana v. Egelhoff, 518 U.S. 37, 41–43, 116 S. Ct. 2013, 135 L. Ed. 2d 361 (1996) (Due Process does not guarantee the right to introduce all relevant evidence and therefore, Federal Rule of Evidence 403 does not violate Due Process).

People v. Holman, 257 Ill. App. 3d 1031, 1033–34, 196 Ill. Dec. 457, 630 N.E.2d 154 (2d Dist. 1994) (evidence is admissible if it is relevant and if the prejudicial impact does not substantially outweigh the probative value of it).

Cunningham v. Millers General Ins. Co., 227 Ill. App. 3d 201, 205, 169 Ill. Dec. 200, 591 N.E.2d 80 (4th Dist. 1992) (if evidence could be prejudicial, it might be prudent to grant a motion in limine until a clear basis for the admission of the evidence appears).

Drews v. Gobel Freight Lines, Inc., 144 Ill. 2d 84, 100-01, 161 Ill. Dec. 324, 578 N.E.2d 970 (1991) (trial judge has discretion to determine whether or not evidence is too gruesome).

Department of Public Works and Bldgs. v. Roehrig, 45 Ill. App. 3d 189, 196, 3 Ill. Dec. 893, 359 N.E.2d 752 (5th Dist. 1976) (exclusion of evidence because the prejudicial impact outweighs the probative value of it).

Hulsebus v. Russian, 118 Ill. App. 2d 174, 180–81, 254 N.E.2d 184 (2d Dist. 1969) (trial judge had discretion to exclude gruesome evidence because it was cumulative and likely to inflame and prejudice the jury).

People v. Lefler, 38 Ill. 2d 216, 221–22, 230 N.E.2d 827 (1967) (evidence should not have been admitted when the nature of the injuries was not disputed and it was likely to arouse strong emotions).

See also 725 ILCS 5/115-7 (2002) (in prosecutions for certain sexual offenses, evidence of the victim's prior sexual activity or reputation is not admissible unless it meets specific relevancy standards and even then, only if the trial judge determines that the probative value of the evidence outweighs the prejudicial impact of it).

§ 2:4 Opposing authorities

Bosco v. Janowitz, 388 Ill.App.3d 450, 463, 903 N.E.2d 756 (1st Dist. 2009) (evidence that the plaintiff failed to follow up with the defendant doctor was relevant to the plaintiff's malpractice claim and was not unfairly prejudicial).

Donnellan v. First Student, Inc, 383 Ill.App.3d 1040, 1051–52, 891 N.E.2d 463 (1st Dist. 2008) (a "day in the life video" was relevant and not unfairly prejudicial merely because it showed the amount of pain that plaintiff was experiencing).

People v. Gonzalez, 379 Ill. App. 3d 941, 318 Ill. Dec. 673, 884 N.E.2d 228, 235–37 (1st Dist. 2008), appeal pending, (May 1, 2008) and appeal denied, 228 Ill. 2d 541, 321 Ill. Dec. 558, 889 N.E.2d 1118 (2008) (evidence of another murder by the defendant was admissible to explain the course of the investigation regarding the charged murder).

Petraski v. Thedos, 382 Ill. App. 3d 22, 320 Ill. Dec. 244, 887 N.E.2d 24 (1st Dist. 2008), appeal denied, 229 Ill. 2d 657, 325 Ill. Dec. 15, 897 N.E.2d 263 (2008) (trial court erred by excluding an expert's opinion regarding the plaintiff's intoxication that was based upon extrapolation from blood that was drawn after the incident in question because the evidence was relevant and reliable and not unfairly prejudicial).

People v. Evans, 373 Ill. App. 3d 948, 958–59, 311 Ill. Dec. 907, 869 N.E.2d 920 (1st Dist. 2007), appeal denied, 225 Ill. 2d 648, 314 Ill. Dec. 830, 875 N.E.2d 1117 (2007) (other crimes evidence was relevant because it placed the defendant in close proximity to the scene of the charged crime).

People v. Dixon, 378 Ill. App. 3d 535, 549–51, 317 Ill. Dec. 788, 882 N.E.2d 668 (1st Dist. 2007), appeal denied, 227 Ill. 2d

587, 321 Ill. Dec. 253, 888 N.E.2d 1186 (2008) (evidence regarding fear of gang retaliation was relevant to the issue of why certain witnesses recanted their prior statements and it was not unfairly prejudicial).

Shaheen v. Advantage Moving and Storage, Inc., 369 Ill. App. 3d 535, 543-44, 307 Ill. Dec. 721, 860 N.E.2d 375 (1st Dist. 2006) (the trial court had discretion to allow an expert to be questioned about the fact that he had been previously hired as an expert by the other party's attorney in a different case).

Shaheen v. Advantage Moving and Storage, Inc., 369 Ill. App. 3d 535, 543-44, 307 Ill. Dec. 721, 860 N.E.2d 375 (1st Dist. 2006) (a party can question a testifying expert about whether he is being compensated for his expert testimony).

People v. Meyers, 367 Ill. App. 3d 402, 416-17, 304 Ill. Dec. 944, 854 N.E.2d 286 (2d Dist. 2006) (in a trial for resisting a peace officer and aggravated battery of a peace officer, impeachment evidence regarding the defendant's prior conviction for aggravated fleeing or attempting to elude a police officer was relevant regarding the issue of his credibility and it was not unfairly prejudicial).

People v. Smith, 362 Ill. App. 3d 1062, 1085–86, 299 Ill. Dec. 77, 841 N.E.2d 489 (1st Dist. 2005) (a photograph depicting the victim in a military uniform was not unduly inflammatory or prejudicial).

People v. Smith, 362 Ill. App. 3d 1062, 1085, 299 Ill. Dec. 77, 841 N.E.2d 489 (1st Dist. 2005) (a witness' testimony that he was currently in the witness protection program was not unduly prejudicial).

People v. Smith, 362 Ill. App. 3d 1062, 1085–86, 299 Ill. Dec. 77, 841 N.E.2d 489 (1st Dist. 2005) (testimony that the murder occurred the day after Palm Sunday was proper to explain why the victim was present at the time of the offense; evidence was not unduly prejudicial).

People v. Baugh, 358 Ill. App. 3d 718, 739–40, 295 Ill. Dec. 453, 832 N.E.2d 903 (1st Dist. 2005) (when the defendant had alleged that his confession was coerced, the prosecutor was entitled to cross-examine the defendant about his state of mind at the time of the confession, over the defendant's objection that the cross-examination was improper harassment and humiliation).

People v. Blankenship, 353 Ill. App. 3d 322, 326, 289 Ill. Dec. 137, 819 N.E.2d 49 (3d Dist. 2004) (trial court did not abuse its discretion by allowing evidence of two prior convictions to be used to impeach defendant, over the defendant's objection that the prior convictions were too similar to the charged offense and thus were unduly prejudicial).

People v. Szudy, 262 Ill. App. 3d 695, 712–14, 200 Ill. Dec. 462, 635 N.E.2d 801 (1st Dist. 1994) (evidence is admissible if it tends to establish a fact in issue, even if it is gruesome, unless the trial judge determines that the prejudicial impact substantially outweighs the probative value of it).

Mack v. First Sec. Bank of Chicago, 158 Ill. App. 3d 497, 504–05, 110 Ill. Dec. 537, 511 N.E.2d 714 (1st Dist. 1987) (trial judge's ruling barring evidence regarding the opinions of the defendant's employee about the race of the plaintiff was improper in that it unduly restricted the plaintiff's presentation of her case).

Burris v. Madison County, 154 Ill. App. 3d 1064, 1070, 107 Ill. Dec. 898, 507 N.E.2d 1267 (5th Dist. 1987) (a trial judge must be cautious in granting a motion in limine so as not to improperly restrict a party's presentation of its case).

Jones v. Greer, 627 F. Supp. 1481, 1487–88 (C.D. Ill. 1986) (Under Federal Rule of Evidence 403, evidence is not prejudicial merely because it harms a party's case; rather the evidence must be of such a character that it suggests a decision based upon an improper basis).

Bradley v. Caterpillar Tractor Co., 75 Ill. App. 3d 890, 899–900, 31 Ill. Dec. 623, 394 N.E.2d 825 (5th Dist. 1979) (trial judge should not enter an order in limine if the order is so complicated that compliance with it would be difficult if that difficulty outweighs the prejudicial impact of failing to grant the motion).

People v. Newbury, 53 Ill. 2d 228, 242, 290 N.E.2d 592 (1972) (trial judge did not improperly admit evidence when it was relevant to demonstrate the manner of death, even if it was capable of arousing strong emotions).

B. MOTION TO EXCLUDE EVIDENCE THAT WILL WASTE TIME

§ 2:5 Suggested motion text

[Name of moving party] hereby moves this Court for an order excluding any and all evidence, references to evidence, testimony or argument relating to *[describe time-wasting evidence]*. The motion is based upon the ground that there is a substantial danger that introduction of the evidence will necessitate an undue consumption of time.

§ 2:6 Motion summary

This motion is used to exclude evidence that threatens to

consume an undue amount of time. It is based on Illinois case law, which provides the authority for the exclusion of such evidence. See e.g. *Trower v. Jones*, 121 Ill. 2d 211, 219, 117 Ill. Dec. 136, 520 N.E.2d 297 (1988).

§ 2:7 Supporting authorities—Exclusion of time-wasting evidence

Federal Rule of Evidence 403 states:

> Although relevant, evidence may be excluded if its probative value is substantially outweighed by the danger of unfair prejudice, confusion of the issues, or misleading the jury, *or by considerations of undue delay, waste of time,* or needless presentation of cumulative evidence. (Emphasis added.)

It must be noted that this Rule has not been codified in Illinois. However, Illinois cases have stated that Illinois has a common-law rule that is comparable to Federal Rule of Evidence 403. See *People v. Walker*, 335 Ill. App. 3d 102, 112, 268 Ill. Dec. 654, 779 N.E.2d 268 (2d Dist. 2002), as modified on denial of reh'g, (Oct. 24, 2002) and judgment aff'd, 211 Ill. 2d 317, 285 Ill. Dec. 519, 812 N.E.2d 339 (2004); and *People v. Peete*, 318 Ill. App. 3d 961, 966–67, 252 Ill. Dec. 821, 743 N.E.2d 689 (4th Dist. 2001). Therefore, it is arguable that Federal Rule of Evidence 403 can be considered as persuasive authority in Illinois.

CFC Investment, L.L.C. v. McLean, 387 Ill.App.3d 520, 530–31, 900 N.E.2d 716 (1st Dist. 2008) (evidence of conduct that was outside of the scope of the complaint was excluded as unduly confusing, misleading and time wasting).

Dillon v. Evanston Hosp., 199 Ill. 2d 483, 494–96, 264 Ill. Dec. 653, 771 N.E.2d 357 (2002) (no abuse of discretion when the trial judge limited cumulative testimony of an expert witness and told the jury that he did so in order to more efficiently use their time).

Kurrack v. American Dist. Telegraph Co., 252 Ill. App. 3d 885, 895–96, 192 Ill. Dec. 520, 625 N.E.2d 675 (1st Dist. 1993) (exclusion of repetitive rebuttal testimony because if there are no limits placed on expert testimony, trials would never conclude).

Palumbo v. Kuiken, 201 Ill. App. 3d 785, 791–92, 147 Ill. Dec. 206, 559 N.E.2d 206 (1st Dist. 1990) (exclusion of a videotape that would have wasted time through the presentation of cumulative evidence).

Trower v. Jones, 121 Ill. 2d 211, 219–21, 117 Ill. Dec. 136,

520 N.E.2d 297 (1988) (proper for a trial judge to limit rehabilitation of an expert witness regarding the witness' credentials, in order to prevent confusion of the issues and undue delay).

§ 2:8 Opposing authorities

Hunt v. Harrison, 303 Ill. App. 3d 54, 57-58, 236 Ill. Dec. 387, 707 N.E.2d 232 (1st Dist. 1999) (trial court should not have barred the only disinterested witness from testifying, even though the testimony of that witness was cumulative of other testimony).

Hubbard v. Sherman Hosp., 292 Ill. App. 3d 148, 155, 226 Ill. Dec. 393, 685 N.E.2d 648 (2d Dist. 1997) (testimony of a disinterested expert was properly allowed in addition to the testimony of the defendant's agents even though the defendant's agents could also qualify as experts).

Burris v. Madison County, 154 Ill. App. 3d 1064, 1070, 107 Ill. Dec. 898, 507 N.E.2d 1267 (5th Dist. 1987) (a trial judge must be cautious in granting a motion in limine so as not to improperly restrict a party's presentation of its case).

People v. Frazier, 129 Ill. App. 3d 704, 710–11, 84 Ill. Dec. 787, 472 N.E.2d 1183 (2d Dist. 1984) (testimony of doctors and others regarding injuries was permitted even though cumulative in part, because each witness added different facts to the case).

Reidelberger v. Highland Body Shop, Inc., 83 Ill. 2d 545, 549–50, 48 Ill. Dec. 237, 416 N.E.2d 268 (1981) (a trial judge must be cautious that its exclusionary order does not improperly restrict the presentation of a party's case).

C. MOTION TO EXCLUDE CONFUSING OR MISLEADING EVIDENCE

§ 2:9 Suggested motion text

[Name of moving party] hereby moves this Court for an order excluding any and all evidence, references to evidence, testimony or argument relating to *[describe confusing evidence]*. The motion is based upon the ground that there is a substantial danger that the evidence will confuse the issues or mislead the jury.

§ 2:10 Motion summary

This motion is used to exclude evidence that will create a substantial danger of confusing the issues or misleading the jury. The motion is based upon Illinois case law. See e.g. *Hulman v. Evanston Hosp. Corp.*, 259 Ill. App. 3d 133, 147–48, 197 Ill. Dec. 319, 631 N.E.2d 322 (1st Dist. 1994).

Motions in limine can and should be used to exclude confusing and misleading evidence to keep the trial focused on the true issues in the case. If a question exists as to how the other party intends to use evidence that appears to be confusing, misleading, or unduly prejudicial, a motion in limine should be presented to exclude the evidence or, at the very least, flush out the other party's intentions with respect to the evidence.

§ 2:11 Supporting authorities—Exclusion of confusing or misleading evidence

Federal Rule of Evidence 403 states:

> Although relevant, evidence may be excluded if its probative value is substantially outweighed by the danger of unfair prejudice, *confusion of the issues, or misleading the jury*, or by considerations of undue delay, waste of time, or needless presentation of cumulative evidence. (Emphasis added.)

It must be noted that this Rule has not been codified in Illinois. However, Illinois cases have stated that Illinois has a common-law rule that is comparable to Federal Rule of Evidence 403. See *People v. Walker*, 335 Ill. App. 3d 102, 112, 268 Ill. Dec. 654, 779 N.E.2d 268 (2d Dist. 2002), as modified on denial of reh'g, (Oct. 24, 2002) and judgment aff'd, 211 Ill. 2d 317, 285 Ill. Dec. 519, 812 N.E.2d 339 (2004); and *People v. Peete*, 318 Ill. App. 3d 961, 966–67, 252 Ill. Dec. 821, 743 N.E.2d 689 (4th Dist. 2001). Therefore, it is arguable that Federal Rule of Evidence 403 can be considered as persuasive authority in Illinois.

Donnellan v. First Student, Inc, 383 Ill.App.3d 1040, 1053–56, 891 N.E.2d 463 (1st Dist. 2008) (a surveillance video was properly excluded as unfairly prejudicial and confusing).

CFC Investment, L.L.C. v. McLean, 387 Ill.App.3d 520, 530–31, 900 N.E.2d 716 (1st Dist. 2008) (evidence of conduct that was outside of the scope of the complaint was excluded as unduly confusing, misleading and time wasting).

Boren v. BOC Group, Inc., 385 Ill.App.3d 248, 255–56, 895 N.E.2d 53 (5th Dist. 2008) (a photograph of a billboard advertisement could not be used as a demonstrative aid to support expert testimony because the expert lacked knowledge of the circumstances surrounding the creation of the billboard and it was confusing and not helpful to explain the expert witness' testimony).

LaSalle Bank N.A. v. C/HCA Development Corp., 384 Ill.App.3d 806, 820–23, 893 N.E.2d 949 (1st Dist. 2008) (trial court had discretion to determine that evidence that a defendant doctor had a general financial incentive to avoid making referrals to specialists was unfairly prejudicial in this case because the defendant doctor had actually made referrals to specialists in other instances).

Boren v. BOC Group, Inc., 385 Ill.App.3d 248, 254–57, 895 N.E.2d 53 (5th Dist. 2008) (photograph of a billboard advertisement which was offered to suggest that cases like the plaintiff's case were solicited and created by lawyers was irrelevant, prejudicial, misleading and confusing and caused grounds for granting a new trial).

Aguirre v. City of Chicago, 382 Ill. App. 3d 89, 320 Ill. Dec. 512, 887 N.E.2d 656 (1st Dist. 2008) (polygraph evidence was excluded as more prejudicial than probative and as confusing to the jury).

Werner v. Nebal, 377 Ill. App. 3d 447, 455–56, 316 Ill. Dec. 89, 878 N.E.2d 811 (1st Dist. 2007) (in a dram shop action, trial court properly excluded evidence of the plaintiff's statements to paramedics regarding how many drinks he had, as confusing to the jury).

Werner v. Nebal, 377 Ill. App. 3d 447, 456, 316 Ill. Dec. 89, 878 N.E.2d 811 (1st Dist. 2007) (trial court properly denied a party's request for a jury instruction that conflicted with the evidence at trial and that would have confused the jury).

Webber v. Wight & Co., 368 Ill. App. 3d 1007, 1023-26, 306 Ill. Dec. 782, 858 N.E.2d 579 (1st Dist. 2006), appeal denied, 223 Ill. 2d 686, 310 Ill. Dec. 258, 865 N.E.2d 978 (2007) (In this retaliatory discharge claim, the trial court did not abuse its discretion by excluding the plaintiff's testimony that the defendant was engaging in "illegal" activities as unreliable and irrelevant).

Spyrka v. County of Cook, 366 Ill. App. 3d 156, 165-69, 303 Ill. Dec. 613, 851 N.E.2d 800 (1st Dist. 2006) (video animation should not have been admitted because it was not used as a demonstrative aid to help the jury understand the testimony but rather was prejudicial and confusing to the jury when it appeared to re-enact the actual incident).

People v. Collins, 366 Ill. App. 3d 885, 897-98, 304 Ill. Dec. 478, 853 N.E.2d 10 (1st Dist. 2006) (details about the actual events underlying the convictions of a witness were properly excluded on the basis that they would "muddy the waters.").

Troyan v. Reyes, 367 Ill. App. 3d 729, 738, 305 Ill. Dec. 451, 855 N.E.2d 967 (3d Dist. 2006) (radiology report with complicated medical terms may be excluded if confusing to the jury).

People v. Bohn, 362 Ill. App. 3d 485, 486–91, 298 Ill. Dec.

649, 840 N.E.2d 762 (2d Dist. 2005) (the trial court did not abuse its discretion by excluding evidence that a witness was arrested for allegedly possessing the same drugs that the defendant was accused of possessing; evidence was irrelevant, prejudicial and confusing).

Chapman v. Hubbard Woods Motors, Inc., 351 Ill. App. 3d 99, 110–11, 285 Ill. Dec. 569, 812 N.E.2d 389 (1st Dist. 2004) (no abuse of discretion to exclude, as confusing and misleading, evidence that a party's expert was originally retained by the opposing party).

Bachman v. General Motors Corp., 332 Ill. App. 3d 760, 785–88, 267 Ill. Dec. 125, 776 N.E.2d 262 (4th Dist. 2002) (exclusion of prior occurrence evidence because the admission of it would confuse and mislead the jury).

Hulman v. Evanston Hosp. Corp., 259 Ill. App. 3d 133, 147–49, 197 Ill. Dec. 319, 631 N.E.2d 322 (1st Dist. 1994) (exclusion of hospital pamphlet because there was already testimony about it and because it included irrelevant material that might confuse the jury).

Congregation of the Passion, Holy Cross Province v. Touche Ross & Co., 224 Ill. App. 3d 559, 578–79, 166 Ill. Dec. 642, 586 N.E.2d 600 (1st Dist. 1991), judgment aff'd, 159 Ill. 2d 137, 201 Ill. Dec. 71, 636 N.E.2d 503 (1994) (proper to exclude relevant evidence to prevent jury confusion).

Pagel v. Yates, 128 Ill. App. 3d 897, 903, 84 Ill. Dec. 180, 471 N.E.2d 946 (4th Dist. 1984) (exclusion of documents regarding misidentification of horse when witness already testified to that fact and the documents would confuse the issues).

§ 2:12 Opposing authorities

Smith v. Joy Marvin, M.D., 377 Ill. App. 3d 562, 567–68, 317 Ill. Dec. 31, 880 N.E.2d 1023 (3d Dist. 2007), appeal pending, (May 1, 2008) and appeal denied, 228 Ill. 2d 554, 321 Ill. Dec. 562, 889 N.E.2d 1122 (2008) (the trial court did not mislead the jury by providing a non-IPI jury instruction that was an accurate statement of the law).

Burris v. Madison County, 154 Ill. App. 3d 1064, 1070, 107 Ill. Dec. 898, 507 N.E.2d 1267 (5th Dist. 1987) (a trial judge must be cautious in granting a motion in limine so as not to improperly restrict a party's presentation of its case).

Reidelberger v. Highland Body Shop, Inc., 83 Ill. 2d 545, 549–50, 48 Ill. Dec. 237, 416 N.E.2d 268 (1981) (a trial judge must be cautious that its exclusionary order does not improperly restrict the presentation of a party's case).

Veer v. Hagemann, 334 Ill. 23, 27–28, 165 N.E. 175 (1929) (trial judge has discretion whether to admit evidence on points that have been conceded or that might confuse the issues).

D. MOTION TO EXCLUDE EVIDENCE USED TO CREATE AN EMOTIONAL BIAS

§ 2:13 Suggested motion text

[Name of moving party] hereby moves this Court for an order excluding any and all evidence, references to evidence, testimony or argument relating to *[describe prejudicial evidence]*. The motion is based upon the ground that there is a substantial danger that the evidence will unfairly inflame the passions or emotions of the jurors.

§ 2:14 Motion summary

This motion is used to exclude evidence that is used to create an unfair emotional bias against a party. The motion is based upon Illinois cases that have approved of the exclusion of evidence that is intended principally to arouse the passions of the jury or inflame juror emotions. See e.g. *Hulsebus v. Russian*, 118 Ill. App. 2d 174, 180–81, 254 N.E.2d 184 (2d Dist. 1969).

§ 2:15 Supporting authorities—Exclusion of prejudicial evidence, generally

Federal Rule of Evidence 403 states:

> Although relevant, evidence may be excluded if its probative value is substantially outweighed by the danger of unfair prejudice, confusion of the issues, or misleading the jury, or by considerations of undue delay, waste of time, or needless presentation of cumulative evidence.

It must be noted that this Rule has not been codified in Illinois. However, Illinois cases have stated that Illinois has a common-law rule that is comparable to Federal Rule of Evidence 403. See and *People v. Walker*, 335 Ill. App. 3d 102, 112, 268 Ill. Dec. 654, 779 N.E.2d 268 (2d Dist. 2002), as modified on denial of reh'g, (Oct. 24, 2002) and judgment aff'd, 211 Ill. 2d 317, 285 Ill. Dec. 519, 812 N.E.2d 339 (2004); *People v. Peete*, 318 Ill. App. 3d 961, 966–67, 252 Ill. Dec. 821, 743 N.E.2d 689 (4th Dist. 2001). Therefore, it is arguable that Federal Rule of Evidence 403 can be considered as persuasive authority in Illinois.

In general, even relevant evidence may be excluded if the probative value is substantially outweighed by the risk of undue prejudice. See *People v. Walker*, 335 Ill. App. 3d 102,

112–13, 268 Ill. Dec. 654, 779 N.E.2d 268 (2d Dist. 2002), as modified on denial of reh'g, (Oct. 24, 2002) and judgment aff'd, 211 Ill. 2d 317, 285 Ill. Dec. 519, 812 N.E.2d 339 (2004); *People v. Peete*, 318 Ill. App. 3d 961, 967–68, 252 Ill. Dec. 821, 743 N.E.2d 689 (4th Dist. 2001); *Gossard v. Kalra*, 291 Ill. App. 3d 180, 182, 225 Ill. Dec. 725, 684 N.E.2d 410 (4th Dist. 1997); and *Rusher v. Smith*, 70 Ill. App. 3d 889, 894, 26 Ill. Dec. 905, 388 N.E.2d 906 (5th Dist. 1979).

For expanded citations on the exclusion of prejudicial evidence, see § 2:1 to § 2:4.

§ 2:16 Supporting authorities—Exclusion of evidence intended to inflame jurors' emotions

Motions to exclude evidence intended to inflame jurors' emotions are especially important for defense counsel in cases involving catastrophic injuries. In cases of close liability, this evidence, if admitted, can sway the jury to find in favor of the plaintiff and against the defendant. In cases with strong proof of liability, this type of evidence can substantially increase the plaintiff's verdict. Even if an objection during trial is sustained, the court's instruction to the jury to disregard the evidence will not, in all likelihood, undo any damage that was done. Therefore, it is important for defense counsel to file a motion in limine to prevent the jury from hearing the evidence in the first place.

Dukes v. Pneumo Abex Corp., 386 Ill.App.3d 425, 438–39, 900 N.E.2d 1128 (4th Dist. 2008) (a letter written by a now deceased employee of a party, on a subject outside of the scope of the individual's employment responsibilities, was inflammatory and prejudicial and should not have been considered as an admission of a party).

Boren v. BOC Group, Inc., 385 Ill.App.3d 248, 256–58, 895 N.E.2d 53 (5th Dist. 2008) (counsel's remarks describing lawsuits like the plaintiff's as a "cottage industry" were inflammatory and prejudicial and caused grounds for granting a new trial).

Yoder v. Ferguson, 381 Ill. App. 3d 353, 319 Ill. Dec. 380, 885 N.E.2d 1060 (1st Dist. 2008), appeal pending, (Sept. 1, 2008) (trial court had discretion to exclude evidence of a derogatory term from a statement because the prejudicial impact of it outweighed the probative value of it).

People v. Schneider, 375 Ill. App. 3d 734, 754–58, 313 Ill. Dec. 890, 873 N.E.2d 514 (2d Dist. 2007), appeal denied, 226 Ill. 2d 604, 316 Ill. Dec. 549, 879 N.E.2d 937 (2007) (closing argument represented an improper appeal to the sympathy of the jury for the victim) (harmless error).

People v. Urdiales, 225 Ill. 2d 354, 312 Ill. Dec. 876, 871 N.E.2d 669 (2007), as modified on denial of reh'g, (May 29, 2007) and cert. denied, 128 S. Ct. 494, 169 L. Ed. 2d 347 (2007) (prosecutor's closing argument, which discussed the families of the murder victims, was inflammatory and improper but constituted harmless error).

People v. Liner, 356 Ill. App. 3d 284, 296–98, 292 Ill. Dec. 838, 826 N.E.2d 1274 (5th Dist. 2005) (prosecutor's closing argument was improper because it was likely to inflame the juror passion regarding the age of the victim).

Elder on Behalf of Finney v. Finney, 256 Ill. App. 3d 424, 427–28, 194 Ill. Dec. 896, 628 N.E.2d 393 (1st Dist. 1993) (tape recordings were properly excluded because they were irrelevant, designed to inflame the fact-finder, and lacked foundation regarding when they were made).

People v. Ford, 113 Ill. App. 3d 659, 662–63, 69 Ill. Dec. 347, 447 N.E.2d 564 (3d Dist. 1983) (not proper to appeal to the fears of the jury by discussing the effect of continued drug dealing on the children in the community).

People v. Witted, 79 Ill. App. 3d 156, 165, 34 Ill. Dec. 393, 398 N.E.2d 68 (1st Dist. 1979) (prosecutor may not make arguments that are designed solely to inflame the emotions of the jury).

Hulsebus v. Russian, 118 Ill. App. 2d 174, 180–81, 254 N.E.2d 184 (2d Dist. 1969) (trial judge had discretion to exclude gruesome evidence because it was cumulative and likely to inflame and prejudice the jury).

People v. Lefler, 38 Ill. 2d 216, 221–22, 230 N.E.2d 827 (1967) (evidence should not have been admitted when the nature of the injuries was not disputed and it was likely to arouse strong emotions).

Brant v. Wabash R. Co., 31 Ill. App. 2d 337, 339–40, 176 N.E.2d 13 (4th Dist. 1961) (improper to appeal to the emotions of the jury by referring to a child without a parent).

People v. Wilson, 400 Ill. 603, 606, 81 N.E.2d 445 (1948) (exclusion of testimony about incidents that were remote and capable of arousing prejudice in the jury).

§ 2:17 Supporting authorities—Jurors' self interest as taxpayers and consumers

Department of Public Works and Buildings For and in Behalf of People v. Sun Oil Co., 66 Ill. App. 3d 64, 68, 22 Ill. Dec. 826, 383 N.E.2d 634 (5th Dist. 1978) (improper to appeal to self-interest of jurors as taxpayers regarding ultimate responsibility to pay for damages in a condemnation suit).

Lukich v. Angeli, 31 Ill. App. 2d 20, 30, 175 N.E.2d 796 (1st Dist. 1961) (improper to argue that the plaintiff's claim is the type that increases the cost of living for everyone).

§ 2:18 Supporting authorities—"Golden rule" argument

Counsel must not ask the jurors to place themselves in the position of one of the parties. This type of argument is commonly referred to as the "Golden Rule" argument. See § 9:48, Supporting authorities—Rejection of "golden rule" argument, infra.

People v. Schneider, 375 Ill. App. 3d 734, 754–58, 313 Ill. Dec. 890, 873 N.E.2d 514 (2d Dist. 2007), appeal denied, 226 Ill. 2d 604, 316 Ill. Dec. 549, 879 N.E.2d 937 (2007) (closing argument represented an improper appeal to the sympathy of the jury for the victim) (harmless error).

Brant v. Wabash R. Co., 31 Ill. App. 2d 337, 339–40, 176 N.E.2d 13 (4th Dist. 1961) (improper to ask jurors to consider how much money they would accept in exchange for incurring the pain and suffering of the victim). It should be noted that this type of argument is sometimes referred to as the "golden rule" argument. See also *Dotson v. Sears, Roebuck and Co.*, 157 Ill. App. 3d 1036, 1042, 110 Ill. Dec. 177, 510 N.E.2d 1208 (1st Dist. 1987).

§ 2:19 Opposing authorities

People v. Urdiales, 225 Ill. 2d 354, 312 Ill. Dec. 876, 871 N.E.2d 669 (2007), as modified on denial of reh'g, (May 29, 2007) and cert. denied, 128 S. Ct. 494, 169 L. Ed. 2d 347 (2007) (prosecutor's closing argument, during sentencing, which stated that he had decided to request the death penalty and it was the jury's job to decide whether to impose it, was not improper).

People v. Smith, 362 Ill. App. 3d 1062, 1085–86, 299 Ill. Dec. 77, 841 N.E.2d 489 (1st Dist. 2005) (a photograph depicting the victim in a military uniform was not unduly inflammatory or prejudicial).

People v. Smith, 362 Ill. App. 3d 1062, 1085, 299 Ill. Dec. 77, 841 N.E.2d 489 (1st Dist. 2005) (a witness' testimony that he was currently in the witness protection program was not unduly prejudicial).

People v. Smith, 362 Ill. App. 3d 1062, 1085–86, 299 Ill. Dec. 77, 841 N.E.2d 489 (1st Dist. 2005) (testimony that the murder occurred the day after Palm Sunday was proper to explain why the victim was present at the time of the offense; evidence was not unduly prejudicial).

People v. Szudy, 262 Ill. App. 3d 695, 706, 200 Ill. Dec. 462, 635 N.E.2d 801 (1st Dist. 1994) (evidence which is admissible for a proper purpose is not made inadmissible solely because it would reflect upon a defendant's propensity to commit crimes).

Burris v. Madison County, 154 Ill. App. 3d 1064, 1070, 107 Ill. Dec. 898, 507 N.E.2d 1267 (5th Dist. 1987) (a trial judge must be cautious in granting a motion in limine so as not to improperly restrict a party's presentation of its case).

Jones v. Greer, 627 F. Supp. 1481, 1487–88 (C.D. Ill. 1986) (Under Federal Rule of Evidence 403, evidence is not prejudicial merely because it harms a party's case; rather the evidence must be of such a character that it suggests a decision based upon an improper basis).

Lundell v. Citrano, 129 Ill. App. 3d 390, 396, 84 Ill. Dec. 581, 472 N.E.2d 541 (1st Dist. 1984) (a motion in limine is designed to limit the prejudicial impact of objecting to questions in front of a jury but a party has no right to use a motion in limine to hamper the presentation of relevant evidence).

Reidelberger v. Highland Body Shop, Inc., 83 Ill. 2d 545, 549–50, 48 Ill. Dec. 237, 416 N.E.2d 268 (1981) (a trial judge must be cautious that its exclusionary order does not improperly restrict the presentation of a party's case).

People v. Newbury, 53 Ill. 2d 228, 242, 290 N.E.2d 592 (1972) (not improper to introduce evidence when it was relevant to demonstrate the manner of death).

Generally, counsel may not ask jurors to put themselves in the place of the plaintiff. However, in this case, the court held that the following question during closing argument was not improper: "Who would trade spots with the decedent as he lay on the ground with his chest moving in and out?" *Clarke v. Medley Moving and Storage, Inc.*, 381 Ill. App. 3d 82, 319 Ill. Dec. 125, 885 N.E.2d 396 (1st Dist. 2008), appeal pending, (May 1, 2008) and appeal denied, 228 Ill. 2d 530, 321 Ill. Dec. 554, 889 N.E.2d 1114 (2008).

E. MOTION TO EXCLUDE OR LIMIT CUMULATIVE EVIDENCE

§ 2:20 Suggested motion text

[Name of moving party] hereby moves this Court for an order

excluding or limiting the introduction of any and all evidence, references to evidence, testimony or argument relating to *[describe cumulative evidence]*. The motion is based upon the ground that that the evidence is cumulative and will therefore necessitate an undue consumption of time and will create a substantial danger of undue prejudice to *[name of moving party]*.

§ 2:21 Motion summary

This motion is used to exclude cumulative evidence. It is based upon the court's inherent discretionary power to exclude prejudicial, irrelevant, and time-consuming evidence, based upon a long line of Illinois cases. See *Swick v. Liautaud*, 169 Ill. 2d 504, 520–21, 215 Ill. Dec. 98, 662 N.E.2d 1238 (1996); *Lundell v. Citrano*, 129 Ill. App. 3d 390, 395–96, 84 Ill. Dec. 581, 472 N.E.2d 541 (1st Dist. 1984); *People v. Peete*, 318 Ill. App. 3d 961, 966–68, 252 Ill. Dec. 821, 743 N.E.2d 689 (4th Dist. 2001); *People v. Walker*, 335 Ill. App. 3d 102, 110–113, 268 Ill. Dec. 654, 779 N.E.2d 268 (2d Dist. 2002), as modified on denial of reh'g, (Oct. 24, 2002) and judgment aff'd, 211 Ill. 2d 317, 285 Ill. Dec. 519, 812 N.E.2d 339 (2004); and *Cochran v. Great Atlantic & Pacific Tea Co., Inc.*, 203 Ill. App. 3d 935, 938, 148 Ill. Dec. 923, 561 N.E.2d 229 (5th Dist. 1990).

There is a fine line between evidence that is considered an "overwhelming amount of evidence" and evidence that is considered "cumulative." An effective argument that is often made by counsel is based upon the number of witnesses that testify to a certain point. In other words, counsel often argue that because so many witnesses testify to a certain point, it must be true. However, at some point, "a lot of evidence" on a certain point becomes "too much evidence" and the line is crossed. The facts of a particular case will determine when evidence will be considered cumulative as opposed to overwhelming and effective.

Note that it might appear to be an uphill battle to prevail on a motion to exclude cumulative evidence *prior to* the commencement of trial, where no other evidence has yet been introduced. However, fact patterns may present themselves to justify an argument that *anticipated* cumulative evidence will prejudice your client. For example, where your opponent lists numerous experts with similar qualifications to render similar opinions, this would appear to be at least arguably cumulative and subject to exclusion under Illinois common law. Other evidence that may raise a red flag includes photographs, newspaper clippings or letters, which may be unduly prejudicial compared to other means of proving the same point.

As a final note, even if a motion in limine is denied, the citations referenced in this section provide a helpful basis for objecting to, and striking, cumulative evidence during trial.

§ 2:22 Supporting authorities—Exclusion of time-wasting evidence

Federal Rule of Evidence 403 states:

> Although relevant, evidence may be excluded if its probative value is substantially outweighed by the danger of unfair prejudice, confusion of the issues, or misleading the jury, *or by considerations of undue delay, waste of time, or needless presentation of cumulative evidence.* (Emphasis added.)

It must be noted that this Rule has not been codified in Illinois. However, Illinois cases have stated that Illinois has a common-law rule that is comparable to Federal Rule of Evidence 403. See *People v. Peete*, 318 Ill. App. 3d 961, 966–67, 252 Ill. Dec. 821, 743 N.E.2d 689 (4th Dist. 2001); and *People v. Walker*, 335 Ill. App. 3d 102, 112, 268 Ill. Dec. 654, 779 N.E.2d 268 (2d Dist. 2002), as modified on denial of reh'g, (Oct. 24, 2002) and judgment aff'd, 211 Ill. 2d 317, 285 Ill. Dec. 519, 812 N.E.2d 339 (2004). Therefore, it is arguable that Federal Rule of Evidence 403 can be considered as persuasive authority in Illinois.

Dillon v. Evanston Hosp., 199 Ill. 2d 483, 494–96, 264 Ill. Dec. 653, 771 N.E.2d 357 (2002) (no abuse of discretion when the trial judge limited cumulative testimony of an expert witness and told the jury that he did so in order to more efficiently use their time).

Kurrack v. American Dist. Telegraph Co., 252 Ill. App. 3d 885, 895–96, 192 Ill. Dec. 520, 625 N.E.2d 675 (1st Dist. 1993) (exclusion of repetitive rebuttal testimony because if there are no limits placed on expert testimony, trials would never conclude).

Palumbo v. Kuiken, 201 Ill. App. 3d 785, 791–92, 147 Ill. Dec. 206, 559 N.E.2d 206 (1st Dist. 1990) (exclusion of a videotape that would have wasted time through the presentation of cumulative evidence).

Trower v. Jones, 121 Ill. 2d 211, 219–21, 117 Ill. Dec. 136, 520 N.E.2d 297 (1988) (proper for a trial judge to limit rehabilitation of an expert witness regarding the witness' credentials, in order to prevent confusion of the issues and undue delay).

See also § 2:5 to § 2:8, supra.

§ 2:23 Supporting authorities—Exclusion of cumulative evidence

In re Detention of Lieberman, 379 Ill. App. 3d 585, 318 Ill. Dec. 605, 884 N.E.2d 160, 179–82 (1st Dist. 2007), appeal denied, 229 Ill. 2d 623, 325 Ill. Dec. 4, 897 N.E.2d 252 (2008) and *cert. denied*, 129 S.Ct. 2050, 77 USLW 3400, 77 USLW 3592, 77 USLW 3594 (U.S.Ill. Apr 27, 2009) (expert testimony that was not disclosed during discovery and that was cumulative of other testimony, was properly excluded).

Simich v. Edgewater Beach Apartments Corp., 368 Ill. App. 3d 394, 411-12, 306 Ill. Dec. 535, 857 N.E.2d 934 (1st Dist. 2006), appeal denied, 223 Ill. 2d 685, 310 Ill. Dec. 257, 865 N.E.2d 977 (2007) (to the extent that evidence of a subsequent remedial measure would have demonstrated a party's knowledge of a condition, it also was cumulative of other testimony proving the same point and thus, the trial court properly barred the evidence).

People v. Hari, 218 Ill. 2d 275, 300 Ill. Dec. 91, 843 N.E.2d 349 (2006) (the trial court did not unduly restrict the defendant from cross-examining a witness regarding alleged bias, where the information was already in evidence).

Dillon v. Evanston Hosp., 199 Ill. 2d 483, 495, 264 Ill. Dec. 653, 771 N.E.2d 357 (2002) (trial court has discretion to exclude cumulative evidence).

Kotvan v. Kirk, 321 Ill. App. 3d 733, 748–49, 254 Ill. Dec. 633, 747 N.E.2d 1045 (1st Dist. 2001) (trial court has discretion to exclude cumulative evidence, even if relevant).

Hunt v. Harrison, 303 Ill. App. 3d 54, 57, 236 Ill. Dec. 387, 707 N.E.2d 232 (1st Dist. 1999) (trial court has considerable discretion to preclude cumulative evidence).

§ 2:24 Supporting authorities—Exclusion of cumulative evidence—Articles, letters and documents

Hulman v. Evanston Hosp. Corp., 259 Ill. App. 3d 133, 147–49, 197 Ill. Dec. 319, 631 N.E.2d 322 (1st Dist. 1994) (exclusion of hospital pamphlet was not error when witnesses were permitted to freely refer to the information in it).

Northern Illinois Medical Center v. Home State Bank of Crystal Lake, 136 Ill. App. 3d 129, 152–53, 90 Ill. Dec. 802, 482 N.E.2d 1085 (2d Dist. 1985) (exclusion of articles of incorporation and bylaws when the information regarding the reorganization of the plaintiff was adequately testified to by other witnesses).

Pagel v. Yates, 128 Ill. App. 3d 897, 903, 84 Ill. Dec. 180, 471 N.E.2d 946 (4th Dist. 1984) (exclusion of documents regarding misidentification of horse when witness already testified to that fact).

Coney v. Rockford Life Ins. Co., 67 Ill. App. 2d 395, 402–03, 214 N.E.2d 1 (3d Dist. 1966) (exclusion of letter regarding lessee's understanding of the meaning of the lease when it was cumulative of other exhibit and self-serving).

§ 2:25 Supporting authorities—Exclusion of cumulative evidence—Credentials

O'Brien v. Meyer, 196 Ill. App. 3d 457, 461–64, 143 Ill. Dec. 322, 554 N.E.2d 257 (1st Dist. 1989) (once an expert has been qualified as an expert, impeachment regarding the expert's failure to pass prior licensing examinations is irrelevant and may be excluded). Although this case was based on the prejudicial influence of the testimony at issue, it arguably could be used to claim that once expertise has been established, any further testimony regarding the expert's qualifications is cumulative, pursuant to the principles described above. For example, in the case of *Canavin v. Pacific Southwest Airlines*, 148 Cal. App. 3d 512, 537–38, 196 Cal. Rptr. 82 (4th Dist. 1983), a California appeals court held that there was no error in excluding extensive credentials and qualifications of scientists employed in the same field as the decedent in a wrongful death action.

Compare *Rockwood v. Singh*, 258 Ill. App. 3d 555, 196 Ill. Dec. 708, 630 N.E.2d 873 (1st Dist. 1993) (when a physician sued for malpractice testifies as an expert, the defendant's failure to pass board certification is relevant and may be admissible.).

§ 2:26 Supporting authorities—Exclusion of cumulative evidence—Number of witnesses

Dillon v. Evanston Hosp., 199 Ill. 2d 483, 495–96, 264 Ill. Dec. 653, 771 N.E.2d 357 (2002) (trial court has discretion to limit the number of expert witnesses in order to exclude cumulative evidence).

Kotvan v. Kirk, 321 Ill. App. 3d 733, 748–49, 254 Ill. Dec. 633, 747 N.E.2d 1045 (1st Dist. 2001) (trial court has discretion to limit the number of witnesses in order to exclude cumulative evidence).

§ 2:27 Supporting authorities—Exclusion of cumulative evidence—Photographs

Swanigan v. Smith, 294 Ill. App. 3d 263, 274, 228 Ill. Dec. 578, 689 N.E.2d 637 (4th Dist. 1998) (trial judge could properly rule that plaintiff could either display his actual injuries or photographs of them but not both, because to allow both would be cumulative).

Davis v. International Harvester Co., 167 Ill. App. 3d 814, 825, 118 Ill. Dec. 589, 521 N.E.2d 1282 (2d Dist. 1988) (court has discretion to exclude photographs that are cumulative of expert testimony).

Simmons v. City of Chicago, 118 Ill. App. 3d 676, 684–85, 74 Ill. Dec. 202, 455 N.E.2d 232 (1st Dist. 1983) (exclusion of overhead slides where the slides were cumulative of the expert's testimony).

Villegas v. Kercher, 11 Ill. App. 2d 282, 290–91, 137 N.E.2d 92 (2d Dist. 1956) (not improper to exclude photograph of plaintiff in traction where witness testimony already established the length of time he was in the hospital and his condition).

§ 2:28 Supporting authorities—Exclusion of cumulative evidence—Reports and records

Carillo v. Ford Motor Co., 325 Ill. App. 3d 955, 966, 259 Ill. Dec. 619, 759 N.E.2d 99 (1st Dist. 2001) (exclusion of statistics from a database when experts already testified regarding them).

Goldstein v. Scott, 108 Ill. App. 3d 867, 879, 64 Ill. Dec. 374, 439 N.E.2d 1039 (1st Dist. 1982) (exclusion of tax return when the plaintiff had already been questioned regarding the contents of it).

§ 2:29 Supporting authorities—Exclusion of cumulative evidence—Videotape evidence

Palumbo v. Kuiken, 201 Ill. App. 3d 785, 791–92, 147 Ill. Dec. 206, 559 N.E.2d 206 (1st Dist. 1990) (exclusion of a videotape of surgery that would have been cumulative of the testimony).

Woodrick v. Smith Gas Service, Inc., 87 Ill. App. 2d 88, 94-95, 230 N.E.2d 508, 4 U.C.C. Rep. Serv. 934 (2d Dist. 1967) (no error in trial court's exclusion of videotape evidence when experts already testified regarding the contents of it).

§ 2:30 Opposing authorities—General authority

People ex rel. Dept. of Transp. v. Kotara, L.L.C., 379 Ill. App. 3d 276, 318 Ill. Dec. 964, 884 N.E.2d 1235, 1244–45 (3d Dist. 2008) (trial court erred by arbitrarily allowing a party to call only one witness and barring other relevant witnesses).

People v. Holman, 257 Ill. App. 3d 1031, 1033–34, 196 Ill. Dec. 457, 630 N.E.2d 154 (2d Dist. 1994) (evidence is admissible if it is relevant and if the prejudicial impact does not substantially outweigh the probative value of it).

Moore v. Swoboda, 213 Ill. App. 3d 217, 241–42, 157 Ill. Dec. 37, 571 N.E.2d 1056 (4th Dist. 1991) (not abuse of discretion to admit relevant evidence, even if it was gruesome and cumulative).

People v. Frazier, 129 Ill. App. 3d 704, 711, 84 Ill. Dec. 787, 472 N.E.2d 1183 (2d Dist. 1984) (a party is permitted to support his or her case with relevant evidence and it is within the trial judge's discretion to assess whether or not there is prejudice related to the accumulation of repetitive evidence).

Lundell v. Citrano, 129 Ill. App. 3d 390, 396, 84 Ill. Dec. 581, 472 N.E.2d 541 (1st Dist. 1984) (a party has no right to hamper the other party's presentation of relevant and admissible evidence by use of a motion in limine).

§ 2:31 Opposing authorities—Number of witnesses

People ex rel. Dept. of Transp. v. Kotara, L.L.C., 379 Ill. App. 3d 276, 318 Ill. Dec. 964, 884 N.E.2d 1235, 1244–45 (3d Dist. 2008) (trial court erred by arbitrarily allowing a party to call only one witness and barring other relevant witnesses).

Hunt v. Harrison, 303 Ill. App. 3d 54, 57-58, 236 Ill. Dec. 387, 707 N.E.2d 232 (1st Dist. 1999) (trial court should not have barred the only disinterested witness from testifying, even though the testimony of that witness was cumulative of other testimony).

People v. Frazier, 129 Ill. App. 3d 704, 710–11, 84 Ill. Dec. 787, 472 N.E.2d 1183 (2d Dist. 1984) (testimony of doctors and others regarding injuries was permitted even though cumulative in part, because each witness added different facts to the case).

Hubbard v. Sherman Hosp., 292 Ill. App. 3d 148, 155, 226 Ill. Dec. 393, 685 N.E.2d 648 (2d Dist. 1997) (testimony of a disinterested expert was properly allowed in addition to the testimony of the defendant's agents even though the defendant's agents could also qualify as experts).

§ 2:32 Opposing authorities—Videotape evidence

Dillon v. Evanston Hosp., 199 Ill. 2d 483, 492–94, 264 Ill. Dec. 653, 771 N.E.2d 357 (2002) (trial court had discretion to allow the jury to view a videotape when an expert testified that it would be helpful in explaining the subject matter of his testimony to the jury).

Montag v. Board of Educ., School Dist. No. 40, Rock Island County, 112 Ill. App. 3d 1039, 1046–47, 68 Ill. Dec. 565, 446 N.E.2d 299, 9 Ed. Law Rep. 989 (3d Dist. 1983) (not an abuse of discretion to admit a videotape which showed the type of movements being made at the time of injury because it was relevant to the issues and helped explain the issues better than live testimony).

Mathias v. Baltimore & O. R. Co., 93 Ill. App. 2d 258, 263–64, 236 N.E.2d 331 (1st Dist. 1968) (error to preclude videotapes of the plaintiff performing work when disability was claimed and the testimony was conflicting about such disability).

§ 2:33 Opposing authorities—Witness credentials

Rockwood v. Singh, 258 Ill. App. 3d 555, 196 Ill. Dec. 708, 630 N.E.2d 873 (1st Dist. 1993) (when a physician sued for malpractice testifies as an expert, the defendant's failure to pass board certification is relevant and may be admissible).

II. SAMPLE MOTIONS

§ 2:34 Motion to exclude confusing evidence

TO: ALL PARTIES AND THEIR RESPECTIVE ATTORNEYS OF RECORD:

PLEASE TAKE NOTICE that plaintiff hereby moves this Court for an order excluding any and all evidence, references to evidence, testimony or argument describing defendant's medical witnesses as "independent" or "independent medical examiners" or any related description.

Plaintiff further moves the Court to instruct defendant and defendant's counsel and to instruct counsel to advise all witnesses:

1. Not to mention, refer to, or attempt to convey to the jury in any manner, either directly or indirectly, any of the facts mentioned in this motion, without first obtaining permission of the Court outside the presence and hearing of the jury;

2. Not to make any reference to the fact that this motion has been filed; and

3. To warn and caution each of defendant's witnesses to strictly follow the same instructions.

This motion is made under the provisions of Illinois case law, which supports this Court's inherent power to limit evidence that would confuse the issues; and is based upon the supporting Memorandum of Points and Authorities, the pleadings and papers on file in this action, and upon such of the argument and evidence as may be presented prior to or at the hearing of this matter.

Dated: *[date]*

MEMORANDUM OF POINTS AND AUTHORITIES

1.
PRELIMINARY STATEMENT

This is a personal injury action arising out of a snorkeling accident that occurred on May 29, 1999. The defendant retained medical doctors to dispute the nature and extent of the plaintiff's injuries and damages. In correspondence, discovery, and prior hearings, the defendant has described the defense medical doctors as "independent." This motion seeks to preclude the defendant from using the term "independent," or any related terminology, to describe said witnesses at the time of trial.

2.
THIS COURT MAY PRECLUDE EVIDENCE THAT IS CONFUSING

Illinois case law provides that evidence may be excluded where it may confuse the issues or mislead the jury. *Congregation of the Passion, Holy Cross Province v. Touche Ross & Co.*, 224 Ill. App. 3d 559, 578–79, 166 Ill. Dec. 642, 586 N.E.2d 600 (1st Dist. 1991), judgment aff'd, 159 Ill. 2d 137, 201 Ill. Dec. 71, 636 N.E.2d 503 (1994). For example, in the case of *Hulman v. Evanston Hosp. Corp.*, 259 Ill. App. 3d 133, 147–48, 197 Ill. Dec. 319, 631 N.E.2d 322 (1st Dist. 1994), the court held that the trial judge properly excluded a hospital pamphlet based upon the fact that there was already testimony about it and the risk that the admission of it might confuse the jury.

In addition, Federal Rule of Evidence 403 states:

> Although relevant, evidence may be excluded if its probative value is substantially outweighed by the danger of unfair prejudice, *confusion of the issues, or misleading the jury*, or by considerations of undue delay, waste of time, or needless presentation of cumulative evidence. (Emphasis added.)

This Rule has not been specifically codified in Illinois. However, Illinois cases have stated that Illinois has a common-law rule that is comparable to Federal Rule of Evidence 403. See *People v. Peete*, 318 Ill. App. 3d 961, 966–67, 252 Ill. Dec. 821, 743 N.E.2d 689 (4th Dist. 2001); and *People v. Walker*, 335 Ill. App. 3d 102, 112, 268 Ill. Dec. 654, 779 N.E.2d 268 (2d Dist. 2002), as modified on denial of reh'g, (Oct. 24, 2002) and judgment aff'd, 211 Ill. 2d 317, 285 Ill. Dec. 519, 812 N.E.2d 339 (2004).

In this case, the probative value of referring to defense medical witnesses as "independent" is nonexistent and would only cause undue confusion and give improper weight and credibility to the defense witnesses. Admission of such evidence will necessitate undue consumption of time to present rebuttal and cross-examination about the lack of independence of the defense witnesses. The jury will be mislead and other relevant issues will be confused by the admission of such evidence.

It should also be noted that the defendant's witnesses do not qualify as independent witnesses under Illinois Supreme Court Rule 213(f) which states in pertinent part:

> *(2) Independent Expert Witnesses.* An 'independent expert witness' is a person giving expert testimony who is not the party, the party's current employee, or the party's retained expert . . .

As such, any references to defendant's physicians as "independent" should be forbidden.

3.

CONCLUSION

Based upon all of the above, exclusion or reference to the defense medical witnesses as "independent" is proper.

Dated: *[date]*

By: ____________________
[name of counsel]
Attorneys for PLAINTIFF,
[name of plaintiff]

§ 2:35 Motion to exclude cumulative evidence

TO: ALL PARTIES AND THEIR RESPECTIVE ATTORNEYS OF RECORD:

PLEASE TAKE NOTICE that defendant hereby moves this Court for an order excluding any and all testimony, evidence, references to evidence or argument relating to the testimony of the following of plaintiff's designated medical experts: 1) Dr.

Superfluous, 2) Dr. Needless, and 3) Dr. Overkill. This motion is based upon the ground that the testimony of each of these witnesses is cumulative to the testimony of other designated witnesses, and therefore should be excluded by the Court.

This motion is made under the provisions of Illinois case law, which supports the Court's inherent powers to exclude such evidence; and is based upon the attached Memorandum of Points and Authorities, the pleadings and papers on file in this action, and upon such of the argument and evidence as may be presented prior to or at the hearing of this matter.

Dated: *[date]*

MEMORANDUM OF POINTS AND AUTHORITIES

1.
PRELIMINARY STATEMENT

This case arises from an alleged excessive use of force by a Cook County Sheriff Deputy. The plaintiff was injured when her vehicle lost control during a high speed police pursuit. The plaintiff claims to have incurred a broken ankle, broken ribs, a bruised kidney and soft tissue neck and back injuries.

In her witness designation list, the plaintiff identified the following medical witnesses: 1) Dr. Cervical [Orthopedic Surgeon]; 2) Dr. Bones [Chiropractor]; 3) Dr. Fixit [General M.D.]; 4) Dr. Organs [Internal Medicine]; 5) Dr. Superfluous [Orthopedic Surgeon]; 6) Dr. Needless [General M.D.]; 7) Dr. Overkill [Internal Medicine]. The plaintiff indicated that the experts' proposed testimony would encompass "the nature and extent of plaintiff's injuries."

By this motion, the defendant seeks to exclude the testimony of Dr. Superfluous, Dr. Needless and Dr. Overkill, based upon the clearly cumulative nature of the expected testimony of these witnesses.

2.
THE COURT MAY LIMIT THE NUMBER OF EXPERT WITNESSES CALLED TO TESTIFY

Illinois case law provides that the Court may limit the number of witnesses called to testify on a single question. *Kotvan v. Kirk*, 321 Ill. App. 3d 733, 748–49, 254 Ill. Dec. 633, 747 N.E.2d 1045 (1st Dist. 2001). Expert testimony that is merely cumulative of prior testimony may be excluded. *Dillon v. Evanston Hosp.*, 199 Ill. 2d 483, 495–96, 264 Ill. Dec. 653, 771 N.E.2d 357 (2002). In *Dillon v. Evanston Hosp.*, 199 Ill. 2d 483,

495–96, 264 Ill. Dec. 653, 771 N.E.2d 357 (2002), the trial judge excluded the testimony of an expert witness whose testimony would be cumulative of the party's other expert.

In the present case, the plaintiff has listed two orthopedic surgeons, two general medical doctors, and two internal medicine specialists. It is unclear how the testimony of these duplicate specialists will differ. What is clear is that Dr. Superfluous, Dr. Needless and Dr. Overkill were not treating physicians, and would not be expected to offer testimony as reliable or material as their treating counterparts.

Allowing the testimony of these witnesses will add hours, if not days, of needless duplicate testimony. Clearly, under the authority of the cases cited above, this Court has the authority to limit the number of plaintiff's experts, as requested herein.

3.
THIS COURT MAY PRECLUDE EVIDENCE THAT WILL WASTE TIME

Illinois case law supports the exclusion of evidence because the evidence would waste the Court's time. For example, in the case of *Dillon v. Evanston Hosp.*, 199 Ill. 2d 483, 494–96, 264 Ill. Dec. 653, 771 N.E.2d 357 (2002), the court found that the trial judge did not abuse its discretion by limiting an expert witness' testimony in order to use the jury's time more efficiently. Similarly, in the case of *Trower v. Jones*, 121 Ill. 2d 211, 219–21, 117 Ill. Dec. 136, 520 N.E.2d 297 (1988), the court held that the trial judge properly limited the rehabilitation of an expert witness in order to prevent undue delay and confusion of the issues.

In addition, Federal Rule of Evidence 403 states:

> Although relevant, evidence may be excluded if its probative value is substantially outweighed by the danger of unfair prejudice, confusion of the issues, or misleading the jury, *or by considerations of undue delay, waste of time*, or needless presentation of cumulative evidence. (Emphasis added.)

This Rule has not been specifically codified in Illinois. However, Illinois cases have stated that Illinois has a common-law rule that is comparable to Federal Rule of Evidence 403. See *People v. Peete*, 318 Ill. App. 3d 961, 966–67, 252 Ill. Dec. 821, 743 N.E.2d 689 (4th Dist. 2001); and *People v. Walker*, 335 Ill. App. 3d 102, 112, 268 Ill. Dec. 654, 779 N.E.2d 268 (2d Dist. 2002), as modified on denial of reh'g, (Oct. 24, 2002) and judgment aff'd, 211 Ill. 2d 317, 285 Ill. Dec. 519, 812 N.E.2d 339 (2004).

As indicated above, three of the plaintiff's seven designated experts are duplicative and clearly unnecessary. Allowing the testimony will prolong this trial significantly, wasting the valuable time and resources of the Court and all other participants, while adding absolutely nothing new to the evidence.

4.
CONCLUSION

Based upon the above Points and Authorities, the defendant respectfully requests that this Court limit the plaintiff's medical experts as requested herein.

Dated: *[date]*

By: ______________________
[name of counsel]
Attorneys for DEFENDANT
[name of defendant]

Chapter 3

Irrelevant Evidence

KeyCite®: Cases and other legal materials listed in KeyCite Scope can be researched through the KeyCite service on Westlaw®. Use KeyCite to check citations for form, parallel references, prior and later history, and comprehensive citator information, including citations to other decisions and secondary materials.

I. MOTION AUTHORITIES

A. MOTION TO EXCLUDE IRRELEVANT EVIDENCE

§ 3:1 Suggested motion text

[Name of moving party] hereby moves this Court for an order excluding any and all evidence, references to evidence, testimony or argument relating to *[describe irrelevant evidence]*. The motion is based upon the ground that the evidence is irrelevant and immaterial to the issues in this action and therefore inadmissible.

§ 3:2 Motion summary

This motion is used to exclude irrelevant evidence, pursuant to the definition contained in Federal Rule of Evidence 401, as adopted through Illinois case law. See *Spencer v. Wandolowski*, 264 Ill. App. 3d 611, 617, 201 Ill. Dec. 422, 636 N.E.2d 854 (1st Dist. 1994); and *People v. Monroe*, 66 Ill. 2d 317, 321–22, 5 Ill. Dec. 824, 362 N.E.2d 295 (1977). Irrelevant evidence may be excluded by an in limine motion. *Swick v. Liautaud*, 169 Ill. 2d 504, 521, 215 Ill. Dec. 98, 662 N.E.2d 1238 (1996). Other evidence that may be excluded under this theory includes that which is speculative [*Modelski v. Navistar Intern. Transp. Corp.*, 302 Ill. App. 3d 879, 885–86, 236 Ill. Dec. 394, 707 N.E.2d 239 (1st Dist. 1999)], outside the pleadings [*Carlyle v. Jaskiewicz*, 124 Ill. App. 3d 487, 496–98, 79 Ill. Dec. 847, 464 N.E.2d 751 (1st Dist. 1984)] or undisputed [*Bullard v. Barnes*, 112 Ill. App. 3d 384, 392–94, 68 Ill. Dec. 37, 445 N.E.2d 485 (4th Dist. 1983), judgment aff'd, 102 Ill. 2d 505, 82 Ill. Dec. 448, 468 N.E.2d 1228 (1984); and *People v. Lefler*, 38 Ill. 2d 216, 221–22, 230 N.E.2d 827 (1967)].

Motions to exclude irrelevant evidence should be used to make sure the evidence presented at trial relates to the true issues in the case. Where counsel has reason to believe that opposing counsel will seek to admit evidence which seems to be irrelevant, counsel should move to exclude the evidence. The court will most likely grant the motion and exclude the evidence. Even if the motion is denied, counsel will have the benefit of learning why the opposition and the Court believe the evidence is relevant and how the opposition plans to use this evidence. Therefore, even if the motion is unsuccessful, counsel will still obtain some benefit from bringing the motion.

§ 3:3 Supporting authorities—Exclusion of irrelevant evidence, generally

Federal Rule of Evidence 401 defines relevancy as,

> evidence having any tendency to make the existence of any fact that is of consequence to the determination of the action more probable or less probable than it would be without the evidence.

Illinois has adopted this definition of relevancy through case law. *Spencer v. Wandolowski*, 264 Ill. App. 3d 611, 617, 201 Ill. Dec. 422, 636 N.E.2d 854 (1st Dist. 1994); and *People v. Monroe*, 66 Ill. 2d 317, 321–22, 5 Ill. Dec. 824, 362 N.E.2d 295 (1977).

Downey v. Dunnington, 384 Ill.App.3d 350, 387–89, 895 N.E.2d 271 (4th Dist. 2008) (evidence that the defendant's father was a minister was irrelevant and prejudicial and should not have been admitted but the error was harmless).

Boren v. BOC Group, Inc., 385 Ill.App.3d 248, 254–57, 895 N.E.2d 53 (5th Dist. 2008) (photograph of a billboard advertisement which was offered to suggest that cases like the plaintiff's case were solicited and created by lawyers was irrelevant, prejudicial, misleading and confusing and caused grounds for granting a new trial).

In re Leona W., 228 Ill. 2d 439, 320 Ill. Dec. 855, 888 N.E.2d 72 (2008) (in a termination of parental rights case, the trial court did not abuse its discretion by granting a motion in limine to exclude evidence regarding the parent's behavior towards other minors, as irrelevant and beyond the scope of the allegations).

Fox v. Seiden, 382 Ill. App. 3d 288, 320 Ill. Dec. 592, 887 N.E.2d 736 (1st Dist. 2008), appeal denied, 229 Ill. 2d 620, 325 Ill. Dec. 2, 897 N.E.2d 250 (2008) (court would not take judicial notice of a bankruptcy court's decision which was issued after the trial court entered the order that was on appeal and therefore, could not have been considered by trial court before it entered the complained of order).

Beard v. Barron, 379 Ill. App. 3d 1, 18-19, 317 Ill. Dec. 906, 882 N.E.2d 1062 (1st Dist. 2008), appeal pending, (May 1, 2008) and appeal denied, 228 Ill. 2d 529, 321 Ill. Dec. 554, 889 N.E.2d 1114 (2008) (trial court properly declined to give an instruction that was irrelevant to the issues).

Bergman v. Kelsey, 375 Ill. App. 3d 612, 635–36, 313 Ill. Dec.

862, 873 N.E.2d 486 (1st Dist. 2007), appeal denied, 226 Ill. 2d 579, 316 Ill. Dec. 541, 879 N.E.2d 929 (2007) (evidence regarding subsequent pregnancies were irrelevant to the issue of the pregnancy at issue in this case and was properly excluded).

People v. Evans, 373 Ill. App. 3d 948, 960–61, 311 Ill. Dec. 907, 869 N.E.2d 920 (1st Dist. 2007), appeal denied, 225 Ill. 2d 648, 314 Ill. Dec. 830, 875 N.E.2d 1117 (2007) (evidence of weapons, other than the murder weapon, should not have been admitted) (harmless error).

Lopez v. Northwestern Memorial Hosp., 375 Ill. App. 3d 637, 649, 313 Ill. Dec. 796, 873 N.E.2d 420 (1st Dist. 2007) (trial court did not err by excluding cross-examination of an expert that was irrelevant to the issues).

People v. Schneider, 375 Ill. App. 3d 734, 751–54, 313 Ill. Dec. 890, 873 N.E.2d 514 (2d Dist. 2007), appeal denied, 226 Ill. 2d 604, 316 Ill. Dec. 549, 879 N.E.2d 937 (2007) (trial court properly excluded irrelevant cross examination about the witness' alleged conduct in another case).

Matthews v. Avalon Petroleum Co., 375 Ill. App. 3d 1, 14-15, 313 Ill. Dec. 132, 871 N.E.2d 859 (1st Dist. 2007) (trial court had discretion to bar evidence that was irrelevant to the issues in the case).

In re Stephen K., 373 Ill. App. 3d 7, 310 Ill. Dec. 768, 867 N.E.2d 81 (1st Dist. 2007) (evidence of a child's hospitalization after being placed in foster care was irrelevant to the issue of whether the child had been medically neglected prior to being placed in foster care).

Alwin v. Village of Wheeling, 371 Ill. App. 3d 898, 309 Ill. Dec. 656, 864 N.E.2d 897 (1st Dist. 2007), appeal denied, 224 Ill. 2d 571, 312 Ill. Dec. 654, 871 N.E.2d 54 (2007) (evidence regarding the conditions in an area managed by the testifying expert were irrelevant to the issue of the safety of the conditions in the area at issue in the case).

Webber v. Wight & Co., 368 Ill. App. 3d 1007, 1023-26, 306 Ill. Dec. 782, 858 N.E.2d 579 (1st Dist. 2006), appeal denied, 223 Ill. 2d 686, 310 Ill. Dec. 258, 865 N.E.2d 978 (2007) (In this retaliatory discharge claim, the trial court did not abuse its discretion by excluding the plaintiff's testimony that the defendant was engaging in "illegal" activities as unreliable and irrelevant).

Ayala v. Murad, 367 Ill. App. 3d 591, 601-02, 305 Ill. Dec. 370, 855 N.E.2d 261 (1st Dist. 2006) (testimony by an expert regarding what he would have done differently than the defendant doctor was irrelevant).

Jones v. Rallos, 373 Ill. App. 3d 439, 311 Ill. Dec. 450, 869 N.E.2d 124 (1st Dist. 2006) (evidence that the defendant specialist had not passed her test for board certification should have been excluded when she was not testifying as an expert), judgment vacated, *Jones v. Rallos*, 225 Ill. 2d 636, 314 Ill. Dec. 13, 873 N.E.2d 943 (2007) ("The appellate court is directed to reconsider its judgment, with additional analysis of whether any error in the trial court's decision to permit plaintiff-appellee to elicit evidence of defendant-appellant's failure to pass board-certification examinations constitutes no more than harmless, non-reversible error.").

Gomez v. The Finishing Co., Inc., 369 Ill. App. 3d 711, 308 Ill. Dec. 124, 861 N.E.2d 189, 201 (1st Dist. 2006) (in a retaliatory discharge case, evidence of cost-cutting measures taken at times other than the time in question was properly excluded as irrelevant).

In re Kenneth D., 364 Ill. App. 3d 797, 301 Ill. Dec. 534, 847 N.E.2d 544 (1st Dist. 2006) (evidence of conduct by a party which occurred after the incidents in question was irrelevant).

Gaston v. Founders Ins. Co., 365 Ill. App. 3d 303, 301 Ill. Dec. 513, 847 N.E.2d 523, 539–40 (1st Dist. 2006) (expert testimony regarding costs that would be involved in fixing an automobile were irrelevant when the insurance company had provided the insured a method of fixing the car at a cost which would not exceed the insured's deductible).

Noakes v. National R.R. Passenger Corp., 363 Ill. App. 3d 851, 859–60, 300 Ill. Dec. 593, 845 N.E.2d 14 (1st Dist. 2006) (testimony regarding the original cause of a person's carpal tunnel syndrome was inadmissible where it was irrelevant and speculative).

Steiner Elec. Co. v. NuLine Technologies, Inc., 364 Ill. App. 3d 876, 882–83, 301 Ill. Dec. 646, 847 N.E.2d 656 (1st Dist. 2006) (when opposing a summary judgment motion, a party could not rely on the party's own answers to requests to admit where answers to request to admit are pleadings and pleadings alone are not sufficient to overcome summary judgment).

Thornton v. Garcini, 364 Ill. App. 3d 612, 618–19, 301 Ill. Dec. 386, 846 N.E.2d 989 (3d Dist. 2006) (damages for loss of society of a stillborn child are not dependant on whether the child survived long enough to have an actual relationship with the family).

Nelson v. Upadhyaya, 361 Ill. App. 3d 415, 422–23, 297 Ill. Dec. 53, 836 N.E.2d 784 (1st Dist. 2005) (trial court erred by admitting articles regarding the proper standard of care that were published after the incident in question where the articles were irrelevant and prejudicial when they were offered to suggest the standard of care at the time of the incident).

People v. Robert P., 354 Ill. App. 3d 1051, 1059, 290 Ill. Dec. 685, 821 N.E.2d 1259 (3d Dist. 2005) (in a sexual assault case, the trial court did not abuse its discretion by excluding evidence that the victim had accused another individual of sexual abuse in the past).

People v. Robert P., 354 Ill. App. 3d 1051, 1060–61, 290 Ill. Dec. 685, 821 N.E.2d 1259 (3d Dist. 2005) (in a sexual assault case, the trial court did not abuse its discretion by excluding evidence that the victim had accused the defendant of biting her in the past; evidence was irrelevant).

People v. Robert P., 354 Ill. App. 3d 1051, 1058–59, 290 Ill. Dec. 685, 821 N.E.2d 1259 (3d Dist. 2005) (the trial court did not abuse its discretion by determining that evidence was irrelevant regarding whether other people were in the house when the defendant allegedly sexually abused the victim).

People v. Robert P., 354 Ill. App. 3d 1051, 1059–60, 290 Ill. Dec. 685, 821 N.E.2d 1259 (3d Dist. 2005) (the trial court did not abuse its discretion by excluding evidence that the defendant's wife had brought the victim for psychological treatment for lying and masturbating; testimony was irrelevant, represented improper lay opinion testimony and disclosed confidential information).

Avery v. State Farm Mut. Auto. Ins. Co., 216 Ill. 2d 100, 141–42, 296 Ill. Dec. 448, 835 N.E.2d 801 (2005) (when a contract was not ambiguous, an internal document of one of the parties was irrelevant when offered to explain the meaning of certain terms in the contract).

People v. Bohn, 362 Ill. App. 3d 485, 486–91, 298 Ill. Dec. 649, 840 N.E.2d 762 (2d Dist. 2005) (the trial court did not abuse its discretion by excluding evidence that a witness was arrested for allegedly possessing the same drugs that the defendant was accused of possessing; evidence was irrelevant, prejudicial and confusing).

People v. Boand, 362 Ill. App. 3d 106, 124–26, 297 Ill. Dec. 880, 838 N.E.2d 367 (2d Dist. 2005) (the trial court erred by admitting evidence of certain uncharged sex offenses in a trial for drug-induced homicide and involuntary manslaughter, where the evidence was irrelevant and prejudicial).

People v. Carini, 357 Ill. App. 3d 103, 115–18, 293 Ill. Dec. 134, 827 N.E.2d 1015 (1st Dist. 2005) (the trial court did not abuse its discretion by determining that the defendant's proposed surrebuttal evidence was collateral).

People v. Cookson, 215 Ill. 2d 194, 213–18, 294 Ill. Dec. 72, 830 N.E.2d 484 (2005) (proffered impeachment evidence suggesting that the victim had allegedly made false abuse allegations against someone other than the defendant was irrelevant).

Mulloy v. American Eagle Airlines, Inc., 358 Ill. App. 3d 706, 295 Ill. Dec. 54, 832 N.E.2d 205, 210 (1st Dist. 2005) (no abuse of discretion to exclude lay witness testimony as irrelevant).

People v. Harvey, 211 Ill. 2d 368, 392, 286 Ill. Dec. 124, 813 N.E.2d 181 (2004) (no abuse of discretion to exclude irrelevant and collateral evidence that victim had previously purchased narcotics from individuals other than defendant).

People v. Hayes, 353 Ill. App. 3d 578, 583–84, 289 Ill. Dec. 184, 819 N.E.2d 341 (3d Dist. 2004) (in a case involving a shooting, no abuse of discretion to exclude witness' testimony that victim had previously attempted to sell the defendant a gun; evidence was remote in time, uncertain, and irrelevant).

In re Marriage of Cianchetti, 351 Ill. App. 3d 832, 837–38, 286 Ill. Dec. 807, 815 N.E.2d 17, 192 Ed. Law Rep. 230 (3d Dist. 2004) (expert testimony regarding costs of education was irrelevant where expert failed to compare similar programs to the one at issue).

Southwestern Illinois Development Authority v. Al-Muhajirum, 348 Ill. App. 3d 398, 401–02, 284 Ill. Dec. 164, 809 N.E.2d 730 (5th Dist. 2004) (in a condemnation proceeding, proposed expert testimony about what a property would be worth if it was developed as a party desired, was properly excluded as irrelevant).

Sullivan-Coughlin v. Palos Country Club, Inc., 349 Ill. App. 3d 553, 559–60, 285 Ill. Dec. 676, 812 N.E.2d 496 (1st Dist. 2004) (language of a golf cart rental agreement was properly excluded as irrelevant, when the plaintiff alleged that she was injured by a golf ball, not the cart).

Preston ex rel. Preston v. Simmons, 321 Ill. App. 3d 789, 803, 254 Ill. Dec. 647, 747 N.E.2d 1059 (1st Dist. 2001) (trial judge should not permit such wide latitude on cross-examination that it undermines the rule that only relevant evidence is admissible).

Carillo v. Ford Motor Co., 325 Ill. App. 3d 955, 968, 259 Ill. Dec. 619, 759 N.E.2d 99 (1st Dist. 2001) (proper to exclude evidence that is irrelevant to the issues being tried).

Vojas v. K mart Corp., 312 Ill. App. 3d 544, 552, 245 Ill. Dec. 144, 727 N.E.2d 397 (5th Dist. 2000) (the burden of establishing relevance is on the party offering the evidence).

Swick v. Liautaud, 169 Ill. 2d 504, 521, 215 Ill. Dec. 98, 662

N.E.2d 1238 (1996) (not an abuse of discretion to exclude evidence of the defendant's conduct towards people other than the plaintiff on the basis of irrelevance).

Cochran v. Great Atlantic & Pacific Tea Co., Inc., 203 Ill. App. 3d 935, 937–38, 148 Ill. Dec. 923, 561 N.E.2d 229 (5th Dist. 1990) (trial judge has inherent power to exclude irrelevant evidence).

Pagel v. Yates, 128 Ill. App. 3d 897, 903, 84 Ill. Dec. 180, 471 N.E.2d 946 (4th Dist. 1984) (exclusion of irrelevant and confusing document).

Benson v. Bradford Mut. Fire Ins. Corp., 121 Ill. App. 3d 500, 510, 76 Ill. Dec. 774, 459 N.E.2d 689, 47 A.L.R.4th 759 (2d Dist. 1984) (trial judge had discretion to exclude irrelevant witness testimony).

§ 3:4 Supporting authorities—Exclusion of irrelevant evidence, generally—Matters not in dispute

Jordan v. Knafel, 378 Ill. App. 3d 219, 235–36, 317 Ill. Dec. 69, 880 N.E.2d 1061 (1st Dist. 2007), appeal denied, 227 Ill. 2d 582, 321 Ill. Dec. 251, 888 N.E.2d 1184 (2008) (trial court had discretion to stay discovery that was irrelevant to the issues in a pending summary judgment motion).

Redelmann v. Claire Sprayway, Inc., 375 Ill. App. 3d 912, 926–27, 314 Ill. Dec. 320, 874 N.E.2d 230 (1st Dist. 2007) (trial court had discretion to stay discovery that was irrelevant to the pending motion to dismiss).

Mulloy v. American Eagle Airlines, Inc., 358 Ill. App. 3d 706, 295 Ill. Dec. 54, 832 N.E.2d 205, 210 (1st Dist. 2005) (trial court did not abuse its discretion by excluding lay witness testimony regarding his own driving habits, where not relevant to the issues of the parties' driving habits or negligence).

Bullard v. Barnes, 112 Ill. App. 3d 384, 392–94, 68 Ill. Dec. 37, 445 N.E.2d 485 (4th Dist. 1983), judgment aff'd, 102 Ill. 2d 505, 82 Ill. Dec. 448, 468 N.E.2d 1228 (1984) (trial judge abused his discretion by admitting photographs of the deceased and testimony regarding the conditions and circumstances surrounding the collision because liability was admitted).

§ 3:5 Supporting authorities—Exclusion of irrelevant evidence, generally—No unlimited inquiry

Lisowski v. MacNeal Memorial Hosp. Ass'n, 381 Ill. App. 3d 275, 319 Ill. Dec. 440, 885 N.E.2d 1120 (1st Dist. 2008), appeal denied, 229 Ill. 2d 626, 325 Ill. Dec. 5, 897 N.E.2d 253 (2008) (cross examination that was hearsay, not based upon the evidence and beyond the scope of direct, was properly stricken).

Bergman v. Kelsey, 375 Ill. App. 3d 612, 635–36, 313 Ill. Dec. 862, 873 N.E.2d 486 (1st Dist. 2007), appeal denied, 226 Ill. 2d 579, 316 Ill. Dec. 541, 879 N.E.2d 929 (2007) (evidence regarding subsequent pregnancies were irrelevant to the issue of the pregnancy at issue in this case and was properly excluded).

Jordan v. Knafel, 378 Ill. App. 3d 219, 235–36, 317 Ill. Dec. 69, 880 N.E.2d 1061 (1st Dist. 2007), appeal denied, 227 Ill. 2d 582, 321 Ill. Dec. 251, 888 N.E.2d 1184 (2008) (trial court had discretion to stay discovery that was irrelevant to the issues in a pending summary judgment motion).

Redelmann v. Claire Sprayway, Inc., 375 Ill. App. 3d 912, 926–27, 314 Ill. Dec. 320, 874 N.E.2d 230 (1st Dist. 2007) (trial court had discretion to stay discovery that was irrelevant to the pending motion to dismiss).

Regency Commercial Associates, LLC v. Lopax, Inc., 373 Ill. App. 3d 270, 285–86, 311 Ill. Dec. 636, 869 N.E.2d 310 (4th Dist. 2007) (trial court had discretion to deny a discovery request for information that was irrelevant to the issues).

Chicago Exhibitors Corp. v. Jeepers! of Illinois, Inc., 376 Ill. App. 3d 599, 606–09, 315 Ill. Dec. 129, 876 N.E.2d 129 (1st Dist. 2007) (trial court properly granted a motion in limine to exclude evidence that was insufficient to establish a defense).

Dillon v. Evanston Hosp., 199 Ill. 2d 483, 494–96, 264 Ill. Dec. 653, 771 N.E.2d 357 (2002) (no abuse of discretion when the trial judge limited cumulative testimony of an expert witness and told the jury that he did so in order to more efficiently use their time).

Kurrack v. American Dist. Telegraph Co., 252 Ill. App. 3d 885, 895–96, 192 Ill. Dec. 520, 625 N.E.2d 675 (1st Dist. 1993) (exclusion of repetitive rebuttal testimony because if there are no limits placed on expert testimony, trials would never conclude).

Jones v. Greer, 627 F. Supp. 1481, 1487–88 (C.D. Ill. 1986) (relevant evidence can be excluded because it wastes time or because it causes an emotional decision or whenever the potential harm from the evidence outweighs the benefits of introducing it).

§ 3:6 Supporting authorities—Exclusion of irrelevant evidence, generally—Other states' laws

Illinois law provides that the trial judge determines the law, while the jury (or trier of fact) determines the facts. *National Bank of Colchester v. Murphy*, 384 Ill. 61, 64–65, 50 N.E.2d 748 (1943). Therefore, reference to other state's laws should be excluded as irrelevant pursuant to the theories discussed in this Chapter.

§ 3:7 Supporting authorities—Exclusion of irrelevant evidence, generally—Outside pleadings

In re Leona W., 228 Ill. 2d 439, 320 Ill. Dec. 855, 888 N.E.2d 72 (2008) (in a termination of parental rights case, the trial court did not abuse its discretion by granting a motion in limine to exclude evidence regarding the parent's behavior towards other minors, as irrelevant and beyond the scope of the allegations).

Bergman v. Kelsey, 375 Ill. App. 3d 612, 635–36, 313 Ill. Dec. 862, 873 N.E.2d 486 (1st Dist. 2007), appeal denied, 226 Ill. 2d 579, 316 Ill. Dec. 541, 879 N.E.2d 929 (2007) (evidence regarding subsequent pregnancies were irrelevant to the issue of the pregnancy at issue in this case and was properly excluded).

Chicago Exhibitors Corp. v. Jeepers! of Illinois, Inc., 376 Ill. App. 3d 599, 606–09, 315 Ill. Dec. 129, 876 N.E.2d 129 (1st Dist. 2007) (trial court properly granted a motion in limine to exclude evidence that was insufficient to establish a defense).

Gerwig v. Bruere, 181 Ill. App. 3d 609, 614–15, 130 Ill. Dec. 515, 537 N.E.2d 844 (2d Dist. 1989) (trial judge properly excluded evidence which was outside of the scope of the pleadings).

Carlyle v. Jaskiewicz, 124 Ill. App. 3d 487, 496–98, 79 Ill. Dec. 847, 464 N.E.2d 751 (1st Dist. 1984) (proper to exclude evidence as irrelevant if it does not bear on an issue in the pleadings).

§ 3:8 Supporting authorities—Exclusion of irrelevant evidence, generally—Prejudicial

Boren v. BOC Group, Inc., 385 Ill.App.3d 248, 254–57, 895 N.E.2d 53 (5th Dist. 2008) (photograph of a billboard advertisement which was offered to suggest that cases like the plaintiff's case were solicited and created by lawyers was irrelevant, prejudicial, misleading and confusing and caused grounds for granting a new trial).

People v. Peete, 318 Ill. App. 3d 961, 966–69, 252 Ill. Dec. 821, 743 N.E.2d 689 (4th Dist. 2001) (trial judge has discretion to exclude relevant evidence if it is more prejudicial than probative).

People v. Holman, 257 Ill. App. 3d 1031, 1034, 196 Ill. Dec. 457, 630 N.E.2d 154 (2d Dist. 1994) (exclusion of prejudicial and irrelevant evidence).

People v. Lefler, 38 Ill. 2d 216, 221–22, 230 N.E.2d 827 (1967) (prejudicial evidence should not have been shown to the jury when the nature of the injuries was not disputed and there was adequate expert testimony regarding the injuries).

See generally § 2:1 to § 2:4, supra.

§ 3:9 Supporting authorities—Exclusion of irrelevant evidence, generally—Speculative evidence

Downey v. Dunnington, 384 Ill.App.3d 350, 386, 895 N.E.2d 271 (4th Dist. 2008) (in a case involving an alleged lack of informed consent, it was improper to allow an expert to testify about what the plaintiff might have done if properly informed because such testimony was speculative and invaded the province of the jury)(harmless error).

CFC Investment, L.L.C. v. McLean, 387 Ill.App.3d 520, 529–30, 900 N.E.2d 716 (1st Dist. 2008) (a party's speculative deposition testimony was not admissible as an admission).

Wiedenbeck v. Searle, 385 Ill.App.3d 289, 895 N.E.2d 1067 (1st Dist. 2008) (speculative expert testimony was insufficient to avoid summary judgment in a case alleging medical malpractice).

Torres v. Midwest Development Co., 383 Ill.App.3d 20, 27–28, 889 N.E.2d 654 (1st Dist. 2008) (expert's opinion lacked a sufficient factual basis and was inadmissible).

Kirkpatrick v. Strosberg, 2008 WL 1795597, 6 (Ill. App. Ct. 2d Dist. 2008), opinion modified and superseded, 385 Ill. App. 3d 119, 323 Ill. Dec. 755, 894 N.E.2d 781 (2d Dist. 2008), appeal denied, 229 Ill. 2d 669, 900 N.E.2d 1118 (2008) and appeal denied, 229 Ill. 2d 669 (2008) (the trial court did not abuse its discretion by determining that an expert appraiser's testimony, which was based upon outdated valuations, was speculative).

Baraniak v. Kurby, 371 Ill. App. 3d 310, 316–18, 308 Ill. Dec. 949, 862 N.E.2d 1152 (1st Dist. 2007), appeal denied, 224 Ill. 2d 571, 312 Ill. Dec. 654, 871 N.E.2d 54 (2007) (without expert testimony to correlate the amount of damage to a vehicle to the amount of personal injuries suffered by the occupants of the vehicle, photographs depicting the damage to the vehicles was irrelevant).

Sobczak v. General Motors Corp., 373 Ill. App. 3d 910, 926–27, 312 Ill. Dec. 682, 871 N.E.2d 82 (1st Dist. 2007), appeal denied, 226 Ill. 2d 609, 316 Ill. Dec. 551, 879 N.E.2d 939 (2007) (Speculative and conclusory opinion, about an issue that the expert lacked personal knowledge of, was properly excluded).

Addis v. Exelon Generation Co., L.L.C., 378 Ill. App. 3d 781, 794, 316 Ill. Dec. 949, 880 N.E.2d 685 (1st Dist. 2007), appeal denied, 228 Ill. 2d 529, 321 Ill. Dec. 554, 889 N.E.2d 1114 (2008) (in a case alleging improper termination, testimony by a supervisor who had left the defendant's company months before the plaintiff was terminated was relevant and admissible).

Jordan v. Knafel, 378 Ill. App. 3d 219, 228, 317 Ill. Dec. 69, 880 N.E.2d 1061 (1st Dist. 2007), appeal denied, 227 Ill. 2d 582, 321 Ill. Dec. 251, 888 N.E.2d 1184 (2008) (speculative and conclusory assertions are insufficient to overcome a motion for summary judgment).

Rose v. Mercedes-Benz U.S.A., LLC, 378 Ill. App. 3d 615, 621–26, 317 Ill. Dec. 538, 882 N.E.2d 112, 64 U.C.C. Rep. Serv. 2d 750 (1st Dist. 2007) (plaintiff's valuation testimony was speculative).

Hussung v. Patel, 369 Ill. App. 3d 924, 308 Ill. Dec. 347, 861 N.E.2d 678, 685-87 (2d Dist. 2007), appeal denied, 223 Ill. 2d 634, 310 Ill. Dec. 248, 865 N.E.2d 968 (2007) (summary judgment was properly granted to the defendant when the plaintiff only presented speculative expert testimony in support of his claim).

Noakes v. National R.R. Passenger Corp., 363 Ill. App. 3d 851, 859–60, 300 Ill. Dec. 593, 845 N.E.2d 14 (1st Dist. 2006) (testimony regarding the original cause of a person's carpal tunnel syndrome was inadmissible where it was irrelevant and speculative).

Foley v. Fletcher, 361 Ill. App. 3d 39, 51, 296 Ill. Dec. 916, 836 N.E.2d 667 (1st Dist. 2005) (because testimony supporting an award for increased risk of future injury was speculative and uncertain; verdict for such damages was vacated on appeal).

Krklus v. Stanley, 359 Ill. App. 3d 471, 295 Ill. Dec. 746, 833 N.E.2d 952, 965–66 (1st Dist. 2005) (suggestion that a party had fabricated evidence as a cover-up attempt was properly excluded as speculative and as more prejudicial than probative).

Perfection Corp. v. Lochinvar Corp., 349 Ill. App. 3d 738, 745–46, 285 Ill. Dec. 645, 812 N.E.2d 465 (1st Dist. 2004) (party's expert opinion regarding damages was unduly speculative and the opposing party was entitled to summary judgment as a result).

People v. Nitz, 353 Ill. App. 3d 978, 985–87, 289 Ill. Dec. 760, 820 N.E.2d 536 (5th Dist. 2004), judgment aff'd in part, rev'd in part, 219 Ill. 2d 400, 302 Ill. Dec. 418, 848 N.E.2d 982 (2006).

People v. Hayes, 353 Ill. App. 3d 578, 583–84, 289 Ill. Dec. 184, 819 N.E.2d 341 (3d Dist. 2004) (in a case involving a shooting, no abuse of discretion to exclude a witness' testimony that victim had previously attempted to sell defendant a gun, where evidence was remote in time, uncertain, and irrelevant).

Modelski v. Navistar Intern. Transp. Corp., 302 Ill. App. 3d 879, 885–86, 236 Ill. Dec. 394, 707 N.E.2d 239 (1st Dist. 1999) (testimony which was based upon speculation and conjecture was irrelevant and should not have been admitted).

Department of Transp. v. Bouy, 69 Ill. App. 3d 29, 37-39, 25 Ill. Dec. 499, 386 N.E.2d 1163 (4th Dist. 1979) (exclusion of expert's opinion testimony when it is based upon a speculative and conjectural method of proof).

People v. Gardner, 47 Ill. App. 3d 529, 537–38, 5 Ill. Dec. 701, 362 N.E.2d 14 (5th Dist. 1977) (trial judge has discretion to exclude evidence that is remote or conjectural).

People v. Newbury, 53 Ill. 2d 228, 239–40, 290 N.E.2d 592 (1972) (trial judge should have excluded evidence when its relevance depended upon unproven assumptions).

§ 3:10 Opposing authorities

Bosco v. Janowitz, 388 Ill.App.3d 450, 463, 903 N.E.2d 756 (1st Dist. 2009) (evidence that the plaintiff failed to follow up with the defendant doctor was relevant to the plaintiff's malpractice claim and was not unfairly prejudicial).

Marston v. Walgreen Co., 389 Ill.App.3d 337, 907 N.E.2d 851 (1st Dist. 2009) (an expert may testify to more than one possible cause of an injury and then it is for the jury to decide causation).

People v. Hogan, 388 Ill.App.3d 885, 896, 904 N.E.2d 1036 (1st Dist. 2009) (a witness' mental health history is relevant for impeachment purposes).

Fronabarger v. Burns, 385 Ill.App.3d 560, 564–65, 895 N.E.2d 1125 (5th Dist. 2008) (trial court had discretion to determine that photographs depicting the amount of damage to vehicles were relevant to suggest the amount of injuries to the occupants of the vehicles).

Johnson v. Johnson, 386 Ill.App.3d 522, 545–46, 898 N.E.2d 145 (1st Dist. 2008) (witness' expert opinion regarding whether a horse was provoked before injuring someone was not improperly speculative).

Grillo v. Yeager Const., 387 Ill.App.3d 577, 600, 900 N.E.2d 1249 (1st Dist. 2008) (a document that provided evidence of conduct that was inconsistent with a party's theory at trial was relevant and admissible).

Donnellan v. First Student, Inc, 383 Ill.App.3d 1040, 1051–52, 891 N.E.2d 463 (1st Dist. 2008) (a "day in the life video" was relevant and not unfairly prejudicial merely because it showed the amount of pain that plaintiff was experiencing).

People ex rel. Dept. of Transp. v. Kotara, L.L.C., 379 Ill.App.3d 276, 284–87, 884 N.E.2d 1235 (3rd Dist. 2008) (evidence that the government agency at issue did not comply with regulations and did not comply with its own policy manual was relevant to the issue of its good-faith in this condemnation case).

Aguirre v. City of Chicago, 382 Ill. App. 3d 89, 320 Ill. Dec. 512, 887 N.E.2d 656 (1st Dist. 2008) (in a case alleging malicious prosecution, testimony from the actual murderer was relevant and admissible).

People v. Gonzalez, 379 Ill. App. 3d 941, 318 Ill. Dec. 673, 884 N.E.2d 228, 235–37 (1st Dist. 2008), appeal pending, (May 1, 2008) and appeal denied, 228 Ill. 2d 541, 321 Ill. Dec. 558, 889 N.E.2d 1118 (2008) (evidence of another murder by the defendant was admissible to explain the course of the investigation regarding the charged murder).

Petraski v. Thedos, 382 Ill. App. 3d 22, 320 Ill. Dec. 244, 887 N.E.2d 24 (1st Dist. 2008), appeal denied, 229 Ill. 2d 657, 325 Ill. Dec. 15, 897 N.E.2d 263 (2008) (evidence regarding whether or not an officer called in a "code" before proceeding at a high rate of speed was relevant to whether his conduct was willful and wanton).

Petraski v. Thedos, 382 Ill. App. 3d 22, 320 Ill. Dec. 244, 887 N.E.2d 24 (1st Dist. 2008), appeal denied, 229 Ill. 2d 657, 325 Ill. Dec. 15, 897 N.E.2d 263 (2008) (trial court erred by excluding an expert's opinion regarding the plaintiff's intoxication that was based upon extrapolation from blood that was drawn after the incident in question because the evidence was relevant and reliable and not unfairly prejudicial).

Bergman v. Kelsey, 375 Ill. App. 3d 612, 630–32, 313 Ill. Dec. 862, 873 N.E.2d 486 (1st Dist. 2007), appeal denied, 226 Ill. 2d 579, 316 Ill. Dec. 541, 879 N.E.2d 929 (2007) (trial court had discretion to allow the plaintiff to introduce post-incident medical literature because it was relevant and not being offered to suggest the standard of care at the time of the incident in question).

Johnson v. Loyola University Medical Center, 2008 WL 919700, 4–8 (Ill. App. Ct. 1st Dist. 2008), opinion modified and superseded on denial of reh'g, 384 Ill. App. 3d 115, 323 Ill. Dec. 253, 893 N.E.2d 267 (1st Dist. 2008), appeal denied, 229 Ill. 2d 669, 900 N.E.2d 1118 (2008) (expert testimony was not speculative and was sufficient to support a jury's finding regarding causation).

McNamee v. Sandore, 373 Ill. App. 3d 636, 648–50, 312 Ill. Dec. 111, 869 N.E.2d 1102 (2d Dist. 2007), appeal denied, 225 Ill. 2d 637, 314 Ill. Dec. 826, 875 N.E.2d 1113 (2007) (admission of agency was a legal conclusion and thus, judicial estoppel would not bar a party from later offering evidence to refute that admission).

People v. Evans, 373 Ill. App. 3d 948, 958–59, 311 Ill. Dec. 907, 869 N.E.2d 920 (1st Dist. 2007), appeal denied, 225 Ill. 2d 648, 314 Ill. Dec. 830, 875 N.E.2d 1117 (2007) (other crimes evidence was relevant because it placed the defendant in close proximity to the scene of the charged crime).

Pancoe v. Singh, 376 Ill. App. 3d 900, 907–08, 315 Ill. Dec. 288, 876 N.E.2d 288 (1st Dist. 2007), appeal denied, 226 Ill. 2d 617, 317 Ill. Dec. 504, 882 N.E.2d 78 (2008) (by presenting evidence in support of an affirmative defense, the defendant waived its claim that the plaintiff had admitted the affirmative defense by failing to file a reply).

Harmon v. Town of Cicero Mun. Officers Electoral Bd., 371 Ill. App. 3d 1111, 1116, 309 Ill. Dec. 755, 864 N.E.2d 996 (1st Dist. 2007), appeal denied, 225 Ill. 2d 632, 314 Ill. Dec. 824, 875 N.E.2d 1111 (2007) (it is proper for a judge to allow cross-examination regarding a witness' preparation for testifying).

People v. Dixon, 378 Ill. App. 3d 535, 549–51, 317 Ill. Dec. 788, 882 N.E.2d 668 (1st Dist. 2007), appeal denied, 227 Ill. 2d 587, 321 Ill. Dec. 253, 888 N.E.2d 1186 (2008) (evidence regarding fear of gang retaliation was relevant to the issue of why certain witnesses recanted their prior statements and it was not unfairly prejudicial).

People v. Flowers, 371 Ill. App. 3d 326, 329-30, 308 Ill. Dec. 882, 862 N.E.2d 1085 (1st Dist. 2007), appeal denied, 224 Ill. 2d 582, 312 Ill. Dec. 658, 871 N.E.2d 58 (2007) (where the witness' records showed that the witness had suffered from hallucinations in the past, witness' mental health history was relevant to the issue of the witness' credibility and should not have been excluded).

Jackson v. Seib, 372 Ill. App. 3d 1061, 310 Ill. Dec. 502, 866 N.E.2d 663 (5th Dist. 2007) (even without expert testimony, photographs depicting little damage to a vehicle were admissible to establish the amount of force involved in the collision).

Jones v. Rallos, 373 Ill. App. 3d 439, 311 Ill. Dec. 450, 869 N.E.2d 124 (1st Dist. 2006) (evidence of the plaintiff's prior bad acts and criminal behavior was relevant to rebut his claim that he began acting in a criminal fashion as a result of the negligence of the defendant), judgment vacated, *Jones v. Rallos*, 225 Ill. 2d 636, 314 Ill. Dec. 13, 873 N.E.2d 943 (2007) ("The appellate court is directed to reconsider its judgment, with additional analysis of whether any error in the trial court's decision to permit plaintiff-appellee to elicit evidence of defendant-appellant's failure to pass board-certification examinations constitutes no more than harmless, non-reversible error.").

Webber v. Wight & Co., 368 Ill. App. 3d 1007, 1027-29, 306 Ill. Dec. 782, 858 N.E.2d 579 (1st Dist. 2006), appeal denied, 223 Ill. 2d 686, 310 Ill. Dec. 258, 865 N.E.2d 978 (2007) (letters written by the plaintiff about the defendants were relevant to impeach the plaintiff's testimony regarding the defendant's alleged improper practices).

In re L.W., 367 Ill. App. 3d 844, 856-59, 305 Ill. Dec. 674, 856 N.E.2d 479 (1st Dist. 2006), appeal allowed, 222 Ill. 2d 608, 308 Ill. Dec. 636, 862 N.E.2d 234 (2007) and judgment rev'd, 228 Ill. 2d 439, 320 Ill. Dec. 855, 888 N.E.2d 72 (2008) (evidence regarding the parent's ability to care for the child's siblings was relevant to the issue of the parent's fitness to care for the child at issue), reversed by *In re Leona W.*, 228 Ill. 2d 439, 320 Ill. Dec. 855, 888 N.E.2d 72 (2008) (in a termination of parental rights case, the trial court did not abuse its discretion by granting a motion in limine to exclude evidence regarding the parent's behavior towards other minors, as irrelevant and beyond the scope of the allegations).

People v. Robinson, 368 Ill. App. 3d 963, 978-79, 307 Ill. Dec. 232, 859 N.E.2d 232 (1st Dist. 2006), appeal denied, 223 Ill. 2d 670, 310 Ill. Dec. 255, 865 N.E.2d 975 (2007) (lay witness' opinion regarding the defendant's sobriety two hours before the alleged DUI was relevant and should not have been excluded).

People v. Meyers, 367 Ill. App. 3d 402, 416-17, 304 Ill. Dec. 944, 854 N.E.2d 286 (2d Dist. 2006) (in a trial for resisting a peace officer and aggravated battery of a peace officer, impeachment evidence regarding the defendant's prior conviction for aggravated fleeing or attempting to elude a police officer was relevant regarding the issue of his credibility and it was not unfairly prejudicial).

Troyan v. Reyes, 367 Ill. App. 3d 729, 732-39, 305 Ill. Dec. 451, 855 N.E.2d 967 (3d Dist. 2006) (certain of the plaintiff's medical records which included diagnoses and opinions were relevant and the trial court erred by excluding them).

People v. Singleton, 367 Ill. App. 3d 182, 189-91, 304 Ill. Dec. 984, 854 N.E.2d 326 (4th Dist. 2006) (evidence that the co-defendant had pled guilty was relevant and admissible as a response to the defendant's implication that the co-defendant had been given full immunity in exchange for testifying against the defendant).

People v. Ursery, 364 Ill. App. 3d 680, 686–87, 302 Ill. Dec. 146, 848 N.E.2d 146 (5th Dist. 2006) (gloves that were found in an apartment approximately six months after the murder, were relevant and admissible in the defendant's murder trial, based upon circumstantial evidence tying the gloves to the defendant).

Thornton v. Garcini, 364 Ill. App. 3d 612, 619–21, 301 Ill. Dec. 386, 846 N.E.2d 989 (3d Dist. 2006) (in a wrongful death case, expert testimony regarding whether a child was likely to have been born with disabilities was relevant to the issue of whether the parents suffered injury from loss of the child's society).

Sharp v. Trans Union L.L.C., 364 Ill. App. 3d 64, 71-75, 300 Ill. Dec. 830, 845 N.E.2d 719 (1st Dist. 2006), as modified on denial of reh'g, (Mar. 1, 2006) (communications between a company and its attorneys were not protected from disclosure under an attorney-client privilege doctrine where the attorney's knowledge of certain facts and issues was relevant to whether a claim existed under the insurance policies).

Village of Oak Park v. Village of Oak Park Firefighters Pension Bd., 362 Ill. App. 3d 357, 372, 298 Ill. Dec. 235, 839 N.E.2d 558 (1st Dist. 2005) (an expert's opinion regarding causation, which was stated in terms of being "more likely than not," was sufficiently certain to support a finding of causation).

Ferro v. Griffiths, 361 Ill. App. 3d 738, 742, 297 Ill. Dec. 194, 836 N.E.2d 925 (3d Dist. 2005) (the trial court had discretion to determine that photographs depicting little damage to the vehicles was relevant to assist the jury in determining the nature of the injuries, even if there was no expert testimony accompanying the photographs).

Camco, Inc. v. Lowery, 362 Ill. App. 3d 421, 435–36, 298 Ill. Dec. 332, 839 N.E.2d 655 (1st Dist. 2005) (evidence regarding an officer's deposition testimony that was based upon the officer's own knowledge and observations was relevant and admissible).

Camco, Inc. v. Lowery, 362 Ill. App. 3d 421, 434–35, 298 Ill. Dec. 332, 839 N.E.2d 655 (1st Dist. 2005) (a lab report was relevant and admissible under a statutory hearsay exception).

People v. Wilder, 356 Ill. App. 3d 712, 720–21, 292 Ill. Dec. 640, 826 N.E.2d 1076 (1st Dist. 2005) (trial court did not err by determining that a bullet cartridge which was found at the apartment of the defendant's co-defendants was relevant).

Quinlan v. Stouffe, 355 Ill. App. 3d 830, 837, 291 Ill. Dec. 305, 823 N.E.2d 597 (4th Dist. 2005) (testimony regarding discussions at a settlement meeting was admissible and relevant to the issue of whether an oral contract was formed and if so, the nature of its terms).

Kimble v. Earle M. Jorgenson Co., 358 Ill. App. 3d 400, 294 Ill. Dec. 402, 830 N.E.2d 814, 829–30 (1st Dist. 2005) (photographs were not unduly gruesome and were relevant to the nature of injury and causation).

In re Kenneth J., 352 Ill. App. 3d 967, 978–82, 288 Ill. Dec. 290, 817 N.E.2d 940 (1st Dist. 2004) (in a termination of parental rights case, a report from a parenting assessment team was relevant to the unfitness portion of the hearing, over the parent's assertion that it applied only to the best interest portion of the hearing).

Hahn v. Union Pacific R. Co., 352 Ill. App. 3d 922, 930–31, 287 Ill. Dec. 867, 816 N.E.2d 834 (5th Dist. 2004) (trial court did not abuse its discretion in allowing an expert to testify about possible causation).

Matuszak v. Cerniak, 346 Ill. App. 3d 766, 772–74, 282 Ill. Dec. 62, 805 N.E.2d 681 (3d Dist. 2004) (expert's testimony regarding causation was not unduly speculative, even though it failed to rule out all possible causes).

People v. Cantlin, 348 Ill. App. 3d 998, 1001–01, 285 Ill. Dec. 29, 811 N.E.2d 270 (2d Dist. 2004) (evidence that the defendant had an open bottle of alcohol in the back seat of his vehicle was relevant in a DUI prosecution).

Tri-G, Inc. v. Burke, Bosselman and Weaver, 353 Ill. App. 3d 197, 221–22, 288 Ill. Dec. 580, 817 N.E.2d 1230 (2d Dist. 2004), judgment aff'd in part, rev'd in part, 222 Ill. 2d 218, 305 Ill. Dec. 584, 856 N.E.2d 389 (2006) (trial court did not err by allowing a witness with experience in the field to testify regarding expected lost profits, over opposition claims that the evidence was speculative) (note that this case was appealed to the Illinois Supreme Court, which did not disturb the Appellate Court's decision regarding this issue; see *Tri-G, Inc. v. Burke, Bosselman & Weaver*, 222 Ill. 2d 218, 305 Ill. Dec. 584, 856 N.E.2d 389 (2006).

People v. Szudy, 262 Ill. App. 3d 695, 712–13, 200 Ill. Dec. 462, 635 N.E.2d 801 (1st Dist. 1994) (prosecutor has the right to prove each element of an offense even if the defendant has stipulated to the facts supporting that element).

Lee v. Chicago Transit Authority, 152 Ill. 2d 432, 461–65, 178 Ill. Dec. 699, 605 N.E.2d 493 (1992) (it is within the trial judge's discretion to admit evidence on a stipulated point and to determine whether evidence might confuse the jury).

O'Brien v. Hertl, 238 Ill. App. 3d 217, 223, 179 Ill. Dec. 393, 606 N.E.2d 225 (1st Dist. 1992) (a party has a right to introduce evidence which assists in the proof of the party's case and also evidence which tends to defeat the other party's theory).

Veer v. Hagemann, 334 Ill. 23, 27–28, 165 N.E. 175 (1929) (trial judge has discretion whether to admit evidence on points that have been conceded or that might confuse the issues).

B. MOTION TO EXCLUDE EVIDENCE OF MATTERS NOT IN CONTROVERSY

§ 3:11 Suggested motion text

[Name of moving party] hereby moves this Court for an order excluding any and all evidence, references to evidence, testimony or argument relating to *[describe matter not in controversy]*. The motion is based upon the ground that the evidence relates to a matter that is not in controversy in this action and is therefore irrelevant, immaterial and inadmissible.

§ 3:12 Motion summary

This motion is based on Illinois cases prohibiting the introduction of evidence of matters not in controversy. See *Bullard v. Barnes*, 112 Ill. App. 3d 384, 392–94, 68 Ill. Dec. 37, 445 N.E.2d 485 (4th Dist. 1983), judgment aff'd, 102 Ill. 2d 505, 82 Ill. Dec. 448, 468 N.E.2d 1228 (1984); and *People v. Lefler*, 38 Ill. 2d 216, 221–22, 230 N.E.2d 827 (1967).

§ 3:13 Supporting authorities—Exclusion of irrelevant evidence, generally

Federal Rule of Evidence 401 defines relevancy as,

> evidence having any tendency to make the existence of any fact that is of consequence to the determination of the action more probable or less probable than it would be without the evidence.

Illinois has adopted this definition of relevancy through case law. *Spencer v. Wandolowski*, 264 Ill. App. 3d 611, 617, 201 Ill. Dec. 422, 636 N.E.2d 854 (1st Dist. 1994); *People v. Monroe*, 66 Ill. 2d 317, 321–22, 5 Ill. Dec. 824, 362 N.E.2d 295 (1977).

Preston ex rel. Preston v. Simmons, 321 Ill. App. 3d 789, 803, 254 Ill. Dec. 647, 747 N.E.2d 1059 (1st Dist. 2001) (trial judge should not permit such wide latitude on cross-examination that it undermines the rule that only relevant evidence is admissible).

For expanded citations on the exclusion of irrelevant evidence, see § 3:1 to § 3:10, supra.

§ 3:14 Supporting authorities—Exclusion of irrelevant evidence, generally—Admitted or uncontroverted matters

Myoda Computer Center Inc. v. American Family Mut. Ins. Co., 2009 WL 884902, 3 (1st Dist. 2009) (a stipulation by a party's attorney was a binding judicial admission by the party).

Downey v. Dunnington, 384 Ill.App.3d 350, 380–81, 895 N.E.2d 271 (4th Dist. 2008) (a party's inconsistent deposition testimony was admissible as an admission).

Jannusch v. Naffziger, 379 Ill. App. 3d 381, 385–87, 318 Ill. Dec. 480, 883 N.E.2d 711, 65 U.C.C. Rep. Serv. 2d 116 (4th Dist. 2008) (party's admission that there was an agreement constituted proof of the existence of an agreement).

Capital One Bank, N.A. v. Czekala, 379 Ill. App. 3d 737, 318 Ill. Dec. 934, 884 N.E.2d 1205, 1212–13 (3d Dist. 2008) (an admission in an affidavit was binding on the party who made the admission).

In re A.W., 373 Ill. App. 3d 574, 577–78, 311 Ill. Dec. 400, 868 N.E.2d 400 (3d Dist. 2007), appeal allowed, 225 Ill. 2d 633, 314 Ill. Dec. 825, 875 N.E.2d 1112 (2007) and judgment aff'd in part, rev'd in part, 231 Ill. 2d 92, 324 Ill. Dec. 530, 896 N.E.2d 316 (2008) (in a neglect proceeding, collateral estoppel barred a parent from attempting to rebut prior allegations of abuse that were previously litigated).

Addis v. Exelon Generation Co., L.L.C., 378 Ill. App. 3d 781, 790, 316 Ill. Dec. 949, 880 N.E.2d 685 (1st Dist. 2007), appeal denied, 228 Ill. 2d 529, 321 Ill. Dec. 554, 889 N.E.2d 1114 (2008) (trial court's instruction that notified the jury that the plaintiff had made an initial admission to one of the relevant issues was based upon the evidence and was not an abuse of discretion).

In re Stephen K., 373 Ill. App. 3d 7, 310 Ill. Dec. 768, 867 N.E.2d 81 (1st Dist. 2007) (a party was estopped from taking a legal and factual position that was contrary to the position that she had taken at the trial court hearing).

Kulchawik v. Durabla Mfg. Co., 371 Ill. App. 3d 964, 309 Ill.

Dec. 503, 864 N.E.2d 744 (1st Dist. 2007) (party was bound by the admission of its attorney in an unverified pleading that the case was settled).

In re Marriage of Mannix and Sheetz, 2007 WL 958574, 4-6 (Ill. App. Ct. 1st Dist. 2007), opinion modified and superseded on denial of reh'g, 374 Ill. App. 3d 76, 311 Ill. Dec. 782, 869 N.E.2d 795 (1st Dist. 2007), as modified on denial of reh'g, (June 18, 2007) and appeal denied, 225 Ill. 2d 637, 314 Ill. Dec. 826, 875 N.E.2d 1113 (2007) (parties each made judicial admissions regarding the paternity of a child, by making factual statements regarding paternity in their verified pleadings).

Alwin v. Village of Wheeling, 371 Ill. App. 3d 898, 309 Ill. Dec. 656, 864 N.E.2d 897 (1st Dist. 2007), appeal denied, 224 Ill. 2d 571, 312 Ill. Dec. 654, 871 N.E.2d 54 (2007) (in a trial after remand, holdings from the prior appeal represented the law of the case).

Sweilem v. Illinois Dept. of Revenue, 372 Ill. App. 3d 475, 310 Ill. Dec. 135, 865 N.E.2d 459 (1st Dist. 2007) (in most circumstances, a fact-finder cannot reject unrebutted testimony that is not inherently incredible or proven to be so).

Roti v. Roti, 364 Ill. App. 3d 191, 199–200, 301 Ill. Dec. 27, 845 N.E.2d 892 (1st Dist. 2006) (allegations in a party's complaint were binding judicial admissions).

Tyler v. Gibbons, 368 Ill. App. 3d 126, 128, 306 Ill. Dec. 486, 857 N.E.2d 885 (3d Dist. 2006) (a verified complaint constitutes an admission by the complaining party).

Knauerhaze v. Nelson, 361 Ill. App. 3d 538, 557–59, 296 Ill. Dec. 889, 836 N.E.2d 640 (1st Dist. 2005) (generally a statement in a verified pleading remains a judicial admission even if it was superseded by a contrary statement in an amended verified pleading).

Steiner Elec. Co. v. NuLine Technologies, Inc., 364 Ill. App. 3d 876, 881–82, 301 Ill. Dec. 646, 847 N.E.2d 656 (1st Dist. 2006) (a party's deposition testimony which denied knowledge of certain facts, constituted a binding admission of the party).

Larson v. O'Donnell, 361 Ill. App. 3d 388, 397–98, 297 Ill. Dec. 132, 836 N.E.2d 863 (1st Dist. 2005) (overruled by, Vision Point of Sale, Inc. v. Haas, 226 Ill. 2d 334, 314 Ill. Dec. 778, 875 N.E.2d 1065 (2007)) (a party was judicially estopped from asserting legal theories which were contrary to the assertions that he had made in prior litigation).

Davis v. International Harvester Co., 167 Ill. App. 3d 814, 824–25, 118 Ill. Dec. 589, 521 N.E.2d 1282 (2d Dist. 1988) (proper to exclude evidence of the feasibility of design changes when there was an admission regarding such feasibility).

Carlyle v. Jaskiewicz, 124 Ill. App. 3d 487, 495–96, 79 Ill. Dec. 847, 464 N.E.2d 751 (1st Dist. 1984) (the trial judge properly took judicial notice of certain facts and then excluded additional proof regarding those facts).

Bullard v. Barnes, 112 Ill. App. 3d 384, 392–94, 68 Ill. Dec. 37, 445 N.E.2d 485 (4th Dist. 1983), judgment aff'd, 102 Ill. 2d 505, 82 Ill. Dec. 448, 468 N.E.2d 1228 (1984) (trial judge abused his discretion by admitting photographs of the deceased and testimony regarding the conditions and circumstances surrounding the collision because liability was admitted).

§ 3:15 Supporting authorities—Exclusion of irrelevant evidence, generally—Collateral issues

In re Leona W., 228 Ill. 2d 439, 320 Ill. Dec. 855, 888 N.E.2d 72 (2008) (in a termination of parental rights case, the trial court did not abuse its discretion by granting a motion in limine to exclude evidence regarding the parent's behavior towards other minors, as irrelevant and beyond the scope of the allegations).

Gaston v. Founders Ins. Co., 365 Ill. App. 3d 303, 301 Ill. Dec. 513, 847 N.E.2d 523, 539–40 (1st Dist. 2006) (expert testimony regarding costs involved in fixing an automobile were irrelevant when the insurance company had provided the insured a method of fixing the car at a cost which would not exceed the insured's deductible).

People v. Carini, 357 Ill. App. 3d 103, 115–18, 293 Ill. Dec. 134, 827 N.E.2d 1015 (1st Dist. 2005) (the trial court did not abuse its discretion by determining that the defendant's proposed surrebuttal evidence was collateral).

People v. Santos, 211 Ill. 2d 395, 401–08, 286 Ill. Dec. 102, 813 N.E.2d 159 (2004) (victim's prior inconsistent statement regarding sexual activity with someone other than the defendant was collateral to the issues in the case).

People v. Harvey, 211 Ill. 2d 368, 392, 286 Ill. Dec. 124, 813 N.E.2d 181 (2004) (no abuse of discretion to exclude irrelevant and collateral evidence that victim had previously purchased narcotics from individuals other than defendant).

People v. Kaczmarek, 243 Ill. App. 3d 1067, 1077–78, 184 Ill. Dec. 661, 613 N.E.2d 1253 (1st Dist. 1993) (exclusion of defendant's proof of prior incidents by other perpetrators as too speculative and dissimilar).

Pagel v. Yates, 128 Ill. App. 3d 897, 903, 84 Ill. Dec. 180, 471 N.E.2d 946 (4th Dist. 1984) (exclusion of irrelevant, collateral and confusing document).

People v. Gardner, 47 Ill. App. 3d 529, 537–38, 5 Ill. Dec. 701, 362 N.E.2d 14 (5th Dist. 1977) (trial judge has discretion to exclude rebuttal evidence that is remote or conjectural).

People v. Wilson, 400 Ill. 603, 605–08, 81 N.E.2d 445 (1948) (testimony regarding past domestic disputes was collateral and remote and therefore, properly excluded).

§ 3:16 Supporting authorities—Exclusion of irrelevant evidence, generally—Unpleaded issues

CFC Investment, L.L.C. v. McLean, 387 Ill.App.3d 520, 530–31, 900 N.E.2d 716 (1st Dist. 2008) (evidence of conduct that was outside of the scope of the complaint was excluded as unduly confusing, misleading and time wasting).

Jones v. O'Brien Tire and Battery Service Center, Inc., 374 Ill. App. 3d 918, 936–37, 312 Ill. Dec. 698, 871 N.E.2d 98 (5th Dist. 2007), appeal denied, 225 Ill. 2d 636, 314 Ill. Dec. 826, 875 N.E.2d 1113 (2007) (trial court had discretion to deny a party's request to amend the complaint shortly before trial to add a new cause of action based on information that had been in the party's possession for a couple of months before the amendment was proposed).

Gerwig v. Bruere, 181 Ill. App. 3d 609, 614–15, 130 Ill. Dec. 515, 537 N.E.2d 844 (2d Dist. 1989) (trial judge properly excluded evidence which was outside of the scope of the pleadings).

Carlyle v. Jaskiewicz, 124 Ill. App. 3d 487, 496–98, 79 Ill. Dec. 847, 464 N.E.2d 751 (1st Dist. 1984) (proper to exclude evidence as irrelevant if it does not bear on an issue in the pleadings).

§ 3:17 Opposing authorities

See § 3:10, Opposing authorities, supra, for additional opposition authorities.

Rath v. Carbondale Nursing and Rehabilitation Center, Inc., 374 Ill. App. 3d 536, 538–43, 312 Ill. Dec. 722, 871 N.E.2d 122 (5th Dist. 2007) (trial court had discretion to allow a party to present evidence regarding an issue, even though the opposing party stipulated to the issue, because it provided the jury with a full understanding of the case).

§ 3:18 Opposing authorities—Collateral issues

People v. Gonzalez, 379 Ill. App. 3d 941, 318 Ill. Dec. 673, 884 N.E.2d 228, 235–37 (1st Dist. 2008), appeal pending, (May

1, 2008) and appeal denied, 228 Ill. 2d 541, 321 Ill. Dec. 558, 889 N.E.2d 1118 (2008) (evidence of another murder by the defendant was admissible to explain the course of the investigation regarding the charged murder).

People v. Evans, 373 Ill. App. 3d 948, 958–59, 311 Ill. Dec. 907, 869 N.E.2d 920 (1st Dist. 2007), appeal denied, 225 Ill. 2d 648, 314 Ill. Dec. 830, 875 N.E.2d 1117 (2007) (other crimes evidence was relevant because it placed the defendant in close proximity to the scene of the charged crime).

Adams v. Sarah Bush Lincoln Health Center, 369 Ill. App. 3d 988, 314 Ill. Dec. 190, 874 N.E.2d 100 (4th Dist. 2007) (trial court properly precluded cross-examination of the plaintiff's treating physician regarding the proper standard of care, where that issue was beyond the scope of direct examination).

People v. Robinson, 368 Ill. App. 3d 963, 980-82, 307 Ill. Dec. 232, 859 N.E.2d 232 (1st Dist. 2006), appeal denied, 223 Ill. 2d 670, 310 Ill. Dec. 255, 865 N.E.2d 975 (2007) (evidence of a witness' contrary grand jury testimony was not collateral and should not have been excluded).

Preston ex rel. Preston v. Simmons, 321 Ill. App. 3d 789, 802–03, 254 Ill. Dec. 647, 747 N.E.2d 1059 (1st Dist. 2001) (it is within the trial judge's discretion to allow inquiry into collateral matters on cross-examination to impeach credibility).

§ 3:19 Opposing authorities—Estoppel: Unpleaded and stipulated issues

Pancoe v. Singh, 376 Ill. App. 3d 900, 907–08, 315 Ill. Dec. 288, 876 N.E.2d 288 (1st Dist. 2007), appeal denied, 226 Ill. 2d 617, 317 Ill. Dec. 504, 882 N.E.2d 78 (2008) (by presenting evidence in support of an affirmative defense, the defendant waived its claim that the plaintiff had admitted the affirmative defense by failing to file a reply).

Cretton v. Protestant Memorial Medical Center, Inc., 371 Ill. App. 3d 841, 309 Ill. Dec. 422, 864 N.E.2d 288, 309-310 (5th Dist. 2007), appeal denied, 224 Ill. 2d 573, 312 Ill. Dec. 655, 871 N.E.2d 55 (2007) (the trial court had discretion to allow the plaintiff to amend the complaint to conform to the trial testimony).

Pullen v. Mulligan, 138 Ill. 2d 21, 73-75, 149 Ill. Dec. 215, 561 N.E.2d 585 (1990) (if a party fails to object to a stipulation when it is entered, the party cannot complain that the legal effect of it was not intended).

People v. Hawkins, 27 Ill. 2d 339, 341–42, 189 N.E.2d 252 (1963) (when the defendant, the court and counsel all understood a stipulation to include proof of ownership, the defendant cannot argue lack of proof of same).

People v. Polk, 19 Ill. 2d 310, 313–15, 167 N.E.2d 185 (1960) (defendant cannot argue regarding the lack of proof of chain of custody of evidence when he stipulated to the admission and identity of the evidence).

First Nat. Bank v. Miller, 235 Ill. 135, 139, 85 N.E. 312 (1908) (defendant is estopped from arguing that there was no plea by taking the matter to trial without objection).

§ 3:20 Opposing authorities—Where relevant to other issues

People ex rel. Dept. of Transp. v. Kotara, L.L.C., 379 Ill.App.3d 276, 284–87, 884 N.E.2d 1235 (3rd Dist. 2008) (evidence that the government agency at issue did not comply with regulations and did not comply with its own policy manual was relevant to the issue of its good-faith in this condemnation case).

Petraski v. Thedos, 382 Ill. App. 3d 22, 320 Ill. Dec. 244, 887 N.E.2d 24 (1st Dist. 2008), appeal denied, 229 Ill. 2d 657, 325 Ill. Dec. 15, 897 N.E.2d 263 (2008) (evidence regarding whether or not an officer called in a "code" before proceeding at a high rate of speed was relevant to whether his conduct was willful and wanton).

Addis v. Exelon Generation Co., L.L.C., 378 Ill. App. 3d 781, 794, 316 Ill. Dec. 949, 880 N.E.2d 685 (1st Dist. 2007), appeal denied, 228 Ill. 2d 529, 321 Ill. Dec. 554, 889 N.E.2d 1114 (2008) (in a case alleging improper termination, testimony by a supervisor who had left the defendant's company months before the plaintiff was terminated was relevant and admissible).

Bergman v. Kelsey, 375 Ill. App. 3d 612, 630–32, 313 Ill. Dec. 862, 873 N.E.2d 486 (1st Dist. 2007), appeal denied, 226 Ill. 2d 579, 316 Ill. Dec. 541, 879 N.E.2d 929 (2007) (trial court had discretion to allow the plaintiff to introduce post-incident medical literature because it was relevant and not being offered to suggest the standard of care at the time of the incident in question).

In re Kenneth J., 352 Ill. App. 3d 967, 978–82, 288 Ill. Dec. 290, 817 N.E.2d 940 (1st Dist. 2004) (in a termination of parental rights case, a report from a parenting assessment team was relevant to the unfitness portion of the hearing, over the parent's assertion that it applied only to the best interest portion of the hearing).

People v. Szudy, 262 Ill. App. 3d 695, 706, 200 Ill. Dec. 462,

635 N.E.2d 801 (1st Dist. 1994) (evidence which is relevant and admissible for one purpose should not be excluded merely because it is irrelevant or inadmissible for another purpose).

Phillips v. Lawrence, 87 Ill. App. 2d 60, 61-63, 230 N.E.2d 505 (5th Dist. 1967) (in action for personal injuries where liability is admitted, evidence of force of impact and surrounding circumstances may be relevant and material to indicate extent of injuries).

§ 3:21 Opposing authorities—Not a binding judicial admission

Stamp v. Sylvan, 906 N.E.2d 1222, 1230 (1st Dist. 2009) (an attorney's statement during closing argument regarding damages was not a judicial admission because it was merely the attorney's opinion regarding the proper amount for any award).

Herman v. Power Maintenance & Constructors, LLC, 388 Ill.App.3d 352, 360–62, 903 N.E.2d 852 (4th Dist. 2009) (an attorney's statement that was made in error and corrected by an amended pleading was not a judicial admission by the party who was represented by the attorney).

CFC Investment, L.L.C. v. McLean, 387 Ill.App.3d 520, 529–30, 900 N.E.2d 716 (1st Dist. 2008) (a party's speculative deposition testimony was not admissible as an admission).

Dukes v. Pneumo Abex Corp., 386 Ill.App.3d 425, 438–39, 900 N.E.2d 1128 (4th Dist. 2008) (a letter written by a now deceased employee of a party, on a subject outside of the scope of the individual's employment responsibilities, was inflammatory and prejudicial and should not have been considered as an admission of a party).

State ex rel. Beeler, Schad and Diamond, P.C. v. Target Corp., 367 Ill. App. 3d 860, 875-76, 306 Ill. Dec. 1, 856 N.E.2d 1096 (1st Dist. 2006), appeal denied, 222 Ill. 2d 624, 308 Ill. Dec. 641, 862 N.E.2d 239 (2007) (the fact-finder can reject the uncontradicted but implausible testimony of a witness who is interested in the outcome of the case).

Jordan v. Knafel, 355 Ill. App. 3d 534, 544, 291 Ill. Dec. 527, 823 N.E.2d 1113 (1st Dist. 2005) (an attorney's statement that the opposing party's pleading did not contain a certain allegation was not a judicial admission that the allegation would have been false if it was alleged).

People ex rel. Dept. of Public Health v. Wiley, 218 Ill. 2d 207, 268–69, 300 Ill. Dec. 1, 843 N.E.2d 259 (2006) (a conclusion of law in a verified complaint is not a binding judicial admission).

Steiner Elec. Co. v. NuLine Technologies, Inc., 364 Ill. App.

3d 876, 882–83, 301 Ill. Dec. 646, 847 N.E.2d 656 (1st Dist. 2006) (when opposing a summary judgment motion, a party could not rely on its own answers to requests to admit where answers to request to admit are pleadings and pleadings alone are not sufficient to overcome summary judgment).

Knauerhaze v. Nelson, 361 Ill. App. 3d 538, 557–59, 296 Ill. Dec. 889, 836 N.E.2d 640 (1st Dist. 2005) (generally a statement in an unverified pleading is a judicial admission unless it was superseded by a contrary statement in an amended verified pleading).

Cianci v. Safeco Ins. Co. of Illinois, 356 Ill. App. 3d 767, 776, 292 Ill. Dec. 407, 826 N.E.2d 548 (1st Dist. 2005) (a party who files a counterclaim or a third-party claim for contribution in a pending case is not admitting liability in the underlying action by filing that pleading).

II. SAMPLE MOTIONS

§ 3:22 Motion to exclude irrelevant evidence

TO: ALL PARTIES AND THEIR RESPECTIVE ATTORNEYS OF RECORD:

PLEASE TAKE NOTICE that plaintiff hereby moves this Court for an order excluding any and all evidence, references to evidence, testimony or argument relating to plaintiff's immigration and/or residence status.

This motion is made under the provisions of Federal Rule of Evidence 401, as adopted through Illinois case law. See *People v. Monroe*, 66 Ill. 2d 317, 321–22, 5 Ill. Dec. 824, 362 N.E.2d 295 (1977); *Spencer v. Wandolowski*, 264 Ill. App. 3d 611, 617, 201 Ill. Dec. 422, 636 N.E.2d 854 (1st Dist. 1994). It is based upon the supporting Memorandum of Points and Authorities, the pleadings and papers on file in this action, and upon such of the argument and evidence as may be presented prior to or at the hearing of this matter.

Dated: *[date]*

MEMORANDUM OF POINTS AND AUTHORITIES

1.

PRELIMINARY STATEMENT

This is a personal injury action arising out of an automobile versus bicycle accident that occurred on January 15, 1997, where the plaintiff incurred a broken left clavicle and two broken ribs. Plaintiff has indicated that he will not be making a claim for recovery of past or future lost earnings. This motion seeks to preclude the defendant from attempting to present prejudicial and irrelevant evidence relating to the plaintiff's immigration status at the time of trial.

2.
PLAINTIFF'S IMMIGRATION STATUS IS NOT RELEVANT TO ANY MATERIAL ISSUE IN THIS CASE

Federal Rule of Evidence 401 defines relevancy as,

> evidence having any tendency to make the existence of any fact that is of consequence to the determination of the action more probable or less probable than it would be without the evidence.

Illinois has adopted this definition of relevancy through case law. *People v. Monroe*, 66 Ill. 2d 317, 321–22, 5 Ill. Dec. 824, 362 N.E.2d 295 (1977); *Spencer v. Wandolowski*, 264 Ill. App. 3d 611, 617, 201 Ill. Dec. 422, 636 N.E.2d 854 (1st Dist. 1994).

Illinois case law provides that evidence may be properly excluded where it is not relevant to matters at issue. See *Pagel v. Yates*, 128 Ill. App. 3d 897, 903, 84 Ill. Dec. 180, 471 N.E.2d 946 (4th Dist. 1984) (exclusion of irrelevant and confusing document); *Cochran v. Great Atlantic & Pacific Tea Co., Inc.*, 203 Ill. App. 3d 935, 937–38, 148 Ill. Dec. 923, 561 N.E.2d 229 (5th Dist. 1990) (trial judge has inherent power to exclude irrelevant evidence); and *Benson v. Bradford Mut. Fire Ins. Corp.*, 121 Ill. App. 3d 500, 510, 76 Ill. Dec. 774, 459 N.E.2d 689, 47 A.L.R.4th 759 (2d Dist. 1984) (trial judge had discretion to exclude irrelevant witness testimony).

In a California case, a court has specifically held that Plaintiff's immigration or residence status is not relevant to the determination of liability. See *Rodriguez v. Kline*, 186 Cal. App. 3d 1145, 232 Cal. Rptr. 157 (2d Dist. 1986). Similarly, Illinois law suggests that a party's life circumstances are not relevant when the party's claim is for compensatory damages only. See e.g. *Chicago Daily News Emp. Credit Union v. Reed*, 42 Ill. App. 2d 336, 340, 192 N.E.2d 447 (1st Dist. 1963) (a party's financial status is not relevant for cross-examination purposes); and *Pagel v. Yates*, 128 Ill. App. 3d 897, 902, 84 Ill. Dec. 180, 471 N.E.2d 946 (4th Dist. 1984) (when the issue is only compensatory damages, a party's financial status is not relevant and is prejudicial). Since the plaintiff is making no claim for past or future loss of earnings, his immigration or residence status is not relevant to the determination of any issues in this case and should properly be excluded.

The instant matter is distinguishable from *People v. Clamuextle*, 255 Ill. App. 3d 504, 511–12, 193 Ill. Dec. 431, 626

N.E.2d 741 (2d Dist. 1994); and *People v. Austin*, 123 Ill. App. 3d 788, 797, 79 Ill. Dec. 103, 463 N.E.2d 444 (2d Dist. 1984), wherein the court held that the defendant could question the State's witnesses about the witnesses' "illegal alien" status, because it potentially showed a bias to testify in favor of the state. Due to the fact that this matter is a civil case, which is between two individuals, there is no such question of bias in favor of a governmental entity. In addition, in the case of *People v. Mancilla*, 250 Ill. App. 3d 353, 358–60, 189 Ill. Dec. 846, 620 N.E.2d 1163 (1st Dist. 1993), the court held that the state should not have been permitted to mention a witness' immigration status when the admission of the information resulted in intimidating a crucial defense witness.

3.
ADMISSION OF PLAINTIFF'S IMMIGRATION STATUS WOULD CREATE UNDUE PREJUDICE TO PLAINTIFF

Federal Rule of Evidence 403 states:

> Although relevant, evidence may be excluded if its probative value is substantially outweighed by the danger of unfair prejudice, confusion of the issues, or misleading the jury, or by considerations of undue delay, waste of time, or needless presentation of cumulative evidence.

Although this rule has not been specifically codified in Illinois, case law has stated that Illinois has a common-law rule that is comparable to Federal Rule of Evidence 403. See *People v. Peete*, 318 Ill. App. 3d 961, 966–67, 252 Ill. Dec. 821, 743 N.E.2d 689 (4th Dist. 2001); *People v. Walker*, 335 Ill. App. 3d 102, 112, 268 Ill. Dec. 654, 779 N.E.2d 268 (2d Dist. 2002), as modified on denial of reh'g, (Oct. 24, 2002) and judgment aff'd, 211 Ill. 2d 317, 285 Ill. Dec. 519, 812 N.E.2d 339 (2004).

Evidence should be excluded when the prejudicial impact of the evidence outweighs the probative value of it. *Department of Public Works and Bldgs. v. Roehrig*, 45 Ill. App. 3d 189, 196, 3 Ill. Dec. 893, 359 N.E.2d 752 (5th Dist. 1976) (exclusion of evidence of prior condemnations in a condemnation case because the prejudicial impact outweighs the probative value of it); *People v. Holman*, 257 Ill. App. 3d 1031, 1033–34, 196 Ill. Dec. 457, 630 N.E.2d 154 (2d Dist. 1994) (evidence is admissible if it is relevant and if the prejudicial impact does not substantially outweigh the probative value of it); and, *Hulsebus v. Russian*, 118 Ill. App. 2d 174, 180–81, 254 N.E.2d 184 (2d Dist. 1969) (trial judge had discretion to exclude a gruesome photograph of the plaintiff during surgery because other evidence established the extent of the injury and because the photograph was likely to inflame and prejudice the jury). In the instant matter there is a strong probability that the admission of the plaintiff's immigration or residency status will create a substantial danger of undue prejudice.

The authorities described above justify the preclusion of the requested evidence in this case. Given the clear lack of relevance, defendant's intention by admitting such evidence can only be to prejudice the plaintiff and cause the jury to look negatively or with ill feelings towards the plaintiff. Certainly, the issues will be confused and the jury will be misled by the admission of such evidence. Moreover, the probative value of the evidence is nonexistent, given the plaintiff's lack of any claim for lost earnings.

4.
CONCLUSION

Based upon all of the above, exclusion or reference to the plaintiff's immigration or residence status is proper.

Dated: *[date]*

By: ______________________
[name of counsel]
Attorneys for PLAINTIFF,
[name of plaintiff]

§ 3:23 Motion to exclude evidence of physical conditions not at issue

TO: ALL PARTIES AND THEIR RESPECTIVE ATTORNEYS OF RECORD:

PLEASE TAKE NOTICE that plaintiff hereby moves this Court for an order excluding any and all evidence, references to evidence, testimony or argument relating to plaintiff's physical conditions that are not at issue in this action.

This motion is made under the provisions of Illinois case law, and is based upon the supporting Memorandum of Points and Authorities, the pleadings and papers on file in this action, and upon such of the argument and evidence as may be presented prior to or at the hearing of this matter.

Dated: *[date]*

MEMORANDUM OF POINTS AND AUTHORITIES

1. PRELIMINARY STATEMENT

The incident which gives rise to this lawsuit for professional negligence occurred on about June 30, 1997, when the plaintiff underwent multiple surgeries by the defendant. Plaintiff alleges and will prove at trial that, during the surgeries, the defendant's conduct fell below the standard of care in the community.

In his proposed witness list, the defendant has included health care practitioners who have treated plaintiff for conditions or injuries in areas of the body *other* than those alleged to have been injured in the within action. By this motion, the plaintiff seeks to exclude the testimony of any witness on such matters.

2. PREJUDICIAL EVIDENCE MAY BE EXCLUDED

Federal Rule of Evidence 403 states:

> Although relevant, evidence may be excluded if its probative value is substantially outweighed by the danger of unfair prejudice, confusion of the issues, or misleading the jury, or by considerations of undue delay, waste of time, or needless presentation of cumulative evidence.

Although this rule has not been specifically codified in Illinois, case law has stated that Illinois has a common-law rule that is comparable to Federal Rule of Evidence 403. See *People v. Peete*, 318 Ill. App. 3d 961, 966–67, 252 Ill. Dec. 821, 743 N.E.2d 689 (4th Dist. 2001); *People v. Walker*, 335 Ill. App. 3d 102, 112, 268 Ill. Dec. 654, 779 N.E.2d 268 (2d Dist. 2002), as modified on denial of reh'g, (Oct. 24, 2002) and judgment aff'd, 211 Ill. 2d 317, 285 Ill. Dec. 519, 812 N.E.2d 339 (2004).

3. ONLY RELEVANT EVIDENCE IS ADMISSIBLE

Federal Rule of Evidence 401 defines relevancy as,

> evidence having any tendency to make the existence of any fact that is of consequence to the determination of the action more probable or less probable than it would be without the evidence.

Illinois has adopted this definition of relevancy through case law. *People v. Monroe*, 66 Ill. 2d 317, 321–22, 5 Ill. Dec. 824, 362 N.E.2d 295 (1977); *Spencer v. Wandolowski*, 264 Ill. App. 3d 611, 617, 201 Ill. Dec. 422, 636 N.E.2d 854 (1st Dist. 1994). In addition, Illinois law is clear that evidence is not admissible when it is irrelevant. See *Preston ex rel. Preston v. Simmons*,

321 Ill. App. 3d 789, 803, 254 Ill. Dec. 647, 747 N.E.2d 1059 (1st Dist. 2001) (trial judge should not permit such wide latitude on cross-examination that it undermines the rule that only relevant evidence is admissible).

4.
EVIDENCE OF PHYSICAL CONDITIONS THAT ARE NOT AT ISSUE ARE PROPERLY EXCLUDED

In *Cancio v. White*, 297 Ill. App. 3d 422, 428–30, 232 Ill. Dec. 7, 697 N.E.2d 749 (1st Dist. 1998), it was error to allow evidence of plaintiff's pre-existing arthritis when there was no clear proof of a direct link to the injury that was at issue in the case.

In *Vojas v. K mart Corp.*, 312 Ill. App. 3d 544, 551–53, 245 Ill. Dec. 144, 727 N.E.2d 397 (5th Dist. 2000), the court held that the party offering the evidence of a prior injury must prove that it is relevant to the current injury.

In addition, in the case of *Obszanski v. Foster Wheeler Const., Inc.*, 328 Ill. App. 3d 550, 558–60, 262 Ill. Dec. 585, 765 N.E.2d 1193 (1st Dist. 2002), the court ruled that the defendant should not have been permitted to introduce evidence of the defendant's subsequent injury unless the defendant could establish that the new injury was the cause of the plaintiff's current distress.

In *Voykin v. Estate of DeBoer*, 192 Ill. 2d 49, 59, 248 Ill. Dec. 277, 733 N.E.2d 1275 (2000), the court held that

> if a defendant wishes to introduce evidence that the plaintiff has suffered a prior injury, . . . the defendant must introduce expert evidence demonstrating why the prior injury is relevant to causation damages or some other issue of consequence. This rule applies unless the trial court, in its discretion, determines that the natures of the prior and current injuries are such that a lay person can readily appraise the relationship, if any, between those injuries without expert assistance.

In this case, the defendant has not identified an expert regarding any relationship between any prior injuries and the injuries at issue. Further, the nature of the injuries is not such that a lay person can readily appraise any relationship between the injuries without the assistance of an expert. See also, *Felber v. London*, 346 Ill. App. 3d 188, 281 Ill. Dec. 482, 803 N.E.2d 1103 (2d Dist. 2004).

Based on the foregoing authorities, this Court should exclude any references to physical injuries or ailments that are not at issue in this case.

5.
DISCUSSION

In the present case, any evidence of a physical condition not alleged to have been caused by the subject incident is completely irrelevant. Allowing the jury to hear this evidence creates a very real danger that the plaintiff will be prejudiced, since the evidence will create a perception that the plaintiff seeks to recover more than he is entitled to by law. This prejudice significantly outweighs any marginal probative value of admitting such irrelevant and inflammatory evidence.

6.
CONCLUSION

Based on the aforementioned authorities and facts, it is respectfully requested that this Court grant this motion and that all witnesses be precluded from testifying regarding injuries other than those at issue in this case.

Dated: *[date]*

Respectfully submitted,
By: ________________________
[name of counsel]
Attorneys for PLAINTIFF,
[name of plaintiff]

Chapter 4

Writings & Physical Evidence

I. MOTION AUTHORITIES

A. MOTION TO EXCLUDE EVIDENCE LACKING FOUNDATION

B. MOTION TO EXCLUDE WRITINGS, GENERALLY

C. MOTION TO EXCLUDE GRUESOME OR INFLAMMATORY PHOTOGRAPHS

D. MOTION TO EXCLUDE PREJUDICIAL FILM OR VIDEOTAPES

E. MOTION TO EXCLUDE PUBLISHED ARTICLES AND TEXTS

F. MOTION TO EXCLUDE POLICE REPORTS AND OTHER TYPES OF ACCIDENT REPORTS

G. MOTION TO EXCLUDE LETTERS

H. MOTION TO EXCLUDE MAPS, MODELS & CHARTS

I. MOTION TO EXCLUDE IMPROPER MEDICAL RECORDS, REPORTS OR BILLS

II. SAMPLE MOTIONS

I. MOTION AUTHORITIES

A. MOTION TO EXCLUDE EVIDENCE LACKING FOUNDATION

§ 4:1 Suggested motion text

[Name of moving party] hereby moves this Court for an order excluding any and all evidence, references to evidence, testimony or argument relating to *[describe evidence lacking foundation]*. The motion is based upon the ground that the evidence lacks a necessary foundation for admission and therefore should be excluded.

§ 4:2 Motion summary

This motion is used to exclude evidence that lacks a required foundation for admission. Counsel should be prepared to demonstrate, where possible, the lack of actual foundational facts and the prejudice that will occur if the evidence is presented to the jury. See e.g. *Anderson v. Human Rights Com'n*, 314 Ill. App. 3d 35, 42-43, 246 Ill. Dec. 843, 731 N.E.2d 371 (1st Dist. 2000) (a foundation is required to prevent improper evidence from being heard by the fact-finder); and *Hopkinson v. Chicago Transit Authority*, 211 Ill. App. 3d 825, 848, 156 Ill. Dec. 240, 570 N.E.2d 716 (1st Dist. 1991) (even if an error in admission of evidence occurred, the party must have been prejudiced by it in order to warrant reversal on appeal). Arguing prejudice to the trial judge is an important element to the motion, since the court has the power to admit evidence conditionally. See *Greig v. Griffel*, 49 Ill. App. 3d 829, 839–41, 7 Ill. Dec. 499, 364 N.E.2d 660 (2d Dist. 1977).

Often, to save time and for the convenience of the parties and witnesses, the parties stipulate to the foundation and/or admission of many types of evidence that is not in dispute. However, where a party plans to admit evidence whose authenticity is in dispute, the proponent of the evidence must make sure that the proper foundation can be laid before seeking admission of the evidence. Where the opponent of the evidence anticipates that counsel will seek admission of evidence and questions its authenticity or believes that an adequate foundation cannot be laid, the opponent should move to exclude the evidence by filing a motion in limine. In the event the motion in limine is denied, to preserve the error for appeal, the unsuccessful party should object at the time the evidence is offered at trial and include the error in a post-trial motion in one becomes necessary.

The sections that follow provide a number of representative cases where general foundational deficiencies were identified. Not all possible evidence types are included in this text.

§ 4:3 Supporting authorities—Exclusion of prejudicial evidence, generally

Federal Rule of Evidence 403 states:

> Although relevant, evidence may be excluded if its probative value is substantially outweighed by the danger of unfair prejudice, confusion of the issues, or misleading the jury, or by considerations of undue delay, waste of time, or needless presentation of cumulative evidence.

It must be noted that this Rule has not been codified in Illinois. However, Illinois cases have stated that Illinois has a common-law rule that is comparable to Federal Rule of Evidence 403. See *People v. Walker*, 335 Ill. App. 3d 102, 112, 268 Ill. Dec. 654, 779 N.E.2d 268 (2d Dist. 2002), as modified on denial of reh'g, (Oct. 24, 2002) and judgment aff'd, 211 Ill. 2d 317, 285 Ill. Dec. 519, 812 N.E.2d 339 (2004); and *People v. Peete*, 318 Ill. App. 3d 961, 966–67, 252 Ill. Dec. 821, 743 N.E.2d 689 (4th Dist. 2001). Therefore, it is arguable that Federal Rule of Evidence 403 can be considered as persuasive authority in Illinois.

People v. Holman, 257 Ill. App. 3d 1031, 1033–34, 196 Ill. Dec. 457, 630 N.E.2d 154 (2d Dist. 1994) (evidence is admissible if it is relevant and if the prejudicial impact does not substantially outweigh the probative value of it).

For expanded citations on the exclusion of prejudicial evidence, see § 2:1 to § 2:4.

§ 4:4 Supporting authorities—Foundations, generally—Definitions

"Foundation" is defined in *Black's Law Dictionary* as follows:

> Preliminary questions to witness to establish admissibility of evidence. "Laying foundation" is a prerequisite to the admission of evidence at trial. It is established by testimony which identifies the evidence sought to be admitted and connects it with the issue in question.

Black's Law Dictionary, 6th Ed. 1990.

Anderson v. Human Rights Com'n, 314 Ill. App. 3d 35, 42-43, 246 Ill. Dec. 843, 731 N.E.2d 371 (1st Dist. 2000) (a proper foundation is one that demonstrates that a given document is actually what it is suggested to be).

§ 4:5 Supporting authorities—Foundations, generally—Offer of proof

Black's defines "Offer of Proof" as follows:

> At a trial or hearing, when an objection to a question has been sustained, the party aggrieved by the ruling may indicate for the record (out of the presence of the jury) the answer which would have been given if the question had not been excluded. The appellate court is then in a position to determine from the record the correctness of the ruling and the prejudice in its exclusion, if any.

Black's Law Dictionary, 6th Ed. 1990 (citing Federal Rule of Evidence 103(a)(2)).

In re Leona W., 228 Ill. 2d 439, 320 Ill. Dec. 855, 888 N.E.2d 72 (2008) (issue regarding the exclusion of evidence was waived for appeal purposes because the party offering the evidence failed to make an offer of proof).

Jones v. DHR Cambridge Homes, Inc., 381 Ill. App. 3d 18, 319 Ill. Dec. 59, 885 N.E.2d 330, 343–44 (1st Dist. 2008) (an offer of proof that did not include the excluded videotape that was at issue on appeal, was insufficient to preserve the objection to its exclusion).

Bergman v. Kelsey, 375 Ill. App. 3d 612, 635, 313 Ill. Dec. 862, 873 N.E.2d 486 (1st Dist. 2007), appeal denied, 226 Ill. 2d 579, 316 Ill. Dec. 541, 879 N.E.2d 929 (2007) (party waived any objection to the exclusion of evidence by failing to make an offer of proof).

People v. Tabb, 374 Ill. App. 3d 680, 690, 312 Ill. Dec. 470, 870 N.E.2d 914 (1st Dist. 2007), appeal denied, 225 Ill. 2d 670, 314 Ill. Dec. 835, 875 N.E.2d 1122 (2007) (offer of proof was not specific enough to preserve an issue for appeal).

Smith v. Black & Decker (U.S.), Inc., 272 Ill. App. 3d 451, 458, 209 Ill. Dec. 135, 650 N.E.2d 1108 (3d Dist. 1995) (appellate court unable to determine whether party was prejudiced by inability to present its evidence when party failed to make an offer of proof regarding evidence).

Allen & Korkowski & Associates v. Pettit, 108 Ill. App. 3d 384, 388, 64 Ill. Dec. 173, 439 N.E.2d 102 (4th Dist. 1982) (an offer of proof is not required to preserve an alleged error in the exclusion of evidence when there is no doubt from the record what the evidence would be).

Scaggs v. Horton, 85 Ill. App. 3d 541, 546, 44 Ill. Dec. 504, 411 N.E.2d 870 (5th Dist. 1980) (in order to preserve an alleged error caused by the exclusion of evidence, the party offering the evidence must make an offer of proof regarding what the expected testimony would be, who would so testify and the purpose of the testimony; however, an offer of proof is unnecessary when, as it was in this case, it is clear that the court and counsel understood the nature of the proposed testimony).

Simon v. Plotkin, 50 Ill. App. 3d 603, 606, 8 Ill. Dec. 636, 365 N.E.2d 1022 (1st Dist. 1977) (to preserve the issue for review, when a trial judge refuses to admit testimony, an offer of proof is required to demonstrate what the proposed testimony is, by whom it would be from, and the purpose of the evidence; in this case, the party waived the issue by failing to make a proper offer of proof).

People v. Eckert, 194 Ill. App. 3d 667, 669–75, 141 Ill. Dec. 633, 551 N.E.2d 820 (5th Dist. 1990) (error in a criminal case to refuse to allow counsel to make an offer of proof in front of the trial judge).

Blazina v. Blazina, 42 Ill. App. 3d 159, 162, 166, 167, 1 Ill. Dec. 164, 356 N.E.2d 164 (2d Dist. 1976) (error in a civil case to prevent a party from making an offer of proof regarding excluded evidence but not prejudicial because it was clear the evidence related to an issue outside the scope of the pleadings).

Note that, in a civil case, if a motion in limine to exclude evidence is *denied*, the opponent of the evidence must generally object at the time the evidence is offered at trial to preserve the error on appeal. However, in a criminal case, a motion in limine, in addition to raising the disputed issue in a post-trial motion, is sufficient to preserve the alleged error for appeal, even without a trial objection. See *People v. Whirl*, 351 Ill. App. 3d 464, 466, 286 Ill. Dec. 646, 814 N.E.2d 872 (2d Dist. 2004); *People v. Barajas*, 322 Ill. App. 3d 541, 552–53, 255 Ill. Dec. 565, 749 N.E.2d 1047 (1st Dist. 2001); and *People v. Hudson*, 157 Ill. 2d 401, 434–35, 193 Ill. Dec. 128, 626 N.E.2d 161 (1993). Also, objecting at trial gives the trial judge an opportunity to reverse his ruling on the original motion in limine and thereby exclude the evidence. If a motion to exclude is granted or a motion to admit is denied on the basis of lack of foundation, the proponent of the evidence must make an offer of proof to preserve the error. Additionally, the proponent of the evidence can ask the court to conditionally admit the evidence, allowing the evidence to be admitted on the condition that at some point during the trial the proper foundation will be laid.

See generally, § 1:5 to § 1:9, supra. See also conditional admissions at § 4:17, Opposing authorities—Conditional admissibility, infra.

§ 4:6 Supporting authorities—Foundations, generally—Determination out of jury presence

Crossman v. Curless, 178 Ill. App. 3d 97, 98, 101, 127 Ill. Dec. 281, 532 N.E.2d 1110 (4th Dist. 1988) (not improper for a party's counsel to say that there will be an offer of proof regarding the party's testimony but that the offer will be outside of the jury's presence. Specifically the statement did not represent an improper attempt to violate a motion in limine preventing the party from testifying about a conversation with the deceased).

Maxwell v. Habel, 92 Ill. App. 510, 1900 WL 3466 (1st Dist. 1900) (if trial judge is concerned that an offer of proof might prejudice the jury, the offer can be made outside the presence of the jury).

Anderson v. Human Rights Com'n, 314 Ill. App. 3d 35, 42-43, 246 Ill. Dec. 843, 731 N.E.2d 371 (1st Dist. 2000) (a foundation is required to prevent improper evidence from being heard by the fact-finder).

Federal Rule of Evidence 103(c) provides:

> Hearing of Jury.—In jury cases, proceedings shall be conducted, to the extent practicable, so as to prevent inadmissible evidence from being suggested to the jury by any means, such as making statements or offers of proof or asking questions in the hearing of the jury.

Although this rule has not been specifically codified in Illinois, Illinois has adopted other Federal Rules of evidence through case law. See e.g. *People v. Monroe*, 66 Ill. 2d 317, 321–22, 5 Ill. Dec. 824, 362 N.E.2d 295 (1977) and *Spencer v. Wandolowski*, 264 Ill. App. 3d 611, 617, 201 Ill. Dec. 422, 636 N.E.2d 854 (1st Dist. 1994) (adopting Federal Rule of Evidence 401). Therefore, cites to the Federal Rules of Evidence can often be cited as persuasive authority in Illinois.

See also Federal Rules of Evidence, Rule 103(a)(2).

§ 4:7 Supporting authorities—Foundations, generally—Inadmissibility of evidence lacking foundation

Dukes v. Pneumo Abex Corp., 386 Ill.App.3d 425, 439–41,

900 N.E.2d 1128 (4th Dist. 2008) (when there was insufficient evidence to support a finding of a conspiracy, statements of the alleged co-conspirators were inadmissible hearsay).

Apa v. National Bank of Commerce, 374 Ill. App. 3d 1082, 1084–88, 313 Ill. Dec. 507, 872 N.E.2d 490 (1st Dist. 2007) (insufficient foundation was provided for the admission of bank statements as business records).

Greaney v. Industrial Com'n, 358 Ill. App. 3d 1002, 1011–12, 295 Ill. Dec. 180, 832 N.E.2d 331 (1st Dist. 2005) (insufficient foundation was provided for the admission of an uncertified doctor's report).

People v. Davis, 322 Ill. App. 3d 762, 765, 256 Ill. Dec. 12, 751 N.E.2d 65 (1st Dist. 2001) (appellate court must reverse if prejudicial documents that lacked foundation were admitted by the trial judge).

Anderson v. Human Rights Com'n, 314 Ill. App. 3d 35, 42-46, 246 Ill. Dec. 843, 731 N.E.2d 371 (1st Dist. 2000) (evidence should not be admitted without a proper foundation).

But see *Holder v. Caselton*, 275 Ill. App. 3d 950, 954–56, 212 Ill. Dec. 479, 657 N.E.2d 680 (4th Dist. 1995) (error regarding exclusion of evidence is waived for purposes of appeal if a party fails to make an offer of proof regarding the nature of the excluded evidence).

§ 4:8 Supporting authorities—Examples of improper foundations—Photographs

Baraniak v. Kurby, 371 Ill. App. 3d 310, 308 Ill. Dec. 949, 862 N.E.2d 1152, 1157-59 (1st Dist. 2007), appeal denied, 224 Ill. 2d 571, 312 Ill. Dec. 654, 871 N.E.2d 54 (2007) (trial court should not have admitted photographs depicting the amount of damage to the vehicle, without expert testimony to show how that correlated to the physical injuries to the person in the vehicle).

Casson v. Nash, 74 Ill. 2d 164, 171–72, 23 Ill. Dec. 571, 384 N.E.2d 365 (1978) (trial judge improperly admitted a photograph over objection when there was no proper foundation to demonstrate that the photograph represented the vehicle immediately after the collision).

Kooyumjian v. Stevens, 10 Ill. App. 2d 378, 387–89, 135 N.E.2d 146 (1st Dist. 1956) (photographs can have a greater impact upon the jury than live testimony and therefore, they should not have been admitted without a proper foundation).

For foundation requirements, see generally, § 4:20 to § 4:38, infra. See § 4:39 to § 4:46, infra, for exclusion of gruesome or inflammatory photographs.

§ 4:9 Supporting authorities—Examples of improper foundations—Tape recordings

Elder on Behalf of Finney v. Finney, 256 Ill. App. 3d 424, 427–28, 194 Ill. Dec. 896, 628 N.E.2d 393 (1st Dist. 1993) (tape recordings were properly excluded because they were irrelevant, designed to inflame the fact-finder, and lacked foundation regarding when they were made).

People v. Melchor, 136 Ill. App. 3d 708, 711–14, 91 Ill. Dec. 485, 483 N.E.2d 971 (1st Dist. 1985) (foundation was proper for a tape recording when a person who overheard the conversation testified to the accuracy of the recording but a typed transcript of the recording was not admissible because no one testified about how it was prepared and someone had added names before each sentence without proof that each name represented the correct speaker on the tape).

For foundation requirements for writings, see § 4:20 to § 4:38, infra.

§ 4:10 Supporting authorities—Examples of improper foundations—Tests and experiments

Carillo v. Ford Motor Co., 325 Ill. App. 3d 955, 967, 259 Ill. Dec. 619, 759 N.E.2d 99 (1st Dist. 2001) (exclusion of experiment evidence when parties disagree if the conditions surrounding the experiment were the same as those surrounding the collision).

Becker v. Aquaslide "N' Dive Corp., 35 Ill. App. 3d 479, 484–85, 341 N.E.2d 369 (4th Dist. 1975) (exclusion of videotaped experiment where there was no foundation to show that the circumstances were identical to those in the actual incident).

Mehochko v. Gold Seal Co., 66 Ill. App. 2d 54, 57-60, 213 N.E.2d 581, 19 A.L.R.3d 1003 (5th Dist. 1966) (improper hearsay and prejudicial to let an expert read from a test report about tests performed by someone else when the expert had no personal knowledge about the tests at issue).

See § 5:1 to § 5:19, infra, for expanded citations supporting the exclusion of experiments and tests.

§ 4:11 Supporting authorities—Examples of improper foundations—Videotapes and motion pictures

Missouri Portland Cement Co. v. United Cement, Lime,

Gypsum and Allied Workers Intern. Union, Div. of Boilermakers, AFL-CIO, Local No. 438, 145 Ill. App. 3d 1023, 1027–29, 99 Ill. Dec. 796, 496 N.E.2d 489 (5th Dist. 1986) (foundation required for a videotape is the same as that for a photograph, i.e. that any witness testifies from personal knowledge that it accurately portrays the events therein and that it is relevant and thus, the videotape was *improperly excluded* in this case on the basis that the videographer did not testify).

Becker v. Aquaslide "N' Dive Corp., 35 Ill. App. 3d 479, 484–85, 341 N.E.2d 369 (4th Dist. 1975) (exclusion of videotaped experiment where there was no foundation to show that the circumstances were identical to those in the actual incident).

For foundation requirements for writings, see § 4:20 to § 4:38, infra.

§ 4:12 Supporting authorities—Examples of improper foundations—Witness testimony—Experts

McWilliams v. Dettore, 387 Ill.App.3d 833, 843–50, 901 N.E.2d 1023 (1st Dist. 2009) (oncologist was not qualified to provide an opinion regarding the standard of care for a surgeon).

Downey v. Dunnington, 384 Ill.App.3d 350, 386, 895 N.E.2d 271 (4th Dist. 2008) (in a case involving an alleged lack of informed consent, it was improper to allow an expert to testify about what the plaintiff might have done if properly informed because such testimony was speculative and invaded the province of the jury)(harmless error).

Ahmed v. Pickwick Place Owners' Ass'n, 385 Ill.App.3d 874, 890–91, 896 N.E.2d 854 (1st Dist. 2008) (police officer was not qualified to provide an expert opinion regarding the cause of certain injuries to a deceased individual).

Torres v. Midwest Development Co., 383 Ill.App.3d 20, 27–28, 889 N.E.2d 654 (1st Dist. 2008) (expert's opinion lacked a sufficient factual basis and was inadmissible).

Boren v. BOC Group, Inc., 385 Ill.App.3d 248, 255–56, 895 N.E.2d 53 (5th Dist. 2008) (a photograph of a billboard advertisement could not be used as a demonstrative aid to support expert testimony because the expert lacked knowledge of the circumstances surrounding the creation of the billboard and it was confusing and not helpful to explain the expert witness' testimony).

Schuler v. Mid-Central Cardiology, 313 Ill. App. 3d 326, 334–36, 246 Ill. Dec. 163, 729 N.E.2d 536 (4th Dist. 2000) (trial judge has discretion to exclude expert testimony that is based upon unsupported and speculative facts).

Hubbard v. Sherman Hosp., 292 Ill. App. 3d 148, 153–55, 226 Ill. Dec. 393, 685 N.E.2d 648 (2d Dist. 1997) (in a medical malpractice case, the trial judge did not abuse its discretion by barring expert testimony when the expert was licensed in the field related to the testimony but did not have the requisite experience related to the subject matter).

People v. Britz, 123 Ill. 2d 446, 457–62, 124 Ill. Dec. 15, 528 N.E.2d 703 (1988) (exclusion of expert testimony when the expert's opinion is based upon a party's own self-serving statements).

Department of Transp. v. Bouy, 69 Ill. App. 3d 29, 33-38, 25 Ill. Dec. 499, 386 N.E.2d 1163 (4th Dist. 1979) (expert's testimony is properly excluded when it is based upon a speculative and conjectural method of proof).

Mehochko v. Gold Seal Co., 66 Ill. App. 2d 54, 57-60, 213 N.E.2d 581, 19 A.L.R.3d 1003 (5th Dist. 1966) (improper hearsay and prejudicial to let an expert read from a test report about tests performed by someone else when the expert had no personal knowledge about the tests at issue).

For expanded citations on the exclusion of expert testimony, see § 8:1 to § 8:22, infra. See § 5:1 to § 5:19, infra, for citations supporting the exclusion of experiments and tests.

§ 4:13 Supporting authorities—Examples of improper foundations—Witness testimony—Lay

Rose v. Mercedes-Benz U.S.A., LLC, 378 Ill. App. 3d 615, 621–26, 317 Ill. Dec. 538, 882 N.E.2d 112, 64 U.C.C. Rep. Serv. 2d 750 (1st Dist. 2007) (lay witness failed to provide sufficient foundation for an opinion regarding what a defective vehicle was actually worth).

People v. Jones, 241 Ill. App. 3d 228, 231–33, 181 Ill. Dec. 702, 608 N.E.2d 953 (4th Dist. 1993) (lay witness testimony must be from personal knowledge of observable facts) (lay witness testimony allowed when based upon personal knowledge and observations of what sex abuse victims often do).

It is important to note that even where a motion to exclude a witness's testimony is unsuccessful (i.e., denied), and the objection to the witness's testimony is overruled at the time of trial, the opponent of the testimony can still argue in the closing argument that the evidence or the testimony lacked foundation or that the foundation was suspect and therefore the evidence is suspect. It is important to remember that many facts go to the weight of the evidence as opposed to its admissibility.

For expanded citations on the exclusion of lay witness testimony, see § 8:29 to § 8:38, infra.

§ 4:14 Supporting authorities—Examples of improper foundations—Writings

Cordeck Sales, Inc. v. Construction Systems, Inc., 382 Ill.App.3d 334, 384–85, 887 N.E.2d 474 (1st Dist. 2008) (insufficient evidence was provided to authenticate a document and it was not considered in a summary judgment ruling).

People v. Urdiales, 225 Ill. 2d 354, 312 Ill. Dec. 876, 871 N.E.2d 669 (2007), as modified on denial of reh'g, (May 29, 2007) and cert. denied, 128 S. Ct. 494, 169 L. Ed. 2d 347 (2007) (trial court had discretion to prohibit the defendant from admitting expert reports during the sentencing hearing without any accompanying testimony that would have been subject to cross-examination).

Camco, Inc. v. Lowery, 362 Ill. App. 3d 421, 435–36, 298 Ill. Dec. 332, 839 N.E.2d 655 (1st Dist. 2005) (evidence regarding an officer's deposition testimony that was based upon information contained in a lab report was improper hearsay) (harmless error).

Hubbert v. Dell Corp., 359 Ill. App. 3d 976, 985, 296 Ill. Dec. 258, 835 N.E.2d 113, 61 U.C.C. Rep. Serv. 2d 114 (5th Dist. 2005) (letters and marketing materials were improperly admitted without a sufficient foundation).

People v. Davis, 322 Ill. App. 3d 762, 765–67, 256 Ill. Dec. 12, 751 N.E.2d 65 (1st Dist. 2001) (in a criminal case, it was reversible error when the trial judge admitted a document without a proper foundation for admission because the person testifying about the document was unable to state when the document was created, how the document was created or that it was made in the regular course of business).

Anderson v. Human Rights Com'n, 314 Ill. App. 3d 35, 42-46, 246 Ill. Dec. 843, 731 N.E.2d 371 (1st Dist. 2000) (documents should not be admitted when the witness testifying about them does not have the personal knowledge to establish a proper foundation).

People v. Melchor, 136 Ill. App. 3d 708, 711–14, 91 Ill. Dec. 485, 483 N.E.2d 971 (1st Dist. 1985) (foundation was proper for a tape recording when a person who overheard the conversation testified to the accuracy of the recording but a typed transcript of the recording was not admissible because no one testified about how it was prepared and someone had added names before each sentence without proof that each name represented the correct speaker on the tape).

For expanded citations on the foundation requirements for writings, see § 4:20 to § 4:38, infra.

§ 4:15 Supporting authorities—Examples of improper foundations—Medical records and reports

The reader is advised to carefully distinguish civil cases and criminal cases with respect to whether hospital and medical records are admissible as business records. The provisions with respect to whether or not hospital and medical records are admissible as business records are different for each type of case.

725 ILCS 5/115-5(a) applies to criminal cases and provides,

> Any writing or record, whether in the form of an entry in a book or otherwise, made as a memorandum or record of any act, transaction, occurrence, or event, shall be admissible as evidence of such act, transaction, occurrence, or event, if made in regular course of any business, and if it was the regular course of such business to make such memorandum or record at the time of such act, transaction, occurrence, or event or within a reasonable time thereafter.
>
> All other circumstances of the making of such writing or record, including lack of personal knowledge by the entrant or maker, may be shown to affect its weight, but such circumstances shall not affect its admissibility.
>
> The term 'business,' as used in this Section, includes business, profession, occupation, and calling of every kind.

However, 725 ILCS 5/115-5(c) provides that 725 ILCS 5/115-5(a) may not be used as the basis for establishing admissibility if,

> such writing or record has been made by anyone in the regular course of any form of hospital or medical business.

Illinois Supreme Court Rule 236(a) provides,

> Any writing or record, whether in the form of any entry in a book or otherwise, made as a memorandum or record of any act, transaction, occurrence, or event, shall be admissible as evidence of the act, transaction, occurrence, or event, if made in the regular course of any business, and if it was the regular course of the business to make such a memorandum or record at the time of such an act, transaction, occurrence, or event or within a reasonable time thereafter. All other circumstances of the making of the writing or record, including lack of personal knowledge by the entrant or maker, may be shown to affect its weight, but shall not affect its admissibility. The term 'business,' as used in this rule, includes business, profession, occupation, and calling of every kind.

Prior to 1992, subsection (b) of Illinois Supreme Court Rule 236 excluded medical records from being admissible if the justification for doing so was based upon subsection (a). However, in 1992, the provision was amended to remove the prohibition against medical records being admitted as business records. See *Williams v. Covenant Medical Center*, 316 Ill. App. 3d 682, 691, 250 Ill. Dec. 40, 737 N.E.2d 662 (4th Dist. 2000); and *Lecroy v. Miller*, 272 Ill. App. 3d 925, 935–36, 209 Ill. Dec. 439, 651 N.E.2d 617 (1st Dist. 1995). Thus, the reader should be careful about using any pre-1992 case to argue about the admissibility of medical records in a civil case. See e.g. *Wilson v. Clark*, 84 Ill. 2d 186, 191–92, 49 Ill. Dec. 308, 417 N.E.2d 1322 (1981) (a proper foundation for admission was not laid when the individuals who made the entries did not testify).

735 ILCS 5/8-401 provides,

> Account books and records. Where in any action or proceeding, the claim or defense is founded on a book account or any other record or document, any party or interested person may testify to his or her account book, or any other record or document and the items therein contained; that the same is a book, record, or document of original entries, and that the entries therein were made by himself or herself, and are true and just; or that the same were made by a deceased person, or by a disinterested person, a non-resident person of the state at the time of the trial, and where made by such deceased or non- resident person in the usual course of trade, and of his or her duty or employment to the party so testifying; and thereupon the account book and entries or any other record or document shall be admitted as evidence in the cause. Where such book of original entries or any other record or document has been photographed, microphotographed, microfilmed, optical imaged, or otherwise reproduced either in the usual course of business, or pursuant to any statute of this State authorizing the reproduction of public records, papers or documents, and the reproduction, in either case, complies with the minimum standards of quality for permanent records approved by the State Records Commission, then such reproduction shall be deemed to be an original record, book or document for all purposes, including introduction in evidence in all courts or administrative agencies.

725 ILCS 5/115-5.1 states,

> In any civil or criminal action the records of the coroner's medical or laboratory examiner summarizing and detailing the performance of his or her official duties in performing medical examinations upon deceased persons or autopsies, or both, and kept in the ordinary course of business of the coroner's office, duly certified by the county coroner or chief supervisory coroner's pathologist or medical examiner, shall be received as competent evi-

> dence in any court of this State, to the extent permitted by this Section. These reports, specifically including but not limited to the pathologist's protocol, autopsy reports and toxicological reports, shall be public documents and thereby may be admissible as prima facie evidence of the facts, findings, opinions, diagnoses and conditions stated therein.
>
> A duly certified coroner's protocol or autopsy report, or both, complying with the requirements of this Section may be duly admitted into evidence as an exception to the hearsay rule as prima facie proof of the cause of death of the person to whom it relates. The records referred to in this Section shall be limited to the records of the results of post-mortem examinations of the findings of autopsy and toxicological laboratory examinations.
>
> Persons who prepare reports or records offered in evidence hereunder may be subpoenaed as witnesses in civil or criminal cases upon the request of either party to the cause. However, if such person is dead, the county coroner or a duly authorized official of the coroner's office may testify to the fact that the examining pathologist, toxicologist or other medical or laboratory examiner is deceased and that the offered report or record was prepared by such deceased person. The witness must further attest that the medical report or record was prepared in the ordinary and usual course of the deceased person's duty or employment in conformity with the provisions of this Section.

For expanded citations on the exclusion of medical records and reports, see § 4:99 to § 4:115, infra.

§ 4:16 Opposing authorities—General

Burlington Northern and Santa Fe Ry. Co. v. ABC-NACO, 906 N.E.2d 83, 95–96 (1st Dist. 2009) (expert could properly give an opinion based upon probabilities or possibilities due to certain assumed facts).

Kunkel v. P.K. Dependable Const., LLC, 387 Ill.App.3d 1153, 1158–59, 902 N.E.2d 769 (5th Dist. 2009) (estimate of cost of repairs from an individual who is experienced in the field is admissible, even if there is no testimony that the estimate is reasonable and the repairs are necessary).

Donnellan v. First Student, Inc., 383 Ill.App.3d 1040, 1052–53, 891 N.E.2d 463 (1st Dist. 2008) (sufficient foundation was laid for admission of a "day in the life video" by the plaintiff's wife who was able to testify that the video accurately represented the plaintiff's functioning ability).

Fronabarger v. Burns, 385 Ill.App.3d 560, 564–65, 895 N.E.2d 1125 (5th Dist. 2008) (even without any expert testimony to correlate vehicle damage to force of impact, trial court had discretion to admit photographs depicting the amount of damage to vehicles to suggest the amount of injuries to the occupants of the vehicles).

Village Discount Outlet v. Department of Employment Sec., 384 Ill.App.3d 522, 524–26, 893 N.E.2d 943 (1st Dist. 2008) (a witness' testimony regarding what he personally observed on a videotape was not hearsay. However, the court noted that the testimony might violate the best evidence rule but that claim was not raised by the parties).

Bergman v. Kelsey, 375 Ill. App. 3d 612, 633–34, 313 Ill. Dec. 862, 873 N.E.2d 486 (1st Dist. 2007), appeal denied, 226 Ill. 2d 579, 316 Ill. Dec. 541, 879 N.E.2d 929 (2007) (proper foundation was laid for the admission of medical literature as authoritative).

Hudson v. City of Chicago, 378 Ill. App. 3d 373, 400–02, 317 Ill. Dec. 262, 881 N.E.2d 430 (1st Dist. 2007), appeal denied, 227 Ill. 2d 580, 321 Ill. Dec. 250, 888 N.E.2d 1183 (2008) (expert testimony was proper because it was supported by the evidence).

Adams v. Sarah Bush Lincoln Health Center, 369 Ill. App. 3d 988, 314 Ill. Dec. 190, 874 N.E.2d 100 (4th Dist. 2007) (an expert witness can be cross-examined by the use of literature if the expert relied on that literature to support his opinion).

First Assist, Inc. v. Industrial Com'n, 371 Ill. App. 3d 488, 311 Ill. Dec. 77, 867 N.E.2d 1063 (4th Dist. 2007) (sufficient foundation was submitted regarding a telephone call when the witness testified that he made the call to the plaintiff's business phone number that was listed in the telephone book and the person who answered discussed the plaintiff's business).

City of Chicago v. Old Colony Partners, L.P., 364 Ill. App. 3d 806, 818–20, 301 Ill. Dec. 555, 847 N.E.2d 565 (1st Dist. 2006) (sufficient foundation was provided for the admission of letters and reports prepared by a third party for a business; documents were admissible as business records).

In re L.W., 367 Ill. App. 3d 844, 856-57, 305 Ill. Dec. 674, 856 N.E.2d 479 (1st Dist. 2006), appeal allowed, 222 Ill. 2d 608, 308 Ill. Dec. 636, 862 N.E.2d 234 (2007) and judgment rev'd, 228 Ill. 2d 439, 320 Ill. Dec. 855, 888 N.E.2d 72 (2008) (an offer of proof was not required to preserve an issue regarding excluded evidence, when the nature of the excluded evidence was clear from the record), reversed by *In re Leona W.*, 228 Ill. 2d 439, 320 Ill. Dec. 855, 888 N.E.2d 72 (2008) (in a termination of parental rights case, the trial court did not abuse its discretion by granting a motion in limine to exclude evidence regarding the parent's behavior towards other minors, as irrelevant and beyond the scope of the allegations).

Schmitz v. Binette, 368 Ill. App. 3d 447, 453-54, 306 Ill. Dec. 447, 857 N.E.2d 846 (1st Dist. 2006) (when the record was sufficiently clear regarding the nature of excluded evidence, even though the party's offer of proof regarding the testimony was defective).

Shaheen v. Advantage Moving and Storage, Inc., 369 Ill. App. 3d 535, 543-45, 307 Ill. Dec. 721, 860 N.E.2d 375 (1st Dist. 2006) (proper foundation was provided for an expert's opinion regarding the plaintiff's lost earning capacity and any defects in the analysis by the expert affected the weight of the evidence, rather than its admissibility).

People v. One 1999 Lexus, VIN JT8BH68X2X0018305, 367 Ill. App. 3d 687, 692-93, 305 Ill. Dec. 303, 855 N.E.2d 194 (2d Dist. 2006) (stipulation to the admission of documents showing that the driver of a vehicle was convicted of DUI established the proper foundation for the documents).

Drews v. Gobel Freight Lines, Inc., 144 Ill. 2d 84, 98-99, 161 Ill. Dec. 324, 578 N.E.2d 970 (1991) (videotapes of the deceased with his family were admissible when there was no claim that the videotapes were inaccurate).

Missouri Portland Cement Co. v. United Cement, Lime, Gypsum and Allied Workers Intern. Union, Div. of Boilermakers, AFL-CIO, Local No. 438, 145 Ill. App. 3d 1023, 1027–29, 99 Ill. Dec. 796, 496 N.E.2d 489 (5th Dist. 1986) (error to exclude a videotape when a witness, other than the videographer, testified from personal knowledge that it accurately portrayed the events therein).

Casson v. Nash, 74 Ill. 2d 164, 171–72, 23 Ill. Dec. 571, 384 N.E.2d 365 (1978) (trial judge did not improperly admit two photographs even though they lacked a proper foundation when the opposing party failed to object to them).

Greig v. Griffel, 49 Ill. App. 3d 829, 834–36, 7 Ill. Dec. 499, 364 N.E.2d 660 (2d Dist. 1977) (parties' stipulation that photographs accurately showed the condition of the vehicle after the collision was sufficient to establish the foundation for admission of the photographs).

Maxwell v. Habel, 92 Ill. App. 510, 1900 WL 3466 (1st Dist. 1900) (if trial judge is concerned that an offer of proof might prejudice the jury, the offer can be made outside the presence of the jury).

§ 4:17 Opposing authorities—Judicial notice

G.I.S. Venture v. Novak, 388 Ill.App.3d 184, 186–87, 902 N.E.2d 744 (2nd Dist. 2009) (court could take judicial notice of the Illinois Administrative Code).

System Development Services, Inc. v. Haarmann, 389 Ill.App.3d 561, 907 N.E.2d 63, 76 (5th Dist. 2009) (court took judicial notice of certain statistical facts about a county).

Green v. Rogers, 384 Ill.App.3d 946, 960–61, 895 N.E.2d 647 (2nd Dist. 2008) (court could take judicial notice of the contents of a county website).

Outcom, Inc. v. Department of Transp., 378 Ill. App. 3d 739, 741, 317 Ill. Dec. 816, 882 N.E.2d 696 (5th Dist. 2008), appeal allowed, (May 29, 2008) (court may take judicial notice of an ordinance).

IFC Credit Corp. v. Rieker Shoe Corp., 378 Ill. App. 3d 77, 81, 317 Ill. Dec. 214, 881 N.E.2d 382 (1st Dist. 2007) (appellate court took judicial notice of unpublished decisions of other courts).

Hermesdorf v. Wu, 372 Ill. App. 3d 842, 310 Ill. Dec. 721, 867 N.E.2d 34 (2d Dist. 2007), appeal denied, 225 Ill. 2d 632, 314 Ill. Dec. 824, 875 N.E.2d 1111 (2007) (appellate court could take judicial notice of the decision of a pension board).

Primax Recoveries, Inc. v. Atherton, 365 Ill. App. 3d 1007, 1012, 303 Ill. Dec. 452, 851 N.E.2d 639 (5th Dist. 2006) (trial court could take judicial notice of a court order from another State's court).

Hoskin v. Union Pacific R.R. Co., 365 Ill. App. 3d 1021, 1024–25, 303 Ill. Dec. 459, 851 N.E.2d 646 (5th Dist. 2006) (appellate court could take judicial notice of the distance between two locations).

§ 4:18 Opposing authorities—Conditional admissibility

Bergman v. Kelsey, 375 Ill. App. 3d 612, 630–33, 313 Ill. Dec. 862, 873 N.E.2d 486 (1st Dist. 2007), appeal denied, 226 Ill. 2d 579, 316 Ill. Dec. 541, 879 N.E.2d 929 (2007) (trial court properly allowed an expert to be cross-examined about literature that was contrary to the expert's opinion).

Greig v. Griffel, 49 Ill. App. 3d 829, 839–41, 7 Ill. Dec. 499, 364 N.E.2d 660 (2d Dist. 1977) (trial judge has discretion to admit evidence based upon a party's promise to provide a foundation for it later).

§ 4:19 Opposing authorities—No offer of proof needed

LaSalle Bank N.A. v. C/HCA Development Corp., 384 Ill.App.3d 806, 823–24, 893 N.E.2d 949 (1st Dist. 2008) (an offer of proof was not required to preserve an error for appeal purposes when the disputed issue was clear from the record).

B. MOTION TO EXCLUDE WRITINGS, GENERALLY

§ 4:20 Suggested motion text

[Name of moving party] hereby moves this Court for an order excluding any and all evidence, references to evidence, testimony or argument relating to *[describe nature of writing or other document to be excluded]*. The motion is based upon the ground that the document *[describe basis for exclusion, e.g., lacks proper authentication, is inadmissible hearsay, etc.]*.

§ 4:21 Motion summary

This motion generally challenges the introduction of writings where the evidence is deficient for one of several commonly encountered reasons, including authenticity, hearsay, or insufficient secondary evidence.

§ 4:22 Supporting authorities—"Writing" defined

Federal Rule of Evidence 1001 defines "writings" and "recordings" as follows:

> "Writings" and "recordings" consist of letters, words, or numbers, or their equivalent, set down by handwriting, typewriting, printing, photostating, photographing, magnetic impulse, mechanical or electronic recording, or other form of data compilation.

Although this Rule has not been specifically codified in Illinois, Illinois case law has referred to this Rule. See e.g. *Kwai Paul Lam v. Northern Illinois Gas Co.*, 114 Ill. App. 3d 325, 332, 70 Ill. Dec. 660, 449 N.E.2d 1007 (1st Dist. 1983); and *People v. Bowman*, 95 Ill. App. 3d 1137, 1142–43, 51 Ill. Dec. 527, 420 N.E.2d 1085 (5th Dist. 1981).

The reader should carefully consider whether any document *or tangible item* that has *any form of communication* on or in it could be excluded because it is hearsay, unauthenticated or not the best evidence. For example, *People v. Thompson*, 327 Ill. App. 3d 1061, 1065, 262 Ill. Dec. 595, 765 N.E.2d 1203 (2d Dist. 2002), defines "hearsay" as, "testimony of an out-of-court statement offered to establish the truth of the matter asserted therein and whose value thus depends upon the credibility of the out-of-court declarant." Such an out of court statement could come in many forms, as the examples in this chapter indicate.

§ 4:23 Supporting authorities—Unauthenticated writings—General authentication requirement

Anderson v. Human Rights Com'n, 314 Ill. App. 3d 35, 42-46, 246 Ill. Dec. 843, 731 N.E.2d 371 (1st Dist. 2000) (evidence should not be admitted without a proper foundation).

People v. Melchor, 136 Ill. App. 3d 708, 711–14, 91 Ill. Dec. 485, 483 N.E.2d 971 (1st Dist. 1985) (foundation was proper for a tape recording when a person who overheard the conversation testified to the accuracy of the recording but a typed transcript of the recording was not admissible because no one testified about how it was prepared and someone had added names before each sentence without proof that each name represented the correct speaker on the tape).

Seward v. Griffin, 116 Ill. App. 3d 749, 763, 72 Ill. Dec. 305, 452 N.E.2d 558 (3d Dist. 1983) (documents must be authenticated before they are admissible as evidence).

§ 4:24 Supporting authorities—Unauthenticated writings—Exclusion of unauthenticated writings

Financial Freedom v. Kirgis, 377 Ill. App. 3d 107, 133–35, 315 Ill. Dec. 537, 877 N.E.2d 24 (1st Dist. 2007), appeal denied, 226 Ill. 2d 614, 317 Ill. Dec. 503, 882 N.E.2d 77 (2008) (unauthenticated documents that contained hearsay, were inadmissible).

CCP Ltd. Partnership v. First Source Financial, Inc., 368 Ill. App. 3d 476, 484-85, 305 Ill. Dec. 687, 856 N.E.2d 492 (1st Dist. 2006) (emails that were attached to a party's motion for summary judgment were not properly authenticated and could not be considered).

Greaney v. Industrial Com'n, 358 Ill. App. 3d 1002, 1011–12, 295 Ill. Dec. 180, 832 N.E.2d 331 (1st Dist. 2005) (an uncertified doctor's report was not sufficiently authenticated).

Anderson v. Human Rights Com'n, 314 Ill. App. 3d 35, 42-46, 246 Ill. Dec. 843, 731 N.E.2d 371 (1st Dist. 2000) (documents should not be admitted when the witness testifying about them does not have the personal knowledge of them to establish a proper foundation).

People v. Melchor, 136 Ill. App. 3d 708, 711–14, 91 Ill. Dec. 485, 483 N.E.2d 971 (1st Dist. 1985) (foundation was proper for a tape recording when a person who overheard the conversation testified to the accuracy of the recording but a typed transcript of the recording was not admissible because no one testified about how it was prepared and someone had added names before each sentence without proof that each name represented the correct speaker on the tape).

Seward v. Griffin, 116 Ill. App. 3d 749, 763, 72 Ill. Dec. 305, 452 N.E.2d 558 (3d Dist. 1983) (exclusion of a repair manual when there was no foundation for its admission).

Roddy v. Chicago and N.W. R. R., 48 Ill. App. 3d 548, 553, 6 Ill. Dec. 536, 363 N.E.2d 65 (1st Dist. 1977) (improper to allow counsel to read hearsay from a National Safety Counsel bulletin without establishing any foundation for the admission of it).

Even when the court denies a motion to exclude a writing based upon the fact that sufficient evidence of authentication has been offered, a party may challenge the authenticity of the writing in closing argument where the authenticity is suspect. Courts will often allow evidence to be admitted with challenges to the evidence going to its weight as opposed to its admissibility.

See § 4:1 to § 4:19, supra, for general citations on foundation requirements.

§ 4:25 Supporting authorities—Inadmissible secondary evidence

Village Discount Outlet v. Department of Employment Sec., 384 Ill.App.3d 522, 524–26, 893 N.E.2d 943 (1st Dist. 2008) (a witness' testimony regarding what he personally observed on a videotape was not hearsay. However, the court noted that the testimony might violate the best evidence rule but that claim was not raised by the parties).

Kwai Paul Lam v. Northern Illinois Gas Co., 114 Ill. App. 3d 325, 332, 70 Ill. Dec. 660, 449 N.E.2d 1007 (1st Dist. 1983) (improper to introduce copies of company records when the party introducing them had destroyed the originals and there was no proof regarding the circumstances surrounding the destruction).

Federal Rule of Evidence 1001 provides in relevant part:

> An "original" of a writing or recording is the writing or recording itself or any counterpart intended to have the same effect by a person executing or issuing it. An 'original' of a photograph includes the negative or any print therefrom. If data are stored in a computer or similar device, any printout or other output readable by sight, shown to reflect the data accurately, is an "original."

> A "duplicate" is a counterpart produced by the same impression as the original, or from the same matrix, or by means of photography, including enlargements and miniatures, or by mechanical or electronic re-recording, or by chemical reproduction, or by other equivalent techniques which accurately reproduces the original.

Federal Rule of Evidence 1003 provides:

> A duplicate is admissible to the same extent as an original unless (1) a genuine question is raised as to the authenticity of the original or (2) in the circumstances it would be unfair to admit the duplicate in lieu of the original.

Although these Rules have not been specifically codified in Illinois, Illinois case law has referred to them. See e.g. *Kwai Paul Lam v. Northern Illinois Gas Co.*, 114 Ill. App. 3d 325, 332, 70 Ill. Dec. 660, 449 N.E.2d 1007 (1st Dist. 1983); and *People v. Bowman*, 95 Ill. App. 3d 1137, 1142–43, 51 Ill. Dec. 527, 420 N.E.2d 1085 (5th Dist. 1981).

§ 4:26 Supporting authorities—Inadmissible written hearsay

Note that hearsay is an expansive area of jurisprudence not covered in a comprehensive fashion in this text. For a detailed discussion, see generally, Robert S. Hunter, Illinois Practice Library, Trial Handbook for Illinois Lawyers Civil 6th Ed. (1989), Chapters 51 and 52.

For additional supporting and opposition citations relating to hearsay, see § 8:78 to § 8:89, infra, in this text.

§ 4:27 Supporting authorities—Inadmissible written hearsay—Generally

People v. Thompson, 327 Ill. App. 3d 1061, 1065, 262 Ill. Dec. 595, 765 N.E.2d 1203 (2d Dist. 2002) (defines "hearsay" as "testimony of an out-of-court statement offered to establish the truth of the matter asserted therein and whose value thus depends upon the credibility of the out-of-court declarant").

§ 4:28 Supporting authorities—Inadmissible written hearsay—Examples of inadmissible written hearsay

Apa v. National Bank of Commerce, 374 Ill. App. 3d 1082, 1084–88, 313 Ill. Dec. 507, 872 N.E.2d 490 (1st Dist. 2007) (insufficient foundation was provided for the admission of bank statements as business records).

Financial Freedom v. Kirgis, 377 Ill. App. 3d 107, 133–35, 315 Ill. Dec. 537, 877 N.E.2d 24 (1st Dist. 2007), appeal denied, 226 Ill. 2d 614, 317 Ill. Dec. 503, 882 N.E.2d 77 (2008) (unauthenticated documents that contained hearsay, were inadmissible).

State ex rel. Beeler, Schad and Diamond, P.C. v. Target Corp., 367 Ill. App. 3d 860, 874-76, 306 Ill. Dec. 1, 856 N.E.2d 1096 (1st Dist. 2006), appeal denied, 222 Ill. 2d 624, 308 Ill. Dec. 641, 862 N.E.2d 239 (2007) (affidavits that were based on hearsay, rather than the personal knowledge of the affiant, would not be considered).

Strino v. Premier Healthcare Associates, P.C., 365 Ill. App. 3d 895, 902-03, 302 Ill. Dec. 784, 850 N.E.2d 221 (1st Dist. 2006) (a witness' deposition testimony was not directly inconsistent with his trial testimony and therefore, it was properly excluded when offered as impeachment evidence).

Camco, Inc. v. Lowery, 362 Ill. App. 3d 421, 435–36, 298 Ill. Dec. 332, 839 N.E.2d 655 (1st Dist. 2005) (evidence regarding an officer's deposition testimony that was based upon information in a lab report was improper hearsay) (harmless error).

Camco, Inc. v. Lowery, 362 Ill. App. 3d 421, 433–34, 298 Ill. Dec. 332, 839 N.E.2d 655 (1st Dist. 2005) (an arrest report was hearsay and should not have been admitted).

Hubbert v. Dell Corp., 359 Ill. App. 3d 976, 985, 296 Ill. Dec. 258, 835 N.E.2d 113, 61 U.C.C. Rep. Serv. 2d 114 (5th Dist. 2005) (letters and marketing materials were improperly admitted where they were hearsay).

Hubbert v. Dell Corp., 359 Ill. App. 3d 976, 985, 296 Ill. Dec. 258, 835 N.E.2d 113, 61 U.C.C. Rep. Serv. 2d 114 (5th Dist. 2005) (the trial court erred by admitting a hearsay newspaper article).

Betts v. Manville Personal Injury Settlement Trust, 225 Ill. App. 3d 882, 924, 167 Ill. Dec. 1063, 588 N.E.2d 1193 (4th Dist. 1992) (improper to introduce inflammatory magazine and newspaper articles which were hearsay).

In re Marriage of Kutinac, 182 Ill. App. 3d 377, 384, 131 Ill. Dec. 487, 538 N.E.2d 862 (2d Dist. 1989) (the contents of a doctor's letter was inadmissible as hearsay when the party offered no proof that a hearsay exception applied).

Roeseke v. Pryor, 152 Ill. App. 3d 771, 779–80, 105 Ill. Dec. 642, 504 N.E.2d 927 (1st Dist. 1987) (officer's police report was hearsay and did not qualify as past recollection recorded when it was not information about which the officer had personal knowledge and the officer could not testify that the information was true and accurate when it was reported).

Roddy v. Chicago and N.W. R. R., 48 Ill. App. 3d 548, 553, 6 Ill. Dec. 536, 363 N.E.2d 65 (1st Dist. 1977) (improper to allow counsel to read hearsay from a National Safety Counsel bulletin without establishing any foundation for the admission of it).

Wilsey v. Schlawin, 35 Ill. App. 3d 892, 895–96, 342 N.E.2d 417 (1st Dist. 1975) (police report was not admissible as a past recollection recorded when the officer did not testify that the facts were true and accurate when they were reported).

Gillson v. Gulf, M. & O. R. Co., 42 Ill. 2d 193, 198–200, 246 N.E.2d 269 (1969) (improper for counsel to refer to the opinion contained in a letter which was inadmissible hearsay and lacked foundation).

Mehochko v. Gold Seal Co., 66 Ill. App. 2d 54, 57-60, 213 N.E.2d 581, 19 A.L.R.3d 1003 (5th Dist. 1966) (improper hearsay and prejudicial to let an expert read from a test report about tests performed by someone else when the expert had no personal knowledge about the tests at issue).

§ 4:29 Opposing authorities—Authentication

Illinois Supreme Court Rule 216(b) allows for a party to serve on the opposing party a request for admission that a document is genuine. If the opposing party fails to reply within the required time then the document is authenticated.

Illinois Supreme Court Rule 216(d) allows for authentication of public records by serving notice of the intent to use it as evidence and then it is authenticated if the opposing party fails to deny the accuracy of the document by affidavit.

Greig v. Griffel, 49 Ill. App. 3d 829, 834–36, 7 Ill. Dec. 499, 364 N.E.2d 660 (2d Dist. 1977) (parties' stipulation that photographs accurately showed the condition of the vehicle after the collision was sufficient to establish the foundation for admission of the photographs).

It is highly recommended that counsel routinely send requests to admit genuineness of documents during the course of discovery to streamline the litigation. Also, again to streamline the trial, counsel should request stipulations from opposing counsel both as to the genuineness of documents and to their admission at trial.

§ 4:30 Opposing authorities—Secondary evidence

People v. Bowman, 95 Ill. App. 3d 1137, 1142–43, 51 Ill. Dec. 527, 420 N.E.2d 1085 (5th Dist. 1981) (a copy of a document should be admissible as an original unless the facts of the case suggest that there is a true question whether the original was authentic or the facts demonstrate that it would be unjust to admit the copy).

§ 4:31 Opposing authorities—Hearsay

Note: for additional supporting and opposition citations relating to hearsay, see § 8:78 to § 8:89, infra.

§ 4:32 Opposing authorities—Hearsay—Impeachment

Lopez v. Northwestern Memorial Hosp., 375 Ill. App. 3d 637, 648, 313 Ill. Dec. 796, 873 N.E.2d 420 (1st Dist. 2007) (individual could be impeached through the use of deposition testimony that was inconsistent with the individual's trial testimony).

Krklus v. Stanley, 359 Ill. App. 3d 471, 295 Ill. Dec. 746, 833 N.E.2d 952, 966–68 (1st Dist. 2005) (deposition testimony was properly admitted to impeach witnesses through prior inconsistent statements).

York v. El-Ganzouri, 353 Ill. App. 3d 1, 17-21, 288 Ill. Dec. 529, 817 N.E.2d 1179 (1st Dist. 2004), judgment aff'd, 222 Ill. 2d 147, 305 Ill. Dec. 43, 854 N.E.2d 635 (2006) (trial court did not err by allowing expert to be impeached with sworn interrogatory answers, even though answers were prepared by and signed by a party's attorney).

People v. Thomas, 354 Ill. App. 3d 868, 883–85, 290 Ill. Dec. 316, 821 N.E.2d 628 (1st Dist. 2004), as modified on denial of reh'g, (Dec. 13, 2004) (witness' prior statement implicating defendant was admissible as a prior inconsistent statement).

Boyce v. Risch, 276 Ill. App. 3d 274, 277–79, 212 Ill. Dec. 800, 657 N.E.2d 1145 (1st Dist. 1995) (a prior inconsistent statement of a witness is admissible for impeachment).

Hapke v. Brandon, 343 Ill. App. 524, 526–29, 99 N.E.2d 636 (4th Dist. 1951) (a witness' written prior inconsistent statements should have been admitted for impeachment of the witness).

Williams v. Matlin, 328 Ill. App. 645, 647–648, 66 N.E.2d 719 (1st Dist. 1946) (proper to introduce a statement prepared by an insurance investigator and signed by the witness as impeachment of that witness' testimony).

§ 4:33 Opposing authorities—Hearsay—Not offered for proof of contents

Brdar v. Cottrell, Inc., 372 Ill. App. 3d 690, 703–04, 311 Ill.

Dec. 99, 867 N.E.2d 1085 (5th Dist. 2007), appeal denied, 224 Ill. 2d 572, 312 Ill. Dec. 654, 871 N.E.2d 54 (2007) (documents that were admitted to show a party's knowledge of a defective condition were not hearsay).

People v. Boand, 362 Ill. App. 3d 106, 126–28, 297 Ill. Dec. 880, 838 N.E.2d 367 (2d Dist. 2005) (the trial court erred by refusing to allow the defendant to cross examine a witness regarding the effect that a note from the prosecutor had on her decision whether or not to testify against the defendant; the note was not being offered for the truth of what was asserted and there was no demonstration of bias on the part of the witness).

People v. Szudy, 262 Ill. App. 3d 695, 711–12, 200 Ill. Dec. 462, 635 N.E.2d 801 (1st Dist. 1994) (improper to exclude a letter from the victim to the defendant as hearsay when it was not offered to prove the truth of its contents).

People v. Lash, 252 Ill. App. 3d 239, 250–51, 191 Ill. Dec. 751, 624 N.E.2d 1129 (1st Dist. 1993) (witness permitted to testify that he received letters and newspapers and about the actions he took as a result of them because existence of the documents was at issue, not the truth of the matters asserted therein).

People v. Vanda, 111 Ill. App. 3d 551, 555–59, 67 Ill. Dec. 373, 444 N.E.2d 609 (1st Dist. 1982) (letters written by the defendant should have been admissible because they were relevant to the issue of his sanity).

Cooper v. Illinois Publishing & Printing Co., 218 Ill. App. 95, 1920 WL 1114, at *9 (1st Dist. 1920) (in libel action where the plaintiff introduced the headlines into evidence, the defendant should have been permitted to introduce the remainder of the article because it was relevant to the case).

§ 4:34 Opposing authorities—Hearsay—Non-hearsay evidence

People v. Fenelon, 14 Ill. App. 3d 622, 623–26, 303 N.E.2d 38 (2d Dist. 1973) (trial judge properly admitted the videotaped portion of the defendant performing sobriety tests; appellate court noted that the videotaped portion was non-testimonial evidence).

§ 4:35 Opposing authorities—Hearsay—Non-assertive conduct

In re E.H., 299 Ill. App. 3d 42, 50-51, 233 Ill. Dec. 336, 700

N.E.2d 1044 (1st Dist. 1998) (officer could testify to another person's hearsay conduct to explain the course of the officer's investigation).

Leonardi v. Loyola University of Chicago, 168 Ill. 2d 83, 98-99, 212 Ill. Dec. 968, 658 N.E.2d 450 (1995) (not hearsay to introduce an out of court statement for the purpose of demonstrating why the witness took certain actions).

§ 4:36 Opposing authorities—Hearsay—Multiple hearsay

Kress Corp. v. Industrial Com'n, 190 Ill. App. 3d 72, 78, 137 Ill. Dec. 285, 545 N.E.2d 1046 (3d Dist. 1989) (two or more exceptions to the hearsay rule may be used to make double or multiple hearsay evidence admissible).

Counsel should keep in mind that evidence often has several levels of hearsay. For the evidence to be admissible, each level must be admissible on its own as an exception to the hearsay rule of exclusion. For example, a plaintiff's statement contained in medical records may be admissible if the records constitute business records (or an admission by a party opponent) and the plaintiff's statement was to a physician for the purpose of medical treatment. If the statement was for another purpose, it may not be admissible even if a proper foundation has been made for the admission of the records themselves.

§ 4:37 Opposing authorities—Hearsay—Relevant

Jackson v. Seib, 372 Ill. App. 3d 1061, 310 Ill. Dec. 502, 866 N.E.2d 663 (5th Dist. 2007) (photographs depicting little damage to a vehicle were relevant to establish the amount of force involved in the collision, with or without accompanying expert testimony).

People v. Lash, 252 Ill. App. 3d 239, 250–51, 191 Ill. Dec. 751, 624 N.E.2d 1129 (1st Dist. 1993) (witness permitted to testify that he received letters and newspapers and about the actions he took as a result of them because existence of the documents was at issue, not the truth of the matters asserted therein).

People v. Vanda, 111 Ill. App. 3d 551, 555–59, 67 Ill. Dec. 373, 444 N.E.2d 609 (1st Dist. 1982) (letters written by the defendant should have been admissible because they were relevant to the issue of his sanity).

Cooper v. Illinois Publishing & Printing Co., 218 Ill. App. 95, 1920 WL 1114, at *9 (1st Dist. 1920) (in libel action where the plaintiff introduced the headlines into evidence, the defendant should have been permitted to introduce the remainder of the article because it was relevant to the case).

§ 4:38 Opposing authorities—Hearsay—Hearsay exceptions

Zaragoza v. Ebenroth, 331 Ill. App. 3d 139, 141–43, 264 Ill. Dec. 542, 770 N.E.2d 1238 (3d Dist. 2002) (exceptions to the hearsay rule are based upon instances where the type of evidence offered is reliable and trustworthy).

Flath v. Madison Metal Services, Inc., 212 Ill. App. 3d 367, 377, 156 Ill. Dec. 496, 570 N.E.2d 1218 (5th Dist. 1991) (party offering hearsay evidence has the burden to establish that it is subject to an exception to the hearsay rule).

Below are several important exceptions applicable to written hearsay. Note that this list is by no means exhaustive. See generally, Robert S. Hunter, Illinois Practice Library, Trial Handbook for Illinois Lawyers Civil 6th Ed. (1989), Chapters 51 and 52. See also Federal Rules of Evidence 803 and 804. Note also that the reader should carefully distinguish between civil and criminal cases in this area.

<u>Business Records Exception</u>:

725 ILCS 5/115-5(a) applies to *criminal cases* and provides:

> Any writing or record, whether in the form of an entry in a book or otherwise, made as a memorandum or record of any act, transaction, occurrence, or event, shall be admissible as evidence of such act, transaction, occurrence, or event, if made in regular course of any business, and if it was the regular course of such business to make such memorandum or record at the time of such act, transaction, occurrence, or event or within a reasonable time thereafter.
>
> All other circumstances of the making of such writing or record, including lack of personal knowledge by the entrant or maker, may be shown to affect its weight, but such circumstances shall not affect its admissibility.
>
> The term "business," as used in this Section, includes business, profession, occupation, and calling of every kind.

725 ILCS 5/115-5(c) provides that the business records as evidence provisions may not be used as the basis for establishing admissibility if,

> such writing or record has been made by anyone during an investigation of an alleged offense or during any investigation relating to pending or anticipated litigation of any kind . . .

725 ILCS 5/115-5(c) provides that 725 ILCS 5/115-5(a) may not be used as the basis for establishing admissibility if,

> such writing or record has been made by anyone in the regular course of any form of hospital or medical business.

Illinois Supreme Court Rule 236, which applies to *civil cases* and provides:

> a) Any writing or record, whether in the form of any entry in a book or otherwise, made as a memorandum or record of any act, transaction, occurrence, or event, shall be admissible as evidence of the act, transaction, occurrence, or event, if made in the regular course of any business, and if it was the regular course of the business to make such a memorandum or record at the time of such an act, transaction, occurrence, or event or within a reasonable time thereafter. All other circumstances of the making of the writing or record, including lack of personal knowledge by the entrant or maker, may be shown to affect its weight, but shall not affect its admissibility. The term "business," as used in this rule, includes business, profession, occupation, and calling of every kind.

Illinois Supreme Court Rule 236(b) provides,

> Although police accident reports may otherwise be admissible in evidence under the law, subsection (a) of this rule [Admission of Business Records in Evidence] does not allow such writings to be admitted as a record or memorandum made in the regular course of business.

Prior to 1992, subsection (b) of Illinois Supreme Court Rule 236 excluded medical records from being admissible if the justification for doing so was based upon subsection (a). However, in 1992, the provision was amended to remove the prohibition against medical records being admitted as business records. See *Williams v. Covenant Medical Center*, 316 Ill. App. 3d 682, 691, 250 Ill. Dec. 40, 737 N.E.2d 662 (4th Dist. 2000); and *Lecroy v. Miller*, 272 Ill. App. 3d 925, 935–36, 209 Ill. Dec. 439, 651 N.E.2d 617 (1st Dist. 1995). Thus, the reader should be careful about using any pre-1992 case to argue about the admissibility of medical records in a civil case. See e.g. *Wilson v. Clark*, 84 Ill. 2d 186, 191–92, 49 Ill. Dec. 308, 417 N.E.2d 1322 (1981) (a proper foundation for admission was not laid when the individuals who made the entries did not testify).

735 ILCS 5/8-401 provides:

> Account books and records. Where in any action or proceeding, the claim or defense is founded on a book account or any other record or document, any party or interested person may testify to his or her account book, or any other record or document and the

items therein contained; that the same is a book, record, or document of original entries, and that the entries therein were made by himself or herself, and are true and just; or that the same were made by a deceased person, or by a disinterested person, a non-resident person of the state at the time of the trial, and where made by such deceased or non- resident person in the usual course of trade, and of his or her duty or employment to the party so testifying; and thereupon the account book and entries or any other record or document shall be admitted as evidence in the cause. Where such book of original entries or any other record or document has been photographed, microphotographed, microfilmed, optical imaged, or otherwise reproduced either in the usual course of business, or pursuant to any statute of this State authorizing the reproduction of public records, papers or documents, and the reproduction, in either case, complies with the minimum standards of quality for permanent records approved by the State Records Commission, then such reproduction shall be deemed to be an original record, book or document for all purposes, including introduction in evidence in all courts or administrative agencies.

Public Records Exception:

725 ILCS 5/115-5(b) provides,

If any business, institution, member of a profession or calling, or any department or agency of government, in the regular course of business or activity has kept or recorded any memorandum, writing, entry, print, representation or combination thereof, of any act, transaction, occurrence, or event, and in the regular course of business has caused any or all of the same to be recorded, copied, or reproduced by any photographic, photostatic, microfilm, micro-card, miniature photographic, optical imaging, or other process which accurately reproduces or forms a medium for so reproducing the original, the original may be destroyed in the regular course of business unless its preservation is required by law. Such reproduction, when satisfactorily identified, is as admissible in evidence as the original itself in any proceeding whether the original is in existence or not and an enlargement or facsimile of such reproduction is likewise admissible in evidence if the original reproduction is in existence and available for inspection under direction of court. The introduction of a reproduced record, enlargement, or facsimile does not preclude admission of the original. This Section shall not be construed to exclude from evidence any document or copy thereof which is otherwise admissible under the rules of evidence.

Coroner's Reports:

725 ILCS 5/115-5.1 states:

In any civil or criminal action the records of the coroner's medical or laboratory examiner summarizing and detailing the performance of his or her official duties in performing medical examinations upon deceased persons or autopsies, or both, and kept in the ordinary course of business of the coroner's office, duly certified by the county coroner or chief supervisory coroner's pathologist or medical examiner, shall be received as competent evidence in any court of this State, to the extent permitted by this Section. These reports, specifically including but not limited to the pathologist's protocol, autopsy reports and toxicological reports, shall be public documents and thereby may be admissible as prima facie evidence of the facts, findings, opinions, diagnoses and conditions stated therein.

A duly certified coroner's protocol or autopsy report, or both, complying with the requirements of this Section may be duly admitted into evidence as an exception to the hearsay rule as prima facie proof of the cause of death of the person to whom it relates. The records referred to in this Section shall be limited to the records of the results of post-mortem examinations of the findings of autopsy and toxicological laboratory examinations.

Persons who prepare reports or records offered in evidence hereunder may be subpoenaed as witnesses in civil or criminal cases upon the request of either party to the cause. However, if such person is dead, the county coroner or a duly authorized official of the coroner's office may testify to the fact that the examining pathologist, toxicologist or other medical or laboratory examiner is deceased and that the offered report or record was prepared by such deceased person. The witness must further attest that the medical report or record was prepared in the ordinary and usual course of the deceased person's duty or employment in conformity with the provisions of this Section.

C. MOTION TO EXCLUDE GRUESOME OR INFLAMMATORY PHOTOGRAPHS

§ 4:39 Suggested motion text

[Name of moving party] hereby moves this Court for an order excluding any and all evidence, references to evidence, testimony or argument relating to photographs depicting *[describe photographic evidence]*. The motion is based upon the ground that the evidence is *[state grounds, e.g., unduly gruesome, intended solely to inflame the jurors' emotions, etc.]* and will therefore create a substantial danger of undue prejudice to *[name of moving party]*.

§ 4:40 Motion summary

We have all heard the expression that a picture is worth a thousand words. No words can describe a scene, the damage to a vehicle, or the severity of injuries better than photographs. Photographs can therefore be the most effective evidence that an attorney can use. Photographs can also be the most unduly prejudicial evidence. In some instances, based upon the facts of a particular case, it is clear that counsel is attempting to use the photographs to gain sympathy or to anger the jurors, rather than to prove a point at issue. In those instances, the evidence should be excluded. The best time to attempt to exclude the photographs is prior to trial, before the jury has had an opportunity to view them.

This motion is used to exclude photographs that are unduly gruesome or inflammatory. The motion is based upon Illinois case law, which has held that photographs may be excluded where the principal effect is to arouse the jury's passion. *Hulsebus v. Russian*, 118 Ill. App. 2d 174, 180–81, 254 N.E.2d 184 (2d Dist. 1969); *People v. Lefler*, 38 Ill. 2d 216, 221–22, 230 N.E.2d 827 (1967). Gruesome photographs may also be excluded where they are cumulative of other, less inflammatory evidence. *Hulsebus v. Russian*, 118 Ill. App. 2d 174, 180–81, 254 N.E.2d 184 (2d Dist. 1969); *People v. Lefler*, 38 Ill. 2d 216, 221–22, 230 N.E.2d 827 (1967).

§ 4:41 Supporting authorities—Exclusion of prejudicial evidence, generally

Federal Rule of Evidence 403 states:

> Although relevant, evidence may be excluded if its probative value is substantially outweighed by the danger of unfair prejudice, confusion of the issues, or misleading the jury, or by considerations of undue delay, waste of time, or needless presentation of cumulative evidence.

It must be noted that this Rule has not been codified in Illinois. However, Illinois cases have stated that Illinois has a common-law rule that is comparable to Federal Rule of Evidence 403. See *People v. Walker*, 335 Ill. App. 3d 102, 112, 268 Ill. Dec. 654, 779 N.E.2d 268 (2d Dist. 2002), as modified on denial of reh'g, (Oct. 24, 2002) and judgment aff'd, 211 Ill. 2d 317, 285 Ill. Dec. 519, 812 N.E.2d 339 (2004); *People v. Peete*, 318 Ill. App. 3d 961, 966–67, 252 Ill. Dec. 821, 743 N.E.2d 689 (4th Dist. 2001). Therefore, it is arguable that Federal Rule of Evidence 403 can be considered as persuasive authority in Illinois.

People v. Holman, 257 Ill. App. 3d 1031, 1033–34, 196 Ill. Dec. 457, 630 N.E.2d 154 (2d Dist. 1994) (evidence is admissible if it is relevant and if the prejudicial impact does not substantially outweigh the probative value of it).

For expanded citations on the exclusion of prejudicial evidence, see § 2:1 to § 2:4.

§ 4:42 Supporting authorities—Exclusion of irrelevant evidence, generally

Federal Rule of Evidence 401 defines relevancy as,

> evidence having any tendency to make the existence of any fact that is of consequence to the determination of the action more probable or less probable than it would be without the evidence.

Illinois has adopted this definition of relevancy through case law. *Spencer v. Wandolowski*, 264 Ill. App. 3d 611, 617, 201 Ill. Dec. 422, 636 N.E.2d 854 (1st Dist. 1994); and *People v. Monroe*, 66 Ill. 2d 317, 321–22, 5 Ill. Dec. 824, 362 N.E.2d 295 (1977).

Baraniak v. Kurby, 371 Ill. App. 3d 310, 316–18, 308 Ill. Dec. 949, 862 N.E.2d 1152 (1st Dist. 2007), appeal denied, 224 Ill. 2d 571, 312 Ill. Dec. 654, 871 N.E.2d 54 (2007) (without expert testimony to correlate the amount of damage to a vehicle to the amount of personal injuries suffered by the occupants of the vehicle, photographs depicting the damage to the vehicles was irrelevant).

Preston ex rel. Preston v. Simmons, 321 Ill. App. 3d 789, 803, 254 Ill. Dec. 647, 747 N.E.2d 1059 (1st Dist. 2001) (trial judge should not permit such wide latitude on cross-examination that it undermines the rule that only relevant evidence is admissible).

Vojas v. K mart Corp., 312 Ill. App. 3d 544, 552, 245 Ill. Dec. 144, 727 N.E.2d 397 (5th Dist. 2000) (the burden of establishing relevance is on the party offering the evidence).

For expanded citations on the exclusion of irrelevant evidence, see § 3:1 to § 3:10.

§ 4:43 Supporting authorities—Gruesome or inflammatory photographs

Hulsebus v. Russian, 118 Ill. App. 2d 174, 180–81, 254 N.E.2d 184 (2d Dist. 1969) (trial judge had discretion to exclude a gruesome photograph of the plaintiff during surgery because other evidence established the extent of the injury and because the photograph was likely to inflame and prejudice the jury).

People v. Lefler, 38 Ill. 2d 216, 221–22, 230 N.E.2d 827 (1967) (autopsy photographs should not have been admitted when the nature of the injuries was not disputed and the photographs were likely to arouse strong emotions).

§ 4:44 Supporting authorities—Purpose to inflame jurors' emotions

Boren v. BOC Group, Inc., 385 Ill.App.3d 248, 254–57, 895

N.E.2d 53 (5th Dist. 2008) (photograph of a billboard advertisement which was offered to suggest that cases like the plaintiff's case were solicited and created by lawyers was irrelevant, prejudicial, misleading and confusing and caused grounds for granting a new trial).

Hulsebus v. Russian, 118 Ill. App. 2d 174, 180–81, 254 N.E.2d 184 (2d Dist. 1969) (trial judge had discretion to exclude a gruesome photograph of the plaintiff during surgery because other evidence established the extent of the injury and because the photograph was likely to inflame and prejudice the jury).

People v. Lefler, 38 Ill. 2d 216, 221–22, 230 N.E.2d 827 (1967) (autopsy photographs should not have been admitted when the nature of the injuries was not disputed and the photographs were likely to arouse strong emotions).

People v. Jackson, 9 Ill. 2d 484, 490–91, 138 N.E.2d 528 (1956) (error to admit an autopsy photograph when the sole purpose was to inflame the jurors' emotions).

§ 4:45 Supporting authorities—Other grounds

Other potential grounds for excluding photographs include the following:

- Confusing or misleading (§ 2:9 to § 2:12)
- Solely intended to create an emotional bias (§ 2:13 to § 2:19)
- Cumulative (§ 2:20 to § 2:33)
- Improper foundation (§ 4:1 to § 4:19)

§ 4:46 Opposing authorities

People v. Tara, 367 Ill. App. 3d 479, 310 Ill. Dec. 910, 867 N.E.2d 961 (2d Dist. 2006) (photographs of an injury were used to help demonstrate the seriousness of the injury to the factfinder).

People v. Smith, 362 Ill. App. 3d 1062, 1085–86, 299 Ill. Dec. 77, 841 N.E.2d 489 (1st Dist. 2005) (a photograph depicting the victim in a military uniform was not unduly inflammatory or prejudicial).

Kimble v. Earle M. Jorgenson Co., 358 Ill. App. 3d 400, 294 Ill. Dec. 402, 830 N.E.2d 814, 829–30 (1st Dist. 2005) (photographs were not unduly gruesome and were relevant to nature of injury and causation).

People v. Szudy, 262 Ill. App. 3d 695, 712–14, 200 Ill. Dec. 462, 635 N.E.2d 801 (1st Dist. 1994) (photographs are admissible if they tend to establish a fact in issue, even if they are gruesome, unless the trial judge determines that the prejudicial impact substantially outweighs the probative value of them).

Drews v. Gobel Freight Lines, Inc., 144 Ill. 2d 84, 100-01, 161 Ill. Dec. 324, 578 N.E.2d 970 (1991) (trial judge has discretion to determine whether or not photographs are too gruesome to be admissible and the trial judge did not abuse that discretion by admitting a morgue photograph).

Moore v. Swoboda, 213 Ill. App. 3d 217, 241–42, 157 Ill. Dec. 37, 571 N.E.2d 1056 (4th Dist. 1991) (not abuse of discretion to admit a photograph of the victim at the scene to show the condition of the victim, even if it was gruesome and cumulative).

Jones v. Greer, 627 F. Supp. 1481, 1487–88 (C.D. Ill. 1986) (Under Federal Rule of Evidence 403, evidence is not prejudicial merely because it harms a party's case; rather, the evidence must be of such a character that it suggests a decision based upon an improper basis).

People v. Newbury, 53 Ill. 2d 228, 242, 290 N.E.2d 592 (1972) (trial judge did not improperly admit photographs of the deceased at the scene of the offense when they were relevant to demonstrate manner of death).

> ◆ **Note:** Gruesome photographs might be more difficult to exclude in criminal cases, where they tend to be relevant to issues arising in murder, mayhem and other prosecutions. See e.g., *People v. Szudy*, 262 Ill. App. 3d 695, 712–14, 200 Ill. Dec. 462, 635 N.E.2d 801 (1st Dist. 1994) (autopsy photographs showing the victim's gunshot wounds were very relevant and admissible to show the manner of death); and *People v. Williams*, 128 Ill. App. 3d 384, 398, 83 Ill. Dec. 720, 470 N.E.2d 1140 (4th Dist. 1984).
>
> It should also be noted that photographs can be admissible for one purpose and inadmissible for another. Additionally, like written documents, a photograph can be redacted to exclude the inadmissible portions of the photograph. These options should always be considered by the proponent of evidence so that total exclusion is avoided.

See also §§ 4:52 et seq. regarding opposition to videotape evidence.

D. MOTION TO EXCLUDE PREJUDICIAL FILM OR VIDEOTAPES

§ 4:47 Suggested motion text

[Name of moving party] hereby moves this Court for an order

excluding any and all evidence, references to evidence, testimony or argument relating to a videotape [or film] made on or about *[date]* depicting *[describe nature of contents of videotape evidence]*. The motion is based upon the ground that the evidence is *[state grounds, e.g., confusing, cumulative, inflammatory, etc.]* and will therefore create a substantial danger of undue prejudice to *[name of moving party]*.

§ 4:48 Motion summary

This motion is used to exclude videotape or related evidence that creates a risk of undue prejudice to the moving party. The motion is based upon Illinois case law that supports the exclusion of prejudicial evidence. See *Woodrick v. Smith Gas Service, Inc.*, 87 Ill. App. 2d 88, 94-95, 230 N.E.2d 508, 4 U.C.C. Rep. Serv. 934 (2d Dist. 1967) [cumulative]; *Hulsebus v. Russian*, 118 Ill. App. 2d 174, 180–81, 254 N.E.2d 184 (2d Dist. 1969) [gruesome and inflammatory photograph]; *Becker v. Aquaslide "N' Dive Corp.*, 35 Ill. App. 3d 479, 484–85, 341 N.E.2d 369 (4th Dist. 1975) [deceptive or confusing].

§ 4:49 Supporting authorities—Exclusion of prejudicial evidence, generally

Federal Rule of Evidence 403 states:

> Although relevant, evidence may be excluded if its probative value is substantially outweighed by the danger of unfair prejudice, confusion of the issues, or misleading the jury, or by considerations of undue delay, waste of time, or needless presentation of cumulative evidence.

It must be noted that this Rule has not been codified in Illinois. However, Illinois cases have stated that Illinois has a common-law rule that is comparable to Federal Rule of Evidence 403. See *People v. Walker*, 335 Ill. App. 3d 102, 112, 268 Ill. Dec. 654, 779 N.E.2d 268 (2d Dist. 2002), as modified on denial of reh'g, (Oct. 24, 2002) and judgment aff'd, 211 Ill. 2d 317, 285 Ill. Dec. 519, 812 N.E.2d 339 (2004); *People v. Peete*, 318 Ill. App. 3d 961, 966–67, 252 Ill. Dec. 821, 743 N.E.2d 689 (4th Dist. 2001). Therefore, it is arguable that Federal Rule of Evidence 403 can be considered as persuasive authority in Illinois.

People v. Holman, 257 Ill. App. 3d 1031, 1033–34, 196 Ill. Dec. 457, 630 N.E.2d 154 (2d Dist. 1994) (evidence is admissible if it is relevant and if the prejudicial impact does not substantially outweigh the probative value of it).

For expanded citations on the exclusion of prejudicial evidence, see § 2:1 to § 2:4.

§ 4:50 Supporting authorities—Exclusion of videotape evidence

Donnellan v. First Student, Inc., 383 Ill.App.3d 1040, 1053–56, 891 N.E.2d 463 (1st Dist. 2008) (a surveillance video was properly excluded as unfairly prejudicial and confusing).

Spyrka v. County of Cook, 366 Ill. App. 3d 156, 165-69, 303 Ill. Dec. 613, 851 N.E.2d 800 (1st Dist. 2006) (video animation should not have been admitted because it was not used as a demonstrative aid to help the jury understand the testimony but rather was prejudicial and confusing to the jury when it appeared to re-enact the actual incident).

Foley v. Fletcher, 361 Ill. App. 3d 39, 50-51, 296 Ill. Dec. 916, 836 N.E.2d 667 (1st Dist. 2005) (the trial court did not abuse its discretion by barring the defendant's request to show a day-in-the-life video of the plaintiff during voir dire).

Waite v. Chicago Transit Authority, 157 Ill. App. 3d 616, 620–21, 110 Ill. Dec. 145, 510 N.E.2d 1176 (1st Dist. 1987) (improper to admit videotape when there was no foundation to show that it represented the plaintiff's physical point of view).

Missouri Portland Cement Co. v. United Cement, Lime, Gypsum and Allied Workers Intern. Union, Div. of Boilermakers, AFL-CIO, Local No. 438, 145 Ill. App. 3d 1023, 1027–29, 99 Ill. Dec. 796, 496 N.E.2d 489 (5th Dist. 1986) (foundation required for a videotape is that a witness testifies from personal knowledge that it accurately portrays the events therein—videotape *improperly* excluded in this case).

French v. City of Springfield, 65 Ill. 2d 74, 81-82, 2 Ill. Dec. 271, 357 N.E.2d 438 (1976) (prejudicial error to present a videotape taken from the plaintiff's perspective and recreating the events because it could unfairly influence the jury).

Becker v. Aquaslide "N' Dive Corp., 35 Ill. App. 3d 479, 484–85, 341 N.E.2d 369 (4th Dist. 1975) (exclusion of videotaped experiment where there was no foundation to show that the circumstances were identical to those in the actual incident).

Hulsebus v. Russian, 118 Ill. App. 2d 174, 180–81, 254 N.E.2d 184 (2d Dist. 1969) (trial judge had discretion to exclude a gruesome photograph of the plaintiff during surgery because other evidence established the extent of the injury and because the photograph was likely to inflame and prejudice the jury).

Woodrick v. Smith Gas Service, Inc., 87 Ill. App. 2d 88, 94-95, 230 N.E.2d 508, 4 U.C.C. Rep. Serv. 934 (2d Dist. 1967) (exclusion of motion picture demonstrating experiments because the evidence was cumulative of other testimony and because the experiments were not performed on an identical vehicle to the one at issue in the case).

§ 4:51 Supporting authorities—Other grounds

Other potential grounds for excluding videotape evidence include:

- Confusing or misleading (§ 2:9 to § 2:12)
- Solely intended to create an emotional bias (§ 2:13 to § 2:19)
- Cumulative (§ 2:20 to § 2:33)
- Irrelevant (§ 3:1 to § 3:10)
- Improper foundation (§ 4:1 to § 4:19)
- Gruesome or inflammatory photographs (§ 4:39 to § 4:46)

§ 4:52 Opposing authorities—Generally

Donnellan v. First Student, Inc., 383 Ill.App.3d 1040, 1052–53, 891 N.E.2d 463 (1st Dist. 2008) (sufficient foundation was laid for admission of a "day in the life video" by the plaintiff's wife who was able to testify that the video accurately represented the plaintiff's functioning ability).

Hudson v. City of Chicago, 378 Ill. App. 3d 373, 400–02, 317 Ill. Dec. 262, 881 N.E.2d 430 (1st Dist. 2007), appeal denied, 227 Ill. 2d 580, 321 Ill. Dec. 250, 888 N.E.2d 1183 (2008) (computer simulation was proper because it was supported by the evidence).

People v. Robert P., 354 Ill. App. 3d 1051, 1064, 290 Ill. Dec. 685, 821 N.E.2d 1259 (3d Dist. 2005) (a videotaped interview of a child was reliable and admissible under 725 ILCS 5/115-10).

Dillon v. Evanston Hosp., 199 Ill. 2d 483, 492–94, 264 Ill. Dec. 653, 771 N.E.2d 357 (2002) (trial court had discretion to allow the jury to view a videotape when an expert testified that it would be helpful in explaining the subject matter of his testimony to the jury).

Brown v. Ford Motor Co., 306 Ill. App. 3d 314, 317–18, 239 Ill. Dec. 637, 714 N.E.2d 556 (1st Dist. 1999) (trial court did not abuse its discretion by admitting videotapes of accident reconstruction, even when some of them were shown in slow motion).

Missouri Portland Cement Co. v. United Cement, Lime, Gypsum and Allied Workers Intern. Union, Div. of Boilermakers, AFL-CIO, Local No. 438, 145 Ill. App. 3d 1023, 1027–29, 99 Ill. Dec. 796, 496 N.E.2d 489 (5th Dist. 1986) (foundation required for a videotape is the same as that for photographs, i.e. that any witness testifies from personal knowledge that it accurately portrays the events therein).

Barenbrugge v. Rich, 141 Ill. App. 3d 1046, 1055–56, 96 Ill. Dec. 163, 490 N.E.2d 1368 (1st Dist. 1986) ("day in the life" video admissible in medical malpractice action, after weighing of probative value and risk of prejudice).

People v. Fenelon, 14 Ill. App. 3d 622, 623–26, 303 N.E.2d 38 (2d Dist. 1973) (trial judge properly admitted the videotaped portion of the defendant performing sobriety tests. The appellate court noted that the videotaped portion was non-testimonial evidence).

Mathias v. Baltimore & O. R. Co., 93 Ill. App. 2d 258, 263–64, 236 N.E.2d 331 (1st Dist. 1968) (error to preclude videotapes of the plaintiff performing work when disability was claimed and the testimony was conflicting about such disability).

§ 4:53 Opposing authorities—Relevance

Donnellan v. First Student, Inc., 383 Ill.App.3d 1040, 1051–52, 891 N.E.2d 463 (1st Dist. 2008) (a "day in the life video" was relevant and not unfairly prejudicial merely because it showed the amount of pain that plaintiff was experiencing).

Missouri Portland Cement Co. v. United Cement, Lime, Gypsum and Allied Workers Intern. Union, Div. of Boilermakers, AFL-CIO, Local No. 438, 145 Ill. App. 3d 1023, 1027–29, 99 Ill. Dec. 796, 496 N.E.2d 489 (5th Dist. 1986) (foundation required for a videotape is the same as that for photographs, i.e. that any witness testifies from personal knowledge that it accurately portrays the events therein).

Montag v. Board of Educ., School Dist. No. 40, Rock Island County, 112 Ill. App. 3d 1039, 1046–47, 68 Ill. Dec. 565, 446 N.E.2d 299, 9 Ed. Law Rep. 989 (3d Dist. 1983) (not an abuse of discretion to admit a videotape which showed the type of movements being made at the time of injury because it was relevant to the issues and helped explain the issues better than live testimony).

Mathias v. Baltimore & O. R. Co., 93 Ill. App. 2d 258, 263–64, 236 N.E.2d 331 (1st Dist. 1968) (error to preclude videotapes of the plaintiff performing work when disability was claimed and the testimony was conflicting about such disability).

§ 4:54 Opposing authorities—Cautionary admonition

Saldana v. Wirtz Cartage Co., 74 Ill. 2d 379, 391, 24 Ill. Dec.

523, 385 N.E.2d 664 (1978) (cautionary admonition can prevent possibility of jury misinterpretation of moving pictures).

E. MOTION TO EXCLUDE PUBLISHED ARTICLES AND TEXTS

§ 4:55 Suggested motion text

[Name of moving party] hereby moves this Court for an order excluding any and all evidence, references to evidence, testimony or argument relating to an article (or text) from the *[date]* issue of *[describe name of publication]*. The motion is based upon the ground that the evidence is *[state ground, e.g., cumulative, hearsay, etc.]* and will create a substantial danger of undue prejudice to *[name of moving party]*.

§ 4:56 Motion summary

This motion is used to exclude newspaper articles and related types of evidence where the prejudicial nature of such evidence outweighs the probative value of them or where they are unduly cumulative or where they contain inadmissible hearsay.

An important issue not addressed in this section relates to published literature either authored by retained experts or relied upon by experts in formulating opinions they express in a case. Readers should be aware that it is *improper* for a witness to simply read literature into evidence at the time of trial because the literature itself, in most cases, is clearly hearsay (unless authored by a party opponent). See § 4:104, Supporting authorities—Medical opinions—Opinions of others—Lack of personal knowledge, and § 8:10, Supporting authorities—Inadmissible hearsay—Treatises, documents & texts, infra. However, an expert *can* base his or her opinion on the literature as long as the literature is reasonably relied upon by similar types of experts in the field at issue. Additionally, it is important to note, that if the article or the literature lacks sufficient foundation for its findings or conclusions, then the article or literature should not even be referred to or relied upon, let alone read into evidence. There are many avenues of attack. See e.g., *Piano v. Davidson* at § 4:58, Supporting authorities—Exclusion of published articles—Hearsay, and § 4:59, Supporting authorities—Exclusion of published articles—Prejudicial, infra.

§ 4:57 Supporting authorities—Exclusion of prejudicial evidence, generally

Federal Rule of Evidence 403 states:

> Although relevant, evidence may be excluded if its probative value is substantially outweighed by the danger of unfair prejudice, confusion of the issues, or misleading the jury, or by considerations of undue delay, waste of time, or needless presentation of cumulative evidence.

It must be noted that this Rule has not been codified in Illinois. However, Illinois cases have stated that Illinois has a common-law rule that is comparable to Federal Rule of Evidence 403. See *People v. Walker*, 335 Ill. App. 3d 102, 112, 268 Ill. Dec. 654, 779 N.E.2d 268 (2d Dist. 2002), as modified on denial of reh'g, (Oct. 24, 2002) and judgment aff'd, 211 Ill. 2d 317, 285 Ill. Dec. 519, 812 N.E.2d 339 (2004); and *People v. Peete*, 318 Ill. App. 3d 961, 966–67, 252 Ill. Dec. 821, 743 N.E.2d 689 (4th Dist. 2001). Therefore, it is arguable that Federal Rule of Evidence 403 can be considered as persuasive authority in Illinois.

People v. Holman, 257 Ill. App. 3d 1031, 1033–34, 196 Ill. Dec. 457, 630 N.E.2d 154 (2d Dist. 1994) (evidence is admissible if it is relevant and if the prejudicial impact does not substantially outweigh the probative value of it).

For expanded citations on the exclusion of prejudicial evidence, see § 2:1 to § 2:4.

§ 4:58 Supporting authorities—Exclusion of published articles—Cumulative

Carillo v. Ford Motor Co., 325 Ill. App. 3d 955, 966, 259 Ill. Dec. 619, 759 N.E.2d 99 (1st Dist. 2001) (exclusion of statistical evidence from a national database when the statistics were cumulative of expert testimony).

For expanded citations on the exclusion of cumulative evidence, see § 2:20 to § 2:33.

§ 4:59 Supporting authorities—Exclusion of published articles—Hearsay

Hubbert v. Dell Corp., 359 Ill. App. 3d 976, 985, 296 Ill. Dec. 258, 835 N.E.2d 113, 61 U.C.C. Rep. Serv. 2d 114 (5th Dist. 2005) (the trial court erred by admitting a hearsay newspaper article).

Betts v. Manville Personal Injury Settlement Trust, 225 Ill. App. 3d 882, 924, 167 Ill. Dec. 1063, 588 N.E.2d 1193 (4th Dist. 1992) (improper to introduce inflammatory magazine and newspaper articles which were hearsay).

Piano v. Davison, 157 Ill. App. 3d 649, 668, 110 Ill. Dec. 35,

510 N.E.2d 1066 (1st Dist. 1987) (proper to exclude medical treatises when there was no proof that they were reliable).

Roddy v. Chicago and N.W. R. R., 48 Ill. App. 3d 548, 553, 6 Ill. Dec. 536, 363 N.E.2d 65 (1st Dist. 1977) (improper to allow counsel to read hearsay from a National Safety Counsel bulletin without establishing any foundation for the admission of it).

Goad v. Grissom, 324 Ill. App. 123, 128–30, 57 N.E.2d 514 (3d Dist. 1944) (improper and prejudicial for counsel to read from a newspaper article which was not in evidence).

For expanded citations on the exclusion of hearsay evidence, see § 8:78 to § 8:89.

§ 4:60 Supporting authorities—Exclusion of published articles—Prejudicial

Thornton v. Garcini, 364 Ill. App. 3d 612, 617–18, 301 Ill. Dec. 386, 846 N.E.2d 989 (3d Dist. 2006) (the trial court erred by failing to grant a mistrial when prejudicial newspaper articles had been seen by some of the jurors).

Nelson v. Upadhyaya, 361 Ill. App. 3d 415, 422–23, 297 Ill. Dec. 53, 836 N.E.2d 784 (1st Dist. 2005) (trial court erred by admitting irrelevant and prejudicial articles regarding the proper standard of care that were published after the incident in question).

Betts v. Manville Personal Injury Settlement Trust, 225 Ill. App. 3d 882, 924, 167 Ill. Dec. 1063, 588 N.E.2d 1193 (4th Dist. 1992) (improper to introduce inflammatory magazine and newspaper articles which were hearsay).

Goad v. Grissom, 324 Ill. App. 123, 128–30, 57 N.E.2d 514 (3d Dist. 1944) (improper and prejudicial for counsel to read from a newspaper article which was not in evidence).

Piano v. Davison, 157 Ill. App. 3d 649, 668, 110 Ill. Dec. 35, 510 N.E.2d 1066 (1st Dist. 1987) (proper to exclude medical treatises when there was no proof that they were reliable).

§ 4:61 Supporting authorities—Exclusion of published articles—Other grounds

Other possible grounds for excluding newspaper articles include:

- Confusing or misleading (§ 2:9 to § 2:12)
- Solely intended to create an emotional bias (§ 2:13 to § 2:19)
- Irrelevant (§ 3:1 to § 3:10)

- Improper foundation (§ 4:1 to § 4:19)
- Inadmissible writings (§ 4:20 to § 4:38)

§ 4:62 Opposition authorities—Where relevant to issues

Cooper v. Illinois Publishing & Printing Co., 218 Ill. App. 95, 1920 WL 1114, at *9 (1st Dist. 1920) (in libel action where the plaintiff introduced the headlines into evidence, the defendant should have been permitted to introduce the remainder of the article because it was relevant to the case).

> ◆ **Comment:** Although the literature is often hearsay and not admissible as substantive evidence, the literature may be relied upon and referred to by experts who reasonably rely upon such literature in their field. See § 4:55, Motion summary, supra.

§ 4:63 Opposition authorities—Nonhearsay

People v. Lash, 252 Ill. App. 3d 239, 250–51, 191 Ill. Dec. 751, 624 N.E.2d 1129 (1st Dist. 1993) (witness permitted to testify that he received letters and newspapers and about the actions he took as a result of them because existence of the documents was at issue, not the truth of the matters asserted therein).

F. MOTION TO EXCLUDE POLICE REPORTS AND OTHER TYPES OF ACCIDENT REPORTS

§ 4:64 Suggested motion text

[Name of moving party] hereby moves this Court for an order excluding any and all evidence, references to evidence, testimony or argument relating to an accident report prepared on *[date]* by *[name of reporting officer]* pertaining to the underlying automobile accident in this case. The motion is based upon the ground that the evidence is inadmissible pursuant to 625 ILCS 5/11-412.

§ 4:65 Motion summary

This motion is used to prevent the introduction of accident reports into evidence. The motion is based upon the express statutory authority of 625 ILCS 5/11-412.

In Illinois, police reports are treated differently than other types of records because they are specifically excluded from the business records exception provided by Supreme Court Rule 236. However, statements or observations contained in a police report can be admissible on other bases (e.g. past recollection recorded, admission by a party opponent, etc.). It should also be noted that although the police report may not be admissible, the police report may be used to refresh a witness's recollection (usually a police officer). Moreover, diagrams contained in police reports are often used for demonstrative purposes.

§ 4:66 Supporting authorities—Exclusion of prejudicial evidence, generally

Federal Rule of Evidence 403 states:

> Although relevant, evidence may be excluded if its probative value is substantially outweighed by the danger of unfair prejudice, confusion of the issues, or misleading the jury, or by considerations of undue delay, waste of time, or needless presentation of cumulative evidence.

It must be noted that this Rule has not been codified in Illinois. However, Illinois cases have stated that Illinois has a common-law rule that is comparable to Federal Rule of Evidence 403. See *People v. Walker*, 335 Ill. App. 3d 102, 112, 268 Ill. Dec. 654, 779 N.E.2d 268 (2d Dist. 2002), as modified on denial of reh'g, (Oct. 24, 2002) and judgment aff'd, 211 Ill. 2d 317, 285 Ill. Dec. 519, 812 N.E.2d 339 (2004); and *People v. Peete*, 318 Ill. App. 3d 961, 966–67, 252 Ill. Dec. 821, 743 N.E.2d 689 (4th Dist. 2001). Therefore, it is arguable that Federal Rule of Evidence 403 can be considered as persuasive authority in Illinois.

People v. Holman, 257 Ill. App. 3d 1031, 1033–34, 196 Ill. Dec. 457, 630 N.E.2d 154 (2d Dist. 1994) (evidence is admissible if it is relevant and if the prejudicial impact does not substantially outweigh the probative value of it).

For expanded citations on the exclusion of prejudicial evidence, see § 2:1 to § 2:4.

§ 4:67 Supporting authorities—Exclusion based upon vehicle code § 5/11-412

625 ILCS 5/11-412 states, in pertinent part, as follows:

> Motor vehicle accident reports confidential. All required written motor vehicle accident reports and supplemental reports shall be without prejudice to the individual so reporting and shall be for the confidential use of the Department and the Secretary of State and, in the case of second division vehicles operated under certificate of convenience and necessity issued by the Illinois Commerce Commission, of the Commission, except that the Administrator or the Secretary of State or the Commission may disclose the identity of a person involved in a motor vehicle accident when such identity is not otherwise known or when such person denies his presence at such motor vehicle accident and the

> Department shall disclose the identity of the insurance carrier, if any, upon demand. The Secretary of State may also disclose notations of accident involvement maintained on individual driving records. The Department may furnish copies of its written accident reports to federal, State, and local agencies that are engaged in highway safety research and studies. Reports furnished to any agency other than the Secretary of State or the Illinois Commerce Commission may be used only for statistical or analytical purposes and shall be held confidential by that agency. No such written report shall be used as evidence in any trial, civil or criminal, arising out of a motor vehicle accident, except that the Administrator shall furnish upon demand of any person who has, or claims to have, made such a written report, or upon demand of any court, a certificate showing that a specified written accident report has or has not been made to the Administrator solely to prove a compliance or a failure to comply with the requirement that such a written report be made to the Administrator.
>
> The Department of Transportation at its discretion may provide for in-depth investigations of accidents involving Department employees. A written report describing the preventability of such an accident may be prepared to enhance the safety of Department employees. *Such reports and any opinions expressed in the review of the accident as to the preventability of the accident shall be for the privileged use of the Department and held confidential and shall not be obtainable or used in any civil or criminal proceeding.* (Emphasis added.)

§ 4:68 Supporting authorities—Inadmissible hearsay

725 ILCS 5/115-5(c) provides that the business records as evidence provisions may not be used as the basis for establishing admissibility if,

> such writing or record has been made by anyone during an investigation of an alleged offense or during any investigation relating to pending or anticipated litigation of any kind . . .

In addition, Illinois Supreme Court Rule 236(b) provides,

> Although police accident reports may otherwise be admissible in evidence under the law, subsection (a) of this rule [Admission of Business Records in Evidence] does not allow such writings to be admitted as a record or memorandum made in the regular course of business.

Berry v. American Standard, Inc., 382 Ill.App.3d 895, 897–905, 888 N.E.2d 740 (5th Dist. 2008) (a deceased party's discovery deposition that was taken prior to the party's death but not under the belief that the party's death was imminent, was inadmissible hearsay).

Camco, Inc. v. Lowery, 362 Ill. App. 3d 421, 433–34, 298 Ill.

Dec. 332, 839 N.E.2d 655 (1st Dist. 2005) (an arrest report was hearsay and should not have been admitted).

People v. Wilder, 356 Ill. App. 3d 712, 724, 292 Ill. Dec. 640, 826 N.E.2d 1076 (1st Dist. 2005) (police reports can be used for certain impeachment purposes but are not generally admissible as substantive evidence).

Horace Mann Ins. Co. v. Brown, 236 Ill. App. 3d 456, 462–63, 177 Ill. Dec. 690, 603 N.E.2d 760 (1st Dist. 1992) (police reports are generally inadmissible as hearsay).

Cranwill v. Donahue, 132 Ill. App. 3d 873, 874–75, 87 Ill. Dec. 883, 478 N.E.2d 22 (3d Dist. 1985) (police reports are generally inadmissible as hearsay).

Wilsey v. Schlawin, 35 Ill. App. 3d 892, 895–96, 342 N.E.2d 417 (1st Dist. 1975) (police report was not admissible as a past recollection recorded when the officer did not testify that the facts were true and accurate when they were reported).

> ◆ **Comment:** Although in *Wilsey* the court did not allow the police report to be admitted as a past recollection recorded, police reports can be admitted as such where the proper foundation is laid. Police reports are often admitted as past recollections recorded because police officers rarely have an independent recollection of the accident. Police reports are also often used to refresh a witness' recollection (usually a police officer).

See § 8:78 to § 8:89 for general hearsay citations.

§ 4:69 Supporting authorities—Statements and opinions in reports

Ahmed v. Pickwick Place Owners' Ass'n, 385 Ill.App.3d 874, 890–91, 896 N.E.2d 854 (1st Dist. 2008) (police officer's opinion regarding the cause of certain injuries to a deceased individual was speculative and based upon hearsay and therefore inadmissible).

Jackson v. Seib, 372 Ill. App. 3d 1061, 310 Ill. Dec. 502, 866 N.E.2d 663 (5th Dist. 2007) (the trial court committed harmless error where it allowed an officer to testify when the officer acknowledged that he had no independent recollection of the occurrence and was relying on his report).

Camco, Inc. v. Lowery, 362 Ill. App. 3d 421, 435–36, 298 Ill. Dec. 332, 839 N.E.2d 655 (1st Dist. 2005) (evidence regarding an officer's deposition testimony based upon information that was contained in a lab report was improper hearsay) (harmless error).

Peterson v. Lou Bachrodt Chevrolet Co., 76 Ill. 2d 353, 362–63, 29 Ill. Dec. 444, 392 N.E.2d 1 (1979) (overruled by, Wills v. Foster, 229 Ill. 2d 393, 323 Ill. Dec. 26, 892 N.E.2d 1018 (2008)) (inaccurate and misleading diagram made at the scene was properly excluded).

Wilsey v. Schlawin, 35 Ill. App. 3d 892, 895–96, 342 N.E.2d 417 (1st Dist. 1975) (police report was not admissible as a past recollection recorded when the officer did not testify that the facts were true and accurate when they were reported).

Allen v. Yancy, 57 Ill. App. 2d 50, 61-62, 206 N.E.2d 452 (1st Dist. 1965) (error to allow counsel to read alleged statements from a police report in an attempt to impeach a witness when the officer who wrote the report had no memory of the statements).

See "Comment" in § 4:68, Supporting authorities—Inadmissible hearsay, supra.

§ 4:70 Supporting authorities—Other grounds

Other possible grounds for excluding traffic accident reports include:

- Cumulative (§ 2:20 to § 2:33)
- Improper foundation (§ 4:1 to § 4:19)
- Inadmissible writings (§ 4:20 to § 4:38)
- Improper impeachment evidence (§ 7:4 to § 7:24)
- Inadmissible hearsay (§ 8:78 to § 8:89)
- Improper evidence of statute violation (§ 10:82 to § 10:92)

§ 4:71 Opposing authorities—Report used to refresh recollection

Tuskey v. Callos, 112 Ill. App. 2d 213, 218–19, 250 N.E.2d 524 (2d Dist. 1969) (police officer could use his report to refresh his recollection regarding the victim's statements).

> ◆ **Note:** For a police report to be admissible as a past recollection recorded, the following foundation must be laid: (1) the witness must have no independent recollection of the occurrence or event recorded; (2) the report must fail to refresh the witness's recollection; (3) the facts in the report must have been recorded at the time of the occurrence or soon thereafter; and (4) the report must be true and accurate. *Jones v. Beker*, 260 Ill. App. 3d 481, 198 Ill. Dec. 214, 632 N.E.2d 273 (1st Dist. 1994).

§ 4:72 Opposing authorities—Diagrams made at scene

Walls v. Jul, 118 Ill. App. 2d 242, 248–49, 254 N.E.2d 173

(2d Dist. 1969) (admission of a police officer's diagram that was attached to his report allowed because it reflected his measurements and observations at the scene).

§ 4:73 Opposing authorities—Business records exception to hearsay rule

725 ILCS 5/115-5(a) provides:

> Any writing or record, whether in the form of an entry in a book or otherwise, made as a memorandum or record of any act, transaction, occurrence, or event, shall be admissible as evidence of such act, transaction, occurrence, or event, if made in regular course of any business, and if it was the regular course of such business to make such memorandum or record at the time of such act, transaction, occurrence, or event or within a reasonable time thereafter.
>
> All other circumstances of the making of such writing or record, including lack of personal knowledge by the entrant or maker, may be shown to affect its weight, but such circumstances shall not affect its admissibility.
>
> The term business, as used in this Section, includes business, profession, occupation, and calling of every kind.

Illinois Supreme Court Rule 236 provides:

> a) Any writing or record, whether in the form of any entry in a book or otherwise, made as a memorandum or record of any act, transaction, occurrence, or event, shall be admissible as evidence of the act, transaction, occurrence, or event, if made in the regular course of any business, and if it was the regular course of the business to make such a memorandum or record at the time of such an act, transaction, occurrence, or event or within a reasonable time thereafter. All other circumstances of the making of the writing or record, including lack of personal knowledge by the entrant or maker, may be shown to affect its weight, but shall not affect its admissibility. The term 'business,' as used in this rule, includes business, profession, occupation, and calling of every kind.

◆ **Note:** It is important to note that although police reports are not admissible as business records pursuant to Supreme Court Rule 236, other accident reports may be.

735 ILCS 5/8-401 provides:

> Account books and records. Where in any action or proceeding, the claim or defense is founded on a book account or any other record or document, any party or interested person may testify to his or her account book, or any other record or document and the items therein contained; that the same is a book, record, or document of original entries, and that the entries therein were made

by himself or herself, and are true and just; or that the same were made by a deceased person, or by a disinterested person, a non-resident person of the state at the time of the trial, and where made by such deceased or non- resident person in the usual course of trade, and of his or her duty or employment to the party so testifying; and thereupon the account book and entries or any other record or document shall be admitted as evidence in the cause. Where such book of original entries or any other record or document has been photographed, microphotographed, microfilmed, optical imaged, or otherwise reproduced either in the usual course of business, or pursuant to any statute of this State authorizing the reproduction of public records, papers or documents, and the reproduction, in either case, complies with the minimum standards of quality for permanent records approved by the State Records Commission, then such reproduction shall be deemed to be an original record, book or document for all purposes, including introduction in evidence in all courts or administrative agencies.

§ 4:74 Opposing authorities—Public records exception to hearsay rule

725 ILCS 5/115-5(b) provides:

If any business, institution, member of a profession or calling, or any department or agency of government, in the regular course of business or activity has kept or recorded any memorandum, writing, entry, print, representation or combination thereof, of any act, transaction, occurrence, or event, and in the regular course of business has caused any or all of the same to be recorded, copied, or reproduced by any photographic, photostatic, microfilm, micro-card, miniature photographic, optical imaging, or other process which accurately reproduces or forms a medium for so reproducing the original, the original may be destroyed in the regular course of business unless its preservation is required by law. Such reproduction, when satisfactorily identified, is as admissible in evidence as the original itself in any proceeding whether the original is in existence or not and an enlargement or facsimile of such reproduction is likewise admissible in evidence if the original reproduction is in existence and available for inspection under direction of court. The introduction of a reproduced record, enlargement, or facsimile does not preclude admission of the original. This Section shall not be construed to exclude from evidence any document or copy thereof which is otherwise admissible under the rules of evidence.

G. MOTION TO EXCLUDE LETTERS

§ 4:75 Suggested motion text

[Name of moving party] hereby moves this Court for an order excluding any and all evidence, references to evidence, testimony or argument relating to a letter written by *[name of author of letter]* pertaining to *[describe nature of content of letter]*. The motion

is based upon the ground that the evidence is *[state ground, e.g., cumulative, irrelevant, collateral, etc.]* and will create a substantial danger of undue prejudice to *[name of moving party]*.

§ 4:76 Motion summary

This motion is used to exclude letters containing irrelevant, collateral or other inappropriate matter that is likely to prejudice the party seeking exclusion. The motion is based upon the authority of Illinois case law. See e.g. *Evans and Associates, Inc. v. Dyer*, 246 Ill. App. 3d 231, 236–38, 185 Ill. Dec. 900, 615 N.E.2d 770 (2d Dist. 1993).

§ 4:77 Supporting authorities—Exclusion of prejudicial evidence, generally

Federal Rule of Evidence 403 states:

> Although relevant, evidence may be excluded if its probative value is substantially outweighed by the danger of unfair prejudice, confusion of the issues, or misleading the jury, or by considerations of undue delay, waste of time, or needless presentation of cumulative evidence.

It must be noted that this Rule has not been codified in Illinois. However, Illinois cases have stated that Illinois has a common-law rule that is comparable to Federal Rule of Evidence 403. See *People v. Walker*, 335 Ill. App. 3d 102, 112, 268 Ill. Dec. 654, 779 N.E.2d 268 (2d Dist. 2002), as modified on denial of reh'g, (Oct. 24, 2002) and judgment aff'd, 211 Ill. 2d 317, 285 Ill. Dec. 519, 812 N.E.2d 339 (2004); *People v. Peete*, 318 Ill. App. 3d 961, 966–67, 252 Ill. Dec. 821, 743 N.E.2d 689 (4th Dist. 2001). Therefore, it is arguable that Federal Rule of Evidence 403 can be considered as persuasive authority in Illinois.

People v. Holman, 257 Ill. App. 3d 1031, 1033–34, 196 Ill. Dec. 457, 630 N.E.2d 154 (2d Dist. 1994) (evidence is admissible if it is relevant and if the prejudicial impact does not substantially outweigh the probative value of it).

For expanded citations on the exclusion of prejudicial evidence, see § 2:1 to § 2:4.

§ 4:78 Supporting authorities—Exclusion of letters—Generally

Liberty Mut. Ins. Co. v. American Home Assur. Co., Inc., 368 Ill. App. 3d 948, 960-61, 306 Ill. Dec. 733, 858 N.E.2d 530 (1st Dist. 2006) (trial court properly excluded a letter from a party's attorney which included evidence of settlement negotiations).

People v. Szudy, 262 Ill. App. 3d 695, 711–12, 200 Ill. Dec. 462, 635 N.E.2d 801 (1st Dist. 1994) (letter properly excluded as irrelevant).

Evans and Associates, Inc. v. Dyer, 246 Ill. App. 3d 231, 236–38, 185 Ill. Dec. 900, 615 N.E.2d 770 (2d Dist. 1993) (proper to exclude letter when it was hearsay and it lacked foundation and no hearsay exception applied to it).

Harris v. Algonquin Ready Mix, Inc., 13 Ill. App. 3d 559, 563–64, 300 N.E.2d 824 (1st Dist. 1973), judgment aff'd in part, appeal dismissed in part, 59 Ill. 2d 445, 322 N.E.2d 58 (1974) (proper to exclude evidence of a form letter when there was no evidence that it was ever sent or received).

Gillson v. Gulf, M. & O. R. Co., 42 Ill. 2d 193, 198–200, 246 N.E.2d 269 (1969) (improper for counsel to refer to the opinion contained in a letter which was inadmissible hearsay and lacked foundation).

§ 4:79 Supporting authorities—Exclusion of letters—Hearsay

Dukes v. Pneumo Abex Corp., 386 Ill.App.3d 425, 438–39, 900 N.E.2d 1128 (4th Dist. 2008) (a letter written by a now deceased employee of a party, on a subject outside of the scope of the individual's employment responsibilities, was inflammatory and prejudicial and should not have been considered as an admission of a party).

Babich v. River Oaks Toyota, 377 Ill. App. 3d 425, 427–29, 316 Ill. Dec. 353, 879 N.E.2d 420 (1st Dist. 2007), appeal denied, 226 Ill. 2d 611, 317 Ill. Dec. 502, 882 N.E.2d 76 (2008) (information in a letter was inadmissible hearsay).

Babich v. River Oaks Toyota, 377 Ill. App. 3d 425, 427–29, 316 Ill. Dec. 353, 879 N.E.2d 420 (1st Dist. 2007), appeal denied, 226 Ill. 2d 611, 317 Ill. Dec. 502, 882 N.E.2d 76 (2008) (a letter was not an admission of a party when there was no proof of who provided the information that was contained in the letter).

Hubbert v. Dell Corp., 359 Ill. App. 3d 976, 985, 296 Ill. Dec. 258, 835 N.E.2d 113, 61 U.C.C. Rep. Serv. 2d 114 (5th Dist. 2005) (letters that were hearsay were improperly admitted).

Evans and Associates, Inc. v. Dyer, 246 Ill. App. 3d 231, 236–38, 185 Ill. Dec. 900, 615 N.E.2d 770 (2d Dist. 1993) (proper to exclude letter when it was hearsay and lacked foundation and no hearsay exception applied).

In re Marriage of Kutinac, 182 Ill. App. 3d 377, 384, 131 Ill.

Dec. 487, 538 N.E.2d 862 (2d Dist. 1989) (the contents of a letter are inadmissible as hearsay unless an exception applies).

Gillson v. Gulf, M. & O. R. Co., 42 Ill. 2d 193, 198–200, 246 N.E.2d 269 (1969) (improper for counsel to refer to the opinion contained in a letter which was inadmissible hearsay and lacked foundation).

For expanded citations on hearsay evidence, see § 8:78 to § 8:89., infra.

§ 4:80 Supporting authorities—Exclusion of letters—Irrelevant

People v. Szudy, 262 Ill. App. 3d 695, 711–12, 200 Ill. Dec. 462, 635 N.E.2d 801 (1st Dist. 1994) (letter properly excluded as irrelevant).

§ 4:81 Supporting authorities—Exclusion of letters—Lack of foundation

Dukes v. Pneumo Abex Corp., 386 Ill.App.3d 425, 438–39, 900 N.E.2d 1128 (4th Dist. 2008) (a letter written by a now deceased employee of a party, on a subject outside of the scope of the individual's employment responsibilities, was inflammatory and prejudicial and should not have been considered as an admission of a party).

Babich v. River Oaks Toyota, 377 Ill. App. 3d 425, 427–29, 316 Ill. Dec. 353, 879 N.E.2d 420 (1st Dist. 2007), appeal denied, 226 Ill. 2d 611, 317 Ill. Dec. 502, 882 N.E.2d 76 (2008) (a witness could not testify to the contents of a letter when the witness had no personal knowledge regarding the information contained in the letter).

Babich v. River Oaks Toyota, 377 Ill. App. 3d 425, 427–29, 316 Ill. Dec. 353, 879 N.E.2d 420 (1st Dist. 2007), appeal denied, 226 Ill. 2d 611, 317 Ill. Dec. 502, 882 N.E.2d 76 (2008) (insufficient foundation was provided for the admission of a letter as a business record).

Hubbert v. Dell Corp., 359 Ill. App. 3d 976, 985, 296 Ill. Dec. 258, 835 N.E.2d 113, 61 U.C.C. Rep. Serv. 2d 114 (5th Dist. 2005) (letters were improperly admitted without a sufficient foundation).

Harris v. Algonquin Ready Mix, Inc., 13 Ill. App. 3d 559, 563–64, 300 N.E.2d 824 (1st Dist. 1973), judgment aff'd in part, appeal dismissed in part, 59 Ill. 2d 445, 322 N.E.2d 58 (1974) (proper to exclude evidence of a form letter when there was no evidence that it was ever sent or received).

Gillson v. Gulf, M. & O. R. Co., 42 Ill. 2d 193, 198–200, 246 N.E.2d 269 (1969) (improper for counsel to refer to the opinion contained in a letter which was inadmissible hearsay and lacked foundation).

§ 4:82 Supporting authorities—Other grounds

Other possible grounds for excluding letters include:

- Collateral to issues in case (§ 2:5 to § 2:8)
- Cumulative (§ 2:20 to § 2:33)
- Irrelevant (§ 3:1 to § 3:10)
- Improper foundation (§ 4:1 to § 4:19)
- Inadmissible writings (§ 4:20 to § 4:38)

§ 4:83 Opposing authorities—Generally—Admissible hearsay or nonhearsay

Townsend v. Fassbinder, 372 Ill. App. 3d 890, 906, 310 Ill. Dec. 470, 866 N.E.2d 631 (2d Dist. 2007) (statement of a party's agent that was contained in a letter was admissible as an admission).

City of Chicago v. Old Colony Partners, L.P., 364 Ill. App. 3d 806, 818–20, 301 Ill. Dec. 555, 847 N.E.2d 565 (1st Dist. 2006) (letters and reports prepared by a third party for a business, were admissible as business records).

People v. Szudy, 262 Ill. App. 3d 695, 711–12, 200 Ill. Dec. 462, 635 N.E.2d 801 (1st Dist. 1994) (improper to exclude a letter from the victim to the defendant as hearsay when it was not offered to prove the truth of its contents) (note, however, letter was properly excluded as irrelevant).

§ 4:84 Opposing authorities—Generally—Relevant

Webber v. Wight & Co., 368 Ill. App. 3d 1007, 1027-29, 306 Ill. Dec. 782, 858 N.E.2d 579 (1st Dist. 2006), appeal denied, 223 Ill. 2d 686, 310 Ill. Dec. 258, 865 N.E.2d 978 (2007) (letters written by the plaintiff about the defendants were relevant to impeach the plaintiff's testimony regarding the defendant's alleged improper practices).

People v. Vanda, 111 Ill. App. 3d 551, 555–59, 67 Ill. Dec. 373, 444 N.E.2d 609 (1st Dist. 1982) (letters written by the defendant should have been admissible because they were relevant to the issue of his sanity).

§ 4:85 Opposing authorities—Generally—Impeachment

Webber v. Wight & Co., 368 Ill. App. 3d 1007, 1027-29, 306

Ill. Dec. 782, 858 N.E.2d 579 (1st Dist. 2006), appeal denied, 223 Ill. 2d 686, 310 Ill. Dec. 258, 865 N.E.2d 978 (2007) (letters written by the plaintiff about the defendants were relevant to impeach the plaintiff's testimony regarding the defendant's alleged improper practices).

Webber v. Wight & Co., 368 Ill. App. 3d 1007, 1028-29, 306 Ill. Dec. 782, 858 N.E.2d 579 (1st Dist. 2006), appeal denied, 223 Ill. 2d 686, 310 Ill. Dec. 258, 865 N.E.2d 978 (2007) (the plaintiff was not unfairly surprised by the introduction of letters that he had signed and that were obtained by the defendant through a subpoena).

Hapke v. Brandon, 343 Ill. App. 524, 526–29, 99 N.E.2d 636 (4th Dist. 1951) (a witness' written prior inconsistent statements should have been admitted for impeachment of the witness).

§ 4:86 Opposing authorities—Exceptions to hearsay rule

Note that letters may be admissible under the business writings or public records exceptions to the hearsay rule. Additionally, note that letters may also be admissible as admissions by a party opponent or as a statement that reflects a witness' state of mind. It may also be persuasive for counsel to note other exceptions to the hearsay rule pursuant to Federal Rules of Evidence 803 and 804. (See generally § 8:77 to § 8:88, infra.)

§ 4:87 Opposing authorities—Exceptions to hearsay rule—Business records exception

725 ILCS 5/115-5(a) provides:

> Any writing or record, whether in the form of an entry in a book or otherwise, made as a memorandum or record of any act, transaction, occurrence, or event, shall be admissible as evidence of such act, transaction, occurrence, or event, if made in regular course of any business, and if it was the regular course of such business to make such memorandum or record at the time of such act, transaction, occurrence, or event or within a reasonable time thereafter.
>
> All other circumstances of the making of such writing or record, including lack of personal knowledge by the entrant or maker, may be shown to affect its weight, but such circumstances shall not affect its admissibility.
>
> The term "business," as used in this Section, includes business, profession, occupation, and calling of every kind.

In addition, Illinois Supreme Court Rule 236 provides:

a) Any writing or record, whether in the form of any entry in a book or otherwise, made as a memorandum or record of any act, transaction, occurrence, or event, shall be admissible as evidence of the act, transaction, occurrence, or event, if made in the regular course of any business, and if it was the regular course of the business to make such a memorandum or record at the time of such an act, transaction, occurrence, or event or within a reasonable time thereafter. All other circumstances of the making of the writing or record, including lack of personal knowledge by the entrant or maker, may be shown to affect its weight, but shall not affect its admissibility. The term 'business,' as used in this rule, includes business, profession, occupation, and calling of every kind.

In addition, 735 ILCS 5/8-401 provides:

Account books and records. Where in any action or proceeding, the claim or defense is founded on a book account or any other record or document, any party or interested person may testify to his or her account book, or any other record or document and the items therein contained; that the same is a book, record, or document of original entries, and that the entries therein were made by himself or herself, and are true and just; or that the same were made by a deceased person, or by a disinterested person, a non-resident person of the state at the time of the trial, and where made by such deceased or non- resident person in the usual course of trade, and of his or her duty or employment to the party so testifying; and thereupon the account book and entries or any other record or document shall be admitted as evidence in the cause. Where such book of original entries or any other record or document has been photographed, microphotographed, microfilmed, optical imaged, or otherwise reproduced either in the usual course of business, or pursuant to any statute of this State authorizing the reproduction of public records, papers or documents, and the reproduction, in either case, complies with the minimum standards of quality for permanent records approved by the State Records Commission, then such reproduction shall be deemed to be an original record, book or document for all purposes, including introduction in evidence in all courts or administrative agencies.

City of Chicago v. Old Colony Partners, L.P., 364 Ill. App. 3d 806, 818–20, 301 Ill. Dec. 555, 847 N.E.2d 565 (1st Dist. 2006) (letters and reports prepared by a third party for a business, were admissible as business records).

City of Chicago v. Old Colony Partners, L.P., 364 Ill. App. 3d 806, 818–20, 301 Ill. Dec. 555, 847 N.E.2d 565 (1st Dist. 2006) (sufficient foundation was provided for the admission of letters and reports prepared by a third party for a business, as business records).

§ 4:88 Opposing authorities—Exceptions to hearsay rule—Public records exception

725 ILCS 5/115-5(b) provides:

> If any business, institution, member of a profession or calling, or any department or agency of government, in the regular course of business or activity has kept or recorded any memorandum, writing, entry, print, representation or combination thereof, of any act, transaction, occurrence, or event, and in the regular course of business has caused any or all of the same to be recorded, copied, or reproduced by any photographic, photostatic, microfilm, micro-card, miniature photographic, optical imaging, or other process which accurately reproduces or forms a medium for so reproducing the original, the original may be destroyed in the regular course of business unless its preservation is required by law. Such reproduction, when satisfactorily identified, is as admissible in evidence as the original itself in any proceeding whether the original is in existence or not and an enlargement or facsimile of such reproduction is likewise admissible in evidence if the original reproduction is in existence and available for inspection under direction of court. The introduction of a reproduced record, enlargement, or facsimile does not preclude admission of the original. This Section shall not be construed to exclude from evidence any document or copy thereof which is otherwise admissible under the rules of evidence.

§ 4:89 Opposing authorities—Inconsistent statement

In civil or criminal matters, prior inconsistent statements of a witness may be used for impeachment purposes. Counsel should note that prior inconsistent statements of a *party* can be used for impeachment purposes and as substantive evidence. It is important for counsel to appreciate that substantive evidence must be admitted to prove a point at issue; counsel cannot simply rely on evidence that has been offered and admitted only for impeachment to prove a point at issue. Evidence used for impeachment purposes is *not* substantive evidence. The filing of a motion in limine will help to reveal the intended uses of a statement and help counsel formulate a strategy with respect to this evidence.

725 ILCS 5/115-10.1 states:

> Admissibility of Prior Inconsistent Statements. In all *criminal cases*, evidence of a statement made by a witness is not made inadmissible by the hearsay rule if
>
> (a) the statement is inconsistent with his testimony at the hearing or trial, and
>
> (b) the witness is subject to cross-examination concerning the statement, and

(c) the statement—

(1) was made under oath at a trial, hearing, or other proceeding, or

(2) narrates, describes, or explains an event or condition of which the witness had personal knowledge, and

(A) the statement is proved to have been written or signed by the witness, or

(B) the witness acknowledged under oath the making of the statement either in his testimony at the hearing or trial in which the admission into evidence of the prior statement is being sought, or at a trial, hearing, or other proceeding, or

(C) the statement is proved to have been accurately recorded by a tape recorder, videotape recording, or any other similar electronic means of sound recording.

Nothing in this Section shall render a prior inconsistent statement inadmissible for purposes of impeachment because such statement was not recorded or otherwise fails to meet the criteria set forth herein. (Emphasis added.)

Boyce v. Risch, 276 Ill. App. 3d 274, 277–79, 212 Ill. Dec. 800, 657 N.E.2d 1145 (1st Dist. 1995) (a prior inconsistent statement of a witness is admissible for impeachment).

Hapke v. Brandon, 343 Ill. App. 524, 526–29, 99 N.E.2d 636 (4th Dist. 1951) (a witness' written prior inconsistent statements should have been admitted for impeachment of the witness).

H. MOTION TO EXCLUDE MAPS, MODELS & CHARTS

§ 4:90 Suggested motion text

[Name of moving party] hereby moves this Court for an order excluding any and all evidence, references to evidence, testimony or argument relating to relating to *[describe map, model or chart]*. The motion is based upon the ground that the evidence is *[state ground, e.g., it is unreliable, not authentic, confusing, etc.]* and will create a substantial danger of undue prejudice to *[name of moving party]*.

§ 4:91 Motion summary

This motion is used to exclude maps, models and charts where the accuracy or reliability of the evidence is in doubt and may cause jury confusion or other prejudice. See e.g. *Peterson v. Lou Bachrodt Chevrolet Co.*, 76 Ill. 2d 353, 362–63, 29 Ill. Dec. 444, 392 N.E.2d 1 (1979) (overruled by, Wills v. Foster, 229 Ill. 2d 393, 323 Ill. Dec. 26, 892 N.E.2d 1018 (2008)).

§ 4:92 Supporting authorities—Exclusion of prejudicial evidence, generally

Federal Rule of Evidence 403 states:

> Although relevant, evidence may be excluded if its probative value is substantially outweighed by the danger of unfair prejudice, confusion of the issues, or misleading the jury, or by considerations of undue delay, waste of time, or needless presentation of cumulative evidence.

It must be noted that this Rule has not been codified in Illinois. However, Illinois cases have stated that Illinois has a common-law rule that is comparable to Federal Rule of Evidence 403. See *People v. Walker*, 335 Ill. App. 3d 102, 112, 268 Ill. Dec. 654, 779 N.E.2d 268 (2d Dist. 2002), as modified on denial of reh'g, (Oct. 24, 2002) and judgment aff'd, 211 Ill. 2d 317, 285 Ill. Dec. 519, 812 N.E.2d 339 (2004); and *People v. Peete*, 318 Ill. App. 3d 961, 966–67, 252 Ill. Dec. 821, 743 N.E.2d 689 (4th Dist. 2001). Therefore, it is arguable that Federal Rule of Evidence 403 can be considered as persuasive authority in Illinois.

Troyan v. Reyes, 367 Ill. App. 3d 729, 738, 305 Ill. Dec. 451, 855 N.E.2d 967 (3d Dist. 2006) (radiology report that included complicated medical terms was properly excluded as confusing to the jury).

People v. Holman, 257 Ill. App. 3d 1031, 1033–34, 196 Ill. Dec. 457, 630 N.E.2d 154 (2d Dist. 1994) (evidence is admissible if it is relevant and if the prejudicial impact does not substantially outweigh the probative value of it).

For expanded citations on the exclusion of prejudicial evidence, see § 2:1 to § 2:4.

§ 4:93 Supporting authorities—Exclusion of maps, models or charts

Nolan v. Elliott, 179 Ill. App. 3d 1077, 1087, 129 Ill. Dec. 288, 535 N.E.2d 1053 (2d Dist. 1989) (no abuse of discretion to exclude an inaccurate and misleading drawing that was made by an eyewitness at the scene of the collision).

Peterson v. Lou Bachrodt Chevrolet Co., 76 Ill. 2d 353, 362–63, 29 Ill. Dec. 444, 392 N.E.2d 1 (1979) (overruled by, Wills v. Foster, 229 Ill. 2d 393, 323 Ill. Dec. 26, 892 N.E.2d 1018 (2008)) (inaccurate and misleading diagram made at the scene was properly excluded).

Hatcher v. Quincy Horse Railway & Carrying Co., 181 Ill. App. 30, 1913 WL 2479, at *2 (3d Dist. 1913) (no error in excluding plat which had drawings and markings added to it that represented the offering party's assertions about the circumstances of the incident).

Zinser v. Sanitary Dist. of Chicago, 175 Ill. App. 9, 1912 WL 2835, at *4 (2d Dist. 1912), cert. denied (proper to exclude plats that have a party's self-serving writings on them and proper to exclude charts and documents that are based upon unproven assumptions).

◆ **Note:** A police officer's diagram contained in a police report that purports to be a "reconstruction" of a motor vehicle accident, can often be excluded based upon a lack of foundation. Common challenges to the foundation are the following: (1) the officer's lack of qualifications; (2) the officer's lack of personal knowledge; and (3) facts upon which the officer's knowledge is based lack credibility or reliability.

§ 4:94 Supporting authorities—Other grounds

Other possible grounds for excluding maps, models or charts include:

- Collateral to issues in case (§ 2:5 to § 2:8)
- Confusing or misleading (§ 2:9 to § 2:12)
- Cumulative (§ 2:20 to § 2:33)
- Improper foundation (§ 4:1 to § 4:19)
- Inadmissible writings (§ 4:20 to § 4:38)
- Inadmissible hearsay (§ 8:78 to § 8:89)

§ 4:95 Opposing authorities—Demonstrative purposes

Maps, models, charts, and other related writings are often used for demonstrative purposes. If the evidence is sought to be used for demonstrative purposes only, the witness who intends to use this evidence must testify that the evidence assists him or her in explaining the testimony. *Schuler v. Mid-Central Cardiology*, 313 Ill. App. 3d 326, 246 Ill. Dec. 163, 729 N.E.2d 536 (4th Dist. 2000). Any risk of confusion of the jury can usually be addressed with a limiting or curative instruction.

Hudson v. City of Chicago, 378 Ill. App. 3d 373, 400–02, 317 Ill. Dec. 262, 881 N.E.2d 430 (1st Dist. 2007), appeal denied, 227 Ill. 2d 580, 321 Ill. Dec. 250, 888 N.E.2d 1183 (2008) (computer simulation was proper because it was supported by the evidence).

Preston ex rel. Preston v. Simmons, 321 Ill. App. 3d 789, 801–02, 254 Ill. Dec. 647, 747 N.E.2d 1059 (1st Dist. 2001) (skeletal model admissible when the expert testified it would be useful to explain his testimony, even though it would have been a better foundation if he had also stated that it accurately portrayed the part of the body at issue).

Schuler v. Mid-Central Cardiology, 313 Ill. App. 3d 326, 337–38, 246 Ill. Dec. 163, 729 N.E.2d 536 (4th Dist. 2000) (trial judge has discretion whether to admit an exhibit to help explain an expert's testimony if it is relevant and fair).

See also *Dillon v. Evanston Hosp.*, 199 Ill. 2d 483, 492–94, 264 Ill. Dec. 653, 771 N.E.2d 357 (2002) (trial court had discretion to allow the jury to view a videotape when an expert testified that it would be helpful in explaining the subject matter of his testimony to the jury).

§ 4:96 Opposing authorities—Where accuracy not disputed

Joynt v. Barnes, 71 Ill. App. 3d 187, 203, 27 Ill. Dec. 249, 388 N.E.2d 1298 (2d Dist. 1979) (not improper to admit a drawing of the plaintiff's tumor that was made by a treating physician and was "reasonably accurate".)

Greig v. Griffel, 49 Ill. App. 3d 829, 834–36, 7 Ill. Dec. 499, 364 N.E.2d 660 (2d Dist. 1977) (parties' stipulation that photographs accurately showed the condition of the vehicle after the collision was sufficient to establish the foundation for admission of the photographs).

Note also that Illinois Supreme Court Rule 216(b) allows for a party to serve on the opposing party a request for admission that a document is genuine. If the opposing party fails to reply within the required time then the document is authenticated. Similarly, Illinois Supreme Court Rule 216(d) allows for authentication of public records by serving notice of the intent to use it as evidence and then it is authenticated if the opposing party fails to deny the accuracy of the document by affidavit.

§ 4:97 Opposing authorities—Relevant to issues

Hudson v. City of Chicago, 378 Ill. App. 3d 373, 400–02, 317 Ill. Dec. 262, 881 N.E.2d 430 (1st Dist. 2007), appeal denied, 227 Ill. 2d 580, 321 Ill. Dec. 250, 888 N.E.2d 1183 (2008) (computer simulation was proper because it was supported by the evidence).

Preston ex rel. Preston v. Simmons, 321 Ill. App. 3d 789, 801–02, 254 Ill. Dec. 647, 747 N.E.2d 1059 (1st Dist. 2001) (skeletal model admissible when the expert testified it would be useful to explain his testimony, even though it would have been a better foundation if he had also stated that it accurately portrayed the part of the body at issue).

§ 4:98 Opposing authorities—As a business record

Kimble v. Earle M. Jorgenson Co., 358 Ill. App. 3d 400, 294 Ill. Dec. 402, 830 N.E.2d 814, 826–28 (1st Dist. 2005) (diagram and accompanying description, made by an employee, was admissible as a business record).

I. MOTION TO EXCLUDE IMPROPER MEDICAL RECORDS, REPORTS OR BILLS

§ 4:99 Suggested motion text

Alternative One (General):

[Name of moving party] hereby moves this Court for an order excluding any and all evidence, references to evidence, testimony or argument relating to *[describe nature of medical report or related document to be excluded]*. The motion is based upon the ground that the document *[describe basis for exclusion, e.g., lacks proper authentication, is inadmissible hearsay, etc.]*.

Alternative Two (Exclusion of Medical History):

[Name of moving party] hereby moves this Court for an order excluding any and all evidence, references to evidence, testimony or argument relating to plaintiff's [or decedent's] medical history and especially any evidence relating to *[describe inflammatory and irrelevant matter in history, e.g., "plaintiff's prior treatment for addiction to alcohol."]* The motion is based upon the ground that the information is irrelevant and intended solely to inflame the jurors' emotions and that any probative value is outweighed by the prejudicial impact of such evidence.

Alternative Three (Billing Records):

[Name of moving party] hereby moves this Court for an order excluding any and all evidence, references to evidence, testimony or argument relating to billing records from *[name of medical provider(s)]* for treatment of plaintiff occurring from *[list treatment dates]*. The motion is based upon the ground that the plaintiff and plaintiff's experts have failed to establish in any pretrial discovery that the billings were reasonable and necessary for treatment arising from the subject incident and therefore a proper foundation cannot be established and jurors would be mislead and confused by the introduction of any such evidence, to the prejudice of the defendant.

Note that if the treatment was not related to the incident at issue, the bills for the said treatment are not related and should not be admissible. Also, where there is no evidence that the treatment was reasonable and necessary and that the bills reflect the usual and customary charges for the types of services rendered, there must be evidence that the bill was paid for the bill to be admissible. *Victory Memorial Hosp. v. Rice*, 143 Ill. App. 3d 621, 97 Ill. Dec. 635, 493 N.E.2d 117 (2d Dist. 1986); *Temesvary v. Houdek*, 301 Ill. App. 3d 560, 234 Ill. Dec. 752, 703 N.E.2d 613 (2d Dist. 1998).

§ 4:100 Motion summary

This motion is used to exclude improper medical reports, medical history, opinions or billing records. The motion may be used to exclude improper hearsay, character evidence, or otherwise inadmissible matter contained in the reports, or, where appropriate, the entire report, record or bill. The motion is based upon the general exclusion of prejudicial evidence, as well as specific challenges to a report's foundation, [*Anderson v. Human Rights Com'n*, 314 Ill. App. 3d 35, 42-46, 246 Ill. Dec. 843, 731 N.E.2d 371 (1st Dist. 2000), hearsay [*Mehochko v. Gold Seal Co.*, 66 Ill. App. 2d 54, 57-60, 213 N.E.2d 581, 19 A.L.R.3d 1003 (5th Dist. 1966)], improper history [*People v. Britz*, 123 Ill. 2d 446, 457–62, 124 Ill. Dec. 15, 528 N.E.2d 703 (1988)], or the reasonableness of billings [*Baker v. Hutson*, 333 Ill. App. 3d 486, 493–94, 266 Ill. Dec. 791, 775 N.E.2d 631 (5th Dist. 2002)].

§ 4:101 Supporting authorities—Exclusion of prejudicial matter, generally

Federal Rule of Evidence 403 states:

> Although relevant, evidence may be excluded if its probative value is substantially outweighed by the danger of unfair prejudice, confusion of the issues, or misleading the jury, or by considerations of undue delay, waste of time, or needless presentation of cumulative evidence.

It must be noted that this Rule has not been codified in Illinois. However, Illinois cases have stated that Illinois has a common-law rule that is comparable to Federal Rule of Evidence 403. See *People v. Walker*, 335 Ill. App. 3d 102, 112, 268 Ill. Dec. 654, 779 N.E.2d 268 (2d Dist. 2002), as modified on denial of reh'g, (Oct. 24, 2002) and judgment aff'd, 211 Ill. 2d 317, 285 Ill. Dec. 519, 812 N.E.2d 339 (2004); and *People v. Peete*, 318 Ill. App. 3d 961, 966–67, 252 Ill. Dec. 821, 743 N.E.2d 689 (4th Dist. 2001). Therefore, it is arguable that

Federal Rule of Evidence 403 can be considered as persuasive authority in Illinois.

People v. Holman, 257 Ill. App. 3d 1031, 1033–34, 196 Ill. Dec. 457, 630 N.E.2d 154 (2d Dist. 1994) (evidence is admissible if it is relevant and if the prejudicial impact does not substantially outweigh the probative value of it).

For expanded citations on the exclusion of prejudicial evidence, see § 2:1 to § 2:4.

§ 4:102 Supporting authorities—Improper foundation, generally

Greaney v. Industrial Com'n, 358 Ill. App. 3d 1002, 1011–12, 295 Ill. Dec. 180, 832 N.E.2d 331 (1st Dist. 2005) (insufficient foundation was provided for the admission of an uncertified doctor's report).

Anderson v. Human Rights Com'n, 314 Ill. App. 3d 35, 42-46, 246 Ill. Dec. 843, 731 N.E.2d 371 (1st Dist. 2000) (documents should not be admitted when the witness testifying about them does not have the personal knowledge of them to establish a proper foundation).

See generally *Piano v. Davison*, 157 Ill. App. 3d 649, 668, 110 Ill. Dec. 35, 510 N.E.2d 1066 (1st Dist. 1987) (proper to exclude expert's use of medical treatises when there was no proof that they were reliable).

§ 4:103 Supporting authorities—Improper foundation, generally—Criminal vs. civil cases

The reader is advised to carefully distinguish civil cases and criminal cases with respect to whether hospital and medical records are admissible as business records. The provisions with respect to whether or not hospital and medical records are admissible as business records are different for each type of case. The following citations may be instructive.

725 ILCS 5/115-5(a) applies to criminal cases and provides:

> Any writing or record, whether in the form of an entry in a book or otherwise, made as a memorandum or record of any act, transaction, occurrence, or event, shall be admissible as evidence of such act, transaction, occurrence, or event, if made in regular course of any business, and if it was the regular course of such business to make such memorandum or record at the time of such act, transaction, occurrence, or event or within a reasonable time thereafter.
>
> All other circumstances of the making of such writing or record, including lack of personal knowledge by the entrant or maker,

> may be shown to affect its weight, but such circumstances shall not affect its admissibility.
> The term 'business,' as used in this Section, includes business, profession, occupation, and calling of every kind.

However, 725 ILCS 5/115-5(c) provides that 725 ILCS 5/115-5(a) may not be used as the basis for establishing admissibility if, "such writing or record has been made by anyone in the regular course of any form of hospital or medical business."

Illinois Supreme Court Rule 236(a) provides:

> Any writing or record, whether in the form of any entry in a book or otherwise, made as a memorandum or record of any act, transaction, occurrence, or event, shall be admissible as evidence of the act, transaction, occurrence, or event, if made in the regular course of any business, and if it was the regular course of the business to make such a memorandum or record at the time of such an act, transaction, occurrence, or event or within a reasonable time thereafter. All other circumstances of the making of the writing or record, including lack of personal knowledge by the entrant or maker, may be shown to affect its weight, but shall not affect its admissibility. The term 'business,' as used in this rule, includes business, profession, occupation, and calling of every kind.

Prior to 1992, subsection (b) of Illinois Supreme Court Rule 236 excluded medical records from being admissible if the justification for doing so was based upon subsection (a). However, in 1992, the provision was amended to remove the prohibition against medical records being admitted as business records. See *Williams v. Covenant Medical Center*, 316 Ill. App. 3d 682, 691, 250 Ill. Dec. 40, 737 N.E.2d 662 (4th Dist. 2000); and *Lecroy v. Miller*, 272 Ill. App. 3d 925, 935–36, 209 Ill. Dec. 439, 651 N.E.2d 617 (1st Dist. 1995). Thus, the reader should be careful about using any pre-1992 case to argue about the admissibility of medical records in a civil case. See e.g. *Wilson v. Clark*, 84 Ill. 2d 186, 191–92, 49 Ill. Dec. 308, 417 N.E.2d 1322 (1981) (a proper foundation for admission was not laid when the individuals who made the entries did not testify).

735 ILCS 5/8-401 provides:

> Account books and records. Where in any action or proceeding, the claim or defense is founded on a book account or any other record or document, any party or interested person may testify to his or her account book, or any other record or document and the items therein contained; that the same is a book, record, or document of original entries, and that the entries therein were made by himself or herself, and are true and just; or that the same were made by a deceased person, or by a disinterested person, a non-resident person of the state at the time of the trial, and

where made by such deceased or non-resident person in the usual course of trade, and of his or her duty or employment to the party so testifying; and thereupon the account book and entries or any other record or document shall be admitted as evidence in the cause. Where such book of original entries or any other record or document has been photographed, microphotographed, microfilmed, optical imaged, or otherwise reproduced either in the usual course of business, or pursuant to any statute of this State authorizing the reproduction of public records, papers or documents, and the reproduction, in either case, complies with the minimum standards of quality for permanent records approved by the State Records Commission, then such reproduction shall be deemed to be an original record, book or document for all purposes, including introduction in evidence in all courts or administrative agencies.

725 ILCS 5/115-5.1 states:

In any civil or criminal action the records of the coroner's medical or laboratory examiner summarizing and detailing the performance of his or her official duties in performing medical examinations upon deceased persons or autopsies, or both, and kept in the ordinary course of business of the coroner's office, duly certified by the county coroner or chief supervisory coroner's pathologist or medical examiner, shall be received as competent evidence in any court of this State, to the extent permitted by this Section. These reports, specifically including but not limited to the pathologist's protocol, autopsy reports and toxicological reports, shall be public documents and thereby may be admissible as prima facie evidence of the facts, findings, opinions, diagnoses and conditions stated therein.

A duly certified coroner's protocol or autopsy report, or both, complying with the requirements of this Section may be duly admitted into evidence as an exception to the hearsay rule as prima facie proof of the cause of death of the person to whom it relates. The records referred to in this Section shall be limited to the records of the results of post-mortem examinations of the findings of autopsy and toxicological laboratory examinations.

Persons who prepare reports or records offered in evidence hereunder may be subpoenaed as witnesses in civil or criminal cases upon the request of either party to the cause. However, if such person is dead, the county coroner or a duly authorized official of the coroner's office may testify to the fact that the examining pathologist, toxicologist or other medical or laboratory examiner is deceased and that the offered report or record was prepared by such deceased person. The witness must further attest that the medical report or record was prepared in the ordinary and usual course of the deceased person's duty or employment in conformity with the provisions of this Section.

Regarding the exclusion of writings in general, see § 4:20 to § 4:38, supra.

§ 4:104 Supporting authorities—Medical opinions—Improper hearsay evidence

725 ILCS 5/115-5(c) provides that in criminal cases, the business records as evidence provisions may not be used as the basis for establishing admissibility if,

> such writing or record has been made by anyone in the regular course of any form of hospital or medical business.

See also Illinois Supreme Court Rule 236(a), discussed supra at § 4:1 to § 4:19.

§ 4:105 Supporting authorities—Medical opinions—Opinions of others—Lack of personal knowledge

Hubbard v. Sherman Hosp., 292 Ill. App. 3d 148, 153–55, 226 Ill. Dec. 393, 685 N.E.2d 648 (2d Dist. 1997) (in a medical malpractice case, the trial court did not abuse its discretion by barring expert testimony when the expert was licensed in the field related to the testimony but did not have the requisite experience related to the subject matter).

People v. Britz, 123 Ill. 2d 446, 457–62, 124 Ill. Dec. 15, 528 N.E.2d 703 (1988) (exclusion of expert when the expert's opinion is based upon a party's own self-serving statements).

Dugan v. Weber, 175 Ill. App. 3d 1088, 1097–99, 125 Ill. Dec. 598, 530 N.E.2d 1007, 77 A.L.R.4th 447 (1st Dist. 1988) (proper to bar a party's expert from relying on a report by another expert that was prepared for the purpose of the litigation because such reports are not the type generally relied upon for treatment and diagnosis).

Piano v. Davison, 157 Ill. App. 3d 649, 668, 110 Ill. Dec. 35, 510 N.E.2d 1066 (1st Dist. 1987) (proper to exclude expert's use of medical treatises when there was no proof that they were reliable).

Mehochko v. Gold Seal Co., 66 Ill. App. 2d 54, 57-60, 213 N.E.2d 581, 19 A.L.R.3d 1003 (5th Dist. 1966) (improper hearsay and prejudicial to let an expert read from a test report about tests performed by someone else when the expert had no personal knowledge about the tests at issue).

> ◆ **Note:** Experts can certainly refer to and rely on authoritative texts in support of their opinions even though the texts themselves may not be admissible. Additionally, counsel may utilize authoritative texts on cross-examination for impeachment purposes. See *Wilson v. Clark*, § 4:110, Op-

position citations—Proper identification, infra. See also § 8:10, Supporting authorities—Inadmissible hearsay—Treatises, documents & texts, infra.

§ 4:106 Supporting authorities—Patient medical history

Counsel should be prepared to challenge irrelevant and prejudicially collateral matters in medical records that were not necessary to form the opinion. Examples might include prior drug or alcohol use or statements regarding how an accident occurred.

Regarding the exclusion of collateral evidence in general, see § 3:15, Supporting authorities—Exclusion of irrelevant evidence, generally—Collateral issues, supra; regarding the exclusion of irrelevant evidence, see § 3:1 to § 3:10.

§ 4:107 Supporting authorities—Billing records—Lack of foundation

Land and Lakes Co. v. Industrial Com'n, 359 Ill. App. 3d 582, 590–91, 296 Ill. Dec. 26, 834 N.E.2d 583 (2d Dist. 2005) (insufficient foundation was provided for the admission of medical billing records, where there was no showing that they were made in the ordinary course of business or that they were reasonable).

Baker v. Hutson, 333 Ill. App. 3d 486, 493–94, 266 Ill. Dec. 791, 775 N.E.2d 631 (5th Dist. 2002) (when a bill is unpaid, the party must establish the reasonableness of the bill and that the services were necessarily related to the injury in question).

Cooper v. Cox, 31 Ill. App. 2d 51, 58-59, 175 N.E.2d 651 (1st Dist. 1961) (improper to admit an unpaid bill when there was no showing that the bill was reasonable).

§ 4:108 Supporting authorities—Billing records—Lack of foundation—Failure to pay medical bill

Baker v. Hutson, 333 Ill. App. 3d 486, 493–94, 266 Ill. Dec. 791, 775 N.E.2d 631 (5th Dist. 2002) (when a bill is unpaid, the party must establish the reasonableness of the bill through other competent evidence).

Cooper v. Cox, 31 Ill. App. 2d 51, 58-59, 175 N.E.2d 651 (1st Dist. 1961) (improper to admit an unpaid bill when there was no showing that the bill was reasonable).

Peterson v. Lou Bachrodt Chevrolet Co., 76 Ill. 2d 353,

362–63, 29 Ill. Dec. 444, 392 N.E.2d 1 (1979) (overruled by, Wills v. Foster, 229 Ill. 2d 393, 323 Ill. Dec. 26, 892 N.E.2d 1018 (2008)) (party is not entitled to damages based upon medical services that were obtained at no charge).

But see *American Nat. Bank & Trust Co. v. Peoples Gas Light & Coke Co.*, 42 Ill. App. 2d 163, 177, 191 N.E.2d 628 (1st Dist. 1963) (competent testimony by the provider and by a hospital billing manager was sufficient proof of reasonableness of charges); and *Williams v. Matlin*, 328 Ill. App. 645, 648, 66 N.E.2d 719 (1st Dist. 1946) (proof of payment of medical bills is evidence that charges were reasonable).

§ 4:109 Supporting authorities—Other grounds

Other possible grounds for excluding medical records or reports include:

- Irrelevant (§ 3:1 to § 3:10)
- Cumulative (§ 2:20 to § 2:33)
- Improper foundation (§ 4:1 to § 4:19)
- Inadmissible writings (§ 4:20 to § 4:38)
- Improper expert opinions (§ 8:1 to § 8:22)
- Inadmissible hearsay (§ 8:78 to § 8:89)

§ 4:110 Opposition citations—Proper authentication

Wilson v. Clark, 84 Ill. 2d 186, 191–92, 49 Ill. Dec. 308, 417 N.E.2d 1322 (1981) (a proper foundation for admission was not laid when the individuals who made the entries did not testify but an expert may still provide an opinion based upon the records if such records are the type relied upon in the expert's field (adopting Federal Rules of Evidence 703 and 705)). It must be noted that this case was decided prior to 1992 when Illinois Supreme Court Rule 236 was amended to remove the provision that "medical records" were not covered by the rule.

Federal Rule of Evidence 703 provides:

> The facts or data in the particular case upon which an expert bases an opinion or inference may be those perceived by or made known to the expert at or before the hearing. If of a type reasonably relied upon by experts in the particular field in forming opinions or inferences upon the subject, the facts or data need not be admissible in evidence in order for the opinion or inference to be admitted. Facts or data that are otherwise inadmissible shall not be disclosed to the jury by the proponent of the opinion or inference unless the court determines that their probative value in assisting the jury to evaluate the expert's opinion substantially outweighs their prejudicial effect.

Federal Rule of Evidence 705 provides:

> The expert may testify in terms of opinion or inference and give reasons therefor without first testifying to the underlying facts or data, unless the court requires otherwise. The expert may in any event be required to disclose the underlying facts or data on cross-examination.

In criminal cases, 725 ILCS 5/115-5(c) provides that the business records as evidence provisions may not be used as the basis for establishing admissibility if,

> such writing or record has been made by anyone in the regular course of any form of hospital or medical business.

See authentication requirements for writings, generally, § 4:20 to § 4:38, supra.

§ 4:111 Opposition citations—Opinions of others—Opinion used in formation of diagnosis and treatment

Williams v. Covenant Medical Center, 316 Ill. App. 3d 682, 691, 250 Ill. Dec. 40, 737 N.E.2d 662 (4th Dist. 2000) (hearsay statements describing a person's medical conditions and the circumstances surrounding the conditions are admissible as an exception to the hearsay rule, when the statements are made in the course of treatment).

People v. Eiskant, 253 Ill. App. 3d 773, 775–76, 192 Ill. Dec. 863, 625 N.E.2d 1018 (5th Dist. 1993) (expert's opinion can be based upon hearsay documents and statements if such documents and statements are normally relied upon in the expert's field).

Melecosky v. McCarthy Bros. Co., 115 Ill. 2d 209, 213–17, 104 Ill. Dec. 798, 503 N.E.2d 355 (1986) (expert opinion based upon party's own statements should have been allowed when such statements are the type of information generally relied upon in the expert's field).

§ 4:112 Opposition citations—Opinions of others—Business records exception

Note that in medical malpractice cases, the records are often admissible as admissions by a party opponent where the defendant prepared the records and made the entries sought to be admitted. Also, medical records are admissible in all types of actions as business records pursuant to Supreme Court Rule 236 as long as the proper foundation is laid. Even where the medical records are not admissible, they can certainly be referred to and relied upon by experts in formulating their opinions. *Wilson v. Clark*, 84 Ill. 2d 186, 191–92, 49 Ill. Dec. 308, 417 N.E.2d 1322 (1981). Additionally, treating physicians can refer to the records to refresh their recollection. If all else fails, the records may be admissible as past recollections recorded.

Troyan v. Reyes, 367 Ill. App. 3d 729, 732-39, 305 Ill. Dec. 451, 855 N.E.2d 967 (3d Dist. 2006) (certain of the plaintiff's medical records which included diagnoses and opinions were admissible as business records and the trial court erred by excluding them).

In re Kenneth J., 352 Ill. App. 3d 967, 982–84, 288 Ill. Dec. 290, 817 N.E.2d 940 (1st Dist. 2004) (in a termination of parental rights case, a report from a parenting assessment team was admissible as a business record).

Williams v. Covenant Medical Center, 316 Ill. App. 3d 682, 691, 250 Ill. Dec. 40, 737 N.E.2d 662 (4th Dist. 2000) (patient chart entries and a nurse's report from a "falls assessment" were admissible as a business record when made in the course of treatment).

Lecroy v. Miller, 272 Ill. App. 3d 925, 935–36, 209 Ill. Dec. 439, 651 N.E.2d 617 (1st Dist. 1995) (discharge summary admissible as a business record in a civil case when a witness who was familiar with the document and the business testified that the document was prepared and kept in the regular course of business).

See generally § 4:1 to § 4:19, supra.

§ 4:113 Opposition citations—Patient history—Observations of physician

Williams v. Covenant Medical Center, 316 Ill. App. 3d 682, 691, 250 Ill. Dec. 40, 737 N.E.2d 662 (4th Dist. 2000) (patient chart entries and a nurse's report from a "falls assessment" were admissible as a business record when made in the course of treatment).

Lecroy v. Miller, 272 Ill. App. 3d 925, 935–36, 209 Ill. Dec. 439, 651 N.E.2d 617 (1st Dist. 1995) (discharge summary admissible as a business record in a civil case when a witness who was familiar with the document and the business testified that the document was prepared and kept in the regular course of business).

People v. Eiskant, 253 Ill. App. 3d 773, 775–76, 192 Ill. Dec. 863, 625 N.E.2d 1018 (5th Dist. 1993) (expert's opinion can be based upon the opinions and records of others if such opinions are normally relied upon in the expert's field).

§ 4:114 Opposition citations—Patient history—Pertinent to medical diagnosis

Note that a patient's statements to a medical provider for the purposes of treatment are inherently reliable and therefore usually admissible as an exception to the hearsay rule. *Rogers v. Chicago & North Western Transp. Co.*, 59 Ill. App. 3d 911, 16 Ill. Dec. 845, 375 N.E.2d 952 (5th Dist. 1978) (statements are admissible on the theory that the desire for proper treatment outweighs any motive to falsify). Because of the inherent reliability of these statements, it is critical for counsel to review the patient's statements made to the initial care providers. The statements made to the initial care providers are the most reliable because of the lack of time to fabricate.

Williams v. Covenant Medical Center, 316 Ill. App. 3d 682, 691, 250 Ill. Dec. 40, 737 N.E.2d 662 (4th Dist. 2000) (hearsay statements describing a person's medical conditions and the circumstances surrounding the conditions are admissible as an exception to the hearsay rule, when the statements are made in the course of treatment).

People v. Eiskant, 253 Ill. App. 3d 773, 775–76, 192 Ill. Dec. 863, 625 N.E.2d 1018 (5th Dist. 1993) (expert's opinion can be based upon the patient's medical records if such records are normally relied upon in the expert's field).

Melecosky v. McCarthy Bros. Co., 115 Ill. 2d 209, 213–17, 104 Ill. Dec. 798, 503 N.E.2d 355 (1986) (expert opinion based upon party's own statements should have been allowed when such statements are the type of information generally relied upon in the expert's field).

§ 4:115 Opposition citations—Medical billing records—Reasonableness of charges

Arthur v. Catour, 216 Ill. 2d 72, 295 Ill. Dec. 641, 833 N.E.2d 847, 849–53 (2005) (a partially paid bill will not establish the reasonableness of the entire amount of the bill, but a plaintiff may still establish the reasonableness of the entire bill through other competent evidence).

American Nat. Bank & Trust Co. v. Peoples Gas Light & Coke Co., 42 Ill. App. 2d 163, 177, 191 N.E.2d 628 (1st Dist. 1963) (competent testimony by the provider and by a hospital billing manager was sufficient proof of reasonableness of charges).

Williams v. Matlin, 328 Ill. App. 645, 648, 66 N.E.2d 719 (1st Dist. 1946) (proof of payment of medical bills is evidence that charges were reasonable).

See also *Kunkel v. P.K. Dependable Const., LLC*, 387 Ill.App.3d 1153, 1158–59, 902 N.E.2d 769 (5th Dist. 2009) (estimate of cost of repairs from an individual who is experienced in the field is admissible, even if there is no testimony that the estimate is reasonable and the repairs are necessary).

II. SAMPLE MOTIONS

§ 4:116 Motion to exclude gruesome photographs

TO: ALL PARTIES AND THEIR RESPECTIVE ATTORNEYS OF RECORD:

PLEASE TAKE NOTICE that defendant hereby moves this Court for an order excluding any and all evidence, references to evidence, testimony or argument relating to three close-up photographs of plaintiff's injuries taken by Peter Snapshot on the date of the subject accident in this case.

This motion is made under the authority of Illinois case law and is based upon the supporting Memorandum of Points and Authorities, the pleadings and papers on file in this action, and upon such of the argument and evidence as may be presented prior to or at the hearing of this matter.

Dated: *[date]*

MEMORANDUM OF POINTS AND AUTHORITIES

1.
INTRODUCTION

This is a personal injury action arising out of an automobile versus pedestrian accident that occurred on January 15, 1997. At the time the incident, the plaintiff incurred certain injuries to his left knee and kneecap. Discovery in this action revealed that a bystander by the name of Peter Snapshot took 14 photographs of the accident scene and eight photographs of plaintiff's injured knee shortly after the incident occurred.

The subject of this motion relates to three close-up photographs taken of the plaintiff's injured knee by Mr. Snapshot. Copies of the three photographs are attached hereto as Exhibits "A," "B" and "C" respectively. The defendant does not object to any other photographs identified by plaintiff in his list of proposed exhibits, including several other shots of plaintiff's knee taken at the scene and several post-operation photographs. Note too that for purposes of this motion, defendant does not challenge the authenticity of the three disputed photographs, but reserves the right to raise this objection at trial.

By this motion, the defendant seeks to preclude each of the three photographs, based upon the clearly prejudicial and cumulative nature of this evidence.

2.

THIS COURT MAY PRECLUDE EVIDENCE WHEN THE PREJUDICIAL EFFECT OF IT OUTWEIGHS ITS PROBATIVE VALUE

Federal Rule of Evidence 403 states:

> Although relevant, evidence may be excluded if its probative value is substantially outweighed by the danger of unfair prejudice, confusion of the issues, or misleading the jury, or by considerations of undue delay, waste of time, or needless presentation of cumulative evidence.

Although this rule has not been specifically codified in Illinois, case law has stated that Illinois has a common-law rule that is comparable to Federal Rule of Evidence 403. See *People v. Peete*, 318 Ill. App. 3d 961, 966–67, 252 Ill. Dec. 821, 743 N.E.2d 689 (4th Dist. 2001); *People v. Walker*, 335 Ill. App. 3d 102, 112, 268 Ill. Dec. 654, 779 N.E.2d 268 (2d Dist. 2002), as modified on denial of reh'g, (Oct. 24, 2002) and judgment aff'd, 211 Ill. 2d 317, 285 Ill. Dec. 519, 812 N.E.2d 339 (2004).

Moreover, Illinois law clearly states that evidence should be excluded when the prejudicial impact of the evidence outweighs the probative value of it. *Hulsebus v. Russian*, 118 Ill. App. 2d 174, 180–81, 254 N.E.2d 184 (2d Dist. 1969) (trial judge had discretion to exclude a gruesome photograph of the plaintiff during surgery because other evidence established the extent of the injury and because the photograph was likely to inflame and prejudice the jury); *Department of Public Works and Bldgs. v. Roehrig*, 45 Ill. App. 3d 189, 196, 3 Ill. Dec. 893, 359 N.E.2d 752 (5th Dist. 1976) (exclusion of evidence of prior condemnations in a condemnation case because the prejudicial impact outweighs the probative value of it); and *People v. Holman*, 257 Ill. App. 3d 1031, 1033–34, 196 Ill. Dec. 457, 630 N.E.2d 154 (2d Dist. 1994) (evidence is admissible if it is relevant and if the prejudicial impact does not substantially outweigh the probative value of it). In the instant matter there is a strong probability that the admission of the above-described photographs will create a substantial danger of undue prejudice. Therefore, the authorities cited herein justify the preclusion of the requested evidence in this case.

3.

GRUESOME PHOTOGRAPHS MAY BE EXCLUDED BECAUSE THEIR PREJUDICIAL IMPACT OUTWEIGHS THEIR PROBATIVE VALUE

A number of courts have held that gruesome photographs may be excluded where offered for no other purpose but to inflame the emotions of the jury. See *Hulsebus v. Russian*, 118 Ill. App. 2d 174, 180–81, 254 N.E.2d 184 (2d Dist. 1969) (trial judge had discretion to exclude a gruesome photograph of the plaintiff during surgery because other evidence established the extent of the injury and because the photograph was likely to inflame and prejudice the jury); and *People v. Lefler*, 38 Ill. 2d 216, 221–22, 230 N.E.2d 827 (1967) (prejudicial photographs should not have been shown to the jury when the nature of the injuries was not disputed and there was adequate expert testimony regarding the injuries).

In the present case, the three disputed photographs show various angles of *extreme close-ups* of plaintiff's injured knee. All three photographs are extremely graphic, but add nothing of relevance to plaintiff's case that could not, and presumably will not, be presented by plaintiff's medical witnesses and other non-objectionable photographs of plaintiff's knee.

The only logical purpose for the introduction of this evidence is to inflame the jury's passions in favor of the plaintiff and against the defendant. Avoiding such a result is the very purpose underlying the cases cited herein.

As such, the defendant respectfully requests that the evidence be excluded.

4.

THE COURT MAY EXCLUDE CUMULATIVE PHOTOGRAPHIC EVIDENCE

Federal Rule of Evidence 403 states:

> Although relevant, evidence may be excluded if its probative value is substantially outweighed by the danger of unfair prejudice, confusion of the issues, or misleading the jury, or by considerations of undue delay, waste of time, or *needless presentation of cumulative evidence*. (Emphasis added.)

This Rule has not been specifically codified in Illinois. However, Illinois cases have stated that Illinois has a common-law rule that is comparable to Federal Rule of Evidence 403. See *People v. Peete*, 318 Ill. App. 3d 961, 966–67, 252 Ill. Dec. 821, 743 N.E.2d 689 (4th Dist. 2001); and *People v. Walker*, 335 Ill. App. 3d 102, 112, 268 Ill. Dec. 654, 779 N.E.2d 268 (2d

Dist. 2002), as modified on denial of reh'g, (Oct. 24, 2002) and judgment aff'd, 211 Ill. 2d 317, 285 Ill. Dec. 519, 812 N.E.2d 339 (2004). In fact, courts have specifically held that cumulative photographs may be excluded where the proponent cannot show how the photographs differ from other evidence. See *Villegas v. Kercher*, 11 Ill. App. 2d 282, 290–91, 137 N.E.2d 92 (2d Dist. 1956) (not improper to exclude photograph of plaintiff in traction where witness testimony already established the length of time he was in the hospital and his condition); *Davis v. International Harvester Co.*, 167 Ill. App. 3d 814, 825, 118 Ill. Dec. 589, 521 N.E.2d 1282 (2d Dist. 1988) (court has discretion to exclude photographs that are cumulative of expert testimony); and *Swanigan v. Smith*, 294 Ill. App. 3d 263, 274, 228 Ill. Dec. 578, 689 N.E.2d 637 (4th Dist. 1998) (trial judge could properly rule that plaintiff could either display his actual injuries or photographs of them but not both, because to allow both would be cumulative).

In the present case, the plaintiff has identified more than a dozen additional photographs of his injured knee. Clearly, the plaintiff will have an opportunity to prove his case for damages with ample photographic evidence that objectively shows the nature and extent of his injuries.

The three disputed photographs add nothing to plaintiff's case that is not presented in the other photographs. What these photographs do add, however, is an extremely bloody *close-up* view of the *inside* of plaintiff's injured knee.

Clearly this evidence is cumulative and intended solely to inflame the jury against the defendant. As such, the defendant requests that the evidence be excluded.

Dated: *[date]*

By: ______________________
[name of counsel]
Attorneys for DEFENDANT,
[name of defendant]

Chapter 5

Tests & Related Scientific Evidence

I. MOTION AUTHORITIES

A. MOTION TO EXCLUDE TESTS, EXPERIMENTS AND RELATED TESTIMONY AND EVIDENCE

B. MOTION TO EXCLUDE "JUNK SCIENCE" AND RELATED EVIDENCE

II. SAMPLE MOTIONS

I. MOTION AUTHORITIES

A. MOTION TO EXCLUDE TESTS, EXPERIMENTS AND RELATED TESTIMONY AND EVIDENCE

§ 5:1 Suggested motion text

[Name of moving party] hereby moves this Court for an order excluding any and all evidence, references to evidence, testimony or argument relating to *[describe nature of test or experiment]* conducted by *[name of witness that conducted test or experiment]*. The motion is based upon the ground that the evidence is *[describe challenges to evidence, e.g., "not generally accepted in the scientific community," "not made under substantially identical conditions to subject incident," "not reliable," etc.]* and is therefore inadmissible.

§ 5:2 Motion summary

This motion is used to exclude evidence of tests and experiments that do not meet established requirements for admissibility. In general, test evidence is admissible where it is 1) relevant, 2) was obtained under conditions substantially similar to those to which it is sought to be applied, and 3) will not cause undue delay or jury confusion. Test evidence may be challenged for a variety of reasons, including lack of proper expert qualifications, dissimilar conditions, lack of general acceptance, too speculative, too unreliable, too many variables and too time consuming. *People v. Acri*, 277 Ill. App. 3d 1030, 1033–34, 214 Ill. Dec. 761, 662 N.E.2d 115 (3d Dist. 1996) (Illinois has adopted the *Frye* standard for the admission of scientific evidence); see also *Donaldson v. Central Illinois Public Service Co.*, 199 Ill. 2d 63, 262 Ill. Dec. 854, 767 N.E.2d 314 (2002) (abrogated by, In re Commitment of Simons, 213 Ill. 2d 523, 290 Ill. Dec. 610, 821 N.E.2d 1184 (2004)) (the exclusive test in Illinois for the admission of expert testimony is governed by the standard announced in *Frye*).

The admission of expert testimony is governed by the standard first expressed in *Frye v. U.S.*, 293 F. 1013, 34 A.L.R. 145 (App. D.C. 1923) (rejected by, State v. Walstad, 119 Wis. 2d 483, 351 N.W.2d 469 (1984)) and (rejected by, State v. Brown, 297 Or. 404, 687 P.2d 751 (1984)) and (rejected by, Nelson v.

State, 628 A.2d 69 (Del. 1993)) and (rejected by, State v. Alberico, 116 N.M. 156, 861 P.2d 192 (1993)) and (rejected by, State v. Moore, 268 Mont. 20, 885 P.2d 457 (1994)) and (rejected by, State v. Faught, 127 Idaho 873, 908 P.2d 566 (1995)) and (rejected by, People v. Shreck, 22 P.3d 68, 90 A.L.R. 5th 765 (Colo. 2001)). The *Frye* standard, commonly called the "general acceptance" test, provides that scientific evidence is only admissible at trial if the methodology or scientific principle upon which the opinion is based is "sufficiently established to have gained general acceptance in a particular field in which it belongs." If any aspect of the *Frye* test is not satisfied, the evidence and/or testimony will be barred. Expert testimony plays a very important role in cases that are litigated these days. In fact, it is rare that a case is not decided by a "battle of experts." Therefore, if counsel can bar an expert or his opinion on any basis, including a *Frye* challenge, it will substantially increase the chances of winning.

◆ ***Important Note:*** Some Courts have suggested that, in the future, Illinois is likely to adopt the Federal *Daubert* holding, which requires a trial judge to perform gatekeeping functions before admitting expert testimony. See *Donnellan v. First Student, Inc.*, 383 Ill.App.3d 1040, 1057–61, 891 N.E.2d 463 (1st Dist. 2008) (the appellate court suggested that in the future, Illinois courts are likely to adopt the *Daubert* holding but also stated that this particular case did not represent the proper circumstances for doing so).

§ 5:3 Supporting authorities—Expert not qualified to testify on subject

Note that there are many ways to attack an expert's qualifications to testify on a particular subject. All avenues of attack should be explored (e.g. lack of experience, training, or knowledge, etc.).

McWilliams v. Dettore, 387 Ill.App.3d 833, 843–50, 901 N.E.2d 1023 (1st Dist. 2009) (oncologist was not qualified to provide an opinion regarding the standard of care for a surgeon).

Ahmed v. Pickwick Place Owners' Ass'n, 385 Ill.App.3d 874, 890–91, 896 N.E.2d 854 (1st Dist. 2008) (police officer was not qualified to provide an expert opinion regarding the cause of certain injuries to a deceased individual).

Alm v. Loyola University Medical Center, 373 Ill. App. 3d 1, 310 Ill. Dec. 641, 866 N.E.2d 1243 (1st Dist. 2007), appeal denied, 225 Ill. 2d 627, 314 Ill. Dec. 822, 875 N.E.2d 1109 (2007) (the trial court did not abuse its discretion by determining that a pathologist lacked the proper qualifications to testify regarding the treatment provided by plastic surgeons and an anesthesiologist).

People v. Swanson, 335 Ill. App. 3d 117, 125–27, 269 Ill. Dec. 157, 780 N.E.2d 342 (2d Dist. 2002) (improper to allow an expert to repeat a hearsay statement of another expert when the statement did not relate to the defendant's condition and was not the type of statement that was normally relied upon in the field).

Hubbard v. Sherman Hosp., 292 Ill. App. 3d 148, 153–55, 226 Ill. Dec. 393, 685 N.E.2d 648 (2d Dist. 1997) (in a medical malpractice case, no abuse of discretion by barring expert testimony when the expert was licensed in the field related to the testimony but did not have the requisite experience related to the specific subject matter of the testimony).

People v. Acri, 277 Ill. App. 3d 1030, 1033–34, 214 Ill. Dec. 761, 662 N.E.2d 115 (3d Dist. 1996) (Illinois has adopted the *Frye* standard for the admission of scientific evidence) (see *Frye v. U.S.*, 293 F. 1013, 34 A.L.R. 145 (App. D.C. 1923) (rejected by, State v. Walstad, 119 Wis. 2d 483, 351 N.W.2d 469 (1984)) and (rejected by, State v. Brown, 297 Or. 404, 687 P.2d 751 (1984)) and (rejected by, Nelson v. State, 628 A.2d 69 (Del. 1993)) and (rejected by, State v. Alberico, 116 N.M. 156, 861 P.2d 192 (1993)) and (rejected by, State v. Moore, 268 Mont. 20, 885 P.2d 457 (1994)) and (rejected by, State v. Faught, 127 Idaho 873, 908 P.2d 566 (1995)) and (rejected by, People v. Shreck, 22 P.3d 68, 90 A.L.R.5th 765 (Colo. 2001))).

People v. Owens, 155 Ill. App. 3d 990, 998–99, 108 Ill. Dec. 511, 508 N.E.2d 1088 (4th Dist. 1987) (trial judge improperly allowed a witness to testify without sufficient proof of the witness' qualifications in the relevant field).

People v. Jordan, 103 Ill. 2d 192, 208, 82 Ill. Dec. 925, 469 N.E.2d 569 (1984) (party offering the evidence has the burden to prove that the expert is qualified [the experts were qualified in this case]; but see also *People v. Eiskant*, 253 Ill. App. 3d 773, 776, 192 Ill. Dec. 863, 625 N.E.2d 1018 (5th Dist. 1993) (party opposing evidence on the basis of its reliability or sufficiency has the burden to challenge the evidence through cross-examination).

Mehochko v. Gold Seal Co., 66 Ill. App. 2d 54, 57-60, 213 N.E.2d 581, 19 A.L.R.3d 1003 (5th Dist. 1966) (improper hearsay and prejudicial to let an expert read from a test report about tests performed by someone else when the expert had no personal knowledge about the tests at issue).

See also *Wilson v. Clark*, 84 Ill. 2d 186, 191–92, 49 Ill. Dec. 308, 417 N.E.2d 1322 (1981) (a proper foundation for admission was not laid when the individuals who made the entries in a record did not testify but an expert may still provide an opinion based upon the record if such record is the type relied upon in the expert's field (adopting Federal Rules of Evidence 703 and 705)).

Federal Rule of Evidence 703 provides:

> The facts or data in the particular case upon which an expert bases an opinion or inference may be those perceived by or made known to the expert at or before the hearing. If of a type reasonably relied upon by experts in the particular field in forming opinions or inferences upon the subject, the facts or data need not be admissible in evidence in order for the opinion or inference to be admitted. Facts or data that are otherwise inadmissible shall not be disclosed to the jury by the proponent of the opinion or inference unless the court determines that their probative value in assisting the jury to evaluate the expert's opinion substantially outweighs their prejudicial effect.

Federal Rule of Evidence 705 provides:

> The expert may testify in terms of opinion or inference and give reasons therefor without first testifying to the underlying facts or data, unless the court requires otherwise. The expert may in any event be required to disclose the underlying facts or data on cross-examination.

See § 8:1 to § 8:23, infra, for challenges to expert qualifications, generally.

§ 5:4 Supporting authorities—Not generally accepted

Bernardoni v. Industrial Com'n, 362 Ill. App. 3d 582, 593–96, 298 Ill. Dec. 530, 840 N.E.2d 300 (3d Dist. 2005) (expert testimony regarding alleged multiple chemical sensitivity (MCS) of a party was properly excluded as not based upon generally accepted methodology under *Frye*).

Agnew v. Shaw, 355 Ill. App. 3d 981, 988–90, 291 Ill. Dec. 460, 823 N.E.2d 1046 (1st Dist. 2005) (trial court correctly found that proponent of expert testimony had failed to demonstrate that backward extrapolation had sufficient acceptance as applied to expert's theory, to be admissible under *Frye*).

Perfection Corp. v. Lochinvar Corp., 349 Ill. App. 3d 738, 745–46, 285 Ill. Dec. 645, 812 N.E.2d 465 (1st Dist. 2004) ("event study methodology" does not have sufficient acceptance in the scientific community to provide a reliable basis for expert opinion).

In re Marriage of Bates, 212 Ill. 2d 489, 518–22, 525, 289 Ill. Dec. 218, 819 N.E.2d 714 (2004) (trial court allowed testimony regarding parental alienation syndrome after a *Frye* hearing; note however, that appellate court discussed conflict in many jurisdictions and in scientific arena surrounding evidence and declined to determine whether evidence was proper because judge did not rely on that term for decision).

People v. Wheeler, 334 Ill. App. 3d 273, 284–86, 268 Ill. Dec. 38, 777 N.E.2d 961 (3d Dist. 2001), as supplemented, (Sept. 27, 2002) (after remand and further opinion, the court held that Leuco-Malachite Green (LMG) testing is not admissible because it is only accepted in the relevant scientific community as a test for the possible presence of blood and it is not accepted as a test which is presumptive for the presence of blood).

People v. Wheeler, 334 Ill. App. 3d 273, 281–82, 268 Ill. Dec. 38, 777 N.E.2d 961 (3d Dist. 2001), as supplemented, (Sept. 27, 2002) (whether a scientific principle has gained general acceptance in the relevant scientific field should be determined in a separate *Frye* hearing) (see Frye v. U.S., 293 F. 1013, 34 A.L.R. 145 (App. D.C. 1923) (rejected by, State v. Walstad, 119 Wis. 2d 483, 351 N.W.2d 469 (1984)) and (rejected by, State v. Brown, 297 Or. 404, 687 P.2d 751 (1984)) and (rejected by, Nelson v. State, 628 A.2d 69 (Del. 1993)) and (rejected by, State v. Alberico, 116 N.M. 156, 861 P.2d 192 (1993)) and (rejected by, State v. Moore, 268 Mont. 20, 885 P.2d 457 (1994)) and (rejected by, State v. Faught, 127 Idaho 873, 908 P.2d 566 (1995)) and (rejected by, People v. Shreck, 22 P.3d 68, 90 A.L.R. 5th 765 (Colo. 2001))).

People v. Wheeler, 334 Ill. App. 3d 273, 282–83, 268 Ill. Dec. 38, 777 N.E.2d 961 (3d Dist. 2001), as supplemented, (Sept. 27, 2002) (a *Frye* hearing should have been conducted regarding the admissibility of Leuco-Malachite Green (LMG) testing for blood when there were no Illinois cases on the issue and the trial judge was unfamiliar with the test and the fact that the subject was taught at a university in Illinois did not prove general acceptance).

People v. Acri, 277 Ill. App. 3d 1030, 1033–34, 214 Ill. Dec. 761, 662 N.E.2d 115 (3d Dist. 1996) (Illinois has adopted the *Frye* standard for the admission of scientific evidence) (see *Frye v. U.S.*, 293 F. 1013, 34 A.L.R. 145 (App. D.C. 1923) (rejected by, State v. Walstad, 119 Wis. 2d 483, 351 N.W.2d 469 (1984)) and (rejected by, State v. Brown, 297 Or. 404, 687 P.2d 751 (1984)) and (rejected by, Nelson v. State, 628 A.2d 69 (Del. 1993)) and (rejected by, State v. Alberico, 116 N.M. 156, 861 P.2d 192 (1993)) and (rejected by, State v. Moore, 268 Mont.

20, 885 P.2d 457 (1994)) and (rejected by, State v. Faught, 127 Idaho 873, 908 P.2d 566 (1995)) and (rejected by, People v. Shreck, 22 P.3d 68, 90 A.L.R.5th 765 (Colo. 2001))).

People v. Acri, 277 Ill. App. 3d 1030, 1033–34, 214 Ill. Dec. 761, 662 N.E.2d 115 (3d Dist. 1996) (proper to exclude evidence of dog alerts when the results were not corroborated by laboratory results because experts disagree whether uncorroborated dog alerts are reliable).

People v. Ferguson, 172 Ill. App. 3d 1, 8-12, 122 Ill. Dec. 266, 526 N.E.2d 525 (2d Dist. 1988) (witness testified that her theories were not generally accepted in the relevant community).

§ 5:5 Supporting authorities—Not generally accepted—*Donaldson* decision

The *Donaldson* decision, cited below, is an important case that answers many questions that may arise in this area. Counsel should be well-versed in the points of law addressed therein.

Donaldson v. Central Illinois Public Service Co., 199 Ill. 2d 63, 77, 262 Ill. Dec. 854, 767 N.E.2d 314 (2002) (abrogated by, In re Commitment of Simons, 213 Ill. 2d 523, 290 Ill. Dec. 610, 821 N.E.2d 1184 (2004)) (the exclusive test in Illinois for the admission of expert testimony is governed by the standard announced in *Frye v. U.S.*, 293 F. 1013, 34 A.L.R. 145 (App. D.C. 1923) (rejected by, State v. Walstad, 119 Wis. 2d 483, 351 N.W.2d 469 (1984)) and (rejected by, State v. Brown, 297 Or. 404, 687 P.2d 751 (1984)) and (rejected by, Nelson v. State, 628 A.2d 69 (Del. 1993)) and (rejected by, State v. Alberico, 116 N.M. 156, 861 P.2d 192 (1993)) and (rejected by, State v. Moore, 268 Mont. 20, 885 P.2d 457 (1994)) and (rejected by, State v. Faught, 127 Idaho 873, 908 P.2d 566 (1995)) and (rejected by, People v. Shreck, 22 P.3d 68, 90 A.L.R.5th 765 (Colo. 2001)), which states that scientific evidence is only admissible at trial if the methodology or scientific principle upon which the opinion is based is sufficiently established to have gained general acceptance in the particular field in which it belongs).

Donaldson v. Central Illinois Public Service Co., 199 Ill. 2d 63, 78-79, 83-84, 262 Ill. Dec. 854, 767 N.E.2d 314 (2002) (abrogated by, In re Commitment of Simons, 213 Ill. 2d 523, 290 Ill. Dec. 610, 821 N.E.2d 1184 (2004)) (after the acceptance of a scientific methodology has been decided through full litigation, that decision applies to later cases).

Donaldson v. Central Illinois Public Service Co., 199 Ill. 2d 63, 80, 262 Ill. Dec. 854, 767 N.E.2d 314 (2002) (abrogated by,

In re Commitment of Simons, 213 Ill. 2d 523, 290 Ill. Dec. 610, 821 N.E.2d 1184 (2004)) (court would not consider whether to adopt the standard for the admission of scientific evidence that was set forth in *Daubert* because the issue was not raised by the parties) (see *Daubert v. Merrell Dow Pharmaceuticals, Inc.*, 509 U.S. 579, 113 S. Ct. 2786, 125 L. Ed. 2d 469, 37, 37 Fed. R. Evid. Serv. 1 (1993)).

Donaldson v. Central Illinois Public Service Co., 199 Ill. 2d 63, 79-82, 262 Ill. Dec. 854, 767 N.E.2d 314 (2002) (abrogated by, In re Commitment of Simons, 213 Ill. 2d 523, 290 Ill. Dec. 610, 821 N.E.2d 1184 (2004)) (Illinois does not follow the "*Frye*-plus reliability" standard and therefore, once a scientific methodology has been determined to be generally accepted in the relevant community, a trial judge should not conduct additional hearings regarding whether the opinion itself is reliable) (see *Daubert v. Merrell Dow Pharmaceuticals, Inc.*, 509 U.S. 579, 113 S. Ct. 2786, 125 L. Ed. 2d 469, 37, 37 Fed. R. Evid. Serv. 1 (1993)).

Donaldson v. Central Illinois Public Service Co., 199 Ill. 2d 63, 79-82, 262 Ill. Dec. 854, 767 N.E.2d 314 (2002) (abrogated by, In re Commitment of Simons, 213 Ill. 2d 523, 290 Ill. Dec. 610, 821 N.E.2d 1184 (2004)) (questions regarding the underlying information the expert used or the manner in which the expert applied a generally accepted methodology go to the weight and not the admissibility of the evidence).

Donaldson v. Central Illinois Public Service Co., 199 Ill. 2d 63, 77-78, 262 Ill. Dec. 854, 767 N.E.2d 314 (2002) (abrogated by, In re Commitment of Simons, 213 Ill. 2d 523, 290 Ill. Dec. 610, 821 N.E.2d 1184 (2004)) (trial judge does not need to conduct a *Frye* hearing when the methodology underlying the evidence is not "novel" or "new").

> ◆ ***Important Note:*** Some Courts have suggested that, in the future, Illinois is likely to adopt the Federal *Daubert* holding, which requires a trial judge to perform gatekeeping functions before admitting expert testimony. See *Donnellan v. First Student, Inc.*, 383 Ill.App.3d 1040, 1057–61, 891 N.E.2d 463 (1st Dist. 2008) (the appellate court suggested that in the future, Illinois courts are likely to adopt the *Daubert* holding but also stated that this particular case did not represent the proper circumstances for doing so).

§ 5:6 Supporting authorities—Test not made under substantially similar conditions

Carillo v. Ford Motor Co., 325 Ill. App. 3d 955, 967, 259 Ill.

Dec. 619, 759 N.E.2d 99 (1st Dist. 2001) (exclusion of experiment evidence when parties disagree if the conditions surrounding the experiment were the same as those surrounding the collision).

Becker v. Aquaslide "N' Dive Corp., 35 Ill. App. 3d 479, 484–85, 341 N.E.2d 369 (4th Dist. 1975) (exclusion of videotaped experiment where there was no foundation to show that the circumstances were identical to those in the actual incident).

Mehochko v. Gold Seal Co., 66 Ill. App. 2d 54, 57-60, 213 N.E.2d 581, 19 A.L.R.3d 1003 (5th Dist. 1966) (improper hearsay and prejudicial to let an expert read from a test report about tests performed by someone else when the expert had no personal knowledge about the tests at issue).

§ 5:7 Supporting authorities—Not reliable

Perfection Corp. v. Lochinvar Corp., 349 Ill. App. 3d 738, 745–46, 285 Ill. Dec. 645, 812 N.E.2d 465 (1st Dist. 2004) ("event study methodology" does not have sufficient acceptance in scientific community to provide reliable basis for expert opinion).

People v. Swanson, 335 Ill. App. 3d 117, 125–27, 269 Ill. Dec. 157, 780 N.E.2d 342 (2d Dist. 2002) (improper to allow an expert to repeat a hearsay statement of another expert when the statement did not relate to the defendant's condition and was not the type of statement that was normally relied upon in the field).

People v. Wheeler, 334 Ill. App. 3d 273, 284–86, 268 Ill. Dec. 38, 777 N.E.2d 961 (3d Dist. 2001), as supplemented, (Sept. 27, 2002) (after remand and further opinion, the court held that LMG testing is not admissible because it is only accepted in the relevant scientific community as a test for the possible presence of blood and it is not accepted as a test which is presumptive for the presence of blood).

People v. Acri, 277 Ill. App. 3d 1030, 1033–34, 214 Ill. Dec. 761, 662 N.E.2d 115 (3d Dist. 1996) (Illinois has adopted the *Frye* standard for the admission of scientific evidence) (see Frye v. U.S., 293 F. 1013, 34 A.L.R. 145 (App. D.C. 1923) (rejected by, State v. Walstad, 119 Wis. 2d 483, 351 N.W.2d 469 (1984)) and (rejected by, State v. Brown, 297 Or. 404, 687 P.2d 751 (1984)) and (rejected by, Nelson v. State, 628 A.2d 69 (Del. 1993)) and (rejected by, State v. Alberico, 116 N.M. 156, 861 P.2d 192 (1993)) and (rejected by, State v. Moore, 268 Mont. 20, 885 P.2d 457 (1994)) and (rejected by, State v.

Faught, 127 Idaho 873, 908 P.2d 566 (1995)) and (rejected by, People v. Shreck, 22 P.3d 68, 90 A.L.R.5th 765 (Colo. 2001))).

People v. Acri, 277 Ill. App. 3d 1030, 1033–34, 214 Ill. Dec. 761, 662 N.E.2d 115 (3d Dist. 1996) (proper to exclude evidence of dog alerts when the results were not corroborated by laboratory results because experts disagree whether uncorroborated dog alerts are reliable).

People v. Britz, 123 Ill. 2d 446, 457–62, 124 Ill. Dec. 15, 528 N.E.2d 703 (1988) (exclusion of expert when the expert's opinion is based upon a party's own self-serving statements).

People v. Owens, 155 Ill. App. 3d 990, 998, 108 Ill. Dec. 511, 508 N.E.2d 1088 (4th Dist. 1987) (trial judge should not have taken judicial notice of whether blood-spatter evidence is reliable without conducting a hearing).

Piano v. Davison, 157 Ill. App. 3d 649, 668, 110 Ill. Dec. 35, 510 N.E.2d 1066 (1st Dist. 1987) (proper to exclude medical treatises when there was no proof that they were reliable).

People v. Miller, 20 Ill. App. 3d 1061, 1063–64, 313 N.E.2d 660 (4th Dist. 1974) (improper to admit evidence of fingerprint comparison when there was insufficient evidence that the sample used for the comparison was actually from the defendant).

See also *Kumho Tire Co., Ltd. v. Carmichael*, 526 U.S. 137, 119 S. Ct. 1167, 143 L. Ed. 2d 238, 50 Fed. R. Evid. Serv. 1373 (1999) (*Daubert* standard for determining reliability of testimony stating scientific conclusions may apply to both scientists and non-scientists).

◆ ***Important Note:*** Some Courts have suggested that, in the future, Illinois is likely to adopt the Federal *Daubert* holding, which requires a trial judge to perform gatekeeping functions before admitting expert testimony. See *Donnellan v. First Student, Inc.*, 383 Ill.App.3d 1040, 1057–61, 891 N.E.2d 463 (1st Dist. 2008)(the appellate court suggested that in the future, Illinois courts are likely to adopt the *Daubert* holding but also stated that this particular case did not represent the proper circumstances for doing so).

§ 5:8 Supporting authorities—Scientific procedures not proper

Ahmed v. Pickwick Place Owners' Ass'n, 385 Ill.App.3d 874, 890–91, 896 N.E.2d 854 (1st Dist. 2008) (police officer's opinion regarding the cause of certain injuries to a deceased individual was speculative and based upon hearsay and therefore inadmissible).

Bernardoni v. Industrial Com'n, 362 Ill. App. 3d 582, 593–96, 298 Ill. Dec. 530, 840 N.E.2d 300 (3d Dist. 2005) (expert testimony regarding alleged multiple chemical sensitivity (MCS) of a party was properly excluded as not based upon generally accepted methodology under *Frye*).

Perfection Corp. v. Lochinvar Corp., 349 Ill. App. 3d 738, 745–46, 285 Ill. Dec. 645, 812 N.E.2d 465 (1st Dist. 2004) ("event study methodology" does not have sufficient acceptance in scientific community to provide reliable basis for expert opinion).

People v. Miller, 20 Ill. App. 3d 1061, 1063–64, 313 N.E.2d 660 (4th Dist. 1974) (improper to admit evidence of fingerprint comparison when there was insufficient evidence that the sample used for the comparison was actually from the defendant).

§ 5:9 Supporting authorities—Speculative or conjectural

Ahmed v. Pickwick Place Owners' Ass'n, 385 Ill.App.3d 874, 890–91, 896 N.E.2d 854 (1st Dist. 2008) (police officer's opinion regarding the cause of certain injuries to a deceased individual was speculative and based upon hearsay and therefore inadmissible).

Torres v. Midwest Development Co., 383 Ill.App.3d 20, 27–28, 889 N.E.2d 654 (1st Dist. 2008) (expert's opinion lacked a sufficient factual basis and was inadmissible).

Torres v. Midwest Development Co., 383 Ill.App.3d 20, 27–28, 889 N.E.2d 654 (1st Dist. 2008) (expert's testimony lacked sufficient certainty and was inadmissible).

Wiedenbeck v. Searle, 385 Ill.App.3d 289, 895 N.E.2d 1067 (1st Dist. 2008) (speculative expert testimony was insufficient to avoid summary judgment in a case alleging medical malpractice).

Kirkpatrick v. Strosberg, 2008 WL 1795597, 6 (Ill. App. Ct. 2d Dist. 2008), opinion modified and superseded, 385 Ill. App. 3d 119, 323 Ill. Dec. 755, 894 N.E.2d 781 (2d Dist. 2008), appeal denied, 229 Ill. 2d 669, 900 N.E.2d 1118 (2008) and appeal denied, 229 Ill. 2d 669 (2008) (the trial court did not abuse its discretion by determining that an expert appraiser's testimony, which was based upon outdated valuations, was speculative).

Rose v. Mercedes-Benz U.S.A., LLC, 378 Ill. App. 3d 615, 621–26, 317 Ill. Dec. 538, 882 N.E.2d 112, 64 U.C.C. Rep. Serv. 2d 750 (1st Dist. 2007) (plaintiff's valuation testimony was speculative).

Avery v. State Farm Mut. Auto. Ins. Co., 216 Ill. 2d 100, 149–50, 296 Ill. Dec. 448, 835 N.E.2d 801 (2005) (where an expert testified on cross-examination that his damage calculation could have been in error by as much as one billion, the damage award was speculative and unconstitutional).

Perfection Corp. v. Lochinvar Corp., 349 Ill. App. 3d 738, 745–46, 285 Ill. Dec. 645, 812 N.E.2d 465 (1st Dist. 2004) (party's expert opinion regarding damages was unduly speculative and, as a result, opposing party was entitled to summary judgment).

Schuler v. Mid-Central Cardiology, 313 Ill. App. 3d 326, 334–36, 246 Ill. Dec. 163, 729 N.E.2d 536 (4th Dist. 2000) (trial judge has discretion to exclude expert testimony that is based upon unsupported and speculative facts).

Modelski v. Navistar Intern. Transp. Corp., 302 Ill. App. 3d 879, 884–86, 236 Ill. Dec. 394, 707 N.E.2d 239 (1st Dist. 1999) (accident reconstruction evidence should not have been admitted when it was based upon the expert's speculation regarding what occurred).

People v. Britz, 123 Ill. 2d 446, 457–62, 124 Ill. Dec. 15, 528 N.E.2d 703 (1988) (exclusion of expert testimony when the expert's opinion was based upon a party's own self-serving statements).

Department of Transp. v. Bouy, 69 Ill. App. 3d 29, 33-38, 25 Ill. Dec. 499, 386 N.E.2d 1163 (4th Dist. 1979) (expert's testimony is properly excluded when it is based upon a speculative and conjectural method of proof).

§ 5:10 Supporting authorities—Too time-consuming

Donaldson v. Central Illinois Public Service Co., 199 Ill. 2d 63, 75-76, 262 Ill. Dec. 854, 767 N.E.2d 314 (2002) (abrogated by, In re Commitment of Simons, 213 Ill. 2d 523, 290 Ill. Dec. 610, 821 N.E.2d 1184 (2004)) (error if any in failing to conduct a *Frye* hearing was harmless when the hearing was requested very close to the trial date and the hearing would have required substantial time and resources).

§ 5:11 Supporting authorities—Appellate review of trial judge's *Frye* decisions

In re Commitment of Simons, 213 Ill. 2d 523, 529–32, 290 Ill. Dec. 610, 821 N.E.2d 1184 (2004) (appellate court will review trial judge's decision regarding qualifications of expert and relevancy of expert's testimony under an abuse of discretion standard; but appellate court will review trial judge's *Frye* analysis *de novo*).

In re Commitment of Simons, 213 Ill. 2d 523, 530–43, 290 Ill. Dec. 610, 821 N.E.2d 1184 (2004) (appellate court can review items outside the record when considering whether a scientific methodology is novel or new, including opinions of other jurisdictions and legal and scientific literature).

§ 5:12 Supporting authorities—Other grounds

Other possible grounds for excluding evidence of tests and experiments include:

- Prejudicial (§ 2:1 to § 2:4)
- Time-wasting (§ 2:5 to § 2:8)
- Confusing or misleading (§ 2:9 to § 2:12)
- Cumulative (§ 2:20 to § 2:33)
- Irrelevant (§ 3:1 to § 3:10)
- Collateral to issues in case (§ 3:11 to § 3:21)
- Improper foundation (§ 4:1 to § 4:19)
- Improper expert opinion (§ 8:1 to § 8:23)
- Improper expert qualifications (§ 8:24 to § 8:28)
- Inadmissible hearsay (§ 8:78 to § 8:89)

§ 5:13 Opposing authorities—Court's discretion

People v. Miller, 173 Ill. 2d 167, 186, 219 Ill. Dec. 43, 670 N.E.2d 721 (1996) (abrogated by, In re Commitment of Simons, 213 Ill. 2d 523, 290 Ill. Dec. 610, 821 N.E.2d 1184 (2004)) (there is no exact rule regarding what combination of knowledge, training and experience qualifies a person as an expert).

People v. Pollard, 225 Ill. App. 3d 970, 976, 168 Ill. Dec. 61, 589 N.E.2d 175 (3d Dist. 1992) (trial judge has discretion to determine whether an individual is qualified as an expert based upon the individual's experience and training in the relevant field).

People v. Williams, 128 Ill. App. 3d 384, 398, 83 Ill. Dec. 720, 470 N.E.2d 1140 (4th Dist. 1984) (the trial judge has discretion to determine whether an individual is qualified to provide expert testimony).

§ 5:14 Opposing authorities—Identical conditions requirement

Hudson v. City of Chicago, 378 Ill. App. 3d 373, 400–02, 317 Ill. Dec. 262, 881 N.E.2d 430 (1st Dist. 2007), appeal denied,

227 Ill. 2d 580, 321 Ill. Dec. 250, 888 N.E.2d 1183 (2008) (computer simulation was proper because it was supported by the evidence).

Rios v. Navistar Intern. Transp. Corp., 200 Ill. App. 3d 526, 532–34, 146 Ill. Dec. 289, 558 N.E.2d 252 (1st Dist. 1990) (an experiment only needs to match the "essential conditions" of the original incident in order for evidence of it to be properly admitted).

§ 5:15 Opposing authorities—General acceptance

Donnellan v. First Student, Inc., 383 Ill.App.3d 1040, 1057–61, 891 N.E.2d 463 (1st Dist. 2008) (SPECT scans are a generally accepted methodology under *Frye*).

Ruffin ex rel. Sanders v. Boler, 384 Ill.App.3d 7, 18–25, 890 N.E.2d 1174 (1st Dist. 2008) (expert's opinion regarding causation that was based upon maternal labor force theory was admissible under *Frye* principles because it rested upon generally accepted methodology).

Wartalski v. JSB Const. and Consulting Co., 384 Ill.App.3d 139, 144–47, 892 N.E.2d 122 (1st Dist. 2008) (a "temporal relationship" is an accepted basis for an expert opinion).

Bowman v. University of Chicago Hospitals, 366 Ill. App. 3d 577, 586-88, 304 Ill. Dec. 133, 852 N.E.2d 383 (1st Dist. 2006) (the trial court did not abuse its discretion by allowing experts to be cross-examined through the use of literature which the experts agreed was "authoritative") (note that the use of the term "authoritative" is not required).

Donaldson v. Central Illinois Public Service Co., 199 Ill. 2d 63, 79-82, 262 Ill. Dec. 854, 767 N.E.2d 314 (2002) (abrogated by, In re Commitment of Simons, 213 Ill. 2d 523, 290 Ill. Dec. 610, 821 N.E.2d 1184 (2004)) (Illinois does not follow the "*Frye*-plus reliability" standard and therefore, once a scientific methodology has been determined to be generally accepted in the relevant community, a trial judge should not conduct additional hearings regarding whether the opinion itself is reliable) (see *Daubert v. Merrell Dow Pharmaceuticals, Inc.*, 509 U.S. 579, 113 S. Ct. 2786, 125 L. Ed. 2d 469, 37, 37 Fed. R. Evid. Serv. 1 (1993)).

Donaldson v. Central Illinois Public Service Co., 199 Ill. 2d 63, 78-79, 83-84, 262 Ill. Dec. 854, 767 N.E.2d 314 (2002) (abrogated by, In re Commitment of Simons, 213 Ill. 2d 523, 290 Ill. Dec. 610, 821 N.E.2d 1184 (2004)) (after the acceptance of a scientific methodology has been decided through full litigation, that decision applies to later cases).

People v. Shanahan, 323 Ill. App. 3d 835, 838–39, 257 Ill. Dec. 402, 753 N.E.2d 1028 (1st Dist. 2001) (trial court does not need to conduct a *Frye* hearing if the same type of scientific evidence has been admitted in other Illinois cases).

§ 5:16 Opposing authorities—General acceptance—Level of acceptance in scientific community

Donnellan v. First Student, Inc, 383 Ill.App.3d 1040, 1057–61, 891 N.E.2d 463 (1st Dist. 2008) (SPECT scans are a generally accepted methodology under *Frye*).

In re Commitment of Sandry, 367 Ill. App. 3d 949, 967-77, 306 Ill. Dec. 202, 857 N.E.2d 295 (2d Dist. 2006) (penile plethysmograph (PPG) test has sufficient acceptance in the scientific community under the *Frye* test to form the basis of an expert's opinion).

People v. Vercolio, 363 Ill. App. 3d 232, 236–37, 300 Ill. Dec. 159, 843 N.E.2d 417 (3d Dist. 2006) ("25 variable test" for sex offender recidivism, which was used by an expert as the basis for an opinion, was sufficiently accepted in the relevant field under a *Frye* analysis).

Donaldson v. Central Illinois Public Service Co., 199 Ill. 2d 63, 76-77, 262 Ill. Dec. 854, 767 N.E.2d 314 (2002) (abrogated by, In re Commitment of Simons, 213 Ill. 2d 523, 290 Ill. Dec. 610, 821 N.E.2d 1184 (2004)) (level of acceptance required for the *Frye* test depends upon whether the technique has general acceptance and not upon whether the conclusion that was reached by the expert has general acceptance).

Donaldson v. Central Illinois Public Service Co., 199 Ill. 2d 63, 77-78, 262 Ill. Dec. 854, 767 N.E.2d 314 (2002) (abrogated by, In re Commitment of Simons, 213 Ill. 2d 523, 290 Ill. Dec. 610, 821 N.E.2d 1184 (2004)) (level of acceptance required for the *Frye* test does not require unanimity or even majority consensus).

Melecosky v. McCarthy Bros. Co., 115 Ill. 2d 209, 213–17, 104 Ill. Dec. 798, 503 N.E.2d 355 (1986) (expert opinion based upon party's own statements should have been allowed when such statements are the type of information generally relied upon in the expert's field).

People v. McGee, 88 Ill. App. 3d 447, 450–51, 43 Ill. Dec. 641, 410 N.E.2d 641 (2d Dist. 1980) (trial judge improperly excluded evidence of an absorption inhibition test on vaginal fluid on the grounds that the experts indicated that the test can lead to inaccurate results, when the experts also testified that the test is generally accepted in the relevant field).

People v. Milone, 43 Ill. App. 3d 385, 395, 2 Ill. Dec. 63, 356 N.E.2d 1350 (2d Dist. 1976) (a scientific method does not need to be unanimously accepted in the field to be admissible).

§ 5:17 Opposing authorities—Weight vs. admissibility

Marston v. Walgreen Co., 389 Ill.App.3d 337, 907 N.E.2d 851 (1st Dist. 2009) (an expert may testify to more than one possible cause of an injury and then it is for the jury to decide causation).

Johnson v. Johnson, 386 Ill.App.3d 522, 545–46, 898 N.E.2d 145 (1st Dist. 2008) (witness' expert opinion regarding whether a horse was provoked before injuring someone was not improperly speculative).

Bergman v. Kelsey, 375 Ill. App. 3d 612, 622–23, 313 Ill. Dec. 862, 873 N.E.2d 486 (1st Dist. 2007), appeal denied, 226 Ill. 2d 579, 316 Ill. Dec. 541, 879 N.E.2d 929 (2007) (conflicting expert testimony regarding the proper standard of care, raised a factual issue for the jury).

Shaheen v. Advantage Moving and Storage, Inc., 369 Ill. App. 3d 535, 543-45, 307 Ill. Dec. 721, 860 N.E.2d 375 (1st Dist. 2006) (proper foundation was provided for an expert's opinion regarding the plaintiff's lost earning capacity and any defects in the analysis by the expert affected the weight of the evidence, rather than its admissibility).

Moller v. Lipov, 368 Ill. App. 3d 333, 344-45, 305 Ill. Dec. 859, 856 N.E.2d 664 (1st Dist. 2006) (factual basis for an expert's opinion affects the weight of the opinion and not its admissibility).

Donaldson v. Central Illinois Public Service Co., 199 Ill. 2d 63, 79-82, 262 Ill. Dec. 854, 767 N.E.2d 314 (2002) (abrogated by, In re Commitment of Simons, 213 Ill. 2d 523, 290 Ill. Dec. 610, 821 N.E.2d 1184 (2004)) (questions regarding the underlying information the expert used or the manner in which the expert applied a generally accepted methodology go to the weight and not the admissibility of the evidence).

People v. Eiskant, 253 Ill. App. 3d 773, 776, 192 Ill. Dec. 863, 625 N.E.2d 1018 (5th Dist. 1993) (as long as information is the type normally relied upon in the expert's field, it is proper to allow an expert to testify about it; the source of information only affects the weight of the expert's testimony, not the admissibility of it).

People v. Pollard, 225 Ill. App. 3d 970, 976–78, 168 Ill. Dec. 61, 589 N.E.2d 175 (3d Dist. 1992) (child sexual abuse accommodation syndrome is a recognized form of post-traumatic stress syndrome and evidence of it is therefore admissible in criminal sexual abuse cases. It is for the jury to determine the weight of the testimony).

People v. Israel, 181 Ill. App. 3d 851, 862, 130 Ill. Dec. 795, 537 N.E.2d 1124 (2d Dist. 1989) (method used by a psychiatric expert to arrive at a diagnosis went to the weight of the opinion and not its admissibility).

People v. Henne, 165 Ill. App. 3d 315, 325–26, 116 Ill. Dec. 296, 518 N.E.2d 1276 (4th Dist. 1988) (fact that in-court measurements of a boot differed from the measurements of the boot print went to the weight of the comparison testimony and not its admissibility).

People v. Jordan, 103 Ill. 2d 192, 208–09, 82 Ill. Dec. 925, 469 N.E.2d 569 (1984) (experts were qualified to testify that "pink tooth theory" demonstrated that strangulation was a *possible* cause of the victim's death).

People v. McGee, 88 Ill. App. 3d 447, 452–53, 43 Ill. Dec. 641, 410 N.E.2d 641 (2d Dist. 1980) (trial judge improperly excluded evidence of an absorption inhibition test on vaginal fluid on the grounds that the experts disagreed about whether the test had been performed in a manner that would produce accurate results because it was for the jury to decide the weight of the evidence).

People v. Singletary, 73 Ill. App. 3d 239, 248–49, 29 Ill. Dec. 177, 391 N.E.2d 440 (1st Dist. 1979) (fact that expert testified that a bullet may have been fired by a gun that was found at the time of the defendant's apprehension but that it also may have come from a similar gun, affected the weight and not the admissibility of the evidence).

§ 5:18 Opposing authorities—Weight vs. admissibility—Improper testing and weight of testimony

Kunkel v. P.K. Dependable Const., LLC, 387 Ill.App.3d 1153, 1158–59, 902 N.E.2d 769 (5th Dist. 2009) (estimate of cost of repairs from an individual who is experienced in the field is admissible, even if there is no testimony that the estimate is reasonable and the repairs are necessary).

Shaheen v. Advantage Moving and Storage, Inc., 369 Ill. App. 3d 535, 543-45, 307 Ill. Dec. 721, 860 N.E.2d 375 (1st Dist. 2006) (proper foundation was provided for an expert's opinion regarding the plaintiff's lost earning capacity and any defects in the analysis by the expert affected the weight of the evidence, rather than its admissibility).

Moller v. Lipov, 368 Ill. App. 3d 333, 344-45, 305 Ill. Dec.

859, 856 N.E.2d 664 (1st Dist. 2006) (factual basis for an expert's opinion affects the weight of the opinion and not its admissibility).

Donaldson v. Central Illinois Public Service Co., 199 Ill. 2d 63, 79-82, 262 Ill. Dec. 854, 767 N.E.2d 314 (2002) (abrogated by, In re Commitment of Simons, 213 Ill. 2d 523, 290 Ill. Dec. 610, 821 N.E.2d 1184 (2004)) (questions regarding the underlying information the expert used or the manner in which the expert applied a generally accepted methodology go to the weight and not the admissibility of the testimony).

People v. Dalcollo, 282 Ill. App. 3d 944, 957, 218 Ill. Dec. 435, 669 N.E.2d 378 (2d Dist. 1996) (disagreements with the actual procedures used in a specific case affect the weight and not the admissibility of the evidence).

People v. Mehlberg, 249 Ill. App. 3d 499, 539–41, 188 Ill. Dec. 598, 618 N.E.2d 1168 (5th Dist. 1993) (allegations of improper testing are the proper subject of cross-examination but they do not render evidence inadmissible when the evidence is based upon a methodology that is generally accepted in the relevant scientific community).

People v. Henne, 165 Ill. App. 3d 315, 325–26, 116 Ill. Dec. 296, 518 N.E.2d 1276 (4th Dist. 1988) (fact that in court measurements of a boot differed from the measurements of the boot print went to the weight of the comparison testimony and not its admissibility).

People v. McGee, 88 Ill. App. 3d 447, 452–53, 43 Ill. Dec. 641, 410 N.E.2d 641 (2d Dist. 1980) (trial judge improperly excluded evidence of an absorption inhibition test on vaginal fluid on the grounds that the experts disagreed about whether the test had been performed in a manner that would produce accurate results, because it was for the jury to decide the weight of the evidence).

§ 5:19 Opposing authorities—Outside realm of *Frye* requirements

Wartalski v. JSB Const. and Consulting Co., 384 Ill.App.3d 139, 144–47, 892 N.E.2d 122 (1st Dist. 2008) (a *Frye* hearing is not required before a treating physician can provide an opinion regarding the cause of the plaintiff's condition).

Jackson v. Seib, 372 Ill. App. 3d 1061, 310 Ill. Dec. 502, 866 N.E.2d 663 (5th Dist. 2007) (experts' testimony was admissible without a *Frye* hearing because the experts relied upon their own deductions which were based upon their own observations and experience, rather than "scientific" evidence).

Noakes v. National R.R. Passenger Corp., 363 Ill. App. 3d 851, 855–57, 300 Ill. Dec. 593, 845 N.E.2d 14 (1st Dist. 2006) (no *Frye* hearing was required where the testimony at issue did not address new or novel theories).

Noakes v. National R.R. Passenger Corp., 363 Ill. App. 3d 851, 855–57, 300 Ill. Dec. 593, 845 N.E.2d 14 (1st Dist. 2006) (the issue of whether or not repetitive motion could cause carpal tunnel syndrome was not new or novel).

Noakes v. National R.R. Passenger Corp., 363 Ill. App. 3d 851, 855–59, 300 Ill. Dec. 593, 845 N.E.2d 14 (1st Dist. 2006) ("pure opinion" testimony based upon the expert's own training and knowledge is not subject to a *Frye* analysis).

In re Marriage of Alexander, 368 Ill. App. 3d 192, 196-203, 306 Ill. Dec. 367, 857 N.E.2d 766 (5th Dist. 2006) (expert's opinion which was based upon the expert's observations and experience was not considered scientific evidence and therefore, was not subject to a *Frye* analysis).

Elam v. Lincoln Elec. Co., 362 Ill. App. 3d 884, 897–98, 299 Ill. Dec. 305, 841 N.E.2d 1037 (5th Dist. 2005) (an expert's opinion that was based upon the expert's own experience and knowledge was not subject to a *Frye* analysis).

In re K.T., 361 Ill. App. 3d 187, 201–03, 297 Ill. Dec. 38, 836 N.E.2d 769 (1st Dist. 2005) (there was no plain error caused when experts were permitted to provide opinions regarding whether a party suffered from factitious disorder by proxy, without a *Frye* hearing, even though there was evidence that there was disagreement among experts about that alleged disorder).

Donaldson v. Central Illinois Public Service Co., 199 Ill. 2d 63, 77-78, 262 Ill. Dec. 854, 767 N.E.2d 314 (2002) (abrogated by, In re Commitment of Simons, 213 Ill. 2d 523, 290 Ill. Dec. 610, 821 N.E.2d 1184 (2004)) (trial judge does not need to conduct a *Frye* hearing when the methodology underlying the evidence is not "novel" or "new").

People v. Shanahan, 323 Ill. App. 3d 835, 838–39, 257 Ill. Dec. 402, 753 N.E.2d 1028 (1st Dist. 2001) (trial court does not need to conduct a *Frye* hearing if the same type of scientific evidence has been admitted in other Illinois cases).

People v. Reeves, 314 Ill. App. 3d 482, 247 Ill. Dec. 305, 732 N.E.2d 21 (1st Dist. 2000) (evidence of dog alerts can be admitted as corroboration for other evidence, even if it is inadmissible to prove an element of an offense).

People v. Eiskant, 253 Ill. App. 3d 773, 774–77, 192 Ill. Dec. 863, 625 N.E.2d 1018 (5th Dist. 1993) (trial judge improperly excluded evidence of rape trauma syndrome from a witness who had sufficient training and experience in the subject matter) (case cites to 725 ILCS 5/115-7.2).

People v. Pollard, 225 Ill. App. 3d 970, 976, 168 Ill. Dec. 61, 589 N.E.2d 175 (3d Dist. 1992) (child sexual abuse accommodation syndrome is a recognized form of post-traumatic stress syndrome and expert testimony regarding evidence of it is therefore admissible in criminal sexual abuse cases).

People v. Thomas, 137 Ill. 2d 500, 517–18, 148 Ill. Dec. 751, 561 N.E.2d 57 (1990) (*Frye* analysis not required when the test has been determined to be reliable in other Illinois cases).

People v. Israel, 181 Ill. App. 3d 851, 861–62, 130 Ill. Dec. 795, 537 N.E.2d 1124 (2d Dist. 1989) (*Frye* analysis not required before admitting testimony that a psychiatric nurse assigned numbers to each factor she considered in forming her opinion because her scoring system did not involve a scientific test or theory).

People v. Milone, 43 Ill. App. 3d 385, 396–99, 2 Ill. Dec. 63, 356 N.E.2d 1350 (2d Dist. 1976) (proper to consider whether the evidence at issue relies upon a novel use of machine-produced results or whether it is based upon visual comparisons that can be readily duplicated by the trial judge).

See also 725 ILCS 5/115-7.2, which provides that in criminal cases for certain sexual offenses and abuse offenses, testimony from an expert who is qualified by the court regarding, "any recognized and accepted form of post-traumatic stress syndrome shall be admissible as evidence"; and, 735 ILCS 5/8-1501, which states:

> Comparison. In all courts of this State it shall be lawful to prove handwriting by comparison made by the witness or jury with writings properly in the files of records of the case, admitted in evidence or treated as genuine or admitted to be genuine, by the party against whom the evidence is offered, or proved to be genuine to the satisfaction of the court.

B. MOTION TO EXCLUDE "JUNK SCIENCE" AND RELATED EVIDENCE

§ 5:20 Suggested motion text

[Name of moving party] hereby moves this Court for an order excluding any and all evidence, references to evidence, testimony or argument relating to *[insert description of test or evidence, e.g., polygraph tests; or, a party's or witness' refusal or willingness to take a polygraph test; or, the results of polygraph tests, etc.]*. The motion is based upon the grounds that such evidence is unreliable and inadmissible pursuant to established laws of this

state and will create a substantial danger of undue prejudice to *[name of moving party]*.

§ 5:21 Motion summary

This section provides a number of citations supporting the exclusion of evidence relating to new scientific techniques or disapproved existing techniques, based upon a failure to satisfy *Frye* requirements for admissibility. See generally *Donaldson v. Central Illinois Public Service Co.*, 199 Ill. 2d 63, 262 Ill. Dec. 854, 767 N.E.2d 314 (2002) (abrogated by, In re Commitment of Simons, 213 Ill. 2d 523, 290 Ill. Dec. 610, 821 N.E.2d 1184 (2004)); *People v. Acri*, 277 Ill. App. 3d 1030, 1033–34, 214 Ill. Dec. 761, 662 N.E.2d 115 (3d Dist. 1996) (Illinois has adopted the *Frye* standard for the admission of scientific evidence); *Frye v. U.S.*, 293 F. 1013, 34 A.L.R. 145 (App. D.C. 1923) (rejected by, State v. Walstad, 119 Wis. 2d 483, 351 N.W.2d 469 (1984)) and (rejected by, State v. Brown, 297 Or. 404, 687 P.2d 751 (1984)) and (rejected by, Nelson v. State, 628 A.2d 69 (Del. 1993)) and (rejected by, State v. Alberico, 116 N.M. 156, 861 P.2d 192 (1993)) and (rejected by, State v. Moore, 268 Mont. 20, 885 P.2d 457 (1994)) and (rejected by, State v. Faught, 127 Idaho 873, 908 P.2d 566 (1995)) and (rejected by, People v. Shreck, 22 P.3d 68, 90 A.L.R.5th 765 (Colo. 2001)) and following cases. Where the matter has not been tested by the appellate courts of this state, citations from other jurisdictions may be helpful. See *Whiting v. Coultrip*, 324 Ill. App. 3d 161, 164–65, 258 Ill. Dec. 111, 755 N.E.2d 494 (3d Dist. 2001), as modified on denial of reh'g, (Sept. 12, 2001); *People v. Dalcollo*, 282 Ill. App. 3d 944, 955, 218 Ill. Dec. 435, 669 N.E.2d 378 (2d Dist. 1996).

§ 5:22 Supporting authorities—Exclusion of new scientific evidence—Generally

People v. Acri, 277 Ill. App. 3d 1030, 1033–34, 214 Ill. Dec. 761, 662 N.E.2d 115 (3d Dist. 1996) (scientific evidence should be admitted only when the technique upon which the evidence is based has gained general acceptance in the relevant scientific community).

People v. Owens, 155 Ill. App. 3d 990, 998, 108 Ill. Dec. 511, 508 N.E.2d 1088 (4th Dist. 1987) (trial judge should not have taken judicial notice of whether blood-spatter evidence is reliable without conducting a hearing).

People v. Milone, 43 Ill. App. 3d 385, 396–99, 2 Ill. Dec. 63, 356 N.E.2d 1350 (2d Dist. 1976) (proper to consider whether the evidence at issue relies upon a novel use of machine-produced results or whether it is based upon visual comparisons that can be readily duplicated by the trial judge).

Note also that scientific evidence may be defeated for reasons other than a failure to satisfy the *Frye* standards, including prejudice, relevance, undue consumption of time, confusion, and lack of foundation. See e.g. *People v. Schulz*, 154 Ill. App. 3d 358, 362–66, 107 Ill. Dec. 288, 506 N.E.2d 1343 (1st Dist. 1987) (scientific evidence was irrelevant when it simply failed to exclude the defendant as a possible perpetrator of the offense).

For additional citations on the exclusion of tests and scientific evidence in general, see § 5:1 to § 5:19, supra.

§ 5:23 Supporting authorities—Hedonic damage evidence

This theory attempts to assign a dollar value to the "loss of enjoyment of life," separate and apart from other recognized forms of damages, typically arising in personal injury and wrongful death cases.

Sherrod v. Berry, 629 F. Supp. 159, 164 (N.D. Ill. 1985), judgment aff'd, 827 F.2d 195, 23 Fed. R. Evid. Serv. 708 (7th Cir. 1987), reh'g granted and opinion vacated, 835 F.2d 1222 (7th Cir. 1988), on reh'g en banc, 856 F.2d 802, 26 Fed. R. Evid. Serv. 875 (7th Cir. 1988) and judgment rev'd, 856 F.2d 802, 26 Fed. R. Evid. Serv. 875 (7th Cir. 1988) (first widely reported case accepting admissibility of hedonic damage testimony); but see *Ayers v. Robinson*, 887 F. Supp. 1049, 1064, 42 Fed. R. Evid. Serv. 308 (N.D. Ill. 1995) (hedonic damage testimony excluded, as falling short of *Daubert* standards).

Fetzer v. Wood, 211 Ill. App. 3d 70, 81-86, 155 Ill. Dec. 626, 569 N.E.2d 1237 (2d Dist. 1991) (statistical evidence not permitted to demonstrate the value of the loss of life because that decision is within the knowledge of an average jury) (noting that *Sherrod* was based upon federal civil rights laws and not state law).

Mercado v. Ahmed, 756 F. Supp. 1097, 1098–1103, 32 Fed. R. Evid. Serv. 397 (N.D. Ill. 1991) (statistical evidence is not admissible in a personal injury action to explain loss of enjoyment of life because that decision is within the knowledge of the average jury).

See also *Johnson v. Inland Steel Co.*, 1992 WL 396296, 3–4 (N.D. Ill. 1992) (decision under *Indiana* law that hedonic damages are not allowed for the decedent's loss of his own life in a wrongful death action).

§ 5:24 Supporting authorities—"Truth-serum" evidence

"Truth Serum" represents various chemical tests, including the administration of sodium amytal and sodium pentathol, to obtain "true" statements from witnesses.

People v. Harper, 111 Ill. App. 2d 204, 205–09, 250 N.E.2d 5 (4th Dist. 1969) (identification by a witness of the defendant as the perpetrator of the offense was not admissible when it resulted from an interview that was conducted when the witness was provided with sodium amobarbital, a so-called "truth-serum").

See also 735 ILCS 5/2-1104, which states,

> Party need not submit to lie detector. In the course of any civil trial or pre-trial proceeding the court shall not require that the plaintiff or defendant submit to a polygraphic detection deception test, commonly known as a lie detector test or require, suggest or request that the plaintiff or defendant submit to questioning under the effect of thiopental sodium or to any other test or questioning by means of any chemical substance.

§ 5:25 Supporting authorities—Polygraph evidence

Polygraph or "lie detector" tests utilize an electronic device that purportedly determines if a witness is telling the truth, based upon increase in heart rate and other data.

Aguirre v. City of Chicago, 382 Ill. App. 3d 89, 320 Ill. Dec. 512, 887 N.E.2d 656 (1st Dist. 2008) (polygraph evidence was excluded as more prejudicial than probative and as confusing to the jury).

People v. Gard, 158 Ill. 2d 191, 200–05, 198 Ill. Dec. 415, 632 N.E.2d 1026 (1994) (polygraph results are unreliable and prejudicial and therefore, should not be admitted as evidence)

People v. Baynes, 88 Ill. 2d 225, 230–45, 58 Ill. Dec. 819, 430 N.E.2d 1070 (1981) (polygraph results are not reliable evidence and thus, they are not admissible into evidence, even if the parties stipulate to them).

735 ILCS 5/2-1104 states,

> Party need not submit to lie detector. In the course of any civil trial or pre-trial proceeding the court shall not require that the plaintiff or defendant submit to a polygraphic detection deception test, commonly known as a lie detector test or require, suggest or request that the plaintiff or defendant submit to questioning under the effect of thiopental sodium or to any other test or questioning by means of any chemical substance.

But see *People v. Avery*, 227 Ill. App. 3d 382, 390–92, 169 Ill. Dec. 542, 592 N.E.2d 29 (1st Dist. 1991) (*not improper* to admit evidence of a polygraph when the issue was the voluntariness of the defendant's statements); see also § 5:47, Opposing authorities—Polygraph evidence—Stipulation or agreement of parties, infra.

§ 5:26 Supporting authorities—Polygraph evidence—Refusal to take polygraph test

People v. Finley, 312 Ill. App. 3d 892, 895–96, 245 Ill. Dec. 370, 728 N.E.2d 101 (4th Dist. 2000) (improper for witness to testify that a criminal defendant refused to take a polygraph test).

735 ILCS 5/2-1104 states,

> Party need not submit to lie detector. In the course of any civil trial or pre-trial proceeding the court shall not require that the plaintiff or defendant submit to a polygraphic detection deception test, commonly known as a lie detector test or require, suggest or request that the plaintiff or defendant submit to questioning under the effect of thiopental sodium or to any other test or questioning by means of any chemical substance.

See also § 5:47, Opposing authorities—Polygraph evidence—Stipulation or agreement of parties, regarding admissibility of voluntary polygraph tests.

§ 5:27 Supporting authorities—Psychological tests and syndromes—In general

In re Marriage of Bates, 212 Ill. 2d 489, 518–22, 525, 289 Ill. Dec. 218, 819 N.E.2d 714 (2004) (trial court allowed testimony regarding parental alienation syndrome after a *Frye* hearing; note however, that appellate court discussed conflict in many jurisdictions and in scientific arena surrounding evidence and declined to determine whether evidence was proper because judge did not rely on that term for decision).

People v. Williams, 332 Ill. App. 3d 693, 697–99, 266 Ill. Dec. 168, 773 N.E.2d 1238 (3d Dist. 2002) (trial judge should not have admitted expert evidence on the issue of the cycle of violence when there was no showing that the testimony was based upon accepted methodology).

In re Marriage of Jawad and Whalen, 326 Ill. App. 3d 141, 150–54, 259 Ill. Dec. 941, 759 N.E.2d 1002 (2d Dist. 2001) (when a psychological opinion relies upon the literature and studies of others in the expert's field, it is scientific evidence and is subject to a *Frye* analysis).

§ 5:28 Supporting authorities—Psychological tests and syndromes—Rape trauma syndrome

People v. Williams, 332 Ill. App. 3d 693, 697–99, 266 Ill. Dec. 168, 773 N.E.2d 1238 (3d Dist. 2002) (trial judge should not have admitted expert evidence on the issue of the cycle of violence because it represented improper comment on the credibility of a witness).

725 ILCS 5/115-7.2 provides that in criminal cases for certain sexual offenses and abuse offenses testimony from an expert who is qualified by the court regarding, "any recognized and accepted form of post-traumatic stress syndrome shall be admissible as evidence."

But see *People v. Eiskant*, 253 Ill. App. 3d 773, 774–77, 192 Ill. Dec. 863, 625 N.E.2d 1018 (5th Dist. 1993) (trial judge *improperly excluded* evidence of rape trauma syndrome from a witness who had sufficient training and experience in the subject matter) (case cites to 725 ILCS 5/115-7.2).

§ 5:29 Supporting authorities—Psychological tests and syndromes—Child molestation syndrome

People v. Williams, 332 Ill. App. 3d 693, 697–99, 266 Ill. Dec. 168, 773 N.E.2d 1238 (3d Dist. 2002) (trial judge should not have admitted expert evidence on the issue of the cycle of violence because it represented improper comment on the credibility of a witness); *People v. Shanahan*, 323 Ill. App. 3d 835, 838–39, 257 Ill. Dec. 402, 753 N.E.2d 1028 (1st Dist. 2001) (Illinois cases have not decided whether battered child syndrome is admissible and therefore, a *Frye* hearing is required before offering such evidence).

725 ILCS 5/115-7.2 provides that in criminal cases for certain sexual offenses and abuse offenses testimony from an expert who is qualified by the court regarding, "any recognized and accepted form of post-traumatic stress syndrome shall be admissible as evidence."

But see *People v. Pollard*, 225 Ill. App. 3d 970, 976, 168 Ill. Dec. 61, 589 N.E.2d 175 (3d Dist. 1992) (child sexual abuse accommodation syndrome is a recognized form of post-traumatic stress syndrome and evidence of it is therefore admissible in criminal sexual abuse cases).

See also *People v. Wasson*, 211 Ill. App. 3d 264, 269–72, 155 Ill. Dec. 710, 569 N.E.2d 1321 (4th Dist. 1991).

§ 5:30 Supporting authorities—Psychological tests and syndromes—Electronic penile plethysmograph test

In re Detention of Hughes, 346 Ill. App. 3d 637, 650–52, 282 Ill. Dec. 106, 805 N.E.2d 725 (2d Dist. 2004) (trial court erred by allowing an expert to base an opinion on a penile plethysmograph test, without first conducting a *Frye* hearing).

People v. Swanson, 335 Ill. App. 3d 117, 127, 269 Ill. Dec. 157, 780 N.E.2d 342 (2d Dist. 2002) (defendant's attorney should have requested a hearing regarding whether or not the results of a penile plethysmograph should have been admitted because Illinois state courts have not yet determined whether the tests are reliable evidence and there is a conflict among courts in other jurisdictions regarding the admissibility of such tests) (citing *Berthiaume v. Caron*, 142 F.3d 12, 17 (1st Cir. 1998); *Walrath v. U.S.*, 830 F. Supp. 444, 447 (N.D. Ill. 1993); and *State v. Riles*, 135 Wash. 2d 326, 343–44, 957 P.2d 655 (1998) (all holding that such tests are reliable) and *In re Mark C.*, 7 Cal. App. 4th 433, 444–45, 8 Cal. Rptr. 2d 856 (4th Dist. 1992); *Gentry v. State*, 213 Ga. App. 24, 25–26, 443 S.E.2d 667 (1994); *State v. Spencer*, 119 N.C. App. 662, 667–68, 459 S.E.2d 812 (1995); and *In Interest of A.V.*, 849 S.W.2d 393, 399 (Tex. App. Fort Worth 1993) (all holding that such tests are not reliable)).

§ 5:31 Supporting authorities—Hypnosis evidence—Civil cases

People v. Sutton, 349 Ill. App. 3d 608, 615–17, 285 Ill. Dec. 723, 812 N.E.2d 543 (1st Dist. 2004) (trial court erred by allowing hypnotically enhanced testimony by a witness when record suggested that hypnosis influenced the testimony).

People v. Lampkin, 193 Ill. App. 3d 570, 575–76, 140 Ill. Dec. 642, 550 N.E.2d 278 (3d Dist. 1990) (identification testimony by a witness which resulted from the witness' hypnotically induced identification of the defendant was improper and prejudicial when the hypnotist was a law enforcement officer who had insufficient training and when the witness had read and heard news reports regarding the offense prior to being hypnotized).

People v. Zayas, 131 Ill. 2d 284, 289–98, 137 Ill. Dec. 568, 546 N.E.2d 513 (1989) (hypnotically induced testimony by anyone other than the accused in a criminal case is "per se" inadmissible as evidence in Illinois).

People v. Zayas, 131 Ill. 2d 284, 297, 137 Ill. Dec. 568, 546

N.E.2d 513 (1989) (pre-hypnotic recall by a witness can be admitted if the proponent of the evidence proves that it was in fact pre-hypnotic recall).

Note that hypnosis evidence may be admissible in criminal cases, when certain conditions have been met. See § 5:51, Opposing authorities—Hypnosis evidence, infra.

§ 5:32 Supporting authorities—Voiceprint identification

People v. Ashford, 121 Ill. 2d 55, 78-79, 117 Ill. Dec. 171, 520 N.E.2d 332 (1988) (the court noted a conflict in jurisdictions regarding whether voiceprint evidence is accepted as reliable and asserted that the issue has not yet been decided in Illinois).

§ 5:33 Supporting authorities—Accident reconstruction evidence

While commonly used as an investigative tool in a number of litigated cases, especially personal injury and criminal matters, accident reconstruction evidence may be subject to exclusion at trial. The following cases provide general support for this proposition. For additional citations and cross-references, see §§ 10:150 et seq., infra.

Glass v. City of Chicago, 323 Ill. App. 3d 158, 166, 256 Ill. Dec. 88, 751 N.E.2d 141 (1st Dist. 2001) (trial judge has discretion to determine whether or not accident reconstruction evidence should be allowed) (note that it *was allowed* in this case because the testimony assisted the jury).

Modelski v. Navistar Intern. Transp. Corp., 302 Ill. App. 3d 879, 884–86, 236 Ill. Dec. 394, 707 N.E.2d 239 (1st Dist. 1999) (accident reconstruction evidence should not have been admitted when it was based upon the expert's speculation regarding what occurred).

Seward v. Griffin, 116 Ill. App. 3d 749, 762–63, 72 Ill. Dec. 305, 452 N.E.2d 558 (3d Dist. 1983) (not improper to exclude accident reconstruction evidence when there was no showing that the vehicle used for the reconstruction adequately resembled the structure of the actual vehicle).

§ 5:34 Supporting authorities—Biomechanical evidence

Biomechanical evidence has been rejected for lack of sufficient foundation under a *Frye* analysis in at least one Illinois case and in several other jurisdictions, as is noted below. For more detailed discussion, see §§ 10:156 et seq., infra.

Whiting v. Coultrip, 324 Ill. App. 3d 161, 164–69, 258 Ill. Dec. 111, 755 N.E.2d 494 (3d Dist. 2001), as modified on denial of reh'g, (Sept. 12, 2001) (biomechanical evidence should not have been admitted when the evidence was not shown to be generally accepted in the relevant scientific community and was not proven reliable. However, the court noted that it was not saying that such evidence could not be admissible if a proper foundation under *Frye* was established).

See also *People v. Dellinger*, 163 Cal. App. 3d 284, 292–93, 209 Cal. Rptr. 503 (4th Dist. 1984) (California reliability standard not met regarding biomechanical testing of anthropomorphic dummy and "finite element analysis" to determine force involved in victim's head injury); cf. *People v. Roehler*, 167 Cal. App. 3d 353, 390, 213 Cal. Rptr. 353 (2d Dist. 1985) (use of test evidence on dummy allowed, not to show cause of injury, but to corroborate conclusions of medical witnesses); *Clemente v. Blumenberg*, 183 Misc. 2d 923, 705 N.Y.S.2d 792, 794–95 (Sup 1999) (studies relied upon by biomechanical expert regarding claimed non-injuries in low speed accident held unreliable); *Smelser v. Norfolk Southern Ry. Co.*, 105 F.3d 299, 301, 46 Fed. R. Evid. Serv. 468, 1997 FED App. 0033P (6th Cir. 1997) (court erred in allowing biomechanical expert to offer opinion regarding medical causation of injury).

§ 5:35 Supporting authorities—Biomechanical evidence—Low-speed impact cases

Accident reconstruction and biomechanical testimony in low-speed cases is often vigorously disputed and, in a growing number of jurisdictions, is being excluded at trial. See *Clemente v. Blumenberg*, 183 Misc. 2d 923, 705 N.Y.S.2d 792, 794–95 (Sup 1999); *Smelser v. Norfolk Southern Ry. Co.*, 105 F.3d 299, 301, 46 Fed. R. Evid. Serv. 468, 1997 FED App. 0033P (6th Cir. 1997). At least one commentator has suggested that evidence in these cases is "junk science" and therefore not reliable. See "Challenging Expert Testimony in Low Speed Cases" by Robert Mahoney, *Trial Excellence*, Vol. 13, No 6 (Esquire One, 2001); see generally *Plaintiffs' Lawyers Guide to Minor Impact Cervical and Lumbar Injury* (Thomson West).

Whiting v. Coultrip, 324 Ill. App. 3d 161, 164–69, 258 Ill. Dec. 111, 755 N.E.2d 494 (3d Dist. 2001), as modified on denial of reh'g, (Sept. 12, 2001) (biomechanical evidence should not have been admitted when the evidence was not shown to be generally accepted in the relevant scientific community and was not proven reliable. However, the court noted that it was not saying that such evidence could not be admissible if a proper foundation under *Frye* was established).

For a more detailed discussion of the exclusion of expert evidence in low-speed cases, see § 10:160, Supporting authorities—Low-speed impact automobile cases, infra.

§ 5:36 Supporting authorities—Statistical evidence—Exclusion of confusing evidence, generally

Federal Rule of Evidence 403 states:

> Although relevant, evidence may be excluded if its probative value is substantially outweighed by the danger of unfair prejudice, *confusion of the issues, or misleading the jury*, or by considerations of undue delay, waste of time, or needless presentation of cumulative evidence. (Emphasis added.)

It must be noted that this Rule has not been codified in Illinois. However, Illinois cases have stated that Illinois has a common-law rule that is comparable to Federal Rule of Evidence 403. See *People v. Walker*, 335 Ill. App. 3d 102, 112, 268 Ill. Dec. 654, 779 N.E.2d 268 (2d Dist. 2002), as modified on denial of reh'g, (Oct. 24, 2002) and judgment aff'd, 211 Ill. 2d 317, 285 Ill. Dec. 519, 812 N.E.2d 339 (2004); and *People v. Peete*, 318 Ill. App. 3d 961, 966–67, 252 Ill. Dec. 821, 743 N.E.2d 689 (4th Dist. 2001). Therefore, it is arguable that Federal Rule of Evidence 403 can be considered as persuasive authority in Illinois.

Congregation of the Passion, Holy Cross Province v. Touche Ross & Co., 224 Ill. App. 3d 559, 578–79, 166 Ill. Dec. 642, 586 N.E.2d 600 (1st Dist. 1991), judgment aff'd, 159 Ill. 2d 137, 201 Ill. Dec. 71, 636 N.E.2d 503 (1994) (proper to exclude relevant evidence to prevent jury confusion).

Regarding confusing evidence, see also § 2:9 to § 2:12, supra.

§ 5:37 Supporting authorities—Statistical evidence—Disapproved statistics evidence

Avery v. State Farm Mut. Auto. Ins. Co., 216 Ill. 2d 100, 149–50, 296 Ill. Dec. 448, 835 N.E.2d 801 (2005) (where an expert testified on cross-examination that his damage calculation could have been in error by as much as one billion, the damage award was speculative and unconstitutional).

In re Marriage of Jawad and Whalen, 326 Ill. App. 3d 141, 150–54, 259 Ill. Dec. 941, 759 N.E.2d 1002 (2d Dist. 2001) (when a psychological opinion relies upon the literature and studies of others, the trial judge must examine the underlying information to determine whether it is reliable).

Fetzer v. Wood, 211 Ill. App. 3d 70, 81-86, 155 Ill. Dec. 626, 569 N.E.2d 1237 (2d Dist. 1991) (statistical evidence not permitted to demonstrate the value of the loss of life because that decision is within the knowledge of an average juror).

Mercado v. Ahmed, 756 F. Supp. 1097, 1098–1103, 32 Fed. R. Evid. Serv. 397 (N.D. Ill. 1991) (statistical evidence is not admissible in a personal injury action to explain loss of enjoyment of life because that decision is within the knowledge of the average jury).

Sherrod v. Berry, 629 F. Supp. 159, 164 (N.D. Ill. 1985), judgment aff'd, 827 F.2d 195, 23 Fed. R. Evid. Serv. 708 (7th Cir. 1987), reh'g granted and opinion vacated, 835 F.2d 1222 (7th Cir. 1988), on reh'g en banc, 856 F.2d 802, 26 Fed. R. Evid. Serv. 875 (7th Cir. 1988) and judgment rev'd, 856 F.2d 802, 26 Fed. R. Evid. Serv. 875 (7th Cir. 1988) (first widely reported case accepting admissibility of hedonic damage testimony); but see *Ayers v. Robinson*, 887 F. Supp. 1049, 1064, 42 Fed. R. Evid. Serv. 308 (N.D. Ill. 1995) (hedonic damage testimony excluded, as falling short of *Daubert* standards).

Department of Transp. v. Bouy, 69 Ill. App. 3d 29, 33-38, 25 Ill. Dec. 499, 386 N.E.2d 1163 (4th Dist. 1979) (expert's testimony was properly excluded when it was based upon a speculative and conjectural method of determining value).

§ 5:38 Supporting authorities—Statistical evidence—Statistics in employment discrimination cases

Walther v. Lone Star Gas Co., 952 F.2d 119, 124 (5th Cir. 1992) (rejected by, Coffey v. Fayette Tubular Products, 929 S.W.2d 326 (Tenn. 1996)) (in age discrimination cases, where innumerable groupings of employees are possible according to ages and divisions within the corporate structure, statistics are easily manipulated and may be deceptive).

Williams v. Cerberonics, Inc., 871 F.2d 452, 455, n. 1 (4th Cir. 1989) ("[R]aw statistics devoid of any context which relates those statistics to the alleged discriminatory practice are of minimal probative value.").

§ 5:39 Supporting authorities—Blood hound evidence

People v. Stewart, 229 Ill. App. 3d 886, 889, 171 Ill. Dec. 577, 594 N.E.2d 429 (5th Dist. 1992) (bloodhound tracking evidence is not admissible in Illinois).

But see the dissent: *People v. Stewart*, 229 Ill. App. 3d 886, 891, 171 Ill. Dec. 577, 594 N.E.2d 429 (5th Dist. 1992) (bloodhound tracking evidence was relevant and the reliability of it should have been considered).

§ 5:40 Opposing authorities—In general

In re Marriage of Bates, 212 Ill. 2d 489, 518–22, 525, 289 Ill. Dec. 218, 819 N.E.2d 714 (2004) (trial court allowed testimony regarding parental alienation syndrome after a *Frye* hearing; note however, that appellate court discussed conflict in many jurisdictions and in scientific arena surrounding evidence and declined to determine whether evidence was proper because judge did not rely on that term for decision).

Donaldson v. Central Illinois Public Service Co., 199 Ill. 2d 63, 80, 262 Ill. Dec. 854, 767 N.E.2d 314 (2002) (abrogated by, In re Commitment of Simons, 213 Ill. 2d 523, 290 Ill. Dec. 610, 821 N.E.2d 1184 (2004)) (court would not consider whether to adopt the standard for the admission of scientific evidence that was set forth in *Daubert* because the issue was not raised by the parties) (See *Daubert v. Merrell Dow Pharmaceuticals, Inc.*, 509 U.S. 579, 113 S. Ct. 2786, 125 L. Ed. 2d 469, 37, 37 Fed. R. Evid. Serv. 1 (1993)).

Donaldson v. Central Illinois Public Service Co., 199 Ill. 2d 63, 79-82, 262 Ill. Dec. 854, 767 N.E.2d 314 (2002) (abrogated by, In re Commitment of Simons, 213 Ill. 2d 523, 290 Ill. Dec. 610, 821 N.E.2d 1184 (2004)) (Illinois does not follow the "*Frye*-plus reliability" standard and therefore, once a scientific methodology has been determined to be generally accepted in the relevant community, a trial judge should not conduct additional hearings regarding whether the opinion itself is reliable) (see *Daubert v. Merrell Dow Pharmaceuticals, Inc.*, 509 U.S. 579, 113 S. Ct. 2786, 125 L. Ed. 2d 469, 37, 37 Fed. R. Evid. Serv. 1 (1993)).

§ 5:41 Opposing authorities—In general—Weight vs. admissibility

Donaldson v. Central Illinois Public Service Co., 199 Ill. 2d 63, 79-82, 262 Ill. Dec. 854, 767 N.E.2d 314 (2002) (abrogated by, In re Commitment of Simons, 213 Ill. 2d 523, 290 Ill. Dec. 610, 821 N.E.2d 1184 (2004)) (questions regarding the underlying information the expert used or the manner in which the expert applied a generally accepted methodology go to the weight and not the admissibility of the evidence).

People v. Dalcollo, 282 Ill. App. 3d 944, 957, 218 Ill. Dec. 435, 669 N.E.2d 378 (2d Dist. 1996) (disagreements with the actual procedures used in a specific case affect the weight and not the admissibility of the evidence).

People v. Henne, 165 Ill. App. 3d 315, 325–26, 116 Ill. Dec. 296, 518 N.E.2d 1276 (4th Dist. 1988) (fact that in court measurements of a boot differed from the measurements of the boot print went to the weight of the comparison testimony and not its admissibility).

People v. McGee, 88 Ill. App. 3d 447, 452–53, 43 Ill. Dec. 641, 410 N.E.2d 641 (2d Dist. 1980) (trial judge improperly excluded evidence of an absorption inhibition test on vaginal fluid on the grounds that the experts disagreed about whether the test had been performed in a manner that would produce accurate results, because it was for the jury to decide the weight of the evidence).

§ 5:42 Opposing authorities—In general—Where *Frye* test not required

Wartalski v. JSB Const. and Consulting Co., 384 Ill.App.3d 139, 144–47, 892 N.E.2d 122 (1st Dist. 2008) (a *Frye* hearing is not required before a treating physician can provide an opinion regarding the cause of the plaintiff's condition).

Noakes v. National R.R. Passenger Corp., 363 Ill. App. 3d 851, 855–57, 300 Ill. Dec. 593, 845 N.E.2d 14 (1st Dist. 2006) (no *Frye* hearing was required where the testimony at issue did not address new or novel theories).

Noakes v. National R.R. Passenger Corp., 363 Ill. App. 3d 851, 855–57, 300 Ill. Dec. 593, 845 N.E.2d 14 (1st Dist. 2006) (the issue of whether or not repetitive motion could cause carpal tunnel syndrome was not new or novel).

Noakes v. National R.R. Passenger Corp., 363 Ill. App. 3d 851, 855–59, 300 Ill. Dec. 593, 845 N.E.2d 14 (1st Dist. 2006) ("pure opinion" testimony based upon the expert's own training and knowledge is not subject to a *Frye* analysis).

Elam v. Lincoln Elec. Co., 362 Ill. App. 3d 884, 897–98, 299 Ill. Dec. 305, 841 N.E.2d 1037 (5th Dist. 2005) (an expert's opinion that was based upon the expert's own experience and knowledge was not subject to a *Frye* analysis).

In re K.T., 361 Ill. App. 3d 187, 201–03, 297 Ill. Dec. 38, 836 N.E.2d 769 (1st Dist. 2005) (there was no plain error caused when experts were permitted to provide opinions regarding whether a party suffered from factitious disorder by proxy, without a *Frye* hearing, even though there was evidence that there was disagreement among experts about that alleged disorder).

Donaldson v. Central Illinois Public Service Co., 199 Ill. 2d 63, 77-78, 262 Ill. Dec. 854, 767 N.E.2d 314 (2002) (abrogated by, In re Commitment of Simons, 213 Ill. 2d 523, 290 Ill. Dec. 610, 821 N.E.2d 1184 (2004)) (trial judge does not need to conduct a *Frye* hearing when the methodology underlying the evidence is not "novel" or "new").

People v. Shanahan, 323 Ill. App. 3d 835, 838–39, 257 Ill. Dec. 402, 753 N.E.2d 1028 (1st Dist. 2001) (trial court does not need to conduct a *Frye* hearing if the same type of scientific evidence has been admitted in other Illinois cases).

People v. Thomas, 137 Ill. 2d 500, 517–18, 148 Ill. Dec. 751, 561 N.E.2d 57 (1990) (*Frye* analysis not required when the test has been determined to be reliable in other Illinois cases).

People v. Israel, 181 Ill. App. 3d 851, 861–62, 130 Ill. Dec. 795, 537 N.E.2d 1124 (2d Dist. 1989) (*Frye* analysis not required before admitting testimony that a psychiatric nurse assigned numbers to each factor she considered in forming her opinion because her scoring system did not involve a scientific test or theory).

See also 725 ILCS 5/115-7.2, which provides that in criminal cases for certain sexual offenses and abuse offenses, testimony by an expert who is qualified by the court regarding, "any recognized and accepted form of post-traumatic stress syndrome shall be admissible as evidence"; and 735 ILCS 5/8-1501, which states,

> Comparison. In all courts of this State it shall be lawful to prove handwriting by comparison made by the witness or jury with writings properly in the files of records of the case, admitted in evidence or treated as genuine or admitted to be genuine, by the party against whom the evidence is offered, or proved to be genuine to the satisfaction of the court.

§ 5:43 Opposing authorities—In general—Approved tests

Note that a number of tests have been approved by appellate courts in this state, and therefore admissible without the need for a *Frye* evaluation [See *Donaldson v. Central Illinois Public Service Co.*, 199 Ill. 2d 63, 78-79, 262 Ill. Dec. 854, 767 N.E.2d 314 (2002) (abrogated by, In re Commitment of Simons, 213 Ill. 2d 523, 290 Ill. Dec. 610, 821 N.E.2d 1184 (2004))]. The following list includes some of the more widely used tests that have met with court approval:

- Maternal Labor Force Theory [*Ruffin ex rel. Sanders v. Boler*, 384 Ill.App.3d 7, 18–25, 890 N.E.2d 1174 (1st Dist. 2008)]
- SPECT scans [*Donnellan v. First Student, Inc*, 383 Ill.App.3d 1040, 1057–61, 891 N.E.2d 463 (1st Dist. 2008)]

- Temporal Relationship [*Wartalski v. JSB Const. and Consulting Co.*, 384 Ill.App.3d 139, 144–47, 892 N.E.2d 122 (1st Dist. 2008)]
- DNA Typing. [*People v. Dalcollo*, 282 Ill. App. 3d 944, 951–60, 218 Ill. Dec. 435, 669 N.E.2d 378 (2d Dist. 1996); *People v. Almighty Four Hundred*, 287 Ill. App. 3d 123, 128–30, 222 Ill. Dec. 533, 677 N.E.2d 1332 (1st Dist. 1997); *People v. Miller*, 173 Ill. 2d 167, 183–90, 219 Ill. Dec. 43, 670 N.E.2d 721 (1996) (abrogated by, In re Commitment of Simons, 213 Ill. 2d 523, 290 Ill. Dec. 610, 821 N.E.2d 1184 (2004))]
- Electrophoretic Testing [*People v. Lopez*, 228 Ill. App. 3d 1061, 1073–74, 170 Ill. Dec. 758, 593 N.E.2d 647 (1st Dist. 1992); *People v. Thomas*, 137 Ill. 2d 500, 517–18, 148 Ill. Dec. 751, 561 N.E.2d 57 (1990); *People v. Partee*, 157 Ill. App. 3d 231, 260–63, 110 Ill. Dec. 845, 511 N.E.2d 1165 (1st Dist. 1987)]
- Footprint Identification [*People v. Henne*, 165 Ill. App. 3d 315, 325–26, 116 Ill. Dec. 296, 518 N.E.2d 1276 (4th Dist. 1988); *People v. Hanson*, 31 Ill. 2d 31, 39-40, 198 N.E.2d 815 (1964)]
- Bite-Mark Identification [*People v. Milone*, 43 Ill. App. 3d 385, 390–99, 2 Ill. Dec. 63, 356 N.E.2d 1350 (2d Dist. 1976); *People v. Williams*, 128 Ill. App. 3d 384, 398, 83 Ill. Dec. 720, 470 N.E.2d 1140 (4th Dist. 1984)]
- Fingerprint Comparison and Testing [*People v. Eyler*, 133 Ill. 2d 173, 214–16, 139 Ill. Dec. 756, 549 N.E.2d 268 (1989); *People v. Jennings*, 252 Ill. 534, 546–51, 96 N.E. 1077 (1911)]
- HGN Sobriety Tests [*People v. Basler*, 193 Ill. 2d 545, 551, 251 Ill. Dec. 171, 740 N.E.2d 1 (2000)]; but see *People v. Herring*, 327 Ill. App. 3d 259, 262, 261 Ill. Dec. 259, 762 N.E.2d 1186 (4th Dist. 2002) (trial court should conduct a *Frye* hearing before admitting HGN sobriety tests)
- Child Abuse Accommodation Syndrome [*People v. Pollard*, 225 Ill. App. 3d 970, 976, 168 Ill. Dec. 61, 589 N.E.2d 175 (3d Dist. 1992); *People v. Wasson*, 211 Ill. App. 3d 264, 269–72, 155 Ill. Dec. 710, 569 N.E.2d 1321 (4th Dist. 1991)]
- Handwriting Analysis [735 ILCS 5/8-1501 states, "Comparison. In all courts of this State it shall be lawful to prove handwriting by comparison made by the witness or jury with writings properly in the files of records of the case, admitted in evidence or treated as genuine or admitted to be genuine, by the party against whom the evidence is offered, or proved to be genuine to the satisfaction of

the court;" see also *People v. Smith*, 318 Ill. 114, 123–27, 149 N.E. 3 (1925).]

- Actuarial Risk Assessment Regarding Recidivism [*In re Commitment of Simons*, 213 Ill. 2d 523, 533–43, 290 Ill. Dec. 610, 821 N.E.2d 1184 (2004)]
- Penile Plethysmograph (PPG) test [*In re Commitment of Sandry*, 367 Ill. App. 3d 949, 967-77, 306 Ill. Dec. 202, 857 N.E.2d 295 (2d Dist. 2006)]

See also 725 ILCS 5/115-7.2, which provides that in criminal cases for certain sexual offenses and abuse offenses, testimony by an expert who is qualified by the court regarding, "any recognized and accepted form of post-traumatic stress syndrome shall be admissible as evidence."

See also *Petraski v. Thedos*, 382 Ill. App. 3d 22, 320 Ill. Dec. 244, 887 N.E.2d 24 (1st Dist. 2008), appeal denied, 229 Ill. 2d 657, 325 Ill. Dec. 15, 897 N.E.2d 263 (2008) (trial court erred by excluding an expert's opinion regarding the plaintiff's intoxication that was based upon extrapolation from blood that was drawn after the incident in question because the evidence was relevant and reliable and not unfairly prejudicial).

§ 5:44 Opposing authorities—In general—Judicial notice

People v. Lopez, 228 Ill. App. 3d 1061, 1073–74, 170 Ill. Dec. 758, 593 N.E.2d 647 (1st Dist. 1992) (trial judge can take judicial notice that a methodology has been determined to be reliable).

People v. Thomas, 137 Ill. 2d 500, 517–18, 148 Ill. Dec. 751, 561 N.E.2d 57 (1990) (proper to take judicial notice of the general acceptance of a scientific test when the test has been accepted as reliable in other Illinois cases).

But see *People v. Owens*, 155 Ill. App. 3d 990, 998, 108 Ill. Dec. 511, 508 N.E.2d 1088 (4th Dist. 1987) (trial judge *should not have* taken judicial notice of whether blood-spatter evidence is reliable without conducting a hearing).

§ 5:45 Opposing authorities—Hedonic damages

Sherrod v. Berry, 629 F. Supp. 159, 164 (N.D. Ill. 1985), judgment aff'd, 827 F.2d 195, 23 Fed. R. Evid. Serv. 708 (7th Cir. 1987), reh'g granted and opinion vacated, 835 F.2d 1222 (7th Cir. 1988), on reh'g en banc, 856 F.2d 802, 26 Fed. R. Evid. Serv. 875 (7th Cir. 1988) and judgment rev'd, 856 F.2d 802, 26 Fed. R. Evid. Serv. 875 (7th Cir. 1988) (first widely reported case accepting admissibility of hedonic damage testimony); but see *Ayers v. Robinson*, 887 F. Supp. 1049, 1064, 42 Fed. R. Evid. Serv. 308 (N.D. Ill. 1995) (hedonic damage testimony excluded, as falling short of *Daubert* standards).

§ 5:46 Opposing authorities—Truth serum

People v. Wolfram, 12 Ill. App. 3d 262, 266, 298 N.E.2d 188 (1st Dist. 1973) (not improper to admit evidence that resulted from a defendant's confession when the confession occurred while the defendant was under the influence of drugs that allegedly had effects that were similar to "truth serum" type drugs).

§ 5:47 Opposing authorities—Polygraph evidence—Stipulation or agreement of parties

Alm v. General Tel. Co. of Illinois, 27 Ill. App. 3d 876, 879, 881–82, 327 N.E.2d 523 (4th Dist. 1975) (not error to cross-examine the plaintiff about the results of a polygraph test when the plaintiff had volunteered to take the test).

Rotheimer v. Rotheimer, 34 Ill. App. 2d 1, 4-6, 180 N.E.2d 356 (1st Dist. 1962) (not improper for a trial judge to order a polygraph test when the party ordered to take it requested the order).

§ 5:48 Opposing authorities—Polygraph evidence—Where used for investigative purposes

People v. Avery, 227 Ill. App. 3d 382, 390–92, 169 Ill. Dec. 542, 592 N.E.2d 29 (1st Dist. 1991) (not improper to admit evidence of a polygraph when the issue was the voluntariness of the defendant's statements).

People v. Thomas, 137 Ill. 2d 500, 516, 148 Ill. Dec. 751, 561 N.E.2d 57 (1990) (polygraph test was properly used for investigative purposes and it did not make the defendant's confession involuntary).

But see *People v. Baynes*, 88 Ill. 2d 225, 230–45, 58 Ill. Dec. 819, 430 N.E.2d 1070 (1981) (polygraph results are not reliable evidence and thus, they are not admissible into evidence even if the parties stipulate to them).

§ 5:49 Opposing authorities—Psychological tests and syndromes—Rape trauma syndrome

People v. Eiskant, 253 Ill. App. 3d 773, 776, 192 Ill. Dec. 863, 625 N.E.2d 1018 (5th Dist. 1993) (trial judge should have allowed evidence that the victim exhibited symptoms that were consistent with the symptoms of rape trauma syndrome).

But see *People v. Williams*, 332 Ill. App. 3d 693, 697–99, 266 Ill. Dec. 168, 773 N.E.2d 1238 (3d Dist. 2002) (trial judge should not have admitted expert evidence on the issue of the cycle of violence because it represented improper comment on the credibility of a witness).

725 ILCS 5/115-7.2 provides that in criminal cases for certain sexual offenses and abuse offenses testimony by an expert who is qualified by the court regarding, "any recognized and accepted form of post-traumatic stress syndrome shall be admissible as evidence").

§ 5:50 Opposing authorities—Psychological tests and syndromes—Child molestation syndrome

People v. Pollard, 225 Ill. App. 3d 970, 976, 168 Ill. Dec. 61, 589 N.E.2d 175 (3d Dist. 1992) (child sexual abuse accommodation syndrome is a recognized form of post-traumatic stress syndrome and evidence of it is therefore, *admissible* in criminal sexual abuse cases) accord *People v. Wasson*, 211 Ill. App. 3d 264, 269–72, 155 Ill. Dec. 710, 569 N.E.2d 1321 (4th Dist. 1991)].

But see *People v. Williams*, 332 Ill. App. 3d 693, 697–99, 266 Ill. Dec. 168, 773 N.E.2d 1238 (3d Dist. 2002) (trial judge should not have admitted expert evidence on the issue of the cycle of violence because it represented improper comment on the credibility of a witness); and *People v. Shanahan*, 323 Ill. App. 3d 835, 838–39, 257 Ill. Dec. 402, 753 N.E.2d 1028 (1st Dist. 2001) (Illinois cases have not decided whether battered child syndrome is admissible and therefore, a *Frye* hearing is required before offering such evidence).

See also 725 ILCS 5/115-7.2, which provides that in criminal cases for certain sexual offenses and abuse offenses testimony from an expert who is qualified by the court regarding, "any recognized and accepted form of post-traumatic stress syndrome shall be admissible as evidence."

§ 5:51 Opposing authorities—Hypnosis evidence

People v. Lampkin, 193 Ill. App. 3d 570, 576–77, 140 Ill. Dec. 642, 550 N.E.2d 278 (3d Dist. 1990) (pre-hypnotic recall by a witness can be admitted if the proponent of the evidence proves that it was in fact pre-hypnotic recall).

People v. Zayas, 131 Ill. 2d 284, 297, 137 Ill. Dec. 568, 546

N.E.2d 513 (1989) (pre-hypnotic recall by a witness can be admitted if the proponent of the evidence proves that it was in fact pre-hypnotic recall).

Rock v. Arkansas, 483 U.S. 44, 57–61, 107 S. Ct. 2704, 97 L. Ed. 2d 37, 22 Fed. R. Evid. Serv. 1128 (1987) (reliability of hypnosis-refreshed testimony generally is uncertain, but certain corroborating evidence, procedural safeguards, and circumstances of the hypnosis may support reliability; a state's legitimate interest in barring unreliable evidence does not extend to per se exclusion of the defendant's right to testify).

§ 5:52 Opposing authorities—Statistics evidence—General acceptance

People v. Vercolio, 363 Ill. App. 3d 232, 236–37, 300 Ill. Dec. 159, 843 N.E.2d 417 (3d Dist. 2006) ("25 variable test" for sex offender recidivism, which was used by an expert as the basis for an opinion, was sufficiently accepted in the relevant field under a *Frye* analysis).

People v. Taylor, 357 Ill. App. 3d 1033, 1034–39, 294 Ill. Dec. 443, 830 N.E.2d 855 (2d Dist. 2005) (expert testimony about actuarial instruments related to whether defendant would reoffend was admissible).

In re Commitment of Simons, 213 Ill. 2d 523, 533–43, 290 Ill. Dec. 610, 821 N.E.2d 1184 (2004) (actuarial risk assessment regarding recidivism of sex offenders has gained sufficient scientific acceptance to be admissible). [*Note that this case resolved a prior conflict among the districts regarding the necessity of a Frye hearing for such instruments.*]

Donaldson v. Central Illinois Public Service Co., 199 Ill. 2d 63, 262 Ill. Dec. 854, 767 N.E.2d 314 (2002) (abrogated by, In re Commitment of Simons, 213 Ill. 2d 523, 290 Ill. Dec. 610, 821 N.E.2d 1184 (2004)) (The exclusive test for admission of expert testimony in Illinois is governed by Frye v. U.S., 293 F. 1013, 34 A.L.R. 145 (App. D.C. 1923) (rejected by, State v. Walstad, 119 Wis. 2d 483, 351 N.W.2d 469 (1984)) and (rejected by, State v. Brown, 297 Or. 404, 687 P.2d 751 (1984)) and (rejected by, Nelson v. State, 628 A.2d 69 (Del. 1993)) and (rejected by, State v. Alberico, 116 N.M. 156, 861 P.2d 192 (1993)) and (rejected by, State v. Moore, 268 Mont. 20, 885 P.2d 457 (1994)) and (rejected by, State v. Faught, 127 Idaho 873, 908 P.2d 566 (1995)) and (rejected by, People v. Shreck, 22 P.3d 68, 90 A.L.R.5th 765 (Colo. 2001)), which provides that scientific evidence is only admissible at trial if the methodology or scientific principle upon which the opinion is based is sufficiently established or gained general acceptance in the particular field in which it belongs).

People v. Almighty Four Hundred, 287 Ill. App. 3d 123, 128–35, 222 Ill. Dec. 533, 677 N.E.2d 1332 (1st Dist. 1997) (method used for statistical probabilities for DNA typing was generally accepted).

People v. Pope, 284 Ill. App. 3d 695, 704–05, 220 Ill. Dec. 309, 672 N.E.2d 1321 (4th Dist. 1996) (when statistics form the basis for an accepted method of arriving at an opinion then the statistical evidence is admissible).

People v. Miller, 173 Ill. 2d 167, 183–90, 219 Ill. Dec. 43, 670 N.E.2d 721 (1996) (abrogated by, In re Commitment of Simons, 213 Ill. 2d 523, 290 Ill. Dec. 610, 821 N.E.2d 1184 (2004)) (methods used for statistical probabilities for DNA typing were generally accepted).

Akiba South Side Jewish Day School and Open Kitchens, Inc. v. State, 36 Ill. Ct. Cl. 119, 1983 WL 507977 (Ill. Ct. Cl. 1983) (statistical evidence allowed despite disagreement among experts regarding the accuracy of them).

§ 5:53 Opposing authorities—Statistics evidence—Weight vs. admissibility relating to statistics issue

People v. Almighty Four Hundred, 287 Ill. App. 3d 123, 128–35, 222 Ill. Dec. 533, 677 N.E.2d 1332 (1st Dist. 1997) (method used for statistical probabilities for DNA typing was generally accepted and any defects in the method of compiling the statistics affected the weight and not the admissibility of the testimony of the expert who relied upon the statistics).

People v. Israel, 181 Ill. App. 3d 851, 862, 130 Ill. Dec. 795, 537 N.E.2d 1124 (2d Dist. 1989) (method used by a psychiatric expert to arrive at a diagnosis went to the weight of the opinion and not its admissibility).

§ 5:54 Opposing authorities—Statistics evidence—Compare: Psychological profiling

People v. Israel, 181 Ill. App. 3d 851, 861–62, 130 Ill. Dec. 795, 537 N.E.2d 1124 (2d Dist. 1989) (*Frye* analysis not required before admitting testimony that a psychiatric nurse assigned numbers to each factor she considered in forming her diagnosis because her scoring system did not involve a scientific test or theory).

§ 5:55 Opposing authorities—Accident reconstruction and biomechanical evidence

Fronabarger v. Burns, 385 Ill.App.3d 560, 565–66, 895 N.E.2d 1125 (5th Dist. 2008) (trial court had discretion to determine that a neurologist was qualified to provide an opinion regarding the correlation between the amount of damage to vehicles and the severity of injury to occupants of the vehicles).

Canopy v. Hentz, 345 Ill. App. 3d 797, 801–03, 281 Ill. Dec. 254, 803 N.E.2d 658 (3d Dist. 2004) (no error in allowing jury to conclude that an impact was not severe, based upon photographs that depicted only a small amount of damage to vehicle, despite plaintiff's claim that impact was severe).

Whiting v. Coultrip, 324 Ill. App. 3d 161, 164–69, 258 Ill. Dec. 111, 755 N.E.2d 494 (3d Dist. 2001), as modified on denial of reh'g, (Sept. 12, 2001) (evidence could be admissible if a proper foundation under *Frye* is established).

Brown v. Ford Motor Co., 306 Ill. App. 3d 314, 317–18, 239 Ill. Dec. 637, 714 N.E.2d 556 (1st Dist. 1999) (trial judge did not abuse its discretion by admitting videotapes of accident reconstruction, even when some of them were shown in slow motion).

Rios v. Navistar Intern. Transp. Corp., 200 Ill. App. 3d 526, 536–37, 146 Ill. Dec. 289, 558 N.E.2d 252 (1st Dist. 1990) (trial judge had discretion to admit accident reconstruction evidence when the evidence was helpful to the trier of fact).

Augenstein v. Pulley, 191 Ill. App. 3d 664, 671–81, 138 Ill. Dec. 724, 547 N.E.2d 1345 (5th Dist. 1989) (whether accident reconstruction evidence should be admissible should be decided in the same fashion as any other type of expert testimony. Specifically, the court should examine whether the expert is qualified in the field and whether the evidence would be helpful to the jury).

For additional opposition citations regarding a motion to exclude accident reconstruction and biomechanical evidence, see §§ 10:166 et seq., infra.

II. SAMPLE MOTIONS

§ 5:56 Motion to exclude evidence of statistical analysis

TO: ALL PARTIES AND THEIR RESPECTIVE ATTORNEYS OF RECORD:

PLEASE TAKE NOTICE that the plaintiff hereby moves

this Court for an order excluding any and all evidence, references to evidence, testimony or argument relating to an internal report prepared by the defendant entitled "Low-Speed Seatback Failure: A Statistical Report," dated May 4, 1999.

This motion is made under the provisions of Illinois case law; and is based on the attached Memorandum of Points and Authorities, the pleadings and papers on file in this action, and upon such of the argument and evidence as may be presented prior to or at the hearing of this matter.

Dated: *[date]*

MEMORANDUM OF POINTS AND AUTHORITIES

1.
PRELIMINARY STATEMENT

This is a products liability action arising from a failed "seatback" on the plaintiff's 1996 Ranchster automobile. The underlying accident occurred on February 2, 1998, when plaintiff's vehicle, which was stopped at a red light, was rear-ended by a mid-sized sedan at a speed of approximately 35 miles. As a result of the accident, the plaintiff's driver-side seatback failed and threw the plaintiff head-first into the rear seat, breaking the plaintiff's C-2 vertebrae.

The issue raised by this motion relates to an internal report prepared by the defendant automobile manufacturer entitled "Low-Speed Seatback Failure: A Statistical Report" ("Report"). This Report is a compilation of repair records for the 1997 and 1998 model years of the Ranchster vehicle, analyzing seatback failure in rear-end accidents at speeds from 1–15 miles per hour. Not surprisingly, this self-serving document, prepared in anticipation of this litigation, shows no seatback failure at such low speeds.

By this motion, the plaintiff seeks to exclude this Report as irrelevant, confusing and prejudicial.

2.
THIS COURT MAY EXCLUDE IRRELEVANT EVIDENCE

Evidence Federal Rule of Evidence 401 defines relevancy as,

> evidence having any tendency to make the existence of any fact that is of consequence to the determination of the action more probable or less probable than it would be without the evidence.

Illinois has adopted this definition of relevancy through case law. *Spencer v. Wandolowski*, 264 Ill. App. 3d 611, 617, 201 Ill. Dec. 422, 636 N.E.2d 854 (1st Dist. 1994); and *People v. Monroe*,

66 Ill. 2d 317, 321–22, 5 Ill. Dec. 824, 362 N.E.2d 295 (1977). See also *Preston ex rel. Preston v. Simmons*, 321 Ill. App. 3d 789, 803, 254 Ill. Dec. 647, 747 N.E.2d 1059 (1st Dist. 2001) (trial judge should not permit such wide latitude on cross-examination that it undermines the rule that only relevant evidence is admissible).

In the present case, defendant's Report is clearly irrelevant and should be excluded. The Report is a compilation of repair records relating to seatback failure for the *1997* and *1998* model years of the Ranchster vehicle. The plaintiff's vehicle is a *1996* model—manufactured *prior to the adoption of a more rigid seatback design* which was added beginning with the 1997 models. Furthermore, the Report focuses on seatback failure in accidents of 1–15 miles per hour. The plaintiff's accident occurred at rate of 35 miles per hour, a much greater rate of speed.

Because the report has no rational bearing on the facts of this case, it is clearly irrelevant and should be excluded. Further, as is discussed below, because of this clear lack of relevance, there is a great danger that the jurors will be confused, to the detriment of the plaintiff.

3.

THIS COURT MAY EXCLUDE CONFUSING OR PREJUDICIAL STATISTICAL EVIDENCE

Evidence Federal Rule of Evidence 403 states:

> Although relevant, evidence may be excluded if its probative value is substantially outweighed by the danger of unfair prejudice, *confusion of the issues, or misleading the jury*, or by considerations of undue delay, waste of time, or needless presentation of cumulative evidence. (Emphasis added.)

Although this Rule has not been specifically codified in Illinois, Illinois cases have stated that Illinois has a common-law rule that is comparable to Federal Rule of Evidence 403. See *People v. Walker*, 335 Ill. App. 3d 102, 112, 268 Ill. Dec. 654, 779 N.E.2d 268 (2d Dist. 2002), as modified on denial of reh'g, (Oct. 24, 2002) and judgment aff'd, 211 Ill. 2d 317, 285 Ill. Dec. 519, 812 N.E.2d 339 (2004); and *People v. Peete*, 318 Ill. App. 3d 961, 966–67, 252 Ill. Dec. 821, 743 N.E.2d 689 (4th Dist. 2001). Therefore, Federal Rule of Evidence 403 should be considered as persuasive authority in Illinois.

The Court may exclude unreliable or potentially confusing evidence. See *Bachman v. General Motors Corp.*, 332 Ill. App. 3d 760, 785–88, 267 Ill. Dec. 125, 776 N.E.2d 262 (4th Dist. 2002) (exclusion of prior occurrence evidence because the admission of it would confuse and mislead the jury); *Whiting v. Coultrip*, 324 Ill. App. 3d 161, 164–69, 258 Ill. Dec. 111, 755 N.E.2d 494 (3d Dist. 2001), as modified on denial of reh'g, (Sept. 12, 2001) (biomechanical evidence should not have been admitted when the evidence was not shown to be generally accepted in the relevant scientific community and was not proven reliable); *Hulman v. Evanston Hosp. Corp.*, 259 Ill. App. 3d 133, 147–49, 197 Ill. Dec. 319, 631 N.E.2d 322 (1st Dist. 1994) (exclusion of hospital pamphlet because there was already testimony about it and because it included irrelevant material that might confuse the jury); and *Congregation of the Passion, Holy Cross Province v. Touche Ross & Co.*, 224 Ill. App. 3d 559, 578–79, 166 Ill. Dec. 642, 586 N.E.2d 600 (1st Dist. 1991), judgment aff'd, 159 Ill. 2d 137, 201 Ill. Dec. 71, 636 N.E.2d 503 (1994) (proper to exclude relevant evidence to prevent jury confusion).

In addition, the Court may look at the evidence underlying the defendant's report in order to determine the admissibility of it. *In re Marriage of Jawad and Whalen*, 326 Ill. App. 3d 141, 150–54, 259 Ill. Dec. 941, 759 N.E.2d 1002 (2d Dist. 2001) (when an opinion relies upon the literature and studies of others, the trial judge must examine the underlying information to determine whether it is reliable); *Modelski v. Navistar Intern. Transp. Corp.*, 302 Ill. App. 3d 879, 884–86, 236 Ill. Dec. 394, 707 N.E.2d 239 (1st Dist. 1999) (accident reconstruction evidence should not have been admitted when it was based upon the expert's speculation regarding what occurred); *Fetzer v. Wood*, 211 Ill. App. 3d 70, 81-86, 155 Ill. Dec. 626, 569 N.E.2d 1237 (2d Dist. 1991) (statistical evidence not permitted to demonstrate the value of the loss of life because that decision is within the knowledge of an average jury); and *Mercado v. Ahmed*, 756 F. Supp. 1097, 1098–1103, 32 Fed. R. Evid. Serv. 397 (N.D. Ill. 1991) (statistical evidence is not admissible in a personal injury action to explain loss of enjoyment of life because that decision is within the knowledge of the average jury).

In the present case, the defendant's Report contains misleading and confusing *pseudoscientific* speculations that should be excluded. The Report contains an internal analysis of seatback failure at rates of speed significantly lower than the speed of the subject accident. In addition, the Report analyzes accidents with newer Ranchster models, manufactured after important safety features were added to prevent exactly the type of failure that occurred in this case. Because of key differences between the analyzed data and the facts of this case, there is a very real danger that the jurors will be confused by the Report's findings, which shows no seatback failure in newer Ranchster vehicles.

The Report, which was prepared in anticipation of this litigation, *excludes key data* regarding the rate of speed and the model year involved in the subject accident. To allow this evidence would create undue prejudice to the plaintiff based upon the danger of jury confusion, while adding absolutely nothing of material value for the jury's consideration.

As such, it is respectfully requested that the Court exclude the Report and any mention of the findings contained therein.

Dated: *[date]*

By: ________________________
[name of counsel]
Attorneys for PLAINTIFF,
[name of plaintiff]

Chapter 6

Discovery Motions

I. MOTION AUTHORITIES

A. MOTION FOR EVIDENTIARY SANCTIONS

B. MOTION TO EXCLUDE EVIDENCE OF CLAIMS DENIED DURING DISCOVERY

C. MOTIONS REGARDING EXPERT DISCLOSURES AND EXPERT DEPOSITIONS

D. MOTION TO EXCLUDE STATUTORILY PRIVILEGED INFORMATION

I. MOTION AUTHORITIES

A. MOTION FOR EVIDENTIARY SANCTIONS

The goal of Illinois civil discovery rules is to avoid unfair surprise and prejudice at trial. The parties should "know" what the case is all about. When a party abuses discovery (intentionally or unintentionally) and the result is unfair surprise or prejudice to the opposition, the sanctions can be very harsh. The sanctions available and the bases therefore are the subjects of this chapter. It should also be noted that motions related to discovery can be used to obtain sanctions and as a preventative measure to avoid any unfair surprise or prejudice. Motions in limine should be routinely used to prevent the other party from offering any evidence, witness, or opinion not previously disclosed.

§ 6:1 Suggested motion text

Alternative One (Sanction Precluding Evidence):

[Name of moving party] hereby moves this Court for an order precluding *[name of party]* from introducing or mentioning evidence relating to *[describe evidence to be excluded]*. The motion is based upon the grounds that [name of party] misused the discovery process by *[describe discovery abuse, e.g. "violating a court order to appear for deposition"]* and therefore an evidence sanction, pursuant to Illinois Supreme Court Rule 219(c)(ii-),(iii),(iv) and (d), is an appropriate remedy.

Alternative Two (Sanction Establishing Facts):

[Name of moving party] hereby moves this Court for an order that *[describe facts to be established]* shall be taken as established at the time of trial in this matter. The motion is based upon the grounds that *[name of party]* misused the discovery process by *[describe discovery abuse, e.g. "violating two court orders to appear for deposition"]* and therefore may be sanctioned by way of an issue sanction, pursuant to Illinois Supreme Court Rule 219(c)(ii),(iii) and (iv).

Alternative Three (Sanction Prohibiting Party From Supporting or Opposing Claim or Defense):

[Name of moving party] hereby moves this Court for an order prohibiting *[name of party]* from supporting or opposing the following *[claims or defenses]*: *[list claims or defenses forming basis of requested sanction, relating to offending party's discovery abuse]*. The motion is based upon the grounds that *[name of party]* misused the discovery process by *[describe discovery abuse, e.g. "violating two court orders to appear for deposition and negligently destroying key evidence"]* and therefore may be sanctioned by way of an issue sanction, pursuant to Illinois Supreme Court Rule 219(c)(ii),(iii) and (iv).

Alternative Four (Terminating Sanction):

[Name of moving party] hereby moves this Court for an order *[describe desired terminating sanction, e.g., striking the pleadings, staying further proceedings, dismissing the action, rendering default judgment, etc.]*. The motion is based upon the grounds that *[name of party]* misused the discovery process in a blatant and egregious fashion by *[describe discovery abuse, e.g. "violating two court orders to appear for deposition and intentionally destroying key evidence"]* and therefore may be sanctioned by

way of a terminating sanction, pursuant to Illinois Supreme Court Rule 219(c) (v) and (vi).

◆ **Comment:** Readers should also note that motions can be filed to request a sanction for not producing evidence or a witness. A motion can also be filed requesting the court to provide a 5.01 instruction which allows for an adverse inference where a party fails to produce evidence or a witness that is within its control. These motions are particularly appropriate where there is evidence of destruction or modification of evidence (especially in violation of a protective order). In some situations, a party may file a motion to amend the complaint to add a spoliation count. See generally, "Spoliation of Evidence," Ch. 24, Illinois Causes of Action-Elements, Forms & Winning Tips: Tort Actions, IICLE 2002. Scott D. Lane and Stephen I. Lane. See also §§ 9:22 et seq., infra.

§ 6:2 Motion summary

This motion is based upon Illinois Supreme Court Rule 219(c) and (d), which provide the authority for evidence, issue and terminating sanctions against parties who have misused the discovery process. See Illinois Supreme Court Rule 219(c) and (d); *Ashpole v. Brunswick Bowling and Billiards Corp.*, 297 Ill. App. 3d 725, 726–30, 232 Ill. Dec. 308, 697 N.E.2d 1238 (2d Dist. 1998) [evidence sanction]; *King v. Clemons*, 264 Ill. App. 3d 138, 140–41, 201 Ill. Dec. 630, 636 N.E.2d 1062 (5th Dist. 1994) and *Golembiewski v. Hallberg Ins. Agency, Inc.*, 262 Ill. App. 3d 1082, 1086–87, 200 Ill. Dec. 113, 635 N.E.2d 452 (1st Dist. 1994) [issue sanction]; *Paquet v. Steiner*, 239 Ill. App. 3d 866, 867–71, 180 Ill. Dec. 546, 607 N.E.2d 615 (2d Dist. 1993) [terminating sanction].

Note: This chapter, at § 6:3, Supporting authorities—General authority [Illinois Supreme Court Rule 219]—Misuse of discovery process, provides general authorities for obtaining discovery sanctions. For abuses arising from the following specific discovery types, see the noted sections:

- Depositions [§ 6:8]
- Interrogatories [§ 6:12]
- Production Requests [§ 6:16]
- Mental and Physical Examinations [§ 6:19]
- Requests for Admission [§ 6:22]

Regarding motions to exclude evidence of claims denied during discovery, see § 6:35 to § 6:42; for motions regarding expert depositions and expert disclosures, see § 6:43 to § 6:54; for exclusion of references to lost or destroyed evidence, see § 9:22 to § 9:31.

§ 6:3 Supporting authorities—General authority [Illinois Supreme Court Rule 219]—Misuse of discovery process

Illinois Supreme Court Rule 201 states in pertinent part as follows:

> (a) Discovery Methods. Information is obtainable as provided in these rules through any of the following discovery methods: depositions upon oral examination or written questions, written interrogatories to parties, discovery of documents, objects or tangible things, inspection of real estate, requests to admit and physical and mental examination of persons. Duplication of discovery methods to obtain the same information should be avoided . . . .
>
> (k) Reasonable Attempt to Resolve Differences Required. The parties shall facilitate discovery under these rules and shall make reasonable attempts to resolve differences over discovery. Every motion with respect to discovery shall incorporate a statement that counsel responsible for trial of the case after personal consultation and reasonable attempts to resolve differences have been unable to reach an accord or that opposing counsel made himself or herself unavailable for personal consultation or was unreasonable in attempts to resolve differences.

Illinois Supreme Court Rule 219 states in pertinent part:

> (c) Failure to Comply with Order or Rules. If a party, or any person at the instance of or in collusion with a party, unreasonably fails to comply with any provision of part E of article II of the rules of this court [Discovery, Requests for Admission, and Pretrial Procedure] or fails to comply with any order entered under these rules, *the court, on motion, may enter, in addition to remedies elsewhere specifically provided, such orders as are just, including, among others, the following:*
>
> (i) That further proceedings be stayed until the order or rule is complied with;
>
> (ii) *That the offending party be debarred from filing any other pleading relating to any issue to which the refusal or failure relates;*
>
> (iii) *That the offending party be debarred from maintaining any particular claim, counterclaim, third-party complaint, or defense relating to that issue*;
>
> (iv) *That a witness be barred from testifying concerning that issue*;
>
> (v) *That, as to claims or defenses asserted in any pleading to which that issue is material, a judgment by default be entered against the offending party or that the offending party's action be dismissed with or without prejudice*; or
>
> (vi) *That any portion of the offending party's pleadings relating to*

> *that issue be stricken and, if thereby made appropriate, judgment be entered as to that issue.*
>
> (vii) That in cases where a money judgment is entered against a party subject to sanctions under this subparagraph, order the offending party to pay interest at the rate provided by law for judgments for any period of pretrial delay attributable to the offending party's conduct.
>
> In lieu of or in addition to the foregoing, the court, upon motion or upon its own initiative, may impose upon the offending party or his or her attorney, or both, an appropriate sanction, which may include an order to pay to the other party or parties the amount of reasonable expenses incurred as a result of the misconduct, including a reasonable attorney fee, and when the misconduct is willful, a monetary penalty. When appropriate, the court may, by contempt proceedings, compel obedience by any party or person to any subpoena issued or order entered under these rules. Notwithstanding the entry of a judgment or an order of dismissal, whether voluntary or involuntary, the trial court shall retain jurisdiction to enforce, on its own motion or on the motion of any party, any order imposing monetary sanctions, including such orders as may be entered on motions which were pending hereunder prior to the filing of a notice or motion seeking a judgment or order of dismissal.
>
> Where a sanction is imposed under this paragraph (c), the judge shall set forth with specificity the reasons and basis of any sanction so imposed either in the judgment order itself or in a separate written order.
>
> (d) Abuse of Discovery Procedures. *The court may order that information obtained through abuse of discovery procedures be suppressed.* If a party willfully obtains or attempts to obtain information by an improper discovery method, willfully obtains or attempts to obtain information to which that party is not entitled, or otherwise abuses these discovery rules, the court may enter any order provided for in paragraph (c) of this rule. (Emphasis added.)

See also *Boren v. BOC Group, Inc.*, 385 Ill.App.3d 248, 258–59, 895 N.E.2d 53 (5th Dist. 2008) (failure of the defendants to provide complete disclosures of key witnesses and information provided grounds for granting a new trial).

§ 6:4 Supporting authorities—General authority [Illinois Supreme Court Rule 219]—Evidence sanction

Somers v. Quinn, 373 Ill. App. 3d 87, 96-99, 310 Ill. Dec. 848, 867 N.E.2d 539 (2d Dist. 2007) (trial court did not abuse its discretion by denying a party's request for a continuance after disqualifying the party's expert because the party had not diligently attempted to secure a new expert after learning the information that led to the eventual disqualification of the expert).

White v. Garlock Sealing Technologies, LLC, 373 Ill. App. 3d 309, 311–30, 311 Ill. Dec. 570, 869 N.E.2d 244 (4th Dist. 2007), appeal denied, 225 Ill. 2d 679, 314 Ill. Dec. 838, 875 N.E.2d 1125 (2007) (trial court had discretion to grant a new trial after an undisclosed expert opinion was provided to the jury and to exclude any mention of that same opinion upon retrial).

Cyclonaire Corp. v. ISG Riverdale, Inc., 378 Ill. App. 3d 554, 561–62, 317 Ill. Dec. 804, 882 N.E.2d 684 (1st Dist. 2007) (trial court had discretion to exclude an exhibit that was not disclosed during the discovery period).

Boyd v. City of Chicago, 378 Ill. App. 3d 57, 67-69, 317 Ill. Dec. 41, 880 N.E.2d 1033 (1st Dist. 2007) (trial court had discretion to bar the testimony of undisclosed witnesses).

Jackson v. Seib, 372 Ill. App. 3d 1061, 310 Ill. Dec. 502, 866 N.E.2d 663 (5th Dist. 2007) (the trial court did not err by excluding certain demonstrative evidence as a sanction for failing to provide the evidence in discovery).

Cretton v. Protestant Memorial Medical Center, Inc., 371 Ill. App. 3d 841, 309 Ill. Dec. 422, 864 N.E.2d 288, 300-03 (5th Dist. 2007), appeal denied, 224 Ill. 2d 573, 312 Ill. Dec. 655, 871 N.E.2d 55 (2007) (the trial court had discretion to bar evidence as a sanction for a party's failure to properly cooperate with discovery).

Spyrka v. County of Cook, 366 Ill. App. 3d 156, 165-66, 303 Ill. Dec. 613, 851 N.E.2d 800 (1st Dist. 2006) (video animation was not timely disclosed and should not have been admitted at trial).

People v. Robert P., 354 Ill. App. 3d 1051, 1058–59, 290 Ill. Dec. 685, 821 N.E.2d 1259 (3d Dist. 2005) (no abuse in barring evidence that other people were in the house when the defendant allegedly sexually abused the victim; witnesses had not been previously disclosed and were irrelevant).

In re Marriage of Vancura, 356 Ill. App. 3d 200, 201–03, 292 Ill. Dec. 89, 825 N.E.2d 345 (2d Dist. 2005) (trial court did not err in striking party's answer and preventing party from presenting evidence regarding asset division as a sanction for failing to comply with discovery).

Chapman v. Hubbard Woods Motors, Inc., 351 Ill. App. 3d 99, 108–10, 285 Ill. Dec. 569, 812 N.E.2d 389 (1st Dist. 2004) (trial court did not err by preventing expert from testifying that he had reviewed certain records where records were not disclosed as basis for opinion during deposition or in responses to interrogatories).

Sullivan v. Edward Hosp., 209 Ill. 2d 100, 107–11, 282 Ill. Dec. 348, 806 N.E.2d 645 (2004) (trial court properly barred testimony of an undisclosed expert).

Bill Marek's The Competitive Edge, Inc. v. Mickelson Group, Inc., 346 Ill. App. 3d 996, 1006–09, 282 Ill. Dec. 305, 806 N.E.2d 280 (2d Dist. 2004) (trial court did not err by striking defendant's witnesses and affidavits, as a discovery sanction, for failing to timely disclose the witnesses and the nature of their testimony).

Ashpole v. Brunswick Bowling and Billiards Corp., 297 Ill. App. 3d 725, 726–30, 232 Ill. Dec. 308, 697 N.E.2d 1238 (2d Dist. 1998) (trial court abused its discretion by allowing testimony by an eyewitness when the party offering the testimony had not disclosed the witness as such in response to an interrogatory).

Harding v. Amsted Industries, Inc., 276 Ill. App. 3d 483, 492–93, 213 Ill. Dec. 187, 658 N.E.2d 1208 (1st Dist. 1995) (trial judge properly excluded testimony obtained by the defendant through contacts with the plaintiff's doctors that was not obtained through the proper formal discovery means).

King v. Clemons, 264 Ill. App. 3d 138, 140–41, 201 Ill. Dec. 630, 636 N.E.2d 1062 (5th Dist. 1994) (trial court did not abuse its discretion by barring evidence after a party had altered it despite the opposing party's request for it to be preserved in tact).

Golembiewski v. Hallberg Ins. Agency, Inc., 262 Ill. App. 3d 1082, 1086–87, 200 Ill. Dec. 113, 635 N.E.2d 452 (1st Dist. 1994) (trial judge properly precluded the testimony of the defendant's president, precluded the defendant from offering a defense and ordered the defendant's attorney to pay the plaintiff's attorney's fees, when the defendant's attorney improperly interfered with the ability of the plaintiff to conduct a full deposition of the defendant's president).

Paquet v. Steiner, 239 Ill. App. 3d 866, 867–71, 180 Ill. Dec. 546, 607 N.E.2d 615 (2d Dist. 1993) (trial judge properly excluded expert testimony when no expert was disclosed in a timely fashion, without any justifiable reason for the delay in disclosure).

Savage v. Martin, 256 Ill. App. 3d 272, 285, 195 Ill. Dec. 142, 628 N.E.2d 606 (1st Dist. 1993) (expert opinion that went beyond opinions stated at deposition was properly excluded, where expert stated that he had no other opinions beyond those in his report).

Lewis v. Illinois Cent. R. Co., 234 Ill. App. 3d 669, 676–81,

175 Ill. Dec. 573, 600 N.E.2d 504 (5th Dist. 1992) (trial judge properly excluded all evidence obtained by the defendant through contacts with the plaintiff's doctors that was not obtained through the proper formal discovery means).

Atwood v. Warner Elec. Brake and Clutch Co., Inc., 239 Ill. App. 3d 81, 88-90, 179 Ill. Dec. 18, 605 N.E.2d 1032 (2d Dist. 1992) (trial judge had discretion to bar evidence and claims for failure to provide the ordered discovery by the trial judge's cut-off date).

Perez v. Hartmann, 187 Ill. App. 3d 1098, 1101–04, 135 Ill. Dec. 455, 543 N.E.2d 1023 (1st Dist. 1989) (trial judge properly excluded evidence based upon a party's failure to produce it in discovery until one month before trial, despite requests for it by the opposing party and a court order to produce it).

Renfro v. Allied Indus. Equipment Corp., 155 Ill. App. 3d 140, 161–63, 107 Ill. Dec. 844, 507 N.E.2d 1213 (5th Dist. 1987) (trial judge properly excluded testimony of undisclosed expert when the expert was not disclosed until after the other party had rested her case and therefore, the opportunity for her to conduct effective discovery, even if a continuance were to be granted, was limited).

Ideal Plumbing Co. v. Shevlin-Manning, Inc., 96 Ill. App. 3d 207, 209–10, 51 Ill. Dec. 927, 421 N.E.2d 562 (3d Dist. 1981) (evidence sanction is proper when the evidence was not disclosed despite requests through multiple means of discovery).

Ideal Plumbing Co. v. Shevlin-Manning, Inc., 96 Ill. App. 3d 207, 209–10, 51 Ill. Dec. 927, 421 N.E.2d 562 (3d Dist. 1981) (evidence sanction is proper when the evidence is crucial for the case and was not disclosed despite requests through multiple means of discovery, even if the non-disclosure was inadvertent).

For exclusion of references to lost or destroyed evidence, see § 9:22 to § 9:31, infra.

§ 6:5 Supporting authorities—General authority [Illinois Supreme Court Rule 219]—Issue sanction

Cretton v. Protestant Memorial Medical Center, Inc., 371 Ill. App. 3d 841, 309 Ill. Dec. 422, 864 N.E.2d 288, 300-03 (5th Dist. 2007), appeal denied, 224 Ill. 2d 573, 312 Ill. Dec. 655, 871 N.E.2d 55 (2007) (the trial court had discretion to consider certain elements of the cause of action as established as a sanction for the defendant's failure to properly cooperate with discovery).

In re Marriage of Vancura, 356 Ill. App. 3d 200, 201–03, 292 Ill. Dec. 89, 825 N.E.2d 345 (2d Dist. 2005) (trial court did not err in striking party's answer and preventing party from presenting evidence regarding asset division as a sanction for failing to comply with discovery).

King v. Clemons, 264 Ill. App. 3d 138, 140–41, 201 Ill. Dec. 630, 636 N.E.2d 1062 (5th Dist. 1994) (trial court did not abuse its discretion by excluding any defense related to certain evidence after a party had altered the evidence despite the opposing party's request for it to be preserved in tact.).

Atwood v. Warner Elec. Brake and Clutch Co., Inc., 239 Ill. App. 3d 81, 88-91, 179 Ill. Dec. 18, 605 N.E.2d 1032 (2d Dist. 1992) (trial judge had discretion to bar evidence and claims for failure to provide the ordered discovery by the trial judge's cutoff date).

§ 6:6 Supporting authorities—General authority [Illinois Supreme Court Rule 219]—Terminating sanction

Koppel v. Michael, 374 Ill. App. 3d 998, 998–1007, 313 Ill. Dec. 161, 871 N.E.2d 888 (1st Dist. 2007) (trial court had discretion to enter a default judgment against a party for the party's repeated failure to comply with discovery).

Robbins v. Allstate Ins. Co., 362 Ill. App. 3d 540, 542–44, 298 Ill. Dec. 879, 841 N.E.2d 22 (2d Dist. 2005) (overruled by, Vision Point of Sale, Inc. v. Haas, 226 Ill. 2d 334, 314 Ill. Dec. 778, 875 N.E.2d 1065 (2007)) (summary judgment was granted after a party failed to file a timely and sufficient answer to requests to admit).

Evitts v. DaimlerChrysler Motors Corp., 359 Ill. App. 3d 504, 513–14, 296 Ill. Dec. 137, 834 N.E.2d 942 (1st Dist. 2005) (the trial court did not abuse its discretion by denying a party's request for additional discovery before ruling on a motion to dismiss).

Heinrich v. Mitchell, 357 Ill. App. 3d 1017, 1021–23, 294 Ill. Dec. 246, 830 N.E.2d 658 (1st Dist. 2005) (trial court did not abuse its discretion by entering a "take-nothing" judgment as a discovery sanction, after a party did not preserve certain evidence as ordered).

Paquet v. Steiner, 239 Ill. App. 3d 866, 867–71, 180 Ill. Dec. 546, 607 N.E.2d 615 (2d Dist. 1993) (trial judge properly excluded expert testimony and then granted summary judgment based upon the lack of expert testimony, when no expert was disclosed in a timely fashion and there was no justifiable reason for the delay in disclosure).

Hartnett v. Stack, 241 Ill. App. 3d 157, 174–76, 180 Ill. Dec. 634, 607 N.E.2d 703 (2d Dist. 1993) (trial court did not abuse its discretion by striking the defendant's pleadings and entering a default judgment when the defendant willfully failed to comply with multiple means of discovery and court orders regarding same).

Chovan v. Floor Covering Associates, Inc., 159 Ill. App. 3d 447, 450–51, 111 Ill. Dec. 412, 512 N.E.2d 801 (3d Dist. 1987) (trial judge did not err by dismissing the cause of action when the plaintiff had completely failed to comply with discovery).

See also *Atwood v. Warner Elec. Brake and Clutch Co., Inc.*, 239 Ill. App. 3d 81, 88-91, 179 Ill. Dec. 18, 605 N.E.2d 1032 (2d Dist. 1992) (trial judge had discretion to bar evidence and claims for failure to provide the ordered discovery by the trial judge's cut-off date).

§ 6:7 Supporting authorities—General authority [Illinois Supreme Court Rule 219]—When prior attempts to resolve discovery issues without court intervention unnecessary [Illinois Supreme Court Rule 201(k)]

Hartnett v. Stack, 241 Ill. App. 3d 157, 172–74, 180 Ill. Dec. 634, 607 N.E.2d 703 (2d Dist. 1993) (plaintiff did not need to comply with rule 201(k) before filing a motion for discovery sanctions when the record clearly showed that the defendant willfully failed to comply with multiple means of discovery).

But see *Brandt v. John S. Tilley Ladders Co.*, 145 Ill. App. 3d 304, 306–07, 99 Ill. Dec. 534, 495 N.E.2d 1269 (1st Dist. 1986) (trial judge should not have dismissed the Plaintiff's case for failure to comply with discovery when the defendant did not allege that it had complied with Illinois Supreme Court Rule 201(k)).

See generally, Illinois Supreme Court Rule 201, at § 6:3, Supporting authorities—General authority [Illinois Supreme Court Rule 219]—Misuse of discovery process, supra.

§ 6:8 Supporting authorities—Depositions—Depositions, generally

The following citations provide general guidance regarding depositions:

Illinois Supreme Court Rule 201 states in pertinent part as follows:

(a) Discovery Methods. Information is obtainable as provided in

> these rules through any of the following discovery methods: *depositions upon oral examination or written questions . . . .* (Emphasis added.)

Illinois Supreme Court Rule 202 states as follows:

> Any party may take the testimony of any party or person by deposition upon oral examination or written questions for the purpose of discovery or for use as evidence in the action. The notice, order, or stipulation to take a deposition shall specify whether the deposition is to be a discovery deposition or an evidence deposition. In the absence of specification a deposition is a discovery deposition only. If both discovery and evidence depositions are desired of the same witness they shall be taken separately, unless the parties stipulate otherwise or the court orders otherwise upon notice and motion. If the evidence deposition of a witness is to be taken within 21 days of trial, a discovery deposition is not permitted unless the parties stipulate otherwise or the court orders otherwise upon notice and motion.

For additional deposition citations, see Illinois Supreme Court Rules 201 through 212 and 217 and 219.

§ 6:9 Supporting authorities—Depositions—Compelling deposition answers

Illinois Supreme Court Rule 219(a) states in pertinent part:

> If a party or other deponent refuses to answer any question propounded upon oral examination, the examination shall be completed on other matters or adjourned, as the proponent of the question may prefer. Thereafter, *on notice to all persons affected thereby, the proponent of the question may move the court for an order compelling an answer.* (Emphasis added.)

§ 6:10 Supporting authorities—Depositions—Failure to comply with discovery order re deposition

Illinois Supreme Court Rule 219(c) provides for evidence and issue sanctions for failing to comply with a court's discovery order; Illinois Supreme Court Rule 219(d) provides for additional sanctions for willful discovery abuses. *See § 6:3, Supporting authorities—General authority [Illinois Supreme Court Rule 219]—Misuse of discovery process, supra, for applicable excerpts from Rule 219(c) to (d).*

Note that prior attempts to resolve differences without court intervention may not be required where such attempts would be futile in remedying the discovery abuse. *See § 6:7, Supporting authorities—General authority [Illinois Supreme Court Rule 219]—When prior attempts to resolve discovery issues without court intervention unnecessary [Illinois Supreme Court Rule 201(k)], supra.*

§ 6:11 Supporting authorities—Depositions—Evidence exclusion arising from deposition misconduct

Harding v. Amsted Industries, Inc., 276 Ill. App. 3d 483, 492, 213 Ill. Dec. 187, 658 N.E.2d 1208 (1st Dist. 1995) (trial judge properly excluded expert testimony that exceeded the opinions expressed by the expert during discovery).

Golembiewski v. Hallberg Ins. Agency, Inc., 262 Ill. App. 3d 1082, 1086–87, 200 Ill. Dec. 113, 635 N.E.2d 452 (1st Dist. 1994) (trial judge properly precluded the testimony of the defendant's president, precluded the defendant from offering a defense and ordered the defendant's attorney to pay the plaintiff's attorney's fees when the defendant's counsel improperly interfered with the ability of the plaintiff to conduct a full deposition of the defendant's president).

Savage v. Martin, 256 Ill. App. 3d 272, 285, 195 Ill. Dec. 142, 628 N.E.2d 606 (1st Dist. 1993) (expert opinion that went beyond opinions stated at deposition was properly excluded, where expert stated that he had no other opinions beyond those in his report).

Perez v. Hartmann, 187 Ill. App. 3d 1098, 1101–04, 135 Ill. Dec. 455, 543 N.E.2d 1023 (1st Dist. 1989) (trial judge properly excluded evidence based upon a party's failure to produce it in discovery until one month before trial, when the party's expert had access to the evidence in preparing for deposition but the opposing party's expert did not).

Ideal Plumbing Co. v. Shevlin-Manning, Inc., 96 Ill. App. 3d 207, 209–10, 51 Ill. Dec. 927, 421 N.E.2d 562 (3d Dist. 1981) (evidence sanction is proper when the evidence was not disclosed despite requests through multiple means of discovery).

See §§ 6:4 et seq., supra, for general case authority supporting a motion to exclude evidence based upon discovery abuses. See § 6:48, Supporting authorities—Opinions not referenced at deposition, infra, regarding exclusion of expert testimony for failure to fully disclose opinions at deposition.

§ 6:12 Supporting authorities—Interrogatories [Illinois Supreme Court Rule 213]—Interrogatories, generally

Illinois Supreme Court Rule 201 states in pertinent part as follows:

> (a) Discovery Methods. Information is obtainable as provided in these rules through any of the following discovery methods: de-

positions upon oral examination or written questions, *written interrogatories to parties* . . . . (Emphasis added.)

Illinois Supreme Court Rule 213 states:

(a) Directing Interrogatories. A party may direct written interrogatories to any other party. A copy of the interrogatories shall be served on all other parties entitled to notice.

(b) Duty of Attorney. It is the duty of an attorney directing interrogatories to restrict them to the subject matter of the particular case, to avoid undue detail, and to avoid the imposition of any unnecessary burden or expense on the answering party.

(c) Number of Interrogatories. Except as provided in subparagraph (j), a party shall not serve more than 30 interrogatories, including sub-parts, on any other party except upon agreement of the parties or leave of court granted upon a showing of good cause. A motion for leave of court to serve more than 30 interrogatories must be in writing and shall set forth the proposed interrogatories and the reasons establishing good cause for their use.

(d) Answers and Objections. Within 28 days after service of the interrogatories upon the party to whom they are directed, the party shall serve a sworn answer or an objection to each interrogatory, with proof of service upon all other parties entitled to notice. *Any objection to an answer or to the refusal to answer an interrogatory shall be heard by the court upon prompt notice and motion of the party propounding the interrogatory.* The answering party shall set forth in full each interrogatory being answered immediately preceding the answer. Sworn answers to interrogatories directed to a public or private corporation, or a partnership or association shall be made by an officer, partner, or agent, who shall furnish such information as is available to the party.

(e) Option to Produce Documents. When the answer to an interrogatory may be obtained from documents in the possession or control of the party on whom the interrogatory was served, it shall be a sufficient answer to the interrogatory to produce those documents responsive to the interrogatory. When a party elects to answer an interrogatory by the production of documents, that production shall comply with the requirements of Rule 214.

(f) Identity and Testimony of Witnesses. Upon written interrogatory, a party must furnish the identities and addresses of witnesses who will testify at trial and must provide the following information:

(1) *Lay Witnesses.* A "lay witness" is a person giving only fact or lay opinion testimony. For each lay witness, the party must identify the subjects on which the witness will testify. An answer is sufficient if it gives reasonable notice of the testimony, taking into account the limitations on the party's knowledge of the facts known by and opinions held by the witness.

(2) *Independent Expert Witnesses.* An "independent expert witness" is a person giving expert testimony who is not the party,

the party's current employee, or the party's retained expert. For each independent expert witness, the party must identify the subjects on which the witness will testify and the opinions the party expects to elicit. An answer is sufficient if it gives reasonable notice of the testimony, taking into account the limitations on the party's knowledge of the facts known by and opinions held by the witness.

(3) *Controlled Expert Witnesses.* A "controlled expert witness" is a person giving expert testimony who is the party, the party's current employee, or the party's retained expert. For each controlled expert witness, the party must identify: (i) the subject matter on which the witness will testify; (ii) the conclusions and opinions of the witness and the bases therefore; (iii) the qualifications of the witness; and (iv) any reports prepared by the witness about the case.

(g) Limitation on Testimony and Freedom to Cross-Examine. The information disclosed in answer to a Rule 213 (f) interrogatory, or at deposition, limits the testimony that can be given by a witness on direct examination. Information expressed in a deposition need not be later specifically identified in a Rule 213(f) answer, but, upon objection at trial, the burden is on the proponent of the witness to prove the information was provided in a Rule 213(f) answer or in the deposition.

Without making disclosure under this rule, however, a cross-examining party can elicit information, including opinions, from the witness. This freedom to cross-examine is subject to a restriction that applies in actions that involve multiple parties and multiple representation. In such actions, the cross- examining party may not elicit undisclosed information, including opinions, from the witness on an issue on which its position is aligned with that of the party doing the direct examination.

(h) Use of Answers to Interrogatories. Answers to interrogatories may be used in evidence to the same extent as a discovery deposition.

(i) Duty to Supplement. A party has a duty to seasonably supplement or amend any prior answer or response whenever new or additional information subsequently becomes known to that party.

(j) The Supreme Court, by administrative order, may approve standard forms of interrogatories for different classes of cases.

(k) Liberal Construction. This rule is to be liberally construed to do substantial justice between or among the parties. (Emphasis added.)

§ 6:13 Supporting authorities—Interrogatories [Illinois Supreme Court Rule 213]—Compelling interrogatory responses

Illinois Supreme Court Rule 219(a) states in pertinent part:

If a party or other deponent refuses to answer any written question upon the taking of his or her deposition or *if a party fails to answer any interrogatory served upon him or her*, or to comply with a request for the production of documents or tangible things or inspection of real property, *the proponent of the question or interrogatory or the party serving the request may on like notice move for an order compelling an answer or compliance with the request.* (Emphasis added.)

§ 6:14 Supporting authorities—Interrogatories [Illinois Supreme Court Rule 213]—Failure to comply with discovery order re interrogatories

Illinois Supreme Court Rule 219(c) provides for evidence and issue sanctions for failing to comply with a court's discovery order; Illinois Supreme Court Rule 219(d) provides for additional sanctions for willful discovery abuses. *See § 6:3, Supporting authorities—General authority [Illinois Supreme Court Rule 219]—Misuse of discovery process, supra, for applicable excerpts from Rule 219(c) to (d).*

Note that prior attempts to resolve differences without court intervention may not be required where such attempts would be futile in remedying the discovery abuse. *See § 6:7, Supporting authorities—General authority [Illinois Supreme Court Rule 219]—When prior attempts to resolve discovery issues without court intervention unnecessary [Illinois Supreme Court Rule 201(k)], supra.*

§ 6:15 Supporting authorities—Interrogatories [Illinois Supreme Court Rule 213]—Evidence exclusion arising from incomplete interrogatory responses

Kim v. Mercedes-Benz, U.S.A., Inc., 353 Ill. App. 3d 444, 453–55, 288 Ill. Dec. 778, 818 N.E.2d 713 (1st Dist. 2004), opinion modified on reh'g, (Oct. 21, 2004) (trial court did not abuse its discretion by excluding lay witness' opinion regarding valuation, when subject matter of opinion had not been disclosed in response to interrogatories).

Ashpole v. Brunswick Bowling and Billiards Corp., 297 Ill. App. 3d 725, 726–30, 232 Ill. Dec. 308, 697 N.E.2d 1238 (2d Dist. 1998) (trial court abused its discretion by allowing testimony by an eyewitness when the party offering the testimony had not disclosed the witness as such in response to an interrogatory).

See §§ 6:4 et seq., supra, for general case authority supporting a motion to exclude evidence based upon discovery abuses.

§ 6:16 Supporting authorities—Production requests [Illinois Supreme Court Rule 214]—Production requests, generally

Illinois Supreme Court Rule 201 states in pertinent part as follows:

> (a) Discovery Methods. Information is obtainable as provided in these rules through any of the following discovery methods: depositions upon oral examination or written questions, written interrogatories to parties, discovery of documents, objects or tangible things, inspection of real estate . . . .

Illinois Supreme Court Rule 214 states:

> Any party may by written request direct any other party to produce for inspection, copying, reproduction photographing, testing or sampling specified documents, objects or tangible things, or to permit access to real estate for the purpose of making surface or subsurface inspections or surveys or photographs, or tests or taking samples, or to disclose information calculated to lead to the discovery of the whereabouts of any of these items, whenever the nature, contents, or condition of such documents, objects, tangible things, or real estate is relevant to the subject matter of the action. The request shall specify a reasonable time, which shall not be less than 28 days except by agreement or by order of court, and the place and manner of making the inspection and performing the related acts. One copy of the request shall be served on all other parties entitled to notice. A party served with the written request shall (1) produce the requested documents as they are kept in the usual course of business or organized and labeled to correspond with the categories in the request, and all retrievable information in computer storage in printed form or (2) serve upon the party so requesting written objections on the ground that the request is improper in whole or in part. *If written objections to a part of the request are made, the remainder of the request shall be complied with. Any objection to the request or the refusal to respond shall be heard by the court upon prompt notice and motion of the party submitting the request.* If the party claims that the item is not in his or her possession or control or that he or she does not have information calculated to lead to the discovery of its whereabouts, the party may be ordered to submit to examination in open court or by deposition regarding such claim. The party producing documents shall furnish an affidavit stating whether the production is complete in accordance with the request.
>
> A party has a duty to seasonably supplement any prior response to the extent of documents, objects or tangible things which subsequently come into that party's possession or control or become known to that party.
>
> This rule does not preclude an independent action against a person not a party for production of documents and things and permission to enter upon real estate. (Emphasis added.)

§ 6:17 Supporting authorities—Production requests [Illinois Supreme Court Rule 214]—Compelling production requests

Illinois Supreme Court Rule 219(a) states in pertinent part:

> (a) Refusal to Answer or Comply with Request for Production. If a party or other deponent refuses to answer any question propounded upon oral examination, the examination shall be completed on other matters or adjourned, as the proponent of the question may prefer. Thereafter, on notice to all persons affected thereby, the proponent of the question may move the court for an order compelling an answer. *If a party* or other deponent *refuses* to answer any written question upon the taking of his or her deposition or if a party fails to answer any interrogatory served upon him or her, or *to comply with a request for the production of documents or tangible things or inspection of real property, the proponent of the question or interrogatory or the party serving the request may on like notice move for an order compelling an answer or compliance with the request.* If the court finds that the refusal or failure was without substantial justification, the court shall require the offending party or deponent, or the party whose attorney advised the conduct complained of, or either of them, to pay to the aggrieved party the amount of the reasonable expenses incurred in obtaining the order, including reasonable attorney's fees. If the motion is denied and the court finds that the motion was made without substantial justification, the court shall require the moving party to pay to the refusing party the amount of the reasonable expenses incurred in opposing the motion, including reasonable attorney's fees.

Tomczak v. Ingalls Memorial Hosp., 359 Ill. App. 3d 448, 456–57, 295 Ill. Dec. 968, 834 N.E.2d 549 (1st Dist. 2005) (the trial court did not abuse its discretion by requiring the defendant hospital to disclose the triage time, treatment time and triage determination of severity, where the information did not violate physician-patient privilege and it was relevant to the action).

Youle v. Ryan, 349 Ill. App. 3d 377, 379–82, 285 Ill. Dec. 402, 811 N.E.2d 1281 (4th Dist. 2004) (trial court should have held an in camera review of certain medical documents for relevancy and privilege before compelling party to produce them during discovery, over party's claim that they were irrelevant).

§ 6:18 Supporting authorities—Production requests [Illinois Supreme Court Rule 214]—Failure to comply with discovery order re production request

Illinois Supreme Court Rule 219(c) provides for evidence and issue sanctions for failing to comply with a court's discovery order; Illinois Supreme Court Rule 219(d) provides for additional sanctions for willful discovery abuses. *See § 6:3, Supporting authorities—General authority [Illinois Supreme Court Rule 219]—Misuse of discovery process, supra, for applicable excerpts from Rule 219(c) to (d).*

Note that prior attempts to resolve differences without court intervention may not be required where such attempts would be futile in remedying the discovery abuse. *See § 6:7, Supporting authorities—General authority [Illinois Supreme Court Rule 219]—When prior attempts to resolve discovery issues without court intervention unnecessary [Illinois Supreme Court Rule 201(k), supra.*

See §§ 6:4 et seq., supra, for general case authority supporting a motion to exclude evidence based upon discovery abuses.

§ 6:19 Supporting authorities—Mental and physical examinations [Illinois Supreme Court Rule 215]—Examinations, generally

Illinois Supreme Court Rule 201 states in pertinent part as follows:

> (a) Discovery Methods. Information is obtainable as provided in these rules through any of the following discovery methods: depositions upon oral examination or written questions, written interrogatories to parties, discovery of documents, objects or tangible things, inspection of real estate, requests to admit and *physical and mental examination of persons.* (Emphasis added.)

§ 6:20 Supporting authorities—Mental and physical examinations [Illinois Supreme Court Rule 215]—Moving to compel examination

Illinois Supreme Court Rule 215 provides:

> Physical and Mental Examination of Parties and Other Persons
>
> (a) Notice; Motion; Order. In any action in which the physical or mental condition of a party or of a person in the party's custody or legal control is in controversy, *the court, upon notice and on motion made within a reasonable time before the trial, may order such party to submit to a physical or mental examination by a licensed professional in a discipline related to the physical or mental condition which is involved.* The motion shall suggest the identity of the examiner and set forth the examiner's specialty or discipline. The court may refuse to order examination by the examiner suggested but in that event shall permit the party seeking the examination to suggest others. A party or person shall not be required to travel an unreasonable distance for the

examination. The order shall fix the time, place, conditions, and scope of the examination and designate the examiner. The party calling an examiner to testify at trial shall disclose the examiner as a controlled expert witness in accordance with these rules.

(b) Examiner's Fee and Compensation for Loss of Earnings. The party requesting the examination shall pay the fee of the examiner and compensation for any loss of earnings incurred or to be incurred by the party or person to be examined in complying with the order for examination, and shall advance all reasonable expenses incurred or to be incurred by the party or person in complying with the order.

(c) Examiner's Report. Within 21 days after the completion of the examination, the examiner shall prepare and mail or deliver to the attorneys for the party requesting the examination and the party examined duplicate originals of a written report of the examination, setting out the examiner's findings, results of all tests made, and the examiner's diagnosis and conclusions. The court may enforce compliance with this requirement. *If the report is not delivered or mailed to the attorney for the party examined within the time herein specified or within any extensions or modifications thereof granted by the court, neither the examiner's report, the examiner's testimony, the examiner's findings, X-ray films, nor the results of any tests the examiner has made may be received in evidence except at the instance of the party examined or who produced the person examined.* No examiner under this rule shall be considered a consultant.

(d) Impartial Medical Examiner.

(1) *Examination Before Trial.* A reasonable time in advance of the trial, the court may on its own motion or that of any party, order an impartial physical or mental examination of a party whose mental or physical condition is in issue, when in the court's discretion it appears that such an examination will materially aid in the just determination of the case. The examination shall be made by a member or members of a panel of physicians chosen for their special qualifications by the Administrative Office of the Illinois Courts.

(2) *Examination During Trial.* Should the court at any time during the trial find that compelling considerations make it advisable to have an examination and report at that time, the court may in its discretion so order.

(3) *Copies of Report.* A copy of the report of examination shall be given to the court and to the attorneys for the parties.

(4) *Testimony of Examining Physician.* Either party or the court may call the examining physician or physicians to testify. Any physician so called shall be subject to cross-examination.

(5) *Costs and Compensation of Physician.* The examination shall be made, and the physician or physicians, if called, shall testify without cost to the parties. The court shall determine the compensation of the physician or physicians.

(6) *Administration of Rule.* The Administrative Director and the

Deputy Administrative Director are charged with the administration of the rule. (Emphasis added.)

Fosse v. Pensabene, 362 Ill. App. 3d 172, 180–89, 297 Ill. Dec. 771, 838 N.E.2d 258 (2d Dist. 2005) (in a medical malpractice action, when the physical condition of the deceased was at issue, the defendant could file a motion for an autopsy as part of the discovery process).

§ 6:21 Supporting authorities—Mental and physical examinations [Illinois Supreme Court Rule 215]—Failure to comply with discovery order re examination

Illinois Supreme Court Rule 219(c) provides for evidence and issue sanctions for failing to comply with a court's discovery order; Illinois Supreme Court Rule 219(d) provides for additional sanctions for willful discovery abuses. *See § 6:3, Supporting authorities—General authority [Illinois Supreme Court Rule 219]—Misuse of discovery process, supra, for applicable excerpts from Rule 219(c) to (d).*

Note that prior attempts to resolve differences without court intervention may not be required where such attempts would be futile in remedying the discovery abuse. See § 6:7, Supporting authorities—General authority [Illinois Supreme Court Rule 219]—When prior attempts to resolve discovery issues without court intervention unnecessary [Illinois Supreme Court Rule 201(k), supra.

See §§ 6:4 et seq., supra, for general case authority supporting a motion to exclude evidence based upon discovery abuses.

§ 6:22 Supporting authorities—Requests for admission [Illinois Supreme Court Rule 216]—Requests for admission, generally

A request for an admission is an under-utilized discovery tool. These requests can and should be used to establish critical facts and the foundation for the admission of evidence. When used properly, this discovery tool can help streamline the litigation. Once the request is admitted or denied, the parties can focus their discovery and trial efforts on the relevant issues truly in dispute.

Illinois Supreme Court Rule 201 states in pertinent part as follows:

> (a) Discovery Methods. Information is obtainable as provided in these rules through any of the following discovery methods: de-

> positions upon oral examination or written questions, written interrogatories to parties, discovery of documents, objects or tangible things, inspection of real estate, *requests to admit* and physical and mental examination of persons. (Emphasis added.)

Illinois Supreme Court Rule 216 provides in pertinent part, as follows:

> (a) Request for Admission of Fact. A party may serve on any other party a written request for the admission by the latter of the truth of any specified relevant fact set forth in the request.
>
> (b) Request for Admission of Genuineness of Document. A party may serve on any other party a written request for admission of the genuineness of any relevant documents described in the request. Copies of the documents shall be served with the request unless copies have already been furnished.

§ 6:23 Supporting authorities—Requests for admission [Illinois Supreme Court Rule 216]—Effect of admission or failure to provide timely denial

Illinois Supreme Court Rule 216 provides in pertinent part, as follows:

> (c) Admission in the Absence of Denial. *Each of the matters of fact and the genuineness of each document of which admission is requested is admitted* unless, within 28 days after service thereof, the party to whom the request is directed serves upon the party requesting the admission either (1) a sworn statement denying specifically the matters of which admission is requested or setting forth in detail the reasons why he cannot truthfully admit or deny those matters or (2) written objections on the ground that some or all of the requested admissions are privileged or irrelevant or that the request is otherwise improper in whole or in part. If written objections to a part of the request are made, the remainder of the request shall be answered within the period designated in the request. A denial shall fairly meet the substance of the requested admission. If good faith requires that a party deny only a part, or requires qualification, of a matter of which an admission is requested, he shall specify so much of it as is true and deny only the remainder. Any objection to a request or to an answer shall be heard by the court upon prompt notice and motion of the party making the request.
>
> (d) Public Records. If any public records are to be used as evidence, the party intending to use them may prepare a copy of them insofar as they are to be used, and may seasonably present the copy to the adverse party by notice in writing, and the copy shall thereupon be admissible in evidence as admitted facts in the case if otherwise admissible, except insofar as its inaccuracy is pointed out under oath by the adverse party in an affidavit filed and served within 14 days after service of the notice.
>
> (e) Effect of Admission. Any admission made by a party pursuant

to request under this rule is for the purpose of the pending action and any action commenced pursuant to the authority of section 13-217 of the Code of Civil Procedure (735 ILCS 5/13-217) only. It does not constitute an admission by him for any other purpose and may not be used against him in any other proceeding. (Emphasis added.)

Brookbank v. Olson, 907 N.E.2d 426, 389 Ill.App.3d 683 (1st Dist. 2009) (a party's attorney cannot provide sworn denials to requests to admit on behalf of a party even when the party cannot be located).

Zwicky v. Freightliner Custom Chassis Corp., 373 Ill. App. 3d 135, 141–42, 310 Ill. Dec. 836, 867 N.E.2d 527 (2d Dist. 2007) (failure to respond to the opposing party's requests to admit resulted in deemed admissions).

Larson v. O'Donnell, 361 Ill. App. 3d 388, 395–96, 297 Ill. Dec. 132, 836 N.E.2d 863 (1st Dist. 2005) (overruled by, Vision Point of Sale, Inc. v. Haas, 226 Ill. 2d 334, 314 Ill. Dec. 778, 875 N.E.2d 1065 (2007)) (the trial court erred by granting the defendant additional time to answer requests to admit, when the defendant had not demonstrated sufficient good cause for the extension).

Robbins v. Allstate Ins. Co., 362 Ill. App. 3d 540, 542–44, 298 Ill. Dec. 879, 841 N.E.2d 22 (2d Dist. 2005) (overruled by, Vision Point of Sale, Inc. v. Haas, 226 Ill. 2d 334, 314 Ill. Dec. 778, 875 N.E.2d 1065 (2007)) (a party who failed to file a proper response to a request to admit was precluded from later denying those facts).

Crichton v. Golden Rule Ins. Co., 358 Ill. App. 3d 1137, 1150–52, 295 Ill. Dec. 393, 832 N.E.2d 843 (5th Dist. 2005) (the trial court did not abuse its discretion by denying the plaintiff's request for additional discovery prior to entering summary judgment for the defendant).

Tires 'N Tracks, Inc. v. Dominic Fiordirosa Const. Co., Inc., 331 Ill. App. 3d 87, 89-94, 264 Ill. Dec. 908, 771 N.E.2d 612 (2d Dist. 2002) (trial judge has no discretion to allow untimely responses or untimely amendments to requests to admit if the responding party does not demonstrate that there was sufficient good cause for the delay).

Bright v. Dicke, 166 Ill. 2d 204, 205–210, 209 Ill. Dec. 735, 652 N.E.2d 275 (1995) (trial judge has no discretion to allow untimely responses to requests to admit if the responding party does not demonstrate that there was sufficient good cause for the delay).

Note that the *Bright* case settled prior conflicts in the district courts regarding Illinois Supreme Court Rule 183, which states as follows:

> Extensions of Time—The court, for good cause shown on motion after notice to the opposite party, may extend the time for filing any pleading or the doing of any act which is required by the rules to be done within a limited period, either before or after the expiration of the time.

See also *Johannsen v. General Foods Corp.*, 146 Ill. App. 3d 296, 297–301, 99 Ill. Dec. 851, 496 N.E.2d 544 (3d Dist. 1986) (discusses the previous conflict in the district courts regarding the issue of the trial judge's discretion to allow late filings for responses to requests to admit).

See also *Vision Point of Sale, Inc. v. Haas*, 226 Ill. 2d 334, 356–58, 314 Ill. Dec. 778, 875 N.E.2d 1065 (2007) (when determining whether good cause exists for an extension of time to respond to requests to admit, a trial court can consider whether there was "mistake, inadvertence, or attorney neglect, but may not engage in an open-ended inquiry which considers conduct that is unrelated to the causes of the party's original noncompliance.") (overruling Hammond v. SBC Communications, Inc., 365 Ill.App.3d 879, 850 N.E.2d 265 (1st Dist. 2006); Robbins v. Allstate Ins. Co., 362 Ill.App.3d 540, 841 N.E.2d 22 (2nd Dist. 2005); Larson v. O'Donnell, 361 Ill.App.3d 388, 836 N.E.2d 863, (1st Dist. 2005); Cothren v. Thompson, 356 Ill.App.3d 279, 826 N.E.2d 534 (4th Dist. 2005); and Glasco v. Marony, 347 Ill.App.3d 1069, 808 N.E.2d 1107 (5th Dist. 2004)).

§ 6:24 Supporting authorities—Requests for admission [Illinois Supreme Court Rule 216]—Evidence preclusion arising from admitted facts and issues

Brookbank v. Olson, 907 N.E.2d 426, 389 Ill.App.3d 683 (1st Dist. 2009) (a party's attorney cannot provide sworn denials to requests to admit on behalf of a party even when the party cannot be located).

Zwicky v. Freightliner Custom Chassis Corp., 373 Ill. App. 3d 135, 141–42, 310 Ill. Dec. 836, 867 N.E.2d 527 (2d Dist. 2007) (failure to respond to the opposing party's requests to admit resulted in deemed admissions).

Robbins v. Allstate Ins. Co., 362 Ill. App. 3d 540, 542–44, 298 Ill. Dec. 879, 841 N.E.2d 22 (2d Dist. 2005) (overruled by, Vision Point of Sale, Inc. v. Haas, 226 Ill. 2d 334, 314 Ill. Dec. 778, 875 N.E.2d 1065 (2007)) (summary judgment was granted after a party failed to file a timely and sufficient answers to requests to admit).

Glasco v. Marony, 347 Ill. App. 3d 1069, 1071–74, 283 Ill. Dec. 819, 808 N.E.2d 1107 (5th Dist. 2004) (overruled by, Vision Point of Sale, Inc. v. Haas, 226 Ill. 2d 334, 314 Ill. Dec. 778, 875 N.E.2d 1065 (2007)) (party failed to demonstrate good cause for providing late responses to requests to admit and, as a result, opposing party was entitled to summary judgment).

Davis v. International Harvester Co., 167 Ill. App. 3d 814, 824–25, 118 Ill. Dec. 589, 521 N.E.2d 1282 (2d Dist. 1988) (proper to exclude evidence of the feasibility of design changes when there was an admission to that issue).

Bullard v. Barnes, 112 Ill. App. 3d 384, 392–94, 68 Ill. Dec. 37, 445 N.E.2d 485 (4th Dist. 1983), judgment aff'd, 102 Ill. 2d 505, 82 Ill. Dec. 448, 468 N.E.2d 1228 (1984) (trial judge abused his discretion by admitting photographs of the deceased and testimony regarding the conditions and circumstances surrounding the collision, because liability was admitted).

See also *P.R.S. Intern., Inc. v. Shred Pax Corp.*, 184 Ill. 2d 224, 233–44, 234 Ill. Dec. 459, 703 N.E.2d 71 (1998) (even facts which, if admitted, would lead to summary judgment as a matter of law, can properly be deemed admitted through requests to admit).

§ 6:25 Supporting authorities—Requests for admission [Illinois Supreme Court Rule 216]—Restriction on amending admissions

Robbins v. Allstate Ins. Co., 362 Ill. App. 3d 540, 542–44, 298 Ill. Dec. 879, 841 N.E.2d 22 (2d Dist. 2005) (overruled by, Vision Point of Sale, Inc. v. Haas, 226 Ill. 2d 334, 314 Ill. Dec. 778, 875 N.E.2d 1065 (2007)) (an unsworn denial of requests to admit were not sufficient and the party could not later deny the facts were contained in the request to admit).

Larson v. O'Donnell, 361 Ill. App. 3d 388, 395–96, 297 Ill. Dec. 132, 836 N.E.2d 863 (1st Dist. 2005) (overruled by, Vision Point of Sale, Inc. v. Haas, 226 Ill. 2d 334, 314 Ill. Dec. 778, 875 N.E.2d 1065 (2007)) (the trial court erred by granting the defendant additional time to answer requests to admit, when the defendant had not demonstrated sufficient good cause for the extension).

Ellis v. American Family Mut. Ins. Co., 322 Ill. App. 3d 1006, 1010–11, 255 Ill. Dec. 902, 750 N.E.2d 1287 (4th Dist. 2001) (Illinois Supreme Court Rule 201(j), which normally would allow discovered evidence to be contradicted by other evidence, does not allow a party to amend previous admissions to requests to admit, because requests to admit are different from other forms of discovery).

Ellis v. American Family Mut. Ins. Co., 322 Ill. App. 3d 1006, 1010–11, 255 Ill. Dec. 902, 750 N.E.2d 1287 (4th Dist. 2001) (admitted responses to requests to admit, in contrast to responses to other forms of discovery, may not later be denied, absent a showing of good cause, because the purpose of requests to admit is to narrow the issues at trial).

§ 6:26 Supporting authorities—Other grounds

Other possible grounds for excluding evidence arising from discovery abuses include:

- Prejudicial (§ 2:1 to § 2:4)
- Confusing or misleading (§ 2:9 to § 2:12)
- Cumulative (§ 2:20 to § 2:33)
- Lost or destroyed evidence (§ 9:22 to § 9:31)

§ 6:27 Opposing authorities—Generally

Badea v. Phillips, 389 Ill.App.3d 292, 906 N.E.2d 615, 618–21 (1st Dist. 2009) (trial court lacked jurisdiction to rule on a motion for discovery sanctions that was filed after the case had been dismissed with prejudice).

Grillo v. Yeager Const., 387 Ill.App.3d 577, 598–600, 900 N.E.2d 1249 (1st Dist. 2008) (trial court had discretion to admit evidence that was not disclosed in a timely fashion because the opposing party was not surprised or prejudiced).

Village of Oak Lawn v. Faber, 378 Ill. App. 3d 458, 475, 316 Ill. Dec. 923, 880 N.E.2d 659 (1st Dist. 2007) (party is not bound by an admission to a conclusion of law).

Apa v. National Bank of Commerce, 374 Ill. App. 3d 1082, 1086, 313 Ill. Dec. 507, 872 N.E.2d 490 (1st Dist. 2007) (trial court had discretion to deny a party's request to bar any evidence of the opposing party's business income, as a sanction for failing to disclose requested tax returns, when the opposing party stated that the tax returns were neither completed nor filed).

Heriford v. Moore, 377 Ill. App. 3d 849, 851–54, 318 Ill. Dec. 247, 883 N.E.2d 81 (4th Dist. 2007), appeal denied, 227 Ill. 2d 580, 321 Ill. Dec. 250, 888 N.E.2d 1183 (2008) (trial court erred by barring evidence and entering a directed verdict as a sanction for a party's failure to properly disclose experts, when the opposing party was not surprised or prejudiced by the improper disclosure).

Matthews v. Avalon Petroleum Co., 375 Ill. App. 3d 1, 11-13, 313 Ill. Dec. 132, 871 N.E.2d 859 (1st Dist. 2007) (party was not required to disclose the basis for a lay witness' opinion).

Webber v. Wight & Co., 368 Ill. App. 3d 1007, 1028-29, 306 Ill. Dec. 782, 858 N.E.2d 579 (1st Dist. 2006), appeal denied, 223 Ill. 2d 686, 310 Ill. Dec. 258, 865 N.E.2d 978 (2007) (the plaintiff was not unfairly surprised by the introduction of letters that he had signed and that were obtained by the defendant through a subpoena).

People v. Calderon, 369 Ill. App. 3d 221, 232-33, 307 Ill. Dec. 486, 859 N.E.2d 1163 (2d Dist. 2006) (trial court should not have excluded the testimony of an undisclosed rebuttal witness) (harmless error).

Gee v. Treece, 365 Ill. App. 3d 1029, 1035-37, 303 Ill. Dec. 418, 851 N.E.2d 605 (5th Dist. 2006) (when the testimony would not surprise the opposing party, trial court had discretion to allow the testimony of an untimely disclosed expert witness).

Fosse v. Pensabene, 362 Ill. App. 3d 172, 180–88, 297 Ill. Dec. 771, 838 N.E.2d 258 (2d Dist. 2005) (the plaintiff did not violate the defendant's right to discovery by having an autopsy performed on the deceased without notice to the defendant).

Fosse v. Pensabene, 362 Ill. App. 3d 172, 180–88, 297 Ill. Dec. 771, 838 N.E.2d 258 (2d Dist. 2005) (the trial court abused its discretion by barring autopsy results when the plaintiff did not violate the defendant's right to discovery by having an autopsy performed on the deceased without notice to the defendant).

Adams v. Bath and Body Works, Inc., 358 Ill. App. 3d 387, 294 Ill. Dec. 233, 830 N.E.2d 645, 651–55 (1st Dist. 2005) (trial court abused its discretion by dismissing cause of action as a sanction for destruction of evidence, when destruction was not a willful attempt to avoid discovery and did not involve crucial evidence).

Atlantic Coast Airlines Holdings v. Bloomington-Normal Airport Authority, 357 Ill. App. 3d 929, 933–34, 294 Ill. Dec. 722, 831 N.E.2d 672 (4th Dist. 2005) (trial court should have found that good cause existed for an extension of time to answer requests to admit, because requests were confusing).

Cirrincione v. Westminster Gardens Ltd. Partnership, 352 Ill. App. 3d 755, 760–65, 287 Ill. Dec. 763, 816 N.E.2d 730 (1st Dist. 2004) (trial court erred by dismissing cause of action as a discovery sanction, after it was discovered that party had altered certain evidence, because effect of alteration and credibility determination regarding it, were issues for jury to determine).

Stringer v. Packaging Corp. of America, 351 Ill. App. 3d 1135,

1138–40, 287 Ill. Dec. 73, 815 N.E.2d 476 (4th Dist. 2004) (trial court did not err in failing to grant opposing party's dismissal request as a discovery sanction for destroyed evidence, when party against whom dismissal was sought did not cause destruction of evidence).

People v. Cantlin, 348 Ill. App. 3d 998, 1000–01, 285 Ill. Dec. 29, 811 N.E.2d 270 (2d Dist. 2004) (the defendant was not denied due process by use of evidence that was destroyed in good faith by the police pursuant to a department policy).

In re Marriage of Bates, 212 Ill. 2d 489, 522–23, 289 Ill. Dec. 218, 819 N.E.2d 714 (2004) (trial court did not err by allowing an undisclosed witness to testify where opposing party was not prejudiced or surprised by nature of testimony).

Phillips v. Gannotti, 327 Ill. App. 3d 512, 518, 261 Ill. Dec. 571, 763 N.E.2d 820 (1st Dist. 2002) (discovery sanctions must be designed to ensure fair discovery and should not be used to punish the non-disclosing party).

Phillips v. Gannotti, 327 Ill. App. 3d 512, 518–21, 261 Ill. Dec. 571, 763 N.E.2d 820 (1st Dist. 2002) (trial judge should not have excluded undisclosed opinion testimony and then granted a directed verdict, when a continuance for further discovery would have alleviated the prejudice from the non-disclosure and the non-disclosure was not the fault of the non-disclosing party).

King v. Clay, 335 Ill. App. 3d 923, 926–28, 269 Ill. Dec. 667, 781 N.E.2d 464 (1st Dist. 2002) (trial judge should not have barred all evidence for failure to comply with depositions, when the opposing party failed to show that he fully pursued the available methods for taking the depositions).

In re Marriage of Booher, 313 Ill. App. 3d 356, 359–61, 245 Ill. Dec. 873, 728 N.E.2d 1230 (4th Dist. 2000) (trial judge should only preclude information related to the issues that the non-complying party failed to disclose during discovery and should not bar all evidence, even that evidence which is related to disclosed matters).

Kimco Corp. v. Murdoch, Coll & Lillibridge, Inc., 313 Ill. App. 3d 768, 775–79, 246 Ill. Dec. 678, 730 N.E.2d 1143 (1st Dist. 2000) (party's statement during the deposition was not unequivocal enough to be considered a binding judicial admission, so as to preclude further proof regarding the issue).

Jarke v. Jackson Products, Inc., 282 Ill. App. 3d 292, 296–98, 217 Ill. Dec. 861, 668 N.E.2d 46 (1st Dist. 1996) (not an abuse of discretion to allow an expert to testify to a theory that was not explicitly disclosed but that was arguably included within a broad term the expert had used in describing his opinion).

Tierney v. Community Memorial General Hosp., 268 Ill. App. 3d 1050, 1055–57, 206 Ill. Dec. 279, 645 N.E.2d 284 (1st Dist. 1994) (no error in permitting party's expert to express opinion that was undisclosed at deposition, when the opposing party knew that the subject matter of the testimony would be an issue at trial and had prepared to respond to the subject matter).

Zimmer v. Melendez, 222 Ill. App. 3d 390, 394–96, 164 Ill. Dec. 836, 583 N.E.2d 1158 (2d Dist. 1991) (trial court abused its discretion by excluding testimony that was undisclosed in interrogatories, when the subject matter of the testimony was not a surprise to the opposing party and when the interrogatory that might have covered the subject matter was open-ended and did not clearly request the information at issue).

Brandt v. John S. Tilley Ladders Co., 145 Ill. App. 3d 304, 306–07, 99 Ill. Dec. 534, 495 N.E.2d 1269 (1st Dist. 1986) (trial judge should not have dismissed the plaintiff's case for failure to comply with discovery when the defendant did not allege that it had complied with Illinois Supreme Court Rule 201(k)).

Williams v. A. E. Staley Mfg. Co., 83 Ill. 2d 559, 562–66, 48 Ill. Dec. 221, 416 N.E.2d 252 (1981) (motion for sanctions should have been denied for failure to comply with Rule 201(k)).

Williams v. A. E. Staley Mfg. Co., 83 Ill. 2d 559, 562–66, 48 Ill. Dec. 221, 416 N.E.2d 252 (1981) (trial judge should not have dismissed plaintiff's complaint for failure to comply with discovery when the defendant did not comply with Rule 201(k) before filing a motion for sanctions).

See also Illinois Supreme Court Rule 201(j), which states:

> Disclosure of any matter obtained by discovery is not conclusive, but may be contradicted by other evidence.

§ 6:28 Opposing authorities—Generally—Other remedies available

Dalan/Jupiter, Inc. ex rel. JRC Midway Marketplace, L.P. v. Draper and Kramer, Inc., 372 Ill. App. 3d 362, 369–71, 310 Ill. Dec. 118, 865 N.E.2d 442 (1st Dist. 2007), appeal denied, 225 Ill. 2d 630, 314 Ill. Dec. 823, 875 N.E.2d 1110 (2007) ($1000.00 instead of $4000.00 was a more appropriate sanction for failure to disclose witnesses in a timely fashion).

Phillips v. Gannotti, 327 Ill. App. 3d 512, 518, 261 Ill. Dec. 571, 763 N.E.2d 820 (1st Dist. 2002) (discovery sanctions must be designed to ensure fair discovery and should not be used to punish the non-disclosing party).

Phillips v. Gannotti, 327 Ill. App. 3d 512, 518–21, 261 Ill.

Dec. 571, 763 N.E.2d 820 (1st Dist. 2002) (trial judge should not have excluded undisclosed *lay witness* opinion testimony and then granted a directed verdict, when a continuance for further discovery would have alleviated the prejudice from the non-disclosure and the non-disclosure was not the fault of the non-disclosing party).

Kurrack v. American Dist. Telegraph Co., 252 Ill. App. 3d 885, 902–04, 192 Ill. Dec. 520, 625 N.E.2d 675 (1st Dist. 1993) (trial court did not abuse its discretion by granting brief continuance to depose expert, instead of excluding the expert's testimony as requested).

See also § 9:29, Supporting authorities—Negative presumption, supra, which may actually support a request to allow references to lost evidence, with a proper limiting instruction.

§ 6:29 Opposing authorities—Depositions

Phillips v. Gannotti, 327 Ill. App. 3d 512, 518–21, 261 Ill. Dec. 571, 763 N.E.2d 820 (1st Dist. 2002) (trial judge should not have excluded undisclosed lay witness opinion testimony and then granted a directed verdict, when a continuance for further discovery would have alleviated the prejudice from the non-disclosure and the non-disclosure was not the fault of the non-disclosing party).

King v. Clay, 335 Ill. App. 3d 923, 926–28, 269 Ill. Dec. 667, 781 N.E.2d 464 (1st Dist. 2002) (trial judge should not have barred all evidence for failure to comply with depositions, when the opposing party failed to show that he fully pursued the available methods for taking the depositions).

Kimco Corp. v. Murdoch, Coll & Lillibridge, Inc., 313 Ill. App. 3d 768, 775–79, 246 Ill. Dec. 678, 730 N.E.2d 1143 (1st Dist. 2000) (party's statement during the deposition was not unequivocal enough to be considered a binding judicial admission, so as to preclude further proof regarding the issue).

Jarke v. Jackson Products, Inc., 282 Ill. App. 3d 292, 296–98, 217 Ill. Dec. 861, 668 N.E.2d 46 (1st Dist. 1996) (not an abuse of discretion to allow an expert to testify to a theory that was not explicitly disclosed but that was arguably included within a broad term the expert had used in describing his opinion).

§ 6:30 Opposing authorities—Interrogatories

Zimmer v. Melendez, 222 Ill. App. 3d 390, 394–96, 164 Ill. Dec. 836, 583 N.E.2d 1158 (2d Dist. 1991) (trial court abused its discretion by excluding testimony that was undisclosed in interrogatories, when the subject matter of the testimony was not a surprise to the opposing party and when the interrogatory that might have covered the subject matter was open-ended and did not clearly request the information at issue).

Gee v. Davidson, 21 Ill. App. 3d 654, 315 N.E.2d 674 (1st Dist. 1974) (only abstract published) (trial judge properly allowed expert testimony that had not been disclosed in response to interrogatories when the same information had been provided by other means of discovery).

§ 6:31 Opposing authorities—Requests for production

Adams v. Bath and Body Works, Inc., 358 Ill. App. 3d 387, 294 Ill. Dec. 233, 830 N.E.2d 645, 651–55 (1st Dist. 2005) (trial court abused its discretion by dismissing cause of action as a sanction for destruction of evidence, when destruction was not a willful attempt to avoid discovery and did not involve crucial evidence).

In re Marriage of Booher, 313 Ill. App. 3d 356, 359–61, 245 Ill. Dec. 873, 728 N.E.2d 1230 (4th Dist. 2000) (trial judge should only preclude information related to the issues that the non-complying party failed to disclose during discovery and should not bar all evidence, even evidence that is related to disclosed matters).

Wiebusch v. Taylor, 97 Ill. App. 3d 210, 211–15, 52 Ill. Dec. 666, 422 N.E.2d 875 (1st Dist. 1981) (sanction which barred any evidence related to the defendant's main defense was improper when the sanction was based upon the defendant's failure to produce evidence that was not within his possession or control).

§ 6:32 Opposing authorities—Requests for admission

Favia v. Ford Motor Co., 381 Ill. App. 3d 809, 320 Ill. Dec. 113, 886 N.E.2d 1182 (1st Dist. 2008), appeal pending, (Sept. 1, 2008) (objections to requests to admit were not required to be sworn).

Favia v. Ford Motor Co., 381 Ill. App. 3d 809, 320 Ill. Dec. 113, 886 N.E.2d 1182 (1st Dist. 2008), appeal pending, (Sept. 1, 2008) (a sworn response to requests to admit by an agent of the party was sufficient).

Vision Point of Sale, Inc. v. Haas, 226 Ill. 2d 334, 354–55, 314 Ill. Dec. 778, 875 N.E.2d 1065 (2007) (party is not required to verify and sign responses to requests to admit in order for the responses to be valid) (overruling *Moy v. Ng*, 341 Ill. App. 3d 984, 276 Ill. Dec. 160, 793 N.E.2d 919 (1st Dist. 2003)).

Vision Point of Sale, Inc. v. Haas, 226 Ill. 2d 334, 356–58, 314 Ill. Dec. 778, 875 N.E.2d 1065 (2007) (trial court erred by finding that responses to requests to admit that complied with the Illinois Supreme Court Rules were nonetheless invalid for failing to comply with a local rule).

Vision Point of Sale, Inc. v. Haas, 226 Ill. 2d 334, 356–58, 314 Ill. Dec. 778, 875 N.E.2d 1065 (2007) (when determining whether good cause exists for an extension of time to respond to requests to admit, a trial court can consider whether there was "mistake, inadvertence, or attorney neglect, but may not engage in an open-minded inquiry which considers conduct that is unrelated to the causes of the party's original noncompliance.") (overruling *Hammond v. SBC Communications, Inc.*, 365 Ill. App. 3d 879, 302 Ill. Dec. 828, 850 N.E.2d 265 (1st Dist. 2006); *Robbins v. Allstate Ins. Co.*, 362 Ill. App. 3d 540, 298 Ill. Dec. 879, 841 N.E.2d 22 (2d Dist. 2005); *Larson v. O'Donnell*, 361 Ill. App. 3d 388, 297 Ill. Dec. 132, 836 N.E.2d 863 (1st Dist. 2005); *Cothren v. Thompson*, 356 Ill. App. 3d 279, 292 Ill. Dec. 393, 826 N.E.2d 534 (4th Dist. 2005); and *Glasco v. Marony*, 347 Ill. App. 3d 1069, 283 Ill. Dec. 819, 808 N.E.2d 1107 (5th Dist. 2004)).

Village of Oak Lawn v. Faber, 378 Ill. App. 3d 458, 475, 316 Ill. Dec. 923, 880 N.E.2d 659 (1st Dist. 2007) (party is not bound by an admission to a conclusion of law).

McNamee v. Sandore, 373 Ill. App. 3d 636, 648–50, 312 Ill. Dec. 111, 869 N.E.2d 1102 (2d Dist. 2007), appeal denied, 225 Ill. 2d 637, 314 Ill. Dec. 826, 875 N.E.2d 1113 (2007) (admission of agency was a legal conclusion and thus, judicial estoppel would not bar a party from later offering evidence to refute that admission).

First Nat. Bank of LaGrange v. Lowrey, 375 Ill. App. 3d 181, 220, 313 Ill. Dec. 464, 872 N.E.2d 447 (1st Dist. 2007), appeal denied, 226 Ill. 2d 583, 316 Ill. Dec. 542, 879 N.E.2d 930 (2007) (party was not required to respond to requests to admit that were speculative).

First Nat. Bank of LaGrange v. Lowrey, 375 Ill. App. 3d 181, 218–20, 313 Ill. Dec. 464, 872 N.E.2d 447 (1st Dist. 2007), appeal denied, 226 Ill. 2d 583, 316 Ill. Dec. 542, 879 N.E.2d 930 (2007) (party was not required to respond to a request to admit that was in dispute and would have conceded the entire case).

Troyan v. Reyes, 367 Ill. App. 3d 729, 739-40, 305 Ill. Dec. 451, 855 N.E.2d 967 (3d Dist. 2006) (rather than find certain issues to be deemed admitted based upon the defendant's failure to answer some of the plaintiff's requests to admit, the appellate court directed that on remand, the trial court should allow the defendant to amend her responses to the plaintiff's requests to admit, even though the defendant had improperly objected to the requests).

Feret v. Schillerstrom, 363 Ill. App. 3d 534, 539–40, 300 Ill. Dec. 449, 844 N.E.2d 447 (2d Dist. 2006) (trial court improperly found that a party had made a judicial admission to a legal conclusion).

Golf Trust of America, L.P. v. Soat, 355 Ill. App. 3d 333, 335–36, 290 Ill. Dec. 977, 822 N.E.2d 562 (2d Dist. 2005) (under tax statute, no pleadings were required beyond initial pleadings, and answers to requests to admit were considered pleadings; because collector was not required to file answers to requests to admit, collector was also permitted to file "untimely" answers to requests).

Szczeblewski v. Gossett, 342 Ill. App. 3d 344, 277 Ill. Dec. 1, 795 N.E.2d 368 (5th Dist. 2003) (requests for legal conclusions are improper; however, requests for admissions of factual questions which might give rise to legal conclusions are not improper).

Walker v. Valor Ins. Co., 314 Ill. App. 3d 55, 61-64, 246 Ill. Dec. 835, 731 N.E.2d 363 (1st Dist. 2000) (a legal conclusion is not the proper subject for a request to admit).

P.R.S. Intern., Inc. v. Shred Pax Corp., 184 Ill. 2d 224, 233–44, 234 Ill. Dec. 459, 703 N.E.2d 71 (1998) (conclusions of law are not the proper subject of requests to admit).

Deboe v. Flick, 172 Ill. App. 3d 673, 677–78, 122 Ill. Dec. 520, 526 N.E.2d 913 (5th Dist. 1988) (party must raise the lack of response by the opposing party to the request to admit in order for the issues to be deemed admitted).

§ 6:33 Opposing authorities—Requests for admission—Waiver by party seeking admission

Magee v. Walbro, Inc., 171 Ill. App. 3d 774, 779–81, 121 Ill. Dec. 668, 525 N.E.2d 975 (1st Dist. 1988) (a party can waive the opposing party's admissions by presenting evidence at trial on the issue that was admitted; however, in this case, the party did not waive the admissions because she was forced to present evidence after the trial judge had improperly allowed the opposing party to file untimely answers to the requests to admit).

§ 6:34 Opposing authorities—Requests for admission—Compare: Binding admissions at deposition

CFC Investment, L.L.C. v. McLean, 387 Ill.App.3d 520, 529–30, 900 N.E.2d 716 (1st Dist. 2008) (a party's speculative deposition testimony was not admissible as an admission).

Kimco Corp. v. Murdoch, Coll & Lillibridge, Inc., 313 Ill. App. 3d 768, 775–79, 246 Ill. Dec. 678, 730 N.E.2d 1143 (1st Dist. 2000) (party's statement during the deposition was not unequivocal enough to be considered a binding judicial admission, so as to preclude further proof regarding the issue).

B. MOTION TO EXCLUDE EVIDENCE OF CLAIMS DENIED DURING DISCOVERY

§ 6:35 Suggested motion text

[Name of moving party] hereby moves this Court for an order prohibiting *[name of party]* from introducing or mentioning any evidence relating to *[describe claim or claims denied during discovery]*. The motion is based upon the ground that *[name of party]* denied that a claim would be pursued on this matter in response to *[describe discovery propounded by moving party]* and therefore *[name of moving party]* assumed the matter would not be litigated. Any introduction of evidence on this issue will create unfair surprise and a substantial danger of undue prejudice to *[name of moving party]*.

§ 6:36 Motion summary

This motion seeks to prevent unfair surprise at trial caused by the introduction of evidence regarding claims denied during discovery. Such surprise can be prejudicial, justifying evidence preclusion. See *Harding v. Amsted Industries, Inc.*, 276 Ill. App. 3d 483, 492, 213 Ill. Dec. 187, 658 N.E.2d 1208 (1st Dist. 1995) (trial judge properly excluded expert testimony that exceeded the opinions expressed by the expert during discovery).

§ 6:37 Supporting authorities—Exclusion of prejudicial evidence, generally

Federal Rule of Evidence 403 states:

> Although relevant, evidence may be excluded if its probative value is substantially outweighed by the danger of unfair prejudice, confusion of the issues, or misleading the jury, or by considerations of undue delay, waste of time, or needless presentation of cumulative evidence.

It must be noted that this Rule has not been codified in

Illinois. However, Illinois cases have stated that Illinois has a common-law rule that is comparable to Federal Rule of Evidence 403. See *People v. Walker*, 335 Ill. App. 3d 102, 112, 268 Ill. Dec. 654, 779 N.E.2d 268 (2d Dist. 2002), as modified on denial of reh'g, (Oct. 24, 2002) and judgment aff'd, 211 Ill. 2d 317, 285 Ill. Dec. 519, 812 N.E.2d 339 (2004); and *People v. Peete*, 318 Ill. App. 3d 961, 966–67, 252 Ill. Dec. 821, 743 N.E.2d 689 (4th Dist. 2001). Therefore, it is arguable that Federal Rule of Evidence 403 can be considered as persuasive authority in Illinois.

Montana v. Egelhoff, 518 U.S. 37, 41–43, 116 S. Ct. 2013, 135 L. Ed. 2d 361 (1996) (Due Process does not guarantee the right to introduce all relevant evidence and therefore, Federal Rule of Evidence 403 does not violate Due Process).

For expanded citations on the exclusion of prejudicial evidence, see § 2:1 to § 2:4.

§ 6:38 Supporting authorities—Exclusion of prejudicial evidence, generally—Unfair surprise

Harding v. Amsted Industries, Inc., 276 Ill. App. 3d 483, 492, 213 Ill. Dec. 187, 658 N.E.2d 1208 (1st Dist. 1995) (trial judge properly excluded expert testimony that exceeded the opinions expressed by the expert during discovery).

Savage v. Martin, 256 Ill. App. 3d 272, 285, 195 Ill. Dec. 142, 628 N.E.2d 606 (1st Dist. 1993) (expert opinion that went beyond opinions stated at deposition was properly excluded, where expert stated that he had no other opinions beyond those in his report).

§ 6:39 Supporting authorities—Exclusion of prejudicial evidence, generally—Where privilege raised during discovery

D.C. v. S.A., 178 Ill. 2d 551, 566–70, 227 Ill. Dec. 550, 687 N.E.2d 1032 (1997) (improper to allow a plaintiff to use the protection of a privilege as an unfair weapon against the other party).

Giampa v. Illinois Civil Service Commission, 89 Ill. App. 3d 606, 613–14, 44 Ill. Dec. 744, 411 N.E.2d 1110 (1st Dist. 1980) (not improper to consider a party's decision not to testify at an administrative hearing, even though it might have incriminated the party in a separate criminal proceeding if the party had testified).

Galante v. Steel City Nat. Bank of Chicago, 66 Ill. App. 3d

476, 477–483, 23 Ill. Dec. 421, 384 N.E.2d 57 (1st Dist. 1978) (plaintiff in a civil suit could be forced to choose between waiving privilege or dismissal of the lawsuit but the same is not true for defendants).

Moore v. Wright, 90 Ill. 470, 1878 WL 10189, at *1–2 (1878) (trial judge improperly instructed the jury regarding inferences from a party failing to testify).

See also 725 ILCS 5/115-16, which states as follows:

> Witness disqualification. No person shall be disqualified as a witness in a criminal case or proceeding by reason of his or her interest in the event of the case or proceeding, as a party or otherwise, or by reason of his or her having been convicted of a crime; but the interest or conviction may be shown for the purpose of affecting the credibility of the witness. *A defendant in a criminal case or proceeding shall only at his or her own request be deemed a competent witness, and the person's neglect to testify shall not create a presumption against the person, nor shall the court permit a reference or comment to be made to or upon that neglect.*
>
> In criminal cases, husband and wife may testify for or against each other. Neither, however, may testify as to any communication or admission made by either of them to the other or as to any conversation between them during marriage, except in cases in which either is charged with an offense against the person or property of the other, in case of spouse abandonment, when the interests of their child or children or of any child or children in either spouse's care, custody, or control are directly involved, when either is charged under Section 12-13, 12-14, 12-14.1, 12-15, or 12-16 of the Criminal Code of 1961 and the victim is a minor under 18 years of age in either spouse's care, custody, or control at the time of the offense, or as to matters in which either has acted as agent of the other. (Emphasis added.)

§ 6:40 Supporting authorities—Other grounds

Other possible grounds for excluding matters denied during discovery include:

- Time-wasting (§ 2:5 to § 2:8)
- Confusing or misleading (§ 2:9 to § 2:12)
- Irrelevant (§ 3:1 to § 3:10)
- Collateral to issues in case (§ 3:11 to § 3:21)
- Admitted matter (§ 6:22)

§ 6:41 Opposing authorities—Generally

Troyan v. Reyes, 367 Ill. App. 3d 729, 739-40, 305 Ill. Dec. 451, 855 N.E.2d 967 (3d Dist. 2006) (rather than find certain issues to be deemed admitted based upon the defendant's failure to answer some of the plaintiff's requests to admit, the appellate court directed that on remand, the trial court should allow the defendant to amend her responses to the plaintiff's requests to admit, even though the defendant had improperly objected to the requests).

Golf Trust of America, L.P. v. Soat, 355 Ill. App. 3d 333, 335–36, 290 Ill. Dec. 977, 822 N.E.2d 562 (2d Dist. 2005) (under tax statute, no pleadings were required beyond initial pleadings, and answers to requests to admit were considered pleadings; because collector was not required to file answers to requests to admit, collector was also permitted to file "untimely" answers to requests).

Walker v. Valor Ins. Co., 314 Ill. App. 3d 55, 61-64, 246 Ill. Dec. 835, 731 N.E.2d 363 (1st Dist. 2000) (a legal conclusion is not the proper subject for a request to admit).

Kimco Corp. v. Murdoch, Coll & Lillibridge, Inc., 313 Ill. App. 3d 768, 775–79, 246 Ill. Dec. 678, 730 N.E.2d 1143 (1st Dist. 2000) (party's statement during the deposition was not unequivocal enough to be considered a binding judicial admission, so as to preclude further proof regarding the issue).

P.R.S. Intern., Inc. v. Shred Pax Corp., 184 Ill. 2d 224, 233–44, 234 Ill. Dec. 459, 703 N.E.2d 71 (1998) (conclusions of law are not the proper subject of requests to admit).

§ 6:42 Opposing authorities—Lack of surprise

Bauer ex rel. Bauer v. Memorial Hosp., 377 Ill. App. 3d 895, 913–15, 316 Ill. Dec. 411, 879 N.E.2d 478 (5th Dist. 2007), appeal denied, 227 Ill. 2d 577, 321 Ill. Dec. 249, 888 N.E.2d 1182 (2008) (absent prejudice to the opposing party, it is not reversible error to admit undisclosed expert opinions).

Tierney v. Community Memorial General Hosp., 268 Ill. App. 3d 1050, 1055–57, 206 Ill. Dec. 279, 645 N.E.2d 284 (1st Dist. 1994) (no error in permitting party's expert to express opinion that was undisclosed at deposition, when the opposing party knew that the subject matter of the testimony would be an issue at trial and had prepared to respond to the subject matter).

Zimmer v. Melendez, 222 Ill. App. 3d 390, 394–96, 164 Ill. Dec. 836, 583 N.E.2d 1158 (2d Dist. 1991) (trial court abused its discretion by excluding testimony that was undisclosed in interrogatories, when the subject matter of the testimony was not a surprise to the opposing party and when the interrogatory that might have covered the subject matter was open-ended and did not clearly request the information at issue).

C. MOTIONS REGARDING EXPERT DISCLOSURES AND EXPERT DEPOSITIONS

The goal of Supreme Court Rule 213 is to avoid unfair surprise and prejudice by requiring the parties to disclose their witnesses, the subject matters of their testimony and any opinions they may have. The parties have an obligation to seasonably supplement their 213 disclosures. The opposition is entitled to rely on the other parties' disclosures. Most cases come down to a "battle of the experts." Therefore, complete disclosure of all expert opinions and the bases therefore are critical. However, it should be noted, that because lay witnesses can offer "opinion evidence," disclosure of all lay witness opinions is also critical. A motion in limine which bars all evidence, witnesses, opinions and bases therefore, and testimony that have not been previously disclosed during the course of discovery is strongly encouraged.

§ 6:43 Suggested motion text

Alternative One [Limiting of Testimony]

[Name of moving party] hereby moves this Court for an order excluding any and all evidence, references to evidence, testimony or argument relating to the testimony of *[name of witness]* with respect to *[describe testimony and evidence to be excluded]*. The motion is based upon the ground that *[describe grounds, e.g., the testimony related to matters not disclosed in the opposition's expert disclosures]* and therefore allowing such testimony would create unfair surprise and prejudice to the moving party.

Alternative Two [Undisclosed Witness]

[Name of moving party] hereby moves this Court for an order precluding *[name of witness]* from testifying at the trial of this matter based upon the fact that *[opposing party]* failed to properly disclose said witness pursuant to Illinois Supreme Court Rule 213. This Court has the clear authority to preclude the testimony of said witness to prevent unfair surprise and prejudice to the moving party.

§ 6:44 Motion summary

This motion seeks to exclude expert witness testimony based upon a deficiency in the required expert witness disclosures [Illinois Supreme Court Rule 213] or improper expert testimony. These challenges typically arise where there has been a non-disclosure of experts [*Paquet v. Steiner*, 239 Ill. App. 3d 866, 867–71, 180 Ill. Dec. 546, 607 N.E.2d 615 (2d Dist. 1993)], improper description of expected testimony [*Savage v. Martin*, 256 Ill. App. 3d 272, 285, 195 Ill. Dec. 142, 628 N.E.2d 606 (1st Dist. 1993)], or the expert fails to provide complete opinions at the time of his or her deposition [*Harding v. Amsted Industries, Inc.*, 276 Ill. App. 3d 483, 492, 213 Ill. Dec. 187, 658 N.E.2d 1208 (1st Dist. 1995)].

§ 6:45 Supporting authorities—Improper expert witness disclosure

Illinois Supreme Court Rule 213 states in relevant part:

> (f) Identity and Testimony of Witnesses. Upon written interrogatory, a party must furnish the identities and addresses of witnesses who will testify at trial and must provide the following information:
>
> (1) *Lay Witnesses.* A "lay witness" is a person giving only fact or lay opinion testimony. For each lay witness, the party must identify the subjects on which the witness will testify. An answer is sufficient if it gives reasonable notice of the testimony, taking into account the limitations on the party's knowledge of the facts known by and opinions held by the witness.
>
> (2) *Independent Expert Witnesses.* An "independent expert witness" is a person giving expert testimony who is not the party, the party's current employee, or the party's retained expert. For each independent expert witness, the party must identify the subjects on which the witness will testify and the opinions the party expects to elicit. An answer is sufficient if it gives reasonable notice of the testimony, taking into account the limitations on the party's knowledge of the facts known by and opinions held by the witness.
>
> (3) *Controlled Expert Witnesses.* A "controlled expert witness" is a person giving expert testimony who is the party, the party's current employee, or the party's retained expert. For each controlled expert witness, the party must identify: (i) the subject matter on which the witness will testify; (ii) the conclusions and opinions of the witness and the bases therefore; (iii) the qualifications of the witness; and (iv) any reports prepared by the witness about the case.
>
> (g) Limitation on Testimony and Freedom to Cross-Examine. *The information disclosed in answer to a Rule 213 (f) interrogatory, or at deposition, limits the testimony that can be given by a witness on direct examination.* Information expressed in a deposition need not be later specifically identified in a Rule 213(f) answer, but, upon objection at trial, the burden is on the proponent of the witness to prove the information was provided in a Rule 213(f) answer or in the deposition.
>
> Without making disclosure under this rule, however, a cross-examining party can elicit information, including opinions, from the witness. This freedom to cross-examine is subject to a restriction that applies in actions that involve multiple parties and

multiple representation. In such actions, the cross- examining party may not elicit undisclosed information, including opinions, from the witness on an issue on which its position is aligned with that of the party doing the direct examination . . . .

(i) Duty to Supplement. A party has a duty to seasonably supplement or amend any prior answer or response whenever new or additional information subsequently becomes known to that party . . . .

(k) Liberal Construction. This rule is to be liberally construed to do substantial justice between or among the parties. (Emphasis added.)

§ 6:46 Supporting authorities—Improper expert witness disclosure—Insufficient expert disclosure

Lopez v. Northwestern Memorial Hosp., 375 Ill. App. 3d 637, 644–46, 313 Ill. Dec. 796, 873 N.E.2d 420 (1st Dist. 2007) (trial court properly excluded an undisclosed expert opinion regarding causation).

In re Detention of Lieberman, 379 Ill. App. 3d 585, 318 Ill. Dec. 605, 884 N.E.2d 160, 179–82 (1st Dist. 2007), appeal denied, 229 Ill. 2d 623, 325 Ill. Dec. 4, 897 N.E.2d 252 (2008) and cert. denied, 129 S.Ct. 2050, 77 USLW 3400, 77 USLW 3592, 77 USLW 3594 (U.S.Ill. Apr 27, 2009) (expert testimony that was not disclosed during discovery and that was cumulative of other testimony, was properly excluded).

Chapman v. Hubbard Woods Motors, Inc., 351 Ill. App. 3d 99, 108–10, 285 Ill. Dec. 569, 812 N.E.2d 389 (1st Dist. 2004) (trial court did not err by preventing expert from testifying that he had reviewed certain records where records were not disclosed as basis for opinion during deposition or in responses to interrogatories).

Harding v. Amsted Industries, Inc., 276 Ill. App. 3d 483, 492, 213 Ill. Dec. 187, 658 N.E.2d 1208 (1st Dist. 1995) (trial judge properly excluded expert testimony that exceeded the opinions expressed by the expert at the expert's deposition).

Paquet v. Steiner, 239 Ill. App. 3d 866, 867–71, 180 Ill. Dec. 546, 607 N.E.2d 615 (2d Dist. 1993) (trial judge properly excluded expert testimony and then granted summary judgment based upon the lack of expert testimony, when no expert was disclosed in a timely fashion and there was no justifiable reason for the delay in disclosure).

Savage v. Martin, 256 Ill. App. 3d 272, 285, 195 Ill. Dec. 142, 628 N.E.2d 606 (1st Dist. 1993) (expert opinion that went beyond opinions stated at deposition was properly excluded, where expert stated that he had no other opinions beyond those in his report).

Perez v. Hartmann, 187 Ill. App. 3d 1098, 1101–04, 135 Ill. Dec. 455, 543 N.E.2d 1023 (1st Dist. 1989) (trial judge properly excluded evidence based upon a party's failure to produce it in discovery until one month before trial, when the party's expert had access to the evidence in preparing for deposition but the opposing party's expert did not).

§ 6:47 Supporting authorities—Improper expert witness disclosure—Undisclosed witness

Lopez v. Northwestern Memorial Hosp., 375 Ill. App. 3d 637, 644–46, 313 Ill. Dec. 796, 873 N.E.2d 420 (1st Dist. 2007) (trial court properly excluded an undisclosed expert opinion regarding causation).

Nedzvekas v. Fung, 374 Ill. App. 3d 618, 619–23, 313 Ill. Dec. 448, 872 N.E.2d 431 (1st Dist. 2007) (trial court had discretion to exclude an undisclosed expert's opinion).

Bill Marek's The Competitive Edge, Inc. v. Mickelson Group, Inc., 346 Ill. App. 3d 996, 1006–09, 282 Ill. Dec. 305, 806 N.E.2d 280 (2d Dist. 2004) (trial court did not err by striking defendant's witnesses and affidavits, as a discovery sanction for failing to timely disclose witnesses and nature of their testimony).

Sullivan v. Edward Hosp., 209 Ill. 2d 100, 107–11, 282 Ill. Dec. 348, 806 N.E.2d 645 (2004) (trial court properly barred testimony of undisclosed expert).

Paquet v. Steiner, 239 Ill. App. 3d 866, 867–71, 180 Ill. Dec. 546, 607 N.E.2d 615 (2d Dist. 1993) (trial judge properly excluded expert testimony and then granted summary judgment based upon the lack of expert testimony, when no expert was disclosed in a timely fashion and there was no justifiable reason for the delay in disclosure).

Renfro v. Allied Indus. Equipment Corp., 155 Ill. App. 3d 140, 161–63, 107 Ill. Dec. 844, 507 N.E.2d 1213 (5th Dist. 1987) (trial judge properly excluded testimony of undisclosed expert when the expert was not disclosed until after the other party had rested).

See also *Atwood v. Warner Elec. Brake and Clutch Co., Inc.*, 239 Ill. App. 3d 81, 88-91, 179 Ill. Dec. 18, 605 N.E.2d 1032 (2d Dist. 1992) (trial judge had discretion to bar evidence and claims for failure to provide the ordered discovery by the trial judge's cut-off date).

§ 6:48 Supporting authorities—Opinions not referenced at deposition

The following citations may support a motion to exclude portions of expert testimony relating to opinions not disclosed at the expert's deposition. The motion is usually made when it is anticipated that the expert will testify to new opinions formed after the deposition, even after responding in the negative to a deposition question such as: "Do you have any other opinions not yet expressed?"

Lisowski v. MacNeal Memorial Hosp. Ass'n, 381 Ill. App. 3d 275, 319 Ill. Dec. 440, 885 N.E.2d 1120 (1st Dist. 2008), appeal denied, 229 Ill. 2d 626, 325 Ill. Dec. 5, 897 N.E.2d 253 (2008) (trial court properly barred the opinions of experts that went beyond the specific opinions that were disclosed in discovery).

In re Detention of Lieberman, 379 Ill. App. 3d 585, 318 Ill. Dec. 605, 884 N.E.2d 160, 179–82 (1st Dist. 2007), appeal denied, 229 Ill. 2d 623, 325 Ill. Dec. 4, 897 N.E.2d 252 (2008) and cert. denied, 129 S.Ct. 2050, 77 USLW 3400, 77 USLW 3592, 77 USLW 3594 (U.S.Ill. Apr 27, 2009) (expert testimony that was not disclosed during discovery and that was cumulative of other testimony, was properly excluded).

Nedzvekas v. Fung, 374 Ill. App. 3d 618, 619–23, 313 Ill. Dec. 448, 872 N.E.2d 431 (1st Dist. 2007) (trial court had discretion to exclude an undisclosed expert's opinion).

Shaheen v. Advantage Moving and Storage, Inc., 369 Ill. App. 3d 535, 542-43, 307 Ill. Dec. 721, 860 N.E.2d 375 (1st Dist. 2006) (the trial court had discretion to bar certain undisclosed portions of an expert's opinion).

Chapman v. Hubbard Woods Motors, Inc., 351 Ill. App. 3d 99, 108–10, 285 Ill. Dec. 569, 812 N.E.2d 389 (1st Dist. 2004) (trial court did not err by preventing expert from testifying that he had reviewed certain records where records were not disclosed as basis for opinion during the deposition or in responses to interrogatories).

Harding v. Amsted Industries, Inc., 276 Ill. App. 3d 483, 492, 213 Ill. Dec. 187, 658 N.E.2d 1208 (1st Dist. 1995) (trial judge properly excluded expert testimony that exceeded the opinions expressed by the expert at the expert's deposition).

Savage v. Martin, 256 Ill. App. 3d 272, 285, 195 Ill. Dec. 142, 628 N.E.2d 606 (1st Dist. 1993) (expert opinion that went beyond opinions stated at deposition was properly excluded, where expert stated that he had no other opinions beyond those in his report).

Savage v. Martin, 256 Ill. App. 3d 272, 285, 195 Ill. Dec. 142,

628 N.E.2d 606 (1st Dist. 1993) (party had obligation to disclose additional opinion of expert beyond that stated at expert's deposition, so that opposing party could determine whether there was a need for an additional deposition).

§ 6:49 Opposing authorities—Expert witness disclosures

Johnson v. Johnson, 386 Ill.App.3d 522, 548–49, 898 N.E.2d 145 (1st Dist. 2008) (trial court had discretion to admit an undisclosed expert opinion that was not a surprise to the opposing party).

Beard v. Barron, 379 Ill. App. 3d 1, 16-18, 317 Ill. Dec. 906, 882 N.E.2d 1062 (1st Dist. 2008), appeal pending, (May 1, 2008) and appeal denied, 228 Ill. 2d 529, 321 Ill. Dec. 554, 889 N.E.2d 1114 (2008) (cross-examination questions that expanded upon an expert's opinion were within the scope of the direct examination about those opinions).

Favia v. Ford Motor Co., 381 Ill. App. 3d 809, 320 Ill. Dec. 113, 886 N.E.2d 1182 (1st Dist. 2008), appeal pending, (Sept. 1, 2008) (trial court had discretion to allow an expert to testify to certain undisclosed opinions).

Pancoe v. Singh, 376 Ill. App. 3d 900, 912–15, 315 Ill. Dec. 288, 876 N.E.2d 288 (1st Dist. 2007), appeal denied, 226 Ill. 2d 617, 317 Ill. Dec. 504, 882 N.E.2d 78 (2008) (trial court did not abuse its discretion by allowing an undisclosed expert to testify when the opposing party was not surprised or prejudiced by the expert's testimony and, in fact, had disclosed the same expert).

Brdar v. Cottrell, Inc., 372 Ill. App. 3d 690, 700–01, 311 Ill. Dec. 99, 867 N.E.2d 1085 (5th Dist. 2007), appeal denied, 224 Ill. 2d 572, 312 Ill. Dec. 654, 871 N.E.2d 54 (2007) (trial court had discretion to allow the testimony of experts who were not timely disclosed because the opposing party was not surprised or prejudiced and because the opposing party did not raise a timely objection and instead waited until the eve of trial to object).

Gee v. Treece, 365 Ill. App. 3d 1029, 1035-37, 303 Ill. Dec. 418, 851 N.E.2d 605 (5th Dist. 2006) (when the testimony would not surprise the opposing party, trial court had discretion to allow the testimony of an untimely disclosed expert witness).

Brax v. Kennedy, 363 Ill. App. 3d 343, 353–56, 298 Ill. Dec. 994, 841 N.E.2d 137 (1st Dist. 2005) (the trial court did not abuse its discretion by allowing a defendant doctor to expand on the opinion that he gave at his deposition).

Foley v. Fletcher, 361 Ill. App. 3d 39, 41-49, 296 Ill. Dec. 916, 836 N.E.2d 667 (1st Dist. 2005) (the trial court did not abuse its discretion by determining that an allegedly undisclosed expert opinion was admissible where it was a logical extension of the expert's disclosed opinion).

In re Marriage of Booher, 313 Ill. App. 3d 356, 359–61, 245 Ill. Dec. 873, 728 N.E.2d 1230 (4th Dist. 2000) (trial judge should only preclude information related to the issues that the non-complying party failed to disclose during discovery and should not bar all evidence, even that which is related to disclosed matters).

Jarke v. Jackson Products, Inc., 282 Ill. App. 3d 292, 296–98, 217 Ill. Dec. 861, 668 N.E.2d 46 (1st Dist. 1996) (not an abuse of discretion to allow an expert to testify to a theory that was not explicitly disclosed but that was arguably included within a broad term the expert had used in describing his opinion).

Zimmer v. Melendez, 222 Ill. App. 3d 390, 394–96, 164 Ill. Dec. 836, 583 N.E.2d 1158 (2d Dist. 1991) (trial court abused its discretion by excluding expert testimony that was undisclosed in interrogatories, when the subject matter of the testimony was not a surprise to the opposing party and when the interrogatory that might have covered the subject matter was open-ended and did not clearly request the information at issue).

Renfro v. Allied Indus. Equipment Corp., 155 Ill. App. 3d 140, 160–61, 107 Ill. Dec. 844, 507 N.E.2d 1213 (5th Dist. 1987) (in a case with multiple defendants, no error in allowing the plaintiff to call an expert witness over the objection of one of the defendants, even where the witness was not properly disclosed where the parties were able to depose the witness prior to the witness' testimony).

Gee v. Davidson, 21 Ill. App. 3d 654, 315 N.E.2d 674 (1st Dist. 1974) (only abstract published) (trial judge properly allowed expert testimony that had not been disclosed in response to interrogatories when the same information had been provided by other means of discovery).

§ 6:50 Opposing authorities—Expert witness disclosures—Continuance to depose or retain expert

Spurgeon v. Mruz, 358 Ill. App. 3d 358, 295 Ill. Dec. 170, 832 N.E.2d 321, 323–24 (1st Dist. 2005) (trial court did not abuse its discretion by refusing to bar expert as discovery sanction for late disclosure when opposing party was not surprised by testimony and refused trial court's offer of continuance).

In re Margaret S., 347 Ill. App. 3d 1091, 1094–96, 283 Ill. Dec. 734, 808 N.E.2d 1022 (5th Dist. 2004) (trial court should have allowed party to obtain independent medical examination, which might have allowed party to have a defense or an opposing expert at the trial).

Phillips v. Gannotti, 327 Ill. App. 3d 512, 518–21, 261 Ill. Dec. 571, 763 N.E.2d 820 (1st Dist. 2002) (trial judge should not have excluded undisclosed lay witness opinion testimony and then granted a directed verdict, when a continuance for further discovery would have alleviated the prejudice from the non-disclosure and the non-disclosure was not the fault of the non-disclosing party).

Kurrack v. American Dist. Telegraph Co., 252 Ill. App. 3d 885, 902–04, 192 Ill. Dec. 520, 625 N.E.2d 675 (1st Dist. 1993) (trial court did not abuse its discretion by granting brief continuance to depose expert, instead of excluding the expert's testimony as requested).

Renfro v. Allied Indus. Equipment Corp., 155 Ill. App. 3d 140, 160–61, 107 Ill. Dec. 844, 507 N.E.2d 1213 (5th Dist. 1987) (in a case with multiple defendants, no error in allowing the plaintiff to call an expert witness over the objection of one of the defendants, even where the witness was not properly disclosed where the parties were able to depose the witness prior to the witness' testimony).

But see *Paquet v. Steiner*, 239 Ill. App. 3d 866, 867–71, 180 Ill. Dec. 546, 607 N.E.2d 615 (2d Dist. 1993) (trial judge properly excluded expert testimony and then granted summary judgment based upon the lack of expert testimony, when no expert was disclosed in a timely fashion and there was no justifiable reason for the delay in disclosure, instead of granting a continuance for the other party to depose the expert); *Renfro v. Allied Indus. Equipment Corp.*, 155 Ill. App. 3d 140, 161–63, 107 Ill. Dec. 844, 507 N.E.2d 1213 (5th Dist. 1987) (trial judge properly excluded testimony of undisclosed expert when the expert was not disclosed until after the other party had rested her case and therefore, the opportunity for her to conduct effective discovery, even if a continuance were to be granted, was limited).

§ 6:51 Opposing authorities—Expert witness disclosures—Compare: Treating physicians

Illinois Supreme Court Rule 213 states in relevant part:

(f) Identity and Testimony of Witnesses. Upon written interrogatory, a party must furnish the identities and addresses of witnesses who will testify at trial and must provide the following information: . . . .

(2) Independent Expert Witnesses. An "independent expert witness" is a person giving expert testimony who is not the party, the party's current employee, or the party's retained expert. For each independent expert witness, the party must identify the subjects on which the witness will testify and the opinions the party expects to elicit. An answer is sufficient if it gives reasonable notice of the testimony, taking into account the limitations on the party's knowledge of the facts known by and opinions held by the witness.

(3) Controlled Expert Witnesses. A "controlled expert witness" is a person giving expert testimony who is the party, the party's current employee, or the party's retained expert. For each controlled expert witness, the party must identify: (i) the subject matter on which the witness will testify; (ii) the conclusions and opinions of the witness and the bases therefor; (iii) the qualifications of the witness; and (iv) any reports prepared by the witness about the case. (Emphasis added).

Nedzvekas v. Fung, 374 Ill. App. 3d 618, 623–24, 313 Ill. Dec. 448, 872 N.E.2d 431 (1st Dist. 2007) (a party does not need to disclose the basis for a treating physician's opinion, because a treating physician is considered an independent expert witness, rather than a controlled expert witness).

§ 6:52 Opposing authorities—Undisclosed opinions of expert—Lack of surprise or partial compliance

Grillo v. Yeager Const., 387 Ill.App.3d 577, 598–600, 900 N.E.2d 1249 (1st Dist. 2008) (trial court had discretion to admit evidence that was not disclosed in a timely fashion because the opposing party was not surprised or prejudiced).

Johnson v. Johnson, 386 Ill.App.3d 522, 548–49, 898 N.E.2d 145 (1st Dist. 2008) (trial court had discretion to admit an undisclosed expert opinion that was not a surprise to the opposing party).

Yoder v. Ferguson, 381 Ill. App. 3d 353, 319 Ill. Dec. 380, 885 N.E.2d 1060 (1st Dist. 2008), appeal pending, (Sept. 1, 2008) (trial court had discretion to allow an expert to elaborate on the opinions that were disclosed during discovery).

Bauer ex rel. Bauer v. Memorial Hosp., 377 Ill. App. 3d 895, 913–15, 316 Ill. Dec. 411, 879 N.E.2d 478 (5th Dist. 2007), appeal denied, 227 Ill. 2d 577, 321 Ill. Dec. 249, 888 N.E.2d 1182 (2008) (absent prejudice to the opposing party, it is not reversible error to admit undisclosed expert opinions).

Heriford v. Moore, 377 Ill. App. 3d 849, 851–54, 318 Ill. Dec. 247, 883 N.E.2d 81 (4th Dist. 2007), appeal denied, 227 Ill. 2d

580, 321 Ill. Dec. 250, 888 N.E.2d 1183 (2008) (trial court erred by barring evidence and entering a directed verdict as a sanction for a party's failure to properly disclose experts, when the opposing party was not surprised or prejudiced by the improper disclosure).

Pancoe v. Singh, 376 Ill. App. 3d 900, 912–15, 315 Ill. Dec. 288, 876 N.E.2d 288 (1st Dist. 2007), appeal denied, 226 Ill. 2d 617, 317 Ill. Dec. 504, 882 N.E.2d 78 (2008) (trial court did not abuse its discretion by allowing an undisclosed expert to testify when the opposing party was not surprised or prejudiced by the expert's testimony and, in fact, had disclosed the same expert).

Brdar v. Cottrell, Inc., 372 Ill. App. 3d 690, 700–01, 311 Ill. Dec. 99, 867 N.E.2d 1085 (5th Dist. 2007), appeal denied, 224 Ill. 2d 572, 312 Ill. Dec. 654, 871 N.E.2d 54 (2007) (trial court had discretion to allow the testimony of experts who were not timely disclosed because the opposing party was not surprised or prejudiced and because the opposing party did not raise a timely objection and instead waited until the eve of trial to object).

Gee v. Treece, 365 Ill. App. 3d 1029, 1035-37, 303 Ill. Dec. 418, 851 N.E.2d 605 (5th Dist. 2006) (when the testimony would not surprise the opposing party, trial court had discretion to allow the testimony of an untimely disclosed expert witness).

Brax v. Kennedy, 363 Ill. App. 3d 343, 353–56, 298 Ill. Dec. 994, 841 N.E.2d 137 (1st Dist. 2005) (the trial court did not abuse its discretion by allowing a defendant doctor to expand on the opinion that he gave at his deposition).

Foley v. Fletcher, 361 Ill. App. 3d 39, 41-49, 296 Ill. Dec. 916, 836 N.E.2d 667 (1st Dist. 2005) (the trial court did not abuse its discretion by determining that an allegedly undisclosed expert opinion was admissible where it was a logical extension of the expert's disclosed opinion).

Spurgeon v. Mruz, 358 Ill. App. 3d 358, 295 Ill. Dec. 170, 832 N.E.2d 321, 323–24 (1st Dist. 2005) (trial court did not abuse discretion by refusing to bar expert as a discovery sanction for late disclosure when opposing party was not surprised by testimony and refused trial court's offer of a continuance).

In re Marriage of Booher, 313 Ill. App. 3d 356, 359–61, 245 Ill. Dec. 873, 728 N.E.2d 1230 (4th Dist. 2000) (trial judge should only preclude information related to the issues that the non-complying party failed to disclose during discovery and should not bar all evidence, even that which is related to disclosed matters).

Jarke v. Jackson Products, Inc., 282 Ill. App. 3d 292, 296–98, 217 Ill. Dec. 861, 668 N.E.2d 46 (1st Dist. 1996) (not an abuse of discretion to allow an expert to testify to a theory that was not explicitly disclosed but that was arguably included within a broad term the expert had used in describing his opinion).

Zimmer v. Melendez, 222 Ill. App. 3d 390, 394–96, 164 Ill. Dec. 836, 583 N.E.2d 1158 (2d Dist. 1991) (trial court abused its discretion by excluding expert testimony that was undisclosed in interrogatories, when the subject matter of the testimony was not a surprise to the opposing party and when the interrogatory that might have covered the subject matter was open-ended and did not clearly request the information at issue).

§ 6:53 Opposing authorities—Undisclosed opinions of expert—No effort to follow up by deposing party

Brdar v. Cottrell, Inc., 372 Ill. App. 3d 690, 700–01, 311 Ill. Dec. 99, 867 N.E.2d 1085 (5th Dist. 2007), appeal denied, 224 Ill. 2d 572, 312 Ill. Dec. 654, 871 N.E.2d 54 (2007) (trial court had discretion to allow the testimony of experts who were not timely disclosed because the opposing party was not surprised or prejudiced and because the opposing party did not raise a timely objection and instead waited until the eve of trial to object).

Shaheen v. Advantage Moving and Storage, Inc., 369 Ill. App. 3d 535, 542-43, 307 Ill. Dec. 721, 860 N.E.2d 375 (1st Dist. 2006) (the trial court had discretion to allow certain undisclosed expert testimony because the opposing party had not been diligent in its attempt to discover the undisclosed part of the testimony).

Spurgeon v. Mruz, 358 Ill. App. 3d 358, 295 Ill. Dec. 170, 832 N.E.2d 321, 323–24 (1st Dist. 2005) (trial court did not abuse discretion by refusing to bar expert as a discovery sanction for late disclosure when opposing party was not surprised by testimony and refused trial court's offer of a continuance).

Hastings v. Gulledge, 272 Ill. App. 3d 861, 867–68, 209 Ill. Dec. 600, 651 N.E.2d 778 (5th Dist. 1995) (trial judge properly declined to strike expert's entire testimony when the opposing party did not take any action to compel answers after the expert refused to provide certain information at the deposition).

Jarke v. Jackson Products, Inc., 282 Ill. App. 3d 292, 296–98, 217 Ill. Dec. 861, 668 N.E.2d 46 (1st Dist. 1996) (not an abuse of discretion to allow an expert to testify to a theory that was not explicitly disclosed but that was arguably included within a broad term the expert had used in describing his opinion).

Tierney v. Community Memorial General Hosp., 268 Ill. App. 3d 1050, 1055–57, 206 Ill. Dec. 279, 645 N.E.2d 284 (1st Dist. 1994) (no error in permitting party's expert to express opinion that was undisclosed at deposition, when the opposing party knew that the subject matter of the testimony would be an issue at trial and had prepared to respond to the subject matter).

Zimmer v. Melendez, 222 Ill. App. 3d 390, 394–96, 164 Ill. Dec. 836, 583 N.E.2d 1158 (2d Dist. 1991) (trial court abused its discretion by excluding expert testimony that was undisclosed in interrogatories, when the subject matter of the testimony was not a surprise to the opposing party and therefore, the opposing party could have asked a clear and specific interrogatory to discover the information but did not do so).

§ 6:54 Opposing authorities—Undisclosed opinions of expert—Opportunity to re-depose experts

The trial judge has broad discretion to control discovery in an effort to achieve justice. Therefore, the court, in its discretion, can order additional discovery, including an additional deposition where justice so requires.

Allowing an additional deposition of the subject expert may be a satisfactory remedy to cure any potential prejudice. In opposing a motion to bar undisclosed additional opinions, counsel should offer to make his or her experts available for additional depositions, as necessary.

Spurgeon v. Mruz, 358 Ill. App. 3d 358, 295 Ill. Dec. 170, 832 N.E.2d 321, 323–24 (1st Dist. 2005) (trial court did not abuse discretion by refusing to bar expert as a discovery sanction for late disclosure when opposing party was not surprised by testimony and refused trial court's offer of a continuance).

D. MOTION TO EXCLUDE STATUTORILY PRIVILEGED INFORMATION

§ 6:55 Suggested motion text

[Name of moving party] hereby moves this court for an order prohibiting *[name of party]* from obtaining, introducing or mentioning any evidence relating to *[describe privileged information]*. The Motion is based upon the grounds that the information is privileged by statute.

§ 6:56 Motion summary

This motion seeks to prevent opposing party from obtaining or disclosing privileged information pursuant to the express language of Illinois Supreme Court Rule 201. Examples of privileged communications include, but are not limited to, therapist, clergy, medical studies, husband-wife, physician-patient, and attorney-client.

§ 6:57 Supporting authorities—Generally

Illinois Supreme Court Rule 201 states in relevant part:

> *All matters that are privileged against disclosure on the trial, including privileged communications between a party or his agent and the attorney for the party, are privileged against disclosure through any discovery procedure.* Material prepared by or for a party in preparation for trial is subject to discovery only if it does not contain or disclose the theories, mental impressions, or litigation plans of the party's attorney. (Emphasis added.)

People v. Bell, 373 Ill. App. 3d 811, 818–20, 311 Ill. Dec. 794, 869 N.E.2d 807 (1st Dist. 2007), appeal denied, 225 Ill. 2d 641, 314 Ill. Dec. 828, 875 N.E.2d 1115 (2007) (trial court had discretion to grant the state's request to protect an officer's secret surveillance location from disclosure to the defendant).

Thomas v. Page, 361 Ill. App. 3d 484, 486–97, 297 Ill. Dec. 400, 837 N.E.2d 483 (2d Dist. 2005) (communications between judges and law clerks are privileged).

§ 6:58 Supporting authorities—740 ILCS 110/10 (therapist privilege)

740 ILCS 110/10 provides in relevant part:

> (a) Except as provided herein, in any civil, criminal, administrative, or legislative proceeding, or in any proceeding preliminary thereto, a recipient, and a therapist on behalf and in the interest of a recipient, has the privilege to refuse to disclose and to prevent the disclosure of the recipient's record or communications.

But see the exceptions in 740 ILCS 110/10 (a)(1) to (12); see also 735 ILCS 5/8-802.1 (confidentiality of statements made to rape crisis personnel)and 735 ILCS 5/8-802.2 (confidentiality of statements made to personnel counseling victims of violent crime).

§ 6:59 Supporting authorities—735 ILCS 5/8-803 (clergy privilege)

735 ILCS 5/8-803, states in relevant part:

> Clergyman or practitioner of any religious denomination accred-

ited by the religious body to which he or she belongs, shall not be compelled to disclose in any court, or to any administrative board or agency, or to any public officer, a confession or admission made to him or her in his or her professional character or as a spiritual advisor in the course of the discipline enjoined by the rules or practices of such religious body or of the religion which he or she professes, nor be compelled to divulge any information which has been obtained by him or her in such professional character or as such spiritual advisor.

§ 6:60 Supporting authorities—735 ILCS 5/8-2101 (Medical Studies Act)

735 ILCS 5/8-2101 states in relevant part:

All information, interviews, reports, statements, memoranda, recommendations, letters of reference or other third party confidential assessments of a health care practitioner's professional competence, or other data of the Illinois Department of Public Health, local health departments, the Department of Human Services (as successor to the Department of Mental Health and Developmental Disabilities), the Mental Health and Developmental Disabilities Medical Review Board, Illinois State Medical Society, allied medical societies, health maintenance organizations, medical organizations under contract with health maintenance organizations or with insurance or other health care delivery entities or facilities, tissue banks, organ procurement agencies, physician-owned insurance companies and their agents, committees of ambulatory surgical treatment centers or post-surgical recovery centers or their medical staffs, or committees of licensed or accredited hospitals or their medical staffs, including Patient Care Audit Committees, Medical Care Evaluation Committees, Utilization Review Committees, Credential Committees and Executive Committees, or their designees (but not the medical records pertaining to the patient), used in the course of internal quality control or of medical study for the purpose of reducing morbidity or mortality, or for improving patient care or increasing organ and tissue donation, *shall be privileged, strictly confidential and shall be used only for medical research*, increasing organ and tissue donation, the evaluation and improvement of quality care, or granting, limiting or revoking staff privileges or agreements for services, except that in any health maintenance organization proceeding to decide upon a physician's services or any hospital or ambulatory surgical treatment center proceeding to decide upon a physician's staff privileges, or in any judicial review of either, the claim of confidentiality shall not be invoked to deny such physician access to or use of data upon which such a decision was based. (Emphasis added.)

§ 6:61 Supporting authorities—735 ILCS 5/8-801 (husband and wife privilege)

735 ILCS 5/8-801 provides in relevant part:

In all actions, husband and wife may testify for or against each other, provided that *neither may testify as to any communication or admission made by either of them to the other or as to any conversation between them during marriage*, except in actions between such husband and wife, and in actions where the custody, support, health or welfare of their children or children in either spouse's care, custody or control is directly in issue, and as to matters in which either has acted as agent for the other. (Emphasis added.)

§ 6:62 Supporting authorities—735 ILCS 5/8-802 (physician and patient privilege)

735 ILCS 5/8-802 provides in relevant part:

No physician or surgeon shall be permitted to disclose any information he or she may have acquired in attending any patient in a professional character, necessary to enable him or her professionally to serve the patient, except only (1) in trials for homicide when the disclosure relates directly to the fact or immediate circumstances of the homicide, (2) in actions, civil or criminal, against the physician for malpractice, (3) with the expressed consent of the patient, or in case of his or her death or disability, of his or her personal representative or other person authorized to sue for personal injury or of the beneficiary of an insurance policy on his or her life, health, or physical condition, (4) in all actions brought by or against the patient, his or her personal representative, a beneficiary under a policy of insurance, or the executor or administrator of his or her estate wherein the patient's physical or mental condition is an issue, (5) upon an issue as to the validity of a document as a will of the patient, (6) in any criminal action where the charge is either first degree murder by abortion, attempted abortion or abortion, (7) in actions, civil or criminal, arising from the filing of a report in compliance with the Abused and Neglected Child Reporting Act, (8) to any department, agency, institution or facility which has custody of the patient pursuant to State statute or any court order of commitment, (9) in prosecutions where written results of blood alcohol tests are admissible pursuant to Section 11-501.4 of the Illinois Vehicle Code, (10) in prosecutions where written results of blood alcohol tests are admissible under Section 5-11a of the Boat Registration and Safety Act, (11) in criminal actions arising from the filing of a report of suspected terrorist offense in compliance with Section 29D-10(p)(7) of the Criminal Code of 1961, or (12) upon the issuance of a subpoena pursuant to Section 38 of the Medical Practice Act of 1987; the issuance of a subpoena pursuant to Section 25.1 of the Illinois Dental Practice Act; or the issuance of a subpoena pursuant to Section 22 of the Nursing Home Administrators Licensing and Disciplinary Act. In the event of a conflict between the application of this Section and the Mental Health and Developmental Disabilities Confidentiality Act to a specific situation, the provisions of the Mental Health and Developmental Disabilities Confidentiality Act shall control.

§ 6:63 Supporting authorities—Illinois Supreme Court Rule 201 (work product/attorney and client)

Illinois Supreme Court Rule 201 states in relevant part:

All matters that are privileged against disclosure on the trial, including privileged communications between a party or his agent and the attorney for the party, *are privileged against disclosure through any discovery procedure. Material prepared by or for a party in preparation for trial is subject to discovery only if it does not contain or disclose the theories, mental impressions, or litigation plans of the party's attorney.* (Emphasis added.)

§ 6:64 Opposing authorities—735 ILCS 5/8-802.3 (informant's privilege)

735 ILCS 5/8-802.3 states:

(a) Except as provided in subsection (b), if an individual (i) submits information concerning a criminal act to a law enforcement agency or to a community organization that acts as an intermediary in reporting to law enforcement and (ii) requests anonymity, then the identity of that individual is privileged and confidential and is not subject to discovery or admissible in evidence in a proceeding.

(b) There is no privilege under subsection (a) if a court, after a hearing in camera, finds that the party seeking discovery or the proponent of the evidence has shown that:

(1) the identity of an individual who submits information concerning a criminal act is sought or offered in a court proceeding involving a felony or misdemeanor;

(2) the evidence is not otherwise available; and

(3) nondisclosure infringes upon a constitutional right of an accused, or there is a need for the evidence that substantially outweighs the interest in protecting confidentiality.

(c) The court may impose such sanctions as are necessary to enforce its order.

§ 6:65 Opposing authorities—740 ILCS 110/10 (therapist privilege)

740 ILCS 110/10(a) provides in relevant part:

(1) Records and communications may be disclosed in a civil, criminal or administrative proceeding in which the recipient introduces his mental condition or any aspect of his services received for such condition as an element of his claim or defense, if and only to the extent the court in which the proceedings have been brought, or, in the case of an administrative proceeding, the court to which an appeal or other action for review of an administrative determination may be taken, finds, after in camera examination of testimony or other evidence, that it is rel-

evant, probative, not unduly prejudicial or inflammatory, and otherwise clearly admissible; that other satisfactory evidence is demonstrably unsatisfactory as evidence of the facts sought to be established by such evidence; and that disclosure is more important to the interests of substantial justice than protection from injury to the therapist-recipient relationship or to the recipient or other whom disclosure is likely to harm. Except in a criminal proceeding in which the recipient, who is accused in that proceeding, raises the defense of insanity, no record or communication between a therapist and a recipient shall be deemed relevant for purposes of this subsection, except the fact of treatment, the cost of services and the ultimate diagnosis unless the party seeking disclosure of the communication clearly establishes in the trial court a compelling need for its production. However, for purposes of this Act, in any action brought or defended under the Illinois Marriage and Dissolution of Marriage Act, or in any action in which pain and suffering is an element of the claim, mental condition shall not be deemed to be introduced merely by making such claim and shall be deemed to be introduced only if the recipient or a witness on his behalf first testifies concerning the record or communication.

(2) Records or communications may be disclosed in a civil proceeding after the recipient's death when the recipient's physical or mental condition has been introduced as an element of a claim or defense by any party claiming or defending through or as a beneficiary of the recipient, provided the court finds, after in camera examination of the evidence, that it is relevant, probative, and otherwise clearly admissible; that other satisfactory evidence is not available regarding the facts sought to be established by such evidence; and that disclosure is more important to the interests of substantial justice than protection from any injury which disclosure is likely to cause.

(3) In the event of a claim made or an action filed by a recipient, or, following the recipient's death, by any party claiming as a beneficiary of the recipient for injury caused in the course of providing services to such recipient, the therapist and other persons whose actions are alleged to have been the cause of injury may disclose pertinent records and communications to an attorney or attorneys engaged to render advice about and to provide representation in connection with such matter and to persons working under the supervision of such attorney or attorneys, and may testify as to such records or communication in any administrative, judicial or discovery proceeding for the purpose of preparing and presenting a defense against such claim or action.

(4) Records and communications made to or by a therapist in the course of examination ordered by a court for good cause shown may, if otherwise relevant and admissible, be disclosed in a civil, criminal, or administrative proceeding in which the recipient is a party or in appropriate pretrial proceedings, provided such court has found that the recipient has been as adequately and as effectively as possible informed before submitting to such examina-

tion that such records and communications would not be considered confidential or privileged. Such records and communications shall be admissible only as to issues involving the recipient's physical or mental condition and only to the extent that these are germane to such proceedings.

(5) Records and communications may be disclosed in a proceeding under the Probate Act of 1975, to determine a recipient's competency or need for guardianship, provided that the disclosure is made only with respect to that issue.

(6) Records and communications may be disclosed when such are made during treatment which the recipient is ordered to undergo to render him fit to stand trial on a criminal charge, provided that the disclosure is made only with respect to the issue of fitness to stand trial.

(7) Records and communications of the recipient may be disclosed in any civil or administrative proceeding involving the validity of or benefits under a life, accident, health or disability insurance policy or certificate, or Health Care Service Plan Contract, insuring the recipient, but only if and to the extent that the recipient's mental condition, or treatment or services in connection therewith, is a material element of any claim or defense of any party, provided that information sought or disclosed shall not be redisclosed except in connection with the proceeding in which disclosure is made.

(8) Records or communications may be disclosed when such are relevant to a matter in issue in any action brought under this Act and proceedings preliminary thereto, provided that any information so disclosed shall not be utilized for any other purpose nor be redisclosed except in connection with such action or preliminary proceedings.

(9) Records and communications of the recipient may be disclosed in investigations of and trials for homicide when the disclosure relates directly to the fact or immediate circumstances of the homicide.

(10) Records and communications of a deceased recipient may be disclosed to a coroner conducting a preliminary investigation into the recipient's death under Section 3-3013 of the Counties Code. However, records and communications of the deceased recipient disclosed in an investigation shall be limited solely to the deceased recipient's records and communications relating to the factual circumstances of the incident being investigated in a mental health facility.

(11) Records and communications of a recipient shall be disclosed in a proceeding where a petition or motion is filed under the Juvenile Court Act of 1987 and the recipient is named as a parent, guardian, or legal custodian of a minor who is the subject of a petition for wardship as described in Section 2-3 of that Act or a minor who is the subject of a petition for wardship as described in Section 2-4 of that Act alleging the minor is abused, neglected, or dependent or the recipient is named as a parent of a child who

is the subject of a petition, supplemental petition, or motion to appoint a guardian with the power to consent to adoption under Section 2-29 of the Juvenile Court Act of 1987.

(12) Records and communications of a recipient may be disclosed when disclosure is necessary to collect sums or receive third party payment representing charges for mental health or developmental disabilities services provided by a therapist or agency to a recipient; however, disclosure shall be limited to information needed to pursue collection, and the information so disclosed may not be used for any other purposes nor may it be redisclosed except in connection with collection activities. Whenever records are disclosed pursuant to this subdivision (12), the recipient of the records shall be advised in writing that any person who discloses mental health records and communications in violation of this Act may be subject to civil liability pursuant to Section 15 of this Act or to criminal penalties pursuant to Section 16 of this Act or both.

(b) Before a disclosure is made under subsection (a), any party to the proceeding or any other interested person may request an in camera review of the record or communications to be disclosed. The court or agency conducting the proceeding may hold an in camera review on its own motion. When, contrary to the express wish of the recipient, the therapist asserts a privilege on behalf and in the interest of a recipient, the court may require that the therapist, in an in camera hearing, establish that disclosure is not in the best interest of the recipient. The court or agency may prevent disclosure or limit disclosure to the extent that other admissible evidence is sufficient to establish the facts in issue. The court or agency may enter such orders as may be necessary in order to protect the confidentiality, privacy, and safety of the recipient or of other persons. Any order to disclose or to not disclose shall be considered a final order for purposes of appeal and shall be subject to interlocutory appeal.

(c) A recipient's records and communications may be disclosed to a duly authorized committee, commission or subcommittee of the General Assembly which possesses subpoena and hearing powers, upon a written request approved by a majority vote of the committee, commission or subcommittee members. The committee, commission or subcommittee may request records only for the purposes of investigating or studying possible violations of recipient rights. The request shall state the purpose for which disclosure is sought.

The facility shall notify the recipient, or his guardian, and therapist in writing of any disclosure request under this subsection within 5 business days after such request. Such notification shall also inform the recipient, or guardian, and therapist of their right to object to the disclosure within 10 business days after receipt of the notification and shall include the name, address and telephone number of the committee, commission or subcommittee member or staff person with whom an objection shall be filed. If no objection has been filed within 15 business days after the request for disclosure, the facility shall disclose the records and communications to the committee, commission or subcommittee. If an objection has been filed within 15 business days after the request for disclosure, the facility shall disclose the records and communications only after the committee, commission or subcommittee has permitted the recipient, guardian or therapist to present his objection in person before it and has renewed its request for disclosure by a majority vote of its members.

Disclosure under this subsection shall not occur until all personally identifiable data of the recipient and provider are removed from the records and communications. Disclosure under this subsection shall not occur in any public proceeding.

(d) No party to any proceeding described under paragraphs (1), (2), (3), (4), (7), or (8) of subsection (a) of this Section, nor his or her attorney, shall serve a subpoena seeking to obtain access to records or communications under this Act unless the subpoena is accompanied by a written order issued by a judge, authorizing the disclosure of the records or the issuance of the subpoena. No person shall comply with a subpoena for records or communications under this Act, unless the subpoena is accompanied by a written order authorizing the issuance of the subpoena or the disclosure of the records.

(e) When a person has been transported by a peace officer to a mental health facility, then upon the request of a peace officer, if the person is allowed to leave the mental health facility within 48 hours of arrival, excluding Saturdays, Sundays, and holidays, the facility director shall notify the local law enforcement authority prior to the release of the person. The local law enforcement authority may re-disclose the information as necessary to alert the appropriate enforcement or prosecuting authority.

(f) A recipient's records and communications shall be disclosed to the Inspector General of the Department of Human Services within 10 business days of a request by the Inspector General (i) in the course of an investigation authorized by the Abused and Neglected Long Term Care Facility Residents Reporting Act and applicable rule or (ii) during the course of an assessment authorized by the Abuse of Adults with Disabilities Intervention Act and applicable rule. The request shall be in writing and signed by the Inspector General or his or her designee. The request shall state the purpose for which disclosure is sought. Any person who knowingly and willfully refuses to comply with such a request is guilty of a Class A misdemeanor.

People v. Robert P., 354 Ill. App. 3d 1051, 1059–60, 290 Ill. Dec. 685, 821 N.E.2d 1259 (3d Dist. 2005) (the trial court did not abuse its discretion by excluding evidence that the defendant's wife had brought the victim for psychological treatment for lying and masturbating, where the testimony was irrelevant, represented improper lay opinion testimony and disclosed confidential information).

§ 6:66 Opposing authorities—735 ILCS 5/8-803 (clergy privilege)

People v. Campobello, 348 Ill. App. 3d 619, 633–36, 284 Ill. Dec. 654, 810 N.E.2d 307, 123 A.L.R.5th 761 (2d Dist. 2004) (clergy privilege was not violated by an order requiring a church to produce records regarding its internal investigation of a priest).

§ 6:67 Opposing authorities—735 ILCS 5/8-801 (husband and wife privilege)

735 ILCS 5/8-801 provides in relevant part:

> In all actions, husband and wife may testify for or against each other, provided that neither may testify as to any communication or admission made by either of them to the other or as to any conversation between them during marriage, *except in actions between such husband and wife, and in actions where the custody, support, health or welfare of their children or children in either spouse's care, custody or control is directly in issue, and as to matters in which either has acted as agent for the other.* (Emphasis added).

§ 6:68 Opposing authorities—735 ILCS 5/8-802 (physician and patient privilege)

735 ILCS 5/8-802 provides in relevant part:

> No physician or surgeon shall be permitted to disclose any information he or she may have acquired in attending any patient in a professional character, necessary to enable him or her professionally to serve the patient, *except only (1) in trials for homicide when the disclosure relates directly to the fact or immediate circumstances of the homicide, (2) in actions, civil or criminal, against the physician for malpractice, (3) with the expressed consent of the patient, or in case of his or her death or disability, of his or her personal representative or other person authorized to sue for personal injury or of the beneficiary of an insurance policy on his or her life, health, or physical condition, (4) in all actions brought by or against the patient, his or her personal representative, a beneficiary under a policy of insurance, or the executor or administrator of his or her estate wherein the patient's physical or mental condition is an issue, (5) upon an issue as to the validity of a document as a will of the patient, (6) in any criminal action where the charge is either first degree murder by abortion, attempted abortion or abortion, (7) in actions, civil or criminal, arising from the filing of a report in compliance with the Abused and Neglected Child Reporting Act, (8) to any department, agency, institution or facility which has custody of the patient pursuant to State statute or any court order of commitment, (9) in prosecutions where written results of blood alcohol tests are admissible*

> *pursuant to Section 11-501.4 of the Illinois Vehicle Code, (10) in prosecutions where written results of blood alcohol tests are admissible under Section 5-11a of the Boat Registration and Safety Act, (11) in criminal actions arising from the filing of a report of suspected terrorist offense in compliance with Section 29D-10(p)(7) of the Criminal Code of 1961, or (12) upon the issuance of a subpoena pursuant to Section 38 of the Medical Practice Act of 1987; the issuance of a subpoena pursuant to Section 25.1 of the Illinois Dental Practice Act; or the issuance of a subpoena pursuant to Section 22 of the Nursing Home Administrators Licensing and Disciplinary Act.*
>
> In the event of a conflict between the application of this Section and the Mental Health and Developmental Disabilities Confidentiality Act to a specific situation, the provisions of the Mental Health and Developmental Disabilities Confidentiality Act shall control. (Emphasis added).

Giangiulio v. Ingalls Memorial Hosp., 365 Ill. App. 3d 823, 832-33, 302 Ill. Dec. 812, 850 N.E.2d 249 (1st Dist. 2006) (information that was not directly related to a third party patient's care was not protected from disclosure under the physician-patient privilege).

Troyan v. Reyes, 367 Ill. App. 3d 729, 739-40, 305 Ill. Dec. 451, 855 N.E.2d 967 (3d Dist. 2006) (party put his physical condition in issue by bringing the lawsuit and therefore could not assert physician/patient privilege as grounds for failing to answer requests to admit).

Tomczak v. Ingalls Memorial Hosp., 359 Ill. App. 3d 448, 456–57, 295 Ill. Dec. 968, 834 N.E.2d 549 (1st Dist. 2005) (the trial court did not abuse its discretion by requiring the defendant hospital to disclose the triage time, treatment time and triage determination of severity, where the information did not violate physician-patient privilege and it was relevant to the action).

§ 6:69 Opposing authorities—735 ILCS 5/8-2101 (Medical Studies Act)

Frigo v. Silver Cross Hosp. and Medical Center, 377 Ill. App. 3d 43, 315 Ill. Dec. 385, 876 N.E.2d 697, 716–18 (1st Dist. 2007), as modified, (Sept. 20, 2007) and appeal denied, 226 Ill. 2d 614, 317 Ill. Dec. 503, 882 N.E.2d 77 (2008) (hospital's credentialing requirements were not protected from disclosure under the Medical Studies Act).

Webb v. Mount Sinai Hosp. and Medical Center of Chicago, Inc., 347 Ill. App. 3d 817, 825–28, 283 Ill. Dec. 185, 807 N.E.2d 1026 (1st Dist. 2004) (documents regarding interviews with the plaintiff were not protected under the Medical Studies Act privilege).

Pietro v. Marriott Senior Living Services, Inc., 348 Ill. App. 3d 541, 546–50, 284 Ill. Dec. 564, 810 N.E.2d 217 (1st Dist. 2004) (assisted living facility did not qualify as an entity subject to the Medical Studies Act privilege).

§ 6:70 Opposing authorities—Relevant to issues

Sharp v. Trans Union L.L.C., 364 Ill. App. 3d 64, 71-75, 300 Ill. Dec. 830, 845 N.E.2d 719 (1st Dist. 2006), as modified on denial of reh'g, (Mar. 1, 2006) (communications between a company and its attorneys were not protected from disclosure under an attorney-client privilege doctrine where the attorney's knowledge of certain facts and issues was relevant to whether or not a claim existed under the insurance policies).

Western States Ins. Co. v. O'Hara, 357 Ill. App. 3d 509, 520–21, 293 Ill. Dec. 532, 828 N.E.2d 842 (4th Dist. 2005) (a party waived the attorney-client privilege regarding communications with counsel, when the party placed the communications into issue).

§ 6:71 Opposing authorities—Work product / attorney and client

Allianz Ins. Co. v. Guidant Corporation, 373 Ill. App. 3d 652, 658–77, 312 Ill. Dec. 51, 869 N.E.2d 1042 (2d Dist. 2007), appeal denied, 225 Ill. 2d 627, 314 Ill. Dec. 822, 875 N.E.2d 1109 (2007) (information in the insured's attorney's file was not protected from discovery by the insurer under the work-product doctrine or the attorney-client privilege).

Lawndale Restoration Ltd. Partnership v. Acordia of Illinois, Inc., 367 Ill. App. 3d 24, 32-33, 304 Ill. Dec. 714, 853 N.E.2d 791 (1st Dist. 2006), appeal denied, 222 Ill. 2d 609, 308 Ill. Dec. 637, 862 N.E.2d 235 (2007) (document prepared by an attorney after a company's internal audit, was not privileged as attorney work product because it was not prepared in anticipation of litigation).

II. SAMPLE MOTIONS

§ 6:72 Motion to exclude evidence of wage loss claim denied during discovery

TO: ALL PARTIES AND THEIR RESPECTIVE ATTORNEYS OF RECORD:

PLEASE TAKE NOTICE that defendant hereby moves this Court for an order excluding any and all evidence, references to evidence, testimony or argument relating to plaintiff's alleged wage loss claim. This motion is based upon the grounds that plaintiff denied the claim during the discovery process and therefore, any evidence related to this claim is irrelevant; and is based upon the supporting Memorandum of Points and Authorities, the pleadings and papers on file in this action, and upon such argument and evidence as may be presented prior to or at the hearing of this matter.

Dated: *[date]*

MEMORANDUM OF POINTS AND AUTHORITIES

1.
PRELIMINARY STATEMENT

This action arises from a rear-end automobile accident between plaintiff and defendant that occurred on September 18, 1998. As a result of the accident, plaintiff claims to have sustained neck and back injuries and lost wages.

On June 12, 1999, defendant noticed plaintiff's deposition. The notice, in part, requested that plaintiff produce documents pertaining to his wage loss claim. A copy of the deposition notice is attached hereto as exhibit "A." When asked at the deposition whether he had any documents to support the claim, plaintiff responded "None." When asked whether he was seeking reimbursement for lost wages, the plaintiff responded, "I'm not sure, no." Relevant portions of plaintiff's deposition transcripts are attached hereto as Exhibit "B." See Exhibit "B" at Lines 10–15.

On August 21, 1999, defendant served his First Demand for Inspection of Documents ("Inspection Demand"), asking, at Request No. 2, for "Any and all documents pertaining to your claim for lost wages or lost earning capacity." A copy of defendant's Inspection Demand is attached hereto as exhibit "C." In plaintiff's response to Request No. 2 of the Inspection Demand, plaintiff responded "None." A copy of plaintiff's response to defendant's Inspection Demand is attached hereto as exhibit "D."

Up until the date of the final pre-trial conference in this matter, just 10 days before trial on January 10, 2000, plaintiff had provided no documents to support a claim for loss of earnings or earning capacity. At the pre-trial conference, plaintiff's counsel indicated that plaintiff would be offering several payroll documents at trial relating to plaintiff's earnings history.

By this motion, defendant seeks an order excluding any and all evidence pertaining to plaintiff's wage loss claim.

2.
THIS COURT MAY EXCLUDE PREJUDICIAL EVIDENCE IN ADVANCE OF TRIAL BY WAY OF AN IN LIMINE MOTION

Evidence should be excluded when the prejudicial impact of the evidence outweighs the probative value of it. Federal Rule of Evidence 403 states:

> Although relevant, evidence may be excluded if its probative value is substantially outweighed by the danger of unfair prejudice, confusion of the issues, or misleading the jury, or by considerations of undue delay, waste of time, or needless presentation of cumulative evidence.

Illinois has a common-law rule that is comparable to Federal Rule of Evidence 403. See *People v. Peete*, 318 Ill. App. 3d 961, 966–67, 252 Ill. Dec. 821, 743 N.E.2d 689 (4th Dist. 2001); *People v. Walker*, 335 Ill. App. 3d 102, 112, 268 Ill. Dec. 654, 779 N.E.2d 268 (2d Dist. 2002), as modified on denial of reh'g, (Oct. 24, 2002) and judgment aff'd, 211 Ill. 2d 317, 285 Ill. Dec. 519, 812 N.E.2d 339 (2004).

Illinois cases have excluded evidence when the prejudicial impact of the evidence outweighed the probative value of it. See e.g. *Department of Public Works and Bldgs. v. Roehrig*, 45 Ill. App. 3d 189, 196, 3 Ill. Dec. 893, 359 N.E.2d 752 (5th Dist. 1976) (exclusion of evidence of prior condemnations in a condemnation case because the prejudicial impact outweighs the probative value of it); *People v. Holman*, 257 Ill. App. 3d 1031, 1033–34, 196 Ill. Dec. 457, 630 N.E.2d 154 (2d Dist. 1994) (evidence is admissible if it is relevant and if the prejudicial impact does not substantially outweigh the probative value of it) and *Hulsebus v. Russian*, 118 Ill. App. 2d 174, 180–81, 254 N.E.2d 184 (2d Dist. 1969) (trial judge had discretion to exclude a gruesome photograph of the plaintiff during surgery because other evidence established the extent of the injury and because the photograph was likely to inflame and prejudice the jury).

Moreover, the Court should determine whether to exclude this evidence outside of the presence of the jury in order to prevent the jury from hearing about inadmissible material. Specifically, Federal Rule of evidence 103(c) provides:

> Hearing of Jury.—In jury cases, proceedings shall be conducted, to the extent practicable, so as to prevent inadmissible evidence from being suggested to the jury by any means, such as making statements or offers of proof or asking questions in the hearing of the jury.

Although this rule has not been specifically codified in Illinois, Illinois has adopted other Federal Rules of evidence through case law. See e.g. *People v. Monroe*, 66 Ill. 2d 317, 321–22, 5 Ill. Dec. 824, 362 N.E.2d 295 (1977); and *Spencer v. Wandolowski*, 264 Ill. App. 3d 611, 617, 201 Ill. Dec. 422, 636 N.E.2d 854 (1st Dist. 1994) (adopting Federal Rule of Evidence 401). In the instant matter, the jury will be prejudiced merely by hearing any reference to the defendant's lost wage claims.

3.
EVIDENCE OF PLAINTIFF'S LOST WAGE CLAIM SHOULD BE EXCLUDED TO PREVENT UNFAIR SURPRISE TO DEFENDANT

To avoid unfair surprise, the Court may exclude evidence on issues where discovery responses and actions of counsel led opposing counsel to believe those issues would not be litigated. See *Harding v. Amsted Industries, Inc.*, 276 Ill. App. 3d 483, 492, 213 Ill. Dec. 187, 658 N.E.2d 1208 (1st Dist. 1995) (trial judge properly excluded expert testimony that exceeded the opinions expressed by the expert during discovery); and *Savage v. Martin*, 256 Ill. App. 3d 272, 285, 195 Ill. Dec. 142, 628 N.E.2d 606 (1st Dist. 1993) (expert opinion that went beyond opinions stated at deposition properly excluded, where expert stated that he had no other opinions beyond those in his report.

The Court is within its power to preclude a party from introducing documents not discovered by the opposing party, where relevant evidence is not disclosed during discovery. See Illinois Supreme Court Rule 219; *King v. Clemons*, 264 Ill. App. 3d 138, 140–41, 201 Ill. Dec. 630, 636 N.E.2d 1062 (5th Dist. 1994); *Golembiewski v. Hallberg Ins. Agency, Inc.*, 262 Ill. App. 3d 1082, 1086–87, 200 Ill. Dec. 113, 635 N.E.2d 452 (1st Dist. 1994); and *Ashpole v. Brunswick Bowling and Billiards Corp.*, 297 Ill. App. 3d 725, 726–30, 232 Ill. Dec. 308, 697 N.E.2d 1238 (2d Dist. 1998).

In the present case, plaintiff's statements and actions led defense counsel to reasonably believe that plaintiff would not be pursuing the wage loss claim. Plaintiff responded at his deposition that he would not be seeking reimbursement for his lost wages claim. See Exhibit "B" at Lines 10–15. Plaintiff produced no documentation that would support the claim, despite several formal discovery requests by the defense. See Exhibits "A," "C," and "D."

The first indication that plaintiff would be offering any evidence on the lost wages claim was at the final pre-trial conference, just days before the commencement of trial and after the discovery cut-off date. Clearly, plaintiff knew or should have known that these documents existed when asked at deposition or through other discovery requests. Failure to produce the documents suggests strongly that they were suppressed by the plaintiff.

The defendant will suffer undue prejudice if plaintiff is permitted to testify or introduce any documentation at trial to support his claim for lost wages. As such, this court should exclude any and all evidence, including any mention of evidence, relating to plaintiff's lost wage claim.

4.
PLAINTIFF'S LOST WAGE EVIDENCE WAS NOT DISPUTED THROUGHOUT DISCOVERY

The wage claim should be excluded because it is not relevant to any issue that was raised during discovery. Federal Rule of Evidence 401 defines relevancy as:

> evidence having any tendency to make the existence of any fact that is of consequence to the determination of the action more probable or less probable than it would be without the evidence.

Illinois has adopted this definition of relevancy through case law. *Spencer v. Wandolowski*, 264 Ill. App. 3d 611, 617, 201 Ill. Dec. 422, 636 N.E.2d 854 (1st Dist. 1994); and *People v. Monroe*, 66 Ill. 2d 317, 321–22, 5 Ill. Dec. 824, 362 N.E.2d 295 (1977).

Evidence may be properly excluded where it is not relevant to matters at issue. See *Cochran v. Great Atlantic & Pacific Tea Co., Inc.*, 203 Ill. App. 3d 935, 937–38, 148 Ill. Dec. 923, 561 N.E.2d 229 (5th Dist. 1990) (trial judge has inherent power to exclude irrelevant evidence); *Benson v. Bradford Mut. Fire Ins. Corp.*, 121 Ill. App. 3d 500, 510, 76 Ill. Dec. 774, 459 N.E.2d 689, 47 A.L.R.4th 759 (2d Dist. 1984) (trial judge had discretion to exclude irrelevant witness testimony) and *Pagel v. Yates*, 128 Ill. App. 3d 897, 903, 84 Ill. Dec. 180, 471 N.E.2d 946 (4th Dist. 1984) (exclusion of irrelevant and confusing document).

In addition, the Court may exclude evidence regarding matters that are not in dispute. *Davis v. International Harvester Co.*, 167 Ill. App. 3d 814, 824–25, 118 Ill. Dec. 589, 521 N.E.2d 1282 (2d Dist. 1988) (proper to exclude evidence of the feasibility of design changes when there was an admission to that ability); and *Bullard v. Barnes*, 112 Ill. App. 3d 384, 392–94, 68 Ill. Dec. 37, 445 N.E.2d 485 (4th Dist. 1983), judgment aff'd, 102 Ill. 2d 505, 82 Ill. Dec. 448, 468 N.E.2d 1228 (1984) (trial judge abused his discretion by admitting photographs of the deceased and testimony regarding the conditions and circumstances surrounding the collision, because liability was admitted).

In the present case, the plaintiff testified under oath, at his deposition, that he was not seeking reimbursement for lost wages. See Exhibit "B" at Lines 10–15. The plaintiff's failure to provide supporting documentation, despite several proper discovery requests by defendant, further supports this fact. See Exhibits "A," "C," and "D."

Plaintiff's clear indication throughout the discovery process, and up until just 10 days before trial, was that he was not seeking reimbursement for lost wages. It would be unfair and prejudicial to allow plaintiff, at this late date, to present evidence on an issue that, until days before the start of trial, was not in dispute.

The Court should therefore exclude any and all evidence, including any mention of evidence, relating to plaintiff's wage loss claim.

5.
CONCLUSION

Based on the foregoing, defendant respectfully requests that this Court exclude any testimony or documentary evidence, or mention of any evidence, regarding plaintiff's claim for wage loss.

Dated: *[date]*

By: ______________________
[name of counsel]
Attorneys for Defendant,
[name of defendant]

§ 6:73 Opposition to defendants' motion to limit plaintiff's expert's opinions

TO: ALL DEFENDANTS AND THEIR RESPECTIVE ATTORNEYS OF RECORD:

Plaintiff hereby submits the following Opposition to Defendants' Motion in Limine Limiting Plaintiff's Expert's Opinion Testimony. This Opposition is based upon the grounds that the defense improperly applies the legal principles applicable to this case, and to limit plaintiff's expert testimony would create unfair prejudice to the plaintiff. In the alternative, plaintiff requests that the Court grant a continuance to allow for the deposition of Plaintiff's experts to properly explore the disputed opinion testimony.

Dated: *[date]*

MEMORANDUM OF POINTS AND AUTHORITIES

1.

PRELIMINARY STATEMENT

This case is a medical malpractice and wrongful death action, whereby it is alleged that defendants negligently misdiagnosed and treated the decedent, allowing decedent to become gravely ill and die from complications from pneumonia.

Expert depositions were conducted for all three of plaintiff's disclosed medical experts approximately two months ago. Each deposition in this serious medical malpractice case took approximately two hours. This motion concerns defendants' attempts to exclude key testimony from plaintiff's expert witnesses. Plaintiff submits that defendants never conducted any meaningful inquiry relating to the disputed testimony when the depositions were taken. Near the conclusion of each of plaintiff's expert depositions, Defendants' counsel asked the following general question: "Do you have any other opinions not yet expressed?"

Defendants' motion seeks to limit plaintiff's expert testimony to those opinions and conclusions testified to at their depositions, and secondly, to exclude testimony based upon material available but not provided to or reviewed by them prior to their depositions.

For the reasons and authorities cited below, plaintiff respectfully urges this Court to reject the defendants' overbroad motions. In the alternative, plaintiff requests a brief continuance to allow defendants to re-depose plaintiff's experts to obtain the information they claim was withheld from them at the time of the original depositions.

2.

THE DEFENSE INTERPRETATION OF THE LAW WOULD REWARD DEFENDANTS FOR TAKING INSUFFICIENTLY THOROUGH DEPOSITIONS

Defendants are asking the Court to preclude plaintiff's expert from saying anything that he has not already said in his deposition. This is clearly contrary to the law. A defendant would simply have to ask very few questions and thereby block the expert from testifying about anything other than what he was asked. Surely, the defendants cannot possibly be asking the Court to make such a ruling.

This is particularly true in instances, such as here, where defendants insisted on asking overbroad, catch-all questions such as "do you have any other opinions not yet expressed," rather than asking questions about the specific areas about which an expert could reasonably have an opinion in this case. Indeed, in numerous instances in this case, the defense asked specific questions over plaintiff's objection and despite plaintiff's statement that they were welcome to inquire into remaining areas. They should not expect to use that catch-all question in a way to rule out other opinions the expert might present at trial.

Even more importantly, this motion is universally propounded by defendants in medical malpractice actions in order to gain an unfair litigation advantage, as follows:

Unlike most other litigation, in medical malpractice actions, the defendants have virtually all the facts regarding the incident in question in their possession or control, while plaintiffs have none. Through discovery, plaintiffs seek to elicit as much of this information as possible, and the defendants typically vigorously resist such discovery. Then, almost without exception, at the time of the deposition of plaintiffs' expert witnesses, there will be some information that plaintiffs have not managed to uncover, and that defendants are withholding, and plan to make part of their trial strategy. Knowing that they plan to introduce such information, they nonetheless intentionally fail to ask plaintiffs' experts questions based upon this withheld information. Alternatively, the defendants insist on priority in taking depositions, and then introduce for the first time at the subsequent deposition of defendants' experts, theories which plaintiffs could not reasonably have foreseen and therefore, for which plaintiffs' experts had formulated no opinion. Then, defendants propound the standard motion to exclude additional expert opinions and seek to use it as an offensive weapon, preventing plaintiffs' experts from responding to new facts which are brought out by defendants in their defense claims for the first time at trial or at subsequent depositions.

In the present case, Defendants' experts concocted totally outlandish theories with absolutely no medical basis, which plaintiff's experts would not have dreamed they should address. These defense opinions, such as the notion that decedent suffered from an encephalitis (inflammation of the brain) and myocarditis (inflammation of the heart muscle) and that these conditions, rather than the pneumonia plaintiffs' experts found as the actual treating physicians, caused decedent's death, were not offered until *after* the depositions of plaintiff's experts were taken.

To the extent no questions were asked on subjects that plaintiff's witnesses could not reasonably be expected to predict, defendants should not be rewarded for taking an insufficiently thorough deposition. Accordingly, at the very least, the ruling on the motion should be deferred until the time a specific question is asked and the Court can determine whether such information was material to the particular questions asked at the expert's deposition in this case.

3.

THE DEFENDANTS SHOULD NOT BE SURPRISED BY THE TESTIMONY OF THE PLAINTIFF'S EXPERT AND THUS, THE TESTIMONY SHOULD BE ADMISSIBLE.

Illinois Law provides authority for allowing the plaintiff's expert to testify in the instant matter, despite the fact that the exact nature of the opinion was not expressed at the plaintiff's expert's deposition because the defendant should not be surprised by the testimony. For example, in the case of *Jarke v. Jackson Products, Inc.*, 282 Ill. App. 3d 292, 296–98, 217 Ill. Dec. 861, 668 N.E.2d 46 (1st Dist. 1996), the court held that it was not an abuse of discretion to allow an expert to testify to a theory that was not explicitly disclosed but that was arguably included within a broad term the expert had used in describing his opinion.

Similarly, in the case of *Zimmer v. Melendez*, 222 Ill. App. 3d 390, 394–96, 164 Ill. Dec. 836, 583 N.E.2d 1158 (2d Dist. 1991), the court held that the trial court abused its discretion by excluding expert testimony that was undisclosed in interrogatories when the subject matter of the testimony was not a surprise to the opposing party and when the interrogatory that might have covered the subject matter was open-ended and did not clearly request the information at issue.

In *Gee v. Davidson*, 21 Ill. App. 3d 654, 315 N.E.2d 674 (1st Dist. 1974) (only abstract published) the trial judge properly allowed expert testimony that had not been disclosed in response to interrogatories when the same information had been provided by other means of discovery.

In the instant matter, plaintiff or his experts have not engaged in any abuse of discovery, or any activity that could be construed as waiver or warrant estoppel. The defendants' motion is clearly a shotgun attempt at excluding relevant expert testimony based upon an overbroad reading of existing case law. To allow the exclusion of plaintiff's expert's testimony would only serve to harm the plaintiff and reward the defendants for an incomplete deposition.

4.
THE DEFENDANT DID NOT COMPLY WITH APPLICABLE DISCOVERY RULES FOR RESOLVING DISPUTES AND THEREFORE, THE PLAINTIFF'S EXPERT TESTIMONY SHOULD NOT BE BARRED.

The defendants did not fully comply with applicable Supreme Court Rules for resolving discovery disputes before trying to bar the plaintiff's expert. In the case of *Phillips v. Gannotti*, 327 Ill. App. 3d 512, 518, 261 Ill. Dec. 571, 763 N.E.2d 820 (1st Dist. 2002), the court stated that discovery sanctions must be designed to ensure fair discovery and should not be used to punish the non-disclosing party.

Sanctions should not be imposed when the party asking for sanctions has not pursued all available means for obtaining the requested information. For example, in the case of *King v. Clay*, 335 Ill. App. 3d 923, 926–28, 269 Ill. Dec. 667, 781 N.E.2d 464 (1st Dist. 2002), the court held that the trial judge should not have barred all evidence for failure to comply with depositions when the opposing party failed to show that he fully pursued the available methods for taking the depositions.

Similarly, in the case of *Brandt v. John S. Tilley Ladders Co.*, 145 Ill. App. 3d 304, 306–07, 99 Ill. Dec. 534, 495 N.E.2d 1269 (1st Dist. 1986), the court held that the trial judge should not have dismissed the Plaintiff's case for failure to comply with discovery when the defendant did not allege that it had complied with Illinois Supreme Court Rule 201(k)).

In the instant matter, the facts suggest that the defendants *deliberately attempted* to limit the plaintiff's expert's opinion so that they could bring this motion. This Court should not reward that type of practice by sanctioning the plaintiff.

5.
ALTERNATIVELY, THIS COURT SHOULD ALLOW DEFENDANTS TO RE-DEPOSE PLAINTIFF'S EXPERTS

If this Court feels that defendants have met their burden regarding this motion, plaintiff respectfully requests that a brief continuance be allowed so that defendants may re-depose plaintiff's medical experts, for the limited purpose of allowing defendants to obtain the alleged missing information that they failed to discover in the first deposition.

A number of cases support plaintiff's request for a continuance. See e.g. *Phillips v. Gannotti*, 327 Ill. App. 3d 512, 518, 261 Ill. Dec. 571, 763 N.E.2d 820 (1st Dist. 2002) (discovery sanctions must be designed to ensure fair discovery and should not be used to punish the non-disclosing party); *Phillips v. Gannotti*, 327 Ill. App. 3d 512, 518–21, 261 Ill. Dec. 571, 763 N.E.2d 820 (1st Dist. 2002) (trial judge should not have excluded undisclosed lay witness opinion testimony and then granted a directed verdict when a continuance for further discovery would have alleviated the prejudice from the non-disclosure and the non-disclosure was not the fault of the non-disclosing party); and *Kurrack v. American Dist. Telegraph Co.*, 252 Ill. App. 3d 885, 902–04, 192 Ill. Dec. 520, 625 N.E.2d 675 (1st Dist. 1993) (trial court did not abuse its discretion by granting a brief continuance to depose expert instead of excluding the expert's testimony as requested).

In this case, good cause exists to allow the requested continuance. Plaintiff has not engaged in any improper behavior and has, in fact, been totally forthright in all discovery. A clear reading of the disputed deposition transcripts shows that plaintiff's experts were similarly forthright in their responses to all of defendants' questions. Plaintiff should not be penalized because defendants intentionally failed to take a thorough deposition the first time around.

Plaintiff does not believe that additional depositions are even necessary. However, in the spirit of cooperation, plaintiff will allow the depositions to be retaken, only for the limited purpose of allowing defendants to do follow up inquiry on those issues addressed in their motion. Questions regarding any additional matters would clearly constitute a last-minute "fishing expedition," and should be restricted.

6.
CONCLUSION

For the foregoing reasons, the Court should deny defendants' motion as overbroad but to the extent that the Court grants defendants' Motion, it should not extend to opinions that plaintiff's experts did not give because they were not asked or because they did not have that information available to them at the time of the taking of their deposition. In the alternative, the Court should order that limited depositions be scheduled for plaintiff's medical experts.

Dated: *[date]*

By: ______________________
[name of counsel]
Attorneys for PLAINTIFF,
[name of plaintiff]

§ 6:74 Motion to exclude evidence of medical bills for services obtained after [Date]

TO: ALL PARTIES AND THEIR RESPECTIVE ATTORNEYS OF RECORD:

PLEASE TAKE NOTICE that defendant hereby moves this Court for an order excluding any and all evidence, references to evidence, testimony or argument relating to plaintiff's alleged medical bills that were incurred for services that were obtained after October 15, 2007. This motion is based upon the grounds that plaintiff failed to timely respond to certain requests to admit that were served upon him during the discovery process. Said requests to admit included a request to admit the fact that there were no medical bills for services that were obtained after October 15, 2007, as a result of the incident that is at issue in this case. The plaintiff's failure to respond to the requests have resulted in deemed admissions of them and therefore, any evidence related to medical bills for services that were obtained after October 15, 2007, is prejudicial, irrelevant and inadmissible. This motion is also based upon the supporting Memorandum of Points and Authorities, the pleadings and papers on file in this action, and upon such argument and evidence as may be presented prior to or at the hearing of this matter.

Dated: *[date]*

MEMORANDUM OF POINTS AND AUTHORITIES

1. PRELIMINARY STATEMENT

This action arises from an incident on May 10, 2006, when the plaintiff allegedly slipped and fell in the defendant's supermarket. As a result of the incident, plaintiff claims to have sustained neck and back injuries and lost wages.

On February of 2008, defendant served upon plaintiff certain requests to admit facts. Said requests to admit included a request to admit the fact that there were no medical bills for services that were obtained after October 15, 2007, as a result of the incident that is at issue in this case. A copy of the Requests to Admit and the Proof of Service of them is attached hereto as Exhibit A. Plaintiff failed to timely respond to the requests to admit that were served upon him. The plaintiff's failure to respond to the requests to admit have resulted in deemed admissions of them and therefore, any evidence related to medical bills for services that were obtained after October 15, 2007, is prejudicial, irrelevant and inadmissible.

This case is now set for trial on March 16, 2009. Up until the date of the final pre-trial on March 9, 2009, just one week before the scheduled trial, plaintiff had provided no evidence of medical bills for services that were obtained after October 15, 2007. At the pre-trial conference, plaintiff's counsel indicated that plaintiff would be offering evidence related to medical bills for services that were obtained after October 15, 2007.

By this motion, defendant seeks an order excluding any and all evidence pertaining to plaintiff's claim related to medical bills for services that were obtained after October 15, 2007.

2. PLAINTIFF'S FAILURE TO RESPOND TO DEFENDANT'S REQUESTS TO ADMIT RESULTED IN DEEMED ADMISSIONS OF THOSE FACTS

Pursuant to Illinois Supreme Court Rule 216, defendant was authorized to serve the requests to admit upon plaintiff. Specifically, Illinois Supreme Court Rule 216 provides in pertinent part, "(a) Request for Admission of Fact. A party may serve on any other party a written request for the admission by the latter of the truth of any specified relevant fact set forth in the request." Once the admissions were served upon plaintiff, he was required by law to respond to them within 28 days. In fact, Illinois Supreme Court Rule 216 further provides, "(c) Admission in the Absence of Denial. Each of the matters of fact and the genuineness of each document of which admission is requested is admitted unless, within 28 days after service thereof, the party to whom the request is directed serves upon the party requesting the admission either (1) a sworn statement denying specifically the matters of which admission is requested or setting forth in detail the reasons why he cannot truthfully admit or deny those matters or (2) written objections on the ground that some or all of the requested admissions are privileged or irrelevant or that the request is otherwise improper in whole or in part. If written objections to a part of the request are made, the remainder of the request shall be answered within the period designated in the request. A denial shall fairly meet the substance of the requested admission. If good faith requires that a party deny only a part, or requires qualification, of a matter of which an admission is requested, he shall specify so much of it as is true and deny only the remainder. Any objection to a request or to an answer shall be heard by the court upon prompt notice and motion of the party making the request."

In the case at bar, plaintiff did not respond to the requests to admit in a timely fashion. Furthermore, he has never provided a good faith basis for an extension of time to answer the requests to admit. As a result, plaintiff must be deemed to have admitted the facts as contained in Exhibit A. See *Zwicky v. Freightliner Custom Chassis Corp.*, 373 Ill.App.3d 135, 141–42, 867 N.E.2d 527 (2nd Dist. 2007) (failure to respond to the opposing party's requests to admit resulted in deemed admissions); *Tires 'N Tracks, Inc. v. Dominic Fiordirosa Const. Co., Inc.*, 331 Ill. App. 3d 87, 89–94, 264 Ill. Dec. 908, 771 N.E.2d 612 (2d Dist. 2002) (trial judge has no discretion to allow untimely responses or untimely amendments to requests to admit if the responding party does not demonstrate that there was sufficient good cause for the delay). See also, *Vision Point of Sale, Inc. v. Haas*, 226 Ill.2d 334, 356–58, 314 Ill.Dec. 778, 875 N.E.2d 1065 (2007) (when determining whether good cause exists for an extension of time to respond to requests to admit, a trial court can consider whether there was "mistake, inadvertence, or attorney neglect, but may not engage in an open-ended inquiry which considers conduct that is unrelated to the causes of the party's original noncompliance.").

For the foregoing reasons, this Court should determine that plaintiff has admitted that there are no medical bills for services that were obtained after October 15, 2007, as a result of the incident that is at issue in this case. As such, any evidence related to such medical bills should be excluded from the trial in this case.

3. PLAINTIFF'S MEDICAL BILLS FOR SERVICES THAT WERE OBTAINED AFTER THE REQUESTED DATE ARE IRRELEVANT TO THIS ACTION

Due to the fact that plaintiff has admitted that there are no medical bills for services that were obtained after October 15, 2007, as a result of the incident that is at issue in this case, any such evidence should be excluded as irrelevant to. Federal Rule of Evidence 401 defines relevancy as: evidence having any tendency to make the existence of any fact that is of consequence to the determination of the action more probable or less probable than it would be without the evidence. Illinois has adopted this definition of relevancy through case law. *Spencer v. Wandolowski*, 264 Ill. App. 3d 611, 617, 201 Ill. Dec. 422, 636 N.E.2d 854 (1st Dist. 1994); and *People v. Monroe*, 66 Ill. 2d 317, 321–22, 5 Ill. Dec. 824, 362 N.E.2d 295 (1977).

Evidence may be properly excluded where it is not relevant to matters at issue. See *Cochran v. Great Atlantic & Pacific Tea Co., Inc.*, 203 Ill. App. 3d 935, 937–38, 148 Ill. Dec. 923, 561 N.E.2d 229 (5th Dist. 1990) (trial judge has inherent power to exclude irrelevant evidence); and *Benson v. Bradford Mut. Fire Ins. Corp.*, 121 Ill. App. 3d 500, 510, 76 Ill. Dec. 774, 459 N.E.2d 689, 47 A.L.R.4th 759 (2d Dist. 1984) (trial judge had discretion to exclude irrelevant witness testimony) and *Pagel v. Yates*, 128 Ill. App. 3d 897, 903, 84 Ill. Dec. 180, 471 N.E.2d 946 (4th Dist. 1984) (exclusion of irrelevant and confusing document). In addition, this Court may exclude evidence regarding matters that are not in dispute. *Davis v. International Harvester Co.*, 167 Ill. App. 3d 814, 824–25, 118 Ill. Dec. 589, 521 N.E.2d 1282 (2d Dist. 1988) (proper to exclude evidence of the feasibility of design changes when there was an admission to that ability); and *Bullard v. Barnes*, 112 Ill. App. 3d 384, 392–94, 68 Ill. Dec. 37, 445 N.E.2d 485 (4th Dist. 1983), judgment aff'd, 102 Ill. 2d 505, 82 Ill. Dec. 448, 468 N.E.2d 1228 (1984) (trial judge abused his discretion by admitting photographs of the deceased and testimony regarding the conditions and circumstances surrounding the collision, because liability was admitted).

In the present case, as was discussed above, the plaintiff has admitted, through deemed admissions, that there are no medical bills for services that were obtained after October 15, 2007, as a result of the incident that is at issue in this case. It would be unfair and prejudicial to allow plaintiff, at this late date, to present evidence on an issue that, until days before the start of trial, was not in dispute. Thus, the Court should therefore exclude any and all evidence, including any mention of evidence, relating to medical bills for services that were obtained after October 15, 2007, as irrelevant to the issues in this case.

4. THIS COURT MAY EXCLUDE PREJUDICIAL EVIDENCE IN ADVANCE OF TRIAL BY WAY OF AN IN LIMINE MOTION

Evidence should be excluded when the prejudicial impact of the evidence outweighs the probative value of it. Federal Rule of Evidence 403 states: Although relevant, evidence may be excluded if its probative value is substantially outweighed by the danger of unfair prejudice, confusion of the issues, or misleading the jury, or by considerations of undue delay, waste of time, or needless presentation of cumulative evidence. Illinois has a common-law rule that is comparable to Federal Rule of Evidence 403. See *People v. Peete*, 318 Ill. App. 3d 961, 966–67, 252 Ill. Dec. 821, 743 N.E.2d 689 (4th Dist. 2001); *People v. Walker*, 335 Ill. App. 3d 102, 112, 268 Ill. Dec. 654, 779 N.E.2d 268 (2d Dist. 2002), as modified on denial of reh'g, (Oct. 24, 2002) and judgment aff'd, 211 Ill. 2d 317, 285 Ill. Dec. 519, 812 N.E.2d 339 (2004).

In fact, Illinois cases have excluded evidence when the prejudicial impact of the evidence outweighed the probative value of it. See e.g. *Department of Public Works and Bldgs. v. Roehrig*, 45 Ill. App. 3d 189, 196, 3 Ill. Dec. 893, 359 N.E.2d 752 (5th Dist. 1976) (exclusion of evidence of prior condemnations in a condemnation case because the prejudicial impact outweighs the probative value of it); and *People v. Holman*, 257 Ill. App. 3d 1031, 1033–34, 196 Ill. Dec. 457, 630 N.E.2d 154 (2d Dist. 1994) (evidence is admissible if it is relevant and if the prejudicial impact does not substantially outweigh the probative value of it).

Moreover, the Court should determine whether to exclude this evidence outside of the presence of the jury in order to prevent the jury from hearing about inadmissible material. Specifically, Federal Rule of evidence 103(c) provides: Hearing of Jury.—In jury cases, proceedings shall be conducted, to the extent practicable, so as to prevent inadmissible evidence from being suggested to the jury by any means, such as making statements or offers of proof or asking questions in the hearing of the jury. Although this rule has not been specifically codified in Illinois, Illinois has adopted other Federal Rules of evidence through case law. See e.g. *People v. Monroe*, 66 Ill. 2d 317, 321–22, 5 Ill. Dec. 824, 362 N.E.2d 295 (1977); and *Spencer v. Wandolowski*, 264 Ill. App. 3d 611, 617, 201 Ill. Dec. 422, 636 N.E.2d 854 (1st Dist. 1994) (adopting Federal Rule of Evidence 401). In the instant matter, the jury will be prejudiced merely by hearing any reference to the medical bills for services that were obtained after October 15, 2007. Furthermore, as was discussed above, plaintiff has admitted, through deemed admissions, that there are no medical bills for services that were obtained after October 15, 2007, as a result of the incident that is at issue in this case. It would be unfair and prejudicial to allow plaintiff, at this late date, to present evidence on an issue that, until days before the start of trial, was not in dispute. Thus, the Court should therefore exclude any and all evidence, including any mention of evidence, relating to medical bills for services that were obtained after October 15, 2007, as unfairly prejudicial to defendant.

5. EVIDENCE OF PLAINTIFF'S MEDICAL BILLS FOR SERVICES THAT WERE OBTAINED AFTER THE REQUESTED DATE SHOULD BE EXCLUDED TO PREVENT UNFAIR SURPRISE TO DEFENDANT

To avoid unfair surprise, the Court may exclude evidence on issues where discovery responses and actions of counsel led opposing counsel to believe those issues would not be litigated. See *Harding v. Amsted Industries, Inc.*, 276 Ill. App. 3d 483, 492, 213 Ill. Dec. 187, 658 N.E.2d 1208 (1st Dist. 1995) (trial judge properly excluded expert testimony that exceeded the opinions expressed by the expert during discovery); and *Savage v. Martin*, 256 Ill. App. 3d 272, 285, 195 Ill. Dec. 142, 628 N.E.2d 606 (1st Dist. 1993) (expert opinion that went beyond opinions stated at deposition properly excluded, where expert stated that he had no other opinions beyond those in his report. Furthermore, the Court is within its power to preclude a party from introducing documents not discovered by the opposing party, where the relevant evidence is not disclosed during discovery. See Illinois Supreme Court Rule 219; *King v. Clemons*, 264 Ill. App. 3d 138, 140–41, 201 Ill. Dec. 630, 636 N.E.2d 1062 (5th Dist. 1994); *Golembiewski v. Hallberg Ins. Agency, Inc.*, 262 Ill. App. 3d 1082, 1086–87, 200 Ill. Dec. 113, 635 N.E.2d 452 (1st Dist. 1994); and *Ashpole v. Brunswick Bowling and Billiards Corp.*, 297 Ill. App. 3d 725, 726–30, 232 Ill. Dec. 308, 697 N.E.2d 1238 (2d Dist. 1998).

In the present case, plaintiff's statements and actions led defense counsel to reasonably believe that plaintiff would not be pursuing a claim for medical bills for services that were obtained after October 15, 2007. The first indication that plaintiff would be offering any evidence on this issue was at the final pre-trial conference, just days before the commencement of trial and after the discovery cut-off date. Moreover, as was discussed above, plaintiff has admitted, through deemed admissions, that there are no medical bills for services that were obtained after October 15, 2007, as a result of the incident that is at issue in this case. It would be unfair and prejudicial to allow plaintiff, at this late date, to present evidence on an issue that, until days before the start of trial, was not in dispute. Thus, the Court should therefore exclude any and all evidence, including any mention of evidence, relating to medical bills for services that were obtained after October 15, 2007, to prevent unfair surprise to defendant

6. CONCLUSION

Based on the foregoing, defendant respectfully requests that this Court exclude any testimony or documentary evidence, or mention of any evidence, regarding plaintiff's claim for medical bills for services that were obtained after October 15, 2007.

Dated: *[date]*

By: __________________
[name of counsel]
Attorneys for Defendant,
[name of defendant]

Chapter 7

Character Evidence

I. MOTION AUTHORITIES

A. OVERVIEW OF CHARACTER EVIDENCE

B. MOTION TO EXCLUDE CHARACTER EVIDENCE USED FOR IMPEACHMENT

C. MOTION TO EXCLUDE CHARACTER EVIDENCE USED TO PROVE CONDUCT

D. MOTION TO EXCLUDE EVIDENCE OF PRIOR FELONY CONVICTION

II. SAMPLE MOTIONS

KeyCite®: Cases and other legal materials listed in KeyCite Scope can be researched through the KeyCite service on Westlaw®. Use KeyCite to check citations for form, parallel references, prior and later history, and comprehensive citator information, including citations to other decisions and secondary materials.

I. MOTION AUTHORITIES

Impeachment of a witness' credibility can be accomplished in a variety of ways. One such way is by admission of a witness' past conduct, which often provides ammunition for effective impeachment. Therefore, one aspect of a party's discovery should be geared towards finding out what the opposition knows about your witnesses. A motion in limine requesting that all undisclosed evidence be precluded at trial will prevent the admission of any undisclosed evidence, including information that may be used to impeach a party's witness. As for known, but harmful evidence about a party's witnesses, a motion in limine should be filed to exclude the evidence or, at the very least, limit the use of the evidence. Even if your motion to exclude is denied, the opposition's response and the arguments related to the motion will provide valuable information as to how the opposition intends to use the evidence.

A. OVERVIEW OF CHARACTER EVIDENCE

Character evidence is defined as "evidence regarding someone's personality traits; evidence of a person's moral standing in a community based on reputation or opinion." *Black's Law Dictionary* (7th Edition, 1999).

Before making a motion to exclude character evidence, users should familiarize themselves with the rules of admissibility of such evidence, which can be confusing. For helpful commentary, see Robert S. Hunter, *Illinois Practice Library, Trial Handbook for Illinois Lawyers—Criminal* (6th Ed. 1989), Chapters 39, 40, 42 and 66.

The following sections provide a brief overview of the basis for admitting or excluding character evidence under Illinois law.

§ 7:1 Admissible character evidence, generally

Federal Rule of Evidence 406 states:

> Evidence of the habit of a person or of the routine practice of an organization, whether corroborated or not and regardless of the presence of eyewitnesses, is relevant to prove that the conduct of the person or organization on a particular occasion was in conformity with the habit or routine practice.

Alvarado v. Goepp, 278 Ill. App. 3d 494, 495–97, 215 Ill. Dec. 313, 663 N.E.2d 63 (1st Dist. 1996) (Illinois has adopted Federal Rule of Evidence 406 through case law, regarding admissibility of habit testimony; however, there was an improper foundation to show habit in this case).

People v. Petitt, 245 Ill. App. 3d 132, 139–41, 146–48, 184 Ill. Dec. 766, 613 N.E.2d 1358 (2d Dist. 1993) (a defendant can offer evidence to suggest a good reputation for a character trait that is relevant to the offense charged. In this case, chastity and morality related to an abuse offense but truthfulness did not).

People v. Petitt, 245 Ill. App. 3d 132, 139–41, 146–48, 184 Ill. Dec. 766, 613 N.E.2d 1358 (2d Dist. 1993) (evidence of other offenses is not admissible when it is introduced to suggest that the defendant committed the charged crime; however, such offenses can be admitted when they are relevant to any other issue, such as intent, motive or modus operandi, as long as the probative value outweighs the prejudicial impact of the evidence) (note: the alleged bad acts were deemed not admissible in this case).

People v. Willy, 301 Ill. 307, 317–21, 133 N.E. 859 (1921) (character evidence, when it is admissible, should be demonstrated only through general reputation evidence and not through specific acts and moreover, the reputation evidence must not be too remote from the incident in question).

People v. Willy, 301 Ill. 307, 317–21, 133 N.E. 859 (1921) (character evidence is admissible by the defendant to show good character and if offered, the state can then offer rebuttal evidence to suggest bad character).

§ 7:2 Character evidence subject to exclusion

People v. Petitt, 245 Ill. App. 3d 132, 147–48, 184 Ill. Dec. 766, 613 N.E.2d 1358 (2d Dist. 1993) (when character evidence is admissible, it must be elicited through general reputation evidence and cannot be established through specific acts or through the witness' personal opinion).

People v. Harris, 224 Ill. App. 3d 649, 651–53, 167 Ill. Dec. 165, 587 N.E.2d 47 (3d Dist. 1992) (evidence of past violent crimes was not admissible in a battery prosecution because the probative value outweighed the prejudicial impact of the evidence, due to the fact that the defendant did not put his good character into issue).

Herget Nat. Bank of Pekin v. Johnson, 21 Ill. App. 3d 1024, 1026–28, 316 N.E.2d 191 (3d Dist. 1974) (evidence suggesting that the victim had acted negligently in the past should not be admitted to suggest that he acted negligently in the instant matter).

People v. Moretti, 6 Ill. 2d 494, 523–24, 129 N.E.2d 709 (1955) (when character evidence is admissible, it must be elicited through general reputation evidence and cannot be established through specific acts or through the witness' personal opinion).

People v. Willy, 301 Ill. 307, 317–21, 133 N.E. 859 (1921) (character evidence, when it is admissible, should be demonstrated only through general reputation evidence and not through specific acts and moreover, the reputation evidence must not be too remote from the incident in question).

Starks v. Schlensky, 128 Ill. App. 1, 1906 WL 2026, at *2 (2d Dist. 1906) (character traits that do not reflect upon the witness' truthfulness and are not relevant to the issues in the case, are not proper subjects for cross-examination).

Specific citations regarding the exclusion of character evidence can be found in the following sections:

- Character evidence improperly used for impeachment (§ 7:4 to § 7:24)
- Character evidence improperly used to prove conduct (§ 7:25 to § 7:36)
- Improper evidence of felony convictions (§ 7:37 to § 7:52)

§ 7:3 Statutory limitations on use in criminal cases

See also 725 ILCS 5/115-7 (2002) (in prosecutions for certain sexual offenses, evidence of the victim's prior sexual activity or reputation is not admissible unless it meets specific relevancy standards and even then, only if the trial judge determines that the probative value of the evidence outweighs the prejudicial impact of it).

B. MOTION TO EXCLUDE CHARACTER EVIDENCE USED FOR IMPEACHMENT

§ 7:4 Suggested motion text

[Name of moving party] hereby moves this Court for an order excluding any and all evidence, references to evidence, testimony or argument relating to the character or trait of *[name of witness]* for *[describe the character or trait evidence at issue, e.g., the witness' habits regarding consumption of alcohol]* where such evidence will be used for impeachment purposes. The motion is based upon the grounds that the evidence is irrelevant to the issues in this case, is expressly prohibited for impeachment purposes by Illinois case law and will create a substantial danger of undue prejudice to *[name of moving party]*.

§ 7:5 Motion summary

This motion is used to exclude character evidence of specific instances of a person's conduct, where used for impeachment purposes. The motion is based upon the authority of Illinois cases such as: *People v. Petitt*, 245 Ill. App. 3d 132, 147–48, 184 Ill. Dec. 766, 613 N.E.2d 1358 (2d Dist. 1993); *People v. Moretti*, 6 Ill. 2d 494, 523–24, 129 N.E.2d 709 (1955); and *Starks v. Schlensky*, 128 Ill. App. 1, 1906 WL 2026, at *2 (2d Dist. 1906). This chapter includes citations for the exclusion of character evidence in commonly disputed areas, such as alcohol and drug use, arrests and misdemeanors, felony convictions, sexual behavior, religious beliefs, etc.

§ 7:6 Supporting authorities—Exclusion of prejudicial evidence, generally

Federal Rule of Evidence 403 states:

> Although relevant, evidence may be excluded if its probative value is substantially outweighed by the danger of unfair prejudice, confusion of the issues, or misleading the jury, or by considerations of undue delay, waste of time, or needless presentation of cumulative evidence.

It must be noted that this Rule has not been codified in Illinois. However, Illinois cases have stated that Illinois has a common-law rule that is comparable to Federal Rule of Evidence 403. See *People v. Walker*, 335 Ill. App. 3d 102, 112, 268 Ill. Dec. 654, 779 N.E.2d 268 (2d Dist. 2002), as modified on denial of reh'g, (Oct. 24, 2002) and judgment aff'd, 211 Ill. 2d 317, 285 Ill. Dec. 519, 812 N.E.2d 339 (2004); and *People v. Peete*, 318 Ill. App. 3d 961, 966–67, 252 Ill. Dec. 821, 743 N.E.2d 689 (4th Dist. 2001). Therefore, it is arguable that Federal Rule of Evidence 403 can be considered as persuasive authority in Illinois.

Montana v. Egelhoff, 518 U.S. 37, 41–43, 116 S. Ct. 2013, 135 L. Ed. 2d 361 (1996) (Due Process does not guarantee the right to introduce all relevant evidence and therefore, Federal Rule of Evidence 403 does not violate Due Process).

For expanded citations on the exclusion of prejudicial evidence, see § 2:1 to § 2:4.

§ 7:7 Supporting authorities—Exclusion of irrelevant evidence, generally

Federal Rule of Evidence 401 defines relevancy as,

> evidence having any tendency to make the existence of any fact

that is of consequence to the determination of the action more probable or less probable than it would be without the evidence.

Illinois has adopted this definition of relevancy through case law. *Spencer v. Wandolowski*, 264 Ill. App. 3d 611, 617, 201 Ill. Dec. 422, 636 N.E.2d 854 (1st Dist. 1994); and *People v. Monroe*, 66 Ill. 2d 317, 321–22, 5 Ill. Dec. 824, 362 N.E.2d 295 (1977).

Preston ex rel. Preston v. Simmons, 321 Ill. App. 3d 789, 803, 254 Ill. Dec. 647, 747 N.E.2d 1059 (1st Dist. 2001) (trial judge should not permit such wide latitude on cross-examination that it undermines the rule that only relevant evidence is admissible).

Vojas v. K mart Corp., 312 Ill. App. 3d 544, 552, 245 Ill. Dec. 144, 727 N.E.2d 397 (5th Dist. 2000) (the burden of establishing relevance is on the party offering the evidence).

Swick v. Liautaud, 169 Ill. 2d 504, 521, 215 Ill. Dec. 98, 662 N.E.2d 1238 (1996) (not an abuse of discretion to exclude evidence of the defendant's conduct towards people other than the plaintiff on the basis of irrelevance).

Cochran v. Great Atlantic & Pacific Tea Co., Inc., 203 Ill. App. 3d 935, 937–38, 148 Ill. Dec. 923, 561 N.E.2d 229 (5th Dist. 1990) (trial judge has inherent power to exclude irrelevant evidence).

For expanded citations on the exclusion of irrelevant evidence, see § 3:1 to § 3:10.

§ 7:8 Supporting authorities—Exclusion of improper impeachment evidence, generally

Reichert v. Board of Fire and Police Com'rs of City of Collinsville, 388 Ill.App.3d 834, 846–47, 905 N.E.2d 861 (5th Dist. 2009) (Illinois law prohibits impeachment by evidence of specific acts and does not have an evidentiary rule similar to Federal Rule of Evidence 608(b)).

People v. Tabb, 374 Ill. App. 3d 680, 690, 312 Ill. Dec. 470, 870 N.E.2d 914 (1st Dist. 2007), appeal denied, 225 Ill. 2d 670, 314 Ill. Dec. 835, 875 N.E.2d 1122 (2007) (the defendant was not denied his Constitutional right to confront witnesses when the trial judge denied his request to impeach a witness with a juvenile adjudication).

People v. Collins, 366 Ill. App. 3d 885, 892-93, 304 Ill. Dec. 478, 853 N.E.2d 10 (1st Dist. 2006) (the trial court did not err by excluding evidence regarding the details of the actual allegations against a witness for a charge that had been stricken with leave to reinstate).

People v. Bohn, 362 Ill. App. 3d 485, 486–91, 298 Ill. Dec. 649, 840 N.E.2d 762 (2d Dist. 2005) (the trial court did not abuse its discretion by excluding evidence that a witness was arrested for allegedly possessing the same drugs that the defendant was accused of possessing, as irrelevant, prejudicial and confusing).

People v. Bohn, 362 Ill. App. 3d 485, 490, 298 Ill. Dec. 649, 840 N.E.2d 762 (2d Dist. 2005) (evidence of an arrest was not admissible for impeachment purposes).

People v. Cookson, 215 Ill. 2d 194, 213–18, 294 Ill. Dec. 72, 830 N.E.2d 484 (2005) (proffered impeachment evidence suggesting that victim had allegedly made false abuse allegations against someone other than defendant was irrelevant).

People v. Nitz, 353 Ill. App. 3d 978, 988–89, 289 Ill. Dec. 760, 820 N.E.2d 536 (5th Dist. 2004), judgment aff'd in part, rev'd in part, 219 Ill. 2d 400, 302 Ill. Dec. 418, 848 N.E.2d 982 (2006).

People v. McGee, 286 Ill. App. 3d 786, 795–96, 222 Ill. Dec. 137, 676 N.E.2d 1341 (1st Dist. 1997) (evidence regarding specific acts of untruthfulness, when not directly at issue in the case, is inadmissible).

People v. Petitt, 245 Ill. App. 3d 132, 147–48, 184 Ill. Dec. 766, 613 N.E.2d 1358 (2d Dist. 1993) (when character evidence is admissible, it must be elicited through general reputation evidence and cannot be established through specific acts or through the witness' personal opinion).

People v. Petitt, 245 Ill. App. 3d 132, 139–41, 146–48, 184 Ill. Dec. 766, 613 N.E.2d 1358 (2d Dist. 1993) (evidence of other offenses is not admissible when introduced to suggest that the defendant committed the charged crime; however, such offenses can be admitted when they are relevant to any other issue, such as intent, motive or modus operandi, as long as the probative value outweighs the prejudicial impact of the evidence) (note: the alleged bad acts were deemed not admissible in this case).

People v. Quick, 236 Ill. App. 3d 446, 455, 177 Ill. Dec. 272, 603 N.E.2d 53 (1st Dist. 1992) ("The court should not permit cross-examination that is designed to insult, degrade, or humiliate a witness or whose only apparent purpose is to demonstrate that the defendant was of bad moral character[sic]."

McWethy v. Lee, 1 Ill. App. 3d 80, 84-85, 272 N.E.2d 663 (4th Dist. 1971) (the purpose of impeachment is to introduce evidence that suggests that the witness is not truthful) (alcohol use or presence not proper impeachment in this case).

People v. Moretti, 6 Ill. 2d 494, 523–24, 129 N.E.2d 709 (1955) (when character evidence is admissible, it must be elicited through general reputation evidence and cannot be established through specific acts or through the witness' personal opinion).

Starks v. Schlensky, 128 Ill. App. 1, 1906 WL 2026, at *2 (2d Dist. 1906) (character traits that do not reflect upon the witness' truthfulness and are not relevant to the issues in the case, are not proper subjects for cross-examination).

See also 725 ILCS 5/115-7 (2002) (in prosecutions for certain sexual offenses, evidence of the victim's prior sexual activity or reputation is not admissible unless it meets specific relevancy standards and even then, only if the trial judge determines that the probative value of the evidence outweighs the prejudicial impact of it).

§ 7:9 Supporting authorities—Exclusion of improper impeachment evidence, generally—Alcohol consumption

People v. Bridgewater, 388 Ill.App.3d 787, 793–94, 904 N.E.2d 171 (4th Dist. 2009) (a juvenile adjudication for consumption of alcohol was not admissible to impeach a witness' testimony).

People v. Collette, 217 Ill. App. 3d 465, 467–71, 160 Ill. Dec. 420, 577 N.E.2d 550 (4th Dist. 1991) (trial court properly restricted certain questions regarding the witness' past alcohol use).

Ryan v. McEvoy, 20 Ill. App. 3d 562, 566–67, 315 N.E.2d 38 (1st Dist. 1974) (asking a witness about past alcohol use was improper).

McWethy v. Lee, 1 Ill. App. 3d 80, 83-85, 272 N.E.2d 663 (4th Dist. 1971) (improper to allow evidence of consumption or presence of alcohol when there was no proof that the witness was intoxicated).

§ 7:10 Supporting authorities—Exclusion of improper impeachment evidence, generally—Arrest or misdemeanor convictions that do not involve truth or dishonesty

Reichert v. Board of Fire and Police Com'rs of City of Collinsville, 388 Ill.App.3d 834, 847–49, 905 N.E.2d 861 (5th Dist. 2009) (a violation of a Federal statute prohibiting selling of goods in commerce at unreasonably low prices eliminating competition was not a crime involving dishonesty and was not admissible in Illinois courts to impeach a witness).

People v. Bridgewater, 388 Ill.App.3d 787, 793–94, 904 N.E.2d 171 (4th Dist. 2009) (a juvenile adjudication for consumption of alcohol was not admissible to impeach a witness' testimony).

People v. Buckner, 376 Ill. App. 3d 251, 254–57, 315 Ill. Dec. 87, 876 N.E.2d 87 (1st Dist. 2007), appeal denied, 226 Ill. 2d 619, 317 Ill. Dec. 505, 882 N.E.2d 79 (2008) and cert. denied, 129 S. Ct. 64, 172 L. Ed. 2d 61 (2008) (the trial court properly prevented the defendant from cross-examining a witness about her guilty plea to misdemeanor theft charge because the witness was on supervision for the offense, meaning that if she finished her supervision successfully, there would be no conviction and because there was no showing that the witness' testimony was biased in favor of the State as a result of that charge).

People v. Evans, 373 Ill. App. 3d 948, 956–58, 311 Ill. Dec. 907, 869 N.E.2d 920 (1st Dist. 2007), appeal denied, 225 Ill. 2d 648, 314 Ill. Dec. 830, 875 N.E.2d 1117 (2007) (cross-examination of a witness regarding a pending charge was improper because there was no showing that the charge caused the witness to be biased or testify falsely) (harmless error).

People v. Bohn, 362 Ill. App. 3d 485, 486–91, 298 Ill. Dec. 649, 840 N.E.2d 762 (2d Dist. 2005) (the trial court did not abuse its discretion by excluding evidence, as irrelevant, prejudicial and confusing, that a witness was arrested for allegedly possessing the same drugs that the defendant was accused of possessing).

People v. Bohn, 362 Ill. App. 3d 485, 490, 298 Ill. Dec. 649, 840 N.E.2d 762 (2d Dist. 2005) (evidence of an arrest was not admissible for impeachment purposes).

People v. Moser, 356 Ill. App. 3d 900, 912–13, 293 Ill. Dec. 230, 827 N.E.2d 1111 (2d Dist. 2005) (trial court properly prevented defendant from impeaching witness with evidence of dismissed indictment).

People v. Nitz, 353 Ill. App. 3d 978, 988–89, 289 Ill. Dec. 760, 820 N.E.2d 536 (5th Dist. 2004), judgment aff'd in part, rev'd in part, 219 Ill. 2d 400, 302 Ill. Dec. 418, 848 N.E.2d 982 (2006).

Young v. Chicago Transit Authority, 209 Ill. App. 3d 84, 94-95, 154 Ill. Dec. 18, 568 N.E.2d 18 (1st Dist. 1990) (trial judge did not abuse discretion by disallowing impeachment evidence that the witness had been convicted of soliciting prostitution, a misdemeanor offense).

People v. Mason, 28 Ill. 2d 396, 399–403, 192 N.E.2d 835 (1963) (arrests, charges and prior acts of misconduct are not generally admissible in evidence; however, pending charges or arrests may be used to impeach a state's witness, to suggest a motive to testify falsely).

§ 7:11 Supporting authorities—Exclusion of improper impeachment evidence, generally—Drug use

People v. Kegley, 227 Ill. App. 3d 48, 54-55, 169 Ill. Dec. 3, 590 N.E.2d 922 (2d Dist. 1992) (trial court did not abuse its discretion by refusing to admit impeachment evidence of a single use of narcotics).

Baldwin v. Huffman Towing Co., 51 Ill. App. 3d 861, 863–64, 9 Ill. Dec. 469, 366 N.E.2d 980 (5th Dist. 1977) (trial judge properly excluded evidence of a witness' conviction for possession of a narcotic, because the prejudicial impact of the evidence outweighed its probative value).

People v. Moretti, 6 Ill. 2d 494, 519–23, 129 N.E.2d 709 (1955) (evidence that the victim was a narcotic addict was not admissible when there was no showing that the victim was still an addict at the time of the incident in question).

§ 7:12 Supporting authorities—Exclusion of improper impeachment evidence, generally—Felony convictions improperly used for impeachment

Note that the general rule is that evidence of certain felony convictions is admissible for the purposes of attacking the credibility of a witness. See Federal Rule of Evidence 609 (proposed Rule 609 adopted in Illinois; see *People v. Montgomery*, 47 Ill. 2d 510, 516–19, 268 N.E.2d 695, 67 A.L.R.3d 816 (1971)). However, Rule 609 has several built-in exceptions that would allow for the exclusion of conviction evidence, as is displayed by the cases below.

People v. Naylor, 372 Ill. App. 3d 1, 309 Ill. Dec. 477, 864 N.E.2d 718 (1st Dist. 2007), appeal allowed, 224 Ill. 2d 587, 312 Ill. Dec. 659, 871 N.E.2d 59 (2007) and judgment aff'd, 229 Ill. 2d 584, 323 Ill. Dec. 381, 893 N.E.2d 653 (2008) (the trial court abused its discretion by allowing the defendant to be impeached with a conviction that occurred thirteen years before the trial).

Baldwin v. Huffman Towing Co., 51 Ill. App. 3d 861, 863–64, 9 Ill. Dec. 469, 366 N.E.2d 980 (5th Dist. 1977) (trial judge properly excluded evidence of a witness' conviction for possession of a narcotic, because the prejudicial impact of the evidence outweighed its probative value).

People v. Montgomery, 47 Ill. 2d 510, 512–19, 268 N.E.2d

695, 67 A.L.R.3d 816 (1971) (a felony conviction that was remote in time should not have been admitted for impeachment).

For expanded citations and commentary on the exclusion of criminal convictions, see § 7:37 to § 7:52, infra.

§ 7:13 Supporting authorities—Exclusion of improper impeachment evidence, generally—Fraudulent acts

Reichert v. Board of Fire and Police Com'rs of City of Collinsville, 388 Ill.App.3d 834, 846–47, 905 N.E.2d 861 (5th Dist. 2009) (Illinois law prohibits impeachment by evidence of specific acts and does not have an evidentiary rule similar to Federal Rule of Evidence 608(b)).

Reichert v. Board of Fire and Police Com'rs of City of Collinsville, 388 Ill.App.3d 834, 847–49, 905 N.E.2d 861 (5th Dist. 2009) (a violation of a Federal statute prohibiting selling of goods in commerce at unreasonably low prices eliminating competition, was not a crime involving dishonesty and was not admissible in Illinois courts to impeach a witness).

People v. McGee, 286 Ill. App. 3d 786, 795–96, 222 Ill. Dec. 137, 676 N.E.2d 1341 (1st Dist. 1997) (evidence of the defendant's past use of an alibi was improper).

Pros v. Mid-America Computer Corp., 142 Ill. App. 3d 453, 472, 96 Ill. Dec. 572, 491 N.E.2d 851 (2d Dist. 1986) (evidence of the witness' prior suspension from the practice of law for embezzlement was not admissible).

See also *People v. McGee*, 286 Ill. App. 3d 786, 795–96, 222 Ill. Dec. 137, 676 N.E.2d 1341 (1st Dist. 1997) (evidence regarding specific acts of untruthfulness, when they are not directly at issue in the case, is inadmissible).

§ 7:14 Supporting authorities—Exclusion of improper impeachment evidence, generally—Good character of witness

People v. Petitt, 245 Ill. App. 3d 132, 139–41, 146–48, 184 Ill. Dec. 766, 613 N.E.2d 1358 (2d Dist. 1993) (a defendant can offer evidence to suggest a good reputation for a character trait that is relevant to the offense charged).

People v. Harris, 224 Ill. App. 3d 649, 650–53, 167 Ill. Dec. 165, 587 N.E.2d 47 (3d Dist. 1992) (state may not use cross-examination to deliberately elicit testimony by the defendant regarding his alleged good character so that the state can then impeach the testimony with evidence of bad character).

People v. Partee, 17 Ill. App. 3d 166, 177–79, 308 N.E.2d 18 (1st Dist. 1974) (defendant was properly precluded from introducing evidence that he did not have a reputation for being a homosexual because, "semantically, homosexuality is not one of the character traits for which one can have a good reputation," and because absence of a specific character trait does not necessarily imply a positive good reputation).

§ 7:15 Supporting authorities—Exclusion of improper impeachment evidence, generally—Religious beliefs

Downey v. Dunnington, 384 Ill.App.3d 350, 387–89, 895 N.E.2d 271 (4th Dist. 2008) (evidence that the defendant's father was a minister was irrelevant and prejudicial and should not have been admitted but the error was harmless in this case).

People v. Quick, 236 Ill. App. 3d 446, 455, 177 Ill. Dec. 272, 603 N.E.2d 53 (1st Dist. 1992) (trial judge erred by allowing cross-examination about a witness' religious beliefs in response to the witness' testimony about participation in activities which were religious in nature).

Starks v. Schlensky, 128 Ill. App. 1, 1906 WL 2026, at *2 (2d Dist. 1906) (trial judge properly disallowed cross-examination about the witness' religion, as that issue is irrelevant to whether the witness is truthful or not).

But see *People v. Baseer*, 90 Ill. App. 3d 866, 871–72, 46 Ill. Dec. 283, 414 N.E.2d 5 (1st Dist. 1980) (although a witness' religion is not ordinarily admissible, the state's questions regarding the defendant's religion were admissible in this case because the defendant had raised the subject in his direct testimony).

§ 7:16 Supporting authorities—Exclusion of improper impeachment evidence, generally—Sexual preference or behavior

People v. Santos, 211 Ill. 2d 395, 401–08, 286 Ill. Dec. 102, 813 N.E.2d 159 (2004) (rape shield statute prevented defendant from introducing impeachment evidence about victim's prior inconsistent statement regarding sexual activity with someone other than defendant) [see 725 ILCS 5/115-7].

Doe v. Lutz, 281 Ill. App. 3d 630, 637–38, 218 Ill. Dec. 80, 668 N.E.2d 564, 112 Ed. Law Rep. 371 (1st Dist. 1996), as modified on denial of reh'g, (June 25, 1996) (evidence of prior inappropriate sexual conduct towards someone other than the alleged victim was not admissible because it was irrelevant and prejudicial and it did not demonstrate sufficiently similar behavior to qualify for modus operandi evidence).

Young v. Chicago Transit Authority, 209 Ill. App. 3d 84, 94-95, 154 Ill. Dec. 18, 568 N.E.2d 18 (1st Dist. 1990) (trial judge did not abuse discretion by disallowing impeachment evidence that the witness had been convicted of soliciting prostitution, a misdemeanor offense).

People v. Partee, 17 Ill. App. 3d 166, 177–79, 308 N.E.2d 18 (1st Dist. 1974) (defendant was properly precluded from introducing evidence that he did not have a reputation for being a homosexual because, "semantically, homosexuality is not one of the character traits for which one can have a good reputation," and because absence of a specific character trait does not necessarily imply a positive good reputation).

Ryan v. McEvoy, 20 Ill. App. 3d 562, 567–68, 315 N.E.2d 38 (1st Dist. 1974) (asking a witness about whether he was married was improper).

People v. Parisie, 5 Ill. App. 3d 1009, 1033–35, 287 N.E.2d 310 (4th Dist. 1972) (evidence of the victim's reputation for homosexuality was not admissible as part of an insanity defense in a homicide case because it was not relevant).

See also 725 ILCS 5/115-7 (2002) (in prosecutions for certain sexual offenses, evidence of the victim's prior sexual activity or reputation is not admissible unless it meets specific relevancy standards and even then, only if the trial judge determines that the probative value of the evidence outweighs the prejudicial impact of it).

§ 7:17 Supporting authorities—Other grounds

Other possible grounds for excluding improper character evidence include:

- Collateral to issues in case (§ 2:5 to § 2:8)
- Confusing or misleading (§ 2:9 to § 2:12)
- Solely intended to create an emotional bias (§ 2:13 to § 2:19)
- Inadmissible hearsay (§ 8:78 to § 8:89)

§ 7:18 Opposing authorities—Impeachment, generally

People v. Hogan, 388 Ill.App.3d 885, 896, 904 N.E.2d 1036 (1st Dist. 2009) (a witness' mental health history is relevant for impeachment purposes).

People v. Hogan, 388 Ill.App.3d 885, 895, 904 N.E.2d 1036

(1st Dist. 2009) (a witness' narcotics addiction at the time of testifying or at the time of the event in question, is a proper subject for impeachment of the witness).

People v. Clay, 379 Ill. App. 3d 470, 318 Ill. Dec. 659, 884 N.E.2d 214, 221–22 (1st Dist. 2008), appeal denied, 228 Ill. 2d 539, 321 Ill. Dec. 558, 889 N.E.2d 1118 (2008) (in a murder case, trial court had discretion to allow the prosecution to impeach the defendant with evidence of his prior murder conviction).

People v. Harris, 375 Ill. App. 3d 398, 405–08, 313 Ill. Dec. 960, 873 N.E.2d 584 (3d Dist. 2007), appeal allowed, 226 Ill. 2d 596, 316 Ill. Dec. 547, 879 N.E.2d 935 (2007) and judgment aff'd, 231 Ill. 2d 582, 2008 WL 5246055 (2008) (after the defendant testified and implied that he was law abiding, evidence of his prior juvenile adjudication was admissible).

People v. Farrell, 377 Ill. App. 3d 249, 250–58, 316 Ill. Dec. 389, 879 N.E.2d 456 (4th Dist. 2007) (in an aggravated robbery case, the trial court had discretion to allow the prosecution to impeach the defendant with his theft conviction).

People v. Farrell, 377 Ill. App. 3d 249, 252, 316 Ill. Dec. 389, 879 N.E.2d 456 (4th Dist. 2007) (". . .Illinois courts allow the introduction of prior convictions within 10 years from release from confinement rather than only allowing prior convictions that are less than 10 years old as calculated from the date of conviction. . .").

People v. Barner, 374 Ill. App. 3d 963, 968–73, 313 Ill. Dec. 122, 871 N.E.2d 849 (1st Dist. 2007), appeal denied, 225 Ill. 2d 641, 314 Ill. Dec. 828, 875 N.E.2d 1115 (2007) (in a sexual assault case, evidence of the defendant's conviction for failing to register as a sex offender was admissible to impeach his testimony).

People v. Flowers, 371 Ill. App. 3d 326, 329-30, 308 Ill. Dec. 882, 862 N.E.2d 1085 (1st Dist. 2007), appeal denied, 224 Ill. 2d 582, 312 Ill. Dec. 658, 871 N.E.2d 58 (2007) (the defendant should have been able to cross-examine a witness about the witness' mental health history, when the witness' records showed that the witness had suffered from hallucinations in the past).

People v. Meyers, 367 Ill. App. 3d 402, 416-17, 304 Ill. Dec. 944, 854 N.E.2d 286 (2d Dist. 2006) (in a trial for resisting a peace officer and aggravated battery of a peace officer, the trial court did not abuse its discretion by permitting the prosecution to impeach the defendant with evidence of his prior conviction for aggravated fleeing or attempting to elude a police officer).

People v. Rojas, 359 Ill. App. 3d 392, 402–03, 295 Ill. Dec. 932, 834 N.E.2d 513 (1st Dist. 2005) (the trial court had discretion to allow a witness to testify about intimidating statements that were made by the defendant, in order to explain the witness' prior inconsistent statement).

People v. Makiel, 358 Ill. App. 3d 102, 294 Ill. Dec. 319, 830 N.E.2d 731, 743–45 (1st Dist. 2005) (defendant should have been allowed to impeach witness with evidence of pending forgery charge where pending charge may have affected witness' credibility).

People v. Evans, 209 Ill. 2d 194, 221–22, 283 Ill. Dec. 651, 808 N.E.2d 939 (2004) (in a murder case, evidence regarding defendant's threat to murder his grandmother admissible for impeachment and to show consciousness of guilt).

McWethy v. Lee, 1 Ill. App. 3d 80, 84-85, 272 N.E.2d 663 (4th Dist. 1971) (the purpose of impeachment is to introduce evidence that suggests that the witness is not truthful) (alcohol use or presence not proper impeachment in this case).

Illinois Supreme Court Rule 238 states:

> Impeachment of Witnesses; Hostile Witnesses
> (a) The credibility of a witness may be attacked by any party, including the party calling the witness.
> (b) If the court determines that a witness is hostile or unwilling, the witness may be examined by the party calling the witness as if under cross- examination.

735 ILCS 5/8-101 states:

> Interested witness. No person shall be disqualified as a witness in any action or proceeding, except as hereinafter stated, by reason of his or her interest in the event thereof, as a party or otherwise, or by reason of his or her conviction of any crime; but such interest or conviction may be shown for the purpose of affecting the credibility of such witness; and the fact of such conviction may be proven like any fact not of record, either by the witness himself or herself (who shall be compelled to testify thereto) or by any other witness cognizant of such conviction, as impeaching testimony, or by any other competent evidence.

§ 7:19 Opposing authorities—Impeachment, generally—Witness veracity

People v. Flowers, 371 Ill. App. 3d 326, 329-30, 308 Ill. Dec. 882, 862 N.E.2d 1085 (1st Dist. 2007), appeal denied, 224 Ill. 2d 582, 312 Ill. Dec. 658, 871 N.E.2d 58 (2007) (trial court erred by preventing the defendant from cross-examining a witness about leniency from the State, because that issue was relevant to suggest the witness' motive to testify falsely).

People v. Robinson, 368 Ill. App. 3d 963, 980-82, 307 Ill. Dec. 232, 859 N.E.2d 232 (1st Dist. 2006), appeal denied, 223 Ill. 2d 670, 310 Ill. Dec. 255, 865 N.E.2d 975 (2007) (trial court should have allowed the defendant to impeach a witness with his contradictory grand jury testimony).

Jones v. Rallos, 373 Ill. App. 3d 439, 311 Ill. Dec. 450, 869 N.E.2d 124 (1st Dist. 2006) (evidence of the plaintiff's prior bad acts and criminal behavior was relevant to rebut his claim that he began acting in a criminal fashion as a result of the negligence of the defendant), judgment vacated, *Jones v. Rallos*, 225 Ill. 2d 636, 314 Ill. Dec. 13, 873 N.E.2d 943 (2007) ("The appellate court is directed to reconsider its judgment, with additional analysis of whether any error in the trial court's decision to permit plaintiff-appellee to elicit evidence of defendant-appellant's failure to pass board-certification examinations constitutes no more than harmless, non-reversible error.").

People v. Collins, 366 Ill. App. 3d 885, 892-93, 304 Ill. Dec. 478, 853 N.E.2d 10 (1st Dist. 2006) (evidence that a witness' charge had been stricken with leave to reinstate it was relevant to suggest that the witness was biased or had a motive to testify falsely).

People v. Calderon, 369 Ill. App. 3d 221, 236, 307 Ill. Dec. 486, 859 N.E.2d 1163 (2d Dist. 2006) (a witness' credibility can be attacked in closing argument if the argument is based upon reasonable inferences from the evidence).

People v. Singleton, 367 Ill. App. 3d 182, 189-91, 304 Ill. Dec. 984, 854 N.E.2d 326 (4th Dist. 2006) (evidence that the co-defendant had pled guilty was relevant and admissible as a response to the defendant's implication that the co-defendant had been given full immunity in exchange for testifying against the defendant).

People v. Makiel, 358 Ill. App. 3d 102, 294 Ill. Dec. 319, 830 N.E.2d 731, 743–45 (1st Dist. 2005) (defendant should have been allowed to impeach witness with evidence of pending forgery charge where pending charge may have affected witness' credibility).

People v. Petitt, 245 Ill. App. 3d 132, 147–48, 184 Ill. Dec. 766, 613 N.E.2d 1358 (2d Dist. 1993) (when character evidence is admissible, it must be elicited through general reputation evidence and cannot be established through specific acts or through the witness' personal opinion).

Knowles v. Panopoulos, 66 Ill. 2d 585, 587–91, 6 Ill. Dec. 858, 363 N.E.2d 805, 97 A.L.R.3d 1144 (1977) (in civil cases, a witness may be impeached with a conviction for a crime that was punishable by death or in excess of one year in prison or for a crime that involved dishonesty and then, only if the probative value of the evidence outweighs its prejudicial value) (holding that *People v. Montgomery*, 47 Ill. 2d 510, 268 N.E.2d 695, 67 A.L.R.3d 816 (1971) applies to civil cases).

McWethy v. Lee, 1 Ill. App. 3d 80, 84-85, 272 N.E.2d 663 (4th Dist. 1971) (the purpose of impeachment is to introduce evidence that suggests that the witness is not truthful) (alcohol use or presence not proper impeachment in this case).

§ 7:20 Opposing authorities—Facts at issue/relevant

People v. Gonzalez, 379 Ill. App. 3d 941, 318 Ill. Dec. 673, 884 N.E.2d 228, 235–37 (1st Dist. 2008), appeal pending, (May 1, 2008) and appeal denied, 228 Ill. 2d 541, 321 Ill. Dec. 558, 889 N.E.2d 1118 (2008) (evidence of another murder by the defendant was admissible to explain the course of the investigation regarding the charged murder).

People v. Evans, 373 Ill. App. 3d 948, 958–59, 311 Ill. Dec. 907, 869 N.E.2d 920 (1st Dist. 2007), appeal denied, 225 Ill. 2d 648, 314 Ill. Dec. 830, 875 N.E.2d 1117 (2007) (other crimes evidence was relevant because it placed the defendant in close proximity to the scene of the charged crime).

People v. Harris, 375 Ill. App. 3d 398, 408–11, 313 Ill. Dec. 960, 873 N.E.2d 584 (3d Dist. 2007), appeal allowed, 226 Ill. 2d 596, 316 Ill. Dec. 547, 879 N.E.2d 935 (2007) and judgment aff'd, 231 Ill. 2d 582, 2008 WL 5246055 (2008) (evidence of the defendant's prior misconduct was admissible at the sentencing hearing).

In re Detention of Lieberman, 379 Ill. App. 3d 585, 318 Ill. Dec. 605, 884 N.E.2d 160, 179–80 (1st Dist. 2007), appeal denied, 229 Ill. 2d 623, 325 Ill. Dec. 4, 897 N.E.2d 252 (2008) and cert. denied, 129 S.Ct. 2050, 77 USLW 3400, 77 USLW 3592, 77 USLW 3594 (U.S.Ill. Apr 27, 2009) (expert was properly permitted to testify about the defendant's prior offenses, because those offenses formed part of the basis of the expert's opinion and because those offenses clarified the expert's opinion for the jury).

People v. One 1999 Lexus, VIN JT8BH68X2X0018305, 367 Ill. App. 3d 687, 693-94, 305 Ill. Dec. 303, 855 N.E.2d 194 (2d Dist. 2006) (evidence of a driver's prior DUI arrests was circumstantial evidence that the relative who let the driver use the car knew that the driver's license was suspended or revoked).

People v. Bock, 357 Ill. App. 3d 160, 167–69, 293 Ill. Dec.

208, 827 N.E.2d 1089 (1st Dist. 2005) (evidence regarding a preliminary breath test that was taken by the defendant was admissible to rebut the defendant's description of the circumstances surrounding her arrest and the reasons for her behavior).

People v. Petitt, 245 Ill. App. 3d 132, 139–41, 146–48, 184 Ill. Dec. 766, 613 N.E.2d 1358 (2d Dist. 1993) (evidence of other offenses is not admissible when it is introduced to suggest that the defendant committed the charged crime; however, such offenses can be admitted when they are relevant to any other issue, such as intent, motive or modus operandi, as long as the probative value outweighs the prejudicial impact of the evidence) (note: the alleged bad acts were deemed not admissible in this case).

Starks v. Schlensky, 128 Ill. App. 1, 1906 WL 2026, at *2 (2d Dist. 1906) (character traits that do not reflect upon the witness' truthfulness and are not relevant to the issues in the case are not proper subjects for cross-examination).

725 ILCS 5/115-20 provides that in prosecutions for certain battery offenses and stalking offenses, evidence of prior convictions for the same type of offenses against the same victim may be admissible in evidence if relevant and if the probative value outweighs the prejudicial impact of the evidence.

§ 7:21 Opposing authorities—Alcohol consumption or narcotics (witness perceptions)

People v. Hogan, 388 Ill.App.3d 885, 895, 904 N.E.2d 1036 (1st Dist. 2009) (a witness' narcotics addiction at the time of testifying or at the time of the event in question is a proper subject for impeachment of the witness).

O'Brien v. Hertl, 238 Ill. App. 3d 217, 222–23, 179 Ill. Dec. 393, 606 N.E.2d 225 (1st Dist. 1992) (evidence of alcohol consumption of the party or a witness was admissible as impeachment when the consumption was at or near the time of the incident because such evidence was relevant to suggest impairment of ability to accurately remember the events in question).

§ 7:22 Opposing authorities—Felony convictions

People v. Clay, 379 Ill. App. 3d 470, 318 Ill. Dec. 659, 884 N.E.2d 214, 221–22 (1st Dist. 2008), appeal denied, 228 Ill. 2d 539, 321 Ill. Dec. 558, 889 N.E.2d 1118 (2008) (in a murder case, trial court had discretion to allow the prosecution to impeach the defendant with evidence of his prior murder conviction).

People v. Farrell, 377 Ill. App. 3d 249, 250–51, 316 Ill. Dec. 389, 879 N.E.2d 456 (4th Dist. 2007) (Illinois courts follow Federal Rule of Evidence 609, as it was proposed at the time of the holding in *People v. Montgomery*, 47 Ill. 2d 510, 268 N.E.2d 695, 67 A.L.R.3d 816 (1971) but Illinois courts do not automatically follow subsequent amendments to Rule 609).

People v. Barner, 374 Ill. App. 3d 963, 968–73, 313 Ill. Dec. 122, 871 N.E.2d 849 (1st Dist. 2007), appeal denied, 225 Ill. 2d 641, 314 Ill. Dec. 828, 875 N.E.2d 1115 (2007) (in a sexual assault case, evidence of the defendant's conviction for failing to register as a sex offender was admissible to impeach his testimony).

People v. Stewart, 366 Ill. App. 3d 101, 112-13, 303 Ill. Dec. 485, 851 N.E.2d 672 (1st Dist. 2006), cert. denied, 128 S. Ct. 89, 169 L. Ed. 2d 68 (2007) (after the defendant stipulated to the admission of his prior convictions for purposes of impeachment, he could not complain that the trial court erred by failing to conduct a full balancing test prior to admitting them).

People v. Montgomery, 47 Ill. 2d 510, 512–19, 268 N.E.2d 695, 67 A.L.R.3d 816 (1971) (a felony conviction that was remote in time should not have been admitted for impeachment).

People v. Montgomery, 47 Ill. 2d 510, 516–19, 268 N.E.2d 695, 67 A.L.R.3d 816 (1971) (proposed Federal Rule of Evidence 609 should be followed regarding whether to admit evidence of convictions to impeach a witness).

People v. Montgomery, 47 Ill. 2d 510, 516–17, 268 N.E.2d 695, 67 A.L.R.3d 816 (1971) (adopts proposed Federal Rule of Evidence 609) (general rule of admissibility of felony convictions).

Regarding the admissibility of felony convictions, see Federal Rule of Evidence 609, infra, at § 7:37 to § 7:52.

§ 7:23 Opposing authorities—Good reputation of witness

People v. Petitt, 245 Ill. App. 3d 132, 139–41, 146–48, 184 Ill. Dec. 766, 613 N.E.2d 1358 (2d Dist. 1993) (a defendant can offer evidence to suggest a good reputation for a character trait that is relevant to the offense charged).

People v. Harris, 224 Ill. App. 3d 649, 651–53, 167 Ill. Dec. 165, 587 N.E.2d 47 (3d Dist. 1992) (when a defendant specifically introduces evidence of his reputation for peacefulness in order to bolster his self defense claim, the state can then introduce prior convictions for violent acts) (note that in this case, the defendant did not clearly introduce such evidence and thus, the rebuttal character evidence was not proper).

People v. Rassmussen, 143 Ill. App. 3d 11, 24, 97 Ill. Dec. 176, 492 N.E.2d 612 (1st Dist. 1986) (in a sexual offense case, the state was permitted to question the defendant regarding homosexuality and past misconduct with boys because the defendant had raised a claim of good character).

§ 7:24 Opposing authorities—Religious beliefs

But see *People v. Baseer*, 90 Ill. App. 3d 866, 871–72, 46 Ill. Dec. 283, 414 N.E.2d 5 (1st Dist. 1980) (although a witness' religion is not ordinarily admissible, the state's questions regarding the defendant's religion were admissible in this case because the defendant had raised the subject in his direct testimony).

C. MOTION TO EXCLUDE CHARACTER EVIDENCE USED TO PROVE CONDUCT

§ 7:25 Suggested motion text

[Name of moving party] hereby moves this Court for an order excluding any and all evidence, references to evidence, testimony or argument relating to the character or trait of *[name of witness]* for *[describe the character or trait evidence at issue, e.g., the prior arrest of defendant for possession of marijuana]*. The motion is based upon the grounds that the character evidence is irrelevant to the issues in this case, is prohibited to prove conduct and will create a substantial danger of undue prejudice to *[name of moving party]*.

§ 7:26 Motion summary

This motion is based on the authority of Illinois case law, which generally makes evidence of person's character or trait inadmissible when offered to prove his or her conduct on a specific occasion. *Doe v. Lutz*, 281 Ill. App. 3d 630, 637–38, 218 Ill. Dec. 80, 668 N.E.2d 564, 112 Ed. Law Rep. 371 (1st Dist. 1996), as modified on denial of reh'g, (June 25, 1996) (prior bad conduct is not generally admissible to prove the likelihood that the defendant acted similarly in the incident in question).

§ 7:27 Supporting authorities—Exclusion of prejudicial evidence, generally

Federal Rule of Evidence 403 states:

> Although relevant, evidence may be excluded if its probative value is substantially outweighed by the danger of unfair prejudice, confusion of the issues, or misleading the jury, or by considerations of undue delay, waste of time, or needless presentation of cumulative evidence.

It must be noted that this Rule has not been codified in Illinois. However, Illinois cases have stated that Illinois has a common-law rule that is comparable to Federal Rule of Evidence 403. See *People v. Walker*, 335 Ill. App. 3d 102, 112, 268 Ill. Dec. 654, 779 N.E.2d 268 (2d Dist. 2002), as modified on denial of reh'g, (Oct. 24, 2002) and judgment aff'd, 211 Ill. 2d 317, 285 Ill. Dec. 519, 812 N.E.2d 339 (2004); and *People v. Peete*, 318 Ill. App. 3d 961, 966–67, 252 Ill. Dec. 821, 743 N.E.2d 689 (4th Dist. 2001). Therefore, it is arguable that Federal Rule of Evidence 403 can be considered as persuasive authority in Illinois.

For expanded citations on the exclusion of prejudicial evidence, see § 2:1 to § 2:4.

§ 7:28 Supporting authorities—Exclusion of irrelevant evidence, generally

Federal Rule of Evidence 401 defines relevancy as,

> evidence having any tendency to make the existence of any fact that is of consequence to the determination of the action more probable or less probable than it would be without the evidence.

Illinois has adopted this definition of relevancy through case law. *Spencer v. Wandolowski*, 264 Ill. App. 3d 611, 617, 201 Ill. Dec. 422, 636 N.E.2d 854 (1st Dist. 1994); and *People v. Monroe*, 66 Ill. 2d 317, 321–22, 5 Ill. Dec. 824, 362 N.E.2d 295 (1977).

Cochran v. Great Atlantic & Pacific Tea Co., Inc., 203 Ill. App. 3d 935, 937–38, 148 Ill. Dec. 923, 561 N.E.2d 229 (5th Dist. 1990) (trial judge has inherent power to exclude irrelevant evidence).

For expanded citations on the exclusion of irrelevant evidence, see § 3:1 to § 3:10.

§ 7:29 Supporting authorities—Exclusion of improper character evidence

Reichert v. Board of Fire and Police Com'rs of City of Collinsville, 388 Ill.App.3d 834, 846–47, 905 N.E.2d 861 (5th Dist. 2009) (Illinois law prohibits impeachment by evidence of specific acts and does not have an evidentiary rule similar to Federal Rule of Evidence 608(b)).

Dukes v. Pneumo Abex Corp., 386 Ill.App.3d 425, 436–37, 900 N.E.2d 1128 (4th Dist. 2008) (evidence of a nolo contendere plea that was entered in a similar case should not have been admitted to suggest wrongdoing in the pending case).

People v. Schneider, 375 Ill. App. 3d 734, 751–54, 313 Ill. Dec. 890, 873 N.E.2d 514 (2d Dist. 2007), appeal denied, 226 Ill. 2d 604, 316 Ill. Dec. 549, 879 N.E.2d 937 (2007) (trial court properly excluded irrelevant cross examination about the witness' alleged conduct in another case).

People v. Evans, 373 Ill. App. 3d 948, 960–61, 311 Ill. Dec. 907, 869 N.E.2d 920 (1st Dist. 2007), appeal denied, 225 Ill. 2d 648, 314 Ill. Dec. 830, 875 N.E.2d 1117 (2007) (evidence of weapons, other than the murder weapon, should not have been admitted) (harmless error).

People v. Robinson, 368 Ill. App. 3d 963, 974-75, 307 Ill. Dec. 232, 859 N.E.2d 232 (1st Dist. 2006), appeal denied, 223 Ill. 2d 670, 310 Ill. Dec. 255, 865 N.E.2d 975 (2007) (in an aggravated DUI case, the trial court erred by admitting evidence of the defendant's two prior DUIs during the guilt portion of the defendant's trial).

People v. Boand, 362 Ill. App. 3d 106, 124–26, 297 Ill. Dec. 880, 838 N.E.2d 367 (2d Dist. 2005) (certain uncharged sex offenses were inadmissible to suggest modus operandi, intent and opportunity for purposes of Drug-Induced Homicide and Involuntary Manslaughter).

People v. Liner, 356 Ill. App. 3d 284, 293–94, 292 Ill. Dec. 838, 826 N.E.2d 1274 (5th Dist. 2005) (prosecutor's question regarding defendant's other bad acts was improper propensity evidence and prejudicial).

People v. McGee, 286 Ill. App. 3d 786, 795–96, 222 Ill. Dec. 137, 676 N.E.2d 1341 (1st Dist. 1997) (evidence regarding specific acts of untruthfulness, when they are not directly at issue in the case, is inadmissible).

Doe v. Lutz, 281 Ill. App. 3d 630, 637–38, 218 Ill. Dec. 80, 668 N.E.2d 564, 112 Ed. Law Rep. 371 (1st Dist. 1996), as modified on denial of reh'g, (June 25, 1996) (evidence of prior inappropriate sexual conduct towards someone other than the alleged victim was not admissible because it was irrelevant and prejudicial and it did not demonstrate sufficiently similar behavior to qualify for modus operandi evidence).

People v. Petitt, 245 Ill. App. 3d 132, 147–48, 184 Ill. Dec. 766, 613 N.E.2d 1358 (2d Dist. 1993) (when character evidence is admissible, it must be elicited through general reputation evidence and cannot be established through specific acts or through the witness' personal opinion).

People v. Petitt, 245 Ill. App. 3d 132, 139–41, 146–48, 184 Ill. Dec. 766, 613 N.E.2d 1358 (2d Dist. 1993) (evidence of other offenses is not admissible when it is introduced to suggest that the defendant committed the charged crime).

People v. Petitt, 245 Ill. App. 3d 132, 139–41, 146–48, 184 Ill. Dec. 766, 613 N.E.2d 1358 (2d Dist. 1993) (a defendant can offer evidence to suggest a good reputation for a character trait that is relevant to the offense charged. In this case, chastity and morality related to abuse but truthfulness did not).

People v. Quick, 236 Ill. App. 3d 446, 455, 177 Ill. Dec. 272, 603 N.E.2d 53 (1st Dist. 1992) ("The court should not permit cross-examination that is designed to insult, degrade, or humiliate a witness or whose only apparent purpose is to demonstrate that the defendant was of bad moral character[sic].")

People v. Harris, 224 Ill. App. 3d 649, 650–53, 167 Ill. Dec. 165, 587 N.E.2d 47 (3d Dist. 1992) (state may not use cross-examination to deliberately elicit testimony by the defendant regarding his alleged good character so that the state can then impeach the testimony with evidence of bad character).

For exclusion of character evidence used for impeachment, see § 7:4 to § 7:24, supra.

§ 7:30 Supporting authorities—Exclusion of improper character evidence—Care or skill in negligence cases

Mulloy v. American Eagle Airlines, Inc., 358 Ill. App. 3d 706, 295 Ill. Dec. 54, 832 N.E.2d 205, 209 (1st Dist. 2005) (trial court did not abuse its discretion by finding that witness was not qualified to provide testimony regarding proper standard of care while driving in the circumstances at issue).

Mulloy v. American Eagle Airlines, Inc., 358 Ill. App. 3d 706, 295 Ill. Dec. 54, 832 N.E.2d 205, 210 (1st Dist. 2005) (trial court did not abuse its discretion by excluding lay witness testimony regarding witness' driving habits, where not relevant to issues of parties' driving habits or negligence).

Hajian v. Holy Family Hosp., 273 Ill. App. 3d 932, 942–43, 210 Ill. Dec. 156, 652 N.E.2d 1132 (1st Dist. 1995) (in order to have evidence of habit admitted, the proponent of the evidence must, "show conduct that becomes semiautomatic, invariably regular and not merely a tendency to act in a given manner.")

Herget Nat. Bank of Pekin v. Johnson, 21 Ill. App. 3d 1024, 1026–28, 316 N.E.2d 191 (3d Dist. 1974) (evidence suggesting that the victim had acted negligently in the past should not be admitted to suggest that he acted negligently in the instant matter).

See also *Alvarado v. Goepp*, 278 Ill. App. 3d 494, 495–97, 215 Ill. Dec. 313, 663 N.E.2d 63 (1st Dist. 1996) (Illinois has adopted Federal Rule of Evidence 406 through case law, regarding admissibility of habit testimony; however, there was an improper foundation to show habit in this case).

See Federal Rule of Evidence 406, which states:

> Evidence of the habit of a person or of the routine practice of an organization, whether corroborated or not and regardless of the presence of eyewitnesses, is relevant to prove that the conduct of the person or organization on a particular occasion was in conformity with the habit or routine practice.

Note also in a wrongful death case, habit of due care on the part of the deceased may be admissible if there were no eyewitnesses to the incident. See *Moore v. Bloomington, D. & C.R. Co.*, 295 Ill. 63, 64–65, 128 N.E. 721 (1920).

§ 7:31 Supporting authorities—Exclusion of improper character evidence—Crimes evidence, generally

People v. Robinson, 368 Ill. App. 3d 963, 974-75, 307 Ill. Dec. 232, 859 N.E.2d 232 (1st Dist. 2006), appeal denied, 223 Ill. 2d 670, 310 Ill. Dec. 255, 865 N.E.2d 975 (2007) (in an aggravated DUI case, the trial court erred by admitting evidence of the defendant's two prior DUIs during the guilt portion of the defendant's trial).

People v. Petitt, 245 Ill. App. 3d 132, 139–41, 146–48, 184 Ill. Dec. 766, 613 N.E.2d 1358 (2d Dist. 1993) (evidence of other offenses is not admissible where introduced to suggest that the defendant committed the charged crime).

For expanded discussion of crimes evidence, see § 7:10 to § 7:12, supra, and § 7:37 to § 7:52, infra.

§ 7:32 Supporting authorities—Other grounds

See the following sections for other possible grounds to support a motion to exclude character evidence:

- Collateral to issues in case (§ 2:5 to § 2:8)
- Confusing or misleading (§ 2:9 to § 2:12)
- Solely intended to create an emotional bias (§ 2:13 to § 2:19)
- Irrelevant (§ 3:1 to § 3:10)
- Improper impeachment evidence (§ 7:4 to § 7:24)
- Improper felony conviction (§ 7:37 to § 7:52)
- Inadmissible hearsay (§ 8:78 to § 8:89)

§ 7:33 Opposing authorities—Court's discretion

People v. Kegley, 227 Ill. App. 3d 48, 54-55, 169 Ill. Dec. 3, 590 N.E.2d 922 (2d Dist. 1992) (trial judge has broad discretion to determine the proper scope of cross-examination) (note: in this case it was held that the trial court did not abuse its discretion by refusing to admit impeachment evidence of a single use of narcotics).

§ 7:34 Opposing authorities—Relevant to material issue

Dukes v. Pneumo Abex Corp., 386 Ill.App.3d 425, 442–43, 900 N.E.2d 1128 (4th Dist. 2008) (evidence of a party's membership in certain trade organizations was relevant to show opportunity to coordinate activities with the other members of the group).

People v. Gonzalez, 379 Ill. App. 3d 941, 318 Ill. Dec. 673, 884 N.E.2d 228, 235–37 (1st Dist. 2008), appeal pending, (May 1, 2008) and appeal denied, 228 Ill. 2d 541, 321 Ill. Dec. 558, 889 N.E.2d 1118 (2008) (evidence of another murder by the defendant was admissible to explain the course of the investigation regarding the charged murder).

People v. Harris, 375 Ill. App. 3d 398, 408–11, 313 Ill. Dec. 960, 873 N.E.2d 584 (3d Dist. 2007), appeal allowed, 226 Ill. 2d 596, 316 Ill. Dec. 547, 879 N.E.2d 935 (2007) and judgment aff'd, 231 Ill. 2d 582, 2008 WL 5246055 (2008) (evidence of the defendant's prior misconduct was admissible at the sentencing hearing).

People v. Evans, 373 Ill. App. 3d 948, 958–59, 311 Ill. Dec. 907, 869 N.E.2d 920 (1st Dist. 2007), appeal denied, 225 Ill. 2d 648, 314 Ill. Dec. 830, 875 N.E.2d 1117 (2007) (other crimes evidence was relevant because it placed the defendant in close proximity to the scene of the charged crime).

In re Detention of Lieberman, 379 Ill. App. 3d 585, 318 Ill. Dec. 605, 884 N.E.2d 160, 179–80 (1st Dist. 2007), appeal denied, 229 Ill. 2d 623, 325 Ill. Dec. 4, 897 N.E.2d 252 (2008) and cert. denied, 129 S.Ct. 2050, 77 USLW 3400, 77 USLW 3592, 77 USLW 3594 (U.S.Ill. Apr 27, 2009) (expert was properly permitted to testify about the defendant's prior offenses, because those offenses formed part of the basis of the expert's opinion and because those offenses clarified the expert's opinion for the jury).

In re L.W., 367 Ill. App. 3d 844, 856-59, 305 Ill. Dec. 674, 856 N.E.2d 479 (1st Dist. 2006), appeal allowed, 222 Ill. 2d 608,

308 Ill. Dec. 636, 862 N.E.2d 234 (2007) and judgment rev'd, 228 Ill. 2d 439, 320 Ill. Dec. 855, 888 N.E.2d 72 (2008) (evidence regarding the parent's ability to care for the child's siblings was relevant to the issue of the parent's fitness to care for the child at issue), reversed by *In re Leona W.*, 228 Ill. 2d 439, 320 Ill. Dec. 855, 888 N.E.2d 72 (2008) (in a termination of parental rights case, the trial court did not abuse its discretion by granting a motion in limine to exclude evidence regarding the parent's behavior towards other minors, as irrelevant and beyond the scope of the allegations).

People v. Boand, 362 Ill. App. 3d 106, 122–24, 297 Ill. Dec. 880, 838 N.E.2d 367 (2d Dist. 2005) (certain uncharged sex offenses were admissible to suggest modus operandi, intent and opportunity for purposes of sexual assault).

People v. Moser, 356 Ill. App. 3d 900, 913, 293 Ill. Dec. 230, 827 N.E.2d 1111 (2d Dist. 2005) (evidence of other offenses committed by defendant properly admitted to demonstrate knowledge).

People v. Cantlin, 348 Ill. App. 3d 998, 1000–01, 285 Ill. Dec. 29, 811 N.E.2d 270 (2d Dist. 2004) (evidence that defendant had open bottle of alcohol in backseat of vehicle was relevant circumstantial evidence in DUI prosecution and was not improper propensity evidence).

People v. Petitt, 245 Ill. App. 3d 132, 139–41, 146–48, 184 Ill. Dec. 766, 613 N.E.2d 1358 (2d Dist. 1993) (a defendant can offer evidence to suggest a good reputation for a character trait that is relevant to the offense charged).

People v. Petitt, 245 Ill. App. 3d 132, 139–41, 146–48, 184 Ill. Dec. 766, 613 N.E.2d 1358 (2d Dist. 1993) (evidence of other offenses is not admissible when it is introduced to suggest that the defendant committed the charged crime; however, such offenses can be admitted when they are relevant to any other issue, such as intent, motive or modus operandi, as long as the probative value outweighs the prejudicial impact of the evidence).

People v. Kimbrough, 138 Ill. App. 3d 481, 484–87, 93 Ill. Dec. 82, 485 N.E.2d 1292 (1st Dist. 1985) (prior bad conduct is admissible, if it is offered to prove a relevant factor, other than the defendant's likelihood to have committed the current offense).

But see *Starks v. Schlensky*, 128 Ill. App. 1, 1906 WL 2026, at *2 (2d Dist. 1906) (character traits that do not reflect upon the witness' truthfulness and are not relevant to the issues in the case, are not proper subjects for cross-examination).

725 ILCS 5/115-20 provides that in prosecutions for certain battery offenses and stalking offenses, evidence of prior convictions for the same type of offenses against the same victim may be admissible in evidence if relevant and if the probative value outweighs the prejudicial impact of the evidence.

§ 7:35 Opposing authorities—Witness impeachment

People v. Harris, 375 Ill. App. 3d 398, 405–08, 313 Ill. Dec. 960, 873 N.E.2d 584 (3d Dist. 2007), appeal allowed, 226 Ill. 2d 596, 316 Ill. Dec. 547, 879 N.E.2d 935 (2007) and judgment aff'd, 231 Ill. 2d 582, 2008 WL 5246055 (2008) (after the defendant testified and implied that he was law abiding, evidence of his prior juvenile adjudication was admissible).

Illinois Supreme Court Rule 238 states:

> Impeachment of Witnesses; Hostile Witnesses
> (a) The credibility of a witness may be attacked by any party, including the party calling the witness.
> (b) If the court determines that a witness is hostile or unwilling, the witness may be examined by the party calling the witness as if under cross- examination.

Schmitz v. Binette, 368 Ill. App. 3d 447, 454-62, 306 Ill. Dec. 447, 857 N.E.2d 846 (1st Dist. 2006) (trial court erred by excluding cross-examination regarding the expert's own practice, when the cross-examination would have impeached the expert's testimony regarding the proper standard of care).

People v. Blankenship, 353 Ill. App. 3d 322, 326, 289 Ill. Dec. 137, 819 N.E.2d 49 (3d Dist. 2004) (trial court did not abuse its discretion by allowing defendant to be impeached with two prior convictions, over defendant's objection that prior convictions were too similar to charged offense).

People v. Evans, 209 Ill. 2d 194, 221–22, 283 Ill. Dec. 651, 808 N.E.2d 939 (2004) (in a murder case, evidence regarding defendant's threat to murder his grandmother admissible for impeachment and to show consciousness of guilt).

People v. Flynn, 341 Ill. App. 3d 813, 275 Ill. Dec. 296, 792 N.E.2d 527 (2d Dist. 2003) (defendant's three prior convictions for home repair fraud were admissible in trial for theft and home repair fraud).

Stokes v. City of Chicago, 333 Ill. App. 3d 272, 266 Ill. Dec. 510, 775 N.E.2d 72 (1st Dist. 2002) (evidence of plaintiff's three burglary convictions was proper in personal injury action).

Torres v. Irving Press, Inc., 303 Ill. App. 3d 151, 236 Ill. Dec. 403, 707 N.E.2d 248 (1st Dist. 1999) (plaintiff should have been allowed to cross-examine defense witness regarding theft conviction).

See also 735 ILCS 5/8-101:

> Interested witness. No person shall be disqualified as a witness in any action or proceeding, except as hereinafter stated, by reason of his or her interest in the event thereof, as a party or otherwise, or by reason of his or her conviction of any crime; but such interest or conviction may be shown for the purpose of affecting the credibility of such witness; and the fact of such conviction may be proven like any fact not of record, either by the witness himself or herself (who shall be compelled to testify thereto) or by any other witness cognizant of such conviction, as impeaching testimony, or by any other competent evidence.

Regarding the use of character evidence for impeachment, see generally, § 7:4 to § 7:24.

§ 7:36 Opposing authorities—Trait at issue

In re L.W., 367 Ill. App. 3d 844, 856-59, 305 Ill. Dec. 674, 856 N.E.2d 479 (1st Dist. 2006), appeal allowed, 222 Ill. 2d 608, 308 Ill. Dec. 636, 862 N.E.2d 234 (2007) and judgment rev'd, 228 Ill. 2d 439, 320 Ill. Dec. 855, 888 N.E.2d 72 (2008) (evidence regarding the parent's ability to care for the child's siblings was relevant to the issue of the parent's fitness to care for the child at issue), reversed by *In re Leona W.*, 228 Ill. 2d 439, 320 Ill. Dec. 855, 888 N.E.2d 72 (2008) (in a termination of parental rights case, the trial court did not abuse its discretion by granting a motion in limine to exclude evidence regarding the parent's behavior towards other minors, as irrelevant and beyond the scope of the allegations).

People v. Petitt, 245 Ill. App. 3d 132, 139–41, 146–48, 184 Ill. Dec. 766, 613 N.E.2d 1358 (2d Dist. 1993) (a defendant can offer evidence to suggest a good reputation for a character trait that is relevant to the offense charged; in this case, chastity and morality related to abuse).

People v. Kimbrough, 138 Ill. App. 3d 481, 484–87, 93 Ill. Dec. 82, 485 N.E.2d 1292 (1st Dist. 1985) (prior bad conduct is admissible if it is offered to prove a relevant factor other than the defendant's likelihood to have committed the current offense).

725 ILCS 5/115-20 provides that in prosecutions for certain battery offenses and stalking offenses, evidence of prior convictions for the same type of offenses against the same victim may be admissible in evidence if relevant and if the probative value outweighs the prejudicial impact of the evidence.

D. MOTION TO EXCLUDE EVIDENCE OF PRIOR FELONY CONVICTION

Many attorneys are under the mistaken belief that *all* misdemeanor convictions are inadmissible and *all* felony convictions are admissible for impeachment. The truth is that some misdemeanors are admissible under certain circumstances while some felonies are not. Counsel must examine the case law and apply the law to the specific facts of the case. In all cases, counsel should approach the use of convictions carefully.

Although a conviction may be technically admissible, the use of a conviction may not be in the best interests of the proponent. For example, in a motor vehicle collision involving minor injuries, the defendant may have a prior conviction for theft at a very young age, but may have later turned his life around. At the time of trial, several years after the conviction, and several years after positively changing his life, plaintiff's counsel may technically be allowed to admit the conviction. However, the jury may view plaintiff's counsel as a bully and see the defendant as the victim whose past is being exposed for no legitimate reason. The jury may conclude that the conviction does not truly reflect on the witness' credibility. As a result, the use of the conviction may create sympathy for the witness and animosity towards counsel.

§ 7:37 Suggested motion text

[Name of moving party] hereby moves this Court for an order excluding any and all evidence, references to evidence, testimony or argument relating to a prior felony conviction by *[name of witness]* for *[describe nature of conviction]* that occurred on or about *[date of conviction]*. The motion is based upon the grounds that the probative value of the evidence is substantially outweighed by the risk of undue prejudice to *[name of moving party] [and—include if applicable—that the conviction is not one that reflects on the witness' credibility]* and therefore should be excluded.

§ 7:38 Motion summary

This motion is used to exclude inadmissible evidence of felony convictions. While Illinois case law allows the use of felony convictions to impeach the credibility of a witness, the court has the discretion to exclude such evidence if the probative value is substantially outweighed by the risk of undue prejudice, or if other exceptions apply. See Federal Rules of Evidence 609; *People v. Medreno*, 99 Ill. App. 3d 449, 450–54, 54 Ill. Dec. 723, 425 N.E.2d 588 (3d Dist. 1981); *Knowles v. Panopoulos*, 66 Ill. 2d 585, 587–91, 6 Ill. Dec. 858, 363 N.E.2d 805, 97

A.L.R.3d 1144 (1977); and *People v. Montgomery*, 47 Ill. 2d 510, 516–19, 268 N.E.2d 695, 67 A.L.R.3d 816 (1971).

Evidence of other crimes may also be excluded where it is used for purposes other than to impeach the witness, such as to prove one's disposition to commit a similar crime or to show "bad moral character." See generally: *People v. Petitt*, 245 Ill. App. 3d 132, 139–41, 146–48, 184 Ill. Dec. 766, 613 N.E.2d 1358 (2d Dist. 1993).

§ 7:39 Motion summary—"General rule" of admissibility of crimes evidence

Before discussing the bases for excluding crimes evidence, counsel should be aware of the general rule that allows such evidence to be used for impeachment purposes. This rule is codified by Federal Rule of Evidence 609, the proposed version of which has been adopted in Illinois. See *People v. Montgomery*, 47 Ill. 2d 510, 516–19, 268 N.E.2d 695, 67 A.L.R.3d 816 (1971); see also *People v. Yost*, 78 Ill. 2d 292, 293–97, 35 Ill. Dec. 755, 399 N.E.2d 1283 (1980). Note that the rule has several exceptions [(Rules 609(a) to (d)] which form the primary ammunition for excluding crimes evidence.

Federal Rule of Evidence 609(a) states as follows:

> (a) General rule.—For the purpose of attacking the character for truthfulness of a witness,
> (1) evidence that a witness other than an accused has been convicted of a crime shall be admitted, subject to Rule 403, if the crime was punishable by death or imprisonment in excess of one year under the law under which the witness was convicted, and evidence that an accused has been convicted of such a crime shall be admitted if the court determines that the probative value of admitting this evidence outweighs its prejudicial effect to the accused; and
> (2) evidence that any witness has been convicted of a crime shall be admitted regardless of the punishment, if it readily can be determined that establishing the elements of the crime required proof or admission of an act of dishonesty or false statement by the witness. (Emphasis added.)

People v. Farrell, 377 Ill. App. 3d 249, 250–51, 316 Ill. Dec. 389, 879 N.E.2d 456 (4th Dist. 2007) (Illinois courts follow Federal Rule of Evidence 609, as it was proposed at the time of the holding in *People v. Montgomery*, 47 Ill. 2d 510, 268 N.E.2d 695, 67 A.L.R.3d 816 (1971) but Illinois courts do not automatically follow subsequent amendments to Rule 609).

People v. Montgomery, 47 Ill. 2d 510, 516–19, 268 N.E.2d 695, 67 A.L.R.3d 816 (1971) (proposed Federal Rule of Evidence 609 should be followed regarding whether to admit evidence of convictions to impeach a witness).

◆ **Important Note:** The case of *People v. Yost*, 78 Ill. 2d 292, 293–97, 35 Ill. Dec. 755, 399 N.E.2d 1283 (1980) clarified that the *Montgomery* case (47 Ill.2d 510, 516–19, supra) only adopted Federal Rule of Evidence 609 *as it was proposed at that time* and that the rule does not change just because the Federal Rule is different or is amended. Counsel should be aware of the subtle differences in the language of current Federal Rule 609, cited above, and the proposed version of the Rule at the time of the *Montgomery* decision. While the two versions are similar, there are subtle, but important, differences which could create fertile areas for argument, depending upon the facts of your case. This is especially true with respect to subdivision (a), which addresses the probative/prejudicial balancing test. The current version of Rule 609(a) would allow the evidence if "the probative value of admitting this evidence outweighs its prejudicial effect;" whereas, the prior proposed version (as adopted by *Montgomery*), would allow the evidence if the "probative value of the evidence of the crime is substantially outweighed by the danger of undue prejudice." For a further discussion, see *People v. Yost*, 78 Ill. 2d 292, 293–97, 35 Ill. Dec. 755, 399 N.E.2d 1283 (1980).

See also *Reichert v. Board of Fire and Police Com'rs of City of Collinsville*, 388 Ill.App.3d 834, 847–49, 905 N.E.2d 861 (5th Dist. 2009) (Illinois only adopted proposed Federal Rule of Evidence 609 and did not adopt subsequent changes to the proposed rule).

See the Opposing Authorities at § 7:50, Opposing authorities—General rule: Admissibility of prior convictions, infra, for cases supporting admissibility under the general rule of Federal Rule of Evidence 609.

§ 7:40 Supporting authorities—Balancing prejudicial impact of felony evidence under FRE Rule 609

Both the current and prior proposed versions of Federal Rules of Evidence Rule 609(a) include a probative/prejudicial balancing test similar to that stated in FRE Rule 403. Note that the current version of Rule 609 would allow the evidence if "the probative value of admitting this evidence outweighs its prejudicial effect;" whereas, the prior proposed version (adopted by *Montgomery*), would allow the evidence if the "probative value of the evidence of the crime is substantially outweighed by the danger of undue prejudice." As clarified by *People v. Yost*, 78 Ill. 2d 292, 293–97, 35 Ill. Dec. 755, 399 N.E.2d 1283

(1980), the *Montgomery* court only adopted the *proposed* version of the Rule, and later changes or amendments would not change that holding.

Federal Rule of Evidence 403 states:

> Although relevant, evidence may be excluded if its probative value is substantially outweighed by the danger of unfair prejudice, confusion of the issues, or misleading the jury, or by considerations of undue delay, waste of time, or needless presentation of cumulative evidence.

It must be noted that this Rule has not been codified in Illinois. However, Illinois cases have stated that Illinois has a common-law rule that is comparable to Federal Rule of Evidence 403. See *People v. Walker*, 335 Ill. App. 3d 102, 112, 268 Ill. Dec. 654, 779 N.E.2d 268 (2d Dist. 2002), as modified on denial of reh'g, (Oct. 24, 2002) and judgment aff'd, 211 Ill. 2d 317, 285 Ill. Dec. 519, 812 N.E.2d 339 (2004); and *People v. Peete*, 318 Ill. App. 3d 961, 966–67, 252 Ill. Dec. 821, 743 N.E.2d 689 (4th Dist. 2001). Therefore, it is arguable that Federal Rule of Evidence 403 can be considered as persuasive authority in Illinois.

People v. Calderon, 369 Ill. App. 3d 221, 228-29, 307 Ill. Dec. 486, 859 N.E.2d 1163 (2d Dist. 2006) (trial court did not abuse its discretion by allowing a witness to be impeached with evidence of his most recent felony conviction and by excluding evidence of his two other felony convictions as more prejudicial than probative).

People v. Whirl, 351 Ill. App. 3d 464, 466–67, 286 Ill. Dec. 646, 814 N.E.2d 872 (2d Dist. 2004) (trial court failed to properly balance prejudicial impact of prior convictions for similar offenses against probative value; trial judge erred by admitting impeachment evidence of so many prior convictions).

People v. Petitt, 245 Ill. App. 3d 132, 139–41, 146–48, 184 Ill. Dec. 766, 613 N.E.2d 1358 (2d Dist. 1993) (evidence of other offenses is not admissible when introduced to suggest that the defendant committed the charged crime).

Baldwin v. Huffman Towing Co., 51 Ill. App. 3d 861, 863–64, 9 Ill. Dec. 469, 366 N.E.2d 980 (5th Dist. 1977) (trial judge properly excluded evidence of a witness' conviction for possession of a narcotic, because the prejudicial impact of the evidence outweighed the probative value of it).

But see *People v. Medreno*, 99 Ill. App. 3d 449, 450–54, 54 Ill. Dec. 723, 425 N.E.2d 588 (3d Dist. 1981) (prior rape conviction was admissible despite similarity to the charged crime because the defendant had been released from custody for it within the past ten years and the probative value outweighed the prejudicial impact of the evidence).

§ 7:41 Supporting authorities—Statutory exceptions [FRE 609(b)–(d)]—Convictions that are too remote

Both the current and prior proposed versions of Federal Rules of Evidence Rule 609(b) limit the use of prior convictions that occurred more than 10 years previous.

People v. Naylor, 372 Ill. App. 3d 1, 309 Ill. Dec. 477, 864 N.E.2d 718 (1st Dist. 2007), appeal allowed, 224 Ill. 2d 587, 312 Ill. Dec. 659, 871 N.E.2d 59 (2007) and judgment aff'd, 229 Ill. 2d 584, 323 Ill. Dec. 381, 893 N.E.2d 653 (2008) (the trial court abused its discretion by allowing the defendant to be impeached with a conviction that occurred thirteen years before the trial).

People v. Montgomery, 47 Ill. 2d 510, 512–19, 268 N.E.2d 695, 67 A.L.R.3d 816 (1971) (a felony conviction that was remote in time should not have been admitted for impeachment)

§ 7:42 Supporting authorities—Statutory exceptions [FRE 609(b)–(d)]—Effect of pardon, annulment or certificate of rehabilitation

Both the current and prior proposed versions of Federal Rules of Evidence Rule 609(c) limit the use of prior convictions that were pardoned, annulled or rehabilitated. The current version of Rule 609(c) states as follows:

> Evidence of a conviction is not admissible under this rule if (1) the conviction has been the subject of a pardon, annulment, certificate of rehabilitation, or other equivalent procedure based on a finding of the rehabilitation of the person convicted, and that person has not been convicted of a subsequent crime which was punishable by death or imprisonment in excess of one year, or (2) the conviction has been the subject of a pardon, annulment, or other equivalent procedure based on a finding of innocence.

Note that the prior proposed version of Rule 609 adopted by *Montgomery* (47 Ill.2d 510, 516–19, supra) *does not* include the language appearing at the end of the current Rule 609(c)(1), which, in the current version, would limit this exception if the person were convicted of a subsequent felony after the pardon, annulment, certificate of rehabilitation or equivalent procedure of a felony. Regarding the applicability of the proposed Rule 609, in general, see *People v. Yost*, 78 Ill. 2d 292, 293–97, 35 Ill. Dec. 755, 399 N.E.2d 1283 (1980), supra.

See also *Reichert v. Board of Fire and Police Com'rs of City of Collinsville*, 388 Ill.App.3d 834, 847–49, 905 N.E.2d 861 (5th Dist. 2009) (Illinois only adopted proposed Federal Rule of Evidence 609 and did not adopt subsequent changes to the proposed rule).

§ 7:43 Supporting authorities—Statutory exceptions [FRE 609(b)–(d)]—Evidence of juvenile adjudications

Both the current and prior proposed versions of Federal Rules of Evidence Rule 609(d) limit the use of juvenile adjudications. Rule 609(d) states as follows:

> *Evidence of juvenile adjudications is generally not admissible* under this rule. The court may, however, in a criminal case allow evidence of a juvenile adjudication of a witness other than the accused if conviction of the offense would be admissible to attack the credibility of an adult and the court is satisfied that admission in evidence is necessary for a fair determination of the issue of guilt or innocence. (Emphasis added.)

People v. Tabb, 374 Ill. App. 3d 680, 690, 312 Ill. Dec. 470, 870 N.E.2d 914 (1st Dist. 2007), appeal denied, 225 Ill. 2d 670, 314 Ill. Dec. 835, 875 N.E.2d 1122 (2007) (the defendant was not denied his Constitutional right to confront witnesses when the trial judge denied his request to impeach a witness with a juvenile adjudication).

§ 7:44 Supporting authorities—Statutory exceptions [FRE 609(b)–(d)]—Pendency of appeal

See also Federal Rule of Evidence 609(e), which states:

> The pendency of an appeal therefrom does not render evidence of a conviction inadmissible. Evidence of the pendency of an appeal is admissible.

§ 7:45 Supporting authorities—Dissimilar behavior

Doe v. Lutz, 281 Ill. App. 3d 630, 637–38, 218 Ill. Dec. 80, 668 N.E.2d 564, 112 Ed. Law Rep. 371 (1st Dist. 1996), as modified on denial of reh'g, (June 25, 1996) (evidence of prior inappropriate sexual conduct towards someone other than the alleged victim was not admissible because it was irrelevant and prejudicial and it did not demonstrate sufficiently similar behavior to qualify for modus operandi evidence).

People v. McGee, 286 Ill. App. 3d 786, 795–96, 222 Ill. Dec. 137, 676 N.E.2d 1341 (1st Dist. 1997) (evidence regarding specific acts of untruthfulness, when they are not directly at issue in the case, is inadmissible).

See also *People v. Petitt*, 245 Ill. App. 3d 132, 139–41, 146–48, 184 Ill. Dec. 766, 613 N.E.2d 1358 (2d Dist. 1993) (evidence of other offenses is not admissible, when introduced to suggest that the defendant committed the charged crime).

§ 7:46 Supporting authorities—Improper impeachment evidence—Must reflect on credibility

People v. Quick, 236 Ill. App. 3d 446, 455, 177 Ill. Dec. 272, 603 N.E.2d 53 (1st Dist. 1992) ("The court should not permit cross-examination that is designed to insult, degrade, or humiliate a witness or whose only apparent purpose is to demonstrate that the defendant was of bad moral character[sic].").

McWethy v. Lee, 1 Ill. App. 3d 80, 84-85, 272 N.E.2d 663 (4th Dist. 1971) (the purpose of impeachment is to introduce evidence that suggests that the witness is not truthful) (alcohol use or presence not proper impeachment in this case).

Starks v. Schlensky, 128 Ill. App. 1, 1906 WL 2026, at *2 (2d Dist. 1906) (character traits that do not reflect upon the witness' truthfulness and are not relevant to the issues in the case are not proper subjects for cross-examination).

§ 7:47 Supporting authorities—Improper impeachment evidence—Impeachment in civil cases

Knowles v. Panopoulos, 66 Ill. 2d 585, 587–91, 6 Ill. Dec. 858, 363 N.E.2d 805, 97 A.L.R.3d 1144 (1977) (in civil cases, a witness may be impeached with a conviction for a crime that was punishable by death or in excess of one year in prison or for a crime that involved dishonesty and then, only if the probative value of the evidence outweighs its prejudicial value) (holding that *People v. Montgomery*, 47 Ill. 2d 510, 268 N.E.2d 695, 67 A.L.R.3d 816 (1971) applies to civil cases).

See also § 7:4 to § 7:24, supra.

§ 7:48 Supporting authorities—Irrelevant character evidence

People v. McGee, 286 Ill. App. 3d 786, 795–96, 222 Ill. Dec. 137, 676 N.E.2d 1341 (1st Dist. 1997) (evidence regarding specific acts of untruthfulness, when not directly at issue in the case, is inadmissible).

Doe v. Lutz, 281 Ill. App. 3d 630, 637–38, 218 Ill. Dec. 80, 668 N.E.2d 564, 112 Ed. Law Rep. 371 (1st Dist. 1996), as modified on denial of reh'g, (June 25, 1996) (evidence of prior inappropriate sexual conduct towards someone, other than the alleged victim, was not admissible because it was irrelevant and prejudicial and it did not demonstrate sufficiently similar behavior to qualify for modus operandi evidence).

Starks v. Schlensky, 128 Ill. App. 1, 1906 WL 2026, at *2 (2d Dist. 1906) (character traits that do not reflect upon the witness' truthfulness and are not relevant to the issues in the case, are not proper subjects for cross-examination).

See also *People v. Petitt*, 245 Ill. App. 3d 132, 139–41, 146–48, 184 Ill. Dec. 766, 613 N.E.2d 1358 (2d Dist. 1993) (evidence of other offenses is not admissible when it is introduced to suggest that the defendant committed the charged crime; however, such offenses can be admitted when they are relevant to any other issue, such as intent, motive or modus operandi, as long as the probative value outweighs the prejudicial impact of the evidence).

See also Chapter 3, generally, and § 7:25 to § 7:36, supra.

§ 7:49 Supporting authorities—Other grounds

See the following sections for other possible grounds to support a motion to exclude crimes evidence:

- Collateral to issues in case (§ 2:5 to § 2:8)
- Confusing or misleading (§ 2:9 to § 2:12)
- Solely intended to create an emotional bias (§ 2:13 to § 2:19)
- Irrelevant (§ 3:1 to § 3:10)
- Improper impeachment evidence (§ 7:4 to § 7:24)
- Inadmissible character evidence used to prove conduct (§ 7:25 to § 7:36)
- Inadmissible hearsay (§ 8:78 to § 8:89)
- Statute violation (§ 10:82 to § 10:92)
- Prior D.U.I. (§ 10:122 to § 10:140)

§ 7:50 Opposing authorities—General rule: Admissibility of prior convictions

A primary tool for opposing a motion to exclude impeachment evidence relating to prior criminal convictions, is the express language of Federal Rule of Evidence 609(a), which provides as follows:

> (a) General rule.—For the purpose of attacking the character for truthfulness of a witness,
>
> (1) evidence that a witness other than an accused has been convicted of a crime shall be admitted, subject to Rule 403, if the

crime was punishable by death or imprisonment in excess of one year under the law under which the witness was convicted, and evidence that an accused has been convicted of such a crime shall be admitted if the court determines that the probative value of admitting this evidence outweighs its prejudicial effect to the accused; and

(2) evidence that any witness has been convicted of a crime shall be admitted regardless of the punishment, if it readily can be determined that establishing the elements of the crime required proof or admission of an act of dishonesty or false statement by the witness. (Emphasis added.)

People v. Clay, 379 Ill. App. 3d 470, 318 Ill. Dec. 659, 884 N.E.2d 214, 221–22 (1st Dist. 2008), appeal denied, 228 Ill. 2d 539, 321 Ill. Dec. 558, 889 N.E.2d 1118 (2008) (in a murder case, trial court had discretion to allow the prosecution to impeach the defendant with evidence of his prior murder conviction).

People v. Farrell, 377 Ill. App. 3d 249, 250–58, 316 Ill. Dec. 389, 879 N.E.2d 456 (4th Dist. 2007) (in an aggravated robbery case, the trial court had discretion to allow the prosecution to impeach the defendant with his theft conviction).

People v. Farrell, 377 Ill. App. 3d 249, 252, 316 Ill. Dec. 389, 879 N.E.2d 456 (4th Dist. 2007) (". . . Illinois courts allow the introduction of prior convictions within 10 years from release from confinement rather than only allowing prior convictions that are less than 10 years old as calculated from the date of conviction . . .").

People v. Calderon, 369 Ill. App. 3d 221, 228-29, 307 Ill. Dec. 486, 859 N.E.2d 1163 (2d Dist. 2006) (trial court did not abuse its discretion by allowing a witness to be impeached with evidence of his most recent felony conviction and by excluding evidence of his two other felony convictions as more prejudicial than probative).

People v. Blankenship, 353 Ill. App. 3d 322, 326, 289 Ill. Dec. 137, 819 N.E.2d 49 (3d Dist. 2004) (trial court did not abuse its discretion by allowing defendant to be impeached with two prior convictions, over defendant's objection that prior convictions were too similar to the charged offense).

People v. Medreno, 99 Ill. App. 3d 449, 450–54, 54 Ill. Dec. 723, 425 N.E.2d 588 (3d Dist. 1981) (commission of a felony shows that a witness is not respectful of the rules of society and therefore, a rape conviction was properly admitted to reflect upon veracity).

People v. Medreno, 99 Ill. App. 3d 449, 450–54, 54 Ill. Dec. 723, 425 N.E.2d 588 (3d Dist. 1981) (prior rape conviction was admissible despite similarity to the charged crime because the defendant had been released from custody for it within the past ten years and the probative value outweighed the prejudicial impact of the evidence).

See also *Knowles v. Panopoulos*, 66 Ill. 2d 585, 587–91, 6 Ill. Dec. 858, 363 N.E.2d 805, 97 A.L.R.3d 1144 (1977) (in civil cases, a witness may be impeached with a conviction for a crime that was punishable by death or in excess of one year in prison or for a crime that involved dishonesty and then, only if the probative value of the evidence outweighs the prejudicial value of it) (holding that *People v. Montgomery*, 47 Ill. 2d 510, 268 N.E.2d 695, 67 A.L.R.3d 816 (1971) applies to civil cases); *People v. Montgomery*, 47 Ill. 2d 510, 516–19, 268 N.E.2d 695, 67 A.L.R.3d 816 (1971) (proposed Federal Rule of Evidence 609 should be followed regarding whether to admit evidence of convictions to impeach a witness).

◆ **Important Note:** The case of *People v. Yost*, 78 Ill. 2d 292, 293–97, 35 Ill. Dec. 755, 399 N.E.2d 1283 (1980) clarified that the *Montgomery* case (47 Ill.2d 510, 516–19, supra) only adopted Federal Rule of Evidence 609 *as it was proposed at that time* and that the rule does not change just because the Federal Rule is different or is amended. Counsel should be aware of the subtle differences in the language of current Federal Rule 609, cited above, and the proposed version of the Rule at the time of the *Montgomery* decision. While the two versions are similar, there are subtle, but important, differences which could create fertile areas for argument, depending upon the facts of your case. This is especially true with respect to subdivision (a), which addresses the probative/prejudicial balancing test. The current version of Rule 609(a) would allow the evidence if "the probative value of admitting this evidence outweighs its prejudicial effect;" whereas, the prior proposed version (as adopted by *Montgomery*), would allow the evidence if the "probative value of the evidence of the crime is substantially outweighed by the danger of undue prejudice." For a further discussion, see *People v. Yost*, 78 Ill. 2d 292, 293–97, 35 Ill. Dec. 755, 399 N.E.2d 1283 (1980).

See also *Reichert v. Board of Fire and Police Com'rs of City of Collinsville*, 388 Ill.App.3d 834, 847–49, 905 N.E.2d 861 (5th Dist. 2009) (Illinois only adopted proposed Federal Rule of Evidence 609 and did not adopt subsequent changes to the proposed rule).

§ 7:51 Opposing authorities—Additional statutory authorities

735 ILCS 5/8-101 states:

> Interested witness. No person shall be disqualified as a witness in any action or proceeding, except as hereinafter stated, by reason of his or her interest in the event thereof, as a party or otherwise, or by reason of his or her conviction of any crime; but such interest or conviction may be shown for the purpose of affecting the credibility of such witness; and the fact of such conviction may be proven like any fact not of record, either by the witness himself or herself (who shall be compelled to testify thereto) or by any other witness cognizant of such conviction, as impeaching testimony, or by any other competent evidence.

Illinois Supreme Court Rule 238 states:

> (a) The credibility of a witness may be attacked by any party, including the party calling the witness.
> (b) If the court determines that a witness is hostile or unwilling, the witness may be examined by the party calling the witness as if under cross- examination.

725 ILCS 5/115-20 provides that in prosecutions for certain battery offenses and stalking offenses, evidence of prior convictions for the same type of offenses against the same victim may be admissible in evidence if relevant and if the probative value outweighs the prejudicial impact of the evidence.

§ 7:52 Opposing authorities—Pendency of appeal

Federal Rule of Evidence 609(e) states as follows:

> The pendency of an appeal therefrom does not render evidence of a conviction inadmissible. Evidence of the pendency of an appeal is admissible.

II. SAMPLE MOTIONS

§ 7:53 Motion to exclude evidence of alcoholism of eyewitness

TO: ALL PARTIES AND THEIR RESPECTIVE ATTORNEYS OF RECORD:

PLEASE TAKE NOTICE that defendant hereby moves this Court for an order excluding any and all evidence, references to evidence, testimony or argument pertaining to a trait or habit of excessive alcohol consumption or alcoholism of defense witness, Esau Something. This motion is based upon the ground that the evidence is irrelevant, prejudicial and improper character evidence.

This motion is made under the provisions of Illinois case law and is based upon the supporting Memorandum of Points and Authorities, the pleadings and papers on file in this action, and upon such of the argument and evidence as may be presented prior to or at the hearing of this matter.

Dated: *[date]*

MEMORANDUM OF POINTS AND AUTHORITIES

1.
INTRODUCTION

This case involves a civil action for damages arising from the alleged wrongful imprisonment of the plaintiff, who was detained for three hours in defendant's department store after witnesses observed him shoplifting.

A key issue in this case relates to the credibility of one of the eyewitnesses, Esau Something, an undercover security guard employed by the defendant. The defendant anticipates that the plaintiff will seek to admit evidence relating to this witness' prior treatment for alcoholism. According to the testimony of this witness, he has been "clean and sober" for three years, and it is undisputed that he was not drinking at the time he observed the plaintiff's actions.

By this motion, the defendant seeks to exclude any alcohol evidence regarding this witness.

2.
THIS COURT MAY EXCLUDE PREJUDICIAL EVIDENCE

This Court has authority to exclude evidence because the prejudicial impact outweighs the probative value of it. Federal Rule of Evidence 403 states:

> Although relevant, evidence may be excluded if its probative value is substantially outweighed by the danger of unfair prejudice, confusion of the issues, or misleading the jury, or by considerations of undue delay, waste of time, or needless presentation of cumulative evidence.

Illinois has a common-law rule that is comparable to Federal Rule of Evidence 403. See *People v. Peete*, 318 Ill. App. 3d 961, 966–67, 252 Ill. Dec. 821, 743 N.E.2d 689 (4th Dist. 2001); *People v. Walker*, 335 Ill. App. 3d 102, 112, 268 Ill. Dec. 654, 779 N.E.2d 268 (2d Dist. 2002), as modified on denial of reh'g, (Oct. 24, 2002) and judgment aff'd, 211 Ill. 2d 317, 285 Ill. Dec. 519, 812 N.E.2d 339 (2004).

Illinois case law is clear that Evidence should be excluded when the prejudicial impact of the evidence outweighs its probative value. *Department of Public Works and Bldgs. v. Roehrig*, 45 Ill. App. 3d 189, 196, 3 Ill. Dec. 893, 359 N.E.2d 752 (5th Dist. 1976) (exclusion of evidence of prior condemnations in a condemnation case because the prejudicial impact outweighs its probative value); *People v. Holman*, 257 Ill. App. 3d 1031, 1033–34, 196 Ill. Dec. 457, 630 N.E.2d 154 (2d Dist. 1994) (evidence is admissible if it is relevant and if the prejudicial impact does not substantially outweigh its probative value) and *Hulsebus v. Russian*, 118 Ill. App. 2d 174, 180–81, 254 N.E.2d 184 (2d Dist. 1969) (trial judge had discretion to exclude a gruesome photograph of the plaintiff during surgery because other evidence established the extent of the injury and because the photograph was likely to inflame and prejudice the jury).

In the instant matter there is a strong probability that the admission of the witness' past alcohol use and treatment will create a substantial danger of undue prejudice. The authorities described above justify the preclusion of the requested evidence in this case. Given the clear lack of relevance, plaintiff's intention by using such evidence can only be to prejudice the defendant and cause the jury to look negatively or with ill feelings towards the defendant. Certainly, the issues will be confused and the jury will be misled by the admission of such evidence. Moreover, the probative value of the evidence is nonexistent, given how remote the evidence is.

3.
THE COURT MAY EXCLUDE IRRELEVANT EVIDENCE

This Court also has authority to exclude the evidence because it is irrelevant. Federal Rule of Evidence 401 defines relevancy as,

> evidence having any tendency to make the existence of any fact that is of consequence to the determination of the action more probable or less probable than it would be without the evidence.

Illinois has adopted this definition of relevancy through case law. *People v. Monroe*, 66 Ill. 2d 317, 321–22, 5 Ill. Dec. 824, 362 N.E.2d 295 (1977); *Spencer v. Wandolowski*, 264 Ill. App. 3d 611, 617, 201 Ill. Dec. 422, 636 N.E.2d 854 (1st Dist. 1994).

Illinois case law provides that evidence may be properly excluded where it is not relevant to matters at issue. See *Preston ex rel. Preston v. Simmons*, 321 Ill. App. 3d 789, 803, 254 Ill. Dec. 647, 747 N.E.2d 1059 (1st Dist. 2001) (trial judge should not permit such wide latitude on cross-examination that it undermines the rule that only relevant evidence is admissible); *Cochran v. Great Atlantic & Pacific Tea Co., Inc.*, 203 Ill. App. 3d 935, 937–38, 148 Ill. Dec. 923, 561 N.E.2d 229 (5th Dist. 1990) (trial judge has inherent power to exclude irrelevant evidence); *Pagel v. Yates*, 128 Ill. App. 3d 897, 903, 84 Ill. Dec. 180, 471 N.E.2d 946 (4th Dist. 1984) (exclusion of irrelevant and confusing document); and *Benson v. Bradford Mut. Fire*

Ins. Corp., 121 Ill. App. 3d 500, 510, 76 Ill. Dec. 774, 459 N.E.2d 689, 47 A.L.R.4th 759 (2d Dist. 1984) (trial judge had discretion to exclude irrelevant witness testimony).

As noted previously, the probative value of the evidence is nonexistent, given how remote the evidence is and the fact that it is undisputed that the witness was not drinking at the time he observed the plaintiff's actions.

4.
THIS COURT MAY EXCLUDE IMPROPER CHARACTER EVIDENCE

Evidence of specific instances of past conduct is generally inadmissible to attack or support the credibility of a witness. See *People v. Petitt*, 245 Ill. App. 3d 132, 147–48, 184 Ill. Dec. 766, 613 N.E.2d 1358 (2d Dist. 1993) (when character evidence is admissible, it must be elicited through general reputation evidence and cannot be established through specific acts or through the witness' personal opinion); *People v. Moretti*, 6 Ill. 2d 494, 523–24, 129 N.E.2d 709 (1955) (when character evidence is admissible, it must be elicited through general reputation evidence and cannot be established through specific acts or through the witness' personal opinion); *People v. Willy*, 301 Ill. 307, 317–21, 133 N.E. 859 (1921) (character evidence, when it is admissible, should be demonstrated only through general reputation evidence and not through specific acts and moreover, the reputation evidence must not be too remote from the incident in question) and *Starks v. Schlensky*, 128 Ill. App. 1, 1906 WL 2026, at *2 (2d Dist. 1906) (character traits that do not reflect upon the witness' truthfulness and are not relevant to the issues in the case, are not proper subjects for cross-examination).

In addition, evidence of the drinking habits of a witness is inadmissible, absent a showing that the witness had been drinking prior to or contemporaneous to the event in question. *People v. Collette*, 217 Ill. App. 3d 465, 467–71, 160 Ill. Dec. 420, 577 N.E.2d 550 (4th Dist. 1991) (trial court properly restricted certain questions regarding the witness' past alcohol use); and *McWethy v. Lee*, 1 Ill. App. 3d 80, 83-85, 272 N.E.2d 663 (4th Dist. 1971) (improper to allow evidence of consumption or presence of alcohol when there was no proof that the witness was intoxicated).

In the present case, any evidence of Mr. Something's prior treatment for alcoholism is clearly irrelevant and inadmissible in this case. There is absolutely no evidence that he had consumed any alcohol prior to observing the plaintiff's actions, and certainly his past conduct has no bearing on the issues in this action. To allow the evidence would raise a devastating red herring regarding the witness' ability to accurately perceive the subject events and his credibility.

To avoid undue prejudice to the defendant, it is respectfully requested that this motion be granted and that any reference to Mr. Something's prior drinking habits be excluded.

Dated: *[date]*

Respectfully submitted,
By: ________________
[name of counsel]
Attorneys for DEFENDANT,
[name of defendant]

Chapter 8

Witness Evidence

I. MOTION AUTHORITIES

A. MOTION TO EXCLUDE IMPROPER OPINIONS

B. MOTION TO EXCLUDE TESTIMONY OF UNQUALIFIED EXPERT

C. MOTION TO EXCLUDE OPINION OF NON-EXPERT

D. MOTION TO EXCLUDE TESTIMONY OF INCOMPETENT WITNESS

E. MOTION TO EXCLUDE TESTIMONY OF JUDGE, ARBITRATOR, MEDIATOR OR JUROR

F. MOTION TO EXCLUDE WITNESS FROM COURTROOM PRIOR TO TESTIFYING

G. MOTION TO EXCLUDE COMMENT ON EXERCISE OF PRIVILEGE (NOT TO TESTIFY)

H. MOTION TO EXCLUDE EVIDENCE OF NON-CALLED WITNESSES

I. MOTION TO EXCLUDE HEARSAY STATEMENTS

II. SAMPLE MOTIONS

I. MOTION AUTHORITIES

We all know that the opinions of witnesses (expert and lay witnesses) often determine the outcome of a case. Successfully barring a witness and/or his or her opinion is often one of the keys to a successful result. It is therefore critical for counsel to remember that opinions may be improper for a variety of reasons and explore all possible bases for exclusion.

A. MOTION TO EXCLUDE IMPROPER OPINIONS

§ 8:1 Suggested motion text

[Name of moving party] hereby moves this Court for an order excluding any and all testimony, references to testimony or argument based upon the testimony of *[name of witness]* relating to *[describe improper opinion sought to be excluded, e.g., the witness' opinion of the legal interpretation of the jury instructions in this case]*. The motion is based upon the ground that the subject matter of the witness' opinion testimony is improper and is therefore inadmissible.

§ 8:2 Motion summary

This motion is used to exclude the opinion of an expert witness that is based upon improper matter. See e.g. *Mehochko v.*

Gold Seal Co., 66 Ill. App. 2d 54, 57-60, 213 N.E.2d 581, 19 A.L.R.3d 1003 (5th Dist. 1966). Under Illinois case law an expert opinion is an opinion from an individual who has experience, training, or education beyond the common individual in a reputable field and which will assist the trier of fact. See *Van Holt v. National R.R. Passenger Corp.*, 283 Ill. App. 3d 62, 70, 218 Ill. Dec. 762, 669 N.E.2d 1288 (1st Dist. 1996); *Wilson v. Clark*, 84 Ill. 2d 186, 191–92, 49 Ill. Dec. 308, 417 N.E.2d 1322 (1981) (adopting Federal Rules of Evidence 703 and 705).

Federal Rule of Evidence 703 provides:

> The facts or data in the particular case upon which an expert bases an opinion or inference may be those perceived by or made known to the expert at or before the hearing. If of a type reasonably relied upon by experts in the particular field in forming opinions or inferences upon the subject, the facts or data need not be admissible in evidence in order for the opinion or inference to be admitted. *Facts or data that are otherwise inadmissible shall not be disclosed to the jury by the proponent of the opinion or inference unless the court determines that their probative value in assisting the jury to evaluate the expert's opinion substantially outweighs their prejudicial effect.* (Emphasis added.)

Federal Rule of Evidence 705 provides:

> The expert may testify in terms of opinion or inference and give reasons therefor without first testifying to the underlying facts or data, unless the court requires otherwise. The expert may in any event be required to disclose the underlying facts or data on cross-examination.

§ 8:3 Supporting authorities—Exclusion of improper opinion, generally

Boren v. BOC Group, Inc., 385 Ill.App.3d 248, 255–56, 895 N.E.2d 53 (5th Dist. 2008) (a photograph of a billboard advertisement could not be used as a demonstrative aid to support expert testimony because the expert lacked knowledge of the circumstances surrounding the creation of the billboard and it was confusing and not helpful to explain the expert witness' testimony).

Sobczak v. General Motors Corp., 373 Ill. App. 3d 910, 926–27, 312 Ill. Dec. 682, 871 N.E.2d 82 (1st Dist. 2007), appeal denied, 226 Ill. 2d 609, 316 Ill. Dec. 551, 879 N.E.2d 939 (2007) (Speculative and conclusory opinion, about an issue that the expert lacked personal knowledge of, was properly excluded).

Ayala v. Murad, 367 Ill. App. 3d 591, 601-02, 305 Ill. Dec. 370, 855 N.E.2d 261 (1st Dist. 2006) (testimony by an expert regarding what he would have done differently than the defendant doctor was irrelevant).

People v. Robert P., 354 Ill. App. 3d 1051, 1061–63, 290 Ill. Dec. 685, 821 N.E.2d 1259 (3d Dist. 2005) (testimony of certain witnesses regarding whether they found the victim to be credible was improper opinion testimony but the error was harmless).

Merritt v. Goldenberg, 362 Ill. App. 3d 902, 10–11, 299 Ill. Dec. 271, 841 N.E.2d 1003 (5th Dist. 2005) (insufficient foundation was provided for an expert's opinion regarding the value of a certain type of lawsuit if it had been filed in a different county, when the expert provided no basis for the opinion and did not have sufficient experience regarding the issues involved in the case).

William Blair and Co., LLC v. FI Liquidation Corp., 358 Ill. App. 3d 324, 294 Ill. Dec. 348, 830 N.E.2d 760, 773–74 (1st Dist. 2005) (trial court properly declined to allow expert testimony to support motion for summary judgment, when proposed testimony pertained to a legal question).

In re Marriage of Cianchetti, 351 Ill. App. 3d 832, 837–38, 286 Ill. Dec. 807, 815 N.E.2d 17, 192 Ed. Law Rep. 230 (3d Dist. 2004) (trial court did not abuse its discretion by excluding irrelevant expert testimony regarding costs of education, where expert failed to compare similar programs to one at issue).

People v. Swanson, 335 Ill. App. 3d 117, 125–27, 269 Ill. Dec. 157, 780 N.E.2d 342 (2d Dist. 2002) (improper to allow an expert to repeat a hearsay statement of another expert when the statement did not relate to the defendant's condition and was not the type of statement that was normally relied upon in the field) (not prejudicial in this case).

Hubbard v. Sherman Hosp., 292 Ill. App. 3d 148, 153–55, 226 Ill. Dec. 393, 685 N.E.2d 648 (2d Dist. 1997) (in a medical malpractice case, the court did not abuse its discretion by barring expert testimony when the expert was licensed in the field related to the testimony but did not have the requisite experience related to the specific subject matter of the testimony).

People v. Acri, 277 Ill. App. 3d 1030, 1033–34, 214 Ill. Dec. 761, 662 N.E.2d 115 (3d Dist. 1996) (Illinois has adopted the *Frye* standard for the admission of scientific evidence) (See *Frye v. U.S.*, 293 F. 1013, 34 A.L.R. 145 (App. D.C. 1923) (rejected by, State v. Walstad, 119 Wis. 2d 483, 351 N.W.2d 469 (1984)) and (rejected by, State v. Brown, 297 Or. 404, 687 P.2d 751 (1984)) and (rejected by, Nelson v. State, 628 A.2d 69 (Del. 1993)) and (rejected by, State v. Alberico, 116 N.M. 156, 861 P.2d 192 (1993)) and (rejected by, State v. Moore, 268 Mont. 20, 885 P.2d 457 (1994)) and (rejected by, State v.

Faught, 127 Idaho 873, 908 P.2d 566 (1995)) and (rejected by, People v. Shreck, 22 P.3d 68, 90 A.L.R.5th 765 (Colo. 2001))).

People v. Solis, 275 Ill. App. 3d 346, 348–52, 211 Ill. Dec. 571, 655 N.E.2d 954 (1st Dist. 1995) (expert should not be permitted to refer to inadmissible evidence to explain the expert's opinion).

People v. Owens, 155 Ill. App. 3d 990, 998–99, 108 Ill. Dec. 511, 508 N.E.2d 1088 (4th Dist. 1987) (trial judge improperly allowed a witness to testify without sufficient proof of the witness' qualifications in the relevant field).

Freeding-Skokie Roll-Off Service, Inc. v. Hamilton, 108 Ill. 2d 217, 219–23, 91 Ill. Dec. 178, 483 N.E.2d 524 (1985) (lay witness opinion regarding whether a party could have avoided the accident should not have been admitted because it was not helpful to the trier of fact, which could have made its own assessment by hearing the relevant facts, without the addition of the opinion testimony) (citing Federal Rules of Evidence 701 and 704).

People v. Jordan, 103 Ill. 2d 192, 208, 82 Ill. Dec. 925, 469 N.E.2d 569 (1984) (party offering the evidence has the burden to prove that the expert is qualified) (the experts were qualified in this case); cf. *People v. Eiskant*, 253 Ill. App. 3d 773, 776, 192 Ill. Dec. 863, 625 N.E.2d 1018 (5th Dist. 1993) (party opposing evidence on the basis of its reliability or sufficiency has the burden to challenge the evidence through cross-examination).

Wilson v. Clark, 84 Ill. 2d 186, 191–92, 49 Ill. Dec. 308, 417 N.E.2d 1322 (1981) (a proper foundation for admission was not laid when the individuals who made the entries in a record did not testify; but, an expert may still provide an opinion based upon the record if such record is the type relied upon in the expert's field) (adopting Federal Rules of Evidence 703 and 705).

Mehochko v. Gold Seal Co., 66 Ill. App. 2d 54, 57-60, 213 N.E.2d 581, 19 A.L.R.3d 1003 (5th Dist. 1966) (improper hearsay and prejudicial to let an expert read from a test report about tests performed by someone else when the expert had no personal knowledge about the tests at issue).

Federal Rule of Evidence 701 provides:

> If the witness is not testifying as an expert, the witness' testimony in the form of opinions or inferences is limited to those opinions or inferences which are (a) rationally based on the perception of the witness, (b) helpful to a clear understanding of the witness' testimony or the determination of a fact in issue,

and (c) not based on scientific, technical, or other specialized knowledge within the scope of Rule 702.

Federal Rule of Evidence Rule 704 states:

(a) Except as provided in subdivision (b), testimony in the form of an opinion or inference otherwise admissible is not objectionable because it embraces an ultimate issue to be decided by the trier of fact.

(b) No expert witness testifying with respect to the mental state or condition of a defendant in a criminal case may state an opinion or inference as to whether the defendant did or did not have the mental state or condition constituting an element of the crime charged or of a defense thereto. Such ultimate issues are matters for the trier of fact alone.

See also Federal Rules of Evidence 703 and 705, supra, at § 8:2, Motion summary.

§ 8:4 Supporting authorities—Exclusion of improper opinion, generally—Exclusion of improperly disclosed opinion

Note that disclosure of an opinion must be made in a timely manner with sufficient specificity as required by Supreme Court Rule 213. Failure to do so can result in the opinion being barred.

Illinois Supreme Court Rule 213 states in relevant part:

(f) Identity and Testimony of Witnesses. Upon written interrogatory, a party must furnish the identities and addresses of witnesses who will testify at trial and must provide the following information:

(1) Lay Witnesses. A "lay witness" is a person giving only fact or lay opinion testimony. For each lay witness, the party must identify the subjects on which the witness will testify. An answer is sufficient if it gives reasonable notice of the testimony, taking into account the limitations on the party's knowledge of the facts known by and opinions held by the witness.

(2) Independent Expert Witnesses. An "independent expert witness" is a person giving expert testimony who is not the party, the party's current employee, or the party's retained expert. For each independent expert witness, the party must identify the subjects on which the witness will testify and the opinions the party expects to elicit. An answer is sufficient if it gives reasonable notice of the testimony, taking into account the limitations on the party's knowledge of the facts known by and opinions held by the witness.

(3) Controlled Expert Witnesses. A "controlled expert witness" is a person giving expert testimony who is the party, the party's current employee, or the party's retained expert. For each con-

trolled expert witness, the party must identify: (i) the subject matter on which the witness will testify; (ii) the conclusions and opinions of the witness and the bases therefor; (iii) the qualifications of the witness; and (iv) any reports prepared by the witness about the case.

(g) Limitation on Testimony and Freedom to Cross-Examine. The information disclosed in answer to a Rule 213 (f) interrogatory, or at deposition, limits the testimony that can be given by a witness on direct examination. Information expressed in a deposition need not be later specifically identified in a Rule 213(f) answer, but, upon objection at trial, the burden is on the proponent of the witness to prove the information was provided in a Rule 213(f) answer or in the deposition.

Without making disclosure under this rule, however, a cross-examining party can elicit information, including opinions, from the witness. This freedom to cross-examine is subject to a restriction that applies in actions that involve multiple parties and multiple representation. In such actions, the cross- examining party may not elicit undisclosed information, including opinions, from the witness on an issue on which its position is aligned with that of the party doing the direct examination.

Lisowski v. MacNeal Memorial Hosp. Ass'n, 381 Ill. App. 3d 275, 319 Ill. Dec. 440, 885 N.E.2d 1120 (1st Dist. 2008), appeal denied, 229 Ill. 2d 626, 325 Ill. Dec. 5, 897 N.E.2d 253 (2008) (trial court properly barred the opinions of experts that went beyond the specific opinions that were disclosed in discovery).

Lopez v. Northwestern Memorial Hosp., 375 Ill. App. 3d 637, 644–46, 313 Ill. Dec. 796, 873 N.E.2d 420 (1st Dist. 2007) (trial court properly excluded an undisclosed expert opinion regarding causation).

Nedzvekas v. Fung, 374 Ill. App. 3d 618, 619–23, 313 Ill. Dec. 448, 872 N.E.2d 431 (1st Dist. 2007) (trial court had discretion to exclude an undisclosed expert's opinion).

In re Detention of Lieberman, 379 Ill. App. 3d 585, 318 Ill. Dec. 605, 884 N.E.2d 160, 179–82 (1st Dist. 2007), appeal denied, 229 Ill. 2d 623, 325 Ill. Dec. 4, 897 N.E.2d 252 (2008) and cert. denied, 129 S.Ct. 2050, 77 USLW 3400, 77 USLW 3592, 77 USLW 3594 (U.S.Ill. Apr 27, 2009) (expert testimony that was not disclosed during discovery and that was cumulative of other testimony, was properly excluded).

Shaheen v. Advantage Moving and Storage, Inc., 369 Ill. App. 3d 535, 542-43, 307 Ill. Dec. 721, 860 N.E.2d 375 (1st Dist. 2006) (the trial court had discretion to bar certain undisclosed portions of an expert's opinion).

Bill Marek's The Competitive Edge, Inc. v. Mickelson Group, Inc., 346 Ill. App. 3d 996, 1006–09, 282 Ill. Dec. 305, 806 N.E.2d

280 (2d Dist. 2004) (trial court did not err by striking defendant's witnesses and affidavits, as a discovery sanction, for failing to timely disclose witnesses and nature of their testimony).

Chapman v. Hubbard Woods Motors, Inc., 351 Ill. App. 3d 99, 108–10, 285 Ill. Dec. 569, 812 N.E.2d 389 (1st Dist. 2004) (trial court did not err by preventing expert from testifying that he had reviewed certain records where records were not disclosed as basis for opinion during deposition or in responses to interrogatories).

Kim v. Mercedes-Benz, U.S.A., Inc., 353 Ill. App. 3d 444, 453–55, 288 Ill. Dec. 778, 818 N.E.2d 713 (1st Dist. 2004), opinion modified on reh'g, (Oct. 21, 2004) (trial court did not abuse its discretion by excluding lay witness' opinion regarding valuation, when subject matter of opinion had not been disclosed during interrogatories).

Sullivan v. Edward Hosp., 209 Ill. 2d 100, 107–11, 282 Ill. Dec. 348, 806 N.E.2d 645 (2004) (trial court properly barred testimony of an undisclosed expert).

Hernandez v. Paschen Contractors, Inc., 335 Ill. App. 3d 936, 945–46, 269 Ill. Dec. 893, 781 N.E.2d 1083 (1st Dist. 2002) (witness who was only disclosed as a factual witness and not an opinion witness could not give opinion testimony regarding causation) (citing Illinois Supreme Court Rule 213).

Adami v. Belmonte, 302 Ill. App. 3d 17, 21-24, 235 Ill. Dec. 135, 704 N.E.2d 708 (1st Dist. 1998) (expert witness was properly barred because the witness was disclosed in an untimely fashion under Illinois Supreme Court Rule 213).

§ 8:5 Supporting authorities—Exclusion of improper opinion, generally—Unqualified expert

See § 8:24 to § 8:28, infra, for detailed discussion of exclusions based on insufficient qualifications.

§ 8:6 Supporting authorities—Hypothetical questions

Grabner v. American Airlines, Inc., 81 Ill. App. 3d 894, 897–98, 37 Ill. Dec. 103, 401 N.E.2d 1196 (1st Dist. 1980) (in order to be proper, hypothetical question must be based upon facts in evidence or reasonable inferences from those facts).

§ 8:7 Supporting authorities—Inadmissible hearsay

People v. Duff, 374 Ill. App. 3d 599, 606–07, 313 Ill. Dec. 286, 872 N.E.2d 46 (1st Dist. 2007) (trial court properly excluded proposed cross-examination regarding the reasons that a co-defendant pled guilty to the offense, as hearsay).

Babich v. River Oaks Toyota, 377 Ill. App. 3d 425, 427–29, 316 Ill. Dec. 353, 879 N.E.2d 420 (1st Dist. 2007), appeal denied, 226 Ill. 2d 611, 317 Ill. Dec. 502, 882 N.E.2d 76 (2008) (information in a letter was inadmissible hearsay).

Giraldi by Giraldi v. Community Consol. School Dist. No. 62, 279 Ill. App. 3d 679, 690, 216 Ill. Dec. 272, 665 N.E.2d 332, 110 Ed. Law Rep. 269 (1st Dist. 1996) (trial judge can exclude hearsay evidence that formed the basis of the expert's opinion if the prejudicial impact of the hearsay evidence would outweigh its probative value).

People v. Solis, 275 Ill. App. 3d 346, 348–52, 211 Ill. Dec. 571, 655 N.E.2d 954 (1st Dist. 1995) (expert should not be permitted to refer to inadmissible evidence to explain the expert's opinion).

People v. Britz, 123 Ill. 2d 446, 457–62, 124 Ill. Dec. 15, 528 N.E.2d 703 (1988) (exclusion of expert testimony when the expert's opinion was based upon a party's own self-serving statements).

Mehochko v. Gold Seal Co., 66 Ill. App. 2d 54, 57-60, 213 N.E.2d 581, 19 A.L.R.3d 1003 (5th Dist. 1966) (improper hearsay and prejudicial to let an expert read from a test report about tests performed by someone else when the expert had no personal knowledge about the tests at issue).

See also § 8:78 to § 8:89, infra, for expanded citations on the exclusion of hearsay evidence.

§ 8:8 Supporting authorities—Inadmissible hearsay—Opinions of others

Hubbard v. Sherman Hosp., 292 Ill. App. 3d 148, 153–55, 226 Ill. Dec. 393, 685 N.E.2d 648 (2d Dist. 1997) (in a medical malpractice case, trial court did not abuse its discretion by barring expert testimony when the expert was licensed in the field related to the testimony but did not have the requisite experience related to the subject matter).

Giraldi by Giraldi v. Community Consol. School Dist. No. 62, 279 Ill. App. 3d 679, 690, 216 Ill. Dec. 272, 665 N.E.2d 332, 110 Ed. Law Rep. 269 (1st Dist. 1996) (trial judge can exclude hearsay evidence that formed the basis of the expert's opinion if the prejudicial impact of the hearsay evidence would outweigh its probative value).

People v. Britz, 123 Ill. 2d 446, 457–62, 124 Ill. Dec. 15, 528

N.E.2d 703 (1988) (exclusion of expert testimony when the expert's opinion was based upon a party's own self-serving statements).

Mehochko v. Gold Seal Co., 66 Ill. App. 2d 54, 57-60, 213 N.E.2d 581, 19 A.L.R.3d 1003 (5th Dist. 1966) (improper hearsay and prejudicial to let an expert read from a test report about tests performed by someone else when the expert had no personal knowledge about the tests at issue).

§ 8:9 Supporting authorities—Inadmissible hearsay—Statements of others

Ahmed v. Pickwick Place Owners' Ass'n, 385 Ill.App.3d 874, 890–91, 896 N.E.2d 854 (1st Dist. 2008) (police officer's opinion regarding the cause of certain injuries to a deceased individual was speculative and based upon hearsay and therefore inadmissible).

Giraldi by Giraldi v. Community Consol. School Dist. No. 62, 279 Ill. App. 3d 679, 690, 216 Ill. Dec. 272, 665 N.E.2d 332, 110 Ed. Law Rep. 269 (1st Dist. 1996) (trial judge can exclude hearsay evidence that formed the basis of the expert's opinion if the prejudicial impact of the hearsay evidence would outweigh its probative value).

People v. Britz, 123 Ill. 2d 446, 457–62, 124 Ill. Dec. 15, 528 N.E.2d 703 (1988) (exclusion of expert testimony when the expert's opinion was based upon a party's own self-serving statements).

§ 8:10 Supporting authorities—Inadmissible hearsay—Treatises, documents & texts

Granberry by Granberry v. Carbondale Clinic, S.C., 285 Ill. App. 3d 54, 60-66, 220 Ill. Dec. 284, 672 N.E.2d 1296 (5th Dist. 1996) (post-occurrence published articles should not be admitted to reflect upon the proper standard of care as it existed at the time of the incident; however, post-occurrence published articles should have been admitted in a medical malpractice case to impeach a witness when the articles related to the ability of a specific technology to diagnose the relevant condition).

Piano v. Davison, 157 Ill. App. 3d 649, 668, 110 Ill. Dec. 35, 510 N.E.2d 1066 (1st Dist. 1987) (proper to exclude medical treatises when there was no proof that they were reliable).

Roddy v. Chicago and N.W. R. R., 48 Ill. App. 3d 548, 553, 6 Ill. Dec. 536, 363 N.E.2d 65 (1st Dist. 1977) (improper to allow counsel to read hearsay from a National Safety Counsel bulletin without establishing any foundation for its admission).

§ 8:11 Supporting authorities—Legal questions

U.S. Bank v. YMCA of Metropolitan Chicago, 2008 WL 5454246, 10 (1st Dist. 2008) (trial court had discretion to exclude an expert's opinion that a collision was unavoidable because that issue was for the jury to determine).

Downey v. Dunnington, 384 Ill.App.3d 350, 386, 895 N.E.2d 271 (4th Dist. 2008) (in a case involving an alleged lack of informed consent, it was improper to allow an expert to testify about what the plaintiff might have done if properly informed because such testimony was speculative and invaded the province of the jury)(harmless error).

Mead Corp. v. Department of Revenue, 371 Ill. App. 3d 108, 308 Ill. Dec. 566, 861 N.E.2d 1131, 1141 (1st Dist. 2007), appeal denied, 222 Ill. 2d 609, 308 Ill. Dec. 637, 862 N.E.2d 235 (2007) and cert. granted, 128 S. Ct. 29, 168 L. Ed. 2d 806 (2007) (an expert cannot provide a legal opinion regarding the meaning of a statute), *vacated by MeadWestvaco Corp. ex rel. Mead Corp. v. Illinois Dept. of Revenue*, 128 S. Ct. 1498, 170 L. Ed. 2d 404 (2008) (on other grounds).

William Blair and Co., LLC v. FI Liquidation Corp., 358 Ill. App. 3d 324, 294 Ill. Dec. 348, 830 N.E.2d 760, 773–74 (1st Dist. 2005) (if a contract is not ambiguous, then interpretation of it is a matter of law for court and expert testimony regarding meaning of contract is improper).

Coyne v. Robert H. Anderson & Associates, Inc., 215 Ill. App. 3d 104, 110–13, 158 Ill. Dec. 750, 574 N.E.2d 863 (2d Dist. 1991) (expert testimony was improper because it represented a legal opinion).

See also *Hernandez v. Paschen Contractors, Inc.*, 335 Ill. App. 3d 936, 945–46, 269 Ill. Dec. 893, 781 N.E.2d 1083 (1st Dist. 2002) (witness who was only disclosed as a factual witness and not an opinion witness could not give opinion testimony regarding causation) (citing Illinois Supreme Court Rule 213).

See generally Illinois Supreme Court Rule 213, supra, at § 8:4, Supporting authorities—Exclusion of improper opinion, generally—Exclusion of improperly disclosed opinion.

§ 8:12 Supporting authorities—Legal questions—Compare: Ultimate issues

Note that Illinois law permits expert testimony on ultimate issues (as opposed to questions of law).

Federal Rule of Evidence Rule 704 states:

(a) Except as provided in subdivision (b), testimony in the form of an opinion or inference otherwise admissible is not objectionable because it embraces an ultimate issue to be decided by the trier of fact.

(b) No expert witness testifying with respect to the mental state or condition of a defendant in a criminal case may state an opinion or inference as to whether the defendant did or did not have the mental state or condition constituting an element of the crime charged or of a defense thereto. Such ultimate issues are matters for the trier of fact alone.

Townsend v. Fassbinder, 372 Ill. App. 3d 890, 905, 310 Ill. Dec. 470, 866 N.E.2d 631 (2d Dist. 2007) (an expert can provide an opinion regarding the ultimate issue if it helps clarify the issue for the jury).

Johnson v. Loyola University Medical Center, 2008 WL 919700, 4–8 (Ill. App. Ct. 1st Dist. 2008), opinion modified and superseded on denial of reh'g, 384 Ill. App. 3d 115, 323 Ill. Dec. 253, 893 N.E.2d 267 (1st Dist. 2008), appeal denied, 229 Ill. 2d 669, 900 N.E.2d 1118 (2008) (expert testimony was not speculative and was sufficient to support a jury's finding regarding causation).

Van Holt v. National R.R. Passenger Corp., 283 Ill. App. 3d 62, 70, 218 Ill. Dec. 762, 669 N.E.2d 1288 (1st Dist. 1996) (expert was permitted to give an opinion that related to the ultimate issue of whether the defendant failed to provide employees with a safe working environment).

Freeding-Skokie Roll-Off Service, Inc. v. Hamilton, 108 Ill. 2d 217, 219–23, 91 Ill. Dec. 178, 483 N.E.2d 524 (1985) (lay witness opinion regarding whether a party could have avoided the accident should not have been admitted because it was not helpful to the trier of fact, which could have made its own assessment by hearing the relevant facts without the addition of the opinion testimony) (citing Federal Rules of Evidence 701 and 704).

§ 8:13 Supporting authorities—Matters of common experience

Van Holt v. National R.R. Passenger Corp., 283 Ill. App. 3d 62, 70, 218 Ill. Dec. 762, 669 N.E.2d 1288 (1st Dist. 1996) (it no longer matters in Illinois if the expert's opinion is about a subject within the knowledge of the jurors, provided that the expert is qualified and the expert's opinion will aid the trier of fact).

But see *Freeding-Skokie Roll-Off Service, Inc. v. Hamilton*, 108 Ill. 2d 217, 219–23, 91 Ill. Dec. 178, 483 N.E.2d 524 (1985) (lay witness opinion regarding whether a party could have avoided the accident should not have been admitted because it was not helpful to the trier of fact, which could have made its own assessment by hearing the relevant facts without the addition of the opinion testimony) (citing Federal Rules of Evidence 701 and 704).

§ 8:14 Supporting authorities—Not reasonably relied upon by experts

People v. Acri, 277 Ill. App. 3d 1030, 1033–34, 214 Ill. Dec. 761, 662 N.E.2d 115 (3d Dist. 1996) (proper to exclude evidence of dog alerts when the results were not corroborated by laboratory results, because experts disagree about whether uncorroborated dog alerts are reliable).

People v. Ferguson, 172 Ill. App. 3d 1, 8-12, 122 Ill. Dec. 266, 526 N.E.2d 525 (2d Dist. 1988) (improper to allow witness to compare wear patterns from shoe prints when the shoe that was used for comparison was not the shoe that made the print at the scene, because the witness testified that her theories were not generally accepted in the relevant community).

Wilson v. Clark, 84 Ill. 2d 186, 191–92, 49 Ill. Dec. 308, 417 N.E.2d 1322 (1981) (a proper foundation for admission was not laid when the individuals who made the entries in the record did not testify; but an expert may still provide an opinion based upon the record if such record is the type reasonably replied upon in the expert's field (adopting Federal Rules of Evidence 703 and 705)).

§ 8:15 Supporting authorities—Not perceived or personally known

Boren v. BOC Group, Inc., 385 Ill.App.3d 248, 255–56, 895 N.E.2d 53 (5th Dist. 2008) (a photograph of a billboard advertisement could not be used as a demonstrative aid to support expert testimony because the expert lacked knowledge of the circumstances surrounding the creation of the billboard and it was confusing and not helpful to explain the expert witness' testimony).

Sobczak v. General Motors Corp., 373 Ill. App. 3d 910, 926–27, 312 Ill. Dec. 682, 871 N.E.2d 82 (1st Dist. 2007), appeal denied, 226 Ill. 2d 609, 316 Ill. Dec. 551, 879 N.E.2d 939 (2007) (Speculative and conclusory opinion, about an issue that the expert lacked personal knowledge of, was properly excluded).

Jackson v. Seib, 372 Ill. App. 3d 1061, 310 Ill. Dec. 502, 866 N.E.2d 663 (5th Dist. 2007) (harmless error where the trial court allowed an officer to testify when the officer acknowledged that he had no independent recollection of the occurrence and was relying on his report).

Merritt v. Goldenberg, 362 Ill. App. 3d 902, 10–11, 299 Ill. Dec. 271, 841 N.E.2d 1003 (5th Dist. 2005) (insufficient foundation was provided for an expert's opinion regarding the value of a certain type of lawsuit if it had been filed in a different county, when the expert provided no basis for the opinion and did not have sufficient experience regarding the issues involved in the case).

Kim v. Mercedes-Benz, U.S.A., Inc., 353 Ill. App. 3d 444, 455–57, 288 Ill. Dec. 778, 818 N.E.2d 713 (1st Dist. 2004), opinion modified on reh'g, (Oct. 21, 2004) (lay witness' opinion was properly excluded when insufficient foundation was provided to show that witness had personal knowledge to support opinion).

People v. Britz, 123 Ill. 2d 446, 457–62, 124 Ill. Dec. 15, 528 N.E.2d 703 (1988) (exclusion of expert testimony when the expert's opinion was based upon a party's own self-serving statements).

Wilson v. Clark, 84 Ill. 2d 186, 191–92, 49 Ill. Dec. 308, 417 N.E.2d 1322 (1981) (a proper foundation for admission was not laid when the individuals who made the entries in a record did not testify but an expert may still provide an opinion based upon the record if such record is the type relied upon in the expert's field, adopting Federal Rules of Evidence 703 and 705).

Mehochko v. Gold Seal Co., 66 Ill. App. 2d 54, 57-60, 213 N.E.2d 581, 19 A.L.R.3d 1003 (5th Dist. 1966) (improper hearsay and prejudicial to let an expert read from a test report about tests performed by someone else when the expert had no personal knowledge about the tests at issue).

See Federal Rule of Evidence 703 which provides:

> The facts or data in the particular case upon which an expert bases an opinion or inference may be those perceived by or made known to the expert at or before the hearing. If of a type reasonably relied upon by experts in the particular field in forming opinions or inferences upon the subject, the facts or data need not be admissible in evidence in order for the opinion or inference to be admitted. Facts or data that are otherwise inadmissible shall not be disclosed to the jury by the proponent of the opinion or inference unless the court determines that their probative value in assisting the jury to evaluate the expert's opinion substantially outweighs their prejudicial effect.

See also Federal Rule of Evidence 705, supra.

§ 8:16 Supporting authorities—Speculation or conjecture

Downey v. Dunnington, 384 Ill.App.3d 350, 386, 895 N.E.2d 271 (4th Dist. 2008) (in a case involving an alleged lack of informed consent, it was improper to allow an expert to testify about what the plaintiff might have done if properly informed because such testimony was speculative and invaded the province of the jury)(harmless error).

Wiedenbeck v. Searle, 385 Ill.App.3d 289, 895 N.E.2d 1067 (1st Dist. 2008) (speculative expert testimony was insufficient to avoid summary judgment in a case alleging medical malpractice).

Kirkpatrick v. Strosberg, 2008 WL 1795597, 6 (Ill. App. Ct. 2d Dist. 2008), opinion modified and superseded, 385 Ill. App. 3d 119, 323 Ill. Dec. 755, 894 N.E.2d 781 (2d Dist. 2008), appeal denied, 229 Ill. 2d 669, 900 N.E.2d 1118 (2008) and appeal denied, 229 Ill. 2d 669 (2008) (the trial court did not abuse its discretion by determining that an expert appraiser's testimony, which was based upon outdated valuations, was speculative).

Sobczak v. General Motors Corp., 373 Ill. App. 3d 910, 926–27, 312 Ill. Dec. 682, 871 N.E.2d 82 (1st Dist. 2007), appeal denied, 226 Ill. 2d 609, 316 Ill. Dec. 551, 879 N.E.2d 939 (2007) (Speculative and conclusory opinion, about an issue that the expert lacked personal knowledge of, was properly excluded).

Jordan v. Knafel, 378 Ill. App. 3d 219, 228, 317 Ill. Dec. 69, 880 N.E.2d 1061 (1st Dist. 2007), appeal denied, 227 Ill. 2d 582, 321 Ill. Dec. 251, 888 N.E.2d 1184 (2008) (speculative and conclusory assertions are insufficient to overcome a motion for summary judgment).

Rose v. Mercedes-Benz U.S.A., LLC, 378 Ill. App. 3d 615, 621–26, 317 Ill. Dec. 538, 882 N.E.2d 112, 64 U.C.C. Rep. Serv. 2d 750 (1st Dist. 2007) (plaintiff's valuation testimony was speculative).

Hussung v. Patel, 369 Ill. App. 3d 924, 308 Ill. Dec. 347, 861 N.E.2d 678, 685-87 (2d Dist. 2007), appeal denied, 223 Ill. 2d 634, 310 Ill. Dec. 248, 865 N.E.2d 968 (2007) (insufficient factual basis was provided to support the opinions of the plaintiff's experts).

Avery v. State Farm Mut. Auto. Ins. Co., 216 Ill. 2d 100, 149–50, 296 Ill. Dec. 448, 835 N.E.2d 801 (2005) (where an expert testified on cross-examination that his damage calculation could have been in error by as much as one billion, the damage award was speculative and unconstitutional).

Merritt v. Goldenberg, 362 Ill. App. 3d 902, 10–11, 299 Ill.

Dec. 271, 841 N.E.2d 1003 (5th Dist. 2005) (insufficient foundation was provided for an expert's opinion regarding the value of a certain type of lawsuit if it had been filed in a different county, when the expert provided no basis for the opinion and did not have sufficient experience regarding the issues involved in the case).

Schuler v. Mid-Central Cardiology, 313 Ill. App. 3d 326, 334–36, 246 Ill. Dec. 163, 729 N.E.2d 536 (4th Dist. 2000) (trial judge has discretion to exclude expert testimony that is based upon unsupported and speculative facts).

People v. Acri, 277 Ill. App. 3d 1030, 1033–34, 214 Ill. Dec. 761, 662 N.E.2d 115 (3d Dist. 1996) (proper to exclude evidence of dog alerts when the results were not corroborated by laboratory results, because experts disagree about whether uncorroborated dog alerts are reliable).

LaSalle Nat. Trust, N.A. v. Swedish Covenant Hosp., 273 Ill. App. 3d 780, 792, 210 Ill. Dec. 113, 652 N.E.2d 1089 (1st Dist. 1995) (speculative opinion of an expert witness was properly excluded).

People v. Britz, 123 Ill. 2d 446, 457–62, 124 Ill. Dec. 15, 528 N.E.2d 703 (1988) (exclusion of expert testimony when the expert's opinion was based upon a party's own self-serving statements).

Department of Transp. v. Bouy, 69 Ill. App. 3d 29, 33-38, 25 Ill. Dec. 499, 386 N.E.2d 1163 (4th Dist. 1979) (expert's testimony is properly excluded when it is based upon a speculative and conjectural method of proof).

Modelski v. Navistar Intern. Transp. Corp., 302 Ill. App. 3d 879, 884–86, 236 Ill. Dec. 394, 707 N.E.2d 239 (1st Dist. 1999) (accident reconstruction evidence should not have been admitted when it was based upon the expert's speculation regarding what occurred).

Freeding-Skokie Roll-Off Service, Inc. v. Hamilton, 108 Ill. 2d 217, 219–23, 91 Ill. Dec. 178, 483 N.E.2d 524 (1985) (lay witness opinion regarding whether a party could have avoided the accident should not have been admitted because it was not helpful to the trier of fact, which could have made its own assessment by hearing the relevant facts without the addition of the opinion testimony) (citing Federal Rules of Evidence 701 and 704).

See also Federal Rule of Evidence Rule 704, supra.

See also §§ 3:9 et seq. for exclusion of speculative evidence, generally.

§ 8:17 Supporting authorities—Other grounds

Other possible grounds for excluding expert testimony include:

- Prejudicial (§ 2:1 to § 2:4)
- Time-wasting (§ 2:5 to § 2:8)
- Confusing or misleading (§ 2:9 to § 2:12)
- Cumulative (§ 2:20 to § 2:33)
- Irrelevant (§ 3:1 to § 3:10)
- Collateral to issues in case (§ 3:11 to § 3:21)
- Improper foundation (§ 4:1 to § 4:19)
- Improper test evidence (§ 5:1 to § 5:19)
- Improper expert qualifications (§ 8:24 to § 8:28)
- Inadmissible hearsay (§ 8:78 to § 8:89)

§ 8:18 Opposing authorities—Generally

Burlington Northern and Santa Fe Ry. Co. v. ABC-NACO, 906 N.E.2d 83, 95–96 (1st Dist. 2009) (expert could properly give an opinion based upon probabilities or possibilities due to certain assumed facts).

Favia v. Ford Motor Co., 381 Ill. App. 3d 809, 320 Ill. Dec. 113, 886 N.E.2d 1182 (1st Dist. 2008), appeal pending, (Sept. 1, 2008) (trial court had discretion to allow an expert to testify to certain undisclosed opinions).

Yoder v. Ferguson, 381 Ill. App. 3d 353, 319 Ill. Dec. 380, 885 N.E.2d 1060 (1st Dist. 2008), appeal pending, (Sept. 1, 2008) (trial court had discretion to allow an expert to elaborate on the opinions that were disclosed during discovery).

Petraski v. Thedos, 382 Ill. App. 3d 22, 320 Ill. Dec. 244, 887 N.E.2d 24 (1st Dist. 2008), appeal denied, 229 Ill. 2d 657, 325 Ill. Dec. 15, 897 N.E.2d 263 (2008) (trial court erred by excluding an expert's opinion regarding the plaintiff's intoxication that was based upon extrapolation from blood that was drawn after the incident in question because the evidence was relevant and reliable and not unfairly prejudicial).

In re Lillie M., 375 Ill. App. 3d 852, 855–58, 314 Ill. Dec. 647, 875 N.E.2d 157 (4th Dist. 2007) (expert's observations and review of an individual's medical records provided a proper and sufficient basis for the expert's opinion regarding the individual's mental competence).

Somers v. Quinn, 373 Ill. App. 3d 87, 88-95, 310 Ill. Dec. 848, 867 N.E.2d 539 (2d Dist. 2007) (an expert is not required to be licensed in order to be competent to testify).

Sobczak v. General Motors Corp., 373 Ill. App. 3d 910, 926–27, 312 Ill. Dec. 682, 871 N.E.2d 82 (1st Dist. 2007), appeal denied, 226 Ill. 2d 609, 316 Ill. Dec. 551, 879 N.E.2d 939 (2007) (expert testimony based upon the expert's review of tests conducted by other experts should have been admitted).

Lange v. Freund, 367 Ill. App. 3d 641, 650-51, 305 Ill. Dec. 271, 855 N.E.2d 162 (1st Dist. 2006) (it is not an improper invasion of the province of the jury to allow an expert to testify that he is certain of a specific fact).

Lange v. Freund, 367 Ill. App. 3d 641, 650-51, 305 Ill. Dec. 271, 855 N.E.2d 162 (1st Dist. 2006) (it is not improper to allow an expert to be cross-examined regarding his level of certainty regarding the opinion).

In re Marriage of Gambla and Woodson, 367 Ill. App. 3d 441, 459-60, 304 Ill. Dec. 770, 853 N.E.2d 847 (2d Dist. 2006), cert. denied, 128 S. Ct. 39, 169 L. Ed. 2d 11 (2007) (psychologist's expert opinion was helpful to the jury in a child custody case).

Troyan v. Reyes, 367 Ill. App. 3d 729, 732-39, 305 Ill. Dec. 451, 855 N.E.2d 967 (3d Dist. 2006) (certain of the plaintiff's medical records which included diagnoses and opinions were admissible as business records and the trial court erred by excluding them).

Gee v. Treece, 365 Ill. App. 3d 1029, 1035-37, 303 Ill. Dec. 418, 851 N.E.2d 605 (5th Dist. 2006) (trial court had discretion to allow the testimony of an untimely disclosed expert witness when the testimony would not surprise the opposing party).

In re Objections to Tax Levies of Freeport School Dist. No. 145, 372 Ill. App. 3d 562, 310 Ill. Dec. 37, 865 N.E.2d 361, 219 Ed. Law Rep. 177 (2d Dist. 2007) (an expert cannot provide a legal opinion regarding the meaning of a statutory term but the expert can provide an opinion regarding the meaning of a term in industry standards).

Noakes v. National R.R. Passenger Corp., 363 Ill. App. 3d 851, 854–59, 300 Ill. Dec. 593, 845 N.E.2d 14 (1st Dist. 2006) (sufficient foundation existed for the admission of expert testimony regarding causation).

Village of Oak Park v. Village of Oak Park Firefighters Pension Bd., 362 Ill. App. 3d 357, 372, 298 Ill. Dec. 235, 839 N.E.2d 558 (1st Dist. 2005) (an expert's opinion regarding causation, which was stated in terms of being "more likely than not," was sufficiently certain to support a finding of causation).

Kimble v. Earle M. Jorgenson Co., 358 Ill. App. 3d 400, 294 Ill. Dec. 402, 830 N.E.2d 814, 826–28 (1st Dist. 2005) (diagram and accompanying description made by employee was admissible as a business record; opposing party's claim that it was not to scale and that employee lacked personal knowledge of situation affected weight of evidence and not its admissibility).

Northern Trust Co. v. University of Chicago Hospitals and Clinics, 355 Ill. App. 3d 230, 241–49, 290 Ill. Dec. 445, 821 N.E.2d 757 (1st Dist. 2004) (expert testimony to a reasonable degree of certainty was not improper or speculative, and, to the extent that other experts disagreed, the issue of the expert's credibility was for jury to resolve).

Hahn v. Union Pacific R. Co., 352 Ill. App. 3d 922, 930–31, 287 Ill. Dec. 867, 816 N.E.2d 834 (5th Dist. 2004) (trial court did not abuse its discretion by allowing an expert to testify about possible causation).

Hahn v. Union Pacific R. Co., 352 Ill. App. 3d 922, 930–31, 287 Ill. Dec. 867, 816 N.E.2d 834 (5th Dist. 2004) (sufficient foundation was provided for expert to testify about possible causation, when expert had examined patient and reviewed patient's medical history).

Bill Marek's The Competitive Edge, Inc. v. Mickelson Group, Inc., 346 Ill. App. 3d 996, 1009–10, 282 Ill. Dec. 305, 806 N.E.2d 280 (2d Dist. 2004) (trial court did not err by finding that affidavits submitted by plaintiff were based upon sufficient personal knowledge of witnesses).

Matuszak v. Cerniak, 346 Ill. App. 3d 766, 772–74, 282 Ill. Dec. 62, 805 N.E.2d 681 (3d Dist. 2004) (expert's testimony regarding causation, by use of differential diagnosis, was not unduly speculative even though it failed to rule out all possible causes).

Tri-G, Inc. v. Burke, Bosselman & Weaver, 222 Ill. 2d 218, 305 Ill. Dec. 584, 856 N.E.2d 389 (2006) (trial court did not err by allowing a witness with experience in field to testify regarding expected profits that were lost, over opposing party's claims that evidence was speculative) (note that this case was appealed to the Illinois Supreme Court, which did not disturb the Appellate Court's decision regarding this issue; see 2006 WL 1702282, 12–14).

Van Holt v. National R.R. Passenger Corp., 283 Ill. App. 3d 62, 70, 218 Ill. Dec. 762, 669 N.E.2d 1288 (1st Dist. 1996) (it no longer matters in Illinois if the expert's opinion is about a subject within the knowledge of the jurors, provided that the expert is qualified and the expert's opinion will aid the trier of fact).

But see *Freeding-Skokie Roll-Off Service, Inc. v. Hamilton*,

108 Ill. 2d 217, 219–23, 91 Ill. Dec. 178, 483 N.E.2d 524 (1985) (lay witness opinion regarding whether a party could have avoided the accident should not have been admitted because it was not helpful to the trier of fact, which could have made its own assessment by hearing the relevant facts without the addition of the opinion testimony) (citing Federal Rules of Evidence 701 and 704).

Wilson v. Clark, 84 Ill. 2d 186, 191–92, 49 Ill. Dec. 308, 417 N.E.2d 1322 (1981) (an expert may still provide an opinion based upon the record, if such record is the type relied upon in the expert's field) (adopting Federal Rules of Evidence 703 and 705).

See Federal Rule of Evidence 703, which provides:

> The facts or data in the particular case upon which an expert bases an opinion or inference may be those perceived by or made known to the expert at or before the hearing. If of a type reasonably relied upon by experts in the particular field in forming opinions or inferences upon the subject, the facts or data need not be admissible in evidence in order for the opinion or inference to be admitted. Facts or data that are otherwise inadmissible shall not be disclosed to the jury by the proponent of the opinion or inference unless the court determines that their probative value in assisting the jury to evaluate the expert's opinion substantially outweighs their prejudicial effect.

See also Federal Rule of Evidence 705, which provides:

> The expert may testify in terms of opinion or inference and give reasons therefor without first testifying to the underlying facts or data, unless the court requires otherwise. The expert may in any event be required to disclose the underlying facts or data on cross-examination.

§ 8:19 Opposing authorities—Hearsay

R.J. Management Co. v. SRLB Development Corp., 346 Ill. App. 3d 957, 969–70, 282 Ill. Dec. 486, 806 N.E.2d 1074 (2d Dist. 2004) (expert could rely on tax returns as a basis for expert's opinion, over opposing party's claim that returns were hearsay).

Wilson v. Clark, 84 Ill. 2d 186, 191–92, 49 Ill. Dec. 308, 417 N.E.2d 1322 (1981) (an expert may still provide an opinion based upon the record, if such record is the type relied upon in the expert's field) (adopting Federal Rules of Evidence 703 and 705).

See also Federal Rule of Evidence 703 and Rule 705.

§ 8:20 Opposing authorities—Hypothetical questions

Granberry by Granberry v. Carbondale Clinic, S.C., 285 Ill.

App. 3d 54, 58-60, 220 Ill. Dec. 284, 672 N.E.2d 1296 (5th Dist. 1996) (trial judge should not have excluded a hypothetical question that was within the bounds of the evidence and the reasonable inferences from it, even though it assumed facts that were in dispute).

Leonardi v. Loyola University of Chicago, 168 Ill. 2d 83, 95-99, 212 Ill. Dec. 968, 658 N.E.2d 450 (1995) (trial judge has discretion to allow a party to ask a hypothetical question that assumes facts not in evidence, if the party can introduce the required foundation at a later point).

Spilotro v. Hugi, 93 Ill. App. 3d 837, 838–41, 49 Ill. Dec. 239, 417 N.E.2d 1066 (2d Dist. 1981) (hypothetical question need not include a statement of all the evidence in the case and it is for the opposing party to demonstrate the missing items through cross-examination).

Grabner v. American Airlines, Inc., 81 Ill. App. 3d 894, 897–98, 37 Ill. Dec. 103, 401 N.E.2d 1196 (1st Dist. 1980) (in order to be proper, hypothetical question must be based upon facts in evidence or reasonable inferences from those facts).

Grabner v. American Airlines, Inc., 81 Ill. App. 3d 894, 897–98, 37 Ill. Dec. 103, 401 N.E.2d 1196 (1st Dist. 1980) (trial judge has discretion to determine whether a hypothetical question is proper).

Chloupek v. Jordan, 49 Ill. App. 3d 809, 814–15, 7 Ill. Dec. 489, 364 N.E.2d 650 (1st Dist. 1977) (hypothetical question need not include a statement of all the evidence in the case and it is for the opposing party to demonstrate the missing items through cross-examination)

§ 8:21 Opposing authorities—Legal questions vs. ultimate issues

Counsel should note the distinction between impermissible expert testimony on legal questions and generally permissible testimony on "ultimate issues." The latter is authorized by Illinois case law. But see § 8:12, Supporting authorities—Legal questions—Compare: Ultimate issues, supra.

Townsend v. Fassbinder, 372 Ill. App. 3d 890, 905, 310 Ill. Dec. 470, 866 N.E.2d 631 (2d Dist. 2007) (an expert can provide an opinion regarding the ultimate issue if it helps clarify the issue for the jury).

Jackson v. Seib, 372 Ill. App. 3d 1061, 310 Ill. Dec. 502, 866 N.E.2d 663 (5th Dist. 2007) (experts were properly allowed to provide an expert opinion regarding the ultimate issue of whether the plaintiff was injured in the collision).

Hernandez v. Paschen Contractors, Inc., 335 Ill. App. 3d 936, 943–45, 269 Ill. Dec. 893, 781 N.E.2d 1083 (1st Dist. 2002) (expert's opinion regarding the meaning of a contractual provision based upon what is standard in the industry, was not an improper legal opinion).

Federal Rule of Evidence Rule 704 states:

> (a) Except as provided in subdivision (b), testimony in the form of an opinion or inference otherwise admissible is not objectionable because it embraces an ultimate issue to be decided by the trier of fact.
>
> (b) No expert witness testifying with respect to the mental state or condition of a defendant in a criminal case may state an opinion or inference as to whether the defendant did or did not have the mental state or condition constituting an element of the crime charged or of a defense thereto. Such ultimate issues are matters for the trier of fact alone.

725 ILCS 5/115-7.2 provides that in criminal cases for certain sexual offenses and abuse offenses, testimony from an expert who is qualified by the court regarding, "any recognized and accepted form of post-traumatic stress syndrome shall be admissible as evidence".

§ 8:22 Opposing authorities—Opinions of others

Sobczak v. General Motors Corp., 373 Ill. App. 3d 910, 926–27, 312 Ill. Dec. 682, 871 N.E.2d 82 (1st Dist. 2007), appeal denied, 226 Ill. 2d 609, 316 Ill. Dec. 551, 879 N.E.2d 939 (2007) (expert testimony based upon the expert's review of tests conducted by other experts should have been admitted).

In re Lillie M., 375 Ill. App. 3d 852, 855–58, 314 Ill. Dec. 647, 875 N.E.2d 157 (4th Dist. 2007) (expert's observations and review of an individual's medical records provided a proper and sufficient basis for the expert's opinion regarding the individual's mental competence).

Mele v. Howmedica, Inc., 348 Ill. App. 3d 1, 13, 283 Ill. Dec. 738, 808 N.E.2d 1026 (1st Dist. 2004) (no error in allowing expert to base an opinion regarding causation on opinions of other experts).

§ 8:23 Opposing authorities—Not speculative, for jury to resolve

Marston v. Walgreen Co., 389 Ill.App.3d 337, 907 N.E.2d 851 (1st Dist. 2009) (an expert may testify to more than one possible cause of an injury and then it is for the jury to decide causation).

Marston v. Walgreen Co., 389 Ill.App.3d 337, 907 N.E.2d 851 (1st Dist. 2009) (an expert may testify to probabilities regarding causation of an injury and then it is for the jury to decide causation).

Johnson v. Johnson, 386 Ill.App.3d 522, 545–46, 898 N.E.2d 145 (1st Dist. 2008) (witness' expert opinion regarding whether a horse was provoked before injuring someone was not improperly speculative).

B. MOTION TO EXCLUDE TESTIMONY OF UNQUALIFIED EXPERT

§ 8:24 Suggested motion text

[Name of moving party] hereby moves this Court for an order excluding any and all testimony, references to testimony or argument relating to the testimony of *[name of witness]* that *[describe improper testimony, e.g., the decedent died as a result of drowning]*. The motion is based upon the ground that the witness lacks the requisite knowledge, skill, experience, training, or education to properly testify on this subject and therefore the testimony is inadmissible.

§ 8:25 Motion summary

This motion is used to exclude expert testimony of a witness lacking the necessary background qualifications to testify on the stated areas of expertise. The motion is based upon Illinois case law, which requires that special knowledge, skill, experience, training, or education be shown before a witness may testify as an expert. *Hubbard v. Sherman Hosp.*, 292 Ill. App. 3d 148, 153–55, 226 Ill. Dec. 393, 685 N.E.2d 648 (2d Dist. 1997); *People v. Owens*, 155 Ill. App. 3d 990, 998–99, 108 Ill. Dec. 511, 508 N.E.2d 1088 (4th Dist. 1987).

§ 8:26 Supporting authorities—Exclusion of unqualified experts

735 ILCS 5/8-2501 states, "Expert Witness Standards. In any case in which the standard of care applicable to a medical professional is at issue, the court shall apply the following standards to determine if a witness qualifies as an expert witness and can testify on the issue of the appropriate standard of care.

(a) Whether the witness is board certified or board eligible, or has completed a residency, in the same or substantially similar medical specialties as the defendant and is otherwise qualified by significant experience with the standard of care, methods, procedures, and treatments relevant to the allegations against the defendant;

(b) Whether the witness has devoted a majority of his or her work time to the practice of medicine, teaching or University based research in relation to the medical care and type of treatment at issue which gave rise to the medical problem of which the plaintiff complains;
(c) whether the witness is licensed in the same profession with the same class of license as the defendant if the defendant is an individual; and
(d) whether, in the case against a nonspecialist, the witness can demonstrate a sufficient familiarity with the standard of care practiced in this State.

An expert shall provide evidence of active practice, teaching, or engaging in university-based research. If retired, an expert must provide evidence of attendance and completion of continuing education courses for 3 years previous to giving testimony. An expert who has not actively practiced, taught, or been engaged in university-based research, or any combination thereof, during the preceding 5 years may not be qualified as an expert witness.

The changes to this Section made by this amendatory Act of the 94th General Assembly apply to causes of action accruing on or after its effective date."

McWilliams v. Dettore, 387 Ill.App.3d 833, 843–50, 901 N.E.2d 1023 (1st Dist. 2009) (oncologist was not qualified to provide an opinion regarding the standard of care for a surgeon).

Ahmed v. Pickwick Place Owners' Ass'n, 385 Ill.App.3d 874, 890–91, 896 N.E.2d 854 (1st Dist. 2008) (police officer was not qualified to provide an expert opinion regarding the cause of certain injuries to a deceased individual).

Somers v. Quinn, 373 Ill. App. 3d 87, 95-96, 310 Ill. Dec. 848, 867 N.E.2d 539 (2d Dist. 2007) (trial court had discretion to determine that an expert who had his medical license revoked for forging prescriptions was not qualified to provide an opinion).

Alm v. Loyola University Medical Center, 373 Ill. App. 3d 1, 310 Ill. Dec. 641, 866 N.E.2d 1243 (1st Dist. 2007), appeal denied, 225 Ill. 2d 627, 314 Ill. Dec. 822, 875 N.E.2d 1109 (2007) (the trial court did not abuse its discretion by determining that a pathologist lacked the proper qualifications to testify regarding the treatment provided by plastic surgeons and an anesthesiologist).

Ruiz v. City of Chicago, 366 Ill. App. 3d 947, 953-55, 304 Ill. Dec. 174, 852 N.E.2d 424 (1st Dist. 2006) (trial court abused its discretion by determining that a witness who was licensed in another state was qualified to provide an expert opinion regarding the standard of care in Illinois).

Merritt v. Goldenberg, 362 Ill. App. 3d 902, 10–11, 299 Ill. Dec. 271, 841 N.E.2d 1003 (5th Dist. 2005) (insufficient foundation was provided for an expert's opinion regarding the value of a certain type of lawsuit if it had been filed in a different county, when the expert provided no basis for the opinion and did not have sufficient experience regarding the issues involved in the case).

Mulloy v. American Eagle Airlines, Inc., 358 Ill. App. 3d 706, 295 Ill. Dec. 54, 832 N.E.2d 205, 209 (1st Dist. 2005) (trial court did not abuse its discretion by finding that a witness was not qualified to provide testimony regarding proper standard of care while driving in circumstances at issue).

Sullivan v. Edward Hosp., 209 Ill. 2d 100, 111–23, 282 Ill. Dec. 348, 806 N.E.2d 645 (2004) (physician was not qualified to give an opinion regarding standard of care for nurses).

Garley v. Columbia LaGrange Memorial Hosp., 351 Ill. App. 3d 398, 404–13, 286 Ill. Dec. 337, 813 N.E.2d 1030 (1st Dist. 2004) (physicians were not qualified to provide opinions regarding the standard of care for nurses).

Hubbard v. Sherman Hosp., 292 Ill. App. 3d 148, 153–55, 226 Ill. Dec. 393, 685 N.E.2d 648 (2d Dist. 1997) (in a medical malpractice case, the trial judge did not abuse its discretion by barring expert testimony when the expert was licensed in the field related to the testimony but did not have the requisite experience related to the specific subject matter of the testimony).

Coyne v. Robert H. Anderson & Associates, Inc., 215 Ill. App. 3d 104, 110–13, 158 Ill. Dec. 750, 574 N.E.2d 863 (2d Dist. 1991) (expert testimony was improper because it concerned a subject about which the expert was no more qualified than the jurors).

People v. Owens, 155 Ill. App. 3d 990, 998–99, 108 Ill. Dec. 511, 508 N.E.2d 1088 (4th Dist. 1987) (trial judge improperly allowed a witness to testify without sufficient proof of the witness' qualifications in the relevant field).

People v. Jordan, 103 Ill. 2d 192, 208, 82 Ill. Dec. 925, 469 N.E.2d 569 (1984) (party offering the evidence has the burden to prove that the expert is qualified). But see *People v. Eiskant*, 253 Ill. App. 3d 773, 776, 192 Ill. Dec. 863, 625 N.E.2d 1018 (5th Dist. 1993) (party opposing evidence on the basis of its reliability or sufficiency has the burden to challenge the evidence through cross-examination).

Mehochko v. Gold Seal Co., 66 Ill. App. 2d 54, 57-60, 213

N.E.2d 581, 19 A.L.R.3d 1003 (5th Dist. 1966) (improper hearsay and prejudicial to let an expert read from a test report about tests performed by someone else when the expert had no personal knowledge about the tests at issue).

See also Federal Rule of Evidence 703 and Rule 705, supra.

§ 8:27 Supporting authorities—Other grounds

Other possible grounds for excluding expert testimony include:

- Prejudicial (§ 2:1 to § 2:4)
- Time-wasting (§ 2:5 to § 2:8)
- Confusing or misleading (§ 2:9 to § 2:12)
- Cumulative (§ 2:20 to § 2:33)
- Irrelevant (§ 3:1 to § 3:10)
- Collateral to issues in case (§ 3:11 to § 3:21)
- Improper foundation (§ 4:1 to § 4:19)
- Improper test evidence (§ 5:1 to § 5:19)
- Improper expert opinion (§ 8:1 to § 8:23)
- Inadmissible hearsay (§ 8:78 to § 8:89)

§ 8:28 Opposing authorities—Generally

Kunkel v. P.K. Dependable Const., LLC, 387 Ill.App.3d 1153, 1158–59, 902 N.E.2d 769 (5th Dist. 2009) (estimate of cost of repairs from an individual who is experienced in the field is admissible, even if there is no testimony that the estimate is reasonable and the repairs are necessary).

Ruffin ex rel. Sanders v. Boler, 384 Ill.App.3d 7, 18–25, 890 N.E.2d 1174 (1st Dist. 2008) (biomedical engineer could provide an expert opinion regarding causation based upon the amount of force occurring during childbirth).

Fronabarger v. Burns, 385 Ill.App.3d 560, 565–66, 895 N.E.2d 1125 (5th Dist. 2008) (trial court had discretion to determine that a neurologist was qualified to provide an opinion regarding the correlation between the amount of damage to vehicles and the severity of injury to occupants of the vehicles).

Petryshyn v. Slotky, 387 Ill.App.3d 1112, 1120–22, 902 N.E.2d 709 (4th Dist. 2008) (obstetrician was qualified to provide an opinion regarding the standard of care for the surgical team nurses during a C-Section operation and the trial court properly admitted the obstetrician's testimony in the trial and improperly granted a new trial after doing so).

Johnson v. Johnson, 386 Ill.App.3d 522, 545–46, 898 N.E.2d

145 (1st Dist. 2008) (witness was qualified by her experience with horse ownership and training to provide an opinion regarding whether a horse was provoked before injuring someone).

Favia v. Ford Motor Co., 381 Ill. App. 3d 809, 320 Ill. Dec. 113, 886 N.E.2d 1182 (1st Dist. 2008), appeal pending, (Sept. 1, 2008) (officers were qualified through their training and experience to provide an opinion regarding the cause of a collision).

Kunz v. Little Co. of Mary Hosp. and Health Care Centers, 373 Ill. App. 3d 615, 624–26, 311 Ill. Dec. 654, 869 N.E.2d 328 (1st Dist. 2007), as modified on denial of reh'g, (May 25, 2007) and appeal denied, 225 Ill. 2d 636, 314 Ill. Dec. 826, 875 N.E.2d 1113 (2007) (expert was qualified to provide an opinion regarding the reasonableness of certain unpaid medical bills).

Meyers v. Woods, 374 Ill. App. 3d 440, 451, 312 Ill. Dec. 760, 871 N.E.2d 160 (3d Dist. 2007) (witnesses were qualified by experience and training as experts regarding in-floor heating systems).

Lopez v. Northwestern Memorial Hosp., 375 Ill. App. 3d 637, 646–47, 313 Ill. Dec. 796, 873 N.E.2d 420 (1st Dist. 2007) (trial court had discretion to determine that an expert, who was more involved in administration than patient care, was qualified to testify as an expert regarding patient care).

Somers v. Quinn, 373 Ill. App. 3d 87, 88-95, 310 Ill. Dec. 848, 867 N.E.2d 539 (2d Dist. 2007) (an expert is not required to be licensed in order to be competent to testify).

Petre v. Cardiovascular Consultants, 373 Ill. App. 3d 929, 939–44, 313 Ill. Dec. 53, 871 N.E.2d 780 (1st Dist. 2007), appeal denied, 226 Ill. 2d 608, 316 Ill. Dec. 550, 879 N.E.2d 938 (2007) (a doctor can testify about the standard of care for a nurse but only if the issue involves what a nurse should communicate to a doctor and if the doctor can show that she is familiar with the procedures in the nurse's place of employment).

Alwin v. Village of Wheeling, 371 Ill. App. 3d 898, 309 Ill. Dec. 656, 864 N.E.2d 897 (1st Dist. 2007), appeal denied, 224 Ill. 2d 571, 312 Ill. Dec. 654, 871 N.E.2d 54 (2007) (person was qualified as an expert through experience).

Thompson v. Gordon, 221 Ill. 2d 414, 428-34, 303 Ill. Dec. 806, 851 N.E.2d 1231 (2006) (whether a witness is licensed is only one factor to consider when assessing whether the witness is qualified to testify as an expert).

Ayala v. Murad, 367 Ill. App. 3d 591, 599-600, 305 Ill. Dec. 370, 855 N.E.2d 261 (1st Dist. 2006) (trial court abused its discretion by determining that a licensed doctor, who was board certified in obstetrics and gynecology and had "extensive experience in management and treatment of cancer patients" was not qualified to testify as expert regarding the likely effect of earlier cancer treatment).

In re Marriage of Gambla and Woodson, 367 Ill. App. 3d 441, 459-60, 304 Ill. Dec. 770, 853 N.E.2d 847 (2d Dist. 2006), cert. denied, 128 S. Ct. 39, 169 L. Ed. 2d 11 (2007) (psychologist was qualified through her education and experience to provide an expert opinion in a child custody case).

Elam v. Lincoln Elec. Co., 362 Ill. App. 3d 884, 896–97, 299 Ill. Dec. 305, 841 N.E.2d 1037 (5th Dist. 2005) (a neurologist and a toxicologist were properly allowed to provide expert opinions regarding causation of the plaintiff's central nervous system damage).

Thompson v. Gordon, 356 Ill. App. 3d 447, 457–62, 293 Ill. Dec. 102, 827 N.E.2d 983 (2d Dist. 2005), aff'd, 221 Ill. 2d 414, 303 Ill. Dec. 806, 851 N.E.2d 1231 (2006) (trial court erred by striking engineer's expert opinion based upon fact that witness did not have an engineering license in the state of Illinois).

Burmac Metal Finishing Co. v. West Bend Mut. Ins. Co., 356 Ill. App. 3d 471, 481–82, 292 Ill. Dec. 235, 825 N.E.2d 1246 (2d Dist. 2005) (expert does not need to be licensed in field to render expert opinion; in this case, it was sufficient that expert was working under supervision of a licensed professional).

Sullivan-Coughlin v. Palos Country Club, Inc., 349 Ill. App. 3d 553, 558–59, 285 Ill. Dec. 676, 812 N.E.2d 496 (1st Dist. 2004) (trial court did not abuse its discretion by allowing architect to testify as an expert, over objection that witness did not have specialized expertise in type of property at issue in case).

People v. Miller, 173 Ill. 2d 167, 186, 219 Ill. Dec. 43, 670 N.E.2d 721 (1996) (abrogated by, In re Commitment of Simons, 213 Ill. 2d 523, 290 Ill. Dec. 610, 821 N.E.2d 1184 (2004)) (there is no exact rule regarding what combination of knowledge, training and experience qualifies a person as an expert).

People v. Pollard, 225 Ill. App. 3d 970, 976, 168 Ill. Dec. 61, 589 N.E.2d 175 (3d Dist. 1992) (trial judge has discretion to determine whether an individual is qualified as an expert based upon the individual's experience and training in the relevant field).

People v. Williams, 128 Ill. App. 3d 384, 398, 83 Ill. Dec. 720, 470 N.E.2d 1140 (4th Dist. 1984) (the trial judge has discretion to determine whether an individual is qualified to provide expert testimony).

See also §§ 8:18 et seq., supra, for opposition to expert opinions.

C. MOTION TO EXCLUDE OPINION OF NON-EXPERT

Counsel should not overlook the fact that lay witnesses are capable of offering opinions that may be the deciding factor in a case (e.g. the speed of a vehicle or the intoxication of a party). Make sure the opposition properly discloses their witnesses and their opinions in a timely manner, pursuant to Supreme Court Rule 213. In the event of improper or untimely disclosure, a motion to bar should be presented. For those witnesses and opinions properly disclosed, examine the foundation of the witness's testimony. Pay careful attention to whether the witness had the opportunity to know the information that he or she claims to know and that forms the basis of any opinions the witness plans to render. For example, a witness may claim to have an opinion as to the speed of a vehicle. However, if the witness did not have a sufficient opportunity to observe the vehicle, the opinion as to speed should be barred. Whether a witness is qualified and competent to testify to a certain matter should be carefully examined while considering any motions in limine.

§ 8:29 Suggested motion text

[Name of moving party] hereby moves this Court for an order excluding any and all testimony, reference to testimony or argument relating to the testimony of *[name of witness]* that *[describe opinion testimony to be excluded, e.g., whether the defendant suffered from Alzheimer's Disease]*. The motion is based upon the ground that a non-expert may not testify on such matters, pursuant to Illinois case law, and therefore this testimony is inadmissible.

§ 8:30 Motion summary

This motion is used to exclude improper opinion testimony of a lay witness. The motion is based upon Illinois case law. See *Freeding-Skokie Roll-Off Service, Inc. v. Hamilton*, 108 Ill. 2d 217, 219–23, 91 Ill. Dec. 178, 483 N.E.2d 524 (1985) (citing Federal Rules of Evidence 701 and 704). Examples of inadmissible lay opinion evidence include testimony on causation, legal conclusions, and matters beyond common experience. See *Freeding-Skokie Roll-Off Service, Inc. v. Hamilton*, 108 Ill. 2d 217, 219–23, 91 Ill. Dec. 178, 483 N.E.2d 524 (1985).

See also § 8:1 to § 8:23 (improper expert opinions) and § 8:24 to § 8:28 (non-qualified experts), supra.

§ 8:31 Supporting authorities—Exclusion of non-expert opinion

Yoder v. Ferguson, 381 Ill. App. 3d 353, 319 Ill. Dec. 380, 885 N.E.2d 1060 (1st Dist. 2008), appeal pending, (Sept. 1, 2008) (a lay witness cannot provide an opinion regarding the speed of a vehicle based upon the damage caused by a collision).

Rose v. Mercedes-Benz U.S.A., LLC, 378 Ill. App. 3d 615, 621–26, 317 Ill. Dec. 538, 882 N.E.2d 112, 64 U.C.C. Rep. Serv. 2d 750 (1st Dist. 2007) (lay witness failed to provide sufficient foundation for an opinion regarding what a defective vehicle was actually worth).

Camco, Inc. v. Lowery, 362 Ill. App. 3d 421, 435–36, 298 Ill. Dec. 332, 839 N.E.2d 655 (1st Dist. 2005) (evidence regarding an officer's deposition testimony that was based upon information contained in a lab report was improper hearsay) (harmless error).

People v. Robert P., 354 Ill. App. 3d 1051, 1059–60, 290 Ill. Dec. 685, 821 N.E.2d 1259 (3d Dist. 2005) (the trial court did not abuse its discretion by excluding evidence that the defendant's wife had brought the victim for psychological treatment for lying and masturbating; testimony was irrelevant, represented improper lay opinion testimony and disclosed confidential information).

Mulloy v. American Eagle Airlines, Inc., 358 Ill. App. 3d 706, 295 Ill. Dec. 54, 832 N.E.2d 205, 210 (1st Dist. 2005) (trial court did not abuse its discretion by excluding lay witness testimony regarding his own driving habits, because that was not relevant to issues of parties' driving habits or negligence).

People v. Jones, 241 Ill. App. 3d 228, 231–33, 181 Ill. Dec. 702, 608 N.E.2d 953 (4th Dist. 1993) (lay witness testimony must be from personal knowledge of observable facts) (lay witness testimony allowed when based upon personal knowledge and observations of what sex abuse victims often do).

Freeding-Skokie Roll-Off Service, Inc. v. Hamilton, 108 Ill. 2d 217, 219–23, 91 Ill. Dec. 178, 483 N.E.2d 524 (1985) (lay witness opinion regarding whether a party could have avoided the accident should not have been admitted because it was not helpful to the trier of fact, which could have made its own assessment by hearing the relevant facts, without the addition of the opinion testimony) (citing Federal Rules of Evidence 701 and 704).

Federal Rule of Evidence 701, states:

If the witness is not testifying as an expert, the witness'

testimony in the form of opinions or inferences is limited to those opinions or inferences which are (a) rationally based on the perception of the witness, (b) helpful to a clear understanding of the witness' testimony or the determination of a fact in issue, and (c) not based on scientific, technical, or other specialized knowledge within the scope of Rule 702.

Federal Rule of Evidence Rule 704 states:

(a) Except as provided in subdivision (b), testimony in the form of an opinion or inference otherwise admissible is not objectionable because it embraces an ultimate issue to be decided by the trier of fact.

(b) No expert witness testifying with respect to the mental state or condition of a defendant in a criminal case may state an opinion or inference as to whether the defendant did or did not have the mental state or condition constituting an element of the crime charged or of a defense thereto. Such ultimate issues are matters for the trier of fact alone.

§ 8:32 Supporting authorities—Exclusion of non-expert opinion—Causation

Yoder v. Ferguson, 381 Ill. App. 3d 353, 319 Ill. Dec. 380, 885 N.E.2d 1060 (1st Dist. 2008), appeal pending, (Sept. 1, 2008) (a lay witness cannot provide an opinion regarding the speed of a vehicle based upon the damage caused by a collision).

Hernandez v. Paschen Contractors, Inc., 335 Ill. App. 3d 936, 945–46, 269 Ill. Dec. 893, 781 N.E.2d 1083 (1st Dist. 2002) (witness who was only disclosed as a factual witness and not an opinion witness could not give opinion testimony regarding causation) (citing Illinois Supreme Court Rule 213).

Freeding-Skokie Roll-Off Service, Inc. v. Hamilton, 108 Ill. 2d 217, 219–23, 91 Ill. Dec. 178, 483 N.E.2d 524 (1985) (lay witness opinion regarding whether a party could have avoided the accident should not have been admitted because it was not helpful to the trier of fact, which could have made its own assessment by hearing the relevant facts without the addition of the opinion testimony) (citing Federal Rules of Evidence 701 and 704).

Illinois Supreme Court Rule 213 states in relevant part:

(f) Identity and Testimony of Witnesses. Upon written interrogatory, a party must furnish the identities and addresses of witnesses who will testify at trial and must provide the following information:

(1) Lay Witnesses. A 'lay witness' is a person giving only fact or lay opinion testimony. For each lay witness, the party must identify the subjects on which the witness will testify. An answer

> is sufficient if it gives reasonable notice of the testimony, taking into account the limitations on the party's knowledge of the facts known by and opinions held by the witness . . . .

§ 8:33 Supporting authorities—Exclusion of non-expert opinion—Legal opinions

People v. Crump, 319 Ill. App. 3d 538, 542–44, 253 Ill. Dec. 569, 745 N.E.2d 692 (3d Dist. 2001) (lay witness should not have been permitted to testify regarding whether he thought that the defendant had committed the offense).

Coyne v. Robert H. Anderson & Associates, Inc., 215 Ill. App. 3d 104, 110–13, 158 Ill. Dec. 750, 574 N.E.2d 863 (2d Dist. 1991) (a witness should not be permitted to testify to a legal opinion).

See also Freeding-Skokie Roll-Off Service, Inc. v. Hamilton, 108 Ill. 2d 217, 219–23, 91 Ill. Dec. 178, 483 N.E.2d 524 (1985).

§ 8:34 Supporting authorities—Exclusion of non-expert opinion—Lay experiments

People v. Kurena, 87 Ill. App. 3d 771, 776, 43 Ill. Dec. 277, 410 N.E.2d 277 (1st Dist. 1980) (a jury should not be permitted to conduct experiments that create evidence that was not received at the trial) (the experiment was proper in this case).

Federal Rule of Evidence 701, states:

> If the witness is not testifying as an expert, the witness' testimony in the form of opinions or inferences is limited to those opinions or inferences which are (a) rationally based on the perception of the witness, (b) helpful to a clear understanding of the witness' testimony or the determination of a fact in issue, and (c) *not based on scientific, technical, or other specialized knowledge within the scope of Rule 702*. (Emphasis added.)

§ 8:35 Supporting authorities—Other grounds

Other possible grounds for excluding lay witness testimony include:

- Prejudicial (§ 2:1 to § 2:4)
- Time-wasting (§ 2:5 to § 2:8)
- Confusing or misleading (§ 2:9 to § 2:12)
- Cumulative (§ 2:20 to § 2:33)
- Irrelevant (§ 3:1 to § 3:10)
- Improper foundation (§ 4:1 to § 4:18)
- Improper expert opinion (§ 8:1 to § 8:23)
- Improper expert qualifications (§ 8:24 to § 8:28)
- Incompetent witness (§ 8:39 to § 8:47)

- Inadmissible hearsay (§ 8:78 to § 8:89)

§ 8:36 Opposing authorities—Perceptions of witness

Village Discount Outlet v. Department of Employment Sec., 384 Ill.App.3d 522, 524–26, 893 N.E.2d 943 (1st Dist. 2008) (a witness' testimony regarding what he personally observed on a videotape was not hearsay. However, the court noted that the testimony might violate the best evidence rule but that claim was not raised by the parties).

Smith v. Joy Marvin, M.D., 377 Ill. App. 3d 562, 571–72, 317 Ill. Dec. 31, 880 N.E.2d 1023 (3d Dist. 2007), appeal pending, (May 1, 2008) and appeal denied, 228 Ill. 2d 554, 321 Ill. Dec. 562, 889 N.E.2d 1122 (2008) (the plaintiff could properly testify about the fact that her injuries reduced her earning capacity).

Cambridge Engineering, Inc. v. Mercury Partners 90 BI, Inc., 378 Ill. App. 3d 437, 451, 316 Ill. Dec. 445, 879 N.E.2d 512 (1st Dist. 2007) (lay witness could properly testify about the meaning of an ambiguous contract).

Razor v. Hyundai Motor America, 222 Ill. 2d 75, 109-110, 305 Ill. Dec. 15, 854 N.E.2d 607, 60 U.C.C. Rep. Serv. 2d 426 (2006), cert. denied, 549 U.S. 1181, 127 S. Ct. 1156, 166 L. Ed. 2d 996 (2007) (trial court erred by excluding a witness' opinion about the value of her car before allowing the witness to attempt to establish a foundation as to her personal knowledge regarding the car).

People v. Robinson, 368 Ill. App. 3d 963, 978-79, 307 Ill. Dec. 232, 859 N.E.2d 232 (1st Dist. 2006), appeal denied, 223 Ill. 2d 670, 310 Ill. Dec. 255, 865 N.E.2d 975 (2007) (trial court erred by denying the defendant's request to have a lay witness provide an opinion regarding the defendant's sobriety).

People v. Tara, 367 Ill. App. 3d 479, 310 Ill. Dec. 910, 867 N.E.2d 961 (2d Dist. 2006) (a lay witness can properly testify regarding the extent of her pain, the general nature of her injury and the appearance of a scar).

Camco, Inc. v. Lowery, 362 Ill. App. 3d 421, 435–36, 298 Ill. Dec. 332, 839 N.E.2d 655 (1st Dist. 2005) (evidence regarding an officer's deposition testimony that was based upon the officer's own knowledge and observations was relevant and admissible).

Village of Lake Villa v. Stokovich, 211 Ill. 2d 106, 134, 284 Ill. Dec. 360, 810 N.E.2d 13 (2004) (witness who is familiar with property and who has knowledge regarding property values in area may provide an opinion regarding value of property).

People v. Jones, 241 Ill. App. 3d 228, 231–33, 181 Ill. Dec. 702, 608 N.E.2d 953 (4th Dist. 1993) (lay witness testimony allowed when based upon personal knowledge and observations of what sex abuse victims often do).

Scheibel v. Groeteka, 183 Ill. App. 3d 120, 131–34, 131 Ill. Dec. 680, 538 N.E.2d 1236 (5th Dist. 1989) (trial judge had discretion to allow the plaintiff to testify about his opinion regarding whether the defendant could have avoided the collision, when the plaintiff testified to the facts that led to this opinion).

Wright v. Callaghan, 50 Ill. App. 2d 157, 161–62, 200 N.E.2d 56 (1st Dist. 1964) (trial court has discretion to allow a lay witness to testify regarding the speed of vehicles, as observed by the witness, if the opinion would assist the trier of fact).

Freeding-Skokie Roll-Off Service, Inc. v. Hamilton, 108 Ill. 2d 217, 219–23, 91 Ill. Dec. 178, 483 N.E.2d 524 (1985) (lay witness opinion regarding whether a party could have avoided the accident should not have been admitted because it was not helpful to the trier of fact, which could have made its own assessment by hearing the relevant facts without the addition of the opinion testimony) (citing Federal Rules of Evidence 701 and 704).

See generally, Federal Rule of Evidence 701, supra.

§ 8:37 Opposing authorities—Perceptions of witness—Sanity and mental state

Clarke v. Medley Moving and Storage, Inc., 381 Ill. App. 3d 82, 319 Ill. Dec. 125, 885 N.E.2d 396 (1st Dist. 2008), appeal pending, (May 1, 2008) and appeal denied, 228 Ill. 2d 530, 321 Ill. Dec. 554, 889 N.E.2d 1114 (2008) (lay witnesses can provide evidence to support a finding that a person experienced conscious pain and suffering).

People v. Robinson, 368 Ill. App. 3d 963, 978-79, 307 Ill. Dec. 232, 859 N.E.2d 232 (1st Dist. 2006), appeal denied, 223 Ill. 2d 670, 310 Ill. Dec. 255, 865 N.E.2d 975 (2007) (trial court erred by denying the defendant's request to have a lay witness provide an opinion regarding the defendant's sobriety).

People v. Beller, 45 Ill. App. 3d 816, 816–19, 4 Ill. Dec. 383, 360 N.E.2d 130 (2d Dist. 1977) (lay witness may give an opinion on the issue of another person's mental state and whether they were intoxicated).

People v. Smothers, 55 Ill. 2d 172, 174, 302 N.E.2d 324 (1973) (a lay witness can give an opinion about another person's sanity when the opinion is based upon the facts as observed by the witness).

See also *Skelton v. Chicago Transit Authority*, 214 Ill. App. 3d 554, 574–76, 158 Ill. Dec. 130, 573 N.E.2d 1315 (1st Dist. 1991) (a witness may not testify about another person's drinking of alcohol unless the witness can support a finding that the person was intoxicated, based upon an observed inability or decreased ability to function at the time of the incident in question).

§ 8:38 Opposing authorities—Helpful to clear understanding

Cambridge Engineering, Inc. v. Mercury Partners 90 BI, Inc., 378 Ill. App. 3d 437, 451, 316 Ill. Dec. 445, 879 N.E.2d 512 (1st Dist. 2007) (lay witness could properly testify about the meaning of an ambiguous contract).

Scheibel v. Groeteka, 183 Ill. App. 3d 120, 131–34, 131 Ill. Dec. 680, 538 N.E.2d 1236 (5th Dist. 1989) (trial judge had discretion to allow the plaintiff to testify about his opinion regarding whether the defendant could have avoided the collision, when the plaintiff testified to the facts that led to this opinion).

Wright v. Callaghan, 50 Ill. App. 2d 157, 161–62, 200 N.E.2d 56 (1st Dist. 1964) (trial court has discretion to allow a lay witness to testify regarding the speed of vehicles, as observed by the witness, if the opinion would assist the trier of fact).

Federal Rule of Evidence 701, states, in pertinent part:

> If the witness is not testifying as an expert, the witness' testimony in the form of opinions or inferences is limited to those opinions or inferences which are (a) rationally based on the perception of the witness, (b) *helpful to a clear understanding of the witness' testimony or the determination of a fact in issue*, and (c) not based on scientific, technical, or other specialized knowledge within the scope of Rule 702. (Emphasis added.)

D. MOTION TO EXCLUDE TESTIMONY OF INCOMPETENT WITNESS

§ 8:39 Suggested motion text

[Name of moving party] hereby moves this Court for an order excluding any and all testimony, reference to testimony or argument relating to the testimony of *[name of witness]*. The motion is based upon the grounds that *[describe facts supporting claim that witness is incompetent to testify, e.g., the witness is only five-years of age and is incapable of understanding the duty to tell the truth]* and therefore the witness is incompetent to testify.

§ 8:40 Motion summary

This motion is used to exclude the testimony of any witness who is incompetent under the law. The motion is based upon 725 ILCS 5/115-14 and supporting case law. 725 ILCS 5/115-14(b)(1) disqualifies a witness who is incapable of expressing himself or herself concerning the matter so as to be understood, either directly or through interpretation by one who can understand him or her and 725 ILCS 5/115-14(b)(2) disqualifies a witness who is incapable of understanding the duty of a witness to tell the truth. Witness testimony is also inadmissible where the witness lacks personal knowledge of the matter in question. See *People v. Jones*, 241 Ill. App. 3d 228, 231–33, 181 Ill. Dec. 702, 608 N.E.2d 953 (4th Dist. 1993).

§ 8:41 Supporting authorities—Generally

725 ILCS 5/115-14 states:

> (a) Every person, irrespective of age, is qualified to be a witness and no person is disqualified to testify to any matter, except as provided in subsection (b).
>
> (b) A person is disqualified to be a witness if he or she is:
>
> (1) Incapable of expressing himself or herself concerning the matter so as to be understood, either directly or through interpretation by one who can understand him or her; or
>
> (2) Incapable of understanding the duty of a witness to tell the truth.
>
> (c) A party may move the court prior to a witness' testimony being received in evidence, requesting that the court make a determination if a witness is competent to testify. The hearing shall be conducted outside the presence of the jury and the burden of proof shall be on the moving party.

Hollaris v. Jankowski, 315 Ill. App. 154, 158–59, 42 N.E.2d 859 (1st Dist. 1942) (8-year-old child was not competent to testify about accident that happened almost four years prior to date of trial when child was not shown to be particularly intelligent and facts showed that he did not have much independent memory of the incident).

Dallas v. Granite City Steel Co., 64 Ill. App. 2d 409, 421–22, 211 N.E.2d 907 (5th Dist. 1965) (trial judge did not err by informing jury that he had found plaintiff, who was a child, incompetent to testify).

Champion v. Knasiak, 25 Ill. App. 3d 192, 204–05, 323 N.E.2d 62 (1st Dist. 1974) (trial court should hold a competency hearing regarding any child under age 14 who is offered as a witness).

§ 8:42 Supporting authorities—Children

The well established rule is that the degree of intelligence of a child is the factor which determines competency, not chronological age.

> In order to determine a child's competence, a court should consider whether the child is sufficiently mature to: (1) receive correct impressions from his senses; (2) recollect these impressions; (3) understand questions and narrate answers intelligently; and (4) appreciate the moral duty to tell the truth.

People v. Edwards, 224 Ill. App. 3d 1017, 167 Ill. Dec. 54, 586 N.E.2d 1326 (2d Dist. 1992).

> It is not incumbent upon a child to give perfect answers to questions asked during the competency determination or at trial to be deemed a competent witness, as one imperfect response to a question is insufficient to invalidate a finding of competency in light of the totality of the responses.

People v. Harris, 389 Ill.App.3d 107, 124–29, 904 N.E.2d 1077 (1st Dist. 2009) (trial court had discretion to determine that a specific six year old witness was unable to understand, perceive and relate events and therefore was incompetent to testify).

People v. Sutherland, 317 Ill. App. 3d 1117, 252 Ill. Dec. 851, 743 N.E.2d 1007 (1st Dist. 2000); *People v. Wright*, 234 Ill. App. 3d 880, 176 Ill. Dec. 119, 601 N.E.2d 817 (1st Dist. 1992) (court found child incompetent to testify, in part, based upon the child's tendency to answer questions in a way that she believed people wanted her to answer the questions); *Hollaris v. Jankowski*, 315 Ill. App. 154, 42 N.E.2d 859 (1st Dist. 1942) (child who suffered injuries not competent to testify where not very smart, or precocious, and where very little independent recollection of the accident); *People v. Sims*, 113 Ill. App. 2d 58, 251 N.E.2d 795 (1st Dist. 1969) (court's failure to conduct a competency hearing before allowing child under 14 years of age to testify constituted an abuse of the court's discretion).

People v. Sutherland, 317 Ill. App. 3d 1117, 1124–25, 252 Ill. Dec. 851, 743 N.E.2d 1007 (1st Dist. 2000) (a witness is presumed competent at any age and it is for the trial judge to determine whether or not the witness is actually competent).

People v. Sutherland, 317 Ill. App. 3d 1117, 1124–25, 252 Ill. Dec. 851, 743 N.E.2d 1007 (1st Dist. 2000) (party opposing the witness' testimony has the burden to prove that the witness is incompetent to testify).

People v. Westpfahl, 295 Ill. App. 3d 327, 330–33, 229 Ill.

Dec. 842, 692 N.E.2d 831 (3d Dist. 1998) (prior statute that required a competency hearing for witnesses under 14 years old was repealed and now, pursuant to statute, all witnesses are presumed competent).

People v. Mason, 219 Ill. App. 3d 76, 80-81, 161 Ill. Dec. 705, 578 N.E.2d 1351 (4th Dist. 1991) (trial judge has discretion to determine whether a child witness is competent to testify).

People v. Velasco, 216 Ill. App. 3d 578, 586, 159 Ill. Dec. 147, 575 N.E.2d 954 (4th Dist. 1991) (party opposing the witness' testimony has the burden to prove that the witness is incompetent to testify).

§ 8:43 Supporting authorities—Lack of personal knowledge of subject matter

Babich v. River Oaks Toyota, 377 Ill. App. 3d 425, 427–29, 316 Ill. Dec. 353, 879 N.E.2d 420 (1st Dist. 2007), appeal denied, 226 Ill. 2d 611, 317 Ill. Dec. 502, 882 N.E.2d 76 (2008) (a witness could not testify to the contents of a letter when the witness had no personal knowledge regarding the information contained in the letter).

Jackson v. Seib, 372 Ill. App. 3d 1061, 310 Ill. Dec. 502, 866 N.E.2d 663 (5th Dist. 2007) (harmless error where trial court allowed an officer to testify when the officer acknowledged that he had no independent recollection of the occurrence and was relying on his report).

State ex rel. Beeler, Schad and Diamond, P.C. v. Target Corp., 367 Ill. App. 3d 860, 874-76, 306 Ill. Dec. 1, 856 N.E.2d 1096 (1st Dist. 2006), appeal denied, 222 Ill. 2d 624, 308 Ill. Dec. 641, 862 N.E.2d 239 (2007) (affidavits that were based on hearsay, rather than the personal knowledge of the affiant, would not be considered).

People v. Morgason, 311 Ill. App. 3d 1005, 244 Ill. Dec. 774, 726 N.E.2d 749 (5th Dist. 2000) (witness' testimony regarding murder inadmissible because not based on personal knowledge).

Anderson v. Human Rights Com'n, 314 Ill. App. 3d 35, 42-46, 246 Ill. Dec. 843, 731 N.E.2d 371 (1st Dist. 2000) (documents should not be admitted when the witness testifying about them does not have the personal knowledge of them to establish a proper foundation).

Watkins v. Schmitt, 172 Ill. 2d 193, 216 Ill. Dec. 822, 665 N.E.2d 1379, 110 Ed. Law Rep. 307 (1996) ("It is well established that speed is recognized as a subject about which a layman can express an opinion. In general, when a witness is familiar with the speed of a vehicle he may testify to the speed he observed, and if a witness is unable to estimate miles per hour he may state it as fast or slow.")

People v. Novak, 163 Ill. 2d 93, 205 Ill. Dec. 471, 643 N.E.2d 762 (1994) (abrogated by, People v. Kolton, 219 Ill. 2d 353, 302 Ill. Dec. 386, 848 N.E.2d 950 (2006)) ("Lay witnesses may relate their opinions or conclusions on what they observed because it is sometimes difficult to describe a person's mental or physical condition, character or reputation, or the emotions manifest by his or her acts; or things that occur and can be observed, including speed, appearance, odor, flavor. The limitation that lay witness opinion testimony be rationally based on the witness' perception reflects the general requirement that a witness must have personal knowledge of the matter to testify to it. The testimony must be based on concrete facts perceived from the witness' own senses.")

People v. Jones, 241 Ill. App. 3d 228, 231–33, 181 Ill. Dec. 702, 608 N.E.2d 953 (4th Dist. 1993) (lay witness testimony must be from personal knowledge of observable facts) (lay witness testimony allowed when based upon personal knowledge and observations of what sex abuse victims often do).

O'Brien v. Hertl, 238 Ill. App. 3d 217, 179 Ill. Dec. 393, 606 N.E.2d 225 (1st Dist. 1992) ("After a proper foundation has been established, a witness can testify as to his opinion regarding the state of intoxication of another person. It is within the discretion of the trial court as to what constitutes a sufficient basis for a non-expert to render an opinion based on intoxication.")

See also *Northern Illinois Gas Co. v. Vincent DiVito Const.*, 214 Ill. App. 3d 203, 157 Ill. Dec. 825, 573 N.E.2d 243 (2d Dist. 1991) (testimony regarding events not observed were stricken because admissible testimony limited to matters of which the witness has personal knowledge through his own senses).

Freeding-Skokie Roll-Off Service, Inc. v. Hamilton, 108 Ill. 2d 217, 219–23, 91 Ill. Dec. 178, 483 N.E.2d 524 (1985) (citing Federal Rules of Evidence 701 and 704) (lay witness opinion regarding whether a party could have avoided the accident should not have been admitted because it was not helpful to the trier of fact, which could have made its own assessment by hearing the relevant facts without the addition of the opinion testimony).

Robinson v. Wieboldt Stores, Inc., 104 Ill. App. 3d 1021, 60 Ill. Dec. 767, 433 N.E.2d 1005 (1st Dist. 1982) (plaintiff not qualified as a medical expert and therefore, incompetent to testify regarding specific medical diagnoses).

People v. Robinson, 102 Ill. App. 3d 884, 58 Ill. Dec. 23, 429 N.E.2d 1356 (1st Dist. 1981) ("The question of whether the witness has related underlying facts and circumstances to serve as a foundation for such testimony is for the trial court to decide, and that decision will not be altered in the absence of a showing of abuse of discretion.")

Wilson v. Clark, 84 Ill. 2d 186, 191–92, 49 Ill. Dec. 308, 417 N.E.2d 1322 (1981) (a proper foundation for admission was not laid when the individuals who made the entries in a record did not testify but an expert may still provide an opinion based upon the record, if such record is the type relied upon in the expert's field (adopting Federal Rules of Evidence 703 and 705)).

Harris v. Algonquin Ready Mix, Inc., 13 Ill. App. 3d 559, 563–64, 300 N.E.2d 824 (1st Dist. 1973), judgment aff'd in part, appeal dismissed in part, 59 Ill. 2d 445, 322 N.E.2d 58 (1974) (proper to exclude evidence of a form letter when there was no evidence that it was ever sent or received).

Mehochko v. Gold Seal Co., 66 Ill. App. 2d 54, 57-60, 213 N.E.2d 581, 19 A.L.R.3d 1003 (5th Dist. 1966) (improper hearsay and prejudicial to let an expert read from a test report about tests performed by someone else, when the expert had no personal knowledge about the tests at issue).

See generally Federal Rule of Evidence 701, which states:

> If the witness is not testifying as an expert, the witness' testimony in the form of opinions or inferences is limited to those opinions or inferences which are (a) rationally based on the perception of the witness, (b) helpful to a clear understanding of the witness' testimony or the determination of a fact in issue, and (c) not based on scientific, technical, or other specialized knowledge within the scope of Rule 702.

§ 8:44 Supporting authorities—Other grounds

Other possible grounds for excluding lay witness testimony include:

- Prejudicial (§ 2:1 to § 2:4)
- Time-wasting (§ 2:5 to § 2:8)
- Confusing or misleading (§ 2:9 to § 2:12)
- Cumulative (§ 2:20 to § 2:33)
- Irrelevant (§ 3:1 to § 3:10)
- Improper foundation (§ 4:1 to § 4:19)
- Improper expert qualifications (§ 8:24 to § 8:28)
- Inadmissible hearsay (§ 8:78 to § 8:89)

§ 8:45 Opposing authorities—General authority

Village of Lake Villa v. Stokovich, 211 Ill. 2d 106, 134, 284 Ill. Dec. 360, 810 N.E.2d 13 (2004) (witness who is familiar with property and who has knowledge regarding property values in area, may provide an opinion regarding value of property).

People v. Sutherland, 317 Ill. App. 3d 1117, 1124–25, 252 Ill. Dec. 851, 743 N.E.2d 1007 (1st Dist. 2000) (a witness is presumed competent at any age and it is for the trial judge to determine whether or not the witness is actually competent).

People v. Sutherland, 317 Ill. App. 3d 1117, 1124–25, 252 Ill. Dec. 851, 743 N.E.2d 1007 (1st Dist. 2000) (party opposing the witness' testimony has the burden to prove that the witness is incompetent to testify).

People v. Jones, 241 Ill. App. 3d 228, 231–33, 181 Ill. Dec. 702, 608 N.E.2d 953 (4th Dist. 1993) (lay witness testimony must be from personal knowledge of observable facts; in this case, lay witness testimony was allowed when it was based upon personal knowledge and observations of what sex abuse victims often do).

People v. Westpfahl, 295 Ill. App. 3d 327, 330–33, 229 Ill. Dec. 842, 692 N.E.2d 831 (3d Dist. 1998) (prior statute that required a competency hearing for witnesses under 14 years old was repealed and now, pursuant to statute, all witnesses are presumed competent).

People v. Mason, 219 Ill. App. 3d 76, 80-81, 161 Ill. Dec. 705, 578 N.E.2d 1351 (4th Dist. 1991) (trial judge has discretion to determine whether a child witness is competent to testify).

People v. Velasco, 216 Ill. App. 3d 578, 586, 159 Ill. Dec. 147, 575 N.E.2d 954 (4th Dist. 1991) (party opposing the witness' testimony has the burden to prove that the witness is incompetent to testify).

§ 8:46 Opposing authorities—Children

People v. Sutherland, 317 Ill. App. 3d 1117, 1124–25, 252 Ill. Dec. 851, 743 N.E.2d 1007 (1st Dist. 2000) (6 year old witness was competent to testify).

People v. Sutherland, 317 Ill. App. 3d 1117, 1124–25, 252 Ill. Dec. 851, 743 N.E.2d 1007 (1st Dist. 2000) (a witness does not need to give completely compatible and non-confusing answers to be competent, provided that the witness understands the duty to tell the truth and understands what a lie is).

People v. Westpfahl, 295 Ill. App. 3d 327, 330–33, 229 Ill.

Dec. 842, 692 N.E.2d 831 (3d Dist. 1998) (prior statute that required a competency hearing for witnesses under 14 years old was repealed and now, pursuant to statute, all witnesses are presumed competent).

People v. Dempsey, 242 Ill. App. 3d 568, 582–85, 182 Ill. Dec. 784, 610 N.E.2d 208 (5th Dist. 1993) (9 year old was competent when overall, his answers showed that he understood the duty to tell the truth and understood what a lie was, even though he testified that he did not know what the difference was between the truth and a lie).

People v. C.H., 237 Ill. App. 3d 462, 475–76, 177 Ill. Dec. 906, 603 N.E.2d 1280 (2d Dist. 1992) (a witness' age is not the critical factor in determining the witness' competency to testify).

People v. Mason, 219 Ill. App. 3d 76, 80-81, 161 Ill. Dec. 705, 578 N.E.2d 1351 (4th Dist. 1991) (a witness' reputation for lying does not render the witness incompetent to testify, provided the witness is capable of understanding the requirement to tell the truth).

§ 8:47 Opposing authorities—Mental competence/insanity

People v. Mason, 219 Ill. App. 3d 76, 80-81, 161 Ill. Dec. 705, 578 N.E.2d 1351 (4th Dist. 1991) (a witness' reputation for lying does not render the witness incompetent to testify provided the witness is capable of understanding the requirement to tell the truth).

People v. Velasco, 216 Ill. App. 3d 578, 586, 159 Ill. Dec. 147, 575 N.E.2d 954 (4th Dist. 1991) (victim with Downs Syndrome was competent to testify because she knew the difference between the truth and a lie and she said she would not lie).

In re Estate of Sutera, 199 Ill. App. 3d 531, 145 Ill. Dec. 601, 557 N.E.2d 371 (1st Dist. 1990) (to establish lack of testamentary capacity, it must be shown that at the time the will was executed the testator lacked sufficient mental ability to know and remember who were the natural objects of his bounty, to comprehend the kind and character of his property and to make disposition of his property according to some plan formed in his mind).

People v. Spencer, 119 Ill. App. 3d 971, 975–79, 75 Ill. Dec. 479, 457 N.E.2d 473 (1st Dist. 1983) (witness who could not verbally communicate, had a low IQ, gave some confusing answers, and became tired after lengthy testimony, was competent to testify because she knew what a lie was and knew she should not tell one, and because she was able to communicate non-verbally).

Applehans v. Jurgenson, 336 Ill. 427, 168 N.E. 327, 67 A.L.R. 851 (1929) (the use of intoxicating liquors does not have the effect of rendering a person incompetent to make a will unless it produces intoxication at the time the will is executed; evidence that the testator was addicted to the habitual use of such liquors, however, is admissible on the issue of mental capacity).

E. MOTION TO EXCLUDE TESTIMONY OF JUDGE, ARBITRATOR, MEDIATOR OR JUROR

Alternative dispute resolution (arbitration, mediation, etc.) is gaining wide acceptance in the legal community. Many litigators now realize the benefits of this form of dispute resolution. The benefits include reduced time and expense, and, in many instances, the increased likelihood of a fair and reasonable result. One of the major concerns that the neutral and/or participating parties may have is the possibility that the neutral may be called to testify in the event the case proceeds to trial. This concern is easily addressed by including specific language in any contract that is entered into and by the rules of our court. However, as a precautionary measure, counsel may file a motion in limine which seeks to bar any testimony by the neutral.

§ 8:48 Suggested motion text

[Name of moving party] hereby moves this Court for an order excluding any and all testimony, reference to testimony or argument relating to the testimony of *[name of witness]*. The motion is based upon the ground that the witness has served as *[a/an]* *[judge/arbitrator/mediator/juror*] in a related proceeding *[or describe date and nature of proceeding]* and therefore the witness is incompetent to testify.

§ 8:49 Motion summary

This motion is used to exclude the testimony of a judge, arbitrator, mediator or juror pursuant to the authority of statutory and case law.

§ 8:50 Supporting authorities—Judge as witness

Illinois Supreme Court Rule 63 states in relevant part:

CANON 3

A Judge Should Perform the Duties of Judicial Office Impartially and Diligently

The judicial duties of a judge take precedence over all the judge's other activities. The judge's judicial duties include all the duties of the judge's office prescribed by law. In the performance of these duties, the following standards apply: . . .

C. Disqualification.

(1) A judge shall disqualify himself or herself in a proceeding in which the judge's impartiality might reasonably be questioned, including but not limited to instances where:

(a) the judge has a personal bias or prejudice concerning a party or a party's lawyer, or personal knowledge of disputed evidentiary facts concerning the proceeding;

(b) the judge served as a lawyer in the matter in controversy, or a lawyer with whom the judge previously practiced law served during such association as a lawyer concerning the matter, or the judge has been a material witness concerning it;

(c) the judge was, within the preceding three years, associated in the private practice of law with any law firm or lawyer currently representing any party in the controversy (provided that referral of cases when no monetary interest was retained shall not be deemed an association within the meaning of this subparagraph) or, for a period of seven years following the last date on which the judge represented any party to the controversy while the judge was an attorney engaged in the private practice of law;

(d) the judge knows that he or she, individually or as a fiduciary, or the judge's spouse, parent or child wherever residing, or any other member of the judge's family residing in the judge's household, has an economic interest in the subject matter in controversy or in a party to the proceeding, or has any other more than *de minimis* interest that could be substantially affected by the proceeding; or

(e) the judge or the judge's spouse, or a person within the third degree of relationship to either of them, or the spouse of such a person:

(i) is a party to the proceeding, or an officer, director, or trustee of a party;

(ii) is acting as a lawyer in the proceeding;

(iii) is known by the judge to have a more than *de minimis* interest that could be substantially affected by the proceeding; or

(iv) *is to the judge's knowledge likely to be a material witness in the proceeding.*

(2) A judge shall keep informed about the judge's personal and fiduciary economic interests, and make a reasonable effort to keep informed about the personal economic interests of the judge's spouse and minor children residing in the judge's household.

D. Remittal of Disqualification. A judge disqualified by the terms of Section 3C may disclose on the record the basis of the judge's disqualification and may ask the parties and their lawyers to consider, out of the presence of the judge, whether to waive

> disqualification. If following disclosure of any basis for disqualification other than personal bias or prejudice concerning a party, the parties and lawyers, without participation by the judge, all agree that the judge should not be disqualified, and the judge is then willing to participate, the judge may participate in the proceeding. This agreement shall be incorporated in the record of the proceeding. (Emphasis added.)

See also *In re Estate of Wilson*, 905 N.E.2d 957, 968–70 (1st Dist. 2009) (trial court erred by conducting extensive questioning of a witness prior to ruling on a motion to transfer judges).

§ 8:51 Supporting authorities—Arbitrator or mediator as witness

Illinois Supreme Court Rule 87 states in relevant part:

> Upon appointment to a case, an arbitrator shall notify the court and withdraw from the case if any grounds appear to exist for disqualification pursuant to the Code of Judicial Conduct.

Illinois Supreme Court Rule 93(b) states in relevant part:

> *An arbitrator may not be called to testify as to what transpired before the arbitrators* and no reference to the fact of the conduct of the arbitration hearing may be made at trial. (Emphasis added.)

710 ILCS 20/6 provides:

> All memoranda, work products, or case files of a qualified dispute resolution center and its mediators shall be confidential and shall not be subject to discovery or other disclosure in any judicial or administrative proceeding. Any communication made during the resolution process by any participant, mediator, or any other person present at the mediation shall be a confidential communication.

§ 8:52 Supporting authorities—Juror as witness

People v. Cobb, 189 Ill. App. 3d 86, 86-90, 136 Ill. Dec. 482, 544 N.E.2d 1257 (4th Dist. 1989) (a juror must be impartial but the burden is on the party challenging the juror to prove lack of impartiality) (in this case, the juror was proper even though he was the father of the prosecutor who signed the complaint, because that prosecutor was not prosecuting the actual trial and the juror testified that he could be fair; however, the court indicated that it would be more concerned if the juror had known one of the parties).

Article 1, Section 8 of the Illinois Constitution states:

> Rights after Indictment

> In *criminal prosecutions*, the accused shall have the right to appear and defend in person and by counsel; to demand the nature and cause of the accusation and have a copy thereof; to be confronted with the witnesses against him or her and to have process to compel the attendance of witnesses in his or her behalf; and to have a speedy public trial *by an impartial jury* of the county in which the offense is alleged to have been committed. (Emphasis added.)

§ 8:53 Supporting authorities—Special witness doctrine

The "special witness doctrine" provides that a party who wants a prosecutor, defense attorney, judge or reporter to testify must state the proposed testimony, demonstrate why the testimony is necessary and relevant, and describe the efforts that the party made to obtain the evidence from other sources. See generally *People v. Palacio*, 240 Ill. App. 3d 1078, 180 Ill. Dec. 862, 607 N.E.2d 1375 (4th Dist. 1993); *People v. Paris*, 295 Ill. App. 3d 372, 229 Ill. Dec. 859, 692 N.E.2d 848 (4th Dist. 1998).

People v. Willis, 349 Ill. App. 3d 1, 284 Ill. Dec. 907, 811 N.E.2d 202 (1st Dist. 2004) (trial court erred by allowing presiding judge at defendant's first trial to testify at second trial; court noted that State failed to prove requisite elements under "special witness doctrine").

See also *People v. Miller*, 363 Ill. App. 3d 67, 79-80, 299 Ill. Dec. 551, 842 N.E.2d 290 (1st Dist. 2005), appeal denied, 222 Ill. 2d 617, 308 Ill. Dec. 639, 862 N.E.2d 237 (2007) (a prosecutor's testimony was admissible to perfect impeachment of a witness regarding a prior inconsistent statement).

§ 8:54 Supporting authorities—Attorney as witness

Brookbank v. Olson, 2009 WL 987409, 1–5, 907 N.E.2d 426 (1st Dist. 2009) (a party's attorney cannot provide sworn denials to requests to admit on behalf of a party even when the party cannot be located).

§ 8:55 Opposing authorities—General authority

Bauer ex rel. Bauer v. Memorial Hosp., 377 Ill. App. 3d 895, 912–13, 316 Ill. Dec. 411, 879 N.E.2d 478 (5th Dist. 2007), appeal denied, 227 Ill. 2d 577, 321 Ill. Dec. 249, 888 N.E.2d 1182 (2008) (trial court had discretion to allow the plaintiffs to call the defendant's attorney in rebuttal to correct a misleading impression by a witness).

People v. Urdiales, 225 Ill. 2d 354, 312 Ill. Dec. 876, 871

N.E.2d 669 (2007), as modified on denial of reh'g, (May 29, 2007) and cert. denied, 128 S. Ct. 494, 169 L. Ed. 2d 347 (2007) (trial court had discretion to admonish an expert who was evading the questions, to answer the questions directly and responsively).

Cretton v. Protestant Memorial Medical Center, Inc., 371 Ill. App. 3d 841, 309 Ill. Dec. 422, 864 N.E.2d 288, 303-04 (5th Dist. 2007), appeal denied, 224 Ill. 2d 573, 312 Ill. Dec. 655, 871 N.E.2d 55 (2007) (the trial court had discretion to correct a misleading impression that was given to the jury by one of the party's attorneys).

F. MOTION TO EXCLUDE WITNESS FROM COURTROOM PRIOR TO TESTIFYING

§ 8:56 Suggested motion text

[Name of moving party] hereby moves this Court for an order restricting *[name of witness(es)]* from entering the courtroom until called to testify. The motion is based upon the ground that *[state basis for exclusion of witness, e.g., the witnesses will be testifying on similar matters and allowing one to hear the questions and answers of another will undermine the moving party's cross-examination]* and therefore this court should exclude the named witness[es] pursuant to its discretionary authority under Illinois case law.

§ 8:57 Motion summary

This motion is used to exclude a witness from the courtroom while another witness is testifying. The principal basis for making the motion is to avoid the risk that the witness will be unfairly educated on the forthcoming interrogation. See *Smith v. City of Chicago*, 299 Ill. App. 3d 1048, 1053, 234 Ill. Dec. 108, 702 N.E.2d 274 (1st Dist. 1998). The motion is based upon the discretionary authority of Illinois case law. *In re J.E.*, 285 Ill. App. 3d 965, 978–81, 221 Ill. Dec. 249, 675 N.E.2d 156 (1st Dist. 1996).

§ 8:58 Supporting authorities—Exclusion of non-party witnesses from courtroom

In re J.E., 285 Ill. App. 3d 965, 978–81, 221 Ill. Dec. 249, 675 N.E.2d 156 (1st Dist. 1996) (trial judge has discretion to determine whether to exclude witnesses from the courtroom).

Friedman by Friedman v. Park Dist. of Highland Park, 151 Ill. App. 3d 374, 390, 104 Ill. Dec. 329, 502 N.E.2d 826 (2d Dist. 1986) (trial judge had discretion to include a party's expert within the order that excluded testifying witnesses from the courtroom) (stating that Federal Rule of Evidence 703, as adopted by *Wilson v. Clark*, 84 Ill. 2d 186, 191–92, 49 Ill. Dec. 308, 417 N.E.2d 1322 (1981), does not deny the trial judge discretion under "Rule 615" to exclude experts from the courtroom).

See also Federal Rule of Evidence 703, which provides:

> The facts or data in the particular case upon which an expert bases an opinion or inference may be those perceived by or made known to the expert *at or before the hearing*. If of a type reasonably relied upon by experts in the particular field in forming opinions or inferences upon the subject, the facts or data need not be admissible in evidence in order for the opinion or inference to be admitted. Facts or data that are otherwise inadmissible shall not be disclosed to the jury by the proponent of the opinion or inference unless the court determines that their probative value in assisting the jury to evaluate the expert's opinion substantially outweighs their prejudicial effect. (Emphasis added.)

Federal Rule of Evidence 615 provides:

> Exclusion of Witnesses
> At the request of a party the court shall order witnesses excluded so that they cannot hear the testimony of other witnesses, and it may make the order of its own motion. This rule does not authorize exclusion of (1) a party who is a natural person, or (2) an officer or employee of a party which is not a natural person designated as its representative by its attorney, or (3) a person whose presence is shown by a party to be essential to the presentation of the party's cause, or (4) a person authorized by statute to be present.

§ 8:59 Opposing authorities—Generally

People v. Taylor, 244 Ill. App. 3d 460, 461–68, 183 Ill. Dec. 891, 612 N.E.2d 543 (2d Dist. 1993) (trial judge improperly denied the defendant his right to a public trial by excluding his non-testifying relatives).

§ 8:60 Opposing authorities—Discretionary decision

In re J.E., 285 Ill. App. 3d 965, 978–81, 221 Ill. Dec. 249, 675 N.E.2d 156 (1st Dist. 1996) (trial judge has discretion to determine whether to exclude witnesses from the courtroom) (in this case the trial court did not abuse its discretion by excluding the minor's parents in a delinquency hearing because the prosecutor indicated that the parents might be called as rebuttal witnesses).

People v. Walls, 84 Ill. App. 2d 124, 125–27, 228 N.E.2d 602

(1st Dist. 1967) (trial judge had discretion to exclude all witnesses except the investigating officer, where the witness was necessary to assist in the trial.

People v. Chennault, 24 Ill. 2d 185, 186–88, 181 N.E.2d 74 (1962) (whether or not to exclude witnesses and whether to exempt a key investigating witness from an exclusion order, are matters for the trial court's discretion).

§ 8:61 Opposing authorities—Cannot exclude party, or related witnesses

Kopplin v. Kopplin, 330 Ill. App. 211, 213–16, 71 N.E.2d 180 (1st Dist. 1946) (it is improper to exclude a party from the courtroom).

> ◆ **Note:** It is important to note that experts may be allowed to sit in the courtroom during trial testimony because opinions that they render may be based, in part, on the testimony given.

Federal Rule of Evidence 615 provides:

> Exclusion of Witnesses
>
> At the request of a party the court shall order witnesses excluded so that they cannot hear the testimony of other witnesses, and it may make the order of its own motion. *This rule does not authorize exclusion of (1) a party who is a natural person*, or (2) an officer or employee of a party which is not a natural person designated as its representative by its attorney, or (3) a person whose presence is shown by a party to be essential to the presentation of the party's cause, or (4) a person authorized by statute to be present. (Emphasis added.)

§ 8:62 Opposing authorities—Proper remedy for exclusion order violation

Smith v. City of Chicago, 299 Ill. App. 3d 1048, 1055, 234 Ill. Dec. 108, 702 N.E.2d 274 (1st Dist. 1998) (trial judge has discretion to determine the proper remedy for a violation of an exclusion order but must make sure the sanction is proportionate and proper for the violation).

People v. Nelson, 33 Ill. 2d 48, 53, 210 N.E.2d 212 (1965) (it is within the trial judge's discretion to determine the proper sanction for violation of an exclusion order, and, in this case, the trial judge did not abuse his discretion by permitting the witness, who had been in the courtroom in violation of the order, to testify).

G. MOTION TO EXCLUDE COMMENT ON EXERCISE OF PRIVILEGE (NOT TO TESTIFY)

A defendant in a criminal case cannot be forced to testify because of the constitutional right against self-incrimination. Accordingly, the prosecution cannot comment on the defendant's failure to testify. In civil cases, the situation is quite different. In a civil case, a party can certainly comment on the opposition's failure to testify. In fact, in a civil case, a party can "force" the opposition to testify in their case in chief by calling him or her as an adverse witness, pursuant to Section 5/2-1102 of the Illinois Code of Civil Procedure. Of course, a party in a civil case may not be forced to testify in a civil matter if his testimony would be potentially self-incriminating.

§ 8:63 Suggested motion text

[Name of moving party] hereby moves this Court for an order excluding any and all evidence, references to evidence, testimony or argument relating to the fact that *[name of party]* exercised a right not to testify. The motion is based upon the ground that the witness has a Constitutional right not to testify and commenting on that fact is restricted.

◆ **Note:** This motion is for use in criminal cases only. See § 8:68, Opposing authorities, infra, regarding civil implications of silence.

§ 8:64 Motion summary

This motion is used to exclude any comment or evidence regarding the exercise of a witness' Constitutional right not to testify. The motion is based upon the express authority of 725 ILCS 5/115-16 and related case authority. *Moore v. Wright*, 90 Ill. 470, 1878 WL 10189, at *1–2 (1878).

◆ **Note:** The general form of this motion may be used to exclude other privileged evidence.

§ 8:65 Supporting authorities—No-comment rule

People v. Peden, 377 Ill. App. 3d 463, 470–74, 316 Ill. Dec. 156, 878 N.E.2d 1180 (1st Dist. 2007), appeal denied, 226 Ill. 2d 627, 317 Ill. Dec. 507, 882 N.E.2d 81 (2008) (trial court's repeated and improper admonitions regarding the defendant's right to testify and the defendant's trial strategy denied the defendant a fair trial).

In re P.M.C., 376 Ill. App. 3d 867, 872–74, 315 Ill. Dec. 471, 876 N.E.2d 1061 (5th Dist. 2007), appeal denied, judgment vacated, 229 Ill. 2d 668, 324 Ill. Dec. 839, 896 N.E.2d 1058 (2008) (terminating a father's parental rights solely because he would not admit to abusing the minor was a violation of the father's right to avoid self-incrimination).

In re A.W., 373 Ill. App. 3d 574, 578–81, 311 Ill. Dec. 400, 868 N.E.2d 400 (3d Dist. 2007), appeal allowed, 225 Ill. 2d 633, 314 Ill. Dec. 825, 875 N.E.2d 1112 (2007) and judgment aff'd in part, rev'd in part, 231 Ill. 2d 92, 324 Ill. Dec. 530, 896 N.E.2d 316 (2008) (a parent of an abused or neglected child cannot be forced to complete a service task that would force the parent to admit abusing the child).

People v. Herrett, 137 Ill. 2d 195, 148 Ill. Dec. 695, 561 N.E.2d 1 (1990) (an accused has a constitutional right not to testify as a witness in his own behalf and the prosecution may not directly or indirectly comment on the defendant's failure to take the stand in his own defense).

Moore v. Wright, 90 Ill. 470, 1878 WL 10189, at *1–2 (1878) (trial judge improperly instructed the jury regarding inferences from a party failing to testify).

725 ILCS 5/115-16 states as follows:

> No person shall be disqualified as a witness in a criminal case or proceeding by reason of his or her interest in the event of the case or proceeding, as a party or otherwise, or by reason of his or her having been convicted of a crime; but the interest or conviction may be shown for the purpose of affecting the credibility of the witness. *A defendant in a criminal case or proceeding shall only at his or her own request be deemed a competent witness, and the person's neglect to testify shall not create a presumption against the person, nor shall the court permit a reference or comment to be made to or upon that neglect.*
>
> In criminal cases, husband and wife may testify for or against each other. Neither, however, may testify as to any communication or admission made by either of them to the other or as to any conversation between them during marriage, except in cases in which either is charged with an offense against the person or property of the other, in case of spouse abandonment, when the interests of their child or children or of any child or children in either spouse's care, custody, or control are directly involved, when either is charged under Section 12-13, 12-14, 12-14.1, 12-15, or 12-16 of the Criminal Code of 1961 and the victim is a minor under 18 years of age in either spouse's care, custody, or control at the time of the offense, or as to matters in which either has acted as agent of the other. (Emphasis added.)

§ 8:66 Opposing authorities

Counsel opposing a motion brought on the grounds referenced in the preceding sections should be prepared to cite to Illinois

Code of Civil Procedure Section 5/2-1102 [735 ILCS 5/2-1102], which allows a party in a civil case to force the opposition to testify as an adverse witness.

§ 8:67 Opposing authorities—Allowable inferences

Note that it can be proper to comment on the evidence as being uncontradicted. *People v. Skorusa*, 55 Ill. 2d 577, 584–85, 304 N.E.2d 630 (1973). However, these inferences may be drawn from the evidence in the case and not from the claim of the privilege itself. *People v. Skorusa*, 55 Ill. 2d 577, 584–85, 304 N.E.2d 630 (1973); *Moore v. Wright*, 90 Ill. 470, 1878 WL 10189, at *1–2 (1878). It may also be proper to comment on the failure to testify when the comment was made in direct response to the argument by the party who chose not to testify. *People v. Franklin*, 135 Ill. 2d 78, 101–02, 142 Ill. Dec. 152, 552 N.E.2d 743 (1990).

See also *People v. Fenelon*, 14 Ill. App. 3d 622, 623–26, 303 N.E.2d 38 (2d Dist. 1973) (trial judge properly admitted the videotaped portion of the defendant performing sobriety tests. The appellate court noted that the videotaped portion was non-testimonial evidence).

§ 8:68 Opposing authorities—Consequences of silence in civil cases

CHB Uptown Properties, LLC v. Financial Place Apartments, LLC, 378 Ill. App. 3d 105, 108–112, 317 Ill. Dec. 255, 881 N.E.2d 423 (1st Dist. 2007) (trial court was not required to stay a civil proceeding pending the outcome of a criminal proceeding, based upon the fact that one party would plead the Fifth Amendment).

People v. Houar, 365 Ill. App. 3d 682, 690-91, 302 Ill. Dec. 890, 850 N.E.2d 327 (2d Dist. 2006) (if the petition for an order of protection alleged sufficient detail, an adverse inference could be drawn against the defendant from the fact that the defendant refused to testify at the hearing for the order for protection, even though the criminal charges were also pending against the defendant at that same time).

D.C. v. S.A., 178 Ill. 2d 551, 566–70, 227 Ill. Dec. 550, 687 N.E.2d 1032 (1997) (improper to allow a plaintiff to use the protection of a privilege as an unfair weapon against the other party).

Giampa v. Illinois Civil Service Commission, 89 Ill. App. 3d 606, 613–14, 44 Ill. Dec. 744, 411 N.E.2d 1110 (1st Dist. 1980) (not improper to consider a party's decision not to testify at an administrative hearing, even though it might have incriminated the party in a separate criminal proceeding if the party had testified).

Galante v. Steel City Nat. Bank of Chicago, 66 Ill. App. 3d 476, 477–483, 23 Ill. Dec. 421, 384 N.E.2d 57 (1st Dist. 1978) (plaintiff in a civil suit could be forced to choose between waiving privilege or dismissal of the lawsuit but the same is not true for defendants).

Moore v. Wright, 90 Ill. 470, 1878 WL 10189, at *1–2 (1878) (trial judge improperly instructed the jury regarding inferences from a party failing to testify).

Note that if the opposition party is forced to testify at trial in a civil case under Section 5/2-1102 of the Illinois Code of Civil Procedure, and fails to appear, that party is subject to sanctions. See Section 5/2-1102 [735 ILCS 5/2-1102].

See also 725 ILCS 5/115-16, supra.

§ 8:69 Opposing authorities—Waiver

D.C. v. S.A., 178 Ill. 2d 551, 566–70, 227 Ill. Dec. 550, 687 N.E.2d 1032 (1997) (privilege was removed for the discovery of portions of plaintiff's psychiatric records that related directly to the incident in question, could have provided a defense, and were not discoverable by other means, even though court did not find that the plaintiff had waived the issue of his mental health by putting it into issue).

H. MOTION TO EXCLUDE EVIDENCE OF NON-CALLED WITNESSES

§ 8:70 Suggested motion text

[Name of moving party] hereby moves this Court for an order excluding any and all evidence, references to evidence, testimony or argument relating to *[name of moving party]*'s decision not to call certain witnesses to testify at trial. The motion is based upon the grounds that the evidence is speculative, irrelevant and the probative value is substantially outweighed by the risk of undue prejudice to *[name of moving party]*.

§ 8:71 Motion summary

This motion is used to exclude evidence or inferences relating to a party's non-calling of a witness. Where a party chooses not to call a certain witness, this fact generally may not be commented upon by the opposition if the witness was equally available to testify for both parties, [*People v. Munday*, 280 Ill. 32, 40–49, 117 N.E. 286 (1917)], where it would invite juror speculation [*Thompson v. Abbott Laboratories*, 193 Ill. App. 3d 188, 204, 140 Ill. Dec. 423, 549 N.E.2d 1295 (2d Dist. 1990); *People v. Munday*, 280 Ill. 32, 40–49, 117 N.E. 286 (1917)], or where other witnesses had already testified on the disputed point [*Thompson v. Abbott Laboratories*, 193 Ill. App. 3d 188, 201–04, 140 Ill. Dec. 423, 549 N.E.2d 1295 (2d Dist. 1990); *Adami v. Belmonte*, 302 Ill. App. 3d 17, 25-26, 235 Ill. Dec. 135, 704 N.E.2d 708 (1st Dist. 1998)].

§ 8:72 Supporting authorities—Exclusion of prejudicial evidence, generally

Federal Rule of Evidence 403 states:

> Although relevant, evidence may be excluded if its probative value is substantially outweighed by the danger of unfair prejudice, confusion of the issues, or misleading the jury, or by considerations of undue delay, waste of time, or needless presentation of cumulative evidence.

It must be noted that this Rule has not been codified in Illinois. However, Illinois cases have stated that Illinois has a common-law rule that is comparable to Federal Rule of Evidence 403. See *People v. Walker*, 335 Ill. App. 3d 102, 112, 268 Ill. Dec. 654, 779 N.E.2d 268 (2d Dist. 2002), as modified on denial of reh'g, (Oct. 24, 2002) and judgment aff'd, 211 Ill. 2d 317, 285 Ill. Dec. 519, 812 N.E.2d 339 (2004); and *People v. Peete*, 318 Ill. App. 3d 961, 966–67, 252 Ill. Dec. 821, 743 N.E.2d 689 (4th Dist. 2001). Therefore, it is arguable that Federal Rule of Evidence 403 can be considered as persuasive authority in Illinois.

People v. Holman, 257 Ill. App. 3d 1031, 1033–34, 196 Ill. Dec. 457, 630 N.E.2d 154 (2d Dist. 1994) (evidence is admissible if it is relevant and if the prejudicial impact does not substantially outweigh its probative value).

For expanded citations on the exclusion of prejudicial evidence, see § 2:1 to § 2:4.

§ 8:73 Supporting authorities—Where witness was equally available to testify

Lisowski v. MacNeal Memorial Hosp. Ass'n, 381 Ill. App. 3d 275, 319 Ill. Dec. 440, 885 N.E.2d 1120 (1st Dist. 2008), appeal denied, 229 Ill. 2d 626, 325 Ill. Dec. 5, 897 N.E.2d 253 (2008) (party was not entitled to the missing witness instruction when that party could have subpoenaed the witness).

Lisowski v. MacNeal Memorial Hosp. Ass'n, 381 Ill. App. 3d

275, 319 Ill. Dec. 440, 885 N.E.2d 1120 (1st Dist. 2008), appeal denied, 229 Ill. 2d 626, 325 Ill. Dec. 5, 897 N.E.2d 253 (2008) (party was not entitled to the missing witness instruction due to the absence of the opposing party's expert when the complaining party could have subpoenaed the witness).

People v. Munday, 280 Ill. 32, 40–49, 117 N.E. 286 (1917) (a party cannot comment upon another party's failure to call a witness, where the witness was equally available to be called to testify by both parties).

See generally, Illinois Pattern Civil Jury Instruction number 5.01, which states:

> FAILURE TO PRODUCE EVIDENCE OR A WITNESS
>
> If a party to this case has failed [to offer evidence] [to produce a witness] within his power to produce, you may infer that the [evidence] [testimony of the witness] would be adverse to that party if you believe each of the following elements:
>
> 1. The [evidence] [witness] was under the control of the party and could have been produced by the exercise of reasonable diligence.
>
> 2. The [evidence] [witness] was not equally available to an adverse party.
>
> 3. A reasonably prudent person under the same or similar circumstances would have [offered the evidence] [produced the witness] if he believed [it to be] [the testimony would be] favorable to him.
>
> 4. No reasonable excuse for the failure has been shown.

§ 8:74 Supporting authorities—Where comments would invite speculation

Adami v. Belmonte, 302 Ill. App. 3d 17, 25-26, 235 Ill. Dec. 135, 704 N.E.2d 708 (1st Dist. 1998) (trial judge properly declined to give Illinois Pattern Jury Instruction 5.01 [the missing witness instruction] when the missing witness was not adverse to the non-producing party and the testimony would have been cumulative).

Thompson v. Abbott Laboratories, 193 Ill. App. 3d 188, 201–04, 140 Ill. Dec. 423, 549 N.E.2d 1295 (2d Dist. 1990) (trial judge properly declined to give the missing witness instruction when the witnesses at issue would have been cumulative to other witnesses and when the instruction could have implied to the jurors that one party was hiding evidence from the other).

People v. Munday, 280 Ill. 32, 40–49, 117 N.E. 286 (1917) (improper to comment on the defendant's failure to call his codefendants to testify and the comment improperly shifted the burden of proof).

See Illinois Pattern Civil Jury Instruction number 5.01, supra.

§ 8:75 Supporting authorities—Where other adequate testimony

Adami v. Belmonte, 302 Ill. App. 3d 17, 25-26, 235 Ill. Dec. 135, 704 N.E.2d 708 (1st Dist. 1998) (trial judge properly declined to give Illinois Pattern Jury Instruction 5.01 [the missing witness instruction] when the missing witness was not adverse to the non-producing party and the testimony would have been cumulative).

Thompson v. Abbott Laboratories, 193 Ill. App. 3d 188, 201–04, 140 Ill. Dec. 423, 549 N.E.2d 1295 (2d Dist. 1990) (trial judge properly declined to give the missing witness instruction when the witnesses at issue would have been cumulative to other witnesses and when the instruction could have implied to the jurors that one party was hiding evidence from the other).

See Illinois Pattern Civil Jury Instruction number 5.01, supra; see also § 2:20 to § 2:33, supra (exclusion of cumulative testimony).

§ 8:76 Supporting authorities—Other grounds

Other possible grounds for excluding comment on non-called witnesses include:

- Confusing or misleading (§ 2:9 to § 2:12)
- Solely intended to create an emotional bias (§ 2:13 to § 2:19)
- Irrelevant (§ 3:1 to § 3:10)
- Collateral to issues in case (§ 3:11 to § 3:21)
- Inadmissible hearsay (§ 8:78 to § 8:89)

§ 8:77 Opposition citations—Generally

White v. Garlock Sealing Technologies, LLC, 373 Ill. App. 3d 309, 330–31, 311 Ill. Dec. 570, 869 N.E.2d 244 (4th Dist. 2007), appeal denied, 225 Ill. 2d 679, 314 Ill. Dec. 838, 875 N.E.2d 1125 (2007) (trial court had discretion to instruct the jury with the missing witness instruction).

Bauer ex rel. Bauer v. Memorial Hosp., 377 Ill. App. 3d 895, 915–17, 316 Ill. Dec. 411, 879 N.E.2d 478 (5th Dist. 2007), appeal denied, 227 Ill. 2d 577, 321 Ill. Dec. 249, 888 N.E.2d 1182 (2008) (missing witness instruction was proper when the defendant failed to produce several of its employees).

Kersey v. Rush Trucking, Inc., 344 Ill. App. 3d 690, 279 Ill. Dec. 559, 800 N.E.2d 847 (2d Dist. 2003) (trial court improperly failed to give missing witness instruction where defense counsel told jury in opening statement that an expert would be called to counter plaintiff's expert but did not present such an expert; the court rejected defendant's argument that the expert's testimony was cumulative where one of the expert's opinions supported plaintiff's theory).

Roeseke v. Pryor, 152 Ill. App. 3d 771, 780–81, 105 Ill. Dec. 642, 504 N.E.2d 927 (1st Dist. 1987) (trial judge has discretion to instruct the jury that they can assume that evidence would be adverse to the party who failed to present it when that party controlled the evidence and did not offer a reason for failing to produce it and when it is clear that the party would have produced such evidence if it was favorable).

Tonarelli v. Gibbons, 121 Ill. App. 3d 1042, 1046–48, 77 Ill. Dec. 408, 460 N.E.2d 464 (1st Dist. 1984) (trial judge properly gave missing witness instruction when the opposing party had access to the witness and had indicated that the witness would be presented and the witness was hostile to the party requesting the instruction).

See Illinois Pattern Civil Jury Instruction number 5.01, supra.

I. MOTION TO EXCLUDE HEARSAY STATEMENTS

◆ **Note:** The hearsay rule and the rule's many exceptions are an expansive area of evidence law that cannot be briefly encapsulated in this text. The citations below provide only general support for a motion to exclude hearsay statements, or an opposition to such a motion. For a detailed discussion of the hearsay rule and hearsay exceptions, see Robert S. Hunter, Illinois Practice Library, Trial Handbook for Illinois Lawyers Civil 6th Ed. (1989), Chapters 51 and 52 and the Federal Rules of Evidence. See also Federal Rules of Evidence 803 and 804.

For citations supporting the exclusion of written hearsay, see §§ 4:26 et seq., supra, in this text.

§ 8:78 Suggested motion text

[Name of moving party] hereby moves this Court for an order excluding any and all evidence, references to evidence, testimony or argument relating to *[describe hearsay evidence to be excluded]*. The motion is based upon the grounds that the evidence is hearsay not within any recognized exception, and is therefore inadmissible.

§ 8:79 Motion summary

This motion is used to exclude hearsay statements that do not fall within one of the recognized hearsay exceptions. The motion is based upon the authority of Illinois case law and certain statutory exceptions to the hearsay rule. *People v. Thompson*, 327 Ill. App. 3d 1061, 1065, 262 Ill. Dec. 595, 765 N.E.2d 1203 (2d Dist. 2002).

§ 8:80 Supporting authorities—General authority for exclusion

Berry v. American Standard, Inc., 382 Ill.App.3d 895, 897–905, 888 N.E.2d 740 (5th Dist. 2008) (a deceased party's discovery deposition that was taken prior to the party's death but not under the belief that the party's death was imminent was inadmissible hearsay).

Dukes v. Pneumo Abex Corp., 386 Ill.App.3d 425, 439–41, 900 N.E.2d 1128 (4th Dist. 2008) (when there was insufficient evidence to support a finding of a conspiracy, statements of the alleged co-conspirators were inadmissible hearsay).

Ahmed v. Pickwick Place Owners' Ass'n, 385 Ill.App.3d 874, 890–91, 896 N.E.2d 854 (1st Dist. 2008) (police officer's opinion regarding the cause of certain injuries to a deceased individual was speculative and based upon hearsay and therefore was inadmissible).

Lisowski v. MacNeal Memorial Hosp. Ass'n, 381 Ill. App. 3d 275, 319 Ill. Dec. 440, 885 N.E.2d 1120 (1st Dist. 2008), appeal denied, 229 Ill. 2d 626, 325 Ill. Dec. 5, 897 N.E.2d 253 (2008) (cross examination that was hearsay, not based upon the evidence and beyond the scope of direct, was properly stricken).

Longstreet v. Cottrell, Inc., 374 Ill. App. 3d 549, 550–57, 312 Ill. Dec. 672, 871 N.E.2d 72 (5th Dist. 2007), appeal denied, 226 Ill. 2d 587, 316 Ill. Dec. 544, 879 N.E.2d 932 (2007) (the discovery deposition of a deceased victim was inadmissible hearsay).

People v. House, 377 Ill. App. 3d 9, 18-20, 316 Ill. Dec. 147, 878 N.E.2d 1171 (1st Dist. 2007), appeal denied, 226 Ill. 2d 623, 317 Ill. Dec. 506, 882 N.E.2d 80 (2008) (prior consistent statement was inadmissible hearsay).

In re E.H., 377 Ill. App. 3d 406, 413–16, 318 Ill. Dec. 167, 883 N.E.2d 1 (1st Dist. 2007), as modified on denial of reh'g, (Dec. 20, 2007) (trial court abused its discretion by admitting the hearsay statements of certain minors without verifying the reliability of the statements as is required by statute).

People v. Evans, 373 Ill. App. 3d 948, 963–66, 311 Ill. Dec. 907, 869 N.E.2d 920 (1st Dist. 2007), appeal denied, 225 Ill. 2d 648, 314 Ill. Dec. 830, 875 N.E.2d 1117 (2007) (testimony regarding what another person at the scene stated was properly excluded as hearsay).

People v. Calderon, 369 Ill. App. 3d 221, 234, 307 Ill. Dec. 486, 859 N.E.2d 1163 (2d Dist. 2006) (trial court properly excluded a witness' prior consistent statement as inadmissible hearsay).

Gunn v. Sobucki, 216 Ill. 2d 602, 297 Ill. Dec. 414, 837 N.E.2d 865, 866–75 (2005) (testimony that was offered to contradict a bill of sale was improper where it violated the Dead-Man's Act).

Camco, Inc. v. Lowery, 362 Ill. App. 3d 421, 435–36, 298 Ill. Dec. 332, 839 N.E.2d 655 (1st Dist. 2005) (evidence regarding an officer's deposition testimony that was based upon information contained in a lab report was improper hearsay) (harmless error).

People v. Thompson, 327 Ill. App. 3d 1061, 1065, 262 Ill. Dec. 595, 765 N.E.2d 1203 (2d Dist. 2002) (defines "hearsay" as "testimony of an out-of-court statement offered to establish the truth of the matter asserted therein and whose value thus depends upon the credibility of the out-of-court declarant").

People v. Velasco, 216 Ill. App. 3d 578, 583–86, 159 Ill. Dec. 147, 575 N.E.2d 954 (4th Dist. 1991) (videotape of an out of court statement of the victim was inadmissible hearsay because no hearsay exception applied which would allow it to be admitted).

§ 8:81 Supporting authorities—Purpose of rule

In re E.H., 299 Ill. App. 3d 42, 50-51, 233 Ill. Dec. 336, 700 N.E.2d 1044 (1st Dist. 1998) (the purpose of the hearsay rule is that hearsay evidence depends upon the credibility determination of a witness who is not in court to be cross-examined as to the evidence, but evidence is not hearsay if it is not offered for the truth of its contents).

§ 8:82 Opposing authorities—Generally

Beard v. Barron, 379 Ill. App. 3d 1, 11-16, 317 Ill. Dec. 906, 882 N.E.2d 1062 (1st Dist. 2008), appeal pending, (May 1, 2008) and appeal denied, 228 Ill. 2d 529, 321 Ill. Dec. 554, 889 N.E.2d 1114 (2008) (plaintiff opened the door to cross examination about conversations with a deceased person).

Townsend v. Fassbinder, 372 Ill. App. 3d 890, 906, 310 Ill. Dec. 470, 866 N.E.2d 631 (2d Dist. 2007) (statement of a party's agent that was contained in a letter was admissible as an admission).

In re E.H., 299 Ill. App. 3d 42, 50-51, 233 Ill. Dec. 336, 700 N.E.2d 1044 (1st Dist. 1998) (the purpose of the hearsay rule is that hearsay evidence depends upon the credibility determination of a witness who is not in court to be cross-examined as to the evidence, but evidence is not hearsay if it is not offered for the truth of its contents).

§ 8:83 Opposing authorities—Non-hearsay evidence

People v. Gonzalez, 379 Ill. App. 3d 941, 318 Ill. Dec. 673, 884 N.E.2d 228, 238–39 (1st Dist. 2008), appeal pending, (May 1, 2008) and appeal denied, 228 Ill. 2d 541, 321 Ill. Dec. 558, 889 N.E.2d 1118 (2008) (evidence of a statement that was not offered for the truth of what was asserted but was offered to demonstrate why the defendant made a subsequent statement, was not hearsay).

Luss v. Village of Forest Park, 377 Ill. App. 3d 318, 333–35, 316 Ill. Dec. 169, 878 N.E.2d 1193 (1st Dist. 2007) (statement that was offered for the purpose of explaining another person's belief, was not offered for the truth of the statement and thus, it was not hearsay).

Adams v. Sarah Bush Lincoln Health Center, 369 Ill. App. 3d 988, 314 Ill. Dec. 190, 874 N.E.2d 100 (4th Dist. 2007) (evidence that was not being offered to prove the truth of the matter asserted did not constitute hearsay).

People v. Fenelon, 14 Ill. App. 3d 622, 623–26, 303 N.E.2d 38 (2d Dist. 1973) (trial judge properly admitted the videotaped portion of the defendant performing sobriety tests. The appellate court noted that the videotaped portion was non-testimonial evidence).

§ 8:84 Opposing authorities—Non-assertive conduct

In re E.H., 299 Ill. App. 3d 42, 50-51, 233 Ill. Dec. 336, 700 N.E.2d 1044 (1st Dist. 1998) (officer could testify to another person's hearsay conduct to explain the course of the officer's investigation).

Leonardi v. Loyola University of Chicago, 168 Ill. 2d 83, 98-99, 212 Ill. Dec. 968, 658 N.E.2d 450 (1995) (not hearsay to introduce an out of court statement for the purpose of demonstrating why the witness took certain actions).

§ 8:85 Opposing authorities—Multiple hearsay

Kress Corp. v. Industrial Com'n, 190 Ill. App. 3d 72, 78, 137 Ill. Dec. 285, 545 N.E.2d 1046 (3d Dist. 1989) (two or more exceptions to the hearsay rule may be used to make double or multiple hearsay evidence admissible).

Counsel should keep in mind that evidence can have several levels of hearsay. For the evidence to be admissible, each level must be admissible on its own, as an exception to the hearsay rule of exclusion. For example, a plaintiff's statement contained in medical records may be admissible if the records constitute business records (or an admission by a party opponent) and the plaintiff's statement was to a physician for the purpose of medical treatment. If the statement was for another purpose, it may not be admissible, even if a proper foundation has been made for the admission of the records themselves.

§ 8:86 Opposing authorities—Hearsay used for impeachment

People v. Gonzalez, 379 Ill. App. 3d 941, 318 Ill. Dec. 673, 884 N.E.2d 228, 240–41 (1st Dist. 2008), appeal pending, (May 1, 2008) and appeal denied, 228 Ill. 2d 541, 321 Ill. Dec. 558, 889 N.E.2d 1118 (2008) (prior consistent statement was admissible to rebut a charge of recent fabrication).

Lopez v. Northwestern Memorial Hosp., 375 Ill. App. 3d 637, 648, 313 Ill. Dec. 796, 873 N.E.2d 420 (1st Dist. 2007) (individual could be impeached through the use of deposition testimony that was inconsistent with the individual's trial testimony).

People v. Ursery, 364 Ill. App. 3d 680, 687–88, 302 Ill. Dec. 146, 848 N.E.2d 146 (5th Dist. 2006) (evidence regarding a prior consistent statement was permissible when it was used to rebut a defendant's claim that the witness had a motive to testify falsely, where the statement was made before the alleged motive arose).

People v. Rojas, 359 Ill. App. 3d 392, 402–03, 295 Ill. Dec. 932, 834 N.E.2d 513 (1st Dist. 2005) (the trial court had discretion to allow a witness to testify about intimidating statements that were made by the defendant where used to explain the witness' prior inconsistent statement).

People v. Cuadrado, 214 Ill. 2d 79, 291 Ill. Dec. 638, 824 N.E.2d 214, 220–21 (2005) (testimony regarding a witness' prior consistent statement was admissible to rebut the defendant's claim that the witness had recently fabricated the testimony and had a motive to lie).

Boyce v. Risch, 276 Ill. App. 3d 274, 277–79, 212 Ill. Dec. 800, 657 N.E.2d 1145 (1st Dist. 1995) (a prior inconsistent statement of a witness is admissible for impeachment).

Hapke v. Brandon, 343 Ill. App. 524, 526–29, 99 N.E.2d 636 (4th Dist. 1951) (a witness' written prior inconsistent statements should have been admitted for impeachment of the witness).

Williams v. Matlin, 328 Ill. App. 645, 647–48, 66 N.E.2d 719 (1st Dist. 1946) (proper to introduce a statement prepared by an insurance investigator and signed by the witness, as impeachment of that witness' testimony).

The following citations may be useful here, but readers are urged to carefully note the differences between usage in civil and criminal cases.

725 ILCS 5/115-10.1 states:

> Admissibility of Prior Inconsistent Statements. In all *criminal cases*, evidence of a statement made by a witness is not made inadmissible by the hearsay rule if
>
> (a) the statement is inconsistent with his testimony at the hearing or trial, and
>
> (b) the witness is subject to cross-examination concerning the statement, and
>
> (c) the statement—
>
> (1) was made under oath at a trial, hearing, or other proceeding, or
>
> (2) narrates, describes, or explains an event or condition of which the witness had personal knowledge, and
>
> (A) the statement is proved to have been written or signed by the witness, or
>
> (B) the witness acknowledged under oath the making of the statement either in his testimony at the hearing or trial in which the admission into evidence of the prior statement is being sought, or at a trial, hearing, or other proceeding, or
>
> (C) the statement is proved to have been accurately recorded by a tape recorder, videotape recording, or any other similar electronic means of sound recording.
>
> Nothing in this Section shall render a prior inconsistent statement inadmissible for purposes of impeachment because such statement was not recorded or otherwise fails to meet the criteria set forth herein. (Emphasis added.)

§ 8:87 Opposing authorities—Hearsay exceptions

◆ **Note:** this text does not explore in detail the vast number of possible exceptions to the hearsay rule. For expanded citations, see Robert S. Hunter, Illinois Practice Library, Trial

Handbook for Illinois Lawyers Civil 6th Ed. (1989), Chapters 51 and 52. See also Federal Rules of Evidence 803 and 804.

Roszak v. Kankakee Firefighters' Pension Bd., 376 Ill. App. 3d 130, 143–45, 314 Ill. Dec. 993, 875 N.E.2d 1280 (3d Dist. 2007) (statements made to treating physicians for the purpose of diagnosis or treatment are admissible as an exception to the hearsay rule).

Townsend v. Fassbinder, 372 Ill. App. 3d 890, 906, 310 Ill. Dec. 470, 866 N.E.2d 631 (2d Dist. 2007) (statement of a party's agent that was contained in a letter was admissible as an admission).

First Assist, Inc. v. Industrial Com'n, 371 Ill. App. 3d 488, 311 Ill. Dec. 77, 867 N.E.2d 1063 (4th Dist. 2007) (an admission made by an employee of a party during a telephone conversation was an admission by a party-opponent and was not hearsay).

People v. Bueno, 358 Ill. App. 3d 143, 157–63, 293 Ill. Dec. 819, 829 N.E.2d 402 (2d Dist. 2005) (a witness' prior inconsistent statement was admissible as substantive evidence under the residual exception to the hearsay rule).

Camco, Inc. v. Lowery, 362 Ill. App. 3d 421, 434–35, 298 Ill. Dec. 332, 839 N.E.2d 655 (1st Dist. 2005) (a lab report was relevant and admissible under a statutory hearsay exception).

Zaragoza v. Ebenroth, 331 Ill. App. 3d 139, 141–43, 264 Ill. Dec. 542, 770 N.E.2d 1238 (3d Dist. 2002)) (exceptions to the hearsay rule are based upon instances where the type of evidence offered is reliable and trustworthy).

People v. Velasco, 216 Ill. App. 3d 578, 583–86, 159 Ill. Dec. 147, 575 N.E.2d 954 (4th Dist. 1991) (videotape of an out of court statement of the victim was inadmissible hearsay because no hearsay exception applied which would allow it to be admitted) (note that this court considered, discussed and rejected application of the following exceptions: excited utterance; spontaneous declaration; and corroborative complaint under 725 ILCS 115-10).

Flath v. Madison Metal Services, Inc., 212 Ill. App. 3d 367, 377, 156 Ill. Dec. 496, 570 N.E.2d 1218 (5th Dist. 1991) (party offering hearsay evidence has the burden to establish that it is subject to an exception to the hearsay rule).

§ 8:88 Opposing authorities—Hearsay exceptions—Purpose of hearsay exceptions

Zaragoza v. Ebenroth, 331 Ill. App. 3d 139, 141–43, 264 Ill.

Dec. 542, 770 N.E.2d 1238 (3d Dist. 2002) (exceptions to the hearsay rule are based upon instances where the type of evidence offered is reliable and trustworthy).

§ 8:89 Opposing authorities—Hearsay exceptions—Examples of exceptions applicable to hearsay statements

Below are several examples of statutory exceptions applicable to hearsay statements. Note that this list is by no means exhaustive and case law provides additional exceptions. See generally, Robert S. Hunter, Illinois Practice Library, Trial Handbook for Illinois Lawyers Civil 6th Ed. (1989), Chapters 51 and 52. See also Federal Rules of Evidence 803 and 804.

Dead Man's Act:

735 ILCS 5/8-201 states:

Dead-Man's Act. In the trial of any action in which any party sues or defends as the representative of a deceased person or person under a legal disability, no adverse party or person directly interested in the action shall be allowed to testify on his or her own behalf to any conversation with the deceased or person under legal disability or to any event which took place in the presence of the deceased or person under legal disability, except in the following instances:

(a) If any person testifies on behalf of the representative to any conversation with the deceased or person under legal disability or to any event which took place in the presence of the deceased or person under legal disability, any adverse party or interested person, if otherwise competent, may testify concerning the same conversation or event.

(b) If the deposition of the deceased or person under legal disability is admitted in evidence on behalf of the representative, any adverse party or interested person, if otherwise competent, may testify concerning the same matters admitted in evidence.

(c) Any testimony competent under Section 8-401 of this Act, is not barred by this Section.

(d) No person shall be barred from testifying as to any fact relating to the heirship of a decedent.

As used in this Section:

(a) "Person under legal disability" means any person who is adjudged by the court in the pending civil action to be unable to testify by reason of mental illness, mental retardation or deterioration of mentality.

(b) "Representative" means any executor, administrator, heir or legatee of a deceased person and any guardian or trustee of any such heir or legatee, or a guardian or guardian ad litem for a person under legal disability.

(c) "Person directly interested in the action" or "interested person" does not include a person who is interested solely as executor, trustee or in any other fiduciary capacity, whether or not he or she receives or expects to receive compensation for acting in that capacity.

(d) This Section applies to proceedings filed on or after October 1, 1973.

People v. $5,608 U.S. Currency, 359 Ill. App. 3d 891, 892–96, 296 Ill. Dec. 567, 835 N.E.2d 920 (2d Dist. 2005) (an officer who had arrested an individual, who later died, was not an interested party for purposes of a forfeiture action and, therefore, the officer's testimony was not prohibited by the Dead-Man's Act).

Statement of Prior Identification:

725 ILCS 5/115-12 states:

Substantive Admissibility of Prior Identification. A statement is not rendered inadmissible by the hearsay rule if (a) the declarant testifies at the trial or hearing, and (b) the declarant is subject to cross-examination concerning the statement, and (c) the statement is one of identification of a person made after perceiving him. (note that this Statute falls within the Code of Criminal Procedure).

Certain Abuse Cases [725 ILCS 5/115-10]:

725 ILCS 5/115-10 states as follows:

Certain hearsay exceptions.

(a) In a prosecution for a physical or sexual act perpetrated upon or against a child under the age of 13, or a person who was a moderately, severely, or profoundly mentally retarded person as defined in this Code and in Section 2-10.1 of the Criminal Code of 1961 at the time the act was committed, including but not limited to prosecutions for violations of Sections 12-13 through 12-16 of the Criminal Code of 1961 and prosecutions for violations of Sections 10-1 (kidnapping), 10-2 (aggravated kidnapping), 10-3 (unlawful restraint), 10-3.1 (aggravated unlawful restraint), 10-4 (forcible detention), 10-5 (child abduction), 10-6 (harboring a runaway), 10-7 (aiding and abetting child abduction), 11-9 (public indecency), 11-11 (sexual relations within families), 11-21 (harmful material), 12-1 (assault), 12-2 (aggravated assault), 12-3 (battery), 12-3.2 (domestic battery), 12-4 (aggravated battery), 12-4.1 (heinous battery), 12-4.2 (aggravated battery with a firearm), 12-4.3 (aggravated battery of a child), 12-4.7 (drug induced infliction of great bodily harm), 12-5 (reckless conduct), 12-6 (intimidation), 12-6.1 (compelling organization membership of persons), 12-7.1 (hate crime), 12-7.3 (stalking), 12-7.4 (aggravated stalking), 12-10 (tattooing body of minor), 12-11 (home invasion), 12-21.5 (child abandonment), 12-21.6 (endangering the life or health of a child) or 12-32 (ritual mutilation) of the Criminal Code of 1961 or any sex offense as defined in subsection (B) of Section 2 of the Sex Offender Registration Act, the following evidence shall be admitted as an exception to the hearsay rule:

(1) testimony by the victim of an out of court statement made by the victim that he or she complained of such act to another; and

(2) testimony of an out of court statement made by the victim describing any complaint of such act or matter or detail pertaining to any act which is an element of an offense which is the subject of a prosecution for a sexual or physical act against that victim.

(b) Such testimony shall only be admitted if:

(1) The court finds in a hearing conducted outside the presence of the jury that the time, content, and circumstances of the statement provide sufficient safeguards of reliability; and

(2) The child or moderately, severely, or profoundly mentally retarded person either:

(A) testifies at the proceeding; or

(B) is unavailable as a witness and there is corroborative evidence of the act which is the subject of the statement; and

(3) In a case involving an offense perpetrated against a child under the age of 13, the out of court statement was made before the victim attained 13 years of age or within 3 months after the commission of the offense, whichever occurs later, but the statement may be admitted regardless of the age of the victim at the time of the proceeding.

(c) If a statement is admitted pursuant to this Section, the court shall instruct the jury that it is for the jury to determine the weight and credibility to be given the statement and that, in making the determination, it shall consider the age and maturity of the child, or the intellectual capabilities of the moderately, severely, or profoundly mentally retarded person, the nature of the statement, the circumstances under which the statement was made, and any other relevant factor.

(d) The proponent of the statement shall give the adverse party reasonable notice of his intention to offer the statement and the particulars of the statement.

(e) Statements described in paragraphs (1) and (2) of subsection (a) shall not be excluded on the basis that they were obtained as a result of interviews conducted pursuant to a protocol adopted by a Child Advocacy Advisory Board as set forth in subsections (c), (d), and (e) of Section 3 of the Children's Advocacy Center Act or that an interviewer or witness to the interview was or is an employee, agent, or investigator of a State's Attorney's office.

◆ **Important note:** In the case of *In re E.H.*, 355 Ill. App.

3d 564, 291 Ill. Dec. 443, 823 N.E.2d 1029 (1st Dist. 2005), judgment vacated, 224 Ill. 2d 172, 309 Ill. Dec. 1, 863 N.E.2d 231 (2006), the Illinois Appellate Court for the First District determined that 725 ILCS 5/115-10 was unconstitutional, pursuant to the holding by the United States Supreme Court in *Crawford v. Washington*, 541 U.S. 36, 124 S. Ct. 1354, 158 L. Ed. 2d 177, 63 Fed. R. Evid. Serv. 1077 (2004). However, the Illinois Supreme Court vacated the appellate court judgment because it should not have reached the issue of constitutionality without exhausting other potential grounds for resolving the case. *In re E.H.*, 224 Ill. 2d 172, 309 Ill. Dec. 1, 863 N.E.2d 231 (2006).

II. SAMPLE MOTIONS

§ 8:90 Motion to exclude testimony of unqualified medical expert witness; physician's assistant

[Insert caption here]

PLAINTIFF'S [NUMBER] MOTION IN LIMINE
The Testimony of Defendants' Expert, [name of expert witness], Should be Barred

NOW COMES the Plaintiff, *[name of Plaintiff]*, Special Administrator of the Estate, by *[his/her]* attorneys, *[name of Plaintiff's attorney]*, and prior to selection of the jury in this case, respectfully moves this Honorable Court, in limine, to enter and order on the following matters:

Factual Summary

This is a medical malpractice action arising from the death of *[name of deceased]* on *[date of death]*. *[Deceased]* was *[age at time of death]* years of age at the time of *[his/her]* death. *[Deceased]* and *[his/her]* family are of African ethnicity hailing from Nigeria. The family immigrated to the United States in 1998.

Prior to coming to the United States, a Nigerian physician diagnosed *[Deceased]* as having "well controlled mild seasonal asthma." Subsequent to the family's arrival in the States, *[Deceased's]* asthma was controlled by *[his/her]* use of an inhaler and steroids on an as needed basis.

It is important to note that after moving to the United States and prior to *[date of death]*, *[Deceased's]* asthma never required *[him/her]* to seek care at an emergency department, urgent care facility or any physician's office.

On the morning of *[date of death]*, however, *[Deceased]* began experiencing asthmatic symptoms. *[He/She]* was unable to eat *[his/her]* breakfast and was wheezing. As a result, *[Deceased's]* mother, *[name of mother]*, took *[Deceased]* to the *[name and location of clinic]*. At the clinic, Defendant, Physician's Assistant *[name of defendant]* undertook *[Deceased's]* care and treatment. Prior to that day, Defendant did not have the opportunity to treat *[Deceased]* for any condition, let alone asthma. *[Deceased's]* mother informed Defendant that *[Deceased]* took medications to manage *[his/her]* seasonal asthma and that *[he/she]* had taken those medications on *[date of death]*. Defendant noted that *[Deceased]* had a history of mild seasonal asthma. On *[date of death]*, Defendant diagnosed *[Deceased]* as having an "acute asthma exacerbation." Subsequently, Defendant administered the first of two nebulizer" breathing treatments to *[Deceased]*. Following the second nebulizer, Defendant discharged *[Deceased]* from *[his/her]* care with prescriptions for a home nebulizer and oral steroids. Defendant testified that upon discharge, *[Deceased]* was "moving around normally" and was improving, but still exhibited signs and symptoms of an acute asthma exacerbation. Defendant agrees that *[Deceased]* was "clearing" but had not cleared at the time of *[his/her]* discharge. Further, Defendant stated that when *[he/she]* discharged *[him/her]*, *[Deceased]* was wheezing.

Subsequent to *[his/her]* discharge, *[Deceased]* and *[Deceased's mother]* traveled to *[name of pharmacy]* pharmacy to pick up the prescribed medication and home nebulizer unit. *[Deceased's mother]* and *[Deceased]* experienced a delay at the pharmacy. An issue arose over whether or not a home nebulizer unit was available at the pharmacy and whether or not the insurance company would approve payment for the device. Ultimately, *[Deceased's mother]* chose to rent a nebulizer unit that *[name of pharmacy]* Pharmacy would deliver later in the day. Thereafter, *[Deceased's mother]* and *[Deceased]* traveled home. Shortly after arriving at their residence, *[Deceased's father]* returned home. At that time, *[Deceased's]* condition had worsened. *[His/Her]* parents immediately decided to take *[Deceased]* back to the clinic. Unfortunately, *[Deceased]* suffered respiratory distress and lost consciousness. An ambulance was summoned and *[Deceased]* was transferred to *[name of hospital]*. *[Deceased]* died later that day. *[His/Her]* cause of death was respiratory distress secondary to acute asthma exacerbation.

I. Defendants' expert, Dr. Finley W. *[name of Witness]*, Jr. cannot testify in this case.

A. Sullivan v. Edward Hosp., 209 Ill. 2d 100, 282 Ill. Dec. 348, 806 N.E.2d 645 (2004) prohibits *[name of Witness]* from testifying as to matters concerning the standard of care applicable to Physician's Assistant Defendant.

1. This Court should enter an order barring the testimony of *[name of Witness]*, M.D. as it relates to the standard of care applicable to Defendant, PA. Dr. *[name of Witness]* was disclosed as defendants' expert witness. Dr. *[name of Witness']* witness disclosure and deposition testimony make it clear that Dr. *[name of Witness]* intends to offer testimony as to the standard of care applicable to Physician's Assistant Defendant's conduct in this case. Obviously, Dr. *[name of Witness]* will opine that Defendant's conduct and actions as a Physician's Assistant were proper and within the standard of care applicable to a practicing Physician's Assistant. However, *[name of Witness]* is not a physician's assistant. Rather, he is a licensed physician practicing family medicine in *[place of practice]*. Consequently, he is incompetent to testify as to matters related to the standard of care of a Physician's Assistant.

2. A Physician's Assistant is a distinct profession, having separate and unique educational obligations, curriculum, practice standards and most importantly, licensure. In Illinois, Physician's Assistants are licensed by the Illinois Department of Financial and Professional Regulation. The Legislature has meticulously regulated the "PA" profession. 225 ILCS 95/11 et. seq. sets forth the statutory requirements for eligibility to legally practice as a PA in Illinois. To say the least, the Legislature has enacted detailed and express laws governing a PA's role and practice in the medical field. There is no question, both legally and practically, that a PA is a separate and distinct entity who crafts *[his/her]* trade pursuant to valid licensure.

3. The Illinois Supreme Court has clearly stated that in order for a medical expert to testify to the standard of care for a particular school of medicine, the expert witness must be licensed within that school of medicine. *Sullivan v. Edward Hosp.*, 209 Ill. 2d 100, 282 Ill. Dec. 348, 806 N.E.2d 645 (2004). The test that a trial court must apply regarding the admissibility of expert testimony is clear: it is a two-step analysis whereby the court must determine (1) whether the expert is a licensed member of the school of medicine about which *[he/she]* proposes to testify; and (2) the expert witness must show that *[he/she]* is familiar with the methods, procedures and

treatments ordinarily observed by other practitioners, in either the defendant practitioner's community or a similar community. *Sullivan v. Edward Hosp.*, 209 Ill. 2d 100, 114, 282 Ill. Dec. 348, 806 N.E.2d 645 (2004); citing, *Purtill v. Hess*, 111 Ill. 2d 229, 95 Ill. Dec. 305, 489 N.E.2d 867 (1986) and *Dolan v. Galluzzo*, 77 Ill. 2d 279, 32 Ill. Dec. 900, 396 N.E.2d 13 (1979). In other words, the party intending to offer the expert's testimony must establish two separate and distinct requisite elements before the expert may testify. These two elements (licensure and familiarity) within the standard of care are mutually exclusive. That is, if the expert physician fails to satisfy either of these foundational requirements, the trial court must disallow the expert's testimony. *Sullivan*, 209 Ill.2d 114-115.

4. In Sullivan, a physician, Dr. Barnhart, was disclosed by the plaintiff to testify as to the standard of care of a registered nurse. Specifically. Dr. Barnhart was to testify that the nurse in question deviated from the standard of care by (1) failing to communicate her concern of a fall risk to the injured plaintiff; and (2) failing to employ the use of a fall preventative device in the case. *Sullivan*, 209 Ill.2d at 106. The trial court deemed Dr. Barnhart incompetent to testify as to the standard of care of a nurse. As a result, it struck Dr. Barnhart's testimony concerning the defendant nurse's alleged deviations from the standard of care. The trial court's rationale was that Dr. Barnhart was not a licensed nurse; therefore, he was incompetent to testify as to the standard of care applicable to a nurse. *Sullivan*, 209 Ill.2d at 106. The Appellate Court affirmed the trial court's ruling. The plaintiff appealed to the Supreme Court of Illinois. Relying on *Purtill* and *Dolan*, the Supreme Court affirmed the lower courts in certain and unequivocal terms. Plaintiff's position before the Supreme Court was that Illinois law no longer required a medical expert to be a licensed member of the school of medicine about which the expert proposes to testify. In support of that argument, plaintiff relied on the Supreme Court's holding in *Jones v. O'Young*, 154 Ill. 2d 39, 180 Ill. Dec. 330, 607 N.E.2d 224 (1992). In sum, the plaintiff's argument was that Jones "retreats from any rigid, formalistic rule that a health professional expert witness must be a licensed member of the school of medicine about which the expert proposed to testify." *Sullivan*, 209 Ill.2d at 114. In summarily rejecting plaintiff's position, the Court astutely stated:

> We cannot accept this argument. *Jones* clearly reaffirms this Court's decision in *Purtill* describing two foundational requirements: that the health care expert witness must be a

> licensed member of the school of medicine about which the expert proposes to testify; and that the expert must be familiar with the methods, procedures and treatments ordinarily observed by other health-care providers in either the defendant's community or a similar community. Indeed, the very next sentences in *Jones* following the italicized sentence upon which the plaintiff relies state: 'If the plaintiff fails to satisfy either of the foundational requirements of *Purtill* the trial court must disallow the expert's testimony.' *Sullivan*, 209 Ill.2d at 115.

5. The Sullivan Court addressed head-on the argument that a physician may testify as to a nursing standard of care because "there is nothing which a nurse can do which a doctor cannot do." *Sullivan*, 209 Ill.2d at 120-121. In form, this argument appears completely logical. However, as the appellate court recognized (and the Supreme Court expressly affirmed), in application, this statement's logic fails:

> Dr. Barnhart is not a licensed member of the nursing profession. To allow a doctor to testify as to the standard of care applicable to the nursing profession implicates the risks raised by Dolan namely the imposition of a higher standard of care and the muddling and mixing of various tenets and practices unique to each profession. *Sullivan*, 209 Ill.2d at 123.

The Court also based its decision on the fact that the Legislature had acted to designate a unique licensing and regulatory scheme for the nursing profession. *Sullivan*, 209 Ill.2d at 122. The Court held that under the Nursing and Advanced Practice Nursing Act, 225 ILCS 65/5-1, a person with a medical degree, who is licensed to practice medicine, would not meet the qualification for licensure as a registered nurse, nor would that person be competent to sit for the nursing license examination, unless that person completed an accredited program in nursing. *Sullivan*, 209 Ill.2d at 122. Because Dr. Barnhart did not meet the qualifications to practice, nor was he licensed as a nurse under the Illinois Statute, he was deemed incompetent to testify as to the standard of care of a nurse.

6. 225 ILCS 95/1 et seq. sets forth the legal requirements to practice as a Physician's Assistant in Illinois. Section 12 of the Act "Qualifications for licensure reads as follows:

> A person shall be qualified for licensure as a physician's assistant if that person:
>
> 1. Has applied in writing in form and substance satisfactory to the Department and has not violated any of the provisions of Section 21 of this Act or the rules promulgated hereunder. The Department may take into consideration any felony conviction of the applicant but such conviction shall not operate as an absolute bar to licensure; and

2. Has successfully completed the examination provided by the National Commission on the Certification of Physicians Assistant or its successor agency.

In addition, Section 14(b) of the Act provides:

Individuals who have successfully completed an approved physician assistant program as determined by rules of the Department, and who have made application to the Department and submitted evidence to the Department of admission to the certifying examination administered by the National Commission on the Certification of Physician Assistants, or its successor agency, shall be issued a temporary license that shall allow the applicant to practice until:

(1) He or she receives certification from the National Commission on the Certification of Physician Assistants or its successor agency; or

(2) Fifteen months have elapsed, whichever comes first. Under no circumstances shall such applicant continue to practice on the temporary license after notification that he or she has failed the examination. Such authorization shall not be renewable.

The sections of the Act cited supra are but a few of the forty sections and subsections regulating the practice of Physicians Assistants in Illinois. It is clear that it is a highly regulated and closely monitored profession carrying with it stringent eligibility requirements.

7. *Sullivan* controls the case at bar. In this case, as in Sullivan a party proposes to offer the testimony of a licensed physician expert concerning the standard of care applicable to a member of a different licensed medical profession. Namely, Dr. *[name of Witness]* is being offered to testify that a Physicians' Assistant's actions were commensurate with the standard of care of a reasonable, prudent and careful PA practicing under the same or similar circumstances. This is in direct contravention of the law of the State of Illinois and cannot be allowed. The only difference between Sullivan and this case (obviously) is the fact that the profession at issue is a Physician's Assistant---not a nurse. Nonetheless, the distinction makes no difference. A Physician's Assistant operates solely at the discretion and whim of the Illinois Legislature. Just like nurses, chiropractors, certified nurse midwifes and the volume of other regulated healthcare professionals, a Physician's Assistant must first obtain the requisite education, then sit for licensing examinations and finally, receive certificate of licensure to legally practice as a Physician Assistant in Illinois.

Plaintiff anticipates that defendants will argue that Dr. [name of Witness] may competently testify as to Defendant's standard of care due to the fact that a Physician's Assistant acts solely under the watchful eye of a "supervising physician" and that a doctor performs everything that a Physician's Assistant can perform, and more. Unfortunately for the defendants, that argument does not carry the day. In fact, the same argument was made in Sullivan with respect to the nursing profession and its working relationship with doctors. As stated, however, the Supreme Court resoundingly rejected that logic and affirmed the lower court's disallowance of the expert's testimony holding that the nursing profession and physicians were separate and distinct schools of medicine.

8. Here, as in *Sullivan*, this Honorable Court must strike Dr. *[name of Witness']* testimony and opinions as they relate to the standard of care applicable to Physician's Assistant Defendant. *[name of Witness]* is not a Physician's Assistant, therefore, *[he / she]* cannot be allowed to testify.

Wherefore, plaintiff respectfully requests that this Honorable Court grant *[his / her]* Motion in Limine barring Dr. *[name of Witness]* from testifying as to any matter, issue or subject concerning the applicable standard of care of a Physician's Assistant, namely, Defendant.

B. In the alternative, [name of Witness] testimony is speculative and cannot be presented.

1. In the alternative, Dr. *[name of Witness']* testimony should he limited to substance that is founded in the evidence and based upon a reasonable degree of medical certainty. It cannot be speculative and conjectural in nature.

2. The primary issue in this case is whether defendant Defendant's decision to discharge *[Deceased]* was appropriate under the given circumstances. In this case, Defendant's defense rests upon her conclusion that *[Deceased's]* discharge was appropriate considering that Defendant had no "baseline data" from which to gauge *[Deceased's]* medical extremis on *[date of death]*. As a result, Defendant testified that *[he / she]* placed more emphasis on [his/her] observations of the patient and *[his / her]* "clinical judgment" At *[his / her]* deposition, *[Defendant]* testified as follows:

Q: Well, you couldn't get a PEF, or at least according to you, you couldn't you couldn't teach him how to do it. The final analysis is basically the pulse ox which you relied upon to discharge him?

A: Pulse ox and *[his / her]* general appearance and auscultation of improving breath sounds.

Q: But he still had several of the indicators and symptoms of asthma and asthma exacerbation, didn't he?

A: He did.

Q: You didn't rely on a decreasing pulse to normal because it was still abnormal, right?

A: Abnormal possibly because he was using Albuterol, which can increase the pulse rate.

Q: You didn't really on the absence of wheezing because he still had wheezing?

A: *[his/her]* wheezing had improved significantly.

Q: So what, besides a pulse ox and just your visual observation, did you rely on?

A: Basically those, pulse ox, lung sounds, visual observation.

Q: And other - - again, you didn't - - get a PEF. You didn't do a pulmonary. You didn't have anything in the way of objective measurements to quantify [his/her] condition when you discharged him, did you?

A: Auscultation, pulse oxygenation and physical findings of the patient.

Q: But basically it was the pulse ox that you were relying on, wasn't it?

A: Not just one thing, no.

(*[name of person giving deposition]* Deposition, p. *[page numbers of deposition]*, attached hereto as Exhibit *[number of exhibit]*)

3. Defendants disclosed Dr. *[name of Witness]* as a controlled expert witness. In their Supreme Court Rule 213(f)(3) witness disclosure, defendants detail Dr. *[name of Witness']* opinions:

"Dr. *[name of Witness]* also notes that, during [his/her] discovery deposition, plaintiff's standard of care expert, *[name of plaintiff's standard of care expert]*, M.D., agreed that, when baseline data is unavailable (as it was on *[date]*), competent health care professionals must necessarily place greater emphasis and reliance upon their clinical assessment of the patient's condition. That is precisely the predicament in which *[Defendant]* found *[him/her]*self when assessing *[Deceased's]* condition on *[date of death]* ..."

"Dr. *[name of witness]* finds it is highly unusual that *[Deceased]* did not have an established physician-patient relationship relative to the regular monitoring of *[his/her]* asthmatic condition prior to *[date of death]*. This is especially significant, considering that *[Deceased's]* father was a licensed physician; and *[his/her]* mother was a licensed pharmacist, with a master's degree level of education and training ... It also appears that the failure to establish a physician-patient relationship for *[Deceased]* prior to *[date of death]* – in which baseline data could have been taken and recorded for future use – also played an important role in the outcome of this unfortunate case.'

(Attached hereto as Exhibit *[number of exhibit]*)

4. It is clear that the crux of the defendant's position is that defendant's actions were justified and within the standard of care because *[Deceased]* had not visited a physician in the United States, nor undergone any pulmonary function tests to establish a medical "baseline" prior to *[date of death]*.

5. It is well established that an expert witness may not guess or state an opinion based upon mere conjecture. *Schuler v. Mid-Central Cardiology*, 313 Ill. App. 3d 326, 246 Ill. Dec. 163, 729 N.E.2d 536 (4th Dist. 2000); citing, *Dyback v. Weber*, 114 Ill. 2d 232, 102 Ill. Dec. 386, 500 N.E.2d 8 (1986). A medical expert must have evidentiary foundation for their assumptions, opinions and conclusions. An expert in a medical malpractice case cannot base her opinion on what may have occurred or what the expert believed might have occurred in a particular case. An expert witness' opinion cannot be based upon speculation, conjecture or guesswork.

6. As stated, Defendant's 213(f)(3) witness disclosure included *[his/her]* opinion that defendant acted like any other "competent health care professional when she "placed greater emphasis and reliance upon her clinical assessment of the patient's condition. Dr. *[name of Witness']* opinion is that this was "precisely the predicament in which Physician's Assistant Defendant found herself when assessing *[Deceased's]* condition on *[date of death]*. At *[his/her]* discovery deposition, however, Dr. *[name of Witness]* departed from the substance of the defendants 213(f)(3) disclosure. In particular, Dr. *[name of Witness]* admitted that he did not have any idea, if baseline data was available to Defendant on *[date of death]*, whether it would have made a difference in this unfortunate outcome. Dr. *[name of Witness]* testified as follows:

> Q: Explain to me how you feel your allegation or your opinion that no physician-patient relationship was established prior to *[date of death]*, affects the outcome in this case.
>
> A: Are you reading from something?
>
> Q: No, I'm looking at No. *[place in notes]*, of your written notes. I can ask the question again. It was probably poorly worded. In fact why don't I do that. Explain to me how your opinion that no physician-patient relationship was established prior to the date of presentation affects the outcome in this case.
>
> A: It may have affected the outcome, it may not have affected the outcome. There's no way of knowing. Had *[Deceased]* been at the *[name of medical center]* Medical Center a year earlier, had the doctors and PA's in the center better known *[Deceased]*, *[his/her]* asthma, what was good for him, what was bad for him, they

might have jacked up *[his/her]* dose pre-*[date of death]* medications. They might have changed *[his/her]* medications. They might have intervened in some other way that either would have prevented the exacerbation that brought him to Wabash on 5/9 in the first place or -- no one can know -- changed the way they treated him based on the information they had obtained in the previous year.

What possibly could have happened, just as a perfect example, is that *[Deceased]* would have been educated and *[his/her]* mom would have known how to use a peak flow meter. They might have identified earl asthma flare, treated it and jumped on it earlier and prevented him from even coming to the Wabash Medical Center in the first place.

Q: Hypothetically speaking, if he had presented a year prior to *[date of death]*, and the physicians and the caregivers at the *[name of medical center]* location had seen him a year prior, what would they have done differently on *[date of death]*?

A: I don't know. I gave you some examples of what could have happened pre-*[date of death]* and how that might have affected the day before, the evening before, the morning of *[date of death]*. Beyond that, I don't know. It's pure speculation.

(*[name of Witness]* deposition, *[page number]*, attached hereto as Exhibit *[number of exhibit]*)

7. Dr. *[name of Witness']* testimony is clear. He cannot state with any degree of certainty whatsoever, let a lone a reasonable degree of medical certainty as to whether baseline medical information would have altered or in any way affected Defendant's actions on *[date of death]*. In fact, he admits that he did not know and would be purely speculating as to whether or not Defendant's course of treatment would have differed. The most that he can say is that Defendant might have or possibly could have acted differently on *[date of death]*. Alas, this does not deem *[his/her]* testimony admissible, as an expert may not base [his/her] testimony on what might have or could possibly occurred. There is no basis for Dr. *[name of Witness]* opinions in this regard. Hence, this Court should disallow *[his/her]* testimony in these respects.

Wherefore, this Honorable Court should disallow and bar Dr. *[name of Witness]* from testifying, mentioning or in any way alluding to the fact that baseline medical data, or in this case the lack thereof; had any connection or causal relationship to Defendant's conduct or the result in this case. Further, Dr. *[name of Witness]* should be prohibited from testifying that the lack of a physician-patient relationship between *[Deceased]* and the caregivers at *[name of medical center]*, including *[Defendant]*, had any connection or causal relationship to Defendant's conduct or the result in this case.

Plaintiff, *[name of plaintiff]*
By: ______________________________
One of *[his/her]* Attorneys
[Attorney of Defendant]
[Address]
[Telephone number]
[Facsimile number]

__________ Granted
__________ Denied
__________ Reserved

§ 8:91 Motion to exclude testimony of unqualified medical expert witness; registered nurse

[Insert caption]

◆ **Important Note:** 225 ILCS 65/5-1, et. seq., the Nursing Practice Act has been repealed. It has been renumbered and amended and is found at 225 ILCS 65/50-1, et. seq., the Nurse Practice Act.

PLAINTIFF'S *[NUMBER]* MOTION IN LIMINE
Barring Testimony of *[Defendant Doctor]*, M.D

NOW COME the Plaintiffs, [name of plaintiff(s)], Co-Administrators of the Estate of [name of deceased], a deceased infant, by their attorneys, [attorneys for plaintiff(s)], and hereby state the following in support of their [number] Motion in Limine:

I. Factual Background

1.) This case arises from the alleged negligence of the nursing staff at Defendant, *[name of defendant hospital]* Hospital ("Defendant Hospital") in rendering care and treatment to Plaintiff, *[name of plaintiff]*, during her hospitalization on *[date of treatment]*. Plaintiff allege that Defendant Hospital nurse, *[Defendant Nurse]*, failed to appropriately monitor Plaintiff during her visit to Defendant Hospital's obstetrical unit by negligently failing to monitor fetal heart rate data, including heart rate monitor strips which indicated ominous signs of fetal distress. Plaintiffs also sued *[Defendant Doctor]* alleging that he was negligent in rendering care to Plaintiff on *[date of treatment]*. The allegations of negligence pled against Dr. *[De-*

fendant Doctor] were identical to the allegations pled against Defendant Hospital nursing staff.

2.) The nurses who cared for Plaintiff have been deposed, including *[Defendant Nurse]*, the nurse who provided the vast majority of care to Plaintiff and who is alleged to have misinterpreted fetal heart rate data. *[Defendant Doctor]* was also deposed. During his deposition, Dr. *[Defendant Doctor]* was asked about his interpretation of the fetal heart rate data that appears on the monitor strips. Both *[Defendant Doctor]* and *[Defendant Nurse]* testified that the data that appears on the monitor strips does not indicate abnormal or non-reassuring fetal heart rates. Dr. *[Defendant Doctor]*'s testimony also established that he visited with Plaintiff for a period of about twelve minutes on *[date of treatment]*, from *[time period]*. He testified that he analyzed the fetal heart rate monitoring strips during that time. Thereafter, Dr. *[Defendant Doctor]* left the hospital and did not again examine the fetal heart rate strips until after the event giving rise to this lawsuit, *[Plaintiff Infant]*'s death.

3.) In addition, both nurse *[Defendant Nurse]* and Dr. *[Defendant Doctor]* recalled a telephone conversation that took place on the evening of *[date of treatment]*. After Dr. *[Defendant Doctor]* left Defendant Hospital, at approximately *[time period]*, nurse *[Defendant Nurse]* paged Dr. *[Defendant Doctor]*. Dr. *[Defendant Doctor]* returned the page ten minutes later by placing a telephone call to nurse *[Defendant Nurse]* at *[Defendant Hospital]* hospital. The witnesses' recollection of the substance of the conversation is almost identical. Dr. *[Defendant Doctor]* testified that during the conversation, nurse *[Defendant Nurse]* provided an "assessment" that everything was fine and that there were no abnormal or non-reassuring heart rate patterns on the strips. (*[Defendant Doctor]* deposition, pages *[deposition pages]*.) Likewise, nurse *[Defendant Nurse]* testified that during the conversation, she informed Dr. *[Defendant Doctor]* that "the baby was moving around a lot" and that there was "good variability in the fetal heart rate." (*[Defendant Nurse]* deposition, page *[deposition page]*). Following the conversation that evening and per Dr. *[Defendant Doctor]*'s orders, Plaintiff was discharged from *[Defendant Hospital]*'s obstetrical unit to her home. Four hours later, Plaintiff returned to Defendant Hospital and delivered a stillborn baby.

4.) Following these depositions, Plaintiffs disclosed *[Plaintiff's Nurse Witness]*, as an expert who will testify that *[Defendant Nurse]* deviated from the standard of care of a reasonably well qualified nurse in her failing to recognize indications of fetal intolerance to labor indicated on the fetal heart rate tracings generated during Plaintiff's *[date of treatment]* visit to Defendant Hospital hospital. Nurse *[Plaintiff's Nurse Witness]* also holds the opinion that during the *[time]* telephone conversation, *[Defendant Nurse]* failed to inform Dr. *[Defendant Doctor]* of the abnormal and non-reassuring signs of fetal compromise. Nurse *[Plaintiff's Nurse Witness]*'s discovery deposition testimony reiterates and develops these opinions. Plaintiffs also disclosed a physician obstetrician to testify as to the deviations from the standard of care committed by Dr. *[Defendant Doctor]*. Dr. *[Plaintiff's Doctor Witness]* was disclosed, and then, deposed. In sum, Dr. *[Plaintiff's Doctor Witness]* opines that Plaintiff should not have been discharged from Defendant Hospital, regardless of the substance of the telephone conversation that occurred between *[Defendant Nurse]* and Dr. *[Defendant Doctor]*. Dr. *[Plaintiff's Doctor Witness]* agrees with *[Plaintiff's Nurse Witness]* that the fetal heart rate tracings indicate telling signs of fetal intolerance to labor and that those indications were misread or went unrecognized by nurse *[Defendant Nurse]*. Accordingly, he disagrees with Dr. *[Defendant Doctor]*'s and nurse *[Defendant Nurse]*'s opinions concerning the fetal heart rate data.

5.) The Court set a deadline for disclosure of Defendants opinion witnesses of *[date of disclosure deadline]*. Defendant Hospital disclosed its opinion witnesses on *[date of disclosure]*. Defendant Hospital did not disclose any "controlled expert witnesses" as defined by Supreme Court Rule 213(0(3). Rather, Defendant Hospital disclosed Dr. *[Defendant Doctor]* as a witness who will testify "consistent with his discovery deposition. More specifically, Defendant Hospital's Rule 213 witness disclosure states:

> *[Defendant Doctor]*, M.D. Defendant anticipates testimony from Dr. *[Defendant Doctor]* consistent with his discovery deposition. Specifically, Defendant anticipates testimony from Dr. *[Defendant Doctor]* concerning his interpretation of the fetal heart rate monitoring strips, as more hilly set forth in his deposition, including but not limited to pages *[deposition pages]*. In Dr. *[Defendant Doctor]*'s opinion, he found nothing which was non-reassuring (deposition page *[deposition page]*), abnormal (deposition pages *[deposition pages]*) or of concern for the well being of Plaintiff's fetus (deposition pages *[deposition pages]*). He will testify that he viewed the fetal heart monitoring strips shortly after the event described in the Complaint, as well as during his discovery deposition as the request of plaintiff's attorney, and that his interpretation of these monitoring strips did not change. Further, he had no concerns over Nurse *[Defendant Nurse]*'s competence. Finally Dr. *[Defendant Doctor]* will describe what fetal heart rate tracing

patterns should be reported to a doctor by a nurse if such patterns are witnessed on fetal heart monitor tracings and under what circumstances, as more fully described at his deposition beginning at page *[deposition page]*.

Defendant Hospital did not disclose any other expert witnesses (other than *[Defendant Nurse]* and Dr. *[Defendant Doctor]*) who will testify in support of nurse *[Defendant Nurse]* and her conduct on *[date of treatment]*. Trial is set to begin in this matter on *[trial date]*.

II. Applicable law and argument

I. Dr. *[Defendant Doctor]* cannot testify in this case as to any issue concerning the standard of care applicable to a registered nurse, namely, *[Defendant Nurse]*.

A. *Sullivan v. Edward Hosp.*, 209 Ill. 2d 100, 282 Ill. Dec. 348, 806 N.E.2d 645 (2004) prohibits Dr. *[Defendant Doctor]* from testifying as to matters concerning the standard of care applicable to a registered nurse.

1.) This Court should enter an order barring any testimony by Dr. *[Defendant Doctor]* as it in any way relates to the standard of care applicable to a registered nurse, in this case, *[Defendant Nurse]*. *[Defendant Hospital]*'s disclosure of Dr. *[Defendant Doctor]* and Dr. *[Defendant Doctor]*'s deposition testimony make it clear that Defendant Hospital intends to offer his testimony in support of *[Defendant Nurse]*'s conduct on *[date of treatment]*. However. Dr. *[Defendant Doctor]* is not a registered nurse. Rather, his professional license is that of a physician, who practices family medicine. Consequently, and according to the Illinois Supreme Court, he is incompetent to testify as to matters related to the standard of care of a registered nurse.

2.) Nursing is a distinct medical profession, having separate and unique educational obligations, curriculum, practice standards and most importantly, licensure. In Illinois, registered nurses are licensed by the Illinois Department of Financial and Professional Regulation. In addition, the Legislature has meticulously regulated the nursing profession. 225 ILCS 65/10 et. seq. sets forth the statutory requirements for eligibility to legally practice as a registered nurse in the State. To say the least, the Legislature has enacted detailed and express laws governing an R.N's role and practice in the medical field. There is no question, both legally and practically, that a nurse is a separate and distinct entity who crafts her trade pursuant to State issued and valid licensure.

3.) It is well established that in order for a medical expert to testify as to the standard of care for a particular school of medicine, the expert must be licensed within that school of medicine. See *Purtill v. Hess*, 111 Ill. 2d 229, 95 Ill. Dec. 305, 489 N.E.2d 867 (1986) and *Dolan v. Galluzzo*, 77 Ill. 2d 279, 32 Ill. Dec. 900, 396 N.E.2d 13 (1979). More recently, in 2002, the Supreme Court clearly upheld the "licensure requirement" previously announced in *Dolan* and *Purtill*. In *Sullivan v. Edward Hosp.*, 209 Ill. 2d 100, 282 Ill. Dec. 348, 806 N.E.2d 645 (2004), the Court established a two-pronged analysis that a trial court must apply regarding the admissibility of expert testimony. The two-step analysis mandates that prior to a medical expert offering testimony, it must be determined that:

(1) the expert is a licensed member of the school of medicine about which he proposes to testify; and

(2) the expert witness must show that he is familiar with the methods, procedures, and treatments ordinarily observed by other practitioners, in either the defendant practitioner's community or a similar community. *Sullivan*, 209 Ill.2d at 114.

The test requires the party intending to offer the expert's testimony to establish these two separate and distinct requisite elements before the expert may testify. These elements (licensure and familiarity within the standard of care) are mutually exclusive. That is, if the expert physician fails to satisfy either of these foundational requirements, the trial court must disallow the expert's testimony. *Sullivan*, 209 Ill.2d at 114-115.

4.) In Sullivan, a physician, Dr. Barnhart, was disclosed by the plaintiff to testify as to the standard of care of a registered nurse. Specifically, Dr. Barnhart was to testify that the nurse in question deviated from the standard of care by: (1) failing to communicate her concern of a fall risk to the injured plaintiff; and (2) failing to employ the use of a fall preventative device in the case. *Sullivan*, 209 Ill.2d at 106. The trial court deemed Dr. Barnhart incompetent to testify as to the standard of care of a nurse. As a result, it struck Dr. Barnhart's testimony concerning defendant nurse's alleged deviations from the standard of care. The trial court's rationale was that Dr. *[Defendant Doctor]* was not a licensed nurse; therefore, he was incompetent to testify as to the standard of care applicable to a nurse. 225 ILCS 65/10 et. seq. The appellate court affirmed the trial court ruling. The plaintiff appealed to the Supreme Court of Illinois. Relying on *Purtill* and *Dolan* the Supreme Court affirmed the lower courts in certain and unequivocal terms. Plaintiff's position before the Supreme Court was that Illinois law no longer required a medical expert to be a licensed member of the school of medicine about which the expert proposes to testify. In support of that argument, plaintiff relied on the Supreme Court's holding in *Jones v. O'Young*, 154 Ill. 2d 39, 180 Ill. Dec. 330, 607 N.E.2d 224 (1992). In sum, the plaintiff's argument was that Jones "retreats from any rigid, formalistic rule that a health professional expert witness must he a licensed member of the school of medicine about which the expert proposed to testify." *Sullivan*, 209 Ill.2d at 114. In summarily rejecting plaintiff's position, the Court astutely stated:

> We cannot accept this argument. *Jones* clearly reaffirms this Court's decision in *Purtill* describing two foundational requirements: that the health care expert witness must be a licensed member of the school of medicine about which the expert proposes to testify; and that the expert must be familiar with the methods, procedures and treatments ordinarily observed by other health-care providers in either the defendant's community or a similar community. Indeed, the very next sentences in *Jones* following the italicized sentence upon which the plaintiff relies states: 'If the plaintiff fails to satisfy either of the foundational requirements of *Purtill* the trial court must disallow the expert's testimony.' *Sullivan*, 209 Ill.2d at 115.

5.) It seems logical that a physician should be considered competent to testify as to the standard of care of a nurse, if for nothing else than a nurse takes her orders from a physician. However, such is not the case in Illinois. The *Sullivan* Court addressed head on the argument that a physician may testify as to a nursing standard of care because "there is nothing which a nurse can do which a doctor cannot do." *Sullivan*, 209 Ill.2d at 120-121. Again, in form this argument appears completely logical. But, as the appellate court recognized (and the Supreme Court expressly affirmed), in application, this statement's logic fails:

> Dr. Barnhart is not a licensed member of the nursing profession. To allow a doctor to testify as to the standard of care applicable to the nursing profession implicates the risks raised by *Dolan* namely the imposition of a higher standard of care and the muddling and mixing of various tenets and practices unique to each profession. *Sullivan*, 209 Ill.2d at 123.

The Court also based its decision on the fact that the Legislature had acted to designate a unique licensing and regulatory scheme for the nursing profession. *Sullivan*, 209 Ill.2d at 122. The Court held that under the Nursing and Advanced Practice Nursing Act, 225 ILCS 65/5-1, a person with a medical degree, who is licensed to practice medicine, would not meet the qualification for licensure as a registered nurse, nor would that person be competent to sit for the nursing license examination, unless that person completed an accredited program in nursing. *Sullivan*, 209 Ill.2d at 122. In *Sullivan*, because Dr. Barnhart did not meet the qualifications to practice, nor was he licensed as a nurse under the Illinois Statute, he was deemed incompetent to testify as to the standard of care of a nurse.

6.) *Sullivan* controls the case at bar. In this case, as in *Sullivan*, Defendant Hospital proposes to offer the testimony of a licensed physician expert concerning the standard of care applicable to a member of a different licensed medical profession. In particular, Dr. *[Defendant Doctor]* is being offered to testily that *[Defendant Nurse]*'s conduct complied with the standard of care of what a reasonable, prudent and careful nurse practicing under the same or similar circumstances would have done on *[date of treatment]*. This is in direct contravention of the law of the State of Illinois and cannot be allowed. A registered nurse operates solely at the discretion and whim of the Illinois Legislature. Just like physician's assistants, chiropractors, certified nurse midwives and the volume of other regulated healthcare professionals, a registered nurse must first obtain the requisite education, sit for licensing examinations and finally, receive certificate of licensure to legally practice as a nurse in Illinois. Because Dr. *[Defendant Doctor]* does not possess the requisite licensure, under Sullivan he is automatically incompetent to testify as to the nursing standard of care.

7.) Plaintiff anticipates that Defendant Hospital will argue that Dr. *[Defendant Doctor]* may competently testify as to *[Defendant Nurse]*'s standard of care either due to the fact that (1) a nurse acts solely under the watchful eye of a physician and that a doctor performs everything that a nurse can perform or (2) that this case involves a "matter of communication" thus allowing Dr. *[Defendant Doctor]*' testimony under *Wingo by Wingo v. Rockford Memorial Hosp.*, 292 Ill. App. 3d 896, 226 Ill. Dec. 939, 686 N.E.2d 722 (2d Dist. 1997). These anticipated arguments are addressed in turn.

First, with regard to the position that a "doctor performs everything that a nurse can perform" thus, the doctor is competent to testify as to the standard of care, the same argument was made in *Sullivan* with respect to the nursing profession and its working relationship with doctors. The Supreme Court resoundingly rejected that logic and affirmed the lower court's disallowance of the expert's testimony holding that the nursing profession and physicians were separate and distinct schools of medicine. In so doing, the Court emphasized that if the expert is not licensed in the same "school" of medicine as the professional he/she is being offered to criticize, the expert is deemed incompetent and is disqualified from testifying. *Sullivan*, 209 Ill.2d at 123.

Second, whether or not Dr. *[Defendant Doctor]*'s testimony concerns matters of "physician-nurse communication" or reporting is of no consequence and does not render Dr. *[Defendant Doctor]* competent to testify as to the nursing standard of care. Again, it is expected that Defendant Hospital will rely upon *Wingo v. Rockford Memorial Hospital* in support of its offering Dr. *[Defendant Doctro]* as an expert witness and will specifically argue that because this ease involves a matter of "hat a nurse should communicate to a physician, *Wingo* controls. *Wingo* lends no assistance in Defendants effort.

a. Facts of Wingo

In *Wingo* a doctor and hospital were sued for the alleged mismanagement of the labor and delivery of the plaintiff's child. The child was born with significant brain damage. When the plaintiff in *Wingo* presented to the defendant hospital, it was noted that she was leaking amniotic fluid. Later, her care was undertaken by Dr. Klink and an employee of the defendant hospital, nurse Welden. Dr. Klink examined the plaintiff, but noted no presence of amniotic fluid leak. Dr. Klink then left the plaintiff in the care of nurse Welden. Over the course of the day, nurse Welden observed the plaintiff. The hospital records and chart recorded that plaintiff had continuous leaking of amniotic fluid after Mink's examination and while under Welden's care. Approximately six hours after Dr. Klink left the plaintiff, he was paged by nurse Welden with an update about the plaintiffs condition. Welden and Dr. Klink had a telephone conversation, during which Welden informed Dr. Klink that "nothing had changed" in the plaintiff's condition, i.e., that no further amniotic fluid had leaked from her body. Based upon that information, Dr. Klink discharged plaintiff to her home. Plaintiff returned the next day, in labor, and delivered a distressed baby. The baby had contracted a se eye infection, allegedly as a result of the lack of amniotic fluid which had leaked from her body. The infection caused the baby's brain damage.

At trial, the plaintiff offered the expert testimony of two obstetricians/physicians. The experts testified that the nurse (Welden) negligently failed to communicate to the doctor that fluid continued to leak and that she should have questioned the doctors discharge order by exercising the nursing "chain of command" to question the discharge. *Wingo*, 292 Ill.App.3d at 903-904. The plaintiff settled with the defendant physician prior to verdict. After deliberations, the jury returned a verdict in favor of the plaintiff. The hospital appealed.

b. The appeal and the Second District's holding.

On appeal, the hospital argued that the plaintiff's expert physicians should not have been permitted to testify as to the standard of care that applied to nurse Welden or any deviations from the standard of care committed by Welden. The hospital relied on the licensing requirement of *Dolan v. Galuzzo* in support of its argument that the plaintiffs expert doctors incompetent to testify because they were not licensed registered nurses- Plaintiff' countered that despite their lack of holding nursing licenses, the experts testimony was proper because (1) it involved a matter of communication between a nurse and a physician and (2) that the allegations of nurses' negligence did not involve a different standard of care from separate areas of medicine.

In affirming the trial court, the court rejected the hospital's argument, holding that the facts in *Wingo* did not "fit within the *Dolan* license requirement." *Wingo*, 292 Ill.App.3d at 906. The court justified its holding by noting: (1) that the expert doctors' testimony did not relate to a matter of "nursing procedure," but rather, to a matter of what a nurse is required to communicate to a physician about what transpired since the physician last saw the patient; (2) the allegations of negligence did not concern an area of medicine about which there would be a different standard between physician and another school of medicine; and (3) it was established that the allegations of [the nurse's] negligence were well within the testifying doctors' knowledge and experience. *Wingo*, 292 Ill.App.3d at 906. The jury verdict and the trial court's rulings were affirmed.

c. Sullivan trumps *Wingo*

The *Sullivan* Court held that *Wingo* was not applicable to the facts in *Sullivan* because: (1) the trial court struck the expert doctor's opinion concerning communication between nurse and physician as a discovery sanction; and (2) that the remaining opinions offered the expert physician related to nursing procedures and not communications. In other words, in the *Sullivan* case, there was no issue at trial that dealt with "what a nurse should tell a doctor. The issues in *Sullivan* centered on nursing protocols and procedure, issues on which a non-nurse could not render opinions. Nonetheless, and despite the issue not centering on physician-nurse communication," the *Sullivan* Court held that the analysis is a clear, two-step process. In order for a medical expert to be competent to testify concerning the standard of care, the expert must first he licensed in the same school of medicine as the professional he/she intends to criticize (the *Dolan* requirement) and second, the expert must be familiar with the applicable standard of care. The *Sullivan* Court's analysis was complete once it was established that the expert physician was not a registered nurse.

Admittedly, the Supreme Court in *Sullivan* did not discuss the merits of *Wingo*. It held that since the issues revolved around nursing procedure. The case "fell squarely within the license requirement of *Dolan* and its progeny." Although *Sullivan* didn't discuss the merits of *Wingo*, *Garley v. Columbia LaGrange Memorial Hosp.*, 351 Ill. App. 3d 398, 286 Ill. Dec. 337, 813 N.E.2d 1030 (1st Dist. 2004) did.

d. *Garley* further develops *Sullivan*, *Garley* addresses physician-nurse communications and the applicability of *Wingo*

After the *Sullivan* decision came down, the First District decided *Garley v. Columbia LaGrange Memorial Hosp.*, 351 Ill. App. 3d 398, 286 Ill. Dec. 337, 813 N.E.2d 1030 (1st Dist. 2004). The issues in *Garley* were nearly identical to those in *Sullivan*. In *Garley*, a patient underwent several abdominal surgeries. Unfortunately, following the procedures, she suffered a pulmonary embolism and died. Plaintiff's widower filed a wrongful death suit alleging medical negligence on the part of the hospital staff nurses in failing to appropriately manage the decedents post surgical care. Plaintiff offered the testimony of three separate expert physicians, none of whom were licensed nurses Those experts criticized the defendant hospital's nursing staffs conduct. As part of their criticisms, plaintiff's experts opined that nursing staff failed to inform the doctors of their inability to ambulate the patient and that the nurses should have suggested to the doctors that an anti-clotting agent be employed during surgery. *Garley*, 351 Ill.App.3d at 403. At the close of evidence, the jury returned a verdict against the hospital. Defendant appealed arguing that since none of plaintiffs experts were licensed nurses. The plaintiff's expert physicians were incompetent to testify and the licensing requirement originally set forth in Dolan and in Sullivan was violated. Specifically:

> Hospital argues that, because none of plaintiff's expert physicians were licensed nurses, they were not competent to testify as to either the applicable standard of care for the nurses attending Mrs. Garley or whether the nursing stall deviated from that standard of care. Plaintiff, on the other hand, contends that his experts were competent based upon their experience working

with and, as to Drs. Duboe and Vasquez, teaching nurses. *Garley*, 351 Ill.App.3d at 405.

On appeal, plaintiff contended that because a matter of nurse-physician communication was at issue, *Wingo* applied, and that as such the plaintiff's physician experts were competent to testify as to the standard of care of a nurse and to any issues of communication between the doctors and nurses. However, the First District rejected plaintiff's argument that *Wingo* controlled and agreed with the defendant hospital the citing the Supreme Court's decision in *Sullivan*:

> Plaintiff's reliance upon *Wingo* is misplaced. First, the initial premise on which *Wingo's* reasoning was based, i.e. that no Illinois court had directly applied the licensing requirement to prevent a physician from establishing the applicable nursing standard of care, is no longer true. (Citing, *Sullivan*). While the reach of the license requirement in the context of a physician testifying as to the nursing standard of care was an open question when *Wingo* was decided, as well as when the trial in this case was held, the supreme court in *Sullivan* left no doubt that having such a license is "unequivocally required." Id. ("We expressly reaffirm the licensure requirement of *Dolan* and its progeny and decline plaintiff's invitation to deviate therefrom"). Second, in *Wingo* three nurses testified that the nurse deviated from the applicable nursing standard of care by failing to communicate the patient's condition to her doctor. (Citing, *Wingo*.) Here, none of plaintiff's witnesses were competent to establish the applicable nursing standard of care. Therefore, we believe that *Wingo* is not applicable to the case at bar. *Garley v. Columbia LaGrange Memorial Hosp.*, 351 Ill. App. 3d 398, 411-412, 286 Ill. Dec. 337, 813 N.E.2d 1030 (1st Dist. 2004).

The *Garley* court went onto state:

> Plaintiff argues that his experts were competent to testify based upon their years of experience observing, working with, and teaching nurses. While such experience would certainly demonstrate that they were familiar with the methods, procedures and treatments ordinarily observed by other physicians, in either the defendant physicians community or a similar community (Citing *Purtill v. Hess*, 111 Ill. 2d 229, 95 Ill. Dec. 305, 489 N.E.2d 867 (1986)), the second foundational requirement for determining the competency of an expert witness, and could be considered by the circuit court in determining, within her sound discretion, whether a physician is qualified and competent to state his opinion as an expert regarding the standard of care (*Purtill*, 111 Ill.2d at 229), the fact remains that they were not licensed in the school of nursing. An expert physician who is not licensed in the particular school of medicine about which he intends to testify is automatically incompetent his knowledge, experience, and level of expertise, no matter how extensive, are simply irrelevant. *Garley v. Columbia LaGrange Memorial Hosp.*, 351 Ill. App. 3d 398, 412, 286 Ill. Dec. 337, 813 N.E.2d 1030 (1st Dist. 2004).

8.) As was true in *Garley*, *Wingo* does not apply to the facts of this case. The pronouncement of the Illinois Supreme Court in *Sullivan* and by the appellate court in *Garley* is absolutely clear: A physician who is not licensed in the particular school of medicine about which he intends to testify is automatically incompetent, his knowledge, experience, and level of expertise, no matter how extensive, are simply irrelevant. *Garley v. Columbia LaGrange Memorial Hosp.*, 351 Ill. App. 3d 398, 412, 286 Ill. Dec. 337, 813 N.E.2d 1030 (1st Dist. 2004) citing *Sullivan*. Therefore, regardless of how Defendant Hospital couches Dr. *[Defendant Doctor]*'s testimony, Dr. *[Defendant Doctor]* cannot be allowed to testify on behalf of *[Defendant Nurse]*.

9.) It is significant that Defendant Hospital did not disclose a "nurse expert" to testify in support of *[Defendant Nurse]*'s conduct on *[date of treatment]*. That point is important inasmuch as it effectively leaves Defendant Hospital to rely on Dr. *[Defendant Doctor]*'s testimony as the only source of evidence supportive of its employee. The majority of Defendant Hospital disclosure of Dr. *[Defendant Doctor]*'s opinions addresses his interpretation of the fetal heart rate monitoring strips. Initially, it must be remembered that the only portion of the strips Dr. *[Defendant Doctor]* examined during the Plaintiffs visit to the hospital corresponded to the first twelve minutes of her stay at Defendant Hospital. Dr. *[Defendant Doctor]* was not present at the hospital for the remaining time Plaintiff was at Defendant Hospital on *[date of treatment]*, approximately four hours. The first time Dr. *[Defendant Doctor]* analyzed the heart rate tracings in their entirety was well after *[name of deceased]* died and then, again, after he was sued. Accordingly, his testimony concerning the strips is pure "hindsight" and his knowledge of the data on the strips was gained after he realized that a stillbirth occurred and later, after a lawsuit was filed. Taking this into account, it is apparent that the only conceivable purpose underlying Defendant Hospitals offer of Dr. *[Defendant Doctor]*'s opinion concerning his interpretation of the monitor strips is to "back door" an opinion that nurse *[Defendant Nurse]* complied with the standard of care on *[date of treatment]*.

An even more glaring attempt to circumvent the *Sullivan* rule of law is Defendant Hospital's offer of Dr. *[Defendant Doctor]*'s opinion that he "had no concerns over nurse *[Defendant Nurse]*'s competence." Such a statement is simply another way of Dr. *[Defendant Doctor]* saying "nurse *[Defendant Nurse]* complied with the standard of care." Defendant Hospital also discloses that Dr. *[Defendant Doctor]* will testify "what fetal heart rate tracing patterns should be reported to a doctor by a nurse if such patterns are witnessed on fetal heart monitor tracings and under what circumstances." Here again, *Sullivan* and *Dolan* quickly strike this opinion as it deals with nursing protocol and/or chain of command. Even if Defendant Hospital argues that this opinion is a mailer of "what should be communicated to a physician" under *Wingo* both *Sullivan* and *Garley* are clear: Regardless of whether or not this matter is one of nurse-physician communication. a physician who is not licensed in the particular school of medicine about which he intends to testify is automatically incompetent and that *Wingo* is no longer good law.

Simply put, there is no way that the Defendant Hospital may present Dr. *[Defendant Doctor]* as an expert witness without violating the Supreme Court's pronouncement in *Sullivan*. Had Defendant Hospital disclosed a nurse expert witness to testify in support of *[Defendant Nurse]*'s conduct, the matter would be very different but such is not the case. Nonetheless, Defendant Hospital may still rely on *[Defendant Doctor]*'s own testimony that her conduct was within the standard of care, however, it certainly may not rely on Dr. *[Defendant Doctor]*'s opinion to that effect.

10.) Here, as in Sullivan, this Honorable Court must strike Dr. *[Defendant Doctor]*'s opinions and bar any testimony that could be construed as supportive of the standard of care applicable to nurse *[Defendant Nurse]*. Dr. *[Defendant Doctor]* is not a nurse and cannot be allowed to testify.

B. In the alternative, Dr. *[Defendant Doctor]*'s testimony concerning his interpretation of the fetal heart rate monitor tracings should be limited to the tracings he actually observed on *[date of treatment]*.

In the alternative, if Dr. *[Defendant Doctor]* is allowed to testily concerning his interpretation of the fetal heart rate monitor tracings, his testimony should be limited to the data he actually examined and had knowledge of during the time he was present at Defendant Hospital on *[date of treatment]*. Any testimony by Dr. *[Defendant Doctor]* concerning data on the monitor strips recorded after *[time]* can be deemed nothing other than an attempt to instruct the jury as to whether or not nurse *[Defendant Nurse]*'s interpretation of the information on the tracings was appropriate.

WHEREFORE, Plaintiffs respectfully request that this Honorable Court grant their Second Motion in Limine barring

Dr. *[Defendant Doctor]* from testifying as to any matter, issue or subject concerning the applicable standard of care of a nurse.

Plaintiffs, *[name of plaintiffs]*
By:______________________________
One of His Attorneys

THE LAW OFFICES OF *[name of attorneys]*
[address of attorneys]
[telephone number of attorneys]
[fax number of attorneys]

__________ Granted
__________ Denied
__________ Reserved

§ 8:92 Motion to exclude speculative expert opinion

TO: ALL PARTIES AND THEIR RESPECTIVE ATTORNEYS OF RECORD:

PLEASE TAKE NOTICE that plaintiff hereby moves this Court for an order excluding any and all evidence, references to evidence, testimony or argument relating to the opinion of defendant's mechanical engineer expert relating to how the accident occurred and the plaintiff's actions immediately prior to the incident.

This motion is made under the provisions of Illinois case law and is based on the supporting Memorandum of Points and Authorities, the pleadings and papers on file in this action, and upon such of the argument and evidence as may be presented prior to or at the hearing of this matter.

Dated: *[date]*

MEMORANDUM OF POINTS AND AUTHORITIES

1.
INTRODUCTION

This matter arises from a serious fall accident that occurred in the defendant's garage on or about December 24, 1998. The accident occurred when the plaintiff slipped and fell in a puddle of oil on the concrete floor of the defendant's garage, striking the back of her head on the ground as she fell. As a result of the accident, the plaintiff has incurred serious head injuries, with long-term memory loss and other neurological deficiencies. She has no recollection of how the fall occurred. There were no witnesses to the accident or the plaintiff's actions immediately prior to the accident.

A major issue in this case is whether the plaintiff was running or walking when the incident occurred. The plaintiff anticipates that defendant's expert witness, a mechanical engineer, will attempt to testify how the fall occurred, based *solely* upon grease stains on the plaintiff's shoes and clothing.

By this motion, the plaintiff seeks to exclude any testimony as to how the fall occurred, since any such testimony would be too speculative to be reliable.

2.
THIS COURT MAY PRECLUDE EVIDENCE WHERE THE PROBATIVE VALUE IS SUBSTANTIALLY OUTWEIGHED BY THE DANGER OF UNDUE PREJUDICE

This Court has authority to exclude evidence because the prejudicial impact outweighs the probative value of it. Federal Rule of Evidence 403 states:

> Although relevant, evidence may be excluded if its probative value is substantially outweighed by the danger of unfair prejudice, confusion of the issues, or misleading the jury, or by considerations of undue delay, waste of time, or needless presentation of cumulative evidence.

Illinois has a common-law rule that is comparable to Federal Rule of Evidence 403. See *People v. Peete*, 318 Ill. App. 3d 961, 966–67, 252 Ill. Dec. 821, 743 N.E.2d 689 (4th Dist. 2001); *People v. Walker*, 335 Ill. App. 3d 102, 112, 268 Ill. Dec. 654, 779 N.E.2d 268 (2d Dist. 2002), as modified on denial of reh'g, (Oct. 24, 2002) and judgment aff'd, 211 Ill. 2d 317, 285 Ill. Dec. 519, 812 N.E.2d 339 (2004).

Illinois case law is clear that evidence should be excluded when the prejudicial impact of the evidence outweighs the probative value of it. *Department of Public Works and Bldgs. v. Roehrig*, 45 Ill. App. 3d 189, 196, 3 Ill. Dec. 893, 359 N.E.2d 752 (5th Dist. 1976) (exclusion of evidence of prior condemnations in a condemnation case because the prejudicial impact outweighs its probative value); *People v. Holman*, 257 Ill. App. 3d 1031, 1033–34, 196 Ill. Dec. 457, 630 N.E.2d 154 (2d Dist. 1994) (evidence is admissible if it is relevant and if the prejudicial impact does not substantially outweigh its probative value); and, *Hulsebus v. Russian*, 118 Ill. App. 2d 174, 180–81, 254 N.E.2d 184 (2d Dist. 1969) (trial judge had discretion to exclude a gruesome photograph of the plaintiff during surgery because other evidence established the extent of the injury and because the photograph was likely to inflame and prejudice the jury).

In the present case, any testimony relating to how the fall occurred would be purely speculative, as is discussed in more detail below. Allowing such evidence would create unfair and significant prejudice to the plaintiff, and therefore, the evidence should be excluded.

3.

THIS COURT MAY EXCLUDE AN EXPERT'S OPINION WHERE BASED UPON SPECULATION OR CONJECTURE

An expert may not base his or her opinion on speculation or conjecture. See *Schuler v. Mid-Central Cardiology*, 313 Ill. App. 3d 326, 334–36, 246 Ill. Dec. 163, 729 N.E.2d 536 (4th Dist. 2000) (trial judge has discretion to exclude expert testimony that is based upon unsupported and speculative facts); *People v. Britz*, 123 Ill. 2d 446, 457–62, 124 Ill. Dec. 15, 528 N.E.2d 703 (1988) (exclusion of expert testimony when the expert's opinion was based upon a party's own self-serving statements); *Department of Transp. v. Bouy*, 69 Ill. App. 3d 29, 33-38, 25 Ill. Dec. 499, 386 N.E.2d 1163 (4th Dist. 1979) (expert's testimony is properly excluded when it is based upon a speculative and conjectural method of proof).

An expert's opinion may also be excluded if it is not shown to be reliable or to be based upon an acceptable method of proof. *People v. Acri*, 277 Ill. App. 3d 1030, 1033–34, 214 Ill. Dec. 761, 662 N.E.2d 115 (3d Dist. 1996) (proper to exclude evidence of dog alerts when the results were not corroborated by laboratory results because experts disagree about whether uncorroborated dog alerts are reliable); *People v. Ferguson*, 172 Ill. App. 3d 1, 8-12, 122 Ill. Dec. 266, 526 N.E.2d 525 (2d Dist. 1988) (improper to allow opinion where witness testified that her theories were not generally accepted in the relevant community); and *Piano v. Davison*, 157 Ill. App. 3d 649, 668, 110 Ill. Dec. 35, 510 N.E.2d 1066 (1st Dist. 1987) (proper to exclude medical treatises when there was no proof that they were reliable).

In the present case, the defense expert will attempt to determine how the fall occurred, and specifically whether the plaintiff was running or walking at the time, based *solely* upon the oil marks on the plaintiff's clothing and shoes.

Too much critical evidence is missing to allow this expert to render a reliable opinion, as follows:

1. There were no witnesses to the accident or the events

leading up to the accident. Due to the severity of the plaintiff's injuries, she has no recollection of how the incident occurred.

2. Immediately after the accident, the defendant cleaned up the oil spill, eliminating the best possible evidence for analysis: the location, direction and length of the slide marks. The defendant has testified that he has no recollection, one way or another, of any slide marks.

3. The expert's tests and analysis on the plaintiff's clothing occurred more than 12 months after the accident date. Prior to conducting the testing, the articles of clothing were stored in a large plastic trash bag in the plaintiff's closet. Since the oil almost certainly transferred to new areas of the clothing while stored in the bag, any tests attempting to reconstruct the incident based upon the location of the stains would be totally speculative.

Based upon the foregoing, it is unclear how the defense expert can render an opinion on this crucial evidence based upon anything other than conjecture, speculation and simple guesswork. As such, it is again requested that the Court exclude any testimony of defendant's expert relating to how the incident occurred.

Dated: *[date]*

Respectfully submitted,
By: ______________________
[name of counsel]
Attorneys for PLAINTIFF,
[name of plaintiff]

§ 8:93 Motion to exclude reference to non-called witnesses

TO: ALL PARTIES AND THEIR RESPECTIVE ATTORNEYS OF RECORD:

PLEASE TAKE NOTICE that plaintiff hereby moves this Court for an order excluding any and all evidence, references to evidence, testimony or argument relating to plaintiff's decision not to call certain treating physicians to testify at the trial on this matter.

This motion is made under the provisions of Illinois case

law, and is based upon the supporting Memorandum of Points and Authorities, the pleadings and papers on file in this action, and upon such of the argument and evidence as may be presented prior to or at the hearing of this matter.

Dated: *[date]*

MEMORANDUM OF POINTS AND AUTHORITIES

1.
PRELIMINARY STATEMENT

This action involves a dog bite incident whereby the plaintiff was injured and permanently disfigured as a result of an attack by the defendant's German Shepherd. Following this incident, the plaintiff sought treatment by five physicians, including the attending emergency room physician (Dr. Carter), plaintiff's primary care doctor (Dr. Kaiser), a plastic surgeon (Dr. Nippentuck), and two orthopedic surgeons (Dr. Bones and Dr. Fixit).

The plaintiff has chosen to call Dr. Carter, Dr. Fixit and Dr. Nippentuck to testify at trial. To avoid needless duplication of evidence, the plaintiff has chosen not to call the remaining witnesses.

This motion seeks to preclude the defendant from making reference to the fact that the other two treating physicians will not be called to testify in this matter, or to speculate as to what the non-called witnesses might have said on the stand.

2.
PREJUDICIAL EVIDENCE MAY BE EXCLUDED

Federal Rule of Evidence 403 states:

> Although relevant, evidence may be excluded if its probative value is substantially outweighed by the danger of unfair prejudice, confusion of the issues, or misleading the jury, or by considerations of undue delay, waste of time, or needless presentation of cumulative evidence.

Illinois has a common-law rule that is comparable to Federal Rule of Evidence 403. See *People v. Peete*, 318 Ill. App. 3d 961, 966–67, 252 Ill. Dec. 821, 743 N.E.2d 689 (4th Dist. 2001); *People v. Walker*, 335 Ill. App. 3d 102, 112, 268 Ill. Dec. 654, 779 N.E.2d 268 (2d Dist. 2002), as modified on denial of reh'g, (Oct. 24, 2002) and judgment aff'd, 211 Ill. 2d 317, 285 Ill. Dec. 519, 812 N.E.2d 339 (2004).

Illinois case law is clear that Evidence should be excluded when the prejudicial impact of the evidence outweighs the probative value of it. *Department of Public Works and Bldgs. v. Roehrig*, 45 Ill. App. 3d 189, 196, 3 Ill. Dec. 893, 359 N.E.2d 752 (5th Dist. 1976) (exclusion of evidence of prior condemnations in a condemnation case because the prejudicial impact outweighs the probative value of it); *People v. Holman*, 257 Ill. App. 3d 1031, 1033–34, 196 Ill. Dec. 457, 630 N.E.2d 154 (2d Dist. 1994) (evidence is admissible if it is relevant and if the prejudicial impact does not substantially outweigh the probative value of it); and, *Hulsebus v. Russian*, 118 Ill. App. 2d 174, 180–81, 254 N.E.2d 184 (2d Dist. 1969) (trial judge had discretion to exclude a gruesome photograph of the plaintiff during surgery because other evidence established the extent of the injury and because the photograph was likely to inflame and prejudice the jury).

Reference to the fact that these doctors were not called is likely to create prejudice against the plaintiff without offering any probative value to the issues.

3.
ANY REFERENCE TO THE TESTIMONY OF NON-CALLED WITNESSES WOULD BE PURE SPECULATION

A party should not be permitted to refer to a non-called witness when the reference would cause the jury to speculate that the other party was hiding evidence. *Thompson v. Abbott Laboratories*, 193 Ill. App. 3d 188, 201–04, 140 Ill. Dec. 423, 549 N.E.2d 1295 (2d Dist. 1990) (trial judge properly declined to give the missing witness instruction when the witnesses at issue would have been cumulative to other witnesses and when the instruction could have implied to the jurors that one party was hiding evidence from the other); *Adami v. Belmonte*, 302 Ill. App. 3d 17, 25-26, 235 Ill. Dec. 135, 704 N.E.2d 708 (1st Dist. 1998) (trial judge properly declined to give Illinois Pattern Jury Instruction 5.01 [the missing witness instruction] when the missing witness was not adverse to the non-producing party and the testimony would have been cumulative); *People v. Munday*, 280 Ill. 32, 40–49, 117 N.E. 286 (1917) (improper to comment on the defendant's failure to call his co-defendants to testify and the comment improperly shifted the burden of proof).

In the present case, any comments regarding the plaintiff's failure to call a treating physician, even without a suggestion as what the witnesses might or might not have said on the stand, would invite exactly the type of speculation forbidden by the above-referenced cases. As such, the evidence should be excluded.

4.
COUNSEL MAY NOT COMMENT ON A PARTY'S FAILURE TO CALL CERTAIN WITNESSES

It is impermissible for a party to attempt to admit evidence or comment upon the fact that another party did not call certain witnesses, where the witnesses were equally available to each party to subpoena. *People v. Munday*, 280 Ill. 32, 40–49, 117 N.E. 286 (1917) (a party cannot comment upon another party's failure to call a witness, where the witness was equally available to be called to testify by each party).

In fact, Illinois Pattern Jury Instruction number 5.01 states:

FAILURE TO PRODUCE EVIDENCE OR A WITNESS

If a party to this case has failed *[to offer evidence] [to produce a witness]* within his power to produce, you may infer that the *[evidence] [testimony of the witness]* would be adverse to that party if you believe each of the following elements:

1. The [evidence] [witness] was under the control of the party and could have been produced by the exercise of reasonable diligence.

2. *The [evidence] [witness] was not equally available to an adverse party.*

3. A reasonably prudent person under the same or similar circumstances would have [offered the evidence] [produced the witness] if he believed [it to be] [the testimony would be] favorable to him.

4. No reasonable excuse for the failure has been shown. (Emphasis added.)

In the present case, the defendant was advised of the identity of all treating physicians early in this action and had ample opportunity to subpoena the witnesses for deposition prior to trial. Having passed on this opportunity, any reference to what the uncalled witnesses might have testified to would be pure speculation, and should be excluded.

5.
CALLING THE OTHER TREATING PHYSICIANS WOULD CREATE NEEDLESS DUPLICATION OF EVIDENCE

As noted previously, Federal Rule of Evidence 403 states:

Although relevant, evidence may be excluded if its probative value is substantially outweighed by the danger of unfair prejudice, confusion of the issues, or misleading the jury, or by considerations of undue delay, waste of time, or needless presentation of cumulative evidence.

Illinois has a common-law rule that is comparable to Federal Rule of Evidence 403. See *People v. Peete*, 318 Ill. App. 3d 961, 966–67, 252 Ill. Dec. 821, 743 N.E.2d 689 (4th Dist. 2001);

People v. Walker, 335 Ill. App. 3d 102, 112, 268 Ill. Dec. 654, 779 N.E.2d 268 (2d Dist. 2002), as modified on denial of reh'g, (Oct. 24, 2002) and judgment aff'd, 211 Ill. 2d 317, 285 Ill. Dec. 519, 812 N.E.2d 339 (2004).

It has been held that no negative presumption should arise from a failure to call witnesses to testify on matters where there were a number of other witnesses to testify on the same matter. See *Adami v. Belmonte*, 302 Ill. App. 3d 17, 25-26, 235 Ill. Dec. 135, 704 N.E.2d 708 (1st Dist. 1998) (trial judge properly declined to give Illinois Pattern Jury Instruction 5.01 [the missing witness instruction] when the missing witness was not adverse to the non-producing party and the testimony would have been cumulative); and *Thompson v. Abbott Laboratories*, 193 Ill. App. 3d 188, 201–04, 140 Ill. Dec. 423, 549 N.E.2d 1295 (2d Dist. 1990) (trial judge properly declined to give the missing witness instruction when the witnesses at issue would have been cumulative to other witnesses and when the instruction could have implied to the jurors that one party was hiding evidence from the other).

In the present case, the witnesses who will testify will provide ample proof of all the plaintiff's claims in this case. To call the additional witnesses would only unnecessarily delay the proceedings and add needless expense to all parties involved. As such, there is no need to call those witnesses and the plaintiff should not be penalized for exercising such judicial economy.

6.
CONCLUSION

Based on the foregoing, it is respectfully requested that the Court issue the accompanying In Limine Order, as prayed.

Dated: *[date]*

By: ______________________
[name of counsel]
Attorneys for PLAINTIFF,
[name of plaintiff]

§ 8:94 Motion to exclude Evidence of computerized valuations of plaintiff's business, with alternative motion for a *Frye* hearing regarding the validity of the methodology

TO: ALL PARTIES AND THEIR RESPECTIVE ATTORNEYS OF RECORD:

PLEASE TAKE NOTICE that defendant hereby moves this Court for an order excluding evidence of computerized valuations of plaintiff's business or in the alternative for a *Frye* hearing regarding the validity of the methodology underlying such computerized valuations. This motion is based upon the grounds that such valuations are speculative and prejudicial and that such testing has not been deemed to be based upon reliable methodology by the courts of this State. This Motion is also based upon the supporting Memorandum of Points and Authorities, the pleadings and papers on file in this action, and upon such argument and evidence as may be presented prior to or at the hearing of this matter.

Dated: *[date]*

MEMORANDUM OF POINTS AND AUTHORITIES

1. PRELIMINARY STATEMENT

This action arises from an incident in August of 2005, when plaintiff claims that defendant removed certain trade secrets from plaintiff's place of business and used them to benefit defendant's business and as a result, diminish and devalue plaintiff's business. Throughout the discovery in this matter, plaintiff has repeatedly referred to and relied upon computer generated evidence to support his claims regarding the value of his business before August of 2005 and after August of 2005.

By this motion, plaintiff seeks an order excluding evidence of computerized valuations of plaintiff's business or in the alternative for a *Frye* hearing regarding the validity of the methodology underlying such computerized valuations.

2. THIS COURT MAY EXCLUDE PREJUDICIAL EVIDENCE IN ADVANCE OF TRIAL BY WAY OF AN IN LIMINE MOTION

This Court has authority to grant a motion in limine, in advance of trial, which excludes inadmissible evidence, as well as any and all reference by the parties, attorneys and witnesses to the inadmissible evidence. *Cunningham v. Millers General Ins. Co.*, 227 Ill.App.3d 201, 205, 591 N.E.2d 80, 169

Ill.Dec. 200 (4th Dist. 1992); *Cochran v. Great Atlantic & Pacific Tea Co.*, 203 Ill.App.3d 935, 937–38, 561 N.E.2d 229, 148 Ill.Dec. 923 (5th Dist 1990). In fact, "[w]here the evidence could be prejudicial, an order granting a motion in limine may be safer than an order denying it; the evidence will then be kept out until it is clear it should be admitted." *Cunningham v. Millers General Ins. Co.*, 227 Ill.App.3d at 205.

Under Illinois law, evidence should be excluded when the prejudicial impact of the evidence outweighs the probative value of it. Federal Rule of Evidence 403 states: Although relevant, evidence may be excluded if its probative value is substantially outweighed by the danger of unfair prejudice, confusion of the issues, or misleading the jury, or by considerations of undue delay, waste of time, or needless presentation of cumulative evidence. Illinois has a common-law rule that is comparable to Federal Rule of Evidence 403. See *People v. Peete*, 318 Ill. App. 3d 961, 966–67, 252 Ill. Dec. 821, 743 N.E.2d 689 (4th Dist. 2001); *People v. Walker*, 335 Ill. App. 3d 102, 112, 268 Ill. Dec. 654, 779 N.E.2d 268 (2d Dist. 2002), as modified on denial of reh'g, (Oct. 24, 2002) and judgment aff'd, 211 Ill. 2d 317, 285 Ill. Dec. 519, 812 N.E.2d 339 (2004).

In fact, Illinois cases have excluded evidence when the prejudicial impact of the evidence outweighed the probative value of it. See e.g. *Department of Public Works and Bldgs. v. Roehrig*, 45 Ill. App. 3d 189, 196, 3 Ill. Dec. 893, 359 N.E.2d 752 (5th Dist. 1976) (exclusion of evidence of prior condemnations in a condemnation case because the prejudicial impact outweighs the probative value of it); and *People v. Holman*, 257 Ill. App. 3d 1031, 1033–34, 196 Ill. Dec. 457, 630 N.E.2d 154 (2d Dist. 1994) (evidence is admissible if it is relevant and if the prejudicial impact does not substantially outweigh the probative value of it).

Moreover, the Court should determine whether to exclude this evidence outside of the presence of the jury in order to prevent the jury from hearing about inadmissible material. Specifically, Federal Rule of evidence 103(c) provides: Hearing of Jury.—In jury cases, proceedings shall be conducted, to the extent practicable, so as to prevent inadmissible evidence from being suggested to the jury by any means, such as making statements or offers of proof or asking questions in the hearing of the jury. Although this rule has not been specifically codified in Illinois, Illinois has adopted other Federal Rules of evidence through case law. See e.g. *People v. Monroe*, 66 Ill. 2d 317, 321–22, 5 Ill. Dec. 824, 362 N.E.2d 295 (1977); and *Spencer v.*

Wandolowski, 264 Ill. App. 3d 611, 617, 201 Ill. Dec. 422, 636 N.E.2d 854 (1st Dist. 1994) (adopting Federal Rule of Evidence 401).

In the instant matter, the jury will be prejudiced merely by hearing any reference to the computerized valuations. Thus, the computerized valuations should be excluded from the trial in this matter.

3. THIS COURT MAY EXCLUDE THE COMPUTERIZED VALUATIONS, AS IMPROPER SPECULATION

It is improper to provide an opinion to the jury that is based upon speculation or conjecture. See *Schuler v. Mid-Central Cardiology*, 313 Ill. App. 3d 326, 334–36, 246 Ill. Dec. 163, 729 N.E.2d 536 (4th Dist. 2000) (trial judge has discretion to exclude expert testimony that is based upon unsupported and speculative facts); *People v. Britz*, 123 Ill. 2d 446, 457–62, 124 Ill. Dec. 15, 528 N.E.2d 703 (1988) (exclusion of expert testimony when the expert's opinion was based upon a party's own self-serving statements); *Department of Transp. v. Bouy*, 69 Ill. App. 3d 29, 33–38, 25 Ill. Dec. 499, 386 N.E.2d 1163 (4th Dist. 1979) (expert's testimony is properly excluded when it is based upon a speculative and conjectural method of proof).

Upon information and belief, in the case at bar, without establishing any foundation for the reliability of computerized valuations, plaintiff will attempt to provide evidence of the valuations to the jury. The plaintiff should be barred from offering evidence of the computerized valuations, because there is no evidence that they represent anything more than pure speculation. In fact, the Illinois Supreme Court has stated that "garbage" into the computer will lead to "garbage" coming out of it. *Grand Liquor Co, Inc. v. Dept. of Revenue*, 67 Ill.2d 195, 198–203, 367 N.E.2d 1238, 10 Ill.Dec. 472 (1977). Without the proper foundation to establish the reliability and accuracy of the computerized valuations, they represent pure speculation and must be excluded.

4. THIS COURT MAY EXCLUDE THE COMPUTERIZED VALUATIONS, AS HEARSAY

The computerized valuations should also be excluded as improper hearsay. Illinois case law creates a distinction between computer-generated and computer-stored records. *People v. Casey*, 225 Ill.App.3d 82, 88–89, 587 N.E.2d 511, 167 Ill.Dec. 242 (1st Dist. 1992). Computer-generated records are records that are created solely by a computer's internal processing. *Anderson v. Alberto-Culver USA*, 337 Ill.App.3d 643, 667–68, 789 N.E.2d 304, 273 Ill.Dec. 404 (1st Dist. 2003). In contrast, computer-stored records are defined as records that were purposefully and manually entered into a computer, through a human being's selection process. *People v. Casey*, 225 Ill.App.3d at 88–89. Printouts of computer-stored records should generally be excluded as hearsay, because the author of the records cannot be subjected to cross-examination. *People v. Casey*, 225 Ill.App.3d at 88–89. Moreover, even if an exception to the hearsay rule applies to the records at issue, they should not be admitted unless there is a foundation provided to indicate the reliability of them. *In re Marriage of DeLarco*, 313 Ill.App.3d 107, 114–15, 728 N.E.2d 1278, 245 Ill.Dec. 921 (2nd Dist. 2000); *Grand Liquor Co, Inc. v. Dept. of Revenue*, 67 Ill.2d 195, 198–203, 367 N.E.2d 1238, 10 Ill.Dec. 472 (1977) ("garbage" into the computer will lead to "garbage" coming out of it). The plaintiff's valuation reports represent inadmissible computer-stored records and should be excluded.

It is true that Illinois law allows an expert to rely on reports of others, if the reports that are relied upon by the expert are generally accepted and relied upon in the expert's field. *Bachman v. General Motors Corp.*, 332 Ill.App.3d 760, 778–80, 776 N.E.2d 262, 267 Ill.Dec. 125 (4th Dist. 2002); *In re Commitment of Simmons*, 213 Ill.2d 523, 529–43, 821 N.E.2d 1184, 290 Ill.Dec. 610 (2004); *Frye v. United States*, 293 F. 1013 (D.C. Cir. 1923). However, if there is insufficient proof that the expert's methodology is generally accepted, then the opinion that was generated as a result of that methodology, should not be admitted into evidence. *People v. Acri*, 277 Ill.App.3d 1030, 1032–34, 662 N.E.2d 115, 214 Ill.Dec. 761 (3rd Dist. 1996). Moreover, an expert should not be permitted to merely read from another expert's report. *Mehochko v. Gold Seal Co.*, 66 Ill.App.2d 54, 57–59, 213 N.E.2d 581 (5th Dist. 1966). In addition, an expert cannot merely repeat hearsay statements made by another expert. *People v. Swanson*, 335 Ill.App.3d 117, 125–26, 780 N.E.2d 342, 269 Ill.Dec. 157 (2nd Dist. 2002).

Based upon the foregoing, the computerized valuations should be excluded from the trial in this matter, as hearsay.

5. IN THE ALTERNATIVE, THIS COURT SHOULD HOLD A *FRYE* HEARING TO DETERMINE WHETHER THE COMPUTERIZED VALUATIONS ARE BASED UPON ACCEPTED METHODOLGY

The authorities, described above, justify the preclusion of

computerized valuation reports. In the alternative, this Court should conduct a *Frye* hearing, to determine the level of acceptance of such computerized valuations. *People v. Wheeler*, 334 Ill.App.3d 273, 282–83, 777 N.E.2d 961, 268 Ill.Dec. 38 (3rd Dist. 2002); *Frye v. United States*, 293 F. 1013 (D.C. Cir. 1923). Moreover, such evidence should not be admitted if it only raises a possibility of accuracy. *People v. Wheeler*, 334 Ill.App.3d at 284–86. In fact, an expert's opinion should be excluded if it is not shown to be reliable or to be based upon an acceptable method of proof. *People v. Acri*, 277 Ill. App. 3d 1030, 1033–34, 214 Ill. Dec. 761, 662 N.E.2d 115 (3d Dist. 1996) (proper to exclude evidence of dog alerts when the results were not corroborated by laboratory results because experts disagree about whether uncorroborated dog alerts are reliable); *People v. Ferguson*, 172 Ill. App. 3d 1, 8–12, 122 Ill. Dec. 266, 526 N.E.2d 525 (2d Dist. 1988) (improper to allow opinion where witness testified that her theories were not generally accepted in the relevant community); and *Piano v. Davison*, 157 Ill. App. 3d 649, 668, 110 Ill. Dec. 35, 510 N.E.2d 1066 (1st Dist. 1987) (proper to exclude medical treatises when there was no proof that they were reliable).

For the foregoing reasons, if the Court declines to enter an order excluding evidence of computerized valuations of plaintiff's business, then the Court should hold a *Frye* hearing regarding the validity of the methodology underlying such computerized valuations.

6. CONCLUSION

Based on the foregoing, defendant respectfully requests that this Court enter an order instructing plaintiff and his counsel not to mention, refer to, interrogate concerning, or attempt to convey to the fact finder, in any manner, either directly or indirectly, any of the above-mentioned facts or information, without first obtaining permission of this Court and further, to instruct plaintiff and his counsel to warn and caution each and every one of his witnesses to follow these instructions. In the alternative, plaintiff requests a *Frye* hearing, prior to the admission of any such evidence and prior to the use of any such evidence by counsel for the parties, the parties or the parties' witnesses.

Dated: *[date]*

By: ______________
[name of counsel]
Attorneys for Defendant,
[name of defendant]

§ 8:95 Motion to exclude testimony and opinions of medical doctor

TO: ALL PARTIES AND THEIR RESPECTIVE ATTORNEYS OF RECORD:

PLEASE TAKE NOTICE that defendant hereby moves this Court for an order excluding any and all evidence, references to evidence, opinions, testimony or argument relating to Dr. Benjamin Smith. This motion is based upon the grounds that Dr. Benjamin Smith's testimony is speculative and was not fully disclosed to defendant. This motion is also based upon the supporting Memorandum of Points and Authorities, the pleadings and papers on file in this action, and upon such argument and evidence as may be presented prior to or at the hearing of this matter.

Dated: *[date]*

MEMORANDUM OF POINTS AND AUTHORITIES

1. PRELIMINARY STATEMENT

This action is a medical malpractice claim wherein plaintiff alleges that she was permanently disabled as a result of surgery that was allegedly improperly performed by defendant on plaintiff's back, on August 13, 2005.

During the discovery of this matter, plaintiff disclosed Dr. Benjamin Smith as an expert witness who would provide an opinion regarding her current physical condition. However, during his deposition, in September of 2007, Dr. Benjamin Smith specifically testified, "I have no knowledge [with regards to her [the Plaintiff's] current condition]." In addition, he stated that his opinion with respect to the Plaintiff's long term prognosis "would be speculative." A copy of the relevant portions of the deposition of Dr. Benjamin Smith is attached hereto, as Exhibit A.

By this motion, plaintiff seeks an order excluding evidence of opinions, testimony or argument relating to Dr. Benjamin Smith.

2. THIS COURT MAY EXCLUDE PREJUDICIAL AND MISLEADING EVIDENCE IN ADVANCE OF TRIAL BY WAY OF AN IN LIMINE MOTION

This Court has authority to grant a motion in limine, in advance of trial, which excludes inadmissible evidence, as well as any and all reference by the parties, attorneys and witnesses to the inadmissible evidence. *Cunningham v. Millers General Ins. Co.*, 227 Ill.App.3d 201, 205, 591 N.E.2d 80, 169 Ill.Dec. 200 (4th Dist. 1992); *Cochran v. Great Atlantic & Pacific Tea Co.*, 203 Ill.App.3d 935, 937–38, 561 N.E.2d 229, 148 Ill.Dec. 923 (5th Dist 1990). In fact, "[w]here the evidence could be prejudicial, an order granting a motion in limine may be safer than an order denying it; the evidence will then be kept out until it is clear it should be admitted." *Cunningham v. Millers General Ins. Co.*, 227 Ill.App.3d at 205.

Under Illinois law, evidence should be excluded when the prejudicial impact of the evidence outweighs the probative value of it. Federal Rule of Evidence 403 states: Although relevant, evidence may be excluded if its probative value is substantially outweighed by the danger of unfair prejudice, confusion of the issues, or misleading the jury, or by considerations of undue delay, waste of time, or needless presentation of cumulative evidence. Illinois has a common-law rule that is comparable to Federal Rule of Evidence 403. See *People v. Peete*, 318 Ill. App. 3d 961, 966–67, 252 Ill. Dec. 821, 743 N.E.2d 689 (4th Dist. 2001); *People v. Walker*, 335 Ill. App. 3d 102, 112, 268 Ill. Dec. 654, 779 N.E.2d 268 (2d Dist. 2002), as modified on denial of reh'g, (Oct. 24, 2002) and judgment aff'd, 211 Ill. 2d 317, 285 Ill. Dec. 519, 812 N.E.2d 339 (2004).

In the instant matter, it is clear that any testimony or opinions of Dr. Benjamin Smith as they relate to the plaintiff's current condition would be prejudicial and misleading to the jury, because he testified, "I have no knowledge [with regards to her [the Plaintiff's] current condition]." Thus, this Court should enter an order excluding any and all evidence, references to evidence, opinions, testimony or argument relating to Dr. Benjamin Smith in the trial for this matter.

3. THIS COURT MAY EXCLUDE THE TESTIMONY AND OPINIONS OF DR. BENJAMIN SMITH AS REPRESENTING IMPROPER SPECULATION

It is improper to provide an opinion to the jury that is based upon speculation or conjecture. See *Schuler v. Mid-Central*

Cardiology, 313 Ill. App. 3d 326, 334–36, 246 Ill. Dec. 163, 729 N.E.2d 536 (4th Dist. 2000) (trial judge has discretion to exclude expert testimony that is based upon unsupported and speculative facts); *People v. Britz*, 123 Ill. 2d 446, 457–62, 124 Ill. Dec. 15, 528 N.E.2d 703 (1988) (exclusion of expert testimony when the expert's opinion was based upon a party's own self-serving statements); *Department of Transp. v. Bouy*, 69 Ill. App. 3d 29, 33–38, 25 Ill. Dec. 499, 386 N.E.2d 1163 (4th Dist. 1979) (expert's testimony is properly excluded when it is based upon a speculative and conjectural method of proof). Moreover, an expert may not provide opinions to the jury if the opinions are based upon speculative and uncertain assumptions. *Modelski v. Navistar Intern. Transp. Corp.*, 302 Ill.App.3d 879, 885–86, 707 N.E.2d 239, 236 Ill.Dec. 394 (1st Dist. 1999); *LaSalle Nat. Trust, N.A. v. Swedish Covenant Hosp.*, 273 Ill.App.3d 780, 791–92, 652 N.E.2d 1089, 210 Ill.Dec. 113 (1st Dist. 1995); *Hussung v. Patel*, 369 Ill.App.3d 924, 931–34, 861 N.E.2d 678, 308 Ill.Dec. 347 (2nd Dist. 2007).

The deposition testimony of Dr. Benjamin Smith, as described above, shows that his opinions are improperly speculative and based upon unproven assumptions and thus, his opinions and testimony should be excluded from the evidence at this trial.

4. EVIDENCE OF THE TESTIMONY AND OPINIONS OF DR. BENJAMIN SMITH SHOULD BE EXCLUDED TO PREVENT UNFAIR SURPRISE TO DEFENDANT

To avoid unfair surprise, the Court may exclude evidence on issues where discovery responses and actions of counsel led opposing counsel to believe those issues would not be litigated. See *Harding v. Amsted Industries, Inc.*, 276 Ill. App. 3d 483, 492, 213 Ill. Dec. 187, 658 N.E.2d 1208 (1st Dist. 1995) (trial judge properly excluded expert testimony that exceeded the opinions expressed by the expert during discovery); and *Savage v. Martin*, 256 Ill. App. 3d 272, 285, 195 Ill. Dec. 142, 628 N.E.2d 606 (1st Dist. 1993) (expert opinion that went beyond opinions stated at deposition properly excluded, where expert stated that he had no other opinions beyond those in his report. Furthermore, the Court is within its power to preclude a party from introducing documents not discovered by the opposing party, where the relevant evidence is not disclosed during discovery. See Illinois Supreme Court Rule 219; *King v. Clemons*, 264 Ill. App. 3d 138, 140–41, 201 Ill. Dec. 630, 636 N.E.2d 1062 (5th Dist. 1994); *Golembiewski v. Hallberg Ins. Agency, Inc.*, 262 Ill. App. 3d 1082, 1086–87, 200 Ill. Dec. 113, 635

N.E.2d 452 (1st Dist. 1994); and *Ashpole v. Brunswick Bowling and Billiards Corp.*, 297 Ill. App. 3d 725, 726–30, 232 Ill. Dec. 308, 697 N.E.2d 1238 (2d Dist. 1998).

In the present case, plaintiff's statements and actions led defense counsel to reasonably believe that Dr. Benjamin Smith had no knowledge regarding plaintiff's condition. It would be unfair and prejudicial to allow plaintiff, at this late date, to present evidence from Dr. Benjamin Smith on that issue. Thus, the Court should therefore exclude any and all evidence, including any mention of evidence, relating to Dr. Benjamin Smith, to prevent unfair surprise to defendant.

5. CONCLUSION

Based on the foregoing, defendant respectfully requests that this Court exclude any testimony or documentary evidence, or mention of any evidence, or argument relating to Dr. Benjamin Smith.

Dated: *[date]*

By: ___________________
[name of counsel]
Attorneys for Defendant,
[name of defendant]

Chapter 9

Trial Presentation

I. MOTION AUTHORITIES

A. MOTION TO PREVENT IMPROPER VOIR DIRE

B. MOTION TO EXCLUDE IMPROPER ARGUMENTS OR COMMENTS IN OPENING STATEMENT

C. MOTION TO BAR PREMATURE REBUTTAL TO AFFIRMATIVE DEFENSES

D. MOTION RE REFERENCE TO LOST OR DESTROYED EVIDENCE

E. MOTION TO EXCLUDE ARBITRATION EVIDENCE AND FINDINGS

F. MOTION TO EXCLUDE EVIDENCE OF DAMAGES OR LIABILITY IN BIFURCATED TRIAL

G. MOTION TO PRECLUDE "GOLDEN RULE ARGUMENT"

I. MOTION AUTHORITIES

A. MOTION TO PREVENT IMPROPER VOIR DIRE

Voir dire is the first opportunity for counsel to speak directly to the jurors. The parties, through their counsel, have an absolute right to directly question the prospective jurors. *Grossman v. Gebarowski*, 315 Ill. App. 3d 213, 247 Ill. Dec. 768, 732 N.E.2d 1100 (1st Dist. 2000). The stated goal of jury selection is selection of an impartial jury who will render a fair and reasonable verdict, based upon the applicable law and evidence presented. We all know, however, that to be successful, counsel must take advantage of this opportunity to personally interact with the jurors (to create a bond) and find out which jurors would be the most supportive of counsel's case. Nevertheless, counsel cannot cross the line by asking improper questions to precondition the jurors. Knowing which questions are appropriate and which are not, is critical. Motions in limine should be used to prevent counsel from "crossing the line" during jury selection.

§ 9:1 Suggested motion text

[Name of moving party] hereby moves this Court for an order

prohibiting counsel for *[name party]* from conducting any voir dire that relates to *[describe anticipated improper voir dire questions, e.g., educating the jury on the state of the governing law in this case]*. The motion is based upon the ground that *[state basis for belief that improper voir dire will occur, e.g., opposing counsel's proposed voir dire questions listed inappropriate matters, including a description of the pleadings and statements of law]*, which, if allowed, would unfairly precondition the jury in this case.

§ 9:2 Motion summary

This motion is used to restrict counsel from preconditioning the jury by asking improper questions during voir dire. The motion is based upon the authority of Illinois Supreme Court Rules 234 and 431 and cases in this area. See *People v. Tenney*, 329 Ill. App. 3d 430, 439–41, 264 Ill. Dec. 26, 769 N.E.2d 528 (2d Dist. 2002), appeal denied, judgment vacated, 206 Ill. 2d 641, 278 Ill. Dec. 813, 799 N.E.2d 678 (2003) and *People v. Dow*, 240 Ill. App. 3d 392, 396–99, 181 Ill. Dec. 186, 608 N.E.2d 259 (1st Dist. 1992).

◆ **Note:** Absent a factual basis to support a claim of preconditioning, this motion may be better suited for a pretrial stipulation. Facts that might warrant a motion on this issue include past attorney misconduct, information on proposed voir dire questionnaires, comments of counsel, etc. Be prepared to support your motion with a detailed declaration, or consider making the motion orally at a sidebar during voir dire, if necessary.

§ 9:3 Supporting authorities—Improper voir dire

◆ **Note:** Before preparing for voir dire, it is important to check the local rules of the jurisdiction where the case is pending, because local rules may put additional restrictions upon the manner of conducting voir dire.

Illinois Supreme Court Rule 234 applies to civil cases and states:

> The court shall conduct the voir dire examination of prospective jurors by putting to them questions it thinks appropriate touching upon their qualifications to serve as jurors in the case on trial. The court may permit the parties to submit additional questions to it for further inquiry if it thinks they are appropriate, and *shall permit the parties to supplement the examination by such direct inquiry as the court deems proper* for a reasonable period of time depending upon the length of examination by the court, the complexity of the case, and the nature and extent of the damages. *Questions shall not directly or indirectly concern*

> *matters of law or instructions*. The court shall acquaint prospective jurors with the general duties and responsibilities of jurors. (Emphasis added.)

Illinois Supreme Court Rule 431 applies to criminal cases and states:

> (a) The court shall conduct voir dire examination of prospective jurors by putting to them questions it thinks appropriate, touching upon their qualifications to serve as jurors in the case at trial. *The court may permit the parties to submit additional questions to it for further inquiry if it thinks they are appropriate and shall permit the parties to supplement the examination by such direct inquiry as the court deems proper for a reasonable period of time depending upon the length of examination by the court, the complexity of the case, and the nature of the charges. Questions shall not directly or indirectly concern matters of law or instructions.* The court shall acquaint prospective jurors with the general duties and responsibilities of jurors.
>
> (b) The court shall ask each potential juror, individually or in a group, whether that juror understands and accepts the following principles: (1) that the defendant is presumed innocent of the charge(s) against him or her; (2) that before a defendant can be convicted the State must prove the defendant guilty beyond a reasonable doubt; (3) that the defendant is not required to offer any evidence on his or her own behalf; and (4) that the defendant's failure to testify cannot be held against him or her; *however, no inquiry of a prospective juror shall be made into the defendant's failure to testify when the defendant objects.*
>
> The court's method of inquiry shall provide each juror an opportunity to respond to specific questions concerning the principles set out in this section. (emphasis added).

725 ILCS 5/114-3 states:

> (a) Any objection to the manner in which a jury panel has been selected or drawn shall be raised by a motion to discharge the jury panel prior to the voir dire examination. For good cause shown the court may entertain the motion after the voir dire has begun but such motion shall not be heard after a jury has been sworn to hear the cause.
>
> (b) The motion shall be in writing supported by affidavit and shall state facts which show that the jury panel was improperly selected or drawn.
>
> (c) If the motion states facts which show that the jury panel has been improperly selected or drawn it shall be the duty of the court to conduct a hearing. The burden of proving that the jury panel was improperly selected or drawn shall be upon the movant.
>
> (d) If the court finds that the jury panel was improperly selected or drawn the court shall order the jury panel discharged and the

selection or drawing of a new panel in the manner provided by law.

See also Federal Rule of Evidence 403, which states:

> Although relevant, evidence may be excluded if its probative value is substantially outweighed by the danger of unfair prejudice, confusion of the issues, or misleading the jury, or by considerations of undue delay, waste of time, or needless presentation of cumulative evidence.

It must be noted that this Rule has not been codified in Illinois. However, Illinois cases have stated that Illinois has a common-law rule that is comparable to Federal Rule of Evidence 403. See *People v. Walker*, 335 Ill. App. 3d 102, 112, 268 Ill. Dec. 654, 779 N.E.2d 268 (2d Dist. 2002), as modified on denial of reh'g, (Oct. 24, 2002) and judgment aff'd, 211 Ill. 2d 317, 285 Ill. Dec. 519, 812 N.E.2d 339 (2004); and *People v. Peete*, 318 Ill. App. 3d 961, 966–67, 252 Ill. Dec. 821, 743 N.E.2d 689 (4th Dist. 2001).

See also *People v. Holman*, 257 Ill. App. 3d 1031, 1033–34, 196 Ill. Dec. 457, 630 N.E.2d 154 (2d Dist. 1994) (evidence is admissible if it is relevant and if the prejudicial impact does not substantially outweigh its probative value).

Foley v. Fletcher, 361 Ill. App. 3d 39, 50-51, 296 Ill. Dec. 916, 836 N.E.2d 667 (1st Dist. 2005) (the trial court did not abuse its discretion by barring the defendant's request to show a day-in-the-life video of the plaintiff during voir dire).

§ 9:4 Supporting authorities—Preconditioning

People v. Tenney, 347 Ill. App. 3d 359, 368–69, 283 Ill. Dec. 100, 807 N.E.2d 705 (2d Dist. 2004) (trial judge properly prohibited the defendant from asking the jurors during voir dire if they knew people with substance abuse problems and about how they would "handle" such problems).

People v. Tenney, 347 Ill. App. 3d 359, 368–69, 283 Ill. Dec. 100, 807 N.E.2d 705 (2d Dist. 2004) (purpose of voir dire is to ensure that the selected jury is not biased or prejudiced against a party).

People v. Dow, 240 Ill. App. 3d 392, 396–99, 181 Ill. Dec. 186, 608 N.E.2d 259 (1st Dist. 1992) (trial judge properly disallowed a question which was designed to precondition the jury to find in the defendant's favor).

Gasiorowski v. Homer, 47 Ill. App. 3d 989, 994, 7 Ill. Dec. 758, 365 N.E.2d 43 (1st Dist. 1977) (in a vehicle and pedestrian collision, the trial judge properly barred voir dire questions regarding whether the jurors had ever crossed in the middle of a block while walking or if they had ever seen anyone do so).

Gasiorowski v. Homer, 47 Ill. App. 3d 989, 991–94, 7 Ill. Dec. 758, 365 N.E.2d 43 (1st Dist. 1977) ("The only legitimate function of voir dire examination is the selection of an impartial jury. Such attempts to go beyond this function and use the process as a means of affecting the minds of jurors and/or of selecting jurors already harboring certain predispositions, threaten in a fundamental way the ideal of a fair trial, and, where possible, should be frustrated at an early stage.").

Christian v. New York Cent. R. Co., 28 Ill. App. 2d 57, 59-69, 170 N.E.2d 183 (4th Dist. 1960) (manner of voir dire was improper when it was too lengthy, directly discussed principles of law, and discussed the issue of the amount of damages that was requested).

§ 9:5 Supporting authorities—Preconditioning—Preconditioning regarding dollar amount of damages

Counsel in personal injury or wrongful death cases may seek to preclude voir dire questions by the opposition referencing a specific dollar figure for damages. (For example, "Would you have any hesitation awarding my client one million dollars if the evidence justified such a recovery?") Authorities include those cited above relating to preconditioning, as well as the following:

Christian v. New York Cent. R. Co., 28 Ill. App. 2d 57, 59-69, 170 N.E.2d 183 (4th Dist. 1960) (manner of voir dire was improper when it was too lengthy, directly discussed principles of law, and discussed the issue of the amount of damages that was requested).

But see *Gowler v. Ferrell-Ross Co.*, 206 Ill. App. 3d 194, 203–04, 150 Ill. Dec. 646, 563 N.E.2d 773 (1st Dist. 1990) (plaintiff's attorney's comment to the jurors during voir dire that the law does not allow "double recovery," was not inaccurate and did not prejudice the defendant); and, *Scully v. Otis Elevator Co.*, 2 Ill. App. 3d 185, 197–98, 275 N.E.2d 905 (1st Dist. 1971) (questions during voir dire which referenced specific dollar amounts for possible damage awards were not improper because they allowed the party to determine if the jurors had a preconceived bias against large damage awards).

§ 9:6 Supporting authorities—Educating jury on the law

Christian v. New York Cent. R. Co., 28 Ill. App. 2d 57, 59-69, 170 N.E.2d 183 (4th Dist. 1960) (manner of voir dire was improper when it was too lengthy, directly discussed principles of law, and discussed the issue of the amount of damages that was requested).

Illinois Supreme Court Rule 234 applies to civil cases and states:

> The court shall conduct the voir dire examination of prospective jurors by putting to them questions it thinks appropriate touching upon their qualifications to serve as jurors in the case on trial. The court may permit the parties to submit additional questions to it for further inquiry if it thinks they are appropriate, and shall permit the parties to supplement the examination by such direct inquiry as the court deems proper for a reasonable period of time depending upon the length of examination by the court, the complexity of the case, and the nature and extent of the damages. *Questions shall not directly or indirectly concern matters of law or instructions.* The court shall acquaint prospective jurors with the general duties and responsibilities of jurors. (Emphasis added.)

Illinois Supreme Court Rule 431 applies to criminal cases and states:

> (a) The court shall conduct voir dire examination of prospective jurors by putting to them questions it thinks appropriate, touching upon their qualifications to serve as jurors in the case at trial. The court may permit the parties to submit additional questions to it for further inquiry if it thinks they are appropriate and shall permit the parties to supplement the examination by such direct inquiry as the court deems proper for a reasonable period of time depending upon the length of examination by the court, the complexity of the case, and the nature of the charges. *Questions shall not directly or indirectly concern matters of law or instructions.* The court shall acquaint prospective jurors with the general duties and responsibilities of jurors.
> (b) The court shall ask each potential juror, individually or in a group, whether that juror understands and accepts the following principles: (1) that the defendant is presumed innocent of the charge(s) against him or her; (2) that before a defendant can be convicted the State must prove the defendant guilty beyond a reasonable doubt; (3) that the defendant is not required to offer any evidence on his or her own behalf; and (4) that the defendant's failure to testify cannot be held against him or her; however, no inquiry of a prospective juror shall be made into the defendant's failure to testify when the defendant objects.
> The court's method of inquiry shall provide each juror an op-

portunity to respond to specific questions concerning the principles set out in this section. (emphasis added).

§ 9:7 Supporting authorities—Other grounds

Other possible grounds for excluding or limiting improper voir dire questions include:

- Prejudicial (§ 2:1 to § 2:4)
- Time-wasting (§ 2:5 to § 2:8)
- Confusing or misleading (§ 2:9 to § 2:12)
- Solely intended to create an emotional bias (§ 2:13 to § 2:19)
- Irrelevant (§ 3:1 to § 3:10)

§ 9:8 Opposition citations—Generally

Rub v. Consolidated Rail Corp., 331 Ill. App. 3d 692, 696–710, 265 Ill. Dec. 56, 771 N.E.2d 1015 (1st Dist. 2002) (permitting extensive questions regarding the juror's opinions about unmarked railroad crossings was not improper because both parties engaged in the questions and neither objected and because it was not found to be a deliberate attempt to indoctrinate the jurors).

People v. Strain, 306 Ill. App. 3d 328, 333–39, 239 Ill. Dec. 516, 714 N.E.2d 74 (1st Dist. 1999), judgment aff'd, 194 Ill. 2d 467, 252 Ill. Dec. 65, 742 N.E.2d 315 (2000) (in a gang related case, the trial judge should have permitted more voir dire questions regarding possible bias against gang members).

People v. Lanter, 230 Ill. App. 3d 72, 73-76, 172 Ill. Dec. 147, 595 N.E.2d 210 (4th Dist. 1992) (trial judge should have permitted more questions aimed at detecting possible bias towards alcohol or drug use, when the defense was going to be intoxication).

Roberts v. Sisters of Saint Francis Health Services, Inc., 198 Ill. App. 3d 891, 899–901, 145 Ill. Dec. 44, 556 N.E.2d 662 (1st Dist. 1990) (rejected by, Lopez v. Southwest Community Health Services, 114 N.M. 2, 833 P.2d 1183 (Ct. App. 1992)) (trial judge had discretion to permit a party to show a "day in the life video" to the potential jurors before voir dire, in order to determine if any of them would have bias).

Gowler v. Ferrell-Ross Co., 206 Ill. App. 3d 194, 203–04, 150 Ill. Dec. 646, 563 N.E.2d 773 (1st Dist. 1990) (plaintiff's attorney's comment to the jurors during voir dire that the law does not allow "double recovery," was not inaccurate and did not prejudice the defendant).

Gowler v. Ferrell-Ross Co., 206 Ill. App. 3d 194, 206–08, 150

Ill. Dec. 646, 563 N.E.2d 773 (1st Dist. 1990) (counsel's description of certain facts of the case during voir dire did not prejudice the opposing party and although it went beyond merely determining bias, it was not an improper attempt to indoctrinate the jury).

Friedman by Friedman v. Park Dist. of Highland Park, 151 Ill. App. 3d 374, 381–82, 104 Ill. Dec. 329, 502 N.E.2d 826 (2d Dist. 1986) (not improper voir dire to inquire whether the juror or the city where the accident had happened was at fault for the juror's prior accident).

Illinois Supreme Court Rule 234 applies to civil cases and states:

> The court shall conduct the voir dire examination of prospective jurors by putting to them questions it thinks appropriate touching upon their qualifications to serve as jurors in the case on trial. *The court may permit the parties to submit additional questions to it for further inquiry if it thinks they are appropriate, and shall permit the parties to supplement the examination by such direct inquiry as the court deems proper for a reasonable period of time depending upon the length of examination by the court, the complexity of the case, and the nature and extent of the damages.* Questions shall not directly or indirectly concern matters of law or instructions. *The court shall acquaint prospective jurors with the general duties and responsibilities of jurors.* (Emphasis added.)

Illinois Supreme Court Rule 431 applies to criminal cases and states:

> (a) The court shall conduct voir dire examination of prospective jurors by putting to them questions it thinks appropriate, touching upon their qualifications to serve as jurors in the case at trial. *The court may permit the parties to submit additional questions to it for further inquiry if it thinks they are appropriate and shall permit the parties to supplement the examination by such direct inquiry as the court deems proper for a reasonable period of time depending upon the length of examination by the court, the complexity of the case, and the nature of the charges.* Questions shall not directly or indirectly concern matters of law or instructions. The court shall acquaint prospective jurors with the general duties and responsibilities of jurors.
>
> *(b) The court shall ask each potential juror, individually or in a group, whether that juror understands and accepts the following principles: (1) that the defendant is presumed innocent of the charge(s) against him or her; (2) that before a defendant can be convicted the State must prove the defendant guilty beyond a reasonable doubt; (3) that the defendant is not required to offer any evidence on his or her own behalf; and (4) that the defendant's failure to testify cannot be held against him or her*; however, no

inquiry of a prospective juror shall be made into the defendant's failure to testify when the defendant objects.

The court's method of inquiry shall provide each juror an opportunity to respond to specific questions concerning the principles set out in this section. (emphasis added).

§ 9:9 Opposition citations—Specific dollar amount

Scully v. Otis Elevator Co., 2 Ill. App. 3d 185, 197–98, 275 N.E.2d 905 (1st Dist. 1971) (questions during voir dire which referenced specific dollar amounts for possible damage awards were not improper because they allowed the party to determine if the jurors had a preconceived bias against large damage awards).

B. MOTION TO EXCLUDE IMPROPER ARGUMENTS OR COMMENTS IN OPENING STATEMENT

The opening statement is often mistakenly referred to as *opening argument*. The purpose of opening statement is to inform the jury of what counsel believes the evidence will show during the trial. This is not the time to *argue* the law, the evidence, or the reasonable inferences therefrom. Counsel will have the opportunity to argue these points during closing arguments. Many attorneys believe that making objections during opening statement is inappropriate. While it is true that counsel should avoid objections whenever possible (because you do not want the jury to think that you are trying to hide something from them), if the comments made are inappropriate and counsel would like to preserve the error for appeal, counsel must make an objection to the comments. If counsel has reason to believe that the opposition intends to make improper comments during opening statement, a motion in limine should be presented. If the court grants counsel's motion, opposing counsel will not be allowed to make the comments, and, as a result, counsel will not be forced to object during the opposition's opening statement. In the event the motion is denied, counsel will have no choice but to object to the comments when they are made to preserve the error on appeal. An objection "for the record" prior to the opening statement may also be sufficient to preserve the error.

◆ **Note:** Prior to opening statements, the court will likely rule on the motions in limine filed by the parties. The judge may reserve ruling on one or more of the motions so that he or she can consider the evidence offered at trial before ruling. When a ruling on a motion is reserved, counsel should ask the court whether or not the evidence sought to be excluded may be mentioned during opening statement. Even if the court allows counsel to mention the evidence in their opening remarks, the most prudent approach is to avoid mentioning the evidence to the jury until the court rules on the motion and allows its admission. Opening statements should be considered a "promise" to the jury of what the evidence will show. If counsel tells the jurors that evidence will be presented and, because of the court's eventual ruling, it is not, counsel's credibility may be undermined in the eyes of the jurors. As we all know, the credibility of the parties *and* their counsel is critical and should always be a top priority during all phases of the trial.

§ 9:10 Suggested motion text

[Name of moving party] hereby moves this Court for an order prohibiting counsel for *[name party]* from mentioning *[describe anticipated improper matter]* during opening statement. The motion is based upon the ground that *[state basis for belief that improper comments will be made, e.g., opposing counsel made several inappropriate comments in the preliminary statement of his trial brief]*, which, if allowed at trial, would create a substantial danger of undue prejudice to *[name of moving party]*.

§ 9:11 Motion summary

This motion is used to prevent counsel from mentioning improper matters in opening statement that would tend to unduly prejudice the moving party. The motion is based upon court's discretionary authority to exclude prejudicial evidence and leading cases. See *People v. Roberts*, 100 Ill. App. 3d 469, 474–76, 55 Ill. Dec. 779, 426 N.E.2d 1104 (1st Dist. 1981); *People v. Weller*, 123 Ill. App. 2d 421, 425–27, 258 N.E.2d 806 (4th Dist. 1970).

◆ **Note:** Absent a factual basis to support a claim of misconduct, this motion may be inappropriate and better suited for a pre-trial stipulation. Facts that might warrant a motion on this issue include past attorney misconduct, comments made by opposing counsel at arbitration, inappropriate material found in a trial brief, etc.

§ 9:12 Supporting authorities—Exclusion of prejudicial evidence, generally

Federal Rule of Evidence 403 states:

Although relevant, evidence may be excluded if its probative value is substantially outweighed by the danger of unfair prejudice, confusion of the issues, or misleading the jury, or by considerations of undue delay, waste of time, or needless presentation of cumulative evidence.

It must be noted that this Rule has not been codified in Illinois. However, Illinois cases have stated that Illinois has a common-law rule that is comparable to Federal Rule of Evidence 403. See *People v. Walker*, 335 Ill. App. 3d 102, 112, 268 Ill. Dec. 654, 779 N.E.2d 268 (2d Dist. 2002), as modified on denial of reh'g, (Oct. 24, 2002) and judgment aff'd, 211 Ill. 2d 317, 285 Ill. Dec. 519, 812 N.E.2d 339 (2004); and *People v. Peete*, 318 Ill. App. 3d 961, 966–67, 252 Ill. Dec. 821, 743 N.E.2d 689 (4th Dist. 2001).

People v. Holman, 257 Ill. App. 3d 1031, 1033–34, 196 Ill. Dec. 457, 630 N.E.2d 154 (2d Dist. 1994) (evidence is admissible if it is relevant and if the prejudicial impact does not substantially outweigh the probative value of it).

For expanded citations on the exclusion of prejudicial evidence, see § 2:1 to § 2:4.

§ 9:13 Supporting authorities—Exclusion of prejudicial matter in opening statement

Sawicki v. Kim, 112 Ill. App. 3d 641, 644–46, 67 Ill. Dec. 771, 445 N.E.2d 63 (2d Dist. 1983) (prejudicial error occurred when one party's counsel in the opening statement referred to the opposing party's offer to settle the case).

People v. Roberts, 100 Ill. App. 3d 469, 474–76, 55 Ill. Dec. 779, 426 N.E.2d 1104 (1st Dist. 1981) (improper to mention testimony or evidence in opening statement that counsel knows will not be received in evidence at the trial and that will prejudice the jury).

People v. Weller, 123 Ill. App. 2d 421, 425–27, 258 N.E.2d 806 (4th Dist. 1970) (opening statement which was argumentative, contained lengthy descriptions of the facts in the case, and also included references to evidence that never was introduced at trial, was improper).

§ 9:14 Supporting authorities—Other grounds

Other possible grounds for excluding improper matter in opening statement include:

- Prejudicial (§ 2:1 to § 2:4)
- Time-wasting (§ 2:5 to § 2:8)
- Confusing or misleading (§ 2:9 to § 2:12)
- Solely intended to create an emotional bias (§ 2:13 to § 2:19)
- Irrelevant (§ 3:1 to § 3:10)

§ 9:15 Opposing authorities

People v. Trent, 315 Ill. App. 3d 437, 448–49, 248 Ill. Dec. 293, 734 N.E.2d 1 (3d Dist. 2000) (trial judge did not abuse his discretion by permitting the prosecutor to display photographs of the victim during the prosecution's opening statement).

Gowler v. Ferrell-Ross Co., 206 Ill. App. 3d 194, 204–06, 150 Ill. Dec. 646, 563 N.E.2d 773 (1st Dist. 1990) (counsel's reference in the opening statement to evidence that was not later established did not prejudice the opposing party).

C. MOTION TO BAR PREMATURE REBUTTAL TO AFFIRMATIVE DEFENSES

§ 9:16 Suggested motion text

Defendant hereby moves this Court for an order prohibiting plaintiff from presenting any and all evidence, references to evidence or testimony rebutting defendant's affirmative defenses during plaintiff's case in chief. The motion is based upon the ground that the moving party is informed and believes that opposing counsel will improperly present evidence out of order based upon *[state facts to support claim regarding improper order of evidence, e.g., opposing counsel's similar conduct at arbitration or in prior trials]*, which would unfairly and prejudicially undermine defendant's case in chief.

§ 9:17 Motion summary

This motion is used to prevent the plaintiff from undermining defendant's evidence by offering rebuttal evidence prior to defendant's case in chief. The motion is based upon the court's discretionary power to regulate the order of proof and to prevent prejudice and jury confusion. See Illinois Supreme Court Rule 233.

◆ **Note:** This motion may be better suited for pre-trial stipulation. Where facts, such as past attorney misconduct, suggest that the motion is warranted, be prepared to include a detailed, fact-based declaration.

§ 9:18 Supporting authorities—Exclusion of prejudicial evidence, generally

Federal Rule of Evidence 403 states:

> Although relevant, evidence may be excluded if its probative value is substantially outweighed by the danger of unfair prejudice, confusion of the issues, or misleading the jury, or by considerations of undue delay, waste of time, or needless presentation of cumulative evidence.

It must be noted that this Rule has not been codified in Illinois. However, Illinois cases have stated that Illinois has a common-law rule that is comparable to Federal Rule of Evidence 403. See *People v. Walker*, 335 Ill. App. 3d 102, 112, 268 Ill. Dec. 654, 779 N.E.2d 268 (2d Dist. 2002), as modified on denial of reh'g, (Oct. 24, 2002) and judgment aff'd, 211 Ill. 2d 317, 285 Ill. Dec. 519, 812 N.E.2d 339 (2004); and *People v. Peete*, 318 Ill. App. 3d 961, 966–67, 252 Ill. Dec. 821, 743 N.E.2d 689 (4th Dist. 2001).

People v. Holman, 257 Ill. App. 3d 1031, 1033–34, 196 Ill. Dec. 457, 630 N.E.2d 154 (2d Dist. 1994) (evidence is admissible if it is relevant and if the prejudicial impact does not substantially outweigh the probative value of it).

For expanded citations on the exclusion of prejudicial evidence, see § 2:1 to § 2:4.

§ 9:19 Supporting authorities—Order of proof

Illinois Supreme Court Rule 233 states:

> The parties shall proceed at all stages of the trial, including the selection of prospective jurors as specified in Rule 234, opening and closing statements, the offering of evidence, and the examination of witnesses, in the order in which they appear in the pleadings unless otherwise agreed by all parties or ordered by the court. In consolidated cases, third-party proceedings, and all other cases not otherwise provided for, the court shall designate the order.

§ 9:20 Supporting authorities—Other grounds

Other possible grounds supporting this motion include:

- Time-wasting (§ 2:5 to § 2:8)
- Confusing or misleading (§ 2:9 to § 2:12)
- Solely intended to create an emotional bias (§ 2:13 to § 2:19)
- Cumulative (§ 2:20 to § 2:33)
- Improper impeachment evidence (§ 7:1 to § 7:3)

§ 9:21 Opposing authorities

Foerster v. Illinois Bell Tel. Co., 20 Ill. App. 3d 656, 660–61, 315 N.E.2d 63 (1st Dist. 1974) (trial judge had discretion to require defendant to present part of its case before the plaintiff had presented medical testimony regarding damages, in order to accommodate the plaintiff's expert, because the jury still heard the whole case before it deliberated and *there was no indication that the jury was confused or misled*). (Emphasis added.)

D. MOTION RE REFERENCE TO LOST OR DESTROYED EVIDENCE

§ 9:22 Suggested motion text

Alternative One: Restricting Culpable Party from Mentioning Lost/Destroyed Evidence

[Name of moving party] hereby moves this Court for an order excluding any and all evidence, references to evidence, testimony or argument relating to *[describe lost or destroyed evidence]*. The motion is based upon this court's authority to impose just evidentiary sanctions for discovery abuses and the ground that *[state basis for belief that evidence was lost or destroyed]*, and therefore, if allowed to be introduced, *[name of moving party]* will be unfairly prejudiced and surprised at trial.

Alternative Two: Allowing Non-Culpable Party to Reference Opposition's Loss or Destruction of Evidence

[Name of moving party] hereby moves this Court for an order expressly allowing the moving party to reference *[name of party]*'s loss or destruction of *[describe lost or destroyed evidence]*. The motion is based upon this court's authority to impose just evidentiary sanctions for discovery abuses and the ground that *[state basis for belief that evidence was lost or destroyed]*. Therefore, the moving party should be entitled to make references to this fact and allow the jurors to make reasonable inferences regarding the missing evidence.

§ 9:23 Motion summary

This motion is used to address the prejudice that can arise from a party's loss or destruction of evidence. Scenarios include: the culpable party's attempt to reference lost or destroyed evidence to advance their case (clearly prejudicial), as well as any restrictions on the non-culpable party's ability to allow the jury to make inferences regarding the motives/credibility of the opposition with respect to that evidence (clearly there should be no such restrictions). The motion flows from the underlying policies relating to the court's authority under Illinois Supreme Court Rule 219 to impose evidence sanctions for discovery abuses. See also *Shelbyville Mut. Ins. Co. v. Sunbeam Leisure Products Co.*, 262 Ill. App. 3d 636, 637–43, 199 Ill. Dec. 965, 634 N.E.2d 1319 (5th Dist. 1994) (rejected by, Adams v. Bath and Body Works, Inc., 358 Ill. App. 3d 387, 294 Ill. Dec. 233, 830 N.E.2d 645 (1st Dist. 2005)) [accidental destruction of evidence]; *American Family Ins. Co. v. Village Pontiac-GMC, Inc.*, 223 Ill. App. 3d 624, 625–30, 166 Ill. Dec. 93, 585 N.E.2d 1115 (2d Dist. 1992) [intentional destruction].

Note that this motion may not be necessary if previously requested as part of a discovery order relating to the underlying abuse. See generally, § 6:1 to § 6:34, supra.

§ 9:24 Supporting authorities—Exclusion of prejudicial evidence, generally

Federal Rule of Evidence 403 states:

> Although relevant, evidence may be excluded if its probative value is substantially outweighed by the danger of unfair prejudice, confusion of the issues, or misleading the jury, or by considerations of undue delay, waste of time, or needless presentation of cumulative evidence.

It must be noted that this Rule has not been codified in Illinois. However, Illinois cases have stated that Illinois has a common-law rule that is comparable to Federal Rule of Evidence 403. See *People v. Walker*, 335 Ill. App. 3d 102, 112, 268 Ill. Dec. 654, 779 N.E.2d 268 (2d Dist. 2002), as modified on denial of reh'g, (Oct. 24, 2002) and judgment aff'd, 211 Ill. 2d 317, 285 Ill. Dec. 519, 812 N.E.2d 339 (2004); and *People v. Peete*, 318 Ill. App. 3d 961, 966–67, 252 Ill. Dec. 821, 743 N.E.2d 689 (4th Dist. 2001).

People v. Holman, 257 Ill. App. 3d 1031, 1033–34, 196 Ill. Dec. 457, 630 N.E.2d 154 (2d Dist. 1994) (evidence is admissible if it is relevant and if the prejudicial impact does not substantially outweigh the probative value of it).

For expanded citations on the exclusion of prejudicial evidence, see § 2:1 to § 2:4.

§ 9:25 Supporting authorities—Authority for evidence sanctions

Illinois Supreme Court Rule 219 states in pertinent part:

> (c) Failure to Comply with Order or Rules. *If a party, or any person at the instance of or in collusion with a party, unreasonably fails to comply with any provision of part E of article II of the rules of this court (Discovery, Requests for Admission, and Pretrial Procedure) or fails to comply with any order entered under these rules, the court, on motion, may enter, in addition to remedies elsewhere specifically provided, such orders as are just,* including, among others, the following:
>
> (i) That further proceedings be stayed until the order or rule is complied with;
>
> (ii) That the offending party be debarred from filing any other pleading relating to any issue to which the refusal or failure relates;

(iii) That the offending party be debarred from maintaining any particular claim, counterclaim, third-party complaint, or defense relating to that issue;

(iv) That a witness be barred from testifying concerning that issue;

(v) That, as to claims or defenses asserted in any pleading to which that issue is material, a judgment by default be entered against the offending party or that the offending party's action be dismissed with or without prejudice; or

(vi) That any portion of the offending party's pleadings relating to that issue be stricken and, if thereby made appropriate, judgment be entered as to that issue.

(vii) That in cases where a money judgment is entered against a party subject to sanctions under this subparagraph, order the offending party to pay interest at the rate provided by law for judgments for any period of pretrial delay attributable to the offending party's conduct.

In lieu of or in addition to the foregoing, the court, upon motion or upon its own initiative, may impose upon the offending party or his or her attorney, or both, an appropriate sanction . . . . (Emphasis added.)

Heinrich v. Mitchell, 357 Ill. App. 3d 1017, 1021–23, 294 Ill. Dec. 246, 830 N.E.2d 658 (1st Dist. 2005) (trial court did not abuse its discretion by entering a "take-nothing" judgment as a discovery sanction, after a party did not preserve certain evidence, as ordered).

For expanded citations on discovery abuse, see § 6:1 to § 6:34, supra.

§ 9:26 Supporting authorities—Authority for evidence sanctions—Accidental destruction of evidence

Shelbyville Mut. Ins. Co. v. Sunbeam Leisure Products Co., 262 Ill. App. 3d 636, 637–43, 199 Ill. Dec. 965, 634 N.E.2d 1319 (5th Dist. 1994) (rejected by, Adams v. Bath and Body Works, Inc., 358 Ill. App. 3d 387, 294 Ill. Dec. 233, 830 N.E.2d 645 (1st Dist. 2005)) (trial judge properly barred all evidence regarding the condition of a product and then granted summary judgment for the opposing party because the product had been unintentionally misplaced or destroyed by the non-moving party and it represented an important piece of evidence).

§ 9:27 Supporting authorities—Authority for evidence sanctions—Intentional destruction or suppression of evidence

American Family Ins. Co. v. Village Pontiac-GMC, Inc., 223

Ill. App. 3d 624, 625–30, 166 Ill. Dec. 93, 585 N.E.2d 1115 (2d Dist. 1992) (trial judge properly barred all evidence regarding the condition of a vehicle and then granted summary judgment for the opposing party because the vehicle had been intentionally destroyed by the non-moving party and it represented an important piece of evidence).

§ 9:28 Supporting authorities—Authority for evidence sanctions—A note on spoliation of evidence

Note that Illinois courts have recognized that a cause of action for negligent spoliation of evidence is authorized under a general negligence theory. See *Boyd v. Travelers Ins. Co.*, 166 Ill. 2d 188, 192–201, 209 Ill. Dec. 727, 652 N.E.2d 267 (1995), as modified on denial of reh'g, (June 22, 1995).

Boyd v. Travelers Ins. Co., 166 Ill. 2d 188, 192–201, 209 Ill. Dec. 727, 652 N.E.2d 267 (1995), as modified on denial of reh'g, (June 22, 1995) (in order to establish a claim for negligent spoliation of evidence, the party must show that the person that destroyed the evidence had a duty to preserve the evidence and breached that duty and that as a result, the aggrieved party was unable to pursue the original legal action in a meaningful way).

Boyd v. Travelers Ins. Co., 166 Ill. 2d 188, 192–201, 209 Ill. Dec. 727, 652 N.E.2d 267 (1995), as modified on denial of reh'g, (June 22, 1995) (trial judge should consider joining the spoliation of evidence case with the original action because the if the aggrieved party is able to succeed in the original action, then it will also be clear that the spoliation of evidence did not cause harm).

Boyd v. Travelers Ins. Co., 166 Ill. 2d 188, 200–01, 209 Ill. Dec. 727, 652 N.E.2d 267 (1995), as modified on denial of reh'g, (June 22, 1995) (the court declined to consider whether there is a tort in Illinois for intentional spoliation of evidence because the plaintiff's allegations were insufficient to allege an intentional act).

See generally "Spoliation of Evidence," Chapter 24, Illinois Causes of Action—Elements, Forms, and Winning Tips: Tort Actions (IICLE, 2002). Scott D. Lane and Stephen I. Lane.

§ 9:29 Supporting authorities—Negative presumption

Illinois Pattern Civil Jury Instruction number 5.01 states:

> If a party to this case has failed [to offer evidence] [to produce a witness] within his power to produce, you may infer that the [ev-

idence] [testimony of the witness] would be adverse to that party if you believe each of the following elements:

1. The [evidence] [witness] was under the control of the party and could have been produced by the exercise of reasonable diligence.

2. The [evidence] [witness] was not equally available to an adverse party.

3. A reasonably prudent person under the same or similar circumstances would have [offered the evidence] [produced the witness] if he believed [it to be] [the testimony would be] favorable to him.

4. No reasonable excuse for the failure has been shown.

Liebert Corp. v. Mazur, 357 Ill. App. 3d 265, 285–86, 293 Ill. Dec. 28, 827 N.E.2d 909 (1st Dist. 2005) (when a party had destroyed a key piece of evidence, it was presumed that the evidence would have been unfavorable to the party).

Fontana v. TLD Builders, Inc., 362 Ill. App. 3d 491, 504–05, 298 Ill. Dec. 654, 840 N.E.2d 767 (2d Dist. 2005) (an unfavorable inference could be raised against a party who failed to produce a check that would have been under the party's control, after the party testified that the check existed).

Roeseke v. Pryor, 152 Ill. App. 3d 771, 780–81, 105 Ill. Dec. 642, 504 N.E.2d 927 (1st Dist. 1987) (trial judge has discretion to instruct the jury that they can assume that evidence would be adverse to the party who failed to present it when that party controlled the evidence and did not offer a reason for failing to produce it and when it is clear that the party would have produced such evidence if it was favorable).

§ 9:30 Supporting authorities—Other grounds

Other possible grounds for excluding references to lost or destroyed evidence may include:

- Time-wasting (§ 2:5 to § 2:8)
- Confusing or misleading (§ 2:9 to § 2:12)
- Solely intended to create an emotional bias (§ 2:13 to § 2:19)
- Cumulative (§ 2:20 to § 2:33)
- Irrelevant (§ 3:1 to § 3:10)
- Improper foundation (§ 4:1 to § 4:19)
- Discovery sanctions (§ 6:1 to § 6:34)

§ 9:31 Opposition citations—Generally

Cirrincione v. Westminster Gardens Ltd. Partnership, 352 Ill.

App. 3d 755, 760–65, 287 Ill. Dec. 763, 816 N.E.2d 730 (1st Dist. 2004) (trial court erred by dismissing cause of action as discovery sanction after it was discovered that party had altered certain evidence, where effect of alteration and related credibility determination were issues for jury).

R.J. Management Co. v. SRLB Development Corp., 346 Ill. App. 3d 957, 964–66, 282 Ill. Dec. 486, 806 N.E.2d 1074 (2d Dist. 2004) (if party intentionally destroys evidence, presumption arises that evidence would be adverse to that party; note however, that in this case, remaining evidence overcame evidence that was presumed to be adverse to party who had destroyed evidence and therefore party who had destroyed evidence still won case regarding issue in question).

People v. Cantlin, 348 Ill. App. 3d 998, 1000–01, 285 Ill. Dec. 29, 811 N.E.2d 270 (2d Dist. 2004) (the defendant was not denied due process by use of evidence that was destroyed in good faith by police pursuant to a department policy).

Adams v. Bath and Body Works, Inc., 358 Ill. App. 3d 387, 294 Ill. Dec. 233, 830 N.E.2d 645, 651–55 (1st Dist. 2005) (trial court abused its discretion by dismissing cause of action as sanction for destruction of evidence, when destruction was not willful attempt to avoid discovery and did not involve crucial evidence).

Stringer v. Packaging Corp. of America, 351 Ill. App. 3d 1135, 1138–40, 287 Ill. Dec. 73, 815 N.E.2d 476 (4th Dist. 2004) (trial court did not err in failing to grant opposing party dismissal as discovery sanction for destroyed evidence, when party against whom dismissal was requested did not cause evidence destruction).

Phillips v. Gannotti, 327 Ill. App. 3d 512, 518, 261 Ill. Dec. 571, 763 N.E.2d 820 (1st Dist. 2002) (discovery sanctions must be designed to ensure fair discovery and should not be used to punish the non-disclosing party).

King v. Clay, 335 Ill. App. 3d 923, 926–28, 269 Ill. Dec. 667, 781 N.E.2d 464 (1st Dist. 2002) (trial judge should not have barred all evidence for failure to comply with depositions when the opposing party failed to show that he fully pursued the available methods for taking the depositions).

Peterson v. Ress Enterprises, Inc., 292 Ill. App. 3d 566, 577–80, 226 Ill. Dec. 848, 686 N.E.2d 631 (1st Dist. 1997) (trial judge did not abuse his discretion by refusing to give the missing evidence instruction [see Illinois Pattern Civil Jury Instruction 5.01, supra] when the evidence was stolen without fault attributable to either party).

Shimanovsky v. General Motors Corp., 271 Ill. App. 3d 1, 6-11, 207 Ill. Dec. 635, 648 N.E.2d 91 (1st Dist. 1994), judgment aff'd, 181 Ill. 2d 112, 229 Ill. Dec. 513, 692 N.E.2d 286 (1998) (the case was remanded because the trial judge imposed dismissal as a sanction for the plaintiff's expert's destruction of evidence, without first considering the prejudice to the defendant from the lack of the evidence and whether a less severe sanction would be more appropriate).

See also *Brandt v. John S. Tilley Ladders Co.*, 145 Ill. App. 3d 304, 306–07, 99 Ill. Dec. 534, 495 N.E.2d 1269 (1st Dist. 1986) (trial judge should not have dismissed the plaintiff's case for failure to comply with discovery when the defendant did not allege that it had complied with Illinois Supreme Court Rule 201(k)).

See also § 6:27, Opposing authorities—Generally, supra.

E. MOTION TO EXCLUDE ARBITRATION EVIDENCE AND FINDINGS

§ 9:32 Suggested motion text

[Name of moving party] hereby moves this Court for an order excluding any and all evidence, references to evidence, testimony or argument relating to the findings, award, evidence or any other matter arising from a prior arbitration in this matter *[or describe specific arbitration and date]*. The motion is based upon the grounds that any such evidence is barred by Illinois Supreme Court Rule 93.

§ 9:33 Motion summary

This motion is used to exclude any evidence, findings or awards arising from a prior arbitration in the subject case. The motion is based upon the authority of Illinois Supreme Court Rule 93.

◆ **Note:** Some attorneys hire court reporters to record the testimony of the parties and witnesses at an arbitration hearing. Recording the testimony at an arbitration hearing is tantamount to taking a deposition. However, pursuant to Supreme Court Rule 89, all discovery "shall be completed *prior to the hearing* in arbitration," and "no discovery shall be permitted after the hearing." Thus, the use of the court reporter's transcript at trial should be barred pursuant to a motion in limine. In fact, in jurisdictions where the courts allow motions in limine prior to arbitration hearings, counsel should file a motion precluding the use of a court reporter at the hearing itself.

§ 9:34 Supporting authorities—Limitation on arbitration evidence

Illinois Supreme Court Rule 93(b) provides:

(b) *Arbitrator May Not Testify. An arbitrator may not be called to testify as to what transpired before the arbitrators and no reference to the fact of the conduct of the arbitration hearing may be made at trial.* (Emphasis added.)

◆ **Note:** A formal motion on the issue of whether arbitration evidence can be admitted at trial may be unnecessary, given the clear authority of Rule 93. Consider a stipulation if you do not anticipate any opposition.

§ 9:35 Supporting authorities—Other grounds

Other possible grounds for excluding arbitration evidence include:

- Prejudicial (§ 2:1 to § 2:4)
- Time-wasting (§ 2:5 to § 2:8)
- Confusing or misleading (§ 2:9 to § 2:12)
- Cumulative (§ 2:20 to § 2:33)
- Irrelevant (§ 3:1 to § 3:10)
- Improper foundation (§ 4:1 to § 4:19)
- Inadmissible hearsay (§ 8:78 to § 8:89)

F. MOTION TO EXCLUDE EVIDENCE OF DAMAGES OR LIABILITY IN BIFURCATED TRIAL

§ 9:36 Suggested motion text

[Name of moving party] hereby moves this Court for an order excluding any and all evidence, references to evidence, testimony or argument relating to plaintiff's damages during the liability phase of this trial. The motion is based upon the grounds that this case has been bifurcated so that liability and damages will be tried separately, and thus any evidence on damages presented during the liability phase is irrelevant and immaterial to the liability issues.

§ 9:37 Motion summary

This motion is used to prevent the potential prejudice that may occur where a plaintiff's damages are referenced in the liability phase of a bifurcated trial. The motion is based upon Illinois case law.

◆ **Note:** This motion presupposes that damages and liability have been bifurcated by prior order. See generally, *Opal v. Material Service Corp.*, 9 Ill. App. 2d 433, 449–50, 133 N.E.2d 733 (1st Dist. 1956) (suggesting that court has authority to order separate trials for the issues of damages and liability); *Lutgert v. Schaeflein*, 318 Ill. App. 83, 93–94, 47 N.E.2d 359 (1st Dist. 1943) (trial judge has authority to order separate trials for claims and counterclaims if the issues might become confusing to the jury if the issues are all tried at once; however, in this case, the issues were not too complicated or confusing); but see *Mason v. Dunn*, 6 Ill. App. 3d 448, 448–51, 285 N.E.2d 191 (2d Dist. 1972) (in absence of a clear statute allowing for split trials for the issues of liability and damages, a trial judge has no authority to order such a split without the agreement of the parties. This court stated that the statute providing that "an action may be severed" did not imply that a single action could be severed into separate issues).

Regarding a motion to exclude evidence of liability, where liability is not at issue (admitted by defendant), see § 10:196 to § 10:202, infra.

§ 9:38 Supporting authorities—Statutory authority

735 ILCS 5/2-1006 states:

> Consolidation and severance of cases. An action may be severed, and actions pending in the same court may be consolidated, as an aid to convenience, whenever it can be done without prejudice to a substantial right.

735 ILCS 5/2-610(d) states, in pertinent part:

> *If a party wishes to raise an issue as to the amount of damages only, he or she may do so by stating in his or her pleading that he or she desires to contest only the amount of the damages.* (Emphasis added.)

§ 9:39 Supporting authorities—Exclusion based upon admitted liability

Davis v. International Harvester Co., 167 Ill. App. 3d 814, 824–25, 118 Ill. Dec. 589, 521 N.E.2d 1282 (2d Dist. 1988) (proper to exclude evidence of the feasibility of design changes when there was an admission to that ability).

Carlyle v. Jaskiewicz, 124 Ill. App. 3d 487, 495–96, 79 Ill. Dec. 847, 464 N.E.2d 751 (1st Dist. 1984) (the trial judge properly took judicial notice of certain facts and then excluded additional proof regarding those facts).

Bullard v. Barnes, 112 Ill. App. 3d 384, 392–94, 68 Ill. Dec. 37, 445 N.E.2d 485 (4th Dist. 1983), judgment aff'd, 102 Ill. 2d 505, 82 Ill. Dec. 448, 468 N.E.2d 1228 (1984) (trial judge abused his discretion by admitting photographs of the deceased and testimony regarding the conditions and circumstances surrounding the collision, because liability was admitted).

Khatib v. McDonald, 87 Ill. App. 3d 1087, 1099–1100, 43 Ill. Dec. 266, 410 N.E.2d 266 (1st Dist. 1980) (case remanded for a new trial on damages only when there were errors at the trial but liability had been fairly established).

§ 9:40 Supporting authorities—Exclusion based upon prior findings of fact

Stamp v. Sylvan, 906 N.E.2d 1222, 1227–33 (1st Dist. 2009) (on remand for a new trial as to damages only, the trial court could properly limit the evidence regarding damages to a specified period of time which was supported by the evidence at the initial trial).

§ 9:41 Supporting authorities—Other grounds

Other possible grounds for excluding damages evidence in the liability phase of trial include:

- Prejudicial (§ 2:1 to § 2:4)
- Time-wasting (§ 2:5 to § 2:8)
- Confusing or misleading (§ 2:9 to § 2:12)
- Solely intended to create an emotional bias (§ 2:13 to § 2:19)
- Cumulative (§ 2:20 to § 2:33)
- Irrelevant (§ 3:1 to § 3:10)

§ 9:42 Opposing authorities—Liability issues relevant to damages

People v. Szudy, 262 Ill. App. 3d 695, 706, 200 Ill. Dec. 462, 635 N.E.2d 801 (1st Dist. 1994) (evidence which is relevant and admissible for one purpose should not be excluded merely because it is irrelevant or inadmissible for another purpose).

Phillips v. Lawrence, 87 Ill. App. 2d 60, 61-63, 230 N.E.2d 505 (5th Dist. 1967) (in action for personal injuries where liability is admitted, evidence of force of impact and surrounding circumstances may be relevant and material to indicate extent of injuries).

§ 9:43 Opposing authorities—Discretion

Lee v. Chicago Transit Authority, 152 Ill. 2d 432, 461–65, 178 Ill. Dec. 699, 605 N.E.2d 493 (1992) (it is within the trial judge's discretion to admit evidence on a stipulated point and to determine whether evidence might confuse the jury).

Veer v. Hagemann, 334 Ill. 23, 27–28, 165 N.E. 175 (1929) (trial judge has discretion whether to admit evidence on points that have been conceded or that might confuse the issues).

Foerster v. Illinois Bell Tel. Co., 20 Ill. App. 3d 656, 660–61, 315 N.E.2d 63 (1st Dist. 1974) (trial judge had discretion to require defendant to present part of its case before the plaintiff had presented medical testimony regarding damages, in order to accommodate the plaintiff's expert, because the jury still heard the whole case before it deliberated and there was no indication that the jury was confused or misled).

§ 9:44 Opposing authorities—Stipulated facts

People v. Szudy, 262 Ill. App. 3d 695, 712–13, 200 Ill. Dec. 462, 635 N.E.2d 801 (1st Dist. 1994) (prosecutor has the right to prove each element of an offense even if the defendant has stipulated to the facts supporting that element).

G. MOTION TO PRECLUDE "GOLDEN RULE ARGUMENT"

§ 9:45 Suggested motion text

[Name of moving party] hereby moves this Court for an order restricting plaintiff's counsel from making any inquiry, comment or argument before the jury that suggests that jurors should base plaintiff's damages on an amount that the jurors' would charge to endure similar injuries. The motion is based upon the ground that *[describe basis for belief that counsel will engage in such conduct, e.g., counsel made this same argument at a prior arbitration]* and that any such argument is prohibited by law and will create a substantial danger of undue prejudice to *[name of moving party]*.

§ 9:46 Motion summary

This motion is used to prevent unfair prejudice where the jury is asked to "put themselves in the shoes" of another person. This motion typically arises in personal injury actions where plaintiff's counsel asks the jury to calculate pain and suffering damages based upon what the jurors would "charge" or accept to endure a similar injury. This practice, known as the "golden rule argument," has been rejected by Illinois courts and is clearly prejudicial under a probative/prejudicial balancing test. See *People v. Walker*, 335 Ill. App. 3d 102, 112, 268 Ill. Dec. 654, 779 N.E.2d 268 (2d Dist. 2002), as modified on denial of reh'g, (Oct. 24, 2002) and judgment aff'd, 211 Ill. 2d 317, 285 Ill. Dec. 519, 812 N.E.2d 339 (2004); and *People v. Peete*, 318 Ill. App. 3d 961, 966–67, 252 Ill. Dec. 821, 743 N.E.2d 689 (4th Dist. 2001).

Spray-Rite Service Corp. v. Monsanto Co., 684 F.2d 1226, 11 Fed. R. Evid. Serv. 226, 34 Fed. R. Serv. 2d 698 (7th Cir. 1982), judgment aff'd, 465 U.S. 752, 104 S. Ct. 1464, 79 L. Ed. 2d 775 (1984) (a "Golden Rule" appeal in which the jury is asked to put itself in the plaintiff's position is universally recognized as improper because it encourages the jury to depart from neutrality and to decide the case on the basis of personal interest and bias, rather than on the evidence"); see also, *Klotz v. Sears, Roebuck & Co.*, 267 F.2d 53 (7th Cir. 1959).

§ 9:47 Supporting authorities—Exclusion of prejudicial evidence, generally

Federal Rule of Evidence 403 states:

> Although relevant, evidence may be excluded if its probative value is substantially outweighed by the danger of unfair prejudice, confusion of the issues, or misleading the jury, or by considerations of undue delay, waste of time, or needless presentation of cumulative evidence.

It must be noted that this Rule has not been codified in Illinois. However, Illinois cases have stated that Illinois has a common-law rule that is comparable to Federal Rule of Evidence 403. See *People v. Walker*, 335 Ill. App. 3d 102, 112, 268 Ill. Dec. 654, 779 N.E.2d 268 (2d Dist. 2002), as modified on denial of reh'g, (Oct. 24, 2002) and judgment aff'd, 211 Ill. 2d 317, 285 Ill. Dec. 519, 812 N.E.2d 339 (2004); and *People v. Peete*, 318 Ill. App. 3d 961, 966–67, 252 Ill. Dec. 821, 743 N.E.2d 689 (4th Dist. 2001).

People v. Holman, 257 Ill. App. 3d 1031, 1033–34, 196 Ill. Dec. 457, 630 N.E.2d 154 (2d Dist. 1994) (evidence is admissible if it is relevant and if the prejudicial impact does not substantially outweigh the probative value of it).

For expanded citations on the exclusion of prejudicial evidence, see § 2:1 to § 2:4.

§ 9:48 Supporting authorities—Rejection of "golden rule" argument

People v. Schneider, 375 Ill. App. 3d 734, 754–58, 313 Ill. Dec. 890, 873 N.E.2d 514 (2d Dist. 2007), appeal denied, 226 Ill. 2d 604, 316 Ill. Dec. 549, 879 N.E.2d 937 (2007) (closing argument represented an improper appeal to the sympathy of the jury for the victim) (harmless error).

Spray-Rite Service Corp. v. Monsanto Co., 684 F.2d 1226, 11 Fed. R. Evid. Serv. 226, 34 Fed. R. Serv. 2d 698 (7th Cir. 1982), judgment aff'd, 465 U.S. 752, 104 S. Ct. 1464, 79 L. Ed. 2d 775 (1984) (a "Golden Rule" appeal in which the jury is asked to put itself in the plaintiff's position is universally recognized as improper because it encourages the jury to depart from neutrality and to decide the case on the basis of personal interest and bias, rather than on the evidence"); see also, *Klotz v. Sears, Roebuck & Co.*, 267 F.2d 53 (7th Cir. 1959).

Copeland v. Johnson, 63 Ill. App. 2d 361, 366–68, 211 N.E.2d 387 (2d Dist. 1965) (improper to ask the jury to consider what it would have done if it was in the position of either party; however, the error was waived in this case because there was no objection and instead, the opposing party chose to respond through argument).

Brant v. Wabash R. Co., 31 Ill. App. 2d 337, 339–40, 176 N.E.2d 13 (4th Dist. 1961) (improper to ask jurors to consider how much money they would accept in exchange for incurring the pain and suffering of the victim). It should be noted that this type of argument is sometimes referred to as the "golden rule" argument. See *Dotson v. Sears, Roebuck and Co.*, 157 Ill. App. 3d 1036, 1042, 110 Ill. Dec. 177, 510 N.E.2d 1208 (1st Dist. 1987).

§ 9:49 Supporting authorities—Other grounds

Other possible grounds for excluding the golden rule argument include:

- Confusing or misleading (§ 2:9 to § 2:12)
- Solely intended to create an emotional bias (§ 2:13 to § 2:19)
- Irrelevant (§ 3:1 to § 3:10)

H. MOTION TO EXCLUDE IMPROPER TERMINOLOGY

§ 9:50 Suggested motion text

[Name of moving party] hereby moves this Court for an order excluding the mention in the presence of the jury, by counsel, witnesses, or any other person in the courtroom, of the following word [or phrase] or words with related meaning or effect: *[describe terms to be excluded, e.g., "independent medical examiner"].* The motion is based upon the grounds that *[describe grounds, e.g., the words are confusing and meaningless and create the improper impression that the witness being referenced is truly "independent" when if in fact he is a paid expert hired by the defense]*, and therefore any mention of this terminology will unfairly prejudice the moving party.

§ 9:51 Motion summary

This motion is used to exclude evidence of improper, irrelevant, confusing or conclusory terms by witnesses, counsel or any other person in the presence of the jury.

Certain "loaded" words may be subject to exclusion, based upon their potential to confuse or create prejudicial inferences. For example, it may be inappropriate for the defense to use the terms "frivolous lawsuit" in describing plaintiff's case to a jury during voir dire or at any time during the presentation of evidence or argument. Or, it may be improper for plaintiff's counsel to use the terms "litigation doctor" to describe a defense medical expert. Similarly, counsel's use of the word "tap" to describe a low-impact automobile accident might be construed as misleading, since the forces and sounds involved in even a very small accident are inconsistent with the commonly understood meaning of the word "tap." *Webster's* says to tap, in this context, is to "strike lightly esp. with a slight sound," citing as a usage example to "*tap* a pencil on the table." One might argue that the crashing thud of two cars colliding, even in a very small accident, has no relationship to the gentle sound of a pencil tapping a table, and thus, any usage of this term during trial has simply too much potential to mislead.

Note also that, in seeking to limit certain terms of art by qualified experts, the moving party should clarify that the motion is not an attempt to prohibit the expert from testifying about facts or opinions that properly touch on ultimate issues, but rather, that the motion seeks to prevent an expert from prejudicially using loaded terminology designed to precondition or confuse the jurors or words that might improperly or prematurely suggest that certain jury questions have already been decided.

The motion is based upon a combination of authorities found throughout this text, including prejudice [§ 2:1 to § 2:4], juror confusion [§ 2:9 to § 2:12], limitations on juror preconditioning [§ 9:4], restrictions against witness testimony on legal issues [§ 8:11, § 8:32] and avoidance of usurping of the jury function [§ 8:17]. In sum, this motion is one that will be extremely fact specific and may rest upon prior attempts by counsel to paint a negative picture with the subtle use of certain words.

§ 9:52 Supporting authorities—Confusing evidence, generally

Federal Rule of Evidence 403 states:

Although relevant, evidence may be excluded if its probative value is substantially outweighed by the danger of unfair prejudice, *confusion of the issues, or misleading the jury*, or by considerations of undue delay, waste of time, or needless presentation of cumulative evidence. (Emphasis added).

It must be noted that this Rule has not been codified in Illinois. However, Illinois cases have stated that Illinois has a common-law rule that is comparable to Federal Rule of Evidence 403. See *People v. Walker*, 335 Ill. App. 3d 102, 112, 268 Ill. Dec. 654, 779 N.E.2d 268 (2d Dist. 2002), as modified on denial of reh'g, (Oct. 24, 2002) and judgment aff'd, 211 Ill. 2d 317, 285 Ill. Dec. 519, 812 N.E.2d 339 (2004); and *People v. Peete*, 318 Ill. App. 3d 961, 966–67, 252 Ill. Dec. 821, 743 N.E.2d 689 (4th Dist. 2001).

Troyan v. Reyes, 367 Ill. App. 3d 729, 738, 305 Ill. Dec. 451, 855 N.E.2d 967 (3d Dist. 2006) (radiology report which included complicated medical terms was properly excluded as confusing to the jury).

Bachman v. General Motors Corp., 332 Ill. App. 3d 760, 785–88, 267 Ill. Dec. 125, 776 N.E.2d 262 (4th Dist. 2002) (exclusion of prior occurrence evidence because the admission of it would confuse and mislead the jury).

Hulman v. Evanston Hosp. Corp., 259 Ill. App. 3d 133, 147–49, 197 Ill. Dec. 319, 631 N.E.2d 322 (1st Dist. 1994) (exclusion of hospital pamphlet because there was already testimony about it and because it included irrelevant material that might confuse the jury).

Congregation of the Passion, Holy Cross Province v. Touche Ross & Co., 224 Ill. App. 3d 559, 578–79, 166 Ill. Dec. 642, 586 N.E.2d 600 (1st Dist. 1991), judgment aff'd, 159 Ill. 2d 137, 201 Ill. Dec. 71, 636 N.E.2d 503 (1994) (proper to exclude relevant evidence to prevent jury confusion).

§ 9:53 Supporting authorities—Terms containing legal conclusions

Coyne v. Robert H. Anderson & Associates, Inc., 215 Ill. App. 3d 104, 110–13, 158 Ill. Dec. 750, 574 N.E.2d 863 (2d Dist. 1991) (expert testimony was improper because it represented a legal opinion).

§ 9:54 Supporting authorities—Testimony on ultimate issues

Under appropriate circumstances, counsel may seek one or both of the following: 1) to limit references to any ultimate issues by non-experts, including counsel, lay witnesses, experts for matters in which they are not qualified to give an opinion, and others; and, 2) to limit *improper* references to ultimate issues by qualified experts.

Freeding-Skokie Roll-Off Service, Inc. v. Hamilton, 108 Ill. 2d 217, 219–23, 91 Ill. Dec. 178, 483 N.E.2d 524 (1985) (citing Federal Rules of Evidence 701 and 704) (lay witness opinion regarding whether a party could have avoided the accident should not have been admitted because it was not helpful to the trier of fact, which could have made its own assessment by hearing the relevant facts without the addition of the opinion testimony).

Federal Rule of Evidence 704 states, in pertinent part, that "ultimate issues are matters for the trier of fact alone." Note that Federal Rule of Evidence 704 references "testimony in the form of an opinion or inference," which arguably suggests this section does not apply to non-experts or those experts who are not qualified to give an opinion on a certain matter.

§ 9:55 Supporting authorities—Misused terms

Counsel may also argue to limit the *misuse* of recognized terminology that might confuse jurors. For example, a California appellate court limited the use of the terms "unusual delay" in a case where the speaker should have said "unnecessary delay"—the actual term of art at issue. See *Kinney v. County of Contra Costa*, 8 Cal. App. 3d 761, 770–71, 87 Cal. Rptr. 638 (1st Dist. 1970).

For an example of motion that seeks to exclude the terms "independent medical examiner" (a term often used by defendants to reference their own "hired gun" experts), see § 2:34, Motion to exclude confusing evidence, supra.

§ 9:56 Supporting authorities—Preconditioning jury

Improperly referring to legal conclusions or other terms of art creates a very real danger of preconditioning the jury. For citations regarding inappropriate preconditioning during voir dire, see § 9:1 to § 9:9, infra.

§ 9:57 Supporting authorities—Usurping jury function

U.S. Bank v. YMCA of Metropolitan Chicago, 2008 WL 5454246, 10 (1st Dist. 2008) (trial court had discretion to exclude an expert's opinion that a collision was unavoidable because that issue was for the jury to determine).

Coyne v. Robert H. Anderson & Associates, Inc., 215 Ill. App.

3d 104, 110–13, 158 Ill. Dec. 750, 574 N.E.2d 863 (2d Dist. 1991) (expert testimony was improper because it represented a legal opinion which was within the jury's province); *Freeding-Skokie Roll-Off Service, Inc. v. Hamilton*, 108 Ill. 2d 217, 219–23, 91 Ill. Dec. 178, 483 N.E.2d 524 (1985) (lay witness opinion should not have been admitted because it was not helpful to the trier of fact, which could have made its own assessment), supra.

§ 9:58 Supporting authorities—Inflammatory language

Boren v. BOC Group, Inc., 385 Ill.App.3d 248, 256–58, 895 N.E.2d 53 (5th Dist. 2008) (counsel's remarks describing lawsuits like the plaintiff's as a "cottage industry" were inflammatory and prejudicial and caused grounds for granting a new trial).

§ 9:59 Opposing authorities—Legal questions vs. ultimate issues

Van Holt v. National R.R. Passenger Corp., 283 Ill. App. 3d 62, 70, 218 Ill. Dec. 762, 669 N.E.2d 1288 (1st Dist. 1996) (expert was permitted to give an opinion that related to the ultimate issue of whether the defendant failed to provide employees with a safe working environment).

II. SAMPLE MOTIONS

§ 9:60 Motion to exclude reference to lost or destroyed evidence

TO: ALL PARTIES AND THEIR RESPECTIVE ATTORNEYS OF RECORD:

PLEASE TAKE NOTICE THAT defendant hereby moves this Court for an order prohibiting the plaintiff from introducing any and all evidence, references to evidence, testimony or argument relating to plaintiff's electronic computer data backup file ("backup data"). The motion is based upon the ground that plaintiff willfully, recklessly or negligently lost or destroyed the above-referenced evidence, rendering it impossible for the defendant to conduct an examination of the contents of the backup data.

This motion is made under the provisions of Illinois case law and is based upon the attached Memorandum of Points and Authorities, the pleadings and papers on file in this action, and upon such of the argument and evidence as may be presented prior to or at the hearing of this matter.

Dated: *[date]*

MEMORANDUM OF POINTS AND AUTHORITIES

1.

INTRODUCTION

This is an unfair competition case in which the plaintiff alleges that the defendant, a former employee, improperly utilized in-house software development information to advance his business interests. A key issue in this case relates to the content of the plaintiff's network server ("server") during the two-week period prior to defendant's departure from plaintiff's place of employment. During discovery, the defendant served a proper request to examine plaintiff's backup data for this crucial time period. Initially, plaintiff was cooperative and a date was set for examination. Then, just 24 hours before the scheduled examination date, plaintiff's counsel advised that the backup data had been accidentally destroyed during the plaintiff's analysis of this evidence. In follow-up discovery, the plaintiff denied having any test results or other analysis relating to this data.

The defendant moves herein for an order excluding any and all reference to the backup data, and any tests or other analysis that plaintiff or plaintiff's expert or other agents may have conducted prior to the accidental destruction.

2.

THIS COURT MAY EXCLUDE PREJUDICIAL EVIDENCE PURSUANT TO FEDERAL RULE OF EVIDENCE 403

Federal Rule of Evidence 403 states:

> Although relevant, evidence may be excluded if its probative value is substantially outweighed by the danger of unfair prejudice, confusion of the issues, or misleading the jury, or by considerations of undue delay, waste of time, or needless presentation of cumulative evidence.

Illinois has a common-law rule that is comparable to Federal Rule of Evidence 403. See *People v. Peete*, 318 Ill. App. 3d 961, 966–67, 252 Ill. Dec. 821, 743 N.E.2d 689 (4th Dist. 2001); *People v. Walker*, 335 Ill. App. 3d 102, 112, 268 Ill. Dec. 654, 779 N.E.2d 268 (2d Dist. 2002), as modified on denial of reh'g, (Oct. 24, 2002) and judgment aff'd, 211 Ill. 2d 317, 285 Ill. Dec. 519, 812 N.E.2d 339 (2004).

The admission of this evidence would be clearly prejudicial to the defendant because the defendant has been unable to discover the evidence in order to prepare to respond to it.

3.
THE COURT MAY EXCLUDE REFERENCE TO EVIDENCE THAT IS DESTROYED BY A PARTY

The court may exclude references to evidence that is accidentally destroyed by another party. See *Shelbyville Mut. Ins. Co. v. Sunbeam Leisure Products Co.*, 262 Ill. App. 3d 636, 637–43, 199 Ill. Dec. 965, 634 N.E.2d 1319 (5th Dist. 1994) (rejected by, Adams v. Bath and Body Works, Inc., 358 Ill. App. 3d 387, 294 Ill. Dec. 233, 830 N.E.2d 645 (1st Dist. 2005)) (trial judge properly barred all evidence regarding the condition of a product and then granted summary judgment for the opposing party because the product had been unintentionally misplaced or destroyed by the non-moving party and it represented an important piece of evidence).

See also *American Family Ins. Co. v. Village Pontiac-GMC, Inc.*, 223 Ill. App. 3d 624, 625–30, 166 Ill. Dec. 93, 585 N.E.2d 1115 (2d Dist. 1992) (trial judge properly barred all evidence regarding the condition of a vehicle and then granted summary judgment for the opposing party because the vehicle had been intentionally destroyed by the non-moving party and it represented an important piece of evidence).

The present case is directly on point to the factual scenarios in the above-mentioned cases. In each of those cases, the evidence was destroyed before the other party could test it.

In addition, this Court may exclude the evidence at issue as a sanction for the plaintiff's failure to provide the destroyed evidence through discovery. See Illinois Supreme Court Rule 219, which states in pertinent part:

> (c) Failure to Comply with Order or Rules. *If a party, or any person at the instance of or in collusion with a party, unreasonably fails to comply with any provision of part E of article II of the rules of this court (Discovery, Requests for Admission, and Pretrial Procedure) or fails to comply with any order entered under these rules, the court, on motion, may enter, in addition to remedies elsewhere specifically provided, such orders as are just, including, among others, the following:*
>
> . . .
>
> (iii) That the offending party be debarred from maintaining any particular claim, counterclaim, third-party complaint, or defense relating to that issue; . . .
>
> (iv) That a witness be barred from testifying concerning that issue . . . (Emphasis added.)

The plaintiff's willful or negligent failure to preserve the backup data rendered it impossible for the defendant to determine the stage of development of the disputed technology at a critically relevant time period in this case. The loss of this evidence has severely prejudiced the defendant in that he has been unable to prepare a complete defense to plaintiff's claim.

Therefore, if the plaintiff is in possession of any test results or other data from the two-week period prior to defendant's departure from plaintiff's place of employment, said test results or other data must be excluded. Allowing the plaintiff to present evidence or comment in any way on this data would unfairly prejudice the defendant and simply should not be allowed.

4.
CONCLUSION

For all the reasons stated above, the defendant requests that this Court exclude any reference at the time of trial to the backup data and any tests or other analysis relating to such evidence.

Dated: *[date]*

By: ______________________
[name of counsel]
Attorneys for DEFENDANT,
[name of defendant]

Chapter 10

Personal Injury Motions

I. MOTION AUTHORITIES

A. MOTION TO EXCLUDE EVIDENCE OF COLLATERAL SOURCE PAYMENTS

B. MOTION TO EXCLUDE EVIDENCE OF INSURANCE

C. MOTION TO EXCLUDE SETTLEMENT EVIDENCE

D. MOTION TO EXCLUDE EVIDENCE OF OTHER ACCIDENTS

E. MOTION TO EXCLUDE EVIDENCE OF SUBSEQUENT REPAIRS

F. MOTION TO EXCLUDE EVIDENCE OF STATUTE VIOLATION

G. MOTION TO EXCLUDE EVIDENCE OF DRIVER'S LICENSE SUSPENSION

H. MOTION TO EXCLUDE EVIDENCE OF FAILURE TO WEAR SEAT BELT

I. MOTION TO EXCLUDE EVIDENCE OF ALCOHOL CONSUMPTION

J. MOTION TO EXCLUDE EVIDENCE OF PRIOR D.U.I.

K. MOTION TO EXCLUDE EVIDENCE OF PARTY'S HEALTH OR INJURIES WHERE NOT AT ISSUE

L. MOTION TO EXCLUDE ACCIDENT RECONSTRUCTION AND BIOMECHANICAL EVIDENCE

M. MOTION TO EXCLUDE EVIDENCE OF PARTY'S FINANCIAL STATUS

N. MOTION TO EXCLUDE TAX EVIDENCE

O. MOTION TO EXCLUDE LIABILITY EVIDENCE WHERE LIABILITY NOT AT ISSUE

II. SAMPLE MOTIONS

I. MOTION AUTHORITIES

A. MOTION TO EXCLUDE EVIDENCE OF COLLATERAL SOURCE PAYMENTS

§ 10:1 Suggested motion text

The plaintiff hereby moves this Court for an order excluding any and all evidence, references to evidence, testimony or argument relating to collateral payments to plaintiff arising from *[describe collateral source payments, e.g., payments under medical payments policy]*. The motion is based upon the grounds that the evidence is irrelevant, immaterial, confusing, prejudicial and is expressly prohibited by the laws of this state.

§ 10:2 Motion summary

This motion is used to exclude evidence of collateral source payments, such as payments under a medical or disability insurance policy. The motion is based upon the court's authority to exclude evidence that is irrelevant [Federal Rule of Evidence 401, as adopted through Illinois case law; see *Spencer v. Wandolowski*, 264 Ill. App. 3d 611, 617, 201 Ill. Dec. 422, 636 N.E.2d 854 (1st Dist. 1994); and *People v. Monroe*, 66 Ill. 2d 317, 321–22, 5 Ill. Dec. 824, 362 N.E.2d 295 (1977)] or prejudicial [*People v. Walker*, 335 Ill. App. 3d 102, 112, 268 Ill. Dec. 654, 779 N.E.2d 268 (2d Dist. 2002), as modified on denial of reh'g, (Oct. 24, 2002) and judgment aff'd, 211 Ill. 2d 317, 285 Ill. Dec. 519, 812 N.E.2d 339 (2004); *People v. Peete*, 318 Ill. App. 3d 961, 966–67, 252 Ill. Dec. 821, 743 N.E.2d 689 (4th Dist. 2001); and *People v. Holman*, 257 Ill. App. 3d 1031, 1033–34, 196 Ill. Dec. 457, 630 N.E.2d 154 (2d Dist. 1994)], and a long line of Illinois cases. See *Muranyi v. Turn Verein Frisch-Auf*, 308 Ill. App. 3d 213, 214–220, 241 Ill. Dec. 505, 719 N.E.2d 366 (2d Dist. 1999); and *Boden v. Crawford*, 196 Ill. App. 3d 71, 76, 142 Ill. Dec. 546, 552 N.E.2d 1287 (4th Dist. 1990).

§ 10:3 Supporting authorities—Exclusion of prejudicial evidence, generally

Federal Rule of Evidence 403 states:

> Although relevant, evidence may be excluded if its probative value is substantially outweighed by the danger of unfair prejudice, confusion of the issues, or misleading the jury, or by considerations of undue delay, waste of time, or needless presentation of cumulative evidence.

It must be noted that this Rule has not been codified in Illinois. However, Illinois cases have stated that Illinois has a common-law rule that is comparable to Federal Rule of Evidence 403. See *People v. Walker*, 335 Ill. App. 3d 102, 112, 268 Ill. Dec. 654, 779 N.E.2d 268 (2d Dist. 2002), as modified on denial of reh'g, (Oct. 24, 2002) and judgment aff'd, 211 Ill. 2d 317, 285 Ill. Dec. 519, 812 N.E.2d 339 (2004); and *People v. Peete*, 318 Ill. App. 3d 961, 966–67, 252 Ill. Dec. 821, 743 N.E.2d 689 (4th Dist. 2001).

People v. Holman, 257 Ill. App. 3d 1031, 1033–34, 196 Ill. Dec. 457, 630 N.E.2d 154 (2d Dist. 1994) (evidence is admissible if it is relevant and if the prejudicial impact does not substantially outweigh the probative value of it).

For expanded citations on the exclusion of prejudicial evidence, see § 2:1 to § 2:4.

§ 10:4 Supporting authorities—Exclusion of irrelevant evidence, generally

Federal Rule of Evidence 401 defines relevancy as,

> evidence having any tendency to make the existence of any fact that is of consequence to the determination of the action more probable or less probable than it would be without the evidence.

Illinois has adopted this definition of relevancy through case law. *Spencer v. Wandolowski*, 264 Ill. App. 3d 611, 617, 201 Ill. Dec. 422, 636 N.E.2d 854 (1st Dist. 1994); and *People v. Monroe*, 66 Ill. 2d 317, 321–22, 5 Ill. Dec. 824, 362 N.E.2d 295 (1977).

Preston ex rel. Preston v. Simmons, 321 Ill. App. 3d 789, 803, 254 Ill. Dec. 647, 747 N.E.2d 1059 (1st Dist. 2001) (trial judge should not permit such wide latitude on cross-examination that it undermines the rule that only relevant evidence is admissible).

For expanded citations on the exclusion of irrelevant evidence, see § 3:1 to § 3:10.

§ 10:5 Supporting authorities—Exclusion of collateral source evidence, generally

Baraniak v. Kurby, 371 Ill. App. 3d 310, 308 Ill. Dec. 949, 862 N.E.2d 1152, 1155-57 (1st Dist. 2007), appeal denied, 224 Ill. 2d 571, 312 Ill. Dec. 654, 871 N.E.2d 54 (2007) (when the jury asked if the plaintiff's medical bills had been paid, the trial judge should have provided a "collateral source" instruction barring the jury from considering the issue).

Arthur v. Catour, 216 Ill. 2d 72, 295 Ill. Dec. 641, 833 N.E.2d 847, 849–53 (2005) (the collateral source rule could be used to prevent the defendant from showing that the plaintiff was only required to pay a portion of the health-care provider's bill due to an agreement between the health-care provider and the plaintiff's insurance company).

Muranyi v. Turn Verein Frisch-Auf, 308 Ill. App. 3d 213, 214–220, 241 Ill. Dec. 505, 719 N.E.2d 366 (2d Dist. 1999) (collateral source rule barred evidence of payments that were received from insurance coverage that was through the plaintiff's spouse's employment).

Boden v. Crawford, 196 Ill. App. 3d 71, 76, 142 Ill. Dec. 546, 552 N.E.2d 1287 (4th Dist. 1990) (evidence of disability payments the plaintiff was receiving from a source independent from the defendant is inadmissible).

Fear v. Smith, 184 Ill. App. 3d 51, 58-59, 132 Ill. Dec. 491, 539 N.E.2d 1297 (5th Dist. 1989) (trial judge improperly denied the plaintiff damages for lost wages that were also recovered through her employer as a benefit of her employment).

§ 10:6 Supporting authorities—Exclusion of collateral source evidence, generally—Gratuitous payments

Longman v. Jasiek, 91 Ill. App. 3d 83, 89-90, 46 Ill. Dec. 636, 414 N.E.2d 520 (3d Dist. 1980) (payments from the plaintiff's parents to cover medical expenses were not admissible in evidence).

Cooney v. Hughes, 310 Ill. App. 371, 34 N.E.2d 566, 570 (1st Dist. 1941) (gratuitous salary payments by a plaintiff's employer are not admissible to set off damages owed by an independent tortfeasor).

See also *Fear v. Smith*, 184 Ill. App. 3d 51, 58-59, 132 Ill. Dec. 491, 539 N.E.2d 1297 (5th Dist. 1989) (trial judge improperly denied the plaintiff damages for lost wages that were also recovered through her employer as a benefit of her employment); but see *Peterson v. Lou Bachrodt Chevrolet Co.*, 76 Ill. 2d 353, 362–64, 29 Ill. Dec. 444, 392 N.E.2d 1 (1979) (overruled by, Wills v. Foster, 229 Ill. 2d 393, 323 Ill. Dec. 26, 892 N.E.2d 1018 (2008)) (a plaintiff may not recover damages for medical treatment that was provided free of charge).

§ 10:7 Supporting authorities—Exclusion of collateral source evidence, generally—Disability benefits

Boden v. Crawford, 196 Ill. App. 3d 71, 76, 142 Ill. Dec. 546, 552 N.E.2d 1287 (4th Dist. 1990) (evidence of disability payments the plaintiff was receiving from a source independent from the defendant is inadmissible).

Fencl-Tufo Chevrolet, Inc. v. Industrial Com'n of Illinois, 169 Ill. App. 3d 510, 519–20, 120 Ill. Dec. 15, 523 N.E.2d 926 (1st Dist. 1988) (evidence of governmental aid, which paid medical bills, but was subject to reimbursement from plaintiff, was not admissible).

§ 10:8 Supporting authorities—Exclusion of collateral source evidence, generally—Wage payments

Boden v. Crawford, 196 Ill. App. 3d 71, 76, 142 Ill. Dec. 546, 552 N.E.2d 1287 (4th Dist. 1990) (evidence of disability payments representing a portion of the plaintiff's wages that the plaintiff was receiving from a source independent from the defendant was inadmissible).

Fear v. Smith, 184 Ill. App. 3d 51, 58-59, 132 Ill. Dec. 491, 539 N.E.2d 1297 (5th Dist. 1989) (trial judge improperly denied the plaintiff damages for lost wages that were also recovered through her employer as a benefit of her employment).

Cooney v. Hughes, 310 Ill. App. 371, 34 N.E.2d 566, 570 (1st Dist. 1941) (gratuitous salary payments by a plaintiff's employer are not admissible to set off damages owed by an independent tortfeasor).

§ 10:9 Supporting authorities—Exclusion of collateral source evidence, generally—Other payments

Muranyi v. Turn Verein Frisch-Auf, 308 Ill. App. 3d 213, 214–220, 241 Ill. Dec. 505, 719 N.E.2d 366 (2d Dist. 1999) (collateral source rule barred evidence of payments that were received from insurance coverage that was through the plaintiff's spouse's employment).

Alvis v. Henderson Obstetrics, S.C., 227 Ill. App. 3d 1012, 1022–23, 170 Ill. Dec. 242, 592 N.E.2d 678 (3d Dist. 1992) (trial judge properly refused evidence that medicare benefits might be available to cover the injured party's future medical expenses).

§ 10:10 Supporting authorities—Other grounds

Other possible grounds for excluding collateral source evidence include:

- Time-wasting (§ 2:5 to § 2:8)
- Confusing or misleading (§ 2:9 to § 2:12)
- Solely intended to create an emotional bias (§ 2:13 to § 2:19)
- Collateral to issues in case (§ 3:11 to § 3:21)
- Improper foundation (§ 4:1 to § 4:19)
- Inadmissible hearsay (§ 8:78 to § 8:89)

§ 10:11 Opposing authorities—Generally

Hamrock v. Henry, 222 Ill. App. 3d 487, 494–95, 165 Ill. Dec. 25, 584 N.E.2d 204 (1st Dist. 1991) (although evidence that a plaintiff has received compensation from a source that is independent of the defendant is ordinarily not admissible, in this case ["collateral source rule"], the plaintiff opened the door to the evidence and was not prejudiced by it).

§ 10:12 Opposing authorities—Not "wholly independent" source

People v. Roop, 276 Ill. App. 3d 191, 192–93, 212 Ill. Dec. 987, 658 N.E.2d 469 (3d Dist. 1995) (criminal case restitution order was not enforceable on its face when the defendant's liability insurance had already covered the injury to the plaintiff).

Kritzen v. Flender Corp., 226 Ill. App. 3d 541, 558–59, 168 Ill. Dec. 509, 589 N.E.2d 909 (2d Dist. 1992) (collateral source rule should not have been used to bar evidence of disability payments when the employer paid the insurance premiums and was also the defendant-tortfeasor).

Tivador (Kenneth) v. State, 40 Ill. Ct. Cl. 48, 1987 WL 960510 (Ill. Ct. Cl. 1987) (award in a separate court action against the driver of the vehicle was deductible from the maximum amount allowable in this court action against the state, even though the total amount of damages the plaintiff suffered was higher than the maximum).

Rogers v. Chicago & North Western Transp. Co., 59 Ill. App. 3d 911, 916–18, 16 Ill. Dec. 845, 375 N.E.2d 952 (5th Dist.

1978) (collateral source rule does not bar evidence of insurance payments when the defendant-tortfeasor was the source for the insurance premiums).

See also 740 ILCS 100/2, which states:

> Right of Contribution. (a) Except as otherwise provided in this Act, where 2 or more persons are subject to liability in tort arising out of the same injury to person or property, or the same wrongful death, there is a right of contribution among them, even though judgment has not been entered against any or all of them.
>
> (b) The right of contribution exists only in favor of a tortfeasor who has paid more than his pro rata share of the common liability, and his total recovery is limited to the amount paid by him in excess of his pro rata share. No tortfeasor is liable to make contribution beyond his own pro rata share of the common liability.
>
> (c) When a release or covenant not to sue or not to enforce judgment is given in good faith to one or more persons liable in tort arising out of the same injury or the same wrongful death, it does not discharge any of the other tortfeasors from liability for the injury or wrongful death unless its terms so provide but it reduces the recovery on any claim against the others to the extent of any amount stated in the release or the covenant, or in the amount of the consideration actually paid for it, whichever is greater.
>
> (d) The tortfeasor who settles with a claimant pursuant to paragraph (c) is discharged from all liability for any contribution to any other tortfeasor.
>
> (e) A tortfeasor who settles with a claimant pursuant to paragraph (c) is not entitled to recover contribution from another tortfeasor whose liability is not extinguished by the settlement.
>
> (f) Anyone who, by payment, has discharged in full or in part the liability of a tortfeasor and has thereby discharged in full his obligation to the tortfeasor, is subrogated to the tortfeasor's right of contribution. This provision does not affect any right of contribution nor any right of subrogation arising from any other relationship.

§ 10:13 Opposing authorities—Relevant to issues in case

Kritzen v. Flender Corp., 226 Ill. App. 3d 541, 558–60, 168 Ill. Dec. 509, 589 N.E.2d 909 (2d Dist. 1992) (collateral source rule should not have been used to bar evidence of disability payments when they could have been related to the issue of damage calculation for the retaliatory discharge claim).

But see *Brumley v. Federal Barge Lines, Inc.*, 78 Ill. App. 3d 799, 806–08, 33 Ill. Dec. 609, 396 N.E.2d 1333 (5th Dist. 1979) (collateral source rule barred evidence of benefits that plaintiff would receive from retirement, despite the defendant's claim that such evidence was relevant to determine the plaintiff's motivation for working past retirement age); *Lang v. Lake Shore Exhibits, Inc.*, 305 Ill. App. 3d 283, 287–90, 238 Ill. Dec. 463, 711 N.E.2d 1124 (1st Dist. 1999) (improper and prejudicial to allow evidence of the plaintiff's receipt of disability payments to suggest malingering).

§ 10:14 Opposing authorities—Relevant to issues in case—Exception: Paternity cases

Jiles v. Spratt, 195 Ill. App. 3d 354, 357–59, 142 Ill. Dec. 21, 552 N.E.2d 371 (4th Dist. 1990) (collateral source rule does not apply in paternity cases to bar evidence that the mother's medical expenses were paid by insurance).

§ 10:15 Opposing authorities—Relevant to issues in case—Exception: Legal malpractice cases

Sterling Radio Stations, Inc. v. Weinstine, 328 Ill. App. 3d 58, 64-65, 262 Ill. Dec. 230, 765 N.E.2d 56 (1st Dist. 2002) (collateral source rule did not apply to legal malpractice action to exclude evidence that another entity had paid the judgment that was entered against the client due to the malpractice).

§ 10:16 Opposing authorities—Relevant to issues in case—Exception: Free medical services

Peterson v. Lou Bachrodt Chevrolet Co., 76 Ill. 2d 353, 362–64, 29 Ill. Dec. 444, 392 N.E.2d 1 (1979) (overruled by, Wills v. Foster, 229 Ill. 2d 393, 323 Ill. Dec. 26, 892 N.E.2d 1018 (2008)) (a plaintiff may not recover damages for medical treatment that was provided free of charge).

§ 10:17 Opposing authorities—Relevant to issues in case—Exception: Contract cases

American Fidelity Fire Ins. Co. v. General Ry. Signal Co., 184 Ill. App. 3d 601, 617–18, 132 Ill. Dec. 817, 540 N.E.2d 557 (1st Dist. 1989) (The collateral source rule does not apply in contract actions unless there is "an element of fraud, tort or willfulness.")

§ 10:18 Opposing authorities—Relevant to issues in case—Exception: Medical malpractice cases

735 ILCS 5/2-1205 provides:

Reduction in amount of recovery. An amount equal to the sum of (i) 50% of the benefits provided for lost wages or private or governmental disability income programs, which have been paid, or which have become payable to the injured person by any other person, corporation, insurance company or fund in relation to a particular injury, and (ii) 100% of the benefits provided for medical charges, hospital charges, or nursing or caretaking charges, which have been paid, or which have become payable to the injured person by any other person, corporation, insurance company or fund in relation to a particular injury, shall be deducted from any judgment in an action to recover for that injury based on an allegation of negligence or other wrongful act, not including intentional torts, on the part of a licensed hospital or physician; provided, however, that:

(1) Application is made within 30 days to reduce the judgment;

(2) Such reduction shall not apply to the extent that there is a right of recoupment through subrogation, trust agreement, lien, or otherwise;

(3) The reduction shall not reduce the judgment by more than 50% of the total amount of the judgment entered on the verdict;

(4) The damages awarded shall be increased by the amount of any insurance premiums or the direct costs paid by the plaintiff for such benefits in the 2 years prior to plaintiff's injury or death or to be paid by the plaintiff in the future for such benefits; and

(5) There shall be no reduction for charges paid for medical expenses which were directly attributable to the adjudged negligent acts or omissions of the defendants found liable.

B. MOTION TO EXCLUDE EVIDENCE OF INSURANCE

Except in very limited circumstances, evidence of insurance should be excluded at trial. The mention of defendant's liability insurance can only have an adverse effect on the defense. If the jury believes that an insurance company will pay any verdict that is rendered (as opposed to the individual defendant), the jury is more likely to render a verdict in favor of the plaintiff and more likely to award a larger verdict to the plaintiff. *Heard v. City of Chicago*, 265 Ill. App. 3d 493, 202 Ill. Dec. 145, 637 N.E.2d 684 (1st Dist. 1994) (evidence of defendant's insurance may result in a higher verdict award than if the jury was unaware of defendant's insurance status). On the other hand, if the plaintiff's health or automobile insurance is mentioned, it can only hurt the plaintiff's chances of obtaining a substantial verdict. If the jury believes that a plaintiff's insurance will pay the plaintiff's medical bills (past and future) a jury is more likely to avoid awarding amounts to cover those expenses in an effort to avoid double recovery to the plaintiff. Evidence of insurance is irrelevant and can only confuse the issues to be decided by the jury. Therefore, in most circumstances, insurance should be excluded. Motions to exclude the mention of insurance are standard and are rarely contested.

§ 10:19 Suggested motion text

Defendant hereby moves this Court for an order excluding any and all evidence, references to evidence, testimony or argument relating to defendant's liability insurance coverage *[or describe name of policy and nature of coverage]*. The motion is based upon the grounds that the evidence is irrelevant, immaterial, prejudicial and expressly inadmissible pursuant to Illinois case law.

§ 10:20 Motion summary

This motion is used to exclude evidence of a defendant's liability insurance coverage. The motion is based upon the express authority of Illinois case law, as well as the court's discretionary authority to exclude evidence that is irrelevant [Federal Rule of Evidence 401, as adopted through Illinois case law; see *Spencer v. Wandolowski*, 264 Ill. App. 3d 611, 617, 201 Ill. Dec. 422, 636 N.E.2d 854 (1st Dist. 1994); and *People v. Monroe*, 66 Ill. 2d 317, 321–22, 5 Ill. Dec. 824, 362 N.E.2d 295 (1977)] or prejudicial [*People v. Walker*, 335 Ill. App. 3d 102, 112, 268 Ill. Dec. 654, 779 N.E.2d 268 (2d Dist. 2002), as modified on denial of reh'g, (Oct. 24, 2002) and judgment aff'd, 211 Ill. 2d 317, 285 Ill. Dec. 519, 812 N.E.2d 339 (2004); *People v. Peete*, 318 Ill. App. 3d 961, 966–67, 252 Ill. Dec. 821, 743 N.E.2d 689 (4th Dist. 2001); and *People v. Holman*, 257 Ill. App. 3d 1031, 1033–34, 196 Ill. Dec. 457, 630 N.E.2d 154 (2d Dist. 1994)]. See *Golden v. Kishwaukee Community Health Services Center, Inc.*, 269 Ill. App. 3d 37, 43-45, 206 Ill. Dec. 314, 645 N.E.2d 319 (1st Dist. 1994); and *Wiersema v. Lockwood & Strickland Co.*, 147 Ill. App. 33, 1909 WL 1743, at *1–5 (1st Dist. 1909).

§ 10:21 Supporting authorities—Exclusion of prejudicial evidence, generally

Federal Rule of Evidence 403 states:

> Although relevant, evidence may be excluded if its probative value is substantially outweighed by the danger of unfair prejudice, confusion of the issues, or misleading the jury, or by considerations of undue delay, waste of time, or needless presentation of cumulative evidence.

It must be noted that this Rule has not been codified in Illinois. However, Illinois cases have stated that Illinois has a common-law rule that is comparable to Federal Rule of Evidence 403. See *People v. Walker*, 335 Ill. App. 3d 102, 112, 268 Ill. Dec. 654, 779 N.E.2d 268 (2d Dist. 2002), as modified on denial of reh'g, (Oct. 24, 2002) and judgment aff'd, 211 Ill. 2d 317, 285 Ill. Dec. 519, 812 N.E.2d 339 (2004); and *People v. Peete*, 318 Ill. App. 3d 961, 966–67, 252 Ill. Dec. 821, 743 N.E.2d 689 (4th Dist. 2001).

People v. Holman, 257 Ill. App. 3d 1031, 1033–34, 196 Ill. Dec. 457, 630 N.E.2d 154 (2d Dist. 1994) (evidence is admissible if it is relevant and if the prejudicial impact does not substantially outweigh the probative value of it).

For expanded citations on the exclusion of prejudicial evidence, see § 2:1 to § 2:4.

§ 10:22 Supporting authorities—Exclusion of irrelevant evidence, generally

Federal Rule of Evidence 401 defines relevancy as,

> evidence having any tendency to make the existence of any fact that is of consequence to the determination of the action more probable or less probable than it would be without the evidence.

Illinois has adopted this definition of relevancy through case law. *Spencer v. Wandolowski*, 264 Ill. App. 3d 611, 617, 201 Ill. Dec. 422, 636 N.E.2d 854 (1st Dist. 1994); and *People v. Monroe*, 66 Ill. 2d 317, 321–22, 5 Ill. Dec. 824, 362 N.E.2d 295 (1977).

Preston ex rel. Preston v. Simmons, 321 Ill. App. 3d 789, 803, 254 Ill. Dec. 647, 747 N.E.2d 1059 (1st Dist. 2001) (trial judge should not permit such wide latitude on cross-examination that it undermines the rule that only relevant evidence is admissible).

For expanded citations on the exclusion of irrelevant evidence, see § 3:1 to § 3:10.

§ 10:23 Supporting authorities—Exclusion of liability insurance evidence

Ruwisch v. Knoebel, 233 Ill. App. 526, 1924 WL 3596, at *3 (4th Dist. 1924) (improper to allow cross-examination which may have suggested that the defendant was insured).

Wiersema v. Lockwood & Strickland Co., 147 Ill. App. 33, 1909 WL 1743, at *1–5 (1st Dist. 1909) (evidence of the fact that the defendant had insurance coverage was irrelevant and improper).

Seldin v. Babendir, 325 Ill. App. 3d 1058, 259 Ill. Dec. 548, 759 N.E.2d 28 (1st Dist. 2001) (informing jury that defendant is insured against liability is inadmissible on grounds of relevance).

See also 735 ILCS 5/8-1901, which states:

> (a) The providing of, or payment for, medical, surgical, hospital, or rehabilitation services, facilities, or equipment by or on behalf of any person, or the offer to provide, or pay for, any one or more of the foregoing, shall not be construed as an admission of any liability by such person or persons. Testimony, writings, records, reports or information with respect to the foregoing shall not be admissible in evidence as an admission of any liability in any action of any kind in any court or before any commission, administrative agency, or other tribunal in this State, except at the instance of the person or persons so making any such provision, payment or offer.
>
> (b) Any expression of grief, apology, or explanation provided by a health care provider, including, but not limited to, a statement that the health care provider is "sorry" for the outcome to a patient, the patient's family, or the patient's legal representative about an inadequate or unanticipated treatment or care outcome that is provided within 72 hours of when the provider knew or should have known of the potential cause of such outcome shall not be admissible as evidence in any action of any kind in any court or before any tribunal, board, agency, or person. The disclosure of any such information, whether proper, or improper, shall not waive or have any effect upon its confidentiality or inadmissibility. As used in this Section, a "health care provider" is any hospital, nursing home or other facility, or employee or agent thereof, a physician, or other licensed health care professional. Nothing in this Section precludes the discovery or admissibility of any other facts regarding the patient's treatment or outcome as otherwise permitted by law.
>
> (c) The changes to this Section made by this amendatory Act of the 94th General Assembly apply to causes of action accruing on or after its effective date.

Note that paragraphs (b) and (c), above, were added to 735 ILCS 5/8-1901 by P.A. 94-677 (2005) and became effective on August 25, 2005. Therefore, be sure to note that pursuant to Section (c), above, expressions of grief, apology, or explanation in causes of action accruing before August 25, 2005 are not covered by this Act.

§ 10:24 Supporting authorities—Exclusion of liability insurance evidence—Evidence of defendant's lack of insurance

Lenz v. Julian, 276 Ill. App. 3d 66, 74-75, 212 Ill. Dec. 511, 657 N.E.2d 712 (2d Dist. 1995) (improper and prejudicial to refer to the defendant's lack of insurance).

But see *Smith v. Raup*, 296 Ill. App. 171, 15 N.E.2d 936 (2d Dist. 1938) (not error to allow the defendant to testify to his lack of insurance when the issue was first raised during his testimony as an adverse witness for the plaintiff).

Regarding the exclusion of evidence of a party's financial status, in general, see § 10:176 to § 10:186, supra.

§ 10:25 Supporting authorities—Irrelevant

Seldin v. Babendir, 325 Ill. App. 3d 1058, 259 Ill. Dec. 548, 759 N.E.2d 28 (1st Dist. 2001) (informing jury that defendant is insured against liability is inadmissible on grounds of relevance).

Wiersema v. Lockwood & Strickland Co., 147 Ill. App. 33, 1909 WL 1743, at *1–5 (1st Dist. 1909) (evidence of the fact that the defendant had insurance coverage was irrelevant and improper).

§ 10:26 Supporting authorities—Other grounds

Other possible grounds for excluding liability insurance evidence include:

- Time-wasting (§ 2:5 to § 2:8)
- Confusing or misleading (§ 2:9 to § 2:12)
- Solely intended to create an emotional bias (§ 2:13 to § 2:19)
- Collateral to issues in case (§ 3:11 to § 3:21)
- Collateral source rule (§ 10:1 to § 10:18)

§ 10:27 Opposing authorities—Impeachment

Golden v. Kishwaukee Community Health Services Center, Inc., 269 Ill. App. 3d 37, 43-45, 206 Ill. Dec. 314, 645 N.E.2d 319 (1st Dist. 1994) (although reference to a defendant's insurance is generally inadmissible, cross-examination of one of the defendant's experts regarding his relationship with the defendant's insurance group was admissible to show possible bias).

Williams v. Matlin, 328 Ill. App. 645, 647–48, 66 N.E.2d 719 (1st Dist. 1946) (plaintiff's witness was permitted to disclose that the statement that the defendant used to impeach him with was prepared by the defendant's insurance adjuster, for the purpose of suggesting interest or bias of the person that prepared the statement).

§ 10:28 Opposing authorities—Where relevant to issues

People v. Barnett, 347 Ill. 127, 128–37, 179 N.E. 450 (1931) (numerous references to insurance were made during a prosecution for a scheme to defraud by collecting insurance from items that were falsely claimed as stolen items).

§ 10:29 Opposing authorities—Incidental reference to insurance

Seldin v. Babendir, 325 Ill. App. 3d 1058, 259 Ill. Dec. 548, 759 N.E.2d 28 (1st Dist. 2001) (not every mention of "insurance" during a personal injury trial requires a mistrial; must be prejudicial to mandate a mistrial).

Stenger v. Germanos, 265 Ill. App. 3d 942, 203 Ill. Dec. 140, 639 N.E.2d 179 (1st Dist. 1994) (mention of insurance is improper, but courts are becoming more tolerant of such mention).

§ 10:30 Opposing authorities—Non-prejudicial references to insurance

Iverson v. Iverson, 56 Ill. App. 3d 297, 301–03, 13 Ill. Dec. 108, 370 N.E.2d 1135 (1st Dist. 1977) (trial judge has discretion to determine whether a reference to insurance prejudiced either party).

Smith v. Raup, 296 Ill. App. 171, 15 N.E.2d 936 (2d Dist. 1938) (not error to allow the defendant to testify to his lack of insurance when the issue was first raised during his testimony as an adverse witness for the plaintiff).

§ 10:31 Opposing authorities—To prove element of case

Vacker v. Yeager, 151 Ill. App. 144, 1909 WL 2232 (3d Dist. 1909) (liability insurance policy admissible to demonstrate the status of the employment relationship, or lack thereof, between the plaintiff and the defendant).

See also *Boettcher v. Fournie Farms, Inc.*, 243 Ill. App. 3d 940, 184 Ill. Dec. 93, 612 N.E.2d 969 (5th Dist. 1993) (insurance policy information may be admissible to demonstrate issues of agenda, ownership, control, bias, etc.).

§ 10:32 Opposing authorities—First raised by adverse witness

Smith v. Raup, 296 Ill. App. 171, 15 N.E.2d 936 (2d Dist. 1938) (not error to allow the defendant to testify to his lack of insurance when the issue was first raised during his testimony as an adverse witness for the plaintiff).

§ 10:33 Opposing authorities—Voir dire questions

Seldin v. Babendir, 325 Ill. App. 3d 1058, 259 Ill. Dec. 548, 759 N.E.2d 28 (1st Dist. 2001) (during voir dire, the parties may interrogate prospective jurors as to their interest and relationship to insurance companies).

C. MOTION TO EXCLUDE SETTLEMENT EVIDENCE

§ 10:34 Suggested motion text

[Name of moving party] hereby moves this Court for an order excluding any and all evidence, references to evidence, testimony or argument relating to prior settlements or settlement negotiations between parties to this action *[or describe parties and specifics of settlement or negotiations]*. The motion is based upon the grounds that the evidence is irrelevant, immaterial, prejudicial and expressly inadmissible pursuant to Illinois case law.

§ 10:35 Motion summary

This motion is used to exclude evidence of settlements and settlement negotiations between parties and former parties to the action. The motion is based on the court's authority to exclude evidence that is irrelevant [Federal Rule of Evidence 401, as adopted through Illinois case law; see *Spencer v. Wandolowski*, 264 Ill. App. 3d 611, 617, 201 Ill. Dec. 422, 636 N.E.2d 854 (1st Dist. 1994); and *People v. Monroe*, 66 Ill. 2d 317, 321–22, 5 Ill. Dec. 824, 362 N.E.2d 295 (1977)] or misleading, confusing or unduly prejudicial [*People v. Walker*, 335 Ill. App. 3d 102, 112, 268 Ill. Dec. 654, 779 N.E.2d 268 (2d Dist. 2002), as modified on denial of reh'g, (Oct. 24, 2002) and judgment aff'd, 211 Ill. 2d 317, 285 Ill. Dec. 519, 812 N.E.2d 339 (2004); *People v. Peete*, 318 Ill. App. 3d 961, 966–67, 252 Ill. Dec. 821, 743 N.E.2d 689 (4th Dist. 2001); and *People v. Holman*, 257 Ill. App. 3d 1031, 1033–34, 196 Ill. Dec. 457, 630 N.E.2d 154 (2d Dist. 1994)], as well as leading cases. See *Sawicki v. Kim*, 112 Ill. App. 3d 641, 644–46, 67 Ill. Dec. 771, 445 N.E.2d 63 (2d Dist. 1983).

§ 10:36 Supporting authorities—Exclusion of prejudicial evidence, generally

Federal Rule of Evidence 403 states:

> Although relevant, evidence may be excluded if its probative value is substantially outweighed by the danger of unfair preju-

dice, confusion of the issues, or misleading the jury, or by considerations of undue delay, waste of time, or needless presentation of cumulative evidence.

It must be noted that this Rule has not been codified in Illinois. However, Illinois cases have stated that Illinois has a common-law rule that is comparable to Federal Rule of Evidence 403. See *People v. Walker*, 335 Ill. App. 3d 102, 112, 268 Ill. Dec. 654, 779 N.E.2d 268 (2d Dist. 2002), as modified on denial of reh'g, (Oct. 24, 2002) and judgment aff'd, 211 Ill. 2d 317, 285 Ill. Dec. 519, 812 N.E.2d 339 (2004); and *People v. Peete*, 318 Ill. App. 3d 961, 966–67, 252 Ill. Dec. 821, 743 N.E.2d 689 (4th Dist. 2001).

People v. Holman, 257 Ill. App. 3d 1031, 1033–34, 196 Ill. Dec. 457, 630 N.E.2d 154 (2d Dist. 1994) (evidence is admissible if it is relevant and if the prejudicial impact does not substantially outweigh the probative value of it).

For expanded citations on the exclusion of prejudicial evidence, see § 2:1 to § 2:4.

§ 10:37 Supporting authorities—Exclusion of irrelevant evidence, generally

Federal Rule of Evidence 401 defines relevancy as,

> evidence having any tendency to make the existence of any fact that is of consequence to the determination of the action more probable or less probable than it would be without the evidence.

Illinois has adopted this definition of relevancy through case law. *Spencer v. Wandolowski*, 264 Ill. App. 3d 611, 617, 201 Ill. Dec. 422, 636 N.E.2d 854 (1st Dist. 1994); and *People v. Monroe*, 66 Ill. 2d 317, 321–22, 5 Ill. Dec. 824, 362 N.E.2d 295 (1977).

Preston ex rel. Preston v. Simmons, 321 Ill. App. 3d 789, 803, 254 Ill. Dec. 647, 747 N.E.2d 1059 (1st Dist. 2001) (trial judge should not permit such wide latitude on cross-examination that it undermines the rule that only relevant evidence is admissible).

For expanded citations on the exclusion of irrelevant evidence, see § 3:1 to § 3:10.

§ 10:38 Supporting authorities—Exclusion of settlement evidence used to show liability

Garcez By and Through Chicago Title and Trust Co. v. Michel, 282 Ill. App. 3d 346, 351–52, 218 Ill. Dec. 31, 668 N.E.2d 194 (1st Dist. 1996) (closing argument was improper that referred to evidence that the plaintiff had settled with other defendants, because the argument represented an attempt to suggest that the other defendants were the liable parties and that the plaintiff should have been content with the settlement already received).

Sawicki v. Kim, 112 Ill. App. 3d 641, 644–46, 67 Ill. Dec. 771, 445 N.E.2d 63 (2d Dist. 1983) (reference in opening statement to the opposing party's offer to settle the matter was reversible error).

Graff v. Fox, 204 Ill. App. 598, 1917 WL 2128, at *3 (3d Dist. 1917) (admissions made by a party during offers to settle a case are inadmissible).

735 ILCS 5/8-1901 states:

> (a) The providing of, or payment for, medical, surgical, hospital, or rehabilitation services, facilities, or equipment by or on behalf of any person, or the offer to provide, or pay for, any one or more of the foregoing, *shall not be construed as an admission of any liability by such person or persons*. Testimony, writings, records, reports or information with respect to the foregoing shall not be admissible in evidence as an admission of any liability in any action of any kind in any court or before any commission, administrative agency, or other tribunal in this State, except at the instance of the person or persons so making any such provision, payment or offer.
>
> (b) Any expression of grief, apology, or explanation provided by a health care provider, including, but not limited to, a statement that the health care provider is "sorry" for the outcome to a patient, the patient's family, or the patient's legal representative about an inadequate or unanticipated treatment or care outcome that is provided within 72 hours of when the provider knew or should have known of the potential cause of such outcome *shall not be admissible as evidence in any action of any kind in any court or before any tribunal, board, agency, or person*. The disclosure of any such information, whether proper, or improper, shall not waive or have any effect upon its confidentiality or inadmissibility. As used in this Section, a "health care provider" is any hospital, nursing home or other facility, or employee or agent thereof, a physician, or other licensed health care professional. Nothing in this Section precludes the discovery or admissibility of any other facts regarding the patient's treatment or outcome as otherwise permitted by law.
>
> (c) The changes to this Section made by this amendatory Act of the 94th General Assembly apply to causes of action accruing on or after its effective date. (Emphasis added.)

Note that paragraphs (b) and (c), above, were added to 735 ILCS 5/8-1901 by P.A. 94-677 (2005) and became effective on August 25, 2005. Therefore, be sure to note that pursuant to Section (c), above, expressions of grief, apology, or explanation in causes of action accruing before August 25, 2005 are not covered by this Act.

§ 10:39 Supporting authorities—Exclusion of settlement evidence used to show liability—Prior settlements

Garcez By and Through Chicago Title and Trust Co. v. Michel, 282 Ill. App. 3d 346, 348–52, 218 Ill. Dec. 31, 668 N.E.2d 194 (1st Dist. 1996) (trial judge improperly allowed the defendant to offer evidence that the plaintiff had settled with other defendants who then testified as witnesses).

§ 10:40 Supporting authorities—Exclusion of settlement evidence used to show liability—Settlement negotiations

Liberty Mut. Ins. Co. v. American Home Assur. Co., Inc., 368 Ill. App. 3d 948, 960-61, 306 Ill. Dec. 733, 858 N.E.2d 530 (1st Dist. 2006) (trial court properly excluded a letter from a party's attorney which included evidence of settlement negotiations).

Graff v. Fox, 204 Ill. App. 598, 1917 WL 2128, at *3 (3d Dist. 1917) (admissions made by a party during offers to settle a case are inadmissible).

See generally, 735 ILCS 5/8-1901, supra.

§ 10:41 Supporting authorities—Exclusion of settlement evidence used to show liability—Settlement with co-defendants

Singh v. Air Illinois, Inc., 165 Ill. App. 3d 923, 935, 117 Ill. Dec. 501, 520 N.E.2d 852 (1st Dist. 1988) (proper to exclude evidence of plaintiff's settlement with co-defendants and allow the trial judge to determine the proper set-off after the jury has returned a verdict).

See also § 10:41, Supporting authorities—Exclusion of settlement evidence used to show liability—Settlement with co-defendants, infra.

§ 10:42 Supporting authorities—Exclusion of settlement evidence used to show liability—Where offer made prior to litigation

Sawicki v. Kim, 112 Ill. App. 3d 641, 644–46, 67 Ill. Dec. 771, 445 N.E.2d 63 (2d Dist. 1983) (reference in opening statement to the opposing party's offer to settle the matter if a lawyer would not be involved, was reversible error).

§ 10:43 Supporting authorities—Court's discretion

Lewis v. Illinois Cent. R. Co., 234 Ill. App. 3d 669, 175 Ill. Dec. 573, 600 N.E.2d 504 (5th Dist. 1992) (settlement evidence between the plaintiff and the third-party defendants was not improperly excluded, because even if it could have been admissible to show bias, the trial judge had the discretion to determine whether or not to admit it for that purpose).

§ 10:44 Supporting authorities—Other grounds

Other possible grounds for excluding settlement evidence include:

- Time-wasting (§ 2:5 to § 2:8)
- Confusing or misleading (§ 2:9 to § 2:12)
- Solely intended to create an emotional bias (§ 2:13 to § 2:19)
- Collateral to issues in case (§ 3:11 to § 3:21)
- Inadmissible hearsay (§ 8:78 to § 8:89)
- Collateral source rule (§ 10:1 to § 10:18)

§ 10:45 Opposing authorities—Purpose other than to show liability—Admission against interest

Williamson County v. Brock, 367 Ill. 159, 160–62, 10 N.E.2d 654 (1937) (party's offer to sell property involved in a condemnation suit for a specific amount was admissible as an admission against interest).

§ 10:46 Opposing authorities—Purpose other than to show liability—Bias or prejudice

Stathis v. Geldermann, Inc., 295 Ill. App. 3d 844, 861, 229 Ill. Dec. 809, 692 N.E.2d 798 (1st Dist. 1998) (settlement discussions admissible to show factors other than an admission of liability, such as bias, state of mind or prior relationship between the parties).

But see *Garcez By and Through Chicago Title and Trust Co. v. Michel*, 282 Ill. App. 3d 346, 348–52, 218 Ill. Dec. 31, 668 N.E.2d 194 (1st Dist. 1996) (trial judge improperly allowed the defendant to offer evidence that the plaintiff had settled with other defendants who then testified as witnesses because there was no evidence that the witnesses were biased as a result of the settlement).

§ 10:47 Opposing authorities—Purpose other than to show liability—Contract issues

Quinlan v. Stouffe, 355 Ill. App. 3d 830, 837, 291 Ill. Dec. 305, 823 N.E.2d 597 (4th Dist. 2005) (testimony regarding discussions at a settlement meeting was admissible and relevant to the issue of whether an oral contract was formed and, if so, the nature of its terms).

Stathis v. Geldermann, Inc., 295 Ill. App. 3d 844, 861, 229 Ill. Dec. 809, 692 N.E.2d 798 (1st Dist. 1998) (settlement discussions admissible to show factors other than an admission of liability, such as prior relationship between the parties).

§ 10:48 Opposing authorities—Purpose other than to show liability—Impeachment

Garcez By and Through Chicago Title and Trust Co. v. Michel, 282 Ill. App. 3d 346, 348–52, 218 Ill. Dec. 31, 668 N.E.2d 194 (1st Dist. 1996) (trial judge improperly allowed the defendant to offer evidence that the plaintiff had settled with other defendants where there was no evidence that the witnesses were biased as a result of the settlement).

§ 10:49 Opposing authorities—Purpose other than to show liability—State of mind

Garcez By and Through Chicago Title and Trust Co. v. Michel, 282 Ill. App. 3d 346, 348–52, 218 Ill. Dec. 31, 668 N.E.2d 194 (1st Dist. 1996) (trial judge improperly allowed the defendant to offer evidence that the plaintiff had settled with other defendants who then testified as witnesses because there was no evidence that the witnesses were biased as a result of the settlement).

Stathis v. Geldermann, Inc., 295 Ill. App. 3d 844, 861, 229 Ill. Dec. 809, 692 N.E.2d 798 (1st Dist. 1998) (settlement discussions admissible to show factors other than an admission of liability, such as bias, state of mind or prior relationship between the parties).

§ 10:50 Opposing authorities—Purpose other than to show liability—Settlement as a set-off or bar to claim

Varelis v. Northwestern Memorial Hosp., 167 Ill. 2d 449, 450–65, 212 Ill. Dec. 652, 657 N.E.2d 997 (1995) (prior judgment in a personal injury action precluded a later claim for wrongful death based upon the same incident).

Wilson v. Hoffman Group, Inc., 131 Ill. 2d 308, 312–324, 137 Ill. Dec. 579, 546 N.E.2d 524 (1989) (Settlement between the plaintiff and the third party defendant, which included a worker's compensation lien waiver, was admissible for purposes of a set-off, when offered by the defendant).

But see *Singh v. Air Illinois, Inc.*, 165 Ill. App. 3d 923, 935, 117 Ill. Dec. 501, 520 N.E.2d 852 (1st Dist. 1988) (proper to exclude evidence of plaintiff's settlement with co-defendants and allow the trial judge to determine the proper set-off after the jury has returned a verdict).

D. MOTION TO EXCLUDE EVIDENCE OF OTHER ACCIDENTS

§ 10:51 Suggested motion text

[Name of moving party] hereby moves this Court for an order excluding any and all evidence, references to evidence, testimony or argument relating to *[describe date and nature of prior or subsequent accident, e.g., a prior automobile accident involving plaintiff and an unrelated party that occurred on or about January 31, 1999]*. The motion is based upon the grounds that the evidence is irrelevant, immaterial, confusing and will create a substantial danger of undue prejudice to *[name of moving party]*.

◆ **Note:** *For a sample motion to exclude prior accidents, see § 1:23, Sample in limine brief, supra.*

§ 10:52 Motion summary

This motion is used to exclude evidence of prior and subsequent accidents where the evidence is irrelevant to the issues in the case. The motion is based upon the court's authority to exclude prejudicial evidence [*People v. Walker*, 335 Ill. App. 3d 102, 112, 268 Ill. Dec. 654, 779 N.E.2d 268 (2d Dist. 2002), as modified on denial of reh'g, (Oct. 24, 2002) and judgment aff'd, 211 Ill. 2d 317, 285 Ill. Dec. 519, 812 N.E.2d 339 (2004); *People v. Peete*, 318 Ill. App. 3d 961, 966–67, 252 Ill. Dec. 821, 743 N.E.2d 689 (4th Dist. 2001); and *People v. Holman*, 257 Ill. App. 3d 1031, 1033–34, 196 Ill. Dec. 457, 630 N.E.2d 154 (2d Dist. 1994)] and evidence that is irrelevant [Federal Rule of Evidence 401, as adopted through Illinois case law; see *Spencer v. Wandolowski*, 264 Ill. App. 3d 611, 617, 201 Ill. Dec. 422, 636 N.E.2d 854 (1st Dist. 1994); and *People v. Monroe*, 66 Ill. 2d 317, 321–22, 5 Ill. Dec. 824, 362 N.E.2d 295 (1977)] and a line of leading cases. See *Henderson by Hudspeth v. Illinois Cent. Gulf R. Co.*, 114 Ill. App. 3d 754, 757–760, 70 Ill. Dec. 595, 449 N.E.2d 942 (4th Dist. 1983); and *Trimble v. Olympic Tavern, Inc.*, 239 Ill. App. 3d 393, 397–99, 180 Ill.

Dec. 199, 606 N.E.2d 1276 (2d Dist. 1993) [discussing prior accidents] and *Bass v. Cincinnati, Inc.*, 180 Ill. App. 3d 1076, 1078–84, 129 Ill. Dec. 781, 536 N.E.2d 831 (1st Dist. 1989) [discussing subsequent accidents]. Evidence of an *absence* of prior accidents may also be excluded in certain cases. See *Parson v. City of Chicago*, 117 Ill. App. 3d 383, 388–89, 72 Ill. Dec. 895, 453 N.E.2d 770 (1st Dist. 1983).

Note that evidence of prior and subsequent accidents may be admissible to show a dangerous condition or defective product, notice or the cause of an accident, provided that the circumstances are similar and not too remote. See *Henderson by Hudspeth v. Illinois Cent. Gulf R. Co.*, 114 Ill. App. 3d 754, 757–760, 70 Ill. Dec. 595, 449 N.E.2d 942 (4th Dist. 1983); and *Bass v. Cincinnati, Inc.*, 180 Ill. App. 3d 1076, 1078–84, 129 Ill. Dec. 781, 536 N.E.2d 831 (1st Dist. 1989).

§ 10:53 Supporting authorities—Exclusion of prejudicial evidence, generally

Federal Rule of Evidence 403 states:

> Although relevant, evidence may be excluded if its probative value is substantially outweighed by the danger of unfair prejudice, confusion of the issues, or misleading the jury, or by considerations of undue delay, waste of time, or needless presentation of cumulative evidence.

It must be noted that this Rule has not been codified in Illinois. However, Illinois cases have stated that Illinois has a common-law rule that is comparable to Federal Rule of Evidence 403. See *People v. Walker*, 335 Ill. App. 3d 102, 112, 268 Ill. Dec. 654, 779 N.E.2d 268 (2d Dist. 2002), as modified on denial of reh'g, (Oct. 24, 2002) and judgment aff'd, 211 Ill. 2d 317, 285 Ill. Dec. 519, 812 N.E.2d 339 (2004); and *People v. Peete*, 318 Ill. App. 3d 961, 966–67, 252 Ill. Dec. 821, 743 N.E.2d 689 (4th Dist. 2001).

People v. Holman, 257 Ill. App. 3d 1031, 1033–34, 196 Ill. Dec. 457, 630 N.E.2d 154 (2d Dist. 1994) (evidence is admissible if it is relevant and if the prejudicial impact does not substantially outweigh the probative value of it).

For expanded citations on the exclusion of prejudicial evidence, see § 2:1 to § 2:4.

§ 10:54 Supporting authorities—Exclusion of irrelevant evidence, generally

Federal Rule of Evidence 401 defines relevancy as,

evidence having any tendency to make the existence of any fact that is of consequence to the determination of the action more probable or less probable than it would be without the evidence.

Illinois has adopted this definition of relevancy through case law. *Spencer v. Wandolowski*, 264 Ill. App. 3d 611, 617, 201 Ill. Dec. 422, 636 N.E.2d 854 (1st Dist. 1994); and *People v. Monroe*, 66 Ill. 2d 317, 321–22, 5 Ill. Dec. 824, 362 N.E.2d 295 (1977).

Preston ex rel. Preston v. Simmons, 321 Ill. App. 3d 789, 803, 254 Ill. Dec. 647, 747 N.E.2d 1059 (1st Dist. 2001) (trial judge should not permit such wide latitude on cross-examination that it undermines the rule that only relevant evidence is admissible).

For expanded citations on the exclusion of irrelevant evidence, see § 3:1 to § 3:10.

§ 10:55 Supporting authorities—Exclusion of prior-accident evidence—Absence of prior accidents

Jones v. DHR Cambridge Homes, Inc., 381 Ill. App. 3d 18, 319 Ill. Dec. 59, 885 N.E.2d 330, 344–45 (1st Dist. 2008) (trial court properly excluded evidence of the fact that there had not been prior OSHA violations).

Parson v. City of Chicago, 117 Ill. App. 3d 383, 388–89, 72 Ill. Dec. 895, 453 N.E.2d 770 (1st Dist. 1983) (the fact that there were no prior accidents at a given location is less probative than if the fact was instead that there were prior similar accidents and for that reason, the fact that there were no accidents is more likely to be excluded based upon possible confusion of the jury).

Parson v. City of Chicago, 117 Ill. App. 3d 383, 388–89, 72 Ill. Dec. 895, 453 N.E.2d 770 (1st Dist. 1983) (absence of prior accidents in the same location was not admissible absent a proper foundation to show that the conditions were similar for the other individuals who did not have accidents).

Hodges v. Bearse, 129 Ill. 87, 89–90, 21 N.E. 613 (1889) (lack of prior accidents in elevator was not admissible to suggest absence of negligence in building and maintaining the elevator and such evidence would be irrelevant and likely to mislead the jury).

§ 10:56 Supporting authorities—Exclusion of prior-accident evidence—Prior accident evidence used to prove negligence

Henderson by Hudspeth v. Illinois Cent. Gulf R. Co., 114 Ill.

App. 3d 754, 757–760, 70 Ill. Dec. 595, 449 N.E.2d 942 (4th Dist. 1983) (prior accidents should not be admitted to show negligence).

Herget Nat. Bank of Pekin v. Johnson, 21 Ill. App. 3d 1024, 1026–28, 316 N.E.2d 191 (3d Dist. 1974) (evidence suggesting that the victim had acted negligently in the past should not be admitted to suggest that he acted negligently in the instant matter).

§ 10:57 Supporting authorities—Exclusion of prior-accident evidence—Lack of similarity: Dangerous condition/defective products

Note that in dangerous condition and defective product cases, prior accident evidence is relevant and generally admissible. See *Trimble v. Olympic Tavern, Inc.*, 239 Ill. App. 3d 393, 397–98, 180 Ill. Dec. 199, 606 N.E.2d 1276 (2d Dist. 1993)]. The following cases provide potential limitations on this general rule.

LoCoco v. XL Disposal Corp., 307 Ill. App. 3d 684, 693–94, 240 Ill. Dec. 474, 717 N.E.2d 823 (3d Dist. 1999), opinion modified on denial of reh'g, (Oct. 22, 1999) (evidence of prior accidents that almost occurred were not relevant because the proposed testimony would have come from drivers that were traveling in a different direction than the plaintiff) (note that the court declined to determine whether such close calls might be admissible if the circumstances were more similar to those in the case).

Trimble v. Olympic Tavern, Inc., 239 Ill. App. 3d 393, 397–98, 180 Ill. Dec. 199, 606 N.E.2d 1276 (2d Dist. 1993) (prior accident evidence can be admissible to show that a condition is dangerous or that the defendant had notice that the location of the accident was dangerous; however, only similar accidents can be used to show that a condition is dangerous and if dissimilar accidents are used to show notice of a dangerous location, then only the fact of the accident and not the details of it are admissible).

Trimble v. Olympic Tavern, Inc., 239 Ill. App. 3d 393, 397–99, 180 Ill. Dec. 199, 606 N.E.2d 1276 (2d Dist. 1993) (prior accident evidence was not admissible because it was not similar and because the prior accident victims did not notify the defendant, so as to put the defendant on notice of the allegedly dangerous condition).

Henderson by Hudspeth v. Illinois Cent. Gulf R. Co., 114 Ill. App. 3d 754, 757–760, 70 Ill. Dec. 595, 449 N.E.2d 942 (4th

Dist. 1983) (prior accident evidence can be admissible to show that a condition is dangerous or that the defendant had notice that the location of the accident was dangerous; only similar accidents can be used to show that a condition is dangerous and if dissimilar accidents are used to show notice of a dangerous location, then only the fact of the accident and not the details of it are admissible).

Moore v. Bloomington, D. & C.R. Co., 295 Ill. 63, 66–68, 128 N.E. 721 (1920) (evidence of accidents from individuals traveling in the opposite direction from the plaintiff was improper and prejudicial).

§ 10:58 Supporting authorities—Exclusion of prior-accident evidence—Irrelevant

Obszanski v. Foster Wheeler Const., Inc., 328 Ill. App. 3d 550, 558–60, 262 Ill. Dec. 585, 765 N.E.2d 1193 (1st Dist. 2002) (the defendant should not have been permitted to introduce evidence of the Plaintiff's subsequent injury unless the defendant could establish that the new injury was the cause of the plaintiff's current distress).

Vojas v. K mart Corp., 312 Ill. App. 3d 544, 551–53, 245 Ill. Dec. 144, 727 N.E.2d 397 (5th Dist. 2000) (the party offering the evidence of a prior injury must prove that it is relevant to the current injury).

Cancio v. White, 297 Ill. App. 3d 422, 428–30, 232 Ill. Dec. 7, 697 N.E.2d 749 (1st Dist. 1998) (error to allow evidence of plaintiff's pre-existing arthritis when there was no clear proof of a direct link to the injury that was at issue in the case).

Parson v. City of Chicago, 117 Ill. App. 3d 383, 388–89, 72 Ill. Dec. 895, 453 N.E.2d 770 (1st Dist. 1983) (absence of prior accidents in the same location was not admissible, absent a proper foundation to show that the conditions were similar for the other individuals who did not have accidents).

Hodges v. Bearse, 129 Ill. 87, 89–90, 21 N.E. 613 (1889) (lack of prior accidents in elevator was not admissible to suggest absence of negligence in building and maintaining the elevator and such evidence would be irrelevant and likely to mislead the jury).

§ 10:59 Supporting authorities—Exclusion of prior-accident evidence—Jury confusion

Hodges v. Bearse, 129 Ill. 87, 89–90, 21 N.E. 613 (1889) (lack of prior accidents in elevator was not admissible to suggest absence of negligence in building and maintaining the elevator and such evidence would be irrelevant and likely to mislead the jury).

§ 10:60 Supporting authorities—Exclusion of subsequent accident evidence—General rule

Note that evidence of similar post-occurrence accidents can be admissible to demonstrate that a product or condition is dangerous or defective. However, such evidence cannot be admitted to show that the defendant acted with disregard for the safety of others, because a subsequent accident does not prove that the defendant had notice of the defect or danger at the time of the original incident. See generally, *Bass v. Cincinnati, Inc.*, 180 Ill. App. 3d 1076, 1078–84, 129 Ill. Dec. 781, 536 N.E.2d 831 (1st Dist. 1989).

§ 10:61 Supporting authorities—Exclusion of subsequent accident evidence—Dangerous condition cases

Alwin v. Village of Wheeling, 371 Ill. App. 3d 898, 309 Ill. Dec. 656, 864 N.E.2d 897 (1st Dist. 2007), appeal denied, 224 Ill. 2d 571, 312 Ill. Dec. 654, 871 N.E.2d 54 (2007) (evidence regarding prior accidents was admissible to show a party's knowledge of a dangerous condition).

Trimble v. Olympic Tavern, Inc., 239 Ill. App. 3d 393, 397–98, 180 Ill. Dec. 199, 606 N.E.2d 1276 (2d Dist. 1993) (prior accident evidence can be admissible to show that a condition is dangerous or that the defendant had notice that the location of the accident was dangerous. However, only similar accidents can be used to show that a condition is dangerous and if dissimilar accidents are used to show notice of a dangerous location, then only the fact of the accident and not the details of it are admissible).

Trimble v. Olympic Tavern, Inc., 239 Ill. App. 3d 393, 397–99, 180 Ill. Dec. 199, 606 N.E.2d 1276 (2d Dist. 1993) (prior accident evidence was not admissible because it was not similar and because the prior accident victims did not notify the defendant so as to put the defendant on notice of the allegedly dangerous condition).

Bass v. Cincinnati, Inc., 180 Ill. App. 3d 1076, 1078–84, 129 Ill. Dec. 781, 536 N.E.2d 831 (1st Dist. 1989) (evidence of similar post-occurrence accidents cannot be admitted to show that the defendant acted with disregard for the safety of others, because a subsequent accident does not prove that the defendant had notice of the defect or danger at the time of the original incident).

§ 10:62 Supporting authorities—Other grounds

Other possible grounds for excluding evidence of other accidents include:

- Time-wasting (§ 2:5 to § 2:8)
- Confusing or misleading (§ 2:9 to § 2:12)
- Solely intended to create an emotional bias (§ 2:13 to § 2:19)
- Collateral to issues in case (§ 3:11 to § 3:21)
- Inadmissible hearsay (§ 8:78 to § 8:89)

§ 10:63 Opposing authorities—Evidence of prior accidents—Absence of prior accidents

Schaffner v. Chicago and North Western Transp. Co., 161 Ill. App. 3d 742, 760–61, 113 Ill. Dec. 489, 515 N.E.2d 298 (1st Dist. 1987), judgment aff'd, 129 Ill. 2d 1, 133 Ill. Dec. 432, 541 N.E.2d 643, 15 A.L.R.5th 1005 (1989) (proper to allow defendant to show absence of prior accidents when an allegedly dangerous product was used under similar conditions as those surrounding the plaintiff's injury).

Gallick v. Novotney, 124 Ill. App. 3d 756, 759, 79 Ill. Dec. 942, 464 N.E.2d 846 (3d Dist. 1984) (absence of prior accidents at the same location, under similar conditions was admissible to show whether the location was dangerous and, even if it was dangerous, whether the defendant had notice that it was).

§ 10:64 Opposing authorities—Evidence of prior accidents—Court's discretion

Carillo v. Ford Motor Co., 325 Ill. App. 3d 955, 966–68, 259 Ill. Dec. 619, 759 N.E.2d 99 (1st Dist. 2001) (decisions regarding the admissibility of evidence are within the trial court's discretion).

§ 10:65 Opposing authorities—Evidence of prior accidents—Similarity: Dangerous condition/ defective products

Carillo v. Ford Motor Co., 325 Ill. App. 3d 955, 966–68, 259 Ill. Dec. 619, 759 N.E.2d 99 (1st Dist. 2001) (prior accidents which involved less severe impact but where the injured individuals were in similar types of seats and sustained similar injuries, were admissible to suggest a dangerous product).

Trimble v. Olympic Tavern, Inc., 239 Ill. App. 3d 393, 397–98, 180 Ill. Dec. 199, 606 N.E.2d 1276 (2d Dist. 1993) (prior accident evidence can be admissible to show that a condition is dangerous or that the defendant had notice that the location of the accident was dangerous).

Bass v. Cincinnati, Inc., 180 Ill. App. 3d 1076, 1078–84, 129 Ill. Dec. 781, 536 N.E.2d 831 (1st Dist. 1989) (evidence of similar post-occurrence accidents can be admissible to demonstrate that a product or condition is dangerous or defective).

Schaffner v. Chicago and North Western Transp. Co., 161 Ill. App. 3d 742, 760–61, 113 Ill. Dec. 489, 515 N.E.2d 298 (1st Dist. 1987), judgment aff'd, 129 Ill. 2d 1, 133 Ill. Dec. 432, 541 N.E.2d 643, 15 A.L.R.5th 1005 (1989) (proper to allow defendant to show absence of prior accidents when an allegedly dangerous product was used under similar conditions as those surrounding the plaintiff's injury).

See also *Henderson by Hudspeth v. Illinois Cent. Gulf R. Co.*, 114 Ill. App. 3d 754, 757–760, 70 Ill. Dec. 595, 449 N.E.2d 942 (4th Dist. 1983) (prior accident may be admissible to show dangerous condition or notice).

§ 10:66 Opposing authorities—Evidence of prior accidents—Notice

Trimble v. Olympic Tavern, Inc., 239 Ill. App. 3d 393, 397–98, 180 Ill. Dec. 199, 606 N.E.2d 1276 (2d Dist. 1993) (prior accident evidence can be admissible to show that a condition is dangerous or that the defendant had notice that the location of the accident was dangerous).

Gallick v. Novotney, 124 Ill. App. 3d 756, 759, 79 Ill. Dec. 942, 464 N.E.2d 846 (3d Dist. 1984) (absence of prior accidents at the same location, under similar conditions was admissible to show whether the location was dangerous and, even if it was dangerous, whether the defendant had notice that it was).

Grant v. Joseph J. Duffy Co., 20 Ill. App. 3d 669, 677–78, 314 N.E.2d 478 (1st Dist. 1974) ("reasonably similar" prior accidents should have been admitted to demonstrate the defendant's knowledge of the unsafe condition).

§ 10:67 Opposing authorities—Evidence of prior accidents—Relevant to issues in case (e.g., similar injuries)

Mikolajczyk v. Ford Motor Co., 374 Ill. App. 3d 646, 668–70, 312 Ill. Dec. 441, 870 N.E.2d 885 (1st Dist. 2007), appeal allowed, 225 Ill. 2d 637, 314 Ill. Dec. 826, 875 N.E.2d 1113 (2007) and judgment rev'd, 231 Ill. 2d 516, 2008 WL 4603565 (2008), opinion modified on denial of reh'g, (Dec. 18, 2008) (evidence of prior accidents that were not identical but involved the same alleged product defect were admissible).

Schaffner v. Chicago and North Western Transp. Co., 161 Ill. App. 3d 742, 760–61, 113 Ill. Dec. 489, 515 N.E.2d 298 (1st Dist. 1987), judgment aff'd, 129 Ill. 2d 1, 133 Ill. Dec. 432, 541 N.E.2d 643, 15 A.L.R.5th 1005 (1989) (proper to allow defendant to show absence of prior accidents when an allegedly dangerous product was used under similar conditions as those surrounding the plaintiff's injury).

Grant v. Joseph J. Duffy Co., 20 Ill. App. 3d 669, 677–78, 314 N.E.2d 478 (1st Dist. 1974) ("reasonably similar" prior accidents should have been admitted to demonstrate the defendant's knowledge of the unsafe condition).

§ 10:68 Opposing authorities—Evidence of prior accidents—Accidents as basis for expert opinion

Wiedemann v. Industrial Erectors, Inc., 137 Ill. App. 3d 47, 56-57, 91 Ill. Dec. 504, 483 N.E.2d 990 (1st Dist. 1985) (trial judge did not err by allowing the plaintiff's expert to testify that he almost fell when conducting testing on the allegedly dangerous product, under circumstances that were similar to those that had injured the plaintiff).

§ 10:69 Opposing authorities—Evidence of prior accidents—Other possible exceptions—Impeachment

In the California case of *Lowenthal v. Mortimer*, 125 Cal. App. 2d 636, 640, 270 P.2d 942 (2d Dist. 1954), in ruling that prior accident evidence is inadmissible to prove negligence [see Section 10:56], the court discussed several exceptions to this rule in other jurisdictions. These cases, summarized below, may provide support in your opposition briefs.

Bachman v. Ambos, 83 Ohio App. 141, 38 Ohio Op. 227, 50 Ohio L. Abs. 97, 79 N.E.2d 177 (2d Dist. Shelby County 1947) (prior accident evidence allowed where eyesight impairment at issue).

Barshfield v. Vucklich, 108 Kan. 761, 197 P. 205 (1921) (evidence allowed on cross-examination to impeach testimony offered in direct examination that driver was careful).

McGuire v. Village of Caledonia, 140 Minn. 151, 167 N.W.

425, 426 (1918) (cross-examination of claimant regarding prior personal injury claims allowed, where fraud was alleged as defense).

§ 10:70 Opposing authorities—Evidence of subsequent accidents—Court's discretion

Carillo v. Ford Motor Co., 325 Ill. App. 3d 955, 966–68, 259 Ill. Dec. 619, 759 N.E.2d 99 (1st Dist. 2001) (decisions regarding the admissibility of evidence are within the trial court's discretion).

§ 10:71 Opposing authorities—Evidence of subsequent accidents—Dangerous condition

Bass v. Cincinnati, Inc., 180 Ill. App. 3d 1076, 1078–84, 129 Ill. Dec. 781, 536 N.E.2d 831 (1st Dist. 1989) (evidence of similar post-occurrence accidents can be admissible to demonstrate that a product or condition is dangerous or defective).

Wiedemann v. Industrial Erectors, Inc., 137 Ill. App. 3d 47, 56-57, 91 Ill. Dec. 504, 483 N.E.2d 990 (1st Dist. 1985) (trial judge did not err by allowing the plaintiff's expert to testify that he almost fell when conducting testing on the allegedly dangerous product, under circumstances that were similar to those that had injured the plaintiff).

§ 10:72 Opposing authorities—Evidence of subsequent accidents—Impeachment

See generally Section 10:69 supra.

E. MOTION TO EXCLUDE EVIDENCE OF SUBSEQUENT REPAIRS

§ 10:73 Suggested motion text

[Name of moving party] hereby moves this Court for an order excluding any and all evidence, references to evidence, testimony or argument relating to subsequent repairs by *[name of party, or describe subsequent repair evidence to be excluded]*. The motion is based upon the grounds that the evidence is irrelevant, immaterial, confusing, prejudicial and expressly precluded by law and public policy.

§ 10:74 Motion summary

This motion is used to exclude evidence of subsequent repairs, where used to prove negligence or culpable conduct. The motion is based upon the authority of Federal Rule of Evidence 407, as cited by Illinois case law [see e.g. *LoCoco v. XL*

Disposal Corp., 307 Ill. App. 3d 684, 692–93, 240 Ill. Dec. 474, 717 N.E.2d 823 (3d Dist. 1999), opinion modified on denial of reh'g, (Oct. 22, 1999)], as well as the court's authority to exclude evidence that is irrelevant [Federal Rule of Evidence 401, as adopted through Illinois case law; see *Spencer v. Wandolowski*, 264 Ill. App. 3d 611, 617, 201 Ill. Dec. 422, 636 N.E.2d 854 (1st Dist. 1994); and *People v. Monroe*, 66 Ill. 2d 317, 321–22, 5 Ill. Dec. 824, 362 N.E.2d 295 (1977)] or prejudicial [*People v. Walker*, 335 Ill. App. 3d 102, 112, 268 Ill. Dec. 654, 779 N.E.2d 268 (2d Dist. 2002), as modified on denial of reh'g, (Oct. 24, 2002) and judgment aff'd, 211 Ill. 2d 317, 285 Ill. Dec. 519, 812 N.E.2d 339 (2004); *People v. Peete*, 318 Ill. App. 3d 961, 966–67, 252 Ill. Dec. 821, 743 N.E.2d 689 (4th Dist. 2001); and *People v. Holman*, 257 Ill. App. 3d 1031, 1033–34, 196 Ill. Dec. 457, 630 N.E.2d 154 (2d Dist. 1994)]. Note that evidence of remedial measures may be admissible in strict products liability cases. See *Davis v. International Harvester Co.*, 167 Ill. App. 3d 814, 821–25, 118 Ill. Dec. 589, 521 N.E.2d 1282 (2d Dist. 1988); and *Burke v. Illinois Power Co.*, 57 Ill. App. 3d 498, 514, 15 Ill. Dec. 670, 373 N.E.2d 1354 (1st Dist. 1978).

§ 10:75 Supporting authorities—Exclusion of prejudicial evidence, generally

Federal Rule of Evidence 403 states:

> Although relevant, evidence may be excluded if its probative value is substantially outweighed by the danger of unfair prejudice, confusion of the issues, or misleading the jury, or by considerations of undue delay, waste of time, or needless presentation of cumulative evidence.

It must be noted that this Rule has not been codified in Illinois. However, Illinois cases have stated that Illinois has a common-law rule that is comparable to Federal Rule of Evidence 403. See *People v. Walker*, 335 Ill. App. 3d 102, 112, 268 Ill. Dec. 654, 779 N.E.2d 268 (2d Dist. 2002), as modified on denial of reh'g, (Oct. 24, 2002) and judgment aff'd, 211 Ill. 2d 317, 285 Ill. Dec. 519, 812 N.E.2d 339 (2004); and *People v. Peete*, 318 Ill. App. 3d 961, 966–67, 252 Ill. Dec. 821, 743 N.E.2d 689 (4th Dist. 2001). Therefore, it is arguable that Federal Rule of Evidence 403 can be considered as persuasive authority in Illinois.

People v. Holman, 257 Ill. App. 3d 1031, 1033–34, 196 Ill. Dec. 457, 630 N.E.2d 154 (2d Dist. 1994) (evidence is admissible if it is relevant and if the prejudicial impact does not substantially outweigh the probative value of it).

For expanded citations on the exclusion of prejudicial evidence, see § 2:1 to § 2:4.

§ 10:76 Supporting authorities—Exclusion of irrelevant evidence, generally

Federal Rule of Evidence 401 defines relevancy as,

> evidence having any tendency to make the existence of any fact that is of consequence to the determination of the action more probable or less probable than it would be without the evidence.

Illinois has adopted this definition of relevancy through case law. *Spencer v. Wandolowski*, 264 Ill. App. 3d 611, 617, 201 Ill. Dec. 422, 636 N.E.2d 854 (1st Dist. 1994); and *People v. Monroe*, 66 Ill. 2d 317, 321–22, 5 Ill. Dec. 824, 362 N.E.2d 295 (1977).

Preston ex rel. Preston v. Simmons, 321 Ill. App. 3d 789, 803, 254 Ill. Dec. 647, 747 N.E.2d 1059 (1st Dist. 2001) (trial judge should not permit such wide latitude on cross-examination that it undermines the rule that only relevant evidence is admissible).

For expanded citations on the exclusion of irrelevant evidence, see § 3:1 to § 3:10.

§ 10:77 Supporting authorities—Exclusion of subsequent repair evidence—Inadmissible to show negligence

Federal Rule of Evidence 407 states:

> When, after an injury or harm allegedly caused by an event, measures are taken that, if taken previously, would have made the injury or harm less likely to occur, evidence of the subsequent measures is not admissible to prove negligence, culpable conduct, a defect in a product, a defect in a product's design, or a need for a warning or instruction. This rule does not require the exclusion of evidence of subsequent measures when offered for another purpose, such as proving ownership, control, or feasibility of precautionary measures, if controverted, or impeachment.

Zavala v. St. Regis Paper Co., 256 Ill. App. 3d 736, 741, 194 Ill. Dec. 908, 628 N.E.2d 405 (1st Dist. 1993) (subsequent remedial measures are not admissible to show liability of the defendant, but in this case, the remedial measures taken by a non-party were admissible on behalf of the defendant to suggest that the non-party was the negligent cause of the injury).

Davis v. International Harvester Co., 167 Ill. App. 3d 814, 821–25, 118 Ill. Dec. 589, 521 N.E.2d 1282 (2d Dist. 1988) (holding that post accident design changes are not admissible to demonstrate liability and are admissible in strict liability cases only to show the feasibility of changes) (citing Federal Rule of Evidence 407) (note that this case stated that it was disagreeing with other cases that held that design changes might be generally admissible in strict liability cases to prove defective design).

McLaughlin v. Rush-Presbyterian St. Luke's Medical Center, 68 Ill. App. 3d 546, 548–52, 25 Ill. Dec. 63, 386 N.E.2d 334 (1st Dist. 1979) (post-occurrence changes in design by the manufacturer were admissible to suggest that the defendant had not been negligent in the use of the item at issue) (citing Federal Rule of Evidence 407).

Simich v. Edgewater Beach Apartments Corp., 368 Ill. App. 3d 394, 411-12, 306 Ill. Dec. 535, 857 N.E.2d 934 (1st Dist. 2006), appeal denied, 223 Ill. 2d 685, 310 Ill. Dec. 257, 865 N.E.2d 977 (2007) (trial court properly barred evidence regarding a subsequent remedial measure that was taken by the defendant).

Schaffner v. Chicago & North Western Transp. Co., 129 Ill. 2d 1, 133 Ill. Dec. 432, 541 N.E.2d 643, 15 A.L.R.5th 1005 (1989) (generally, evidence of subsequent remedial measures is not admissible to prove negligence so that correction of an unsafe condition is not deterred by the possibility that it will constitute an admission of negligence and because a post occurrence change is not sufficiently probative of prior negligence since later carefulness does not necessarily imply prior negligence).

LoCoco v. XL Disposal Corp., 307 Ill. App. 3d 684, 692–93, 240 Ill. Dec. 474, 717 N.E.2d 823 (3d Dist. 1999), opinion modified on denial of reh'g, (Oct. 22, 1999) (evidence of subsequent repairs was inadmissible because the defendant had participated, along with other independent parties, in making the subsequent repairs; however, the court noted that without the defendant's involvement, the repairs might have been admissible).

Smith v. Black & Decker (U.S.), Inc., 272 Ill. App. 3d 451, 455–57, 209 Ill. Dec. 135, 650 N.E.2d 1108 (3d Dist. 1995) (pre and post-injury safety modifications are inadmissible in negligence and product liability cases unless offered for the sole purpose of showing that such changes were feasible).

§ 10:78 Supporting authorities—Other grounds

Other possible grounds for excluding subsequent repair evidence include:

- Time-wasting (§ 2:5 to § 2:8)
- Confusing or misleading (§ 2:9 to § 2:12)
- Solely intended to create an emotional bias (§ 2:13 to § 2:19)
- Collateral to issues in case (§ 3:11 to § 3:21)
- Inadmissible hearsay (§ 8:78 to § 8:89)

§ 10:79 Opposing authorities—Impeachment

Turgeon v. Commonwealth Edison Co., 258 Ill. App. 3d 234, 245, 197 Ill. Dec. 194, 630 N.E.2d 1318 (2d Dist. 1994) (stating that post-occurrence repairs can be used as impeachment but finding that they did not have impeachment value in this case).

McLaughlin v. Rush-Presbyterian St. Luke's Medical Center, 68 Ill. App. 3d 546, 548–52, 25 Ill. Dec. 63, 386 N.E.2d 334 (1st Dist. 1979) (post-occurrence changes in design by the manufacturer were admissible to suggest that the defendant had not been negligent in the use of the item at issue) (citing Federal Rule of Evidence 407).

Federal Rule of Evidence 407 states:

> When, after an injury or harm allegedly caused by an event, measures are taken that, if taken previously, would have made the injury or harm less likely to occur, evidence of the subsequent measures is not admissible to prove negligence, culpable conduct, a defect in a product, a defect in a product's design, or a need for a warning or instruction. *This rule does not require the exclusion of evidence of subsequent measures when offered for another purpose, such as proving ownership, control, or feasibility of precautionary measures, if controverted, or impeachment.* (Emphasis added.)

§ 10:80 Opposing authorities—Relevant to issues

Herzog v. Lexington Tp., 167 Ill. 2d 288, 212 Ill. Dec. 581, 657 N.E.2d 926 (1995) (evidence of subsequent remedial measures may be admissible for the purpose of proving ownership or control of property where disputed by the defendant or to prove feasibility of precautionary measures where disputed by the defendant).

Worsley v. Farmington Pizza Co., Inc., 322 Ill. App. 3d 371, 372–74, 255 Ill. Dec. 857, 750 N.E.2d 1242 (3d Dist. 2001) (evidence that the defendant had removed certain safety warning devices before the plaintiff was injured was relevant to show that the defendant had prior notice of the dangerous condition. Note that there was a dissent in this case that disagreed with the holding).

Zavala v. St. Regis Paper Co., 256 Ill. App. 3d 736, 741, 194 Ill. Dec. 908, 628 N.E.2d 405 (1st Dist. 1993) (subsequent remedial measures are not admissible to show liability of the defendant, but in this case, the remedial measures taken by a non-party were admissible on behalf of the defendant to suggest that the non-party was the negligent cause of the injury).

Schaffner v. Chicago and North Western Transp. Co., 161 Ill. App. 3d 742, 753–54, 113 Ill. Dec. 489, 515 N.E.2d 298 (1st Dist. 1987), judgment aff'd, 129 Ill. 2d 1, 133 Ill. Dec. 432, 541 N.E.2d 643, 15 A.L.R.5th 1005 (1989) (evidence of subsequent design changes may be admissible to show "wilful [sic] and wanton conduct" by the defendant.)

McLaughlin v. Rush-Presbyterian St. Luke's Medical Center, 68 Ill. App. 3d 546, 548–52, 25 Ill. Dec. 63, 386 N.E.2d 334 (1st Dist. 1979) (post-occurrence changes in design by the manufacturer were admissible to suggest that the defendant had not been negligent in the use of the item at issue) (citing Federal Rule of Evidence 407).

See generally, Federal Rule of Evidence 407, supra.

§ 10:81 Opposing authorities—Strict products liability

Stallings v. Black and Decker (U.S.), Inc., 342 Ill. App. 3d 676, 277 Ill. Dec. 428, 796 N.E.2d 143 (5th Dist. 2003) (evidence of an alternative feasible design may not be excluded on the basis of an admission by the defendant because this would deprive a plaintiff of important proof that the product was unreasonably dangerous due to a design defect).

Smith v. Black & Decker (U.S.), Inc., 272 Ill. App. 3d 451, 455–57, 209 Ill. Dec. 135, 650 N.E.2d 1108 (3d Dist. 1995) (pre and post-injury safety modifications are inadmissible in negligence and product liability cases unless offered for the sole purpose of showing that such changes were feasible).

McLaughlin v. Rush-Presbyterian St. Luke's Medical Center, 68 Ill. App. 3d 546, 548–52, 25 Ill. Dec. 63, 386 N.E.2d 334 (1st Dist. 1979) (post-occurrence changes in design by the manufacturer were admissible to suggest that the defendant had not been negligent in the use of the item at issue) (citing Federal Rule of Evidence 407).

Burke v. Illinois Power Co., 57 Ill. App. 3d 498, 514, 15 Ill. Dec. 670, 373 N.E.2d 1354 (1st Dist. 1978) (post-occurrence design changes may be admissible in strict liability cases).

F. MOTION TO EXCLUDE EVIDENCE OF STATUTE VIOLATION

§ 10:82 Suggested motion text

[Name of moving party] hereby moves this Court for an order excluding any and all evidence, references to evidence, testimony or argument relating to *[describe date and nature of violation]* by *[name of party]*. The motion is based upon the grounds that the evidence is irrelevant, immaterial, confusing and will create a substantial danger of undue prejudice to *[name of moving party]*.

§ 10:83 Motion summary

This motion is used to exclude evidence of the violation of a statue, ordinance, code or other provision, where the violation was not the proximate cause of the subject incident and evidence of it would, therefore, be highly prejudicial if admitted. The motion is based upon the court's authority to exclude evidence that is irrelevant [Federal Rule of Evidence 401, as adopted through Illinois case law; see *Spencer v. Wandolowski*, 264 Ill. App. 3d 611, 617, 201 Ill. Dec. 422, 636 N.E.2d 854 (1st Dist. 1994); and *People v. Monroe*, 66 Ill. 2d 317, 321–22, 5 Ill. Dec. 824, 362 N.E.2d 295 (1977)] or misleading, confusing or unduly prejudicial [*People v. Walker*, 335 Ill. App. 3d 102, 112, 268 Ill. Dec. 654, 779 N.E.2d 268 (2d Dist. 2002), as modified on denial of reh'g, (Oct. 24, 2002) and judgment aff'd, 211 Ill. 2d 317, 285 Ill. Dec. 519, 812 N.E.2d 339 (2004); *People v. Peete*, 318 Ill. App. 3d 961, 966–67, 252 Ill. Dec. 821, 743 N.E.2d 689 (4th Dist. 2001); and *People v. Holman*, 257 Ill. App. 3d 1031, 1033–34, 196 Ill. Dec. 457, 630 N.E.2d 154 (2d Dist. 1994)]. See *Salcik v. Tassone*, 236 Ill. App. 3d 548, 555–56, 177 Ill. Dec. 723, 603 N.E.2d 793 (1st Dist. 1992).

§ 10:84 Supporting authorities—Exclusion of prejudicial evidence, generally

Federal Rule of Evidence 403 states:

> Although relevant, evidence may be excluded if its probative value is substantially outweighed by the danger of unfair prejudice, confusion of the issues, or misleading the jury, or by considerations of undue delay, waste of time, or needless presentation of cumulative evidence.

It must be noted that this Rule has not been codified in Illinois. However, Illinois cases have stated that Illinois has a common-law rule that is comparable to Federal Rule of Evidence 403. See *People v. Walker*, 335 Ill. App. 3d 102, 112, 268 Ill. Dec. 654, 779 N.E.2d 268 (2d Dist. 2002), as modified on denial of reh'g, (Oct. 24, 2002) and judgment aff'd, 211 Ill. 2d 317, 285 Ill. Dec. 519, 812 N.E.2d 339 (2004); and *People v. Peete*, 318 Ill. App. 3d 961, 966–67, 252 Ill. Dec. 821, 743 N.E.2d 689 (4th Dist. 2001).

People v. Holman, 257 Ill. App. 3d 1031, 1033–34, 196 Ill. Dec. 457, 630 N.E.2d 154 (2d Dist. 1994) (evidence is admissible if it is relevant and if the prejudicial impact does not substantially outweigh the probative value of it).

For expanded citations on the exclusion of prejudicial evidence, see § 2:1 to § 2:4.

§ 10:85 Supporting authorities—Exclusion of irrelevant evidence, generally

Federal Rule of Evidence 401 defines relevancy as,

> evidence having any tendency to make the existence of any fact that is of consequence to the determination of the action more probable or less probable than it would be without the evidence.

Illinois has adopted this definition of relevancy through case law. *Spencer v. Wandolowski*, 264 Ill. App. 3d 611, 617, 201 Ill. Dec. 422, 636 N.E.2d 854 (1st Dist. 1994); and *People v. Monroe*, 66 Ill. 2d 317, 321–22, 5 Ill. Dec. 824, 362 N.E.2d 295 (1977).

Preston ex rel. Preston v. Simmons, 321 Ill. App. 3d 789, 803, 254 Ill. Dec. 647, 747 N.E.2d 1059 (1st Dist. 2001) (trial judge should not permit such wide latitude on cross-examination that it undermines the rule that only relevant evidence is admissible).

For expanded citations on the exclusion of irrelevant evidence, see § 3:1 to § 3:10.

§ 10:86 Supporting authorities—Not proximate cause

Eyrich v. Estate of Waldemar, 327 Ill. App. 3d 1095, 1099, 262 Ill. Dec. 367, 765 N.E.2d 504 (3d Dist. 2002) (failure to have a license is not evidence that the individual was driving in a negligent manner).

Wade v. City of Chicago Heights, 216 Ill. App. 3d 418, 421–440, 159 Ill. Dec. 228, 575 N.E.2d 1288 (1st Dist. 1991) (instructing the jury on a specific statute is proper if the evidence supports that the violation occurred and may have caused the injury but it is improper if the evidence does not support such claims); see also *Hitt v. Langel*, 93 Ill. App. 2d 386, 391–97, 236 N.E.2d 118 (5th Dist. 1968) ("a violation of the Motor Vehicle Act does not constitute 'negligence per se,'" but a jury may consider the violation if it is supported by the evidence); and *Ruwisch v. Knoebel*, 233 Ill. App. 526, 1924 WL 3596, at *1–2 (4th Dist. 1924) (trial judge improperly instructed the jury that if they found that the defendant had violated the statute regarding excessive speed then the plaintiff had made a "prima facie case," by demonstrating proof of an injury).

§ 10:87 Supporting authorities—Not proximate cause—Prior violations

Herget Nat. Bank of Pekin v. Johnson, 21 Ill. App. 3d 1024, 1026–28, 316 N.E.2d 191 (3d Dist. 1974) (evidence suggesting that the victim had acted negligently in the past should not be admitted to suggest that he acted negligently in the instant matter).

See also § 7:10, Supporting authorities—Exclusion of improper impeachment evidence, generally—Arrest or misdemeanor convictions that do not involve truth or dishonesty, regarding exclusion of arrests and misdemeanors; § 7:37 to § 7:52 regarding exclusion of prior felonies; and § 10:51 to § 10:72 regarding exclusion of prior accident evidence.

§ 10:88 Supporting authorities—Other grounds

Other possible grounds for excluding evidence of traffic violations include:

- Time-wasting (§ 2:5 to § 2:8)
- Confusing or misleading (§ 2:9 to § 2:12)
- Solely intended to create an emotional bias (§ 2:13 to § 2:19)
- Collateral to issues in case (§ 3:11 to § 3:21)
- Accident reports (§ 4:64 to § 4:74)
- Impermissible impeachment evidence (§ 7:4 to § 7:24)
- Inadmissible hearsay (§ 8:78 to § 8:89)

§ 10:89 Opposing authorities—Impeachment

Note that felony criminal convictions or misdemeanor convictions involving truth or dishonesty may be used for impeachment. See § 7:18, Opposing authorities—Impeachment, generally, § 7:50, Opposing authorities—General rule: Admissibility of prior convictions, and Chapter 7, generally.

§ 10:90 Opposing authorities—Proximate cause

Wade v. City of Chicago Heights, 216 Ill. App. 3d 418, 421–440, 159 Ill. Dec. 228, 575 N.E.2d 1288 (1st Dist. 1991) (instructing the jury on a specific statute is proper if the evidence supports a claim that the violation occurred and may have caused the injury but it is improper if the evidence does not support such claims).

Schultz v. Siddens, 191 Ill. App. 3d 622, 625–27, 138 Ill. Dec. 857, 548 N.E.2d 87 (5th Dist. 1989) (trial judge erred in barring evidence of the defendant's alleged statute violation because it took away from the jury the issue of whether the violation was the proximate cause of the plaintiff's injuries).

Hitt v. Langel, 93 Ill. App. 2d 386, 391–97, 236 N.E.2d 118 (5th Dist. 1968) ("a violation of the Motor Vehicle Act does not constitute 'negligence per se,'" but a jury may consider the violation if it is supported by the evidence).

Cooney v. Hughes, 310 Ill. App. 371, 34 N.E.2d 566, 571 (1st Dist. 1941) (evidence supported instruction regarding statute that defendant had allegedly violated when he injured the plaintiff).

See Illinois Pattern Jury Instruction Civil Number 60.01, which states:

> VIOLATION OF STATUTE, ORDINANCE, OR ADMINISTRATIVE REGULATION
>
> There was in force in the [State of Illinois] [City of ________] at the time of the occurrence in question a certain e.g., Peoria [statute] [ordinance] [administrative (regulation)(rule)(order)] which provided that:
>
> [*Quote or paraphrase applicable part of statute, ordinance or regulation as construed by the courts.*]
>
> If you decide that [a party] [the parties] [________] violated the [statute] [ordinance] [regulation] [rule] [order] on the occasion in question, then you may consider that fact together with all the other facts and circumstances in evidence in determining whether and to what extent, if any, [a party] [the parties] [________________] [was] [were] negligent before and at the time of the occurrence.

§ 10:91 Opposing authorities—Proximate cause—Negligence per se—Presumption of negligence

Loschiavo v. Greco Contractors, Inc., 106 Ill. App. 3d 556, 557–60, 61 Ill. Dec. 861, 435 N.E.2d 702 (1st Dist. 1981) (evidence of a violation of a statute is only conclusive proof of negligence if the statute creates a specific cause of action; however, if the statute is merely designed to provide protection to the public, without providing a specific cause of action, then a violation is only prima facie evidence of negligence).

Hitt v. Langel, 93 Ill. App. 2d 386, 391–97, 236 N.E.2d 118

(5th Dist. 1968) ("a violation of the Motor Vehicle Act does not constitute 'negligence per se,'" but a jury may consider the violation if it is supported by the evidence).

See Illinois Pattern Jury Instruction Civil Number 60.01, supra.

§ 10:92 Opposing authorities—Proximate cause—Movant's reply argument: Gatekeeping provisions

Where the opposition relies upon negligence per se or the violation of a statutory provision as a basis for admission of the disputed statutory violation evidence, the moving party should consider requesting a preliminary showing regarding the validity of the claim. Analogy may be made to other "gatekeeping" cases, addressing the danger of prejudice that is likely if the statutory violation is presented to the jury without a sufficient basis of proof of the applicability of the statute.

G. MOTION TO EXCLUDE EVIDENCE OF DRIVER'S LICENSE SUSPENSION

§ 10:93 Suggested motion text

> *[Name of moving party]* hereby moves this Court for an order excluding any and all evidence, references to evidence, testimony or argument relating to *[describe evidence, e.g., the fact that defendant's license was suspended at the time of the subject incident] [or, describe date and nature of suspension]*. The motion is based upon the grounds that the evidence is expressly prohibited by law and is irrelevant, immaterial, confusing and will create a substantial danger of undue prejudice to *[name of moving party]*.

§ 10:94 Motion summary

This motion is used to exclude evidence that a driver was unlicensed or had his or her license suspended or revoked. The motion is based upon the authority of Illinois case law. See *Eyrich v. Estate of Waldemar*, 327 Ill. App. 3d 1095, 1099, 262 Ill. Dec. 367, 765 N.E.2d 504 (3d Dist. 2002).

§ 10:95 Supporting authorities—Exclusion of evidence of license suspension or revocation

Eyrich v. Estate of Waldemar, 327 Ill. App. 3d 1095, 1099, 262 Ill. Dec. 367, 765 N.E.2d 504 (3d Dist. 2002) (failure to have a license is not evidence that the individual was driving in a negligent manner).

Compare *Wade v. City of Chicago Heights*, 216 Ill. App. 3d

418, 421–440, 159 Ill. Dec. 228, 575 N.E.2d 1288 (1st Dist. 1991) (instructing the jury on a specific statute is proper if the evidence supports the claim that the violation occurred and may have caused the injury but it is improper if the evidence does not support such claims); and *Hitt v. Langel*, 93 Ill. App. 2d 386, 391–97, 236 N.E.2d 118 (5th Dist. 1968) ("a violation of the Motor Vehicle Act does not constitute 'negligence per se,'" but a jury may consider the violation if it is supported by the evidence).

§ 10:96 Supporting authorities—Not evidence of negligence

Eyrich v. Estate of Waldemar, 327 Ill. App. 3d 1095, 1099, 262 Ill. Dec. 367, 765 N.E.2d 504 (3d Dist. 2002) (failure to have a license is not evidence that the individual was driving in a negligent manner).

§ 10:97 Supporting authorities—Other grounds

Other possible grounds for excluding license evidence include:

- Time-wasting (§ 2:5 to § 2:8)
- Confusing or misleading (§ 2:9 to § 2:12)
- Solely intended to create an emotional bias (§ 2:13 to § 2:19)
- Collateral to issues in case (§ 3:11 to § 3:21)
- Impermissible character evidence (§ 7:1 to § 7:3)
- Inadmissible hearsay (§ 8:78 to § 8:89)

§ 10:98 Opposing authorities—Relevant to issues—Negligent entrustment

People v. One 1999 Lexus, VIN JT8BH68X2X0018305, 367 Ill. App. 3d 687, 693-94, 305 Ill. Dec. 303, 855 N.E.2d 194 (2d Dist. 2006) (evidence of a driver's prior DUI arrests was circumstantial evidence that the relative who let the driver use the car knew that the driver's license was suspended or revoked).

Eyrich v. Estate of Waldemar, 327 Ill. App. 3d 1095, 1099, 262 Ill. Dec. 367, 765 N.E.2d 504 (3d Dist. 2002) (no negligent entrustment in this case because there was no evidence to suggest that the seller knew or should have known that the driver did not have a motorcycle license).

But see *Small v. St. Francis Hosp.*, 220 Ill. App. 3d 537, 538–43, 163 Ill. Dec. 203, 581 N.E.2d 154 (1st Dist. 1991) (court held that a car dealership could be held liable for negligent entrustment for selling a vehicle to an underage driver where the dealership had reason to know that the driver was unlicensed).

H. MOTION TO EXCLUDE EVIDENCE OF FAILURE TO WEAR SEAT BELT

§ 10:99 Suggested motion text

[Name of moving party] hereby moves this Court for an order excluding any and all evidence, references to evidence, testimony or argument relating to *[name of party's or witness']* failure to wear a seat belt at the time of the subject accident in this case. The motion is based upon the grounds that the evidence is irrelevant, immaterial, confusing and will create a substantial danger of undue prejudice to *[name of moving party]*.

§ 10:100 Motion summary

This motion is used to exclude evidence of a plaintiff's failure to wear a seat belt or other restraining device at the time of the subject incident. *Clarkson v. Wright*, 108 Ill. 2d 129, 133–34, 90 Ill. Dec. 950, 483 N.E.2d 268 (1985) (rejected by, Law v. Superior Court In and For Maricopa County, 157 Ariz. 147, 755 P.2d 1135 (1988)) (evidence of failure to wear seat belts should not be admitted with respect to either the question of liability or damages); compare *Moore v. Swoboda*, 213 Ill. App. 3d 217, 157 Ill. Dec. 37, 571 N.E.2d 1056 (4th Dist. 1991).

§ 10:101 Supporting authorities—Exclusion of prejudicial evidence, generally

Federal Rule of Evidence 403 states:

> Although relevant, evidence may be excluded if its probative value is substantially outweighed by the danger of unfair prejudice, confusion of the issues, or misleading the jury, or by considerations of undue delay, waste of time, or needless presentation of cumulative evidence.

It must be noted that this Rule has not been codified in Illinois. However, Illinois cases have stated that Illinois has a common-law rule that is comparable to Federal Rule of Evidence 403. See *People v. Walker*, 335 Ill. App. 3d 102, 112, 268 Ill. Dec. 654, 779 N.E.2d 268 (2d Dist. 2002), as modified on denial of reh'g, (Oct. 24, 2002) and judgment aff'd, 211 Ill. 2d 317, 285 Ill. Dec. 519, 812 N.E.2d 339 (2004); and *People v. Peete*, 318 Ill. App. 3d 961, 966–67, 252 Ill. Dec. 821, 743 N.E.2d 689 (4th Dist. 2001).

People v. Holman, 257 Ill. App. 3d 1031, 1033–34, 196 Ill. Dec. 457, 630 N.E.2d 154 (2d Dist. 1994) (evidence is admissible if it is relevant and if the prejudicial impact does not substantially outweigh the probative value of it).

For expanded citations on the exclusion of prejudicial evidence, see § 2:1 to § 2:4.

§ 10:102 Supporting authorities—Exclusion of irrelevant evidence, generally

Federal Rule of Evidence 401 defines relevancy as,

> evidence having any tendency to make the existence of any fact that is of consequence to the determination of the action more probable or less probable than it would be without the evidence.

Illinois has adopted this definition of relevancy through case law. *Spencer v. Wandolowski*, 264 Ill. App. 3d 611, 617, 201 Ill. Dec. 422, 636 N.E.2d 854 (1st Dist. 1994); and *People v. Monroe*, 66 Ill. 2d 317, 321–22, 5 Ill. Dec. 824, 362 N.E.2d 295 (1977).

Preston ex rel. Preston v. Simmons, 321 Ill. App. 3d 789, 803, 254 Ill. Dec. 647, 747 N.E.2d 1059 (1st Dist. 2001) (trial judge should not permit such wide latitude on cross-examination that it undermines the rule that only relevant evidence is admissible).

For expanded citations on the exclusion of irrelevant evidence, see § 3:1 to § 3:10.

§ 10:103 Supporting authorities—Exclusion of seat-belt evidence, generally

Clarkson v. Wright, 108 Ill. 2d 129, 133–34, 90 Ill. Dec. 950, 483 N.E.2d 268 (1985) (rejected by, Law v. Superior Court In and For Maricopa County, 157 Ariz. 147, 755 P.2d 1135 (1988)) (evidence of failure to wear seat belts should not be admitted with respect to either the question of liability or damages); *Moore v. Swoboda*, 213 Ill. App. 3d 217, 157 Ill. Dec. 37, 571 N.E.2d 1056 (4th Dist. 1991).

Wagner v. Zboncak, 111 Ill. App. 3d 268, 271–72, 66 Ill. Dec. 922, 443 N.E.2d 1085 (2d Dist. 1982) (in order to invoke the "seat belt defense," defendant must demonstrate that the plaintiff's injuries would have been lessened if the seat belt had been used).

Kassela v. Stonitsch, 57 Ill. App. 3d 817, 820–22, 15 Ill. Dec. 262, 373 N.E.2d 608 (1st Dist. 1978) (non-use of the seat belt by the plaintiff should not have been admitted when there was no expert evidence to demonstrate a causal connection between the lack of a seat belt and the extent of the plaintiff's injuries).

Kassela v. Stonitsch, 57 Ill. App. 3d 817, 822, 15 Ill. Dec. 262, 373 N.E.2d 608 (1st Dist. 1978) (impeachment on the plaintiff's non-use of a seat belt would be improper impeachment on a collateral issue).

625 ILCS 5/12-603.1(c) provides as follows:

> Failure to wear a seat safety belt in violation of this Section shall not be considered evidence of negligence, shall not limit the liability of an insurer, and shall not diminish any recovery for damages arising out of the ownership, maintenance, or operation of a motor vehicle.

See also 625 ILCS 25/5, which states:

> In no event shall a person's failure to secure a child under 8 years of age in an approved child restraint system constitute contributory negligence or be admissible as evidence in the trial of any civil action. (Effective January 1, 2004.)

§ 10:104 Supporting authorities—Exclusion of seat-belt evidence, generally—Expert testimony required

Wagner v. Zboncak, 111 Ill. App. 3d 268, 271–72, 66 Ill. Dec. 922, 443 N.E.2d 1085 (2d Dist. 1982) (in order to invoke the "seat belt defense," defendant must demonstrate through "competent evidence" that the plaintiff's injuries would have been lessened if the seat belt had been used).

Kassela v. Stonitsch, 57 Ill. App. 3d 817, 820–22, 15 Ill. Dec. 262, 373 N.E.2d 608 (1st Dist. 1978) (non-use of the seat belt by the plaintiff should not have been admitted when there was no expert evidence to demonstrate a causal connection between the lack of a seat belt and the extent of the plaintiff's injuries).

§ 10:105 Supporting authorities—Exclusion of seat-belt evidence, generally—Exclusion in strict liability cases

Note that contributory negligence is not a defense to strict liability. *Arellano v. SGL Abrasives*, 246 Ill. App. 3d 1002, 1010, 186 Ill. Dec. 891, 617 N.E.2d 130 (1st Dist. 1993); *Simpson v. General Motors Corp.*, 108 Ill. 2d 146, 90 Ill. Dec. 854, 483 N.E.2d 1 (1985).

The following California case provides a nice discussion of this issue: *Horn v. General Motors Corp.*, 17 Cal. 3d 359, 369–71, 131 Cal. Rptr. 78, 551 P.2d 398 (1976) (court properly excluded expert testimony on plaintiff's failure to use seat belts in strict liability action against automobile manufacturer where plaintiff was injured by defective horn cap cover on steering wheel).

§ 10:106 Supporting authorities—Exclusion of seat-belt evidence, generally—Defendant's burden regarding seatbelt defense

Note that Illinois Statutes provide for penalties for failure to comply with the mandatory seat belt provisions. See § 10:111 to § 10:121, infra. The following citations address the use of such evidence at trial.

Wagner v. Zboncak, 111 Ill. App. 3d 268, 271–72, 66 Ill. Dec. 922, 443 N.E.2d 1085 (2d Dist. 1982) (in order to invoke the "seat belt defense," defendant must demonstrate that the plaintiff's injuries would have been lessened if the seat belt had been used).

See also *Kassela v. Stonitsch*, 57 Ill. App. 3d 817, 820–22, 15 Ill. Dec. 262, 373 N.E.2d 608 (1st Dist. 1978) (non-use of the seat belt by the plaintiff should not have been admitted when there was no expert evidence to demonstrate a causal connection between the lack of a seat belt and the extent of the plaintiff's injuries).

See also § 10:82 to § 10:92, supra, regarding the exclusion of evidence of a statutory violation.

§ 10:107 Supporting authorities—Other grounds

Other possible grounds for excluding seat belt evidence include:

- Time-wasting (§ 2:5 to § 2:8)
- Confusing or misleading (§ 2:9 to § 2:12)
- Solely intended to create an emotional bias (§ 2:13 to § 2:19)
- Collateral to issues in case (§ 3:11 to § 3:21)
- Impermissible character evidence (§ 7:1 to § 7:3)

§ 10:108 Opposing authorities—Relevant to issues

Bachman v. General Motors Corp., 332 Ill. App. 3d 760, 267 Ill. Dec. 125, 776 N.E.2d 262 (4th Dist. 2002) (allowed the defendant to use seatbelt evidence to suggest forward movement and defeat the claim of alleged premature airbag deployment).

§ 10:109 Opposing authorities—Where use would have reduced injuries

Wagner v. Zboncak, 111 Ill. App. 3d 268, 271–72, 66 Ill. Dec. 922, 443 N.E.2d 1085 (2d Dist. 1982) (in order to invoke the "seat belt defense," defendant must demonstrate through "competent evidence" that the plaintiff's injuries would have been lessened if the seat belt had been used; there was not enough evidence to demonstrate that the injuries would have been reduced in this case).

Kassela v. Stonitsch, 57 Ill. App. 3d 817, 820–22, 15 Ill. Dec. 262, 373 N.E.2d 608 (1st Dist. 1978) (non-use of the seat belt by the plaintiff should not have been admitted when there was no expert evidence to demonstrate a causal connection between the lack of a seat belt and the extent of the plaintiff's injuries).

§ 10:110 Opposing authorities—A note on mandatory seatbelt laws

625 ILCS 25/4a states:

> Every person, when transporting a child 8 years of age or older but under the age of 16, as provided in Section 4 of this Act, shall be responsible for securing that child in either a child restraint system or seat belts.

625 ILCS 25/4b states:

> Every person under the age of 18 years, when transporting a child 8 years of age or older but under the age of 19 years, as provided in Section 4 of this Act, shall be responsible for securing that child in a properly adjusted and fastened seat safety belt or an appropriate child restraint system.

See also 625 ILCS 5/12-603.1.

625 ILCS 5/12-603.1(c) states as follows:

> Failure to wear a seat safety belt in violation of this Section shall not be considered evidence of negligence, shall not limit the liability of an insurer, and shall not diminish any recovery for damages arising out of the ownership, maintenance, or operation of a motor vehicle.

See generally 625 ILCS 5/12-603.1; see also § 10:82 to § 10:92, supra, regarding the exclusion of statute violation evidence.

I. MOTION TO EXCLUDE EVIDENCE OF ALCOHOL CONSUMPTION

§ 10:111 Suggested motion text

> *[Name of moving party]* hereby moves this Court for an order excluding any and all evidence, references to evidence, testimony or argument relating to alcohol consumption by *[name of party or witness] [or describe nature of alcohol-related evidence to be excluded]*. The motion is based upon the grounds that the evidence is irrelevant, immaterial, confusing and will create a substantial danger of undue prejudice to *[name of moving party]*.

§ 10:112 Motion summary

This motion is used to exclude evidence of a party or witness' consumption of alcohol where unrelated to issues in the case. The motion is based upon the court's authority to exclude evidence that is irrelevant [Federal Rule of Evidence 401, as adopted through Illinois case law; see *Spencer v. Wandolowski*, 264 Ill. App. 3d 611, 617, 201 Ill. Dec. 422, 636 N.E.2d 854 (1st Dist. 1994); and *People v. Monroe*, 66 Ill. 2d 317, 321–22, 5 Ill. Dec. 824, 362 N.E.2d 295 (1977)] or misleading, confusing or unduly prejudicial [*People v. Walker*, 335 Ill. App. 3d 102, 112, 268 Ill. Dec. 654, 779 N.E.2d 268 (2d Dist. 2002), as modified on denial of reh'g, (Oct. 24, 2002) and judgment aff'd, 211 Ill. 2d 317, 285 Ill. Dec. 519, 812 N.E.2d 339 (2004); *People v. Peete*, 318 Ill. App. 3d 961, 966–67, 252 Ill. Dec. 821, 743 N.E.2d 689 (4th Dist. 2001); and *People v. Holman*, 257 Ill. App. 3d 1031, 1033–34, 196 Ill. Dec. 457, 630 N.E.2d 154 (2d Dist. 1994)] and leading cases that exclude alcohol evidence where there is no foundational showing of relevance or causation. See *Wagner v. Zboncak*, 111 Ill. App. 3d 268, 269–71, 66 Ill. Dec. 922, 443 N.E.2d 1085 (2d Dist. 1982) [automobile driver]; *McWethy v. Lee*, 1 Ill. App. 3d 80, 82-85, 272 N.E.2d 663 (4th Dist. 1971) [automobile passenger]; and *Ryan v. McEvoy*, 20 Ill. App. 3d 562, 566–67, 315 N.E.2d 38 (1st Dist. 1974) [general intemperance].

§ 10:113 Supporting authorities—Exclusion of prejudicial evidence, generally

Federal Rule of Evidence 403 states:

> Although relevant, evidence may be excluded if its probative value is substantially outweighed by the danger of unfair prejudice, confusion of the issues, or misleading the jury, or by considerations of undue delay, waste of time, or needless presentation of cumulative evidence.

It must be noted that this Rule has not been codified in Illinois. However, Illinois cases have stated that Illinois has a common-law rule that is comparable to Federal Rule of Evidence 403. See *People v. Walker*, 335 Ill. App. 3d 102, 112, 268 Ill. Dec. 654, 779 N.E.2d 268 (2d Dist. 2002), as modified on denial of reh'g, (Oct. 24, 2002) and judgment aff'd, 211 Ill. 2d 317, 285 Ill. Dec. 519, 812 N.E.2d 339 (2004); and *People v. Peete*, 318 Ill. App. 3d 961, 966–67, 252 Ill. Dec. 821, 743 N.E.2d 689 (4th Dist. 2001).

People v. Holman, 257 Ill. App. 3d 1031, 1033–34, 196 Ill. Dec. 457, 630 N.E.2d 154 (2d Dist. 1994) (evidence is admissible if it is relevant and if the prejudicial impact does not substantially outweigh the probative value of it).

For expanded citations on the exclusion of prejudicial evidence, see § 2:1 to § 2:4.

§ 10:114 Supporting authorities—Exclusion of irrelevant evidence, generally

Federal Rule of Evidence 401 defines relevancy as,

> evidence having any tendency to make the existence of any fact that is of consequence to the determination of the action more probable or less probable than it would be without the evidence.

Illinois has adopted this definition of relevancy through case law. *Spencer v. Wandolowski*, 264 Ill. App. 3d 611, 617, 201 Ill. Dec. 422, 636 N.E.2d 854 (1st Dist. 1994); and *People v. Monroe*, 66 Ill. 2d 317, 321–22, 5 Ill. Dec. 824, 362 N.E.2d 295 (1977).

Preston ex rel. Preston v. Simmons, 321 Ill. App. 3d 789, 803, 254 Ill. Dec. 647, 747 N.E.2d 1059 (1st Dist. 2001) (trial judge should not permit such wide latitude on cross-examination that it undermines the rule that only relevant evidence is admissible).

For expanded citations on the exclusion of irrelevant evidence, see § 3:1 to § 3:10.

§ 10:115 Supporting authorities—Intoxication not relevant to issues in case

Werner v. Nebal, 377 Ill. App. 3d 447, 455–56, 316 Ill. Dec. 89, 878 N.E.2d 811 (1st Dist. 2007) (in a dram shop action, trial court properly excluded evidence of the plaintiff's statements to paramedics regarding how many drinks he had, as confusing to the jury).

Carillo v. Ford Motor Co., 325 Ill. App. 3d 955, 968, 259 Ill. Dec. 619, 759 N.E.2d 99 (1st Dist. 2001) (intoxication of the driver of the vehicle that collided with the plaintiff should not have been admitted when that driver had already admitted negligence and the issue for decision was whether the plaintiff's seat was defective or dangerous).

McWethy v. Lee, 1 Ill. App. 3d 80, 83-85, 272 N.E.2d 663 (4th Dist. 1971) (improper to allow evidence of consumption or presence of alcohol when there was no proof that the witness was intoxicated).

Kitten v. Stodden, 76 Ill. App. 2d 177, 180–82, 221 N.E.2d 511 (5th Dist. 1966) (error to admit evidence of drinking and instruct the jury on the issue of intoxication when there was no evidence that the plaintiff, who had admitted to drinking, was intoxicated).

§ 10:116 Supporting authorities—Exclusion in automobile cases—Consumption by driver where no impairment

Wagner v. Zboncak, 111 Ill. App. 3d 268, 269–71, 66 Ill. Dec. 922, 443 N.E.2d 1085 (2d Dist. 1982) (improper and prejudicial to refer to consumption of alcohol by the plaintiff when there was no evidence that the plaintiff was intoxicated or that the plaintiff's driving was impaired).

Bohnen v. Wingereid, 80 Ill. App. 3d 232, 237–39, 35 Ill. Dec. 254, 398 N.E.2d 1204 (1st Dist. 1979) (evidence of alcohol use should only be admitted when there is a sufficient showing that the use may have impaired the driver and contributed to the collision. Note that in this case, the evidence was properly admitted).

But see Illinois Pattern Jury Instruction Civil number 12.01, infra.

> ◆ **Note:** While evidence of a driver's intoxication in automobile negligence cases is relevant in the determination of negligence [see § 10:120, Opposing authorities—Where relevant to issues—Driving under the influence of alcohol as proof of negligence, infra], an in limine motion may be appropriate to exclude alcohol evidence where there is no foundational showing that the driver was *under the influence* at the time of the incident, pursuant to the above authorities.

§ 10:117 Supporting authorities—Exclusion in automobile cases—Consumption by plaintiff-passenger

Of course, even if an individual is intoxicated, the intoxication must be relevant to an issue in the case. It is unusual for a plaintiff-passenger's intoxication to truly be relevant to the issue of negligence or causation. Unless the plaintiff-passenger's impairment is at issue, that party's intoxication should be excluded. Of course, if the plaintiff-passenger's ability to observe is at issue, evidence of his or her intoxication is relevant and admissible. See § 10:121, Opposing authorities—Where relevant to issues—Witness perceptions.

McWethy v. Lee, 1 Ill. App. 3d 80, 82-85, 272 N.E.2d 663 (4th Dist. 1971) (error to allow evidence of consumption or presence of alcohol by passengers when there was no indication that the passengers were intoxicated).

§ 10:118 Supporting authorities—Past alcohol use

People v. Collette, 217 Ill. App. 3d 465, 467–71, 160 Ill. Dec. 420, 577 N.E.2d 550 (4th Dist. 1991) (trial court properly restricted certain questions regarding the witness' past alcohol use).

Ryan v. McEvoy, 20 Ill. App. 3d 562, 566–67, 315 N.E.2d 38 (1st Dist. 1974) (asking a witness about past alcohol use was improper).

See also *People v. Kegley*, 227 Ill. App. 3d 48, 54-55, 169 Ill. Dec. 3, 590 N.E.2d 922 (2d Dist. 1992) (trial court did not abuse its discretion by refusing to admit impeachment evidence of a single use of narcotics); *Baldwin v. Huffman Towing Co.*, 51 Ill. App. 3d 861, 863–64, 9 Ill. Dec. 469, 366 N.E.2d 980 (5th Dist. 1977) (trial judge properly excluded evidence of a witness' conviction for possession of a narcotic, because the prejudicial impact of the evidence outweighed the probative value of it).

See also Chapter 7, regarding character evidence.

§ 10:119 Supporting authorities—Other grounds

Other possible grounds for excluding alcohol evidence include:

- Time-wasting (§ 2:5 to § 2:8)
- Confusing or misleading (§ 2:9 to § 2:12)
- Solely intended to create an emotional bias (§ 2:13 to § 2:19)
- Collateral to issues in case (§ 3:11 to § 3:21)
- Impermissible character evidence (§ 7:1 to § 7:3)

§ 10:120 Opposing authorities—Where relevant to issues—Driving under the influence of alcohol as proof of negligence

Illinois Pattern Jury Instruction Civil number 12.01 states:

> INTOXICATION AS NEGLIGENCE
>
> Whether or not a person involved in the occurrence was intoxicated at the time is a proper question for the jury to consider together with other facts and circumstances in evidence in determining whether or not he was [negligent] [or] [contributorily negligent]. Intoxication is no excuse for failure to act as a reasonably careful person would act. An intoxicated person is held to the same standard of care as a sober person.

Wade v. City of Chicago Heights, 216 Ill. App. 3d 418, 421–440, 159 Ill. Dec. 228, 575 N.E.2d 1288 (1st Dist. 1991) (instructing the jury on a specific statute [in this case certain DUI statutory provisions] is proper if the evidence supports that the violation occurred and may have caused the injury but it is improper if the evidence does not support such claims).

Lindsay v. Appleby, 91 Ill. App. 3d 705, 711, 46 Ill. Dec. 832, 414 N.E.2d 885 (2d Dist. 1980) (trial judge properly allowed a witness to testify to evidence that suggested that the defendant driver was intoxicated at the time of the collision).

Patarozzi v. Prairie States Oil & Grease Co., 71 Ill. App. 2d 155, 157–60, 218 N.E.2d 113 (3d Dist. 1966) (intoxication of the plaintiff driver should have been admissible to allow the jury to consider whether the plaintiff was contributorily negligent).

§ 10:121 Opposing authorities—Where relevant to issues—Witness perceptions

O'Brien v. Hertl, 238 Ill. App. 3d 217, 222–23, 179 Ill. Dec. 393, 606 N.E.2d 225 (1st Dist. 1992) (evidence of alcohol consumption of the party or a witness was admissible as impeachment when the consumption was at or near the time of the incident because such evidence was relevant to suggest impairment of ability to accurately remember the events in question).

J. MOTION TO EXCLUDE EVIDENCE OF PRIOR D.U.I.

§ 10:122 Suggested motion text

[Name of moving party] hereby moves this Court for an order excluding any and all evidence, references to evidence, testimony or argument relating to prior criminal convictions for driving under the influence by *[name of party] [or, describe nature and date of violation]*. The motion is based upon the grounds that the evidence is inadmissible to prove wrongful conduct or impeachment and is irrelevant, immaterial, confusing and will create a substantial danger of undue prejudice to *[name of moving party]*.

§ 10:123 Motion summary

This motion is used to exclude evidence of prior convictions for driving under the influence of alcohol ("D.U.I.") where used for impeachment or to prove wrongful conduct in civil cases. The motion is based upon case law authorities precluding the use of most misdemeanors and certain felony convictions. See generally *People v. Montgomery*, 47 Ill. 2d 510, 516–19, 268

N.E.2d 695, 67 A.L.R.3d 816 (1971) (proposed Federal Rule of Evidence 609 should be followed regarding whether to admit evidence of convictions to impeach a witness); but see *People v. Yost*, 78 Ill. 2d 292, 293–97, 35 Ill. Dec. 755, 399 N.E.2d 1283 (1980), infra.

Current Federal Rule of Evidence 609 states as follows:

(a) General rule.—For the purpose of attacking the character for truthfulness of a witness,

(1) evidence that a witness other than an accused has been convicted of a crime shall be admitted, subject to Rule 403, if the crime was punishable by death or imprisonment in excess of one year under the law under which the witness was convicted, and evidence that an accused has been convicted of such a crime shall be admitted if the court determines that the probative value of admitting this evidence outweighs its prejudicial effect to the accused; and

(2) evidence that any witness has been convicted of a crime shall be admitted regardless of the punishment, if it readily can be determined that establishing the elements of the crime required proof or admission of an act of dishonesty or false statement by the witness.

(b) Time limit. Evidence of a conviction under this rule is not admissible if a period of more than ten years has elapsed since the date of the conviction or of the release of the witness from the confinement imposed for that conviction, whichever is the later date, unless the court determines, in the interests of justice, that the probative value of the conviction supported by specific facts and circumstances substantially outweighs its prejudicial effect. However, evidence of a conviction more than 10 years old as calculated herein, is not admissible unless the proponent gives to the adverse party sufficient advance written notice of intent to use such evidence to provide the adverse party with a fair opportunity to contest the use of such evidence.

(c) Effect of pardon, annulment, or certificate of rehabilitation.—Evidence of a conviction is not admissible under this rule if (1) the conviction has been the subject of a pardon, annulment, certificate of rehabilitation, or other equivalent procedure based on a finding of the rehabilitation of the person convicted, and that person has not been convicted of a subsequent crime that was punishable by death or imprisonment in excess of one year, or (2) the conviction has been the subject of a pardon, annulment, or other equivalent procedure based on a finding of innocence.

(d) Juvenile adjudications. Evidence of juvenile adjudications is generally not admissible under this rule. The court may, however, in a criminal case allow evidence of a juvenile adjudication of a witness other than the accused if conviction of the offense would be admissible to attack the credibility of an adult and the court is satisfied that admission in evidence is necessary for a fair determination of the issue of guilt or innocence.

(e) Pendency of appeal. The pendency of an appeal therefrom does not render evidence of a conviction inadmissible. Evidence of the pendency of an appeal is admissible.

◆ **Important Note:** The case of *People v. Yost*, 78 Ill. 2d 292, 293–97, 35 Ill. Dec. 755, 399 N.E.2d 1283 (1980) clarified that the *Montgomery* case (47 Ill.2d 510, 516–19, supra) only adopted Federal Rule of Evidence 609 *as it was proposed at that time* and that the rule does not change just because the Federal Rule is different or is amended. Counsel should be aware of the subtle differences in the language of current Federal Rule 609, cited above, and the proposed version of the Rule at the time of the *Montgomery* decision. While the two versions are similar, there are subtle, but important, differences which could create fertile areas for argument, depending upon the facts of your case. This is especially true with respect to subdivision (a), which addresses the probative/prejudicial balancing test. The current version of Rule 609(a) would allow the evidence if "the probative value of admitting this evidence outweighs its prejudicial effect;" whereas, the prior proposed version (as adopted by *Montgomery*), would allow the evidence if the "probative value of the evidence of the crime is substantially outweighed by the danger of undue prejudice." For a further discussion, see *People v. Yost*, 78 Ill. 2d 292, 293–97, 35 Ill. Dec. 755, 399 N.E.2d 1283 (1980).

For expanded citations on this topic, see § 7:4 to § 7:24, supra.

§ 10:124 Supporting authorities—Exclusion of prejudicial evidence, generally

Federal Rule of Evidence 403 states:

Although relevant, evidence may be excluded if its probative value is substantially outweighed by the danger of unfair prejudice, confusion of the issues, or misleading the jury, or by considerations of undue delay, waste of time, or needless presentation of cumulative evidence.

It must be noted that this Rule has not been codified in Illinois. However, Illinois cases have stated that Illinois has a common-law rule that is comparable to Federal Rule of Evidence 403. See *People v. Walker*, 335 Ill. App. 3d 102, 112, 268 Ill. Dec. 654, 779 N.E.2d 268 (2d Dist. 2002), as modified on denial of reh'g, (Oct. 24, 2002) and judgment aff'd, 211 Ill. 2d 317, 285 Ill. Dec. 519, 812 N.E.2d 339 (2004); and *People v. Peete*, 318 Ill. App. 3d 961, 966–67, 252 Ill. Dec. 821, 743 N.E.2d 689 (4th Dist. 2001).

People v. Holman, 257 Ill. App. 3d 1031, 1033–34, 196 Ill.

Dec. 457, 630 N.E.2d 154 (2d Dist. 1994) (evidence is admissible if it is relevant and if the prejudicial impact does not substantially outweigh the probative value of it).

For expanded citations on the exclusion of prejudicial evidence, see § 2:1 to § 2:4.

§ 10:125 Supporting authorities—Exclusion of irrelevant evidence, generally

Federal Rule of Evidence 401 defines relevancy as,

> evidence having any tendency to make the existence of any fact that is of consequence to the determination of the action more probable or less probable than it would be without the evidence.

Illinois has adopted this definition of relevancy through case law. *Spencer v. Wandolowski*, 264 Ill. App. 3d 611, 617, 201 Ill. Dec. 422, 636 N.E.2d 854 (1st Dist. 1994); and *People v. Monroe*, 66 Ill. 2d 317, 321–22, 5 Ill. Dec. 824, 362 N.E.2d 295 (1977).

Preston ex rel. Preston v. Simmons, 321 Ill. App. 3d 789, 803, 254 Ill. Dec. 647, 747 N.E.2d 1059 (1st Dist. 2001) (trial judge should not permit such wide latitude on cross-examination that it undermines the rule that only relevant evidence is admissible).

For expanded citations on the exclusion of irrelevant evidence, see § 3:1 to § 3:10.

§ 10:126 Supporting authorities—Blood alcohol evidence—Generally

People v. Beck, 295 Ill. App. 3d 1050, 1060–62, 230 Ill. Dec. 419, 693 N.E.2d 897 (2d Dist. 1998) (after the defendant had successfully received a suppression order regarding a police-ordered blood-alcohol test, the trial judge properly denied the defendant's last-minute request at trial to admit the test results because the late admission of the evidence would cause prejudice to the State).

People v. Rose, 268 Ill. App. 3d 174, 174–83, 205 Ill. Dec. 574, 643 N.E.2d 865 (4th Dist. 1994) (preliminary breath screening test (PBT) results are not admissible in the State's case in chief and the trial judge properly granted the defendant's motion in limine to exclude the results).

People v. Kane, 223 Ill. App. 3d 377, 382–86, 165 Ill. Dec. 610, 584 N.E.2d 1044 (4th Dist. 1991) (trial judge did not abuse his discretion by excluding, as irrelevant and speculative, the defendant's proffered expert testimony regarding his blood alcohol level at the time of his arrest).

People v. Wisbrock, 223 Ill. App. 3d 173, 174–75, 165 Ill. Dec. 334, 584 N.E.2d 513 (3d Dist. 1991) (State was estopped from offering the defendant's breathalyzer results at trial because at the summary suspension hearing, the State had taken the position that the defendant had refused to provide a sample because the sample was deficient).

See also *People v. Lambert*, 249 Ill. App. 3d 726, 727–29, 188 Ill. Dec. 909, 619 N.E.2d 534 (3d Dist. 1993) (the indictment properly notified the defendant that his prior DUI arrests would be used by the State to enhance the classification of his offense. The appellate court noted that the prior offenses were not elements of the charged offense and should not be disclosed to the jury unless such disclosure was otherwise permitted by the rules of evidence).

§ 10:127 Supporting authorities—Blood alcohol evidence—Lack of foundation

People v. Smith, 248 Ill. App. 3d 351, 352–61, 187 Ill. Dec. 380, 617 N.E.2d 837 (2d Dist. 1993) (trial court properly excluded evidence regarding the defendant's blood-alcohol test that was taken at the hospital when the State was unable to lay a foundation to show that an emergency room doctor had ordered the test in the course of treatment to assist with diagnosis or treatment).

People v. Kane, 223 Ill. App. 3d 377, 382–86, 165 Ill. Dec. 610, 584 N.E.2d 1044 (4th Dist. 1991) (no foundation to show that the expert was qualified and there was no proof that the evidence was reliable and helpful to the jury).

People v. Keith, 206 Ill. App. 3d 414, 417–21, 151 Ill. Dec. 446, 564 N.E.2d 901 (3d Dist. 1990), judgment aff'd, 148 Ill. 2d 32, 169 Ill. Dec. 276, 591 N.E.2d 449 (1992) (trial court did not abuse its discretion by granting a motion in limine to exclude evidence of breathalyzer test results when the State was unable to lay a foundation for the results because the officer who administered the test was not certified to perform it at the time the test was taken).

§ 10:128 Supporting authorities—Exclusion of crimes evidence used for impeachment—Generally

People v. Petitt, 245 Ill. App. 3d 132, 139–41, 146–48, 184 Ill. Dec. 766, 613 N.E.2d 1358 (2d Dist. 1993) (evidence of other offenses is not admissible when introduced to suggest that the defendant committed the charged crime).

People v. Mason, 28 Ill. 2d 396, 399–403, 192 N.E.2d 835

(1963) (arrests, charges and prior acts of misconduct are not generally admissible in evidence).

Starks v. Schlensky, 128 Ill. App. 1, 1906 WL 2026, at *2 (2d Dist. 1906) (character traits that do not reflect upon the witness' truthfulness and are not relevant to the issues in the case are not proper subjects for cross-examination).

See *People v. Montgomery*, 47 Ill. 2d 510, 516–17, 268 N.E.2d 695, 67 A.L.R.3d 816 (1971) (adopts proposed Federal Rule of Evidence 609 regarding use of convictions for impeachment.

§ 10:129 Supporting authorities—Exclusion of crimes evidence used for impeachment—Exclusion of arrests and misdemeanor convictions

Where the D.U.I. evidence is a misdemeanor conviction, the motion may be based upon case law precluding the use of such evidence for impeachment.

Young v. Chicago Transit Authority, 209 Ill. App. 3d 84, 94-95, 154 Ill. Dec. 18, 568 N.E.2d 18 (1st Dist. 1990) (trial judge did not abuse discretion by disallowing impeachment evidence that the witness had been convicted of soliciting prostitution, a misdemeanor offense).

Knowles v. Panopoulos, 66 Ill. 2d 585, 587–91, 6 Ill. Dec. 858, 363 N.E.2d 805, 97 A.L.R.3d 1144 (1977) (in civil cases, a witness may be impeached with a conviction for a crime that was punishable by death or in excess of one year in prison or for a crime that involved dishonesty only if the probative value of the evidence outweighs the prejudicial value of it) (holding that *People v. Montgomery*, 47 Ill. 2d 510, 268 N.E.2d 695, 67 A.L.R.3d 816 (1971) applies to civil cases).

People v. Yost, 78 Ill. 2d 292, 293–97, 35 Ill. Dec. 755, 399 N.E.2d 1283 (1980) (in *People v. Montgomery*, 47 Ill. 2d 510, 516–19, 268 N.E.2d 695, 67 A.L.R.3d 816 (1971), the Court only adopted the Federal Rule of Evidence 609 as it was proposed at the time and the rule does not change just because the Federal Rule is different or is amended).

See also *Reichert v. Board of Fire and Police Com'rs of City of Collinsville*, 388 Ill.App.3d 834, 847–49, 905 N.E.2d 861 (5th Dist. 2009) (Illinois only adopted proposed Federal Rule of Evidence 609 and did not adopt subsequent changes to the proposed rule).

People v. Mason, 28 Ill. 2d 396, 399–403, 192 N.E.2d 835 (1963) (arrests, charges and prior acts of misconduct are not generally admissible in evidence).

§ 10:130 Supporting authorities—Exclusion of crimes evidence used for impeachment—Exclusion of felony convictions

People v. Montgomery, 47 Ill. 2d 510, 516–19, 268 N.E.2d 695, 67 A.L.R.3d 816 (1971) (Proposed Federal Rule of Evidence 609 should be followed regarding whether to admit evidence of convictions to impeach a witness).

People v. Montgomery, 47 Ill. 2d 510, 512–19, 268 N.E.2d 695, 67 A.L.R.3d 816 (1971) (a felony conviction that was remote in time should not have been admitted for impeachment).

People v. Yost, 78 Ill. 2d 292, 293–97, 35 Ill. Dec. 755, 399 N.E.2d 1283 (1980) (in *People v. Montgomery*, 47 Ill. 2d 510, 516–19, 268 N.E.2d 695, 67 A.L.R.3d 816 (1971), the Court only adopted the Federal Rule of Evidence 609 as it was proposed at the time and the rule does not change just because the Federal Rule is different or is amended).

See also *Reichert v. Board of Fire and Police Com'rs of City of Collinsville*, 388 Ill.App.3d 834, 847–49, 905 N.E.2d 861 (5th Dist. 2009) (Illinois only adopted proposed Federal Rule of Evidence 609 and did not adopt subsequent changes to the proposed rule).

See generally, § 10:123, Motion summary, supra, for full text of Rule 609.

§ 10:131 Supporting authorities—Exclusion of crimes evidence used for impeachment—Where probative value outweighed by risk of undue prejudice

People v. Petitt, 245 Ill. App. 3d 132, 139–41, 146–48, 184 Ill. Dec. 766, 613 N.E.2d 1358 (2d Dist. 1993) (evidence of other offenses is not admissible when it is introduced to suggest that the defendant committed the charged crime).

People v. Medreno, 99 Ill. App. 3d 449, 450–54, 54 Ill. Dec. 723, 425 N.E.2d 588 (3d Dist. 1981) (prior rape conviction was admissible despite similarity to the charged crime because the defendant had been released from custody for it within the past ten years and the probative value outweighed the prejudicial impact of the evidence).

Baldwin v. Huffman Towing Co., 51 Ill. App. 3d 861, 863–64, 9 Ill. Dec. 469, 366 N.E.2d 980 (5th Dist. 1977) (trial judge properly excluded evidence of a witness' conviction for possession of a narcotic, because the prejudicial impact of the evidence outweighed the probative value).

§ 10:132 Supporting authorities—Exclusion of D.U.I. evidence where used to prove improper conduct—Generally

Where the D.U.I. evidence is used to prove a person's conduct in conformity with the prior conviction, it may be excludable under the authority of Illinois case law upholding the exclusion of such evidence. In that regard, the following cases may be instructive.

People v. Robinson, 368 Ill. App. 3d 963, 974-75, 307 Ill. Dec. 232, 859 N.E.2d 232 (1st Dist. 2006), appeal denied, 223 Ill. 2d 670, 310 Ill. Dec. 255, 865 N.E.2d 975 (2007) (in an aggravated DUI case, evidence of the defendant's two prior DUIs was unfairly prejudicial and should not have been admitted).

Doe v. Lutz, 281 Ill. App. 3d 630, 637–38, 218 Ill. Dec. 80, 668 N.E.2d 564, 112 Ed. Law Rep. 371 (1st Dist. 1996), as modified on denial of reh'g, (June 25, 1996) (evidence of prior inappropriate sexual conduct towards someone other than the alleged victim was not admissible because it was irrelevant and prejudicial and it did not demonstrate sufficiently similar behavior to qualify for modus operandi evidence).

People v. Petitt, 245 Ill. App. 3d 132, 139–41, 146–48, 184 Ill. Dec. 766, 613 N.E.2d 1358 (2d Dist. 1993) (evidence of other offenses is not admissible when it is introduced to suggest that the defendant committed the charged crime).

For expanded citations on this topic, see § 7:25 to § 7:36, supra.

§ 10:133 Supporting authorities—Other grounds

Other possible grounds for excluding D.U.I. evidence:

- Time-wasting (§ 2:5 to § 2:8)
- Confusing or misleading (§ 2:9 to § 2:12)
- Solely intended to create an emotional bias (§ 2:13 to § 2:19)
- Collateral to issues in case (§ 3:11 to § 3:21)
- Improper impeachment evidence (§ 7:4 to § 7:24)
- Improper felony conviction (§ 7:25 to § 7:36)
- Inadmissible hearsay (§ 8:78 to § 8:89)
- Impermissible evidence of statute violation (§ 10:82 to § 10:92)
- Impermissible alcohol evidence (§ 10:111 to § 10:121)

§ 10:134 Opposing authorities

See § 7:18, Opposing authorities—Impeachment, generally,

§ 7:33, Opposing authorities—Court's discretion, and § 7:50, Opposing authorities—General rule: Admissibility of prior convictions, supra, for expanded citations opposing the introduction of character and crimes evidence in general.

§ 10:135 Opposing authorities—Blood alcohol evidence—Generally

Petraski v. Thedos, 382 Ill. App. 3d 22, 320 Ill. Dec. 244, 887 N.E.2d 24 (1st Dist. 2008), appeal denied, 229 Ill. 2d 657, 325 Ill. Dec. 15, 897 N.E.2d 263 (2008) (trial court erred by excluding an expert's opinion regarding the plaintiff's intoxication that was based upon extrapolation from blood that was drawn after the incident in question because the evidence was relevant and reliable and not unfairly prejudicial).

Sobczak v. General Motors Corp., 373 Ill. App. 3d 910, 924–26, 312 Ill. Dec. 682, 871 N.E.2d 82 (1st Dist. 2007), appeal denied, 226 Ill. 2d 609, 316 Ill. Dec. 551, 879 N.E.2d 939 (2007) (trial court had discretion to allow an expert to testify regarding the plaintiff's intoxication at the time of the incident, based upon retrograde extrapolation from blood tests that were taken after the incident).

People v. Basler, 193 Ill. 2d 545, 550–51, 251 Ill. Dec. 171, 740 N.E.2d 1 (2000) (Horizontal Gaze Nystagmus (HGN) tests are not "novel" and therefore, the State does not need to establish their validity. The defendant bears the burden to demonstrate that the results in his case were flawed if he wants to have them excluded).

Ford v. Herman, 316 Ill. App. 3d 726, 735–36, 249 Ill. Dec. 942, 737 N.E.2d 332 (5th Dist. 2000)(the defendant waived his objection to the trial court's refusal to grant his motion in limine to exclude evidence of his DUI convictions by failing to object to the evidence at trial and by eliciting some of the information for rehabilitation purposes).

People v. Davis, 296 Ill. App. 3d 923, 924–39, 231 Ill. Dec. 244, 695 N.E.2d 1363 (3d Dist. 1998) (trial court erred by excluding evidence of the defendant's preliminary breath screening test at the hearing on the defendant's motion to quash arrest and suppress evidence).

People v. Brodack, 296 Ill. App. 3d 71, 76-77, 230 Ill. Dec. 540, 693 N.E.2d 1291 (2d Dist. 1998) (any error caused by the officer's testimony that at the time of his arrest for DUI, the defendant stated that he "had been through this before," was not harmful, despite a prior order in limine precluding evidence of the defendant's prior DUIs).

People v. Giere, 192 Ill. App. 3d 520, 524–26, 139 Ill. Dec. 548, 548 N.E.2d 1104 (2d Dist. 1989) (trial judge had discretion to deny a requested hearing on a motion in limine to exclude blood-alcohol test results and decide the issue during the trial instead, in order to avoid duplication of witness testimony).

§ 10:136 Opposing authorities—Blood alcohol evidence—Relevant

Petraski v. Thedos, 382 Ill. App. 3d 22, 320 Ill. Dec. 244, 887 N.E.2d 24 (1st Dist. 2008), appeal denied, 229 Ill. 2d 657, 325 Ill. Dec. 15, 897 N.E.2d 263 (2008) (trial court erred by excluding an expert's opinion regarding the plaintiff's intoxication that was based upon extrapolation from blood that was drawn after the incident in question because the evidence was relevant and reliable and not unfairly prejudicial).

Sobczak v. General Motors Corp., 373 Ill. App. 3d 910, 924–26, 312 Ill. Dec. 682, 871 N.E.2d 82 (1st Dist. 2007), appeal denied, 226 Ill. 2d 609, 316 Ill. Dec. 551, 879 N.E.2d 939 (2007) (trial court had discretion to allow an expert to testify regarding the plaintiff's intoxication at the time of the incident, based upon retrograde extrapolation from blood tests that were taken after the incident).

People v. One 1999 Lexus, VIN JT8BH68X2X0018305, 367 Ill. App. 3d 687, 693-94, 305 Ill. Dec. 303, 855 N.E.2d 194 (2d Dist. 2006) (evidence of a driver's prior DUI arrests was circumstantial evidence that the relative who let the driver use the car knew that the driver's license was suspended or revoked).

People v. Heineman, 260 Ill. App. 3d 476, 478–80, 198 Ill. Dec. 211, 632 N.E.2d 270 (1st Dist. 1994) (prior DUI arrests and convictions were properly considered as aggravating factors during the defendant's sentencing hearing).

People v. Garriott, 253 Ill. App. 3d 1048, 1048–54, 192 Ill. Dec. 625, 625 N.E.2d 780 (4th Dist. 1993) (trial court erred by excluding evidence of the defendant's failure to submit to a breathalyzer test. The appellate court held that such evidence is relevant and admissible to suggest consciousness of guilt and added that the evidence is admissible for that purpose whether or not the DUI occurred on public or private land).

People v. Smith, 162 Ill. App. 3d 739, 742–43, 114 Ill. Dec. 180, 516 N.E.2d 335 (5th Dist. 1987) (certified copies of the Secretary of State's order revoking the defendant's driver's license for DUI was relevant and admissible in a prosecution against the defendant for the offense of driving while his license was revoked).

§ 10:137 Opposing authorities—Blood alcohol evidence—Foundation

Petraski v. Thedos, 382 Ill. App. 3d 22, 320 Ill. Dec. 244, 887 N.E.2d 24 (1st Dist. 2008), appeal denied, 229 Ill. 2d 657, 325 Ill. Dec. 15, 897 N.E.2d 263 (2008) (trial court erred by excluding an expert's opinion regarding the plaintiff's intoxication that was based upon extrapolation from blood that was drawn after the incident in question because the evidence was relevant and reliable and not unfairly prejudicial).

People v. Buening, 229 Ill. App. 3d 538, 539–46, 170 Ill. Dec. 542, 592 N.E.2d 1222 (5th Dist. 1992) (trial court erred by excluding HGN tests. The appellate court stated that such tests are admissible, provided that the proper foundation is laid, to demonstrate the training and experience of the test provider).

See also *People v. Giere*, 192 Ill. App. 3d 520, 524–26, 139 Ill. Dec. 548, 548 N.E.2d 1104 (2d Dist. 1989) (trial judge correctly determined that for purposes of a reckless homicide charge, the tests only needed to meet ordinary foundation requirements in order to be admissible and they did not need to meet the statutory requirement for the tests when they are to be used in a DUI prosecution).

People v. Sides, 199 Ill. App. 3d 203, 204–07, 145 Ill. Dec. 160, 556 N.E.2d 778 (4th Dist. 1990) (no scientific foundation is needed to establish the reliability of the "finger-to-nose," "one leg stand," and "walk and turn" sobriety tests because the issues are not beyond the jury's ability to understand and analyze).

People v. Vega, 145 Ill. App. 3d 996, 1001, 99 Ill. Dec. 808, 496 N.E.2d 501 (4th Dist. 1986) (the "one leg stand," "finger-to-nose," and "walk the line" sobriety tests "are not so abstruse to require a foundation other than the experience of the officer administering them.").

§ 10:138 Opposing authorities—Impeachment, generally

People v. Prevo, 302 Ill. App. 3d 1038, 1045–50, 235 Ill. Dec. 950, 706 N.E.2d 505 (4th Dist. 1999) (trial judge should have permitted the defendant to impeach the victim of the battery with his DUI conviction when the DUI arose from the same incident and the defendant had testified against the victim at the trial).

§ 10:139 Opposing authorities—Impeachment, generally—Use of felony convictions for impeachment expressly allowed

People v. Medreno, 99 Ill. App. 3d 449, 450–54, 54 Ill. Dec. 723, 425 N.E.2d 588 (3d Dist. 1981) (commission of a felony shows that a witness is not respectful of the rules of society and therefore, a rape conviction was properly admitted to reflect upon veracity).

People v. Medreno, 99 Ill. App. 3d 449, 450–54, 54 Ill. Dec. 723, 425 N.E.2d 588 (3d Dist. 1981) (prior rape conviction was admissible despite similarity to the charged crime because the defendant had been released from custody for it within the past ten years and the probative value outweighed the prejudicial impact of the evidence).

Knowles v. Panopoulos, 66 Ill. 2d 585, 587–91, 6 Ill. Dec. 858, 363 N.E.2d 805, 97 A.L.R.3d 1144 (1977) (in civil cases, a witness may be impeached with a conviction for a crime that was punishable by death or in excess of one year in prison or for a crime that involved dishonesty) (holding that *People v. Montgomery*, 47 Ill. 2d 510, 268 N.E.2d 695, 67 A.L.R.3d 816 (1971) applies to civil cases).

People v. Montgomery, 47 Ill. 2d 510, 516–19, 268 N.E.2d 695, 67 A.L.R.3d 816 (1971) (Proposed Federal Rule of Evidence 609 should be followed regarding whether to admit evidence of convictions to impeach a witness).

People v. Montgomery, 47 Ill. 2d 510, 516–17, 268 N.E.2d 695, 67 A.L.R.3d 816 (1971) (adopts proposed Federal Rule of Evidence 609, "Impeachment by Evidence of Conviction of Crime.")

Federal Rule of Evidence 609 states as follows:

> (a) General rule.—For the purpose of attacking the character for truthfulness of a witness,
>
> (1) evidence that a witness other than an accused has been convicted of a crime shall be admitted, subject to Rule 403, if the crime was punishable by death or imprisonment in excess of one year under the law under which the witness was convicted, and evidence that an accused has been convicted of such a crime shall be admitted if the court determines that the probative value of admitting this evidence outweighs its prejudicial effect to the accused; and
>
> (2) evidence that any witness has been convicted of a crime shall

be admitted regardless of the punishment, if it readily can be determined that establishing the elements of the crime required proof or admission of an act of dishonesty or false statement by the witness.

(b) Time limit. Evidence of a conviction under this rule is not admissible if a period of more than ten years has elapsed since the date of the conviction or of the release of the witness from the confinement imposed for that conviction, whichever is the later date, unless the court determines, in the interests of justice, that the probative value of the conviction supported by specific facts and circumstances substantially outweighs its prejudicial effect. However, evidence of a conviction more than 10 years old as calculated herein, is not admissible unless the proponent gives to the adverse party sufficient advance written notice of intent to use such evidence to provide the adverse party with a fair opportunity to contest the use of such evidence.

(c) Effect of pardon, annulment, or certificate of rehabilitation.—Evidence of a conviction is not admissible under this rule if (1) the conviction has been the subject of a pardon, annulment, certificate of rehabilitation, or other equivalent procedure based on a finding of the rehabilitation of the person convicted, and that person has not been convicted of a subsequent crime that was punishable by death or imprisonment in excess of one year, or (2) the conviction has been the subject of a pardon, annulment, or other equivalent procedure based on a finding of innocence.

(d) Juvenile adjudications. Evidence of juvenile adjudications is generally not admissible under this rule. The court may, however, in a criminal case allow evidence of a juvenile adjudication of a witness other than the accused if conviction of the offense would be admissible to attack the credibility of an adult and the court is satisfied that admission in evidence is necessary for a fair determination of the issue of guilt or innocence.

(e) Pendency of appeal. The pendency of an appeal therefrom does not render evidence of a conviction inadmissible. Evidence of the pendency of an appeal is admissible.

§ 10:140 Opposing authorities—Impeachment, generally—D.U.I. as felony

◆ **Important Note:** The case of *People v. Yost*, 78 Ill. 2d 292, 293–97, 35 Ill. Dec. 755, 399 N.E.2d 1283 (1980) clarified that the *Montgomery* case (47 Ill.2d 510, 516–19, supra) only adopted Federal Rule of Evidence 609 *as it was proposed at that time* and that the rule does not change just because the Federal Rule is different or is amended. Counsel should be aware of the subtle differences in the language of current Federal Rule 609, cited above, and the proposed version of the Rule at the time of the *Montgomery* decision. While the two versions are similar, there are subtle, but important, differences which could create fertile areas for argument, depending upon the facts of your case. This is especially true with respect to subdivision (a), which addresses the probative/prejudicial balancing test. The current version of Rule 609(a) would allow the evidence if "the probative value of admitting this evidence outweighs its prejudicial effect;" whereas, the prior proposed version (as adopted by *Montgomery*), would allow the evidence if the "probative value of the evidence of the crime is substantially outweighed by the danger of undue prejudice." For a further discussion, see *People v. Yost*, 78 Ill. 2d 292, 293–97, 35 Ill. Dec. 755, 399 N.E.2d 1283 (1980).

See also *Reichert v. Board of Fire and Police Com'rs of City of Collinsville*, 388 Ill.App.3d 834, 847–49, 905 N.E.2d 861 (5th Dist. 2009) (Illinois only adopted proposed Federal Rule of Evidence 609 and did not adopt subsequent changes to the proposed rule).

Note that D.U.I convictions may be felonies, under certain circumstances which would fall under the express impeachment provisions of proposed Federal Rule 609, supra.

625 ILCS 5/11-501 states:

> Driving while under the influence of alcohol, other drug or drugs, intoxicating compound or compounds or any combination thereof.
>
> (a) A person shall not drive or be in actual physical control of any vehicle within this State while:
>
> (1) the alcohol concentration in the person's blood or breath is 0.08 or more based on the definition of blood and breath units in Section 11-501.2;
>
> (2) under the influence of alcohol;
>
> (3) under the influence of any intoxicating compound or combination of intoxicating compounds to a degree that renders the person incapable of driving safely;
>
> (4) under the influence of any other drug or combination of drugs to a degree that renders the person incapable of safely driving;
>
> (5) under the combined influence of alcohol, other drug or drugs, or intoxicating compound or compounds to a degree that renders the person incapable of safely driving; or
>
> (6) there is any amount of a drug, substance, or compound in the person's breath, blood, or urine resulting from the unlawful use or consumption of cannabis listed in the Cannabis Control Act, a controlled substance listed in the Illinois Controlled Substances Act, an intoxicating compound listed in the Use of Intoxicating Compounds Act, or methamphetamine as listed in the Methamphetamine Control and Community Protection Act.
>
> (b) The fact that any person charged with violating this Section is or has been legally entitled to use alcohol, other drug or drugs, or intoxicating compound or compounds, or any combination thereof, shall not constitute a defense against any charge of violating this Section.

(c) Penalties.

(1) Except as otherwise provided in this Section, any person convicted of violating subsection (a) of this Section is guilty of a Class A misdemeanor.

(2) A person who violates subsection (a) or a similar provision a second time shall be sentenced to a mandatory minimum term of either 5 days of imprisonment or 240 hours of community service in addition to any other criminal or administrative sanction.

(3) A person who violates subsection (a) is subject to 6 months of imprisonment, an additional mandatory minimum fine of $1,000, and 25 days of community service in a program benefiting children if the person was transporting a person under the age of 16 at the time of the violation.

(4) A person who violates subsection (a) a first time, if the alcohol concentration in his or her blood, breath, or urine was 0.16 or more based on the definition of blood, breath, or urine units in Section 11-501.2, shall be subject, in addition to any other penalty that may be imposed, to a mandatory minimum of 100 hours of community service and a mandatory minimum fine of $500.

(5) A person who violates subsection (a) a second time, if at the time of the second violation the alcohol concentration in his or her blood, breath, or urine was 0.16 or more based on the definition of blood, breath, or urine units in Section 11-501.2, shall be subject, in addition to any other penalty that may be imposed, to a mandatory minimum of 2 days of imprisonment and a mandatory minimum fine of $1,250.

(d) Aggravated driving under the influence of alcohol, other drug or drugs, or intoxicating compound or compounds, or any combination thereof.

(1) Every person convicted of committing a violation of this Section shall be guilty of aggravated driving under the influence of alcohol, other drug or drugs, or intoxicating compound or compounds, or any combination thereof if:

(A) the person committed a violation of subsection (a) or a similar provision for the third or subsequent time;

(B) the person committed a violation of subsection (a) while driving a school bus with persons 18 years of age or younger on board;

(C) the person in committing a violation of subsection (a) was involved in a motor vehicle accident that resulted in great bodily harm or permanent disability or disfigurement to another, when the violation was a proximate cause of the injuries;

(D) the person committed a violation of subsection (a) for a second time and has been previously convicted of violating Section 9-3 of the Criminal Code of 1961 or a similar provision of a law of another state relating to reckless homicide in which the person was determined to have been under the influence of alcohol, other drug or drugs, or intoxicating compound or compounds as an element of the offense or the person has previously been convicted under subparagraph (C) or subparagraph (F) of this paragraph (1);

(E) the person, in committing a violation of subsection (a) while driving at any speed in a school speed zone at a time when a speed limit of 20 miles per hour was in effect under subsection (a) of Section 11-605 of this Code, was involved in a motor vehicle accident that resulted in bodily harm, other than great bodily harm or permanent disability or disfigurement, to another person, when the violation of subsection (a) was a proximate cause of the bodily harm;

(F) the person, in committing a violation of subsection (a), was involved in a motor vehicle, snowmobile, all-terrain vehicle, or watercraft accident that resulted in the death of another person, when the violation of subsection (a) was a proximate cause of the death;

(G) the person committed a violation of subsection (a) during a period in which the defendant's driving privileges are revoked or suspended, where the revocation or suspension was for a violation of subsection (a), or a similar provision, Section 11-501.1, paragraph (b) of Section 11-401, or for reckless homicide as defined in Section 9-3 of the Criminal Code of 1961;

(H) the person committed the violation while he or she did not possess a driver's license or permit or a restricted driving permit or a judicial driving permit or a monitoring device driving permit;

(I) the person committed the violation while he or she knew or should have known that the vehicle he or she was driving was not covered by a liability insurance policy;

(J) the person in committing a violation of subsection (a) was involved in a motor vehicle accident that resulted in bodily harm, but not great bodily harm, to the child under the age of 16 being transported by the person, if the violation was the proximate cause of the injury; or

(K) the person in committing a second violation of subsection (a) or a similar provision was transporting a person under the age of 16.

(2)(A) *Except as provided otherwise, a person convicted of aggravated driving under the influence of alcohol, other drug or drugs, or intoxicating compound or compounds, or any combination thereof is guilty of a Class 4 felony.*

(B) A third violation of this Section or a similar provision is a Class 2 felony. If at the time of the third violation the alcohol concentration in his or her blood, breath, or urine was 0.16 or more based on the definition of blood, breath, or urine units in Section 11-501.2, a mandatory minimum of 90 days of imprisonment and a mandatory minimum fine of $2,500 shall be imposed in addition to any other criminal or administrative sanction. If at the time of the third violation, the defendant was transporting a person under the age of 16, a mandatory fine of $25,000 and 25 days of community service in a program benefiting children shall

be imposed in addition to any other criminal or administrative sanction.

(C) *A fourth violation of this Section or a similar provision is a Class 2 felony, for which a sentence of probation or conditional discharge may not be imposed.* If at the time of the violation, the alcohol concentration in the defendant's blood, breath, or urine was 0.16 or more based on the definition of blood, breath, or urine units in Section 11-501.2, a mandatory minimum fine of $5,000 shall be imposed in addition to any other criminal or administrative sanction. If at the time of the fourth violation, the defendant was transporting a person under the age of 16 a mandatory fine of $25,000 and 25 days of community service in a program benefiting children shall be imposed in addition to any other criminal or administrative sanction.

(D) *A fifth violation of this Section or a similar provision is a Class 1 felony, for which a sentence of probation or conditional discharge may not be imposed.* If at the time of the violation, the alcohol concentration in the defendant's blood, breath, or urine was 0.16 or more based on the definition of blood, breath, or urine units in Section 11-501.2, a mandatory minimum fine of $5,000 shall be imposed in addition to any other criminal or administrative sanction. If at the time of the fifth violation, the defendant was transporting a person under the age of 16, a mandatory fine of $25,000, and 25 days of community service in a program benefiting children shall be imposed in addition to any other criminal or administrative sanction.

(E) *A sixth or subsequent violation of this Section or similar provision is a Class X felony.* If at the time of the violation, the alcohol concentration in the defendant's blood, breath, or urine was 0.16 or more based on the definition of blood, breath, or urine units in Section 11-501.2, a mandatory minimum fine of $5,000 shall be imposed in addition to any other criminal or administrative sanction. If at the time of the violation, the defendant was transporting a person under the age of 16, a mandatory fine of $25,000 and 25 days of community service in a program benefiting children shall be imposed in addition to any other criminal or administrative sanction.

(F) *For a violation of subparagraph (C) of paragraph (1) of this subsection (d), the defendant, if sentenced to a term of imprisonment, shall be sentenced to not less than one year nor more than 12 years.*

(G) *A violation of subparagraph (F) of paragraph (1) of this subsection (d) is a Class 2 felony, for which the defendant, unless the court determines that extraordinary circumstances exist and require probation, shall be sentenced to: (i) a term of imprisonment of not less than 3 years and not more than 14 years if the violation resulted in the death of one person; or (ii) a term of imprisonment of not less than 6 years and not more than 28 years if the violation resulted in the deaths of 2 or more persons.*

(H) For a violation of subparagraph (J) of paragraph (1) of this subsection (d), a mandatory fine of $2,500, and 25 days of community service in a program benefiting children shall be imposed in addition to any other criminal or administrative sanction.

(I) *A violation of subparagraph (K) of paragraph (1) of this subsection (d), is a Class 2 felony* and a mandatory fine of $2,500, and 25 days of community service in a program benefiting children shall be imposed in addition to any other criminal or administrative sanction. If the child being transported suffered bodily harm, but not great bodily harm, in a motor vehicle accident, and the violation was the proximate cause of that injury, a mandatory fine of $5,000 and 25 days of community service in a program benefiting children shall be imposed in addition to any other criminal or administrative sanction.

(3) Any person sentenced under this subsection (d) who receives a term of probation or conditional discharge must serve a minimum term of either 480 hours of community service or 10 days of imprisonment as a condition of the probation or conditional discharge in addition to any other criminal or administrative sanction.

(e) Any reference to a prior violation of subsection (a) or a similar provision includes any violation of a provision of a local ordinance or a provision of a law of another state or an offense committed on a military installation that is similar to a violation of subsection (a) of this Section.

(f) The imposition of a mandatory term of imprisonment or assignment of community service for a violation of this Section shall not be suspended or reduced by the court.

(g) Any penalty imposed for driving with a license that has been revoked for a previous violation of subsection (a) of this Section shall be in addition to the penalty imposed for any subsequent violation of subsection (a).

(h) *For any prosecution under this Section, a certified copy of the driving abstract of the defendant shall be admitted as proof of any prior conviction.* (Emphasis added).

See generally People v. Montgomery, 47 Ill. 2d 510, 516–17, 268 N.E.2d 695, 67 A.L.R.3d 816 (1971) (adopts proposed Federal Rule of Evidence 609); see § 7:34, Opposing authorities—Relevant to material issue, supra, for expanded citations.

K. MOTION TO EXCLUDE EVIDENCE OF PARTY'S HEALTH OR INJURIES WHERE NOT AT ISSUE

§ 10:141 Suggested motion text

[Name of moving party] hereby moves this Court for an order excluding any and all evidence, references to evidence, testimony or argument relating to the physical or mental health of *[name of party] [or, describe health or physical condition to be excluded].* The motion is based upon the grounds that the evidence is irrelevant, immaterial, confusing and will create a substantial danger of undue prejudice to *[name of moving party].*

§ 10:142 Motion summary

This motion is used to exclude evidence of a party's health or injuries where not at issue or not disputed. The motion is based upon the court's authority under Illinois case law to exclude evidence that is irrelevant, as well as leading cases. *Voykin v. Estate of DeBoer*, 192 Ill. 2d 49, 248 Ill. Dec. 277, 733 N.E.2d 1275 (2000) (whether the plaintiff has suffered a prior injury to the same part of the body at issue, the defendant must introduce expert evidence demonstrating why the prior injury is relevant to causation, damages or some other issue of consequence); *Felber v. London*, 346 Ill. App. 3d 188, 281 Ill. Dec. 482, 803 N.E.2d 1103 (2d Dist. 2004); *Obszanski v. Foster Wheeler Const., Inc.*, 328 Ill. App. 3d 550, 558–60, 262 Ill. Dec. 585, 765 N.E.2d 1193 (1st Dist. 2002); and *Vojas v. K mart Corp.*, 312 Ill. App. 3d 544, 551–53, 245 Ill. Dec. 144, 727 N.E.2d 397 (5th Dist. 2000).

Note that prior injuries can be relevant to the nature and extent of plaintiff's claimed injuries in personal injury actions if they are shown to be *related* to the current distress. See *Brown v. Moawad*, 211 Ill. App. 3d 516, 533, 156 Ill. Dec. 14, 570 N.E.2d 490 (1st Dist. 1991); *Lindsay v. Appleby*, 91 Ill. App. 3d 705, 711–12, 46 Ill. Dec. 832, 414 N.E.2d 885 (2d Dist. 1980). The cases cited in this section support exclusion where the other injuries are *not* at issue or *not* disputed.

§ 10:143 Supporting authorities—Exclusion of prejudicial evidence, generally

Federal Rule of Evidence 403 states:

> Although relevant, evidence may be excluded if its probative value is substantially outweighed by the danger of unfair prejudice, confusion of the issues, or misleading the jury, or by considerations of undue delay, waste of time, or needless presentation of cumulative evidence.

It must be noted that this Rule has not been codified in Illinois. However, Illinois cases have stated that Illinois has a common-law rule that is comparable to Federal Rule of Evidence 403. See *People v. Walker*, 335 Ill. App. 3d 102, 112, 268 Ill. Dec. 654, 779 N.E.2d 268 (2d Dist. 2002), as modified on denial of reh'g, (Oct. 24, 2002) and judgment aff'd, 211 Ill. 2d 317, 285 Ill. Dec. 519, 812 N.E.2d 339 (2004); and *People v. Peete*, 318 Ill. App. 3d 961, 966–67, 252 Ill. Dec. 821, 743 N.E.2d 689 (4th Dist. 2001).

People v. Holman, 257 Ill. App. 3d 1031, 1033–34, 196 Ill.

Dec. 457, 630 N.E.2d 154 (2d Dist. 1994) (evidence is admissible if it is relevant and if the prejudicial impact does not substantially outweigh the probative value of it).

For expanded citations on the exclusion of prejudicial evidence, see § 2:1 to § 2:4.

§ 10:144 Supporting authorities—Exclusion of irrelevant evidence, generally

Federal Rule of Evidence 401 defines relevancy as,

> evidence having any tendency to make the existence of any fact that is of consequence to the determination of the action more probable or less probable than it would be without the evidence.

Illinois has adopted this definition of relevancy through case law. *Spencer v. Wandolowski*, 264 Ill. App. 3d 611, 617, 201 Ill. Dec. 422, 636 N.E.2d 854 (1st Dist. 1994); and *People v. Monroe*, 66 Ill. 2d 317, 321–22, 5 Ill. Dec. 824, 362 N.E.2d 295 (1977).

Preston ex rel. Preston v. Simmons, 321 Ill. App. 3d 789, 803, 254 Ill. Dec. 647, 747 N.E.2d 1059 (1st Dist. 2001) (trial judge should not permit such wide latitude on cross-examination that it undermines the rule that only relevant evidence is admissible).

For expanded citations on the exclusion of irrelevant evidence, see § 3:1 to § 3:10.

§ 10:145 Supporting authorities—Exclusion of evidence of party's health or injuries where not at issue

Felber v. London, 346 Ill. App. 3d 188, 281 Ill. Dec. 482, 803 N.E.2d 1103 (2d Dist. 2004); *Obszanski v. Foster Wheeler Const., Inc.*, 328 Ill. App. 3d 550, 558–60, 262 Ill. Dec. 585, 765 N.E.2d 1193 (1st Dist. 2002) (defendant should not have been permitted to introduce evidence of the plaintiff's subsequent injury unless the defendant could establish that the new injury was the cause of the plaintiff's current distress).

Voykin v. Estate of DeBoer, 192 Ill. 2d 49, 248 Ill. Dec. 277, 733 N.E.2d 1275 (2000) (whether the plaintiff has suffered a prior injury to the same part of the body at issue, the defendant must introduce expert evidence demonstrating why the prior injury is relevant to causation, damages or some other issue of consequence).

Vojas v. K mart Corp., 312 Ill. App. 3d 544, 551–53, 245 Ill. Dec. 144, 727 N.E.2d 397 (5th Dist. 2000) (the party offering evidence of a prior injury must prove that it is relevant to the current injury).

Cancio v. White, 297 Ill. App. 3d 422, 428–30, 232 Ill. Dec. 7, 697 N.E.2d 749 (1st Dist. 1998) (error to allow evidence of plaintiff's pre-existing arthritis when there was no clear proof of a direct link to the injury that was at issue in the case).

Fear v. Smith, 184 Ill. App. 3d 51, 56-58, 132 Ill. Dec. 491, 539 N.E.2d 1297 (5th Dist. 1989) (trial judge did not abuse his discretion by determining that new trial was not warranted for newly discovered evidence of the plaintiff's prior conditions on the grounds that the defendant failed to show that the conditions related to the current injury or that evidence of them would have affected the outcome of the case).

See also *Boatmen's Nat. Bank of Belleville v. Martin*, 223 Ill. App. 3d 740, 744–45, 166 Ill. Dec. 306, 585 N.E.2d 1328 (5th Dist. 1992), judgment aff'd, 155 Ill. 2d 305, 185 Ill. Dec. 509, 614 N.E.2d 1194 (1993) (evidence of statistical data was properly barred when it was not shown to correlate to the plaintiff's condition).

§ 10:146 Supporting authorities—Other grounds

Other possible grounds for excluding evidence of unrelated injuries or health conditions include:

- Time-wasting (§ 2:5 to § 2:8)
- Confusing or misleading (§ 2:9 to § 2:12)
- Solely intended to create an emotional bias (§ 2:13 to § 2:19)
- Collateral to issues in case (§ 3:11 to § 3:21)
- Improper foundation (§ 4:1 to § 4:18)
- Improper character evidence (§ 7:1 to § 7:3)
- Inadmissible hearsay (§ 8:78 to § 8:89)

§ 10:147 Opposing authorities—Relevant to issues in case

Felber v. London, 346 Ill. App. 3d 188, 281 Ill. Dec. 482, 803 N.E.2d 1103 (2d Dist. 2004) (court allowed evidence of prior injuries without expert testimony where the jury could reliably appraise the relationship between the injuries at issue and the prior injuries).

Brown v. Moawad, 211 Ill. App. 3d 516, 533, 156 Ill. Dec. 14, 570 N.E.2d 490 (1st Dist. 1991) (defendant was permitted to argue that the plaintiff's decedent's condition was the cause of her death when there was evidence to support that claim).

Lindsay v. Appleby, 91 Ill. App. 3d 705, 711–12, 46 Ill. Dec. 832, 414 N.E.2d 885 (2d Dist. 1980) (the plaintiff's conditions were relevant to possible causation and to damage issues).

L. MOTION TO EXCLUDE ACCIDENT RECONSTRUCTION AND BIOMECHANICAL EVIDENCE

§ 10:148 Suggested motion text

[Name of moving party] hereby moves this Court for an order excluding any and all evidence, references to evidence, testimony or argument relating to *[describe nature of test, experiment or expected testimony, e.g., "any tests or demonstrations comparing the impact forces in the subject accident with every day activities such as plopping into a chair, stepping off of a curb, etc."]* conducted or described by [name of witness]. The motion is based upon the ground that the evidence is *[describe challenges to evidence, e.g., "not generally accepted in the scientific community," "not made under substantially similar conditions to subject incident," "not reliable," etc.]* and therefore does not meet the standards required by *Frye v. U.S.*, 293 F. 1013, 34 A.L.R. 145 (App. D.C. 1923) (rejected by, State v. Walstad, 119 Wis. 2d 483, 351 N.W.2d 469 (1984)) and (rejected by, State v. Brown, 297 Or. 404, 687 P.2d 751 (1984)) and (rejected by, Nelson v. State, 628 A.2d 69 (Del. 1993)) and (rejected by, State v. Alberico, 116 N.M. 156, 861 P.2d 192 (1993)) and (rejected by, State v. Moore, 268 Mont. 20, 885 P.2d 457 (1994)) and (rejected by, State v. Faught, 127 Idaho 873, 908 P.2d 566 (1995)) and (rejected by, People v. Shreck, 22 P.3d 68, 90 A.L.R.5th 765 (Colo. 2001)) and should be excluded. See *People v. Acri*, 277 Ill. App. 3d 1030, 1033–34, 214 Ill. Dec. 761, 662 N.E.2d 115 (3d Dist. 1996) (Illinois has adopted the *Frye* standard for the admission of scientific evidence).

§ 10:149 Motion summary

This motion is used to exclude inadmissible accident reconstruction and/or biomechanical evidence, typically arising in automobile accident litigation. The motion is based upon a series of authorities that have supported the exclusion of such evidence where it lacks sufficient foundation or reliability to be admissible.

In general, accident reconstruction evidence has been excluded where the evidence lacks sufficient evidentiary foundation, is based upon speculation or relies upon hearsay statements. *Hiscott v. Peters*, 324 Ill. App. 3d 114, 123–24, 257 Ill. Dec. 847, 754 N.E.2d 839 (2d Dist. 2001). Biomechanical evidence is often challenged under *Frye* principles, where the proposed test lacks sufficient reliability. See *Whiting v. Coultrip*, 324 Ill. App. 3d 161, 164–69, 258 Ill. Dec. 111, 755 N.E.2d 494 (3d Dist. 2001), as modified on denial of reh'g, (Sept. 12, 2001).

This section also includes a detailed discussion regarding the exclusion of test evidence in low impact automobile cases, which is an area of intense dispute in personal injury litigation.

Since case law is scarce, the authors have provided references to several commentators and provided analogous and out-of-state case support, which may be of assistance in attempting to exclude questionable tests and experiments.

§ 10:150 Supporting authorities—Excluding accident reconstruction evidence

Loseke v. Mables, 217 Ill. App. 3d 521, 524, 160 Ill. Dec. 471, 577 N.E.2d 796 (3d Dist. 1991) ("reconstruction testimony, as it is generally understood, seeks to recreate the accident: who hit whom, where was the impact and how fast the parties were going . . . .") (citations omitted)).

§ 10:151 Supporting authorities—Excluding accident reconstruction evidence—Generally

Kimble v. Earle M. Jorgenson Co., 358 Ill. App. 3d 400, 294 Ill. Dec. 402, 830 N.E.2d 814, 822–24 (1st Dist. 2005) (trial court properly excluded accident reconstruction testimony, when there was adequate eyewitness testimony).

Bachman v. General Motors Corp., 332 Ill. App. 3d 760, 782–85, 267 Ill. Dec. 125, 776 N.E.2d 262 (4th Dist. 2002) (trial court did not abuse its discretion by prohibiting plaintiff's expert from testifying that the injury was caused by premature airbag deployment because the opinion was not within the expert's area of expertise, was based upon hearsay and was not helpful to the jury).

Freeding-Skokie Roll-Off Service, Inc. v. Hamilton, 108 Ill. 2d 217, 219–23, 91 Ill. Dec. 178, 483 N.E.2d 524 (1985) (citing Federal Rules of Evidence 701 and 704) (lay witness opinion regarding whether a party could have avoided the accident should not have been admitted because it was not helpful to the trier of fact, which could have made its own assessment by hearing the relevant facts without the addition of the opinion testimony).

Seward v. Griffin, 116 Ill. App. 3d 749, 762–63, 72 Ill. Dec. 305, 452 N.E.2d 558 (3d Dist. 1983) (not improper to exclude accident reconstruction evidence when there was no showing that the vehicle used for the reconstruction adequately resembled the structure of the actual vehicle).

Peterson v. Lou Bachrodt Chevrolet Co., 76 Ill. 2d 353, 359–60, 29 Ill. Dec. 444, 392 N.E.2d 1 (1979) (overruled by, Wills v. Foster, 229 Ill. 2d 393, 323 Ill. Dec. 26, 892 N.E.2d 1018 (2008)) (trial court should not have admitted accident reconstruction testimony about the speed of the vehicles because there was adequate witness testimony for the jury to determine the issue on its own).

§ 10:152 Supporting authorities—Excluding accident reconstruction evidence—Incomplete facts/ speculation

Williams v. City of Evanston, 378 Ill. App. 3d 590, 599, 318 Ill. Dec. 251, 883 N.E.2d 85 (1st Dist. 2007) (court had discretion to exclude photographs depicting damage to vehicles when offered to suggest the extent of personal injuries without expert testimony to support the inference).

Williams v. City of Evanston, 378 Ill. App. 3d 590, 599–600, 318 Ill. Dec. 251, 883 N.E.2d 85 (1st Dist. 2007) (lay witness could not provide an opinion regarding the speed of another vehicle based solely upon how an impact with that other vehicle felt).

Baraniak v. Kurby, 371 Ill. App. 3d 310, 308 Ill. Dec. 949, 862 N.E.2d 1152, 1157-59 (1st Dist. 2007), appeal denied, 224 Ill. 2d 571, 312 Ill. Dec. 654, 871 N.E.2d 54 (2007) (trial court should not have admitted photographs depicting the amount of damage to the vehicle without expert testimony to show how the damage correlated to the physical injuries to the person in the vehicle).

Hiscott v. Peters, 324 Ill. App. 3d 114, 123–24, 257 Ill. Dec. 847, 754 N.E.2d 839 (2d Dist. 2001) (trial judge erred in allowing speculative reconstruction evidence that was based upon hearsay, when there was no physical evidence to support the testimony).

Modelski v. Navistar Intern. Transp. Corp., 302 Ill. App. 3d 879, 884–86, 236 Ill. Dec. 394, 707 N.E.2d 239 (1st Dist. 1999) (accident reconstruction evidence should not have been admitted when it was based upon the expert's speculation regarding what occurred).

Salcik v. Tassone, 236 Ill. App. 3d 548, 550–53, 177 Ill. Dec. 723, 603 N.E.2d 793 (1st Dist. 1992) (trial judge did not abuse his discretion by barring officer's testimony regarding skid marks when the officer was merely speculating that the skid marks had come from the defendant's vehicle).

Seward v. Griffin, 116 Ill. App. 3d 749, 762–63, 72 Ill. Dec. 305, 452 N.E.2d 558 (3d Dist. 1983) (not improper to exclude accident reconstruction evidence when there was no showing that the vehicle used for the reconstruction adequately resembled the structure of the actual vehicle).

§ 10:153 Supporting authorities—Excluding accident reconstruction evidence—Reliance on observations of others (hearsay)

Bachman v. General Motors Corp., 332 Ill. App. 3d 760, 782–85, 267 Ill. Dec. 125, 776 N.E.2d 262 (4th Dist. 2002) (trial judge did not abuse its discretion by prohibiting plaintiff's expert from testifying that the injury was caused by premature airbag deployment because the opinion was not within the expert's area of expertise, it was based upon hearsay and was not helpful to the jury).

Hiscott v. Peters, 324 Ill. App. 3d 114, 123–24, 257 Ill. Dec. 847, 754 N.E.2d 839 (2d Dist. 2001) (trial judge erred in allowing speculative reconstruction evidence that was based upon hearsay, when there was no physical evidence to support the testimony).

Giraldi by Giraldi v. Community Consol. School Dist. No. 62, 279 Ill. App. 3d 679, 690, 216 Ill. Dec. 272, 665 N.E.2d 332, 110 Ed. Law Rep. 269 (1st Dist. 1996) (trial judge can exclude hearsay evidence that formed the basis of the expert's opinion if the prejudicial impact of the hearsay evidence outweighs its probative value).

People v. Britz, 123 Ill. 2d 446, 457–62, 124 Ill. Dec. 15, 528 N.E.2d 703 (1988) (exclusion of expert testimony when the expert's opinion was based upon a party's own self-serving statements).

Mehochko v. Gold Seal Co., 66 Ill. App. 2d 54, 57-60, 213 N.E.2d 581, 19 A.L.R.3d 1003 (5th Dist. 1966) (improper hearsay and prejudicial to let an expert read from a test report about tests performed by someone else when the expert had no personal knowledge about the tests at issue).

See generally *People v. Solis*, 275 Ill. App. 3d 346, 348–52, 211 Ill. Dec. 571, 655 N.E.2d 954 (1st Dist. 1995) (expert should not be permitted to refer to inadmissible evidence to explain the expert's opinion).

§ 10:154 Supporting authorities—Excluding accident reconstruction evidence—Improper foundation or qualification

Williams v. City of Evanston, 378 Ill. App. 3d 590, 599, 318 Ill. Dec. 251, 883 N.E.2d 85 (1st Dist. 2007) (court had discretion to exclude photographs depicting damage to vehicles when offered to suggest the extent of personal injuries without expert testimony to support the inference).

Williams v. City of Evanston, 378 Ill. App. 3d 590, 599–600, 318 Ill. Dec. 251, 883 N.E.2d 85 (1st Dist. 2007) (lay witness could not provide an opinion regarding the speed of another vehicle based solely upon how an impact with that other vehicle felt).

Baraniak v. Kurby, 371 Ill. App. 3d 310, 308 Ill. Dec. 949, 862 N.E.2d 1152, 1157-59 (1st Dist. 2007), appeal denied, 224 Ill. 2d 571, 312 Ill. Dec. 654, 871 N.E.2d 54 (2007) (trial court should not have admitted photographs depicting the amount of damage to the vehicle without expert testimony to show how the damage correlated to the physical injuries to the person in the vehicle).

Kimble v. Earle M. Jorgenson Co., 358 Ill. App. 3d 400, 294 Ill. Dec. 402, 830 N.E.2d 814, 822–24 (1st Dist. 2005) (expert failed to provide proper foundation for expert testimony where there was no showing that the testimony would help jury).

DiCosola v. Bowman, 342 Ill. App. 3d 530, 276 Ill. Dec. 625, 794 N.E.2d 875 (1st Dist. 2003) (trial court did not abuse its discretion by requiring expert testimony to show a correlation between the extent of the vehicular damage and the extent of plaintiff's injuries).

Bachman v. General Motors Corp., 332 Ill. App. 3d 760, 782–85, 267 Ill. Dec. 125, 776 N.E.2d 262 (4th Dist. 2002) (trial judge did not abuse its discretion by prohibiting plaintiff's expert from testifying that the injury was caused by premature airbag deployment, in part, because the opinion was not within the expert's area of expertise).

Seward v. Griffin, 116 Ill. App. 3d 749, 762–63, 72 Ill. Dec. 305, 452 N.E.2d 558 (3d Dist. 1983) (not improper to exclude accident reconstruction evidence when there was no showing that the vehicle used for the reconstruction adequately resembled the structure of the actual vehicle).

Regarding qualifications of experts, generally, see § 8:24 to § 8:28, supra.

§ 10:155 Supporting authorities—Excluding accident reconstruction evidence—Vehicle speed determinations

Yoder v. Ferguson, 381 Ill. App. 3d 353, 319 Ill. Dec. 380, 885 N.E.2d 1060 (1st Dist. 2008), appeal pending, (Sept. 1, 2008) (a lay witness cannot provide an opinion regarding the speed of a vehicle based upon the damage caused by a collision).

Williams v. City of Evanston, 378 Ill. App. 3d 590, 599–600, 318 Ill. Dec. 251, 883 N.E.2d 85 (1st Dist. 2007) (lay witness could not provide an opinion regarding the speed of another vehicle based solely upon how an impact with that other vehicle felt).

Watkins v. Schmitt, 172 Ill. 2d 193, 204–09, 216 Ill. Dec. 822, 665 N.E.2d 1379, 110 Ed. Law Rep. 307 (1996) (officer was properly prohibited from providing reconstruction testimony regarding vehicle speed because there was sufficient other evidence from which the jury could make its own conclusion).

Peterson v. Lou Bachrodt Chevrolet Co., 76 Ill. 2d 353, 359–60, 29 Ill. Dec. 444, 392 N.E.2d 1 (1979) (overruled by, Wills v. Foster, 229 Ill. 2d 393, 323 Ill. Dec. 26, 892 N.E.2d 1018 (2008)) (trial court should not have admitted accident reconstruction testimony about the speed of the vehicles because there was adequate witness testimony for the jury to determine the issue on its own).

But see *Kassela v. Stonitsch*, 57 Ill. App. 3d 817, 822–24, 15 Ill. Dec. 262, 373 N.E.2d 608 (1st Dist. 1978) (officer testimony regarding point of impact and expert testimony regarding speed based upon the debris found at the scene would be proper even if there were eyewitnesses who could testify to these issues because the testimony would assist the jury).

§ 10:156 Supporting authorities—Excluding biomechanical evidence

"Biomechanics" is defined as the study of "the mechanics of biological and esp. muscular activity." *Webster's Ninth Collegiate Dictionary* 152 (1989). It has also been defined as "the understanding or the application of engineering and physics principles to biological systems." See *Pineda v. Los Angeles Turf Club, Inc.*, 112 Cal. App. 3d 53, 58, 169 Cal. Rptr. 66 (2d Dist. 1980). The following cases address the exclusion of biomechanical evidence. Because of the limited number of Illinois cases on point, the authors have included out-of-state cases, which can be used for illustrative purposes.

Baraniak v. Kurby, 371 Ill. App. 3d 310, 308 Ill. Dec. 949, 862 N.E.2d 1152, 1157-59 (1st Dist. 2007), appeal denied, 224 Ill. 2d 571, 312 Ill. Dec. 654, 871 N.E.2d 54 (2007) (trial court should not have admitted photographs depicting the amount of damage to the vehicle without expert testimony to show how the damage correlated to the physical injuries to the person in the vehicle).

Whiting v. Coultrip, 324 Ill. App. 3d 161, 164–69, 258 Ill. Dec. 111, 755 N.E.2d 494 (3d Dist. 2001), as modified on denial of reh'g, (Sept. 12, 2001) (photos of vehicles and cost of repair were not proven to be an accepted method for determining gravitational forces ("G-forces) experienced by the plaintiff and therefore, the biomechanics expert should not have been permitted to testify).

See also *People v. Dellinger*, 163 Cal. App. 3d 284, 292–93, 209 Cal. Rptr. 503 (4th Dist. 1984) ([*Frye*] test not met regarding biomechanical testing of anthropomorphic dummy and "finite element analysis" to determine the force involved in victim's head injury); *Clemente v. Blumenberg*, 183 Misc. 2d 923, 705 N.Y.S.2d 792, 794–95 (Sup 1999) (studies relied upon by biomechanical expert regarding claimed non-injuries in low speed accident held unreliable); *Smelser v. Norfolk Southern Ry. Co.*, 105 F.3d 299, 301, 46 Fed. R. Evid. Serv. 468, 1997 FED App. 0033P (6th Cir. 1997) (court erred in allowing biomechanical expert to offer opinion regarding medical causation of injury).

§ 10:157 Supporting authorities—Excluding biomechanical evidence—Anthropomorphic dummies

People v. Dellinger, 163 Cal. App. 3d 284, 292–93, 209 Cal. Rptr. 503 (4th Dist. 1984) ([*Frye* test not met regarding biomechanical testing of anthropomorphic dummy to determine the force involved in victim's head injury).

But see *People v. Roehler*, 167 Cal. App. 3d 353, 390, 213 Cal. Rptr. 353 (2d Dist. 1985) (in dicta, court concluded that trial court properly allowed evidence of tests on dummy to determine cause of injury; note that dissent disagreed with this conclusion).

§ 10:158 Supporting authorities—Excluding biomechanical evidence—"Finite element analysis" tests

"Finite Element Analysis" is a method used by biomechanical experts whereby the structure of the body (such as the brain and skull) are fed into the computer and a force is mathematically applied so that the computer can determine the pressures and stresses on the structure. The method was rejected as unreliable in the following case.

People v. Dellinger, 163 Cal. App. 3d 284, 292–93, 209 Cal. Rptr. 503 (4th Dist. 1984) ([*Frye*] test not met regarding "finite element analysis" to determine the force involved in victim's head injury).

§ 10:159 Supporting authorities—Excluding biomechanical evidence—"Pattern of injury" tests

The "pattern of injury" test was discussed, and disapproved, in the *Roehler* case, below. This test sought to establish how the injury occurred based upon the pattern of injury to the decedent's skull.

People v. Roehler, 167 Cal. App. 3d 353, 390, 213 Cal. Rptr. 353 (2d Dist. 1985) (biomechanic's testing and conclusions regarding "pattern of injury" to skull as a basis for proving causation of injury not reliable under *Kelly/Frye*; evidence should not have been admitted, but error was harmless).

§ 10:160 Supporting authorities—Low-speed impact automobile cases

Low speed impact cases provide fertile ground for evidentiary disputes, especially regarding accident reconstruction and biomechanical expert testimony. In these cases, the defense may attempt to put forth expert testimony that occupants of vehicles involved in minor impact accidents could not have been injured, based upon supposedly reliable tests and studies. Other disputed evidence in these cases may include comparisons of low speed accidents to the forces involved with everyday activities (such as "plopping" in a chair), photographs of the purportedly "undamaged" vehicles, and testimony of uninjured experts or witnesses who participated in low speed accident tests.

Several commentators have stated that much of the expert evidence in these cases is "junk science" and should be excluded under *Frye* reliability challenges. See R. Mahoney, "Challenging Expert Testimony in Low Speed Cases" *Trial Excellence* (Esquire One, 2001), Vol. 13, No 6; see also Chapter A-13, "Overcoming Junk Science Defenses," *Plaintiffs' Lawyers Guide to Minor Impact Cervical and Lumbar Injury* (Thomson West 2003).

Several appellate courts outside of Illinois have supported this view, upholding the exclusion of defense biomechanical testimony in low speed cases. See *Clemente v. Blumenberg*, 183 Misc. 2d 923, 705 N.Y.S.2d 792, 794–95 (Sup 1999) (studies relied upon by biomechanical expert regarding claimed non-injuries in low speed accident held unreliable); *Smelser v. Norfolk Southern Ry. Co.*, 105 F.3d 299, 301, 46 Fed. R. Evid. Serv. 468, 1997 FED App. 0033P (6th Cir. 1997) (court erred in allowing biomechanical expert to offer opinion regarding medical causation of injury).

The following sections provide suggested challenges to expert evidence in low impact cases. Since case law is scarce in this area, and most of the proffered testimony is based upon novel "science," the primary argument should rest upon the *Frye* analysis. Other significant factors will often include the prejudice and potential for jury confusion arising from the alluring, but often deceptive evidence.

See also *Whiting v. Coultrip*, 324 Ill. App. 3d 161, 164–69, 258 Ill. Dec. 111, 755 N.E.2d 494 (3d Dist. 2001), as modified on denial of reh'g, (Sept. 12, 2001) (photos of vehicles and cost of repair were not proven to be an accepted method for determining gravitational forces ("G-forces) experienced by the plaintiff and therefore, the biomechanics expert should not have been permitted to testify. Note, however, that there was a dissent in this case that argued that the evidence was properly admitted); and see § 10:150, Supporting authorities—Excluding accident reconstruction evidence, and § 10:156, Supporting authorities—Excluding biomechanical evidence, supra.

§ 10:161 Supporting authorities—Low-speed impact automobile cases—Excluding "Delta V" testimony

A defense accident reconstruction expert may attempt to testify that there is a threshold "Delta-V" for injury at approximately 5 MPH. According to this theory, if a vehicle was not accelerated by the impact to that threshold level, then the occupant could not have been injured.

This theory originated in a 1993 study by Whitman McConnell, entitled "Analysis of Human Test Subject Kinematic Responses to Low Velocity Rear End Impacts" (SAE, 1993), Technical Paper No. 930889 ("McConnell Study"), which concluded that the threshold of a "very mild, single event musculoskeletal cervical strain injury" was at a Delta-V of 4-5 MPH. This paper, and one that followed by McConnell two years later, served as the cornerstone for subsequent research by others in the field by postulating the existence of a 5-MPH Delta-V threshold for injury.

Counsel confronted with biomechanical experts who relied upon the McConnell or related studies should make a motion to exclude testimony that no injury could have occurred. This evidence is not reliable under a *Frye* evaluation and will likely create jury confusion. See *Clemente v. Blumenberg*, 183 Misc. 2d 923, 705 N.Y.S.2d 792, 794–95 (Sup 1999); *Smelser v. Norfolk Southern Ry. Co.*, 105 F.3d 299, 301, 46 Fed. R. Evid. Serv. 468, 1997 FED App. 0033P (6th Cir. 1997).

The following points highlight key deficiencies with the McConnell study, as noted by several commentators:

1. The crash test volunteers in the study were all employees of Biodynamic Research Corporation, which funded the study. This creates questions of bias and "anticipatory response" defects in the results. See R. Mahoney, "Challenging Expert Testimony in Low Speed Cases" *Trial Excellence* (Esquire One, 2001), Vol. 13, No 6, pp. 2–3.
2. All of the crash test volunteers were males; thus the study ignores female occupants who have been shown to suffer cervical injuries at a 2:1 ratio, compared to men. See Temming, J. (Volkswagen AG): "Human Factors in Relation to Whiplash Injuries in Rear End Collisions of Passenger Cars," Technical Paper No 981191 (SAE 1998).
3. It has been revealed that Biodynamics Research Corporation was paid millions of dollars by a major insurer, raising objectivity and bias questions about the study. These payments were identified in the Arizona case *Druz v. State Farm Insurance Company*. See Defendant's Supplemental Response to the Court's Order of January 6, 1997, *Druz v. State Farm Insurance Company*, Maricopa County Superior Court, State of Arizona, Civil Action No. CV95-21280; Low Speed Automobile Accidents, 2d (L&J Pub.), pp. 583–86.

But see *Bachman v. General Motors Corp.*, 332 Ill. App. 3d 760, 765–82, 788–89, 267 Ill. Dec. 125, 776 N.E.2d 262 (4th Dist. 2002) (Delta V evidence and SDM ("Sensor and Diagnostic Module") evidence was allowed to suggest that the injury was not caused by premature airbag deployment).

For an expanded discussion of criticisms of this evidence, see Chapter A-3, "The Delta V Myth," *Plaintiffs' Lawyers Guide to Minor Impact Cervical and Lumbar Injury* (Thomson West); See R. Mahoney, "Challenging Expert Testimony in Low Speed Cases" *Trial Excellence* (Esquire One, 2001), Vol. 13, No 6, pp. 2–3.

§ 10:162 Supporting authorities—Low-speed impact automobile cases—Challenging "plopping into a chair" testimony

The "plopping into a chair" theory is another commonly encountered expert technique in low speed cases. In sum, the expert, after performing a series of calculations relating to the Delta-V of the vehicle, will compare these accelerations to everyday activities, such as "plopping" into a chair. Such comparisons originated in a 1994 article in the journal *Spine*. See Allen, M., et al, "Acceleration Perturbations of Daily Living; A Comparison to Whiplash," *Spine* Volume 19, Number 11, pp. 1285–90 (1994). In this article, the authors make comparisons of the "G" forces involved in the subject collision with those encountered in everyday living activities.

Counsel confronted with this testimony may seek to exclude the evidence based upon *Frye* reliability challenges and especially the fact that the test has not been accepted within the scientific community. (See generally, § 5:1 to § 5:19, supra, regarding the exclusion of new scientific evidence.) The test creates a real potential that jurors will be confused by this enticing, but flawed evidence.

Commentators have stated that there is no scientific basis for making the "G" force comparisons, rendering the evidence deceptive and unreliable. According to a recent article by Robert Mahoney, an accident reconstruction expert, at first look the test appears to provide a means of comparing the forces to those with which we are already familiar. However, unless the position, velocity, and acceleration traces of the daily activities and the collision are compared, then it is difficult for the jury to recognize that two dissimilar events are being compared. See R. Mahoney, "Challenging Expert Testimony in Low Speed Cases" *Trial Excellence* (Esquire One, 2001), Vol. 13, No 6, pp. 6–7.

Another reconstruction expert, Sal Fariello, has identified seven "fatal flaws" with the Allen study based upon the significant differences in the two events:

> (1) Flopping into a chair does not induce the high rate of differential acceleration between T1 and the head center of gravity that produces the so-called *retraction* injury mechanism. . . . .
>
> (2) The potentially high angular acceleration of the head that can lead to brain injury does not occur in a flop into a chair [citation].
>
> (3) A flop into a chair does not produce the head acceleration multiplication factor [citation].
>
> (4) A flop into a chair produces no likelihood of C5-C6 nonphysiologic misalignment which can lead to disc herniation [citation].
>
> (5) The acceleration vector diagram included in the SPINE article [citation] reveals acceleration that does not compare to that occurring in a whiplash event. . . .
>
> (6) The aforementioned vector diagram in SPINE shows peak resolved head acceleration of 10.1 G. Actually, peak head acceleration can reach over 17 G's in a 6 mph Delta V crash [citation].

> (7) T1 vertebra acceleration can reach over 7 G's in a 5.9 mph Delta V crash because of the seat backrest slamming into the torso. . . . In the study reported in SPINE, no T1 acceleration was even measured, and the back of the chair into which a person plops does not slam into the torso as it does in a rear end crash.

Excerpted from Chapter A-13, "Overcoming Junk Science Defenses," *Plaintiffs' Lawyers Guide to Minor Impact Cervical and Lumbar Injury* (Thomson West).

Portions of the Allen study itself identify additional limitations, as follows:

> Note that this study was limited in the number of volunteers. The full spectrum of the population, with a presumed wide variance in physical and psychologic [sic] profiles, was not tested.

Allen, M., et al, "Acceleration Perturbations of Daily Living; A Comparison to Whiplash," *Spine* Volume 19, Number 11, pp. 1285–90 (1994).

See also *Whiting v. Coultrip*, 324 Ill. App. 3d 161, 164–69, 258 Ill. Dec. 111, 755 N.E.2d 494 (3d Dist. 2001), as modified on denial of reh'g, (Sept. 12, 2001) (photos of vehicles and cost of repair were not proven to be an accepted method for determining gravitational forces ("G-forces) experienced by the plaintiff and therefore, the biomechanics expert should not have been permitted to testify. The dissent in this case argued that the evidence should have been admitted).

§ 10:163 Supporting authorities—Low-speed impact automobile cases—"Human crash test dummy" testimony

Some accident reconstruction experts will actually subject themselves to repeated low-speed rear-end impacts in an attempt to prove that one cannot be injured in such a collision. According to the Mahoney article referenced above, human volunteer tests of this type are "nothing more than anecdotal," and are confusing and deceptive. The primary flaw is that the test subject *anticipates* the impact, which renders the results dissimilar to most real life automobile impacts and reduces the likelihood of injury. See R. Mahoney, "Challenging Expert Testimony in Low Speed Cases" *Trial Excellence* (Esquire One, 2001), Vol. 13, No 6, pp. 7–8.

Counsel may seek to exclude testimony of this type based upon its deceptive and confusing nature, as well as *Frye* reliability problems. See *Clemente v. Blumenberg*, 183 Misc. 2d 923, 705 N.Y.S.2d 792, 794–95 (Sup 1999) (studies relied upon by biomechanical expert regarding claimed non-injuries in low speed accident held unreliable); *Smelser v. Norfolk Southern Ry. Co.*, 105 F.3d 299, 301, 46 Fed. R. Evid. Serv. 468, 1997 FED App. 0033P (6th Cir. 1997) (court erred in allowing biomechanical expert to offer opinion regarding medical causation of injury).

§ 10:164 Supporting authorities—Low-speed impact automobile cases—Photographs depicting "no damage" to vehicles

Williams v. City of Evanston, 378 Ill. App. 3d 590, 599, 318 Ill. Dec. 251, 883 N.E.2d 85 (1st Dist. 2007) (court had discretion to exclude photographs depicting damage to vehicles when offered to suggest the extent of personal injuries without expert testimony to support the inference).

Baraniak v. Kurby, 371 Ill. App. 3d 310, 308 Ill. Dec. 949, 862 N.E.2d 1152, 1157-59 (1st Dist. 2007), appeal denied, 224 Ill. 2d 571, 312 Ill. Dec. 654, 871 N.E.2d 54 (2007) (trial court should not have admitted photographs depicting the amount of damage to the vehicle without expert testimony to show how the damage correlated to the physical injuries to the person in the vehicle).

DiCosola v. Bowman, 342 Ill. App. 3d 530, 276 Ill. Dec. 625, 794 N.E.2d 875 (1st Dist. 2003) (trial court did not abuse its discretion by requiring expert testimony to show a correlation between the extent of the vehicular damage and the extent of plaintiff's injuries).

Defense counsel in low speed rear-end impact cases often utilize a blown-up photograph of the rear of the plaintiff vehicle, pointing to the lack of *visible* damages. This exhibit is typically used to support expert testimony that, due to the apparent lack of damages, the plaintiff could not have been injured.

Commentators on low impact accidents have indicated that such evidence is misleading and unreliable. See R. Mahoney, "Challenging Expert Testimony in Low Speed Cases" *Trial Excellence* (Esquire One, 2001), Vol. 13, No 6, pp. 8–9; Chapter A-2, "The Undamaged Bumper Scam," *Plaintiffs' Lawyers Guide to Minor Impact Cervical and Lumbar Injury* (Thomson West). At least one out-of-state court has excluded biomechanical testimony in a low speed case, where the expert relied upon vehicle photographs to formulate his opinion. See *Clemente v. Blumenberg*, 183 Misc. 2d 923, 705 N.Y.S.2d 792, 800 (Sup 1999) (using repair costs and photographs to calculate change in velocity "is not a generally accepted method in any relevant field of engineering or under the laws of physics").

In the *Trial Excellence* article, Mahoney points out that an expert cannot determine, merely from looking at a photograph of a vehicle, what the Delta V for that incident might have been. R. Mahoney, "Challenging Expert Testimony in Low Speed Cases" *Trial Excellence* (Esquire One, 2001), Vol. 13, No 6, p. 8. Such speculative evidence may be excluded. See § 3:9, Supporting authoritites—Exclusion of irrelevant evidence, generally—Speculative evidence, supra. Mahoney further states that vehicles with no observable damages often have hidden damages, including damage to the frame. R. Mahoney, "Challenging Expert Testimony in Low Speed Cases" *Trial Excellence* (Esquire One, 2001), Vol. 13, No 6, p. 9. By its very nature, this evidence has the potential to mislead jurors.

Counsel may also wish to consider a motion to exclude the word "undamaged" or related terminology in connection with the subject vehicle or any photographic or other depictions of the vehicle. Because of potential or actual non-visible damages, using this terminology would be inaccurate and clearly misleading. For citations excluding improper terminology in general, see § 9:50 to § 9:59, supra.

See also *Whiting v. Coultrip*, 324 Ill. App. 3d 161, 164–69, 258 Ill. Dec. 111, 755 N.E.2d 494 (3d Dist. 2001), as modified on denial of reh'g, (Sept. 12, 2001) (photos of vehicles and cost of repair were not proven to be an accepted method for determining gravitational forces ("G-forces) experienced by the plaintiff and therefore, the biomechanics expert should not have been permitted to testify.)

§ 10:165 Supporting authorities—Low-speed impact automobile cases—Other unreliable tests

Other tests that may arise in low impact cases, include but are not limited to, the following:

Use of the "Abbreviated Injury Scale" to measure whiplash injury

Use of the "Injury Assessment Reference Value" to determine if injury has occurred

Use of published bumper height data

For a discussion of additional challenges to these and other tests, see Chapter 13, "Overcoming Junk Science Defenses," *Plaintiffs' Lawyers Guide to Minor Impact Cervical and Lumbar Injury* (Thomson West), pages 13-1 et seq.; see also *Low Speed Automobile Accidents, 2d* (L&J Pub.), pp. 339 et seq.

§ 10:166 Opposition—Tests and scientific testimony, generally

Regarding opposition to motions to exclude tests and scientific evidence, see generally §§ 5:13 et seq., supra; regarding opposition to motions to exclude expert testimony, see generally §§ 8:18 et seq., supra.

§ 10:167 Opposition—Accident reconstruction evidence

Ferro v. Griffiths, 361 Ill. App. 3d 738, 742, 297 Ill. Dec. 194, 836 N.E.2d 925 (3d Dist. 2005) (the trial court had discretion to determine that photographs depicting little damage to vehicles was relevant to assist the jury in determining the nature of the injuries, even if there was no expert testimony accompanying the photographs).

Glass v. City of Chicago, 323 Ill. App. 3d 158, 166, 256 Ill. Dec. 88, 751 N.E.2d 141 (1st Dist. 2001) (trial judge has discretion to determine whether or not accident reconstruction evidence should be allowed) (testimony allowed in this case because it assisted the jury).

Rios v. Navistar Intern. Transp. Corp., 200 Ill. App. 3d 526, 536–37, 146 Ill. Dec. 289, 558 N.E.2d 252 (1st Dist. 1990) (trial judge had discretion to admit accident reconstruction evidence when the evidence was helpful to the trier of fact).

Augenstein v. Pulley, 191 Ill. App. 3d 664, 671–81, 138 Ill. Dec. 724, 547 N.E.2d 1345 (5th Dist. 1989) (whether accident reconstruction evidence should be admissible should be decided in the same fashion as any other type of expert testimony. Specifically, the court should examine whether the expert is qualified in the field and whether the evidence would be helpful to the jury).

Wiedemann v. Industrial Erectors, Inc., 137 Ill. App. 3d 47, 55-56, 91 Ill. Dec. 504, 483 N.E.2d 990 (1st Dist. 1985) (accident reconstruction evidence can be admissible if it is based upon post-occurrence investigation, provided that the circumstances surrounding the investigation are similar to those surrounding the occurrence. Note that the evidence was allowed in this case).

Kassela v. Stonitsch, 57 Ill. App. 3d 817, 822–24, 15 Ill. Dec. 262, 373 N.E.2d 608 (1st Dist. 1978) (officer testimony regarding point of impact and expert testimony regarding speed based upon the debris found at the scene would be proper even if there were eyewitnesses who could testify to these issues because the testimony would assist the jury).

§ 10:168 Opposition—Accident reconstruction evidence—Proper basis for opinion

Favia v. Ford Motor Co., 381 Ill. App. 3d 809, 320 Ill. Dec. 113, 886 N.E.2d 1182 (1st Dist. 2008), appeal pending, (Sept. 1, 2008) (officers were qualified through their training and experience to provide an opinion regarding the cause of a collision).

Whiting v. Coultrip, 324 Ill. App. 3d 161, 164–69, 258 Ill. Dec. 111, 755 N.E.2d 494 (3d Dist. 2001), as modified on denial of reh'g, (Sept. 12, 2001) (biomechanical evidence could be admissible if a proper foundation under *Frye* is established).

Brown v. Ford Motor Co., 306 Ill. App. 3d 314, 317–18, 239 Ill. Dec. 637, 714 N.E.2d 556 (1st Dist. 1999) (trial judge did not abuse its discretion by admitting videotapes of accident reconstruction, even when some of them were shown in slow motion).

Van Holt v. National R.R. Passenger Corp., 283 Ill. App. 3d 62, 70, 218 Ill. Dec. 762, 669 N.E.2d 1288 (1st Dist. 1996) (it no longer matters in Illinois if the expert's opinion is about a subject within the knowledge of the jurors, provided that the expert is qualified and the expert's opinion will aid the trier of fact).

Zavala v. Powermatic, Inc., 167 Ill. 2d 542, 544–47, 212 Ill. Dec. 889, 658 N.E.2d 371 (1995) (expert in "human factors engineering" properly gave reconstruction testimony in a products liability case, after the expert had reviewed the discovery and tested the product).

Loseke v. Mables, 217 Ill. App. 3d 521, 523–26, 160 Ill. Dec. 471, 577 N.E.2d 796 (3d Dist. 1991) (testimony of officer trained in investigating accidents may be admissible as to point of impact).

Rios v. Navistar Intern. Transp. Corp., 200 Ill. App. 3d 526, 536–37, 146 Ill. Dec. 289, 558 N.E.2d 252 (1st Dist. 1990) (trial judge had discretion to admit accident reconstruction evidence when the evidence was helpful to the trier of fact).

Augenstein v. Pulley, 191 Ill. App. 3d 664, 671–81, 138 Ill. Dec. 724, 547 N.E.2d 1345 (5th Dist. 1989) (whether accident reconstruction evidence should be admissible should be decided in the same fashion as any other type of expert testimony. Specifically, the court should examine whether the expert is qualified in the field and whether the evidence would be helpful to the jury).

Wiedemann v. Industrial Erectors, Inc., 137 Ill. App. 3d 47,

55-56, 91 Ill. Dec. 504, 483 N.E.2d 990 (1st Dist. 1985) (accident reconstruction evidence can be admissible if it is based upon post-occurrence investigation, provided that the circumstances surrounding the investigation are similar to those surrounding the occurrence).

Kassela v. Stonitsch, 57 Ill. App. 3d 817, 822–24, 15 Ill. Dec. 262, 373 N.E.2d 608 (1st Dist. 1978) (officer testimony regarding point of impact and expert testimony regarding speed based upon the debris found at the scene would be proper even if there were eyewitnesses who could testify to these issues because the testimony would assist the jury).

See generally Federal Rule of Evidence Rule 704, supra.

§ 10:169 Opposition—Accident reconstruction evidence—Competent facts/foundation

Ferro v. Griffiths, 361 Ill. App. 3d 738, 742, 297 Ill. Dec. 194, 836 N.E.2d 925 (3d Dist. 2005) (the trial court had discretion to determine that photographs depicting little damage to vehicles was relevant to assist the jury in determining the nature of the injuries, even if there was no expert testimony accompanying the photographs).

Whiting v. Coultrip, 324 Ill. App. 3d 161, 164–69, 258 Ill. Dec. 111, 755 N.E.2d 494 (3d Dist. 2001), as modified on denial of reh'g, (Sept. 12, 2001) (biomechanical evidence could be admissible if a proper foundation under *Frye* is established).

Loseke v. Mables, 217 Ill. App. 3d 521, 523–26, 160 Ill. Dec. 471, 577 N.E.2d 796 (3d Dist. 1991) (testimony of officer trained in investigating accidents may be admissible as to point of impact).

Augenstein v. Pulley, 191 Ill. App. 3d 664, 671–81, 138 Ill. Dec. 724, 547 N.E.2d 1345 (5th Dist. 1989) (whether accident reconstruction evidence should be admissible should be decided in the same fashion as any other type of expert testimony. Specifically, the court should examine whether the expert is qualified in the field and whether the evidence would be helpful to the jury).

§ 10:170 Opposition—Accident reconstruction evidence—Vehicle speed

Kassela v. Stonitsch, 57 Ill. App. 3d 817, 822–24, 15 Ill. Dec. 262, 373 N.E.2d 608 (1st Dist. 1978) (officer testimony regarding point of impact and expert testimony regarding speed based upon the debris found at the scene would be proper even if there were eyewitnesses who could testify to these issues because the testimony would assist the jury).

§ 10:171 Opposition—Accident reconstruction evidence—Skid mark analysis

Watkins v. Schmitt, 172 Ill. 2d 193, 207–08, 216 Ill. Dec. 822, 665 N.E.2d 1379, 110 Ed. Law Rep. 307 (1996) (officer should be permitted to describe the skid marks that were at the scene because such testimony would merely involve a description of physical evidence).

See also Kassela v. Stonitsch, 57 Ill. App. 3d 817, 822–24, 15 Ill. Dec. 262, 373 N.E.2d 608 (1st Dist. 1978), supra.

§ 10:172 Opposition—Accident reconstruction evidence—Point of impact

Loseke v. Mables, 217 Ill. App. 3d 521, 523–26, 160 Ill. Dec. 471, 577 N.E.2d 796 (3d Dist. 1991) (testimony of experienced officer trained in investigating accidents may be admissible as to point of impact).

Kassela v. Stonitsch, 57 Ill. App. 3d 817, 822–24, 15 Ill. Dec. 262, 373 N.E.2d 608 (1st Dist. 1978) (officer testimony regarding point of impact and expert testimony regarding speed based upon the debris found at the scene would be proper even if there were eyewitnesses who could testify to these issues because the testimony would assist the jury).

§ 10:173 Opposition—Biomechanical evidence—Cases where admitted

Ruffin ex rel. Sanders v. Boler, 384 Ill.App.3d 7, 18–25, 890 N.E.2d 1174 (1st Dist. 2008) (biomedical engineer could provide an expert opinion regarding causation based upon the amount of force occurring during childbirth).

Bachman v. General Motors Corp., 332 Ill. App. 3d 760, 765–82, 788–89, 267 Ill. Dec. 125, 776 N.E.2d 262 (4th Dist. 2002) (Delta V evidence and SDM ("Sensor and Diagnostic Module") evidence was allowed to suggest that the injury was not caused by premature airbag deployment).

Zavala v. Powermatic, Inc., 167 Ill. 2d 542, 544–47, 212 Ill. Dec. 889, 658 N.E.2d 371 (1995) (expert in "human factors engineering," [the study of how humans interact with machines, including reaction time and coordination] properly gave reconstruction testimony in a products liability case after the expert had reviewed the discovery and tested the product).

See also *Pineda v. Los Angeles Turf Club, Inc.*, 112 Cal. App. 3d 53, 62, 169 Cal. Rptr. 66 (2d Dist. 1980) (no error in allowing biomechanic testimony); but see *People v. Dellinger*, 163 Cal. App. 3d 284, 292–93, 209 Cal. Rptr. 503 (4th Dist. 1984) (neither reliability of field of biomechanics nor qualifications of expert were challenged in *Pineda*; case did not purport to accept the scientific validity of general field of biomechanical engineering).

§ 10:174 Opposition—Admission of photographs depicting "no damage" to vehicles

Fronabarger v. Burns, 385 Ill.App.3d 560, 565–66, 895 N.E.2d 1125 (5th Dist. 2008) (trial court had discretion to determine that a neurologist was qualified to provide an opinion regarding the correlation between the amount of damage to vehicles in an accident and the amount of injury to occupants of the vehicles).

Fronabarger v. Burns, 385 Ill.App.3d 560, 564–65, 895 N.E.2d 1125 (5th Dist. 2008) (trial court had discretion to admit photographs depicting the amount of damage to vehicles to suggest the amount of injuries to the occupants of the vehicles, without any expert testimony to correlate vehicle damage to force of impact).

Jackson v. Seib, 372 Ill. App. 3d 1061, 310 Ill. Dec. 502, 866 N.E.2d 663 (5th Dist. 2007) (photographs depicting little damage to a vehicle were relevant to establish the amount of force involved in the collision with or without accompanying expert testimony).

Ferro v. Griffiths, 361 Ill. App. 3d 738, 742, 297 Ill. Dec. 194, 836 N.E.2d 925 (3d Dist. 2005) (the trial court had discretion to determine that photographs depicting little damage to vehicles was relevant to assist the jury in determining the nature of the injuries, even if there was no expert testimony accompanying the photographs).

Ferro v. Griffiths, 361 Ill. App. 3d 738, 742, 297 Ill. Dec. 194, 836 N.E.2d 925 (3d Dist. 2005) (the court stated in relevant part: "[W]e refuse to adopt a rigid rule that proscribes the admission of pictures without an expert. The critical question in admitting these photographs is whether the jury can properly relate the vehicular damage depicted in the pictures to the injury without the aid of an expert.").

§ 10:175 Opposition—A note on opposing motions to exclude low-impact tests

Defense counsel faced with plaintiff motions in limine seeking to exclude low-impact tests and other scientific evidence should be prepared to establish the reliability of the proffered evidence and the general acceptance within the scientific community. See Frye v. U.S., 293 F. 1013, 34 A.L.R. 145 (App. D.C. 1923) (rejected by, State v. Walstad, 119 Wis. 2d 483, 351 N.W.2d 469 (1984)) and (rejected by, State v. Brown, 297 Or. 404, 687 P.2d 751 (1984)) and (rejected by, Nelson v. State, 628 A.2d 69 (Del. 1993)) and (rejected by, State v. Alberico, 116 N.M. 156, 861 P.2d 192 (1993)) and (rejected by, State v. Moore, 268 Mont. 20, 885 P.2d 457 (1994)) and (rejected by, State v. Faught, 127 Idaho 873, 908 P.2d 566 (1995)) and (rejected by, People v. Shreck, 22 P.3d 68, 90 A.L.R.5th 765 (Colo. 2001)); and *People v. Acri*, 277 Ill. App. 3d 1030, 1033–34, 214 Ill. Dec. 761, 662 N.E.2d 115 (3d Dist. 1996) (Illinois has adopted the *Frye* standard for the admission of scientific evidence). Of some assistance on this end is Chapter 23, *Low Speed Automobile Accidents* (L&J Pub.), pp. 351 et seq., which addresses generally how to survive reliability attacks. Counsel should also seek to invoke the court's broad discretionary authority to allow expert testimony. See e.g., *Bachman v. General Motors Corp.*, 332 Ill. App. 3d 760, 765–82, 788–89, 267 Ill. Dec. 125, 776 N.E.2d 262 (4th Dist. 2002).

Counsel may also invoke the "weight vs. admissibility" argument, urging the court to allow the evidence in and let the jurors decide its weight. See e.g., *Donaldson v. Central Illinois Public Service Co.*, 199 Ill. 2d 63, 79-82, 262 Ill. Dec. 854, 767 N.E.2d 314 (2002) (abrogated by, In re Commitment of Simons, 213 Ill. 2d 523, 290 Ill. Dec. 610, 821 N.E.2d 1184 (2004)) (questions regarding the underlying information the expert used or the manner in which the expert applied a generally accepted methodology go to the weight and not the admissibility of the evidence); and *People v. Eiskant*, 253 Ill. App. 3d 773, 776, 192 Ill. Dec. 863, 625 N.E.2d 1018 (5th Dist. 1993) (as long as information is the type normally relied upon in the expert's field, it is proper to allow an expert to testify about it and the source of the information only affects the weight of the expert's testimony, not its admissibility).

For additional citations on the opposition of motions seeking to exclude tests and scientific evidence, see generally §§ 5:13 et seq., supra.

M. MOTION TO EXCLUDE EVIDENCE OF PARTY'S FINANCIAL STATUS

§ 10:176 Suggested motion text

[Name of moving party] hereby moves this Court for an order

excluding any and all evidence, references to evidence, testimony or argument relating to the wealth or poverty of *[name of party]*. The motion is based upon the grounds that the evidence is irrelevant, immaterial, confusing and will create a substantial danger of undue prejudice to *[name of moving party]*.

§ 10:177 Motion summary

This motion is used to prevent unfair prejudice where irrelevant evidence of a party's financial status is referenced at trial. The motion is based upon the court's authority to exclude irrelevant and prejudicial evidence and leading cases on this subject. See, e.g., *Dupay v. New York Cent. R. Co.*, 110 Ill. App. 2d 146, 154–55, 249 N.E.2d 179 (1st Dist. 1969). Note that evidence of a defendant's financial status *is* relevant but not required in punitive damages cases [*Deal v. Byford*, 127 Ill. 2d 192, 204, 130 Ill. Dec. 200, 537 N.E.2d 267 (1989)].

See also § 10:189, Supporting authorities—Exclusion of prejudicial evidence, generally, infra.

§ 10:178 Supporting authorities—Exclusion of prejudicial evidence, generally

Federal Rule of Evidence 403 states:

> Although relevant, evidence may be excluded if its probative value is substantially outweighed by the danger of unfair prejudice, confusion of the issues, or misleading the jury, or by considerations of undue delay, waste of time, or needless presentation of cumulative evidence.

It must be noted that this Rule has not been codified in Illinois. However, Illinois cases have stated that Illinois has a common-law rule that is comparable to Federal Rule of Evidence 403. See *People v. Walker*, 335 Ill. App. 3d 102, 112, 268 Ill. Dec. 654, 779 N.E.2d 268 (2d Dist. 2002), as modified on denial of reh'g, (Oct. 24, 2002) and judgment aff'd, 211 Ill. 2d 317, 285 Ill. Dec. 519, 812 N.E.2d 339 (2004); and *People v. Peete*, 318 Ill. App. 3d 961, 966–67, 252 Ill. Dec. 821, 743 N.E.2d 689 (4th Dist. 2001).

People v. Holman, 257 Ill. App. 3d 1031, 1033–34, 196 Ill. Dec. 457, 630 N.E.2d 154 (2d Dist. 1994) (evidence is admissible if it is relevant and if the prejudicial impact does not substantially outweigh the probative value of it).

For expanded citations on the exclusion of prejudicial evidence, see § 2:1 to § 2:4.

§ 10:179 Supporting authorities—Exclusion of irrelevant evidence, generally

Federal Rule of Evidence 401 defines relevancy as,

> evidence having any tendency to make the existence of any fact that is of consequence to the determination of the action more probable or less probable than it would be without the evidence.

Illinois has adopted this definition of relevancy through case law. *Spencer v. Wandolowski*, 264 Ill. App. 3d 611, 617, 201 Ill. Dec. 422, 636 N.E.2d 854 (1st Dist. 1994); and *People v. Monroe*, 66 Ill. 2d 317, 321–22, 5 Ill. Dec. 824, 362 N.E.2d 295 (1977).

Preston ex rel. Preston v. Simmons, 321 Ill. App. 3d 789, 803, 254 Ill. Dec. 647, 747 N.E.2d 1059 (1st Dist. 2001) (trial judge should not permit such wide latitude on cross-examination that it undermines the rule that only relevant evidence is admissible).

For expanded citations on the exclusion of irrelevant evidence, see § 3:1 to § 3:10.

§ 10:180 Supporting authorities—Exclusion of financial status evidence, generally

Lenz v. Julian, 276 Ill. App. 3d 66, 74-75, 212 Ill. Dec. 511, 657 N.E.2d 712 (2d Dist. 1995) (improper and prejudicial to refer to the defendant's lack of insurance and the length of time it would require for him to pay any judgment).

DiPaolo v. Johnson, 15 Ill. App. 3d 735, 738–39, 305 N.E.2d 194 (1st Dist. 1973) (comments about the wealth of a party are improper but they were not prejudicial in this case).

Dupay v. New York Cent. R. Co., 110 Ill. App. 2d 146, 154–55, 249 N.E.2d 179 (1st Dist. 1969) (comments regarding a party's financial condition, even if the condition is obvious, are improper).

See also §§ 10:189 et seq., infra.

§ 10:181 Supporting authorities—Exclusion of financial status evidence, generally—Plaintiff's financial status

DiPaolo v. Johnson, 15 Ill. App. 3d 735, 738–39, 305 N.E.2d 194 (1st Dist. 1973) (comments about the plaintiff's financial condition were improper but they were not prejudicial in this case).

§ 10:182 Supporting authorities—Exclusion of financial status evidence, generally—Defendant's financial status

Schultz v. Siddens, 191 Ill. App. 3d 622, 628–29, 138 Ill. Dec. 857, 548 N.E.2d 87 (5th Dist. 1989) (comments regarding the defendant's financial circumstances were improper).

Smith v. Raup, 296 Ill. App. 171, 15 N.E.2d 936 (2d Dist. 1938) (improper, but cured by the sustaining of an objection, to refer to evidence which suggests the financial status of the defendant).

Smith v. Raup, 296 Ill. App. 171, 15 N.E.2d 936 (2d Dist. 1938) (improper to appeal to jury sympathy by referencing defendant's lack of wealth).

Dupay v. New York Cent. R. Co., 110 Ill. App. 2d 146, 154–55, 249 N.E.2d 179 (1st Dist. 1969) (comments regarding the defendant's financial condition, even if the condition is obvious, were improper).

§ 10:183 Supporting authorities—Punitive damages cases

Evidence of defendant's financial status is relevant but not required in cases where exemplary damages are sought. See *Ford v. Herman*, 316 Ill. App. 3d 726, 733–34, 249 Ill. Dec. 942, 737 N.E.2d 332 (5th Dist. 2000); *Deal v. Byford*, 127 Ill. 2d 192, 204, 130 Ill. Dec. 200, 537 N.E.2d 267 (1989).

§ 10:184 Supporting authorities—Other grounds

Other possible grounds for excluding financial evidence include:

- Time-wasting (§ 2:5 to § 2:8)
- Confusing or misleading (§ 2:9 to § 2:12)
- Solely intended to create an emotional bias (§ 2:13 to § 2:19)
- Collateral to issues in case (§ 3:11 to § 3:21)
- Improper character evidence (§ 7:1 to § 7:3)
- Inadmissible hearsay (§ 8:78 to § 8:89)
- Improper tax evidence (§ 10:187 to § 10:195)

§ 10:185 Opposing authorities—Relevant to issues—Generally

Fettson v. James, 298 Ill. App. 3d 77, 81-82, 232 Ill. Dec. 201, 697 N.E.2d 1131 (1st Dist. 1997) (brief testimony regarding the plaintiff's tax returns for the year of the injury was proper because it reflected upon the issue of lost wages but extensive questioning regarding the plaintiff's other tax returns was properly prohibited).

C.L. Maddox, Inc. v. Royal Ins. Co. of America, 208 Ill. App. 3d 1042, 1050–52, 153 Ill. Dec. 791, 567 N.E.2d 749 (5th Dist. 1991) (evidence of the plaintiff's sole shareholder's financial condition should have been admitted in an action to collect on an insurance policy in order to support the defendant's affirmative defense of arson).

People v. Nearn, 178 Ill. App. 3d 480, 493–94, 127 Ill. Dec. 637, 533 N.E.2d 509 (1st Dist. 1988) (trial judge properly allowed cross-examination regarding the defendant's failure to file tax returns, despite the previous order in limine prohibiting the information, after the defendant had opened the door to the information by claiming that he always paid his debts).

§ 10:186 Opposing authorities—Relevant to issues—To support punitive damages claim

Ford v. Herman, 316 Ill. App. 3d 726, 733–34, 249 Ill. Dec. 942, 737 N.E.2d 332 (5th Dist. 2000) (evidence of the defendant's financial condition is relevant and admissible but not required to support a punitive damages claim). *Deal v. Byford*, 127 Ill. 2d 192, 204, 130 Ill. Dec. 200, 537 N.E.2d 267 (1989) (same).

See also §§ 10:195 et seq., infra.

N. MOTION TO EXCLUDE TAX EVIDENCE

§ 10:187 Suggested motion text

[Name of moving party] hereby moves this Court for an order excluding any and all evidence, references to evidence, testimony or argument relating to *[describe tax evidence to be excluded, e.g., the fact that the plaintiff was fined for failing to pay taxes in 1999]*. The motion is based upon the grounds that the evidence is irrelevant, immaterial, confusing and will create a substantial danger of undue prejudice to *[name of moving party]*.

§ 10:188 Motion summary

This motion is used to exclude irrelevant and prejudicial tax evidence. The motion is based upon the court's authority to exclude irrelevant and prejudicial evidence and leading cases in this area. See e.g., *Singh v. Air Illinois, Inc.*, 165 Ill. App. 3d 923, 934, 117 Ill. Dec. 501, 520 N.E.2d 852 (1st Dist. 1988).

See also § 10:176 to § 10:186, supra, regarding improper financial evidence.

§ 10:189 Supporting authorities—Exclusion of prejudicial evidence, generally

Federal Rule of Evidence 403 states:

> Although relevant, evidence may be excluded if its probative value is substantially outweighed by the danger of unfair prejudice, confusion of the issues, or misleading the jury, or by considerations of undue delay, waste of time, or needless presentation of cumulative evidence.

It must be noted that this Rule has not been codified in Illinois. However, Illinois cases have stated that Illinois has a common-law rule that is comparable to Federal Rule of Evidence 403. See *People v. Walker*, 335 Ill. App. 3d 102, 112, 268 Ill. Dec. 654, 779 N.E.2d 268 (2d Dist. 2002), as modified on denial of reh'g, (Oct. 24, 2002) and judgment aff'd, 211 Ill. 2d 317, 285 Ill. Dec. 519, 812 N.E.2d 339 (2004); and *People v. Peete*, 318 Ill. App. 3d 961, 966–67, 252 Ill. Dec. 821, 743 N.E.2d 689 (4th Dist. 2001).

People v. Holman, 257 Ill. App. 3d 1031, 1033–34, 196 Ill. Dec. 457, 630 N.E.2d 154 (2d Dist. 1994) (evidence is admissible if it is relevant and if the prejudicial impact does not substantially outweigh the probative value of it).

For expanded citations on the exclusion of prejudicial evidence, see § 2:1 to § 2:4.

§ 10:190 Supporting authorities—Exclusion of irrelevant evidence, generally

Federal Rule of Evidence 401 defines relevancy as,

> evidence having any tendency to make the existence of any fact that is of consequence to the determination of the action more probable or less probable than it would be without the evidence.

Illinois has adopted this definition of relevancy through case law. *Spencer v. Wandolowski*, 264 Ill. App. 3d 611, 617, 201 Ill. Dec. 422, 636 N.E.2d 854 (1st Dist. 1994); and *People v. Monroe*, 66 Ill. 2d 317, 321–22, 5 Ill. Dec. 824, 362 N.E.2d 295 (1977).

Preston ex rel. Preston v. Simmons, 321 Ill. App. 3d 789, 803, 254 Ill. Dec. 647, 747 N.E.2d 1059 (1st Dist. 2001) (trial judge should not permit such wide latitude on cross-examination that it undermines the rule that only relevant evidence is admissible).

For expanded citations on the exclusion of irrelevant evidence, see § 3:1 to § 3:10.

§ 10:191 Supporting authorities—Exclusion of tax evidence—Tax implications on damages

Singh v. Air Illinois, Inc., 165 Ill. App. 3d 923, 934, 117 Ill. Dec. 501, 520 N.E.2d 852 (1st Dist. 1988) (evidence of future tax consequences of any award is inadmissible).

Klawonn v. Mitchell, 105 Ill. 2d 450, 452–58, 86 Ill. Dec. 478, 475 N.E.2d 857 (1985) (improper for a trial judge to instruct a jury about the tax consequences, or lack thereof, of a damage award).

§ 10:192 Supporting authorities—Exclusion of tax evidence—Tax returns or failure to file tax returns

Dupay v. New York Cent. R. Co., 110 Ill. App. 2d 146, 154–55, 249 N.E.2d 179 (1st Dist. 1969) (comments regarding a party's financial condition, even if the condition is obvious, are improper).

See also *Fettson v. James*, 298 Ill. App. 3d 77, 81-82, 232 Ill. Dec. 201, 697 N.E.2d 1131 (1st Dist. 1997) (brief testimony regarding the plaintiff's tax returns for the year of the injury was proper, because it reflected upon the issue of lost wages but extensive questioning regarding the plaintiff's other tax returns was properly prohibited); *People v. Nearn*, 178 Ill. App. 3d 480, 493–94, 127 Ill. Dec. 637, 533 N.E.2d 509 (1st Dist. 1988) (trial judge properly allowed cross-examination regarding the defendant's failure to file tax returns, despite the previous order in limine prohibiting the information, after the defendant had opened the door to the information by claiming that he always paid his debts).

§ 10:193 Supporting authorities—Improper appeal to jurors as taxpayers

Department of Public Works and Buildings For and in Behalf of People v. Sun Oil Co., 66 Ill. App. 3d 64, 68, 22 Ill. Dec. 826, 383 N.E.2d 634 (5th Dist. 1978) (improper to appeal to self-interest of jurors as taxpayers regarding ultimate responsibility to pay for damages in a condemnation suit).

Lukich v. Angeli, 31 Ill. App. 2d 20, 30, 175 N.E.2d 796 (1st Dist. 1961) (improper to argue that the plaintiff's claim is the type that increases the cost of living for everyone).

§ 10:194 Supporting authorities—Other grounds

Other possible grounds for excluding tax evidence include:

- Time-wasting (§ 2:5 to § 2:8)
- Confusing or misleading (§ 2:9 to § 2:12)
- Solely intended to create an emotional bias (§ 2:13 to § 2:19)
- Collateral to issues in case (§ 3:11 to § 3:21)
- Improper character evidence (§ 7:1 to § 7:3)
- Inadmissible hearsay (§ 8:78 to § 8:89)
- Improper financial evidence (§ 10:176 to § 10:186)

§ 10:195 Opposing authorities—Relevant to issues

R.J. Management Co. v. SRLB Development Corp., 346 Ill. App. 3d 957, 969–70, 282 Ill. Dec. 486, 806 N.E.2d 1074 (2d Dist. 2004) (expert could rely on tax returns as basis for opinion, over opposing party's claim that returns were hearsay).

Fettson v. James, 298 Ill. App. 3d 77, 81-82, 232 Ill. Dec. 201, 697 N.E.2d 1131 (1st Dist. 1997) (brief testimony regarding the plaintiff's tax returns for the year of the injury was proper because it reflected upon the issue of lost wages) (but extensive questioning regarding the plaintiff's other tax returns was properly prohibited).

People v. Clay, 167 Ill. App. 3d 628, 118 Ill. Dec. 175, 521 N.E.2d 243 (2d Dist. 1988) (evidence of failure to file a tax return was admitted in this case where the defendant was charged with willfully failing to file his tax return).

O. MOTION TO EXCLUDE LIABILITY EVIDENCE WHERE LIABILITY NOT AT ISSUE

§ 10:196 Suggested motion text

[Name of moving party] hereby moves this Court for an order excluding any and all evidence, references to evidence, testimony or argument relating to defendant's liability in this action. The motion is based upon the grounds that the evidence is irrelevant, immaterial, confusing and will create a substantial danger of undue prejudice to *[name of moving party]*.

§ 10:197 Motion summary

This motion is used to exclude evidence of defendant's liability, where admitted or undisputed by defendant. The motion is based upon the court's authority to exclude irrelevant and prejudicial evidence, and cases excluding evidence of admitted matters. See e.g. *Davis v. International Harvester Co.*, 167 Ill. App. 3d 814, 824–25, 118 Ill. Dec. 589, 521 N.E.2d 1282 (2d Dist. 1988).

◆ **Note:** In a case of clear liability, defense counsel can increase the credibility of their client (and counsel) in the eyes of the jury, if they admit liability and contest damages only. This approach often results in lower verdicts than if liability is also contested. Where a defendant admits liability, evidence of defendant's negligent conduct during the incident may not be admissible on the basis that the conduct is not relevant to the issue of damages. *Bullard v. Barnes*, 102 Ill. 2d 505, 82 Ill. Dec. 448, 468 N.E.2d 1228 (1984). Evidence of negligent conduct, especially if it borders on egregious, can only increase the verdict for the plaintiff. Consequently, if the jury never learns of the defendant's conduct, the end result will probably be a lower verdict than if such evidence had been admitted.

Of course, where defendant's conduct is relevant to prove damages (e.g. speed of defendant's vehicle to explain mechanisms of plaintiff's injury), some aspects of defendant's conduct may be admissible, even when liability is admitted. Admitting liability can also streamline the case, which results in a shorter trial and less costs. For a variety of reasons, therefore, admitting liability can be a very effective defense tactic.

§ 10:198 Supporting authorities—Exclusion of prejudicial evidence, generally

Federal Rule of Evidence 403 states:

> Although relevant, evidence may be excluded if its probative value is substantially outweighed by the danger of unfair prejudice, confusion of the issues, or misleading the jury, or by considerations of undue delay, waste of time, or needless presentation of cumulative evidence.

It must be noted that this Rule has not been codified in Illinois. However, Illinois cases have stated that Illinois has a common-law rule that is comparable to Federal Rule of Evidence 403. See *People v. Walker*, 335 Ill. App. 3d 102, 112, 268 Ill. Dec. 654, 779 N.E.2d 268 (2d Dist. 2002), as modified on denial of reh'g, (Oct. 24, 2002) and judgment aff'd, 211 Ill. 2d 317, 285 Ill. Dec. 519, 812 N.E.2d 339 (2004); and *People v. Peete*, 318 Ill. App. 3d 961, 966–67, 252 Ill. Dec. 821, 743 N.E.2d 689 (4th Dist. 2001).

People v. Holman, 257 Ill. App. 3d 1031, 1033–34, 196 Ill. Dec. 457, 630 N.E.2d 154 (2d Dist. 1994) (evidence is admissible if it is relevant and if the prejudicial impact does not substantially outweigh the probative value of it).

For expanded citations on the exclusion of prejudicial evidence, see § 2:1 to § 2:4.

§ 10:199 Supporting authorities—Exclusion of irrelevant evidence, generally

Federal Rule of Evidence 401 defines relevancy as,

> evidence having any tendency to make the existence of any fact that is of consequence to the determination of the action more probable or less probable than it would be without the evidence.

Illinois has adopted this definition of relevancy through case law. *Spencer v. Wandolowski*, 264 Ill. App. 3d 611, 617, 201 Ill. Dec. 422, 636 N.E.2d 854 (1st Dist. 1994); and *People v. Monroe*, 66 Ill. 2d 317, 321–22, 5 Ill. Dec. 824, 362 N.E.2d 295 (1977).

Preston ex rel. Preston v. Simmons, 321 Ill. App. 3d 789, 803, 254 Ill. Dec. 647, 747 N.E.2d 1059 (1st Dist. 2001) (trial judge should not permit such wide latitude on cross-examination that it undermines the rule that only relevant evidence is admissible).

For expanded citations on the exclusion of irrelevant evidence, see § 3:1 to § 3:10.

§ 10:200 Supporting authorities—Exclusion of admitted matters

Addis v. Exelon Generation Co., L.L.C., 378 Ill. App. 3d 781, 790, 316 Ill. Dec. 949, 880 N.E.2d 685 (1st Dist. 2007), appeal denied, 228 Ill. 2d 529, 321 Ill. Dec. 554, 889 N.E.2d 1114 (2008) (trial court's instruction that notified the jury that the plaintiff had made an initial admission to one of the relevant issues was based upon the evidence and was not an abuse of discretion).

Davis v. International Harvester Co., 167 Ill. App. 3d 814, 824–25, 118 Ill. Dec. 589, 521 N.E.2d 1282 (2d Dist. 1988) (proper to exclude evidence of the feasibility of design changes when there was an admission to that ability).

Bullard v. Barnes, 112 Ill. App. 3d 384, 392–94, 68 Ill. Dec. 37, 445 N.E.2d 485 (4th Dist. 1983), judgment aff'd, 102 Ill. 2d 505, 82 Ill. Dec. 448, 468 N.E.2d 1228 (1984) (trial judge abused his discretion by admitting photographs of the deceased and testimony regarding the conditions and circumstances surrounding the collision because liability was admitted).

Carlyle v. Jaskiewicz, 124 Ill. App. 3d 487, 495–96, 79 Ill. Dec. 847, 464 N.E.2d 751 (1st Dist. 1984) (the trial judge properly took judicial notice of certain facts and then excluded additional proof regarding those facts).

Khatib v. McDonald, 87 Ill. App. 3d 1087, 1099–1100, 43 Ill.

Dec. 266, 410 N.E.2d 266 (1st Dist. 1980) (case remanded for a new trial on damages only, when there were errors at the trial but liability had been fairly established).

Opal v. Material Service Corp., 9 Ill. App. 2d 433, 449–50, 133 N.E.2d 733 (1st Dist. 1956) (suggesting that court has authority to order separate trials for the issues of damages and liability).

Lutgert v. Schaeflein, 318 Ill. App. 83, 93–94, 47 N.E.2d 359 (1st Dist. 1943) (trial judge has authority to order separate trials for claims and counterclaims if the issues might become confusing to the jury if the issues are all tried at once; however, in this case, the issues were not too complicated or confusing).

But see *Mason v. Dunn*, 6 Ill. App. 3d 448, 448–51, 285 N.E.2d 191 (2d Dist. 1972) (in absence of a clear statute allowing for split trials for the issues of liability and damages, a trial judge has no authority to order such a split without the agreement of the parties. This court stated that the statute providing that "an action may be severed" did not imply that a single action could be severed into separate issues).

735 ILCS 5/2-1006 states:

> Consolidation and severance of cases. An action may be severed, and actions pending in the same court may be consolidated, as an aid to convenience, whenever it can be done without prejudice to a substantial right.

735 ILCS 5/2-610 states:

> Pleadings to be specific. (a) Every answer and subsequent pleading shall contain an explicit admission or denial of each allegation of the pleading to which it relates.
>
> (b) Every allegation, except allegations of damages, not explicitly denied is admitted, unless the party states in his or her pleading that he or she has no knowledge thereof sufficient to form a belief, and attaches an affidavit of the truth of the statement of want of knowledge, or unless the party has had no opportunity to deny.
>
> (c) Denials must not be evasive, but must fairly answer the substance of the allegation denied.
>
> (d) *If a party wishes to raise an issue as to the amount of damages only, he or she may do so by stating in his or her pleading that he or she desires to contest only the amount of the damages.* (Emphasis added.)

See also § 6:22, Supporting authorities—Requests for admission [Illinois Supreme Court Rule 216]—Requests for admission, generally, and § 6:37, Supporting authorities—Exclusion of prejudicial evidence, generally, supra.

§ 10:201 Supporting authorities—Other grounds

Other possible grounds for excluding liability evidence include:

- Time-wasting (§ 2:5 to § 2:8)
- Confusing or misleading (§ 2:9 to § 2:12)
- Solely intended to create an emotional bias (§ 2:13 to § 2:19)
- Collateral to issues in case (§ 3:11 to § 3:21)
- Improper impeachment evidence (§ 7:1 to § 7:3)
- Inadmissible hearsay (§ 8:78 to § 8:89)

§ 10:202 Opposing authorities

People v. Szudy, 262 Ill. App. 3d 695, 706, 200 Ill. Dec. 462, 635 N.E.2d 801 (1st Dist. 1994) (evidence which is relevant and admissible for one purpose should not be excluded merely because it is irrelevant or inadmissible for another purpose).

People v. Szudy, 262 Ill. App. 3d 695, 712–13, 200 Ill. Dec. 462, 635 N.E.2d 801 (1st Dist. 1994) (prosecutor has the right to prove each element of an offense, even if the defendant has stipulated to the facts supporting that element).

Tierney v. Community Memorial General Hosp., 268 Ill. App. 3d 1050, 1055–57, 206 Ill. Dec. 279, 645 N.E.2d 284 (1st Dist. 1994) (no error in permitting party's expert to express opinion that was undisclosed at deposition when the opposing party knew that the subject matter of the testimony would be an issue at trial and had prepared to respond to the subject matter).

Lee v. Chicago Transit Authority, 152 Ill. 2d 432, 461–65, 178 Ill. Dec. 699, 605 N.E.2d 493 (1992) (it is within the trial judge's discretion to admit evidence on a stipulated point and to determine whether evidence might confuse the jury).

Zimmer v. Melendez, 222 Ill. App. 3d 390, 394–96, 164 Ill. Dec. 836, 583 N.E.2d 1158 (2d Dist. 1991) (trial court abused its discretion by excluding testimony that was undisclosed in interrogatories, when the subject matter of the testimony was not a surprise to the opposing party and when the interrogatory that might have covered the subject matter was open-ended and did not clearly request the information at issue).

Phillips v. Lawrence, 87 Ill. App. 2d 60, 61-63, 230 N.E.2d 505 (5th Dist. 1967) (in action for personal injuries where liability is admitted, evidence of force of impact and surrounding circumstances may be relevant and material to indicate extent of injuries).

Veer v. Hagemann, 334 Ill. 23, 27–28, 165 N.E. 175 (1929)

(trial judge has discretion whether to admit evidence on points that have been conceded or that might confuse the issues).

See also *Ellis v. American Family Mut. Ins. Co.*, 322 Ill. App. 3d 1006, 1010–11, 255 Ill. Dec. 902, 750 N.E.2d 1287 (4th Dist. 2001) (Illinois Supreme Court Rule 201(j) does not allow a party to amend previous admissions to requests to admit because requests to admit are different from other forms of discovery).

II. SAMPLE MOTIONS

§ 10:203 Sample motion in limine to exclude collateral source payments under the federal medicare program

[insert caption]

PLAINTIFFS' *[number]* MOTION IN LIMINE

Now come the Plaintiffs, *[name of plaintiffs]*, individually and as the Administrator of the Estate of *[name of deceased]*, deceased, by *[name of attorney]*, their attorneys, and in support of the Plaintiffs' *[number]* Motion in Limine states:

1. Attached hereto and incorporated herewith as Exhibits A and B is a compilation of Plaintiffs' medical bills. Upon information and belief, the parties anticipate that a Stipulation will be presented to this Court, whereby the parties will stipulate that the amount charged by the care providers represent the usual and customary charges for the same or similar services and that the foundational requirements for the admission of said bills to the jury have been satisfied.

2. Pursuant to the Stipulation of the parties, the medical bills set forth in Exhibits A and B have been paid in part by the Federal Medicare program and said bills were subject to certain discounts.

3. Medicare has a right under federal law to recover sums it paid for *[name of deceased]*'s medical bills from the Plaintiffs. See 42 USCA 1395y(b)(2).

4. Pursuant to the Federal Medicare Program, after allowing for discounts in the medical bills, the decedent, *[name of deceased]*, and her parents were responsible for a copay equal to 20% of the medicare approved bill.

5. Portions of the copay referenced in the previous paragraph were paid by private health insurance companies under contracts between GREG and SHARON POTTER and those private health insurance companies. Pursuant to the terms of

said contract, the insurance companies enjoy a right of subrogation to the payments made on behalf of *[name of deceased]*.

6. *[name of deceased]* worked at the Rehab Products and Services and received pay for her work. *[name of deceased]*'s employer took regular deductions from her paycheck for Medicare. See Affidavit of *[name of affiant]* attached hereto and incorporated herewith as Exhibit C.

7. In addition to the amounts deducted from *[name of deceased]*'s paychecks, *[name of plaintiffs]* made quarterly payments to the Medicare program in the amount of $*[dollar amount]*, in order to maintain *[name of deceased]*'s enrolment in the Federal Medicare Program. See Affidavit of *[name of plaintiff]* attached hereto and incorporated herewith as Exhibit D.

8. The Federal Medicare Program is a government insurance program and discounts to medical bills incurred by participants in the program and the payments of benefits under the program are subject to the collateral source rule. See *Arthur v. Catour*, 216 Ill. 2d 72, 295 Ill. Dec. 641, 833 N.E.2d 847 (2005) and the Plaintiff's Memorandum of Law, which is attached hereto and incorporated herewith as it fully set forth in this Motion.

9. Under the Illinois collateral source rule, as established in *Arthur v. Catour*, the Defendant should be barred from any evidence, argument, or inference that *[name of deceased]* participated in the Federal Medicare Program, that her medical bills were discounted under that program, that she received benefits under that program or any other inference concerning the payment of benefits or of benefits received by *[name of deceased]* from any source that is not collateral to the Defendants in this cause.

WHEREFORE, the Plaintiffs, individually and as the Administrator of the Estate of *[name of deceased]*, deceased, pray that this Court will exercise its inherent authority over the conduct of trial in this cause and enter an Order in Limine barring the Defendants from eliciting testimony, arguing or inferring that *[name of deceased]* was a participant in the Federal Medicare Program, that she received benefits under that program, that her medical bills were discounted pursuant to contracts between her heath care providers and the Medicare Program and for such other and further relief as the Court deems appropriate.

Dated this ____________ day of ____________.

[name of plaintiffs] Plaintiffs
BY:_______________________________________
[name of attorney]
Of *[name of firm]*

AFFIDAVIT OF SERVICE BY MAILING

The undersigned, being first duly sworn on oath, deposes and says that she served the within document on all parties, or their attorneys, who have appeared and not heretofore been found by the court to be in default for failure to plead, on the ___________ day of ___________, at ___________ by depositing true copies thereof, with proper First Class postage prepaid, enclosed in envelopes legibly addressed in the United States Post Office at Mattoon, Illinois.

TO: *[Attorneys for Defendant]*
[Address]

Subscribed and sworn to before me this _____________ day of ______________.

____
Notary Public

Note: Thanks to Bill Tapella of Hefner, Eberspacher & Tapella for providing this sample motion.

§ 10:204 Sample memorandum of law supporting motion in limine to exclude collateral source payments under the federal medicare program

[insert caption]

MEMORANDUM OF LAW
IN SUPPORT OF PLAINTIFFS' FIFTH MOTION IN LIMINE

MAY IT PLEASE THE COURT:

The Plaintiff's *[number]* Motion in Limine raises two issues under the Supreme Court's decision in *Arthur v. Catour*, 216 Ill. 2d 72, 295 Ill. Dec. 641, 833 N.E.2d 847 (2005) ("hereinafter Arthur") First, does Arthur apply to governmental program payments like Medicare and second, if so, what is the scope of permissible cross examination and evidence from the Defendant. For the reasons set forth below, Arthur applies to medical expenses paid by governmental programs like Medicare and bars the admission of evidence concerning the existence of the collateral source or the receipt of benefits from that source, including discounts of the medical bill.

In Arthur, the Supreme Court recited the long established application of the collateral source rule under Illinois law. The court held that "[t]he collateral source rule protects collateral payments made to or benefits conferred on the plaintiff by denying the defendant any corresponding offset or credit. Such collateral benefits do not reduce the defendant's tort liability, even though they reduce the plaintiff's loss." *Arthur*, 216 Ill.2d at 78. The Court then cited the Restatement (Second) of Torts, section 920A, comment b, for the proposition that:

> [payments by a collateral source] do not have the effect of reducing the recovery against the defendant. The injured party's net loss may have been reduced correspondingly, and to the extent that the defendant is required to pay the total amount there may be a double compensation for a part of the plaintiff's injury. But it is the position of the law that a benefit that is directed to the injured party should not be shifted so as to become a windfall for the tortfeasor.

Arthur v. Catour, 216 Ill. 2d 72, 78-79, 295 Ill. Dec. 641, 833 N.E.2d 847 (2005).

The Court further addressed the plaintiff's right to introduce into evidence the full value of a medical bill, despite discounts provided for under private insurance contracts. The court's decision does not specifically address governmental payments made under the Medicare program.

The Arthur Court relied heavily upon the separate components of the collateral source rule. The Court noted that the rule has both a substantive and an evidentiary component and held that:

> [t]he substantive component is a rule of damages. This component bars a defendant from reducing the plaintiff's compensatory award by the amount the plaintiff received from the collateral source. The evidentiary component bars admission of evidence of the existence of the collateral source or the receipt of benefits. The concern here is that the trier of fact may use the evidence improperly to deny the plaintiff the full recovery to which he is entitled.

Arthur, 216 Ill.2d at 80. The issues raised by the Plaintiffs *[number]* Motion in Limine requires this court to consider both the substantive and the evidentiary components of the collateral source rule.

I. The Collateral Source Rule Applies to Medicare Payments

With regard to the substantive portion of the collateral

source rule, the law in Illinois demonstrates that the collateral source rule applies with equal vigor to both private pay insurance contracts and Medicare payments made under the federal Medicare program.

Illinois law has long held that government payments under federal benefit programs are subject to the collateral source rule. See *Fencl-Tufo Chevrolet, Inc. v. Industrial Com'n of Illinois*, 169 Ill. App. 3d 510, 120 Ill. Dec. 15, 523 N.E.2d 926 (1st Dist. 1988) (holding that payment of medical bills by the Michigan Department of Social Services fall outside of Peterson and are subject to the collateral source rule); and *Boden v. Crawford*, 196 Ill. App. 3d 71, 142 Ill. Dec. 546, 552 N.E.2d 1287 (4th Dist. 1990) (holding the police disability payments are subject to the collateral source rule). See also, The Restatement of Torts, Second Section 920A, comment (c)(4), (providing that: "The rule that collateral benefits are not subtracted from the plaintiff's recovery applies to the following types of benefits ... social legislation benefits, social security benefits, welfare payments, pensions under special retirement acts, all are subject to the collateral-source rule.") and *Eichel v. New York Cent. R. Co.*, 375 U.S. 253, 84 S. Ct. 316, 11 L. Ed. 2d 307 (1963) (addressing the payment of disability payments under the Railroad Retirement Act and holding that; "we must recognize that the petitioner's receipt of collateral social insurance benefits involves a substantial likelihood of prejudicial impact.").

There is no Illinois appellate or Supreme Court case to suggest that the collateral source rule does not apply to payments by Medicare for medical bills caused by the defendant's negligence.

The payments at issue in this case are not collateral to the Defendants nor does any exception exist to the collateral source rule under the facts of this case. By definition, payments and benefits that are made by the Defendant fall outside the collateral source rule. See *Kirkland v. U.S.*, 1998 WL 895658 (N.D. Ill. 1998). Thus, where the defendant is both the source of medical payments and the source of the judgment, the medical expense payments are not covered by the rule. Illinois has also recognized one exceptions to the collateral source rule: the charitable exclusion established under *Peterson v. Lou Bachrodt Chevrolet Co.*, 76 Ill. 2d 353, 29 Ill. Dec. 444, 392 N.E.2d 1 (1979) (overruled by, Wills v. Foster, 229 Ill. 2d 393, 323 Ill. Dec. 26, 892 N.E.2d 1018 (2008)). Otherwise, the collateral source rule applies with equal vigor to any collateral source, including governmental payments under Medicare. No Illinois case suggests otherwise.

Medicare payments are not collateral to the Defendant in this cause. In *Kirkland v. U.S.*, 1998 WL 895658 (N.D. Ill. 1998), the District Court for the Northern District of Illinois discussed the definition of "collateral" as used in the collateral source rule. Kirkland noted that several federal courts have "considered two factors: (1) whether the injured party contributed to the federal program; and (2) the nature of the programs funding." *Kirkland*, 1998 WL at 2. The court further noted that:

> [t]he Illinois Supreme Court has also emphasized the importance of the contribution factor when deciding whether a source is collateral. . . [In *Wilson v. Hoffman Group, Inc.*, 131 Ill. 2d 308, 137 Ill. Dec. 579, 546 N.E.2d 524 (1989),]the court states that the wrongdoer should not benefit from the expenditures made by the injured party. *Kirkland*, 1998 WL at 2.

In *Kirkland*, the court ruled that "[b]ecause the plaintiff did not contribute to the program, the Illinois Supreme Court would not deem CHAMPUS collateral under this consideration."

[name of deceased] contributed to the Medicare Program through her work. See affidavits of *[name of affiant]* and *[name of plaintiff]* and the Stipulation of the parties, attached hereto as Exhibit C, D and E.

The structure and the source of funding for Medicare demonstrates that program is insurance and not a charitable source of medical payments. Medicare constitutes and insurance contract funded through compulsory employee contribution, such as those made by *[name of deceased]*. As noted by the Ohio Supreme Court:

> [p]ayment into the (Medicare) trust fund, though involuntary, is in exchange for health care coverage, and gives rise to a duty on the part of the government to pay benefits when required. in addition, the language of the statute specifically refers to "policy or contract" of insurance. In shod Medicare, Part A, is funded by payments made by the beneficiaries and their employers, is actuarily determined, and is described by its enabling statute as insurance. *Hodge v. Middletown Hospital Assn.*, 62 Ohio St. 3d 236, 240-241, 581 N.E.2d 529 (1991).

Under the Medicare Act and Hodge Medicare represents an insurance contract and not a charitable contribution, like that at issue in *Peterson v. Lou Bachrodt Chevrolet Co.*, 76 Ill. 2d 353, 29 Ill. Dec. 444, 392 N.E.2d 1 (1979) (overruled by, Wills v. Foster, 229 Ill. 2d 393, 323 Ill. Dec. 26, 892 N.E.2d 1018 (2008)).

Medicare and private insurance contracts share four critical similarities. First, a participant receives benefits based upon c premium payment. See 42 USCA 1395c and 42 USCA 426.

Second, the payments by the program are subject to both deductibles and co-pays. See 42 USCA 1395e. Third, the insurer contracts with health care providers for a reduction in the cost of medical services. See 42 USCA 1395cc and Arthur. Fourth, the plan enjoys a right of subrogation in third party claims of the participant. See 42 USCA 395y(b)(2). Based upon these similarities, the collateral source rule must apply to Medicare.

Other jurisdictions have addressed the application of the collateral source rule to Medicare payments. A review of those opinions reveals that the majority of jurisdiction that have addressed the issue, outside the context of statutory mandates, apply the collateral source rule to Medicare. Indeed, only one state has found Medicare to fall outside of the collateral source rule. See cases in table attached as Exhibit F.

Based upon the nature of the Medicare program, existing Illinois case law and the weight of opinion from other jurisdictions, this court should find that the substantive element of the collateral source rule as defined under Arthur applies to payments made under the federal Medicare program.

II. The Collateral Source Rule Bars the Introduction of Evidence Concerning Medicare or any reduction in Bill by Medicare

The evidentiary component of the rule bars evidence of the existence of the collateral source or the receipt of benefits. *Arthur*, 216 lll.2d at 80. Nothing in the Arthur decision vitiates this well established rule of law. As such the Defendants in this case must be barred from any evidence or argument concerning Medicare's role in paying *[name of deceased]* medical bills or any reduction in those bills.

In their effort to inject Medicare into the trial, the Defendants will almost certainly rely upon Iwo brief passages in Arthur concerning the Defendants right to "rebut the prima facie reasonableness of the medical expense," *Arthur*, 216 lll.2d at 52. The Defendants reliance on these passages is misplaced.

In sum, the Arthur court statements on the Defendants' evidence consisted solely of the following two statements:

> [t]he defendant may rebut the prima fade reasonableness of the medical expense by presenting proper evidence casting suspicion upon the transaction ...
>
> Defendants, of course, are free to challenge plaintiff's proof on cross examination and to offer their own evidence pertaining to the reasonableness of the charges. *Arthur*, 216 Ill.2d at 82-83.

These statements do not represent a change of Illinois law concerning the collateral sources rule.

The language in Arthur permits only proper evidence. The Arthur case, when read as a whole, offers a very clear definition of what is not proper evidence. The court stated that:

> The rule prevents the jury from learning anything about collateral income.
>
> Calling attention to the fact that a plaintiff had such insurance can be prejudicial error because the jury may conclude that the plaintiff sustained no damages for which he was entitled to recover if his medical bills were paid by insurance.
>
> The evidentiary component bars the admission of the existence of the collateral source or the receipt of benefits. The concern here is that the trier of fact may use the evidence improperly to deny the plaintiff the full recovery to which he is entitled. *Arthur*, 216 Ill.2d at 79-80.

As noted by attorney M. Todd Melton, "the very fact that the Arthur court determined that provider discounts were subject to the collateral source rule, necessarily means that any evidence of those discounts is inadmissible." See "A Labyrinth in Arthur's court," Trial Journal, Vol. 8, Number 2 (Illinois Trial Lawyer's Association, 2006), attached hereto and incorporated herewith as Exhibit G. Under Arthur the Supreme Court prohibits the introduction of the existence of the collateral source, the discounts and benefits paid. Nothing in the majority's opinion concerning defense evidence changes the Court's otherwise clear decision.

Justice McMorrow noted in her dissent that, "the majority would allow defendants 'to challenge plaintiff's proof on cross-examination and to offer their own evidence pertaining to the reasonableness of the charges,' but provides no insight as to what that evidence might be." *Arthur*, 216 lll.2d at 96. Justice McMorrow's critique, while valid in some respects, ignores the majority's statement concerning the nature of the evidence excluded under the majority's decision. While, the result may be problematic for defendants, neither Justice McMorrow's dissent or the majority decision suggest that the evidentiary bar of the collateral source rule has been removed by Arthur. Indeed, one cannot read Arthur to both expand and then eliminate the collateral source rule. No other court has suggested that a defendant may present evidence concerning the collateral source or the benefits received by plaintiff. This court should not do so.

III. Conclusion

For the reasons set forth in Plaintiffs' *[number]* Motion in Limine and this Memorandum of Law, the Plaintiffs pray that this court will bar the introduction of any evidence, comment or argument stating, suggesting or implying that Plaintiffs medical bills were paid under by the Medicare Program or any statement or suggestion concerning the discount afforded to the Plaintiffs under the program or benefits received under the program.

Dated this ____________ day of ____________.

[Plaintiffs], individually and as the Administrator of the Estate of *[name of deceased]*, deceased, Plaintiffs,
BY:____
[name of attorney]
Of *[name of firm]*

[attorneys for defendant]
[address]
[telephone number]
[fax number]

Note: Thanks to Bill Tapella of Hefner, Eberspacher & Tapella for providing this sample motion.

§ 10:205 Sample motion in limine to exclude collateral evidence

[insert caption]

MOTIONS IN LIMINE

NOW COMES the Plaintiff, *[Plaintiff]* individually and as Special Administrator of the ESTATE OF *[name of deceased]*, a minor, by and through their attorneys, *[name of attorneys]*, and moves this Court in Limine to prohibit Defendant, *[Defendant]*, her agents and employees, defense counsel and any witness presented or questioned by defense counsel from making statements, offering evidence, testimony, remarks, arguments, or from conveying to the panel information regarding any of the following matters:

1. That Plaintiff has or may have received benefits or payments from a collateral source including private health insurance, medical payments insurance or from the *Wilson v. Hoffman Group, Inc.*, 131 Ill. 2d 308, 137 Ill. Dec. 579, 546 N.E.2d 524 (1989).

2. The fact that there are any or no injuries sustained to any of the other occupants in either vehicle. The details about the nature and severity of personal injuries to non-litigants in automobile cases are not admissible. *Martin v. Sally*, 341 Ill. App. 3d 308, 275 Ill. Dec. 285, 792 N.E.2d 516 (2d Dist. 2003).

3. Evidence of Plaintiff or Plaintiffs family financial condition. *Pagel v. Yates*, 128 Ill. App. 3d 897, 84 Ill. Dec. 180, 471 N.E.2d 946 (4th Dist. 1984).

4. That the Defendant be barred from asking questions of any witness involving similar or dissimilar injuries from prior or subsequent accidents, unless there is a showing by the defendant, that there will be a connection between this line of questioning and the plaintiffs injury by competent medical testimony. *Marut v. Costello*, 53 Ill. App. 2d 340, 202 N.E.2d 853 (1st Dist. 1964), judgment aff'd, 34 Ill. 2d 125, 214 N.E.2d 768 (1965).

5. That any recovery by Plaintiff is not subject to taxation. *Klawonn v. Mitchell*, 105 Ill. 2d 450, 86 Ill. Dec. 478, 475 N.E.2d 857 (1985); 26 USCA § 104(a)(2).

6. That all witnesses, with the exception of those declared under Supreme Court Rule 213(f)(3), are excluded from the proceedings until called to testify. *Friedman by Friedman v. Park Dist. of Highland Park*, 151 Ill. App. 3d 374, 104 Ill. Dec. 329, 502 N.E.2d 826 (2d Dist. 1986).

7. That Plaintiff was referred to any treating physicians by any lawyer or that any of the treating physicians have treated other clients of the Plaintiffs attorneys as this is not relevant to any fact or consequence in the above captioned case. *In re Elias*, 114 Ill. 2d 321, 102 Ill. Dec. 314, 499 N.E.2d 1327 (1986).

8. That Plaintiff retained legal counsel after the accident which is contained in her medical records as this is not relevant to any fact of consequence in the above captioned case. *In re Elias*, 114 Ill. 2d 321, 102 Ill. Dec. 314, 499 N.E.2d 1327 (1986).

9. Any mention or inference that any award to Plaintiff will have to be paid out of the personal assets of the Defendant or that it will ruin the Defendant's life.

10. The immigration or naturalization status of any of the Plaintiffs as such is not relevant or material to any issue before the court and the danger of unfair prejudice outweighs any probative value.

11. That the Defendant not be allowed to argue in closing argument that Plaintiff is asking for a greater amount of money than he actually expects to be awarded. *Kallas v. Lee*, 22 Ill. App. 3d 496, 317 N.E.2d 704 (1st Dist. 1974).

12. That the Defendant be prohibited from arguing in closing arguments that the Plaintiff's injuries or medical treatment were not reasonable or that Plaintiff's injuries were not treated

by qualified medical providers without presenting competent medical testimony or evidence to support such argument and factual assertions.

13. Evidence of the Defendant's safe driving habits.

14. Any argument by counsel or testimonial evidence from any witness in support of a contribution action or an allegation of contributory negligence against *[name of deceased]* for any act, as a minor under seven years of age is incapable of contributory negligence and the contributory negligence of others cannot be imputed to the minor. *Chu v. Bowers*, 275 Ill. App. 3d 861, 212 Ill. Dec. 113, 656 N.E.2d 436 (3d Dist. 1995); IPI 11.03; 11.05.

15. Any argument by counsel or testimonial evidence from any witness in support of a contribution action or allegation of contributory negligence against *[plaintiff]* based upon his failure to properly secure *[name of deceased]* in a seatbelt as under Illinois law a motorist who fails to properly restrain a passenger cannot be held liable for contribution to a second motorist whose alleged negligence caused the accident. *Brager v. Fee*, 750 F. Supp. 364 (C.D. Ill. 1990). As a matter of law, there is no duty imposed upon the driver of an automobile to guard against the negligence of others. The evidence of seatbelt use is inadmissible in a personal injury action with respect to either the question of negligence or damages. *Clarkson v. Wright*, 108 Ill. 2d 129, 90 Ill. Dec. 950, 483 N.E.2d 268 (1985) (rejected by, Law v. Superior Court In and For Maricopa County, 157 Ariz. 147, 755 P.2d 1135 (1988)); 625 ILCS 5/12-603.1 (2001); 625 ILCS 25/5 (2001) (see memorandum in support of Motion In Limine).

16. Any argument by counselor testimonial evidence from any witness in support of a contribution action against *[Plaintiff]* based upon his positioning of *[name of deceased]* in the front seat of his non-air bag equipped motor vehicle or on the lap of her sister. As a matter of law, there is no duty imposed upon the driver of an automobile to guard against the negligence of others. Under Illinois law, the children riding in the front seat or on each other's lap, does not constitute negligence which was the proximate cause of the accident. *Brager v. Fee*, 750 F. Supp. 364 (C.D. Ill. 1990); *Clarkson v. Wright*, 108 Ill. 2d 129, 90 Ill. Dec. 950, 483 N.E.2d 268 (1985) (rejected by, Law v. Superior Court In and For Maricopa County, 157 Ariz. 147, 755 P.2d 1135 (1988)); (see memorandum in support of Motion In Limine).

17. That any argument or evidence of, or inquiry into *[Plain-*

tiff]'s guilty plea and conviction for child endangerment or seatbelt violation be prohibited as the only evidence supporting the plea was the fact that he improperly placed two children in a single seatbelt. No other evidence of wrongdoing on the part of *[Plaintiff]* formed the basis of the charge of child endangerment. (see attached testimony of arresting Officer *[police report]* attached as Exhibits A & B). As noted above, under Illinois law a motorist who fails to properly restrain a passenger cannot be held liable for contribution to a second motorist whose alleged negligence caused the accident. *Brager v. Fee*, 750 F. Supp. 364 (C.D. Ill. 1990). As a matter of law, there is no duty imposed upon the driver of an automobile to guard against the negligence of others. The evidence of seatbelt use is inadmissible in a personal injury action with respect to either the question of negligence or damages. *Clarkson v. Wright*, 108 Ill. 2d 129, 90 Ill. Dec. 950, 483 N.E.2d 268 (1985) (rejected by, Law v. Superior Court In and For Maricopa County, 157 Ariz. 147, 755 P.2d 1135 (1988)); 625 ILCS 5/12-603.1 (2001) (see memorandum in support of Motion In Limine). Where the predicate act of the misuse of a seatbelt is inadmissible the plea of guilty to an offense based solely on the inadmissible evidence should be also excluded as it is not relevant to any mailer before the court and the danger of unfair prejudice outweighs any probative value.

Relevant evidence, that which "tends to either prove a fact in controversy or render a matter in issue more or less probable," is generally admissible. *Hiscott v. Peters*, 324 Ill. App. 3d 114, 257 Ill. Dec. 847, 754 N.E.2d 839 (2d Dist. 2001), quoting *Galowich v. Beech Aircraft Corp.*, 209 Ill. App. 3d 128, 154 Ill. Dec. 46, 568 N.E.2d 46 (1st Dist. 1991). However, when the probative value of the evidence a party seeks to introduce is outweighed by its prejudicial effect, the trial court may properly deny its introduction. *Koonce ex rel. Koonce v. Pacilio*, 307 Ill. App. 3d 449, 463, 241 Ill. Dec. 57, 718 N.E.2d 628 (1st Dist. 1999). *[Plaintiff]*'s failure to properly seat belt his children is not at issue and not admissible. It cannot be the subject of a claim for contribution and is specifically precluded by statute and caselaw. Accordingly, it clearly is not relevant in the present case.

18. The fact that on prior occasions minors *[name of deceased]* had ridden in the back seat of the *[Plaintiff]*'s vehicles. Said evidence of what they did on prior occasions is not relevant to any issue before the court as to where they were seated at the time of the accident and their positioning on the day of the accident cannot form the basis of an action for contributory

negligence. (See memo in support.) Furthermore, a minor under age seven is conclusively incapable of contributory negligence. *Chu v. Bowers*, 275 Ill. App. 3d 861, 212 Ill. Dec. 113, 656 N.E.2d 436 (3d Dist. 1995).

19. That 213(f)(2) witness, Dr. *[name of witness]*, restrict and limit his testimony to disclosed opinions within his area of expertise as a forensic pathology expert and not be allowed to offer opinions in the area of bio-medical or bio-mechanical engineering concerning testimony that the positioning and manner in which *[name of deceased]* were seated with a motorized shoulder belt contributed to the fatal injuries sustained in this accident. Dr. *[name of witness]* is admittedly not an expert in the field of human factors, bio-medical or bio-mechanical engineering and is clearly not qualified to testify regarding specific occupant kinematics, positioning and directional forces of occupants in relation to safety equipment within the vehicle. *Martin v. Sally*, 341 Ill. App. 3d 308, 275 Ill. Dec. 285, 792 N.E.2d 516 (2d Dist. 2003). Moreover, evidence of failure to proper seatbelt is inadmissible as noted above and may not be admitted or relied upon for the issue of liability or damages or submitted in mitigation of damages. Furthermore Defendant has admitted in a Rule 216 admission that "the defendant does not dispute that the accident in question resulted in the death of *[name of deceased]*." (See defendant's 216 admission to request to admit No. *[number]* attached as Exhibit C.)

20. Any evidence that Defendant, was treated by any psychiatrist or any other mental health professional for any psychiatric or mental injuries related to this accident as Defendant's mental state following this incident is not relevant to any issue before the court thus the probative value of such evidence would be outweighed by the danger of unfair prejudice.

21. The fact that *[Plaintiff]* voluntarily dismissed his case prior to trial as such was by agreement of defense counsel and is not relevant to any issue before the court.

22. Any statements allegedly made by unidentified witnesses to the occurrence as such constitute impermissible hearsay are unreliable and are not relevant to any issue before the court.

WHEREFORE, Plaintiff, *[Plaintiff]* individually and as Special Administrator of the ESTATE OF *[name of deceased]*, a minor, respectfully request that this Court instruct Defendant, defense counsel and any witness presented or questioned by defense counsel not to offer evidence, elicit testimony or make remarks, comments or arguments on matters herein argue that should be excluded and further that each counsel be instructed to inform each and every witness appearing in their phase of this suit to strictly comply with the rulings of this court.

Respectfully submitted,

____

[Attorney for Plaintiff]
[Firm]
[Address]
[Telephone number]
[Fax number]

§ 10:206 Sample memorandum of law and authorities in support of motion in limine to exclude collateral evidence

[insert caption]

MEMORANDUM IN SUPPORT OF ESTATE OF *[name of deceased]* MOTIONS IN LIMINE

NOW COMES the Plaintiff, *[name of Plaintiff]* individually and as Special Administrator of the ESTATE OF *[name of deceased]*, a minor, by and through her parent and next friend, *[name of Plaintiffs]*, individually, by and through their attorneys, by and through her attorneys, *[name of attorneys]*, and submits the following Memorandum of Law in support of their Motion in Limine.

FACTUAL SUMMARY

On *[date of accident]*, at approximately *[time]*, Plaintiff, *[name of plaintiff]*, a *[age of plaintiff]* year old male, was driving his *[make and model of vehicle]* in a westbound direction on *[location of accident]*. *[Plaintiff]* was returning from his part-time position with *[employer]* where he worked to provide additional income for his young family. That evening, *[Plaintiff]* brought his two daughters to the *[employer]* to participate in "Family Night" recreational activities while he performed his duties. The *[employer]* was located approximately 3 miles from *[Plaintiff]*'s home in *[Plaintiff's place of residence]*. *[Plaintiff]*'s daughters, *[names of deceased]*, were riding as passengers in the right front passenger seat. Both children were buckled with the same motorized shoulder belt, with the younger *[name of deceased]* seated on *[name of deceased]*'s lap. In this model year *[vehicle]*, the lap belt was independent from the motorized shoulder belt and was not used in the accident. *[Plaintiff]*'s *[vehicle]* did not have a passenger side airbag.

The three were traveling in the westbound curb lane of *[location of accident]*. As they approached that intersection, a vehicle in front of them driven by *[name of driver]* began to slow and signal to make a right hand turn northbound on *[location of accident]*. *[Plaintiff]* then changed to the median lane of traffic and began to enter the intersection. At approximately the same time, a *[make and model of defendant's vehicle]* driven by Defendant, *[name of defendant]*, was traveling in the opposite direction. As *[Plaintiff]* entered the intersection on a yellow light, Defendant was following a vehicle with several friends to a party in *[location]*, failed to wait for traffic to clear and initiated a left-hand turn northbound on the yellow. A collision between the two vehicles occurred. Sadly, as a result of the collision *[Plaintiff]*'s youngest daughter, *[name of deceased]*, received fatal injuries.

Following the occurrence *[Plaintiff]* was charged with a misdemeanor of endangering the life of a child, 720 ILCS 5/12-21.6 and failure to properly secure the children in a seatbelt, 625 ILCS 5/12-603.1. Unrepresented by counsel, and mentally unsound due to the stress of having just lost his six year old daughter, *[Plaintiff]* pled guilty to the endangering the life of a child charge. Defendant was charged with failure to yield to oncoming traffic when making her left hand turn.

The Estate of *[name of deceased]* initiated a civil action against Defendant as a result of her failure to yield on a left hand turn to Plaintiff's vehicle which was traveling through the intersection on a solid yellow light.

On *[date of filing]*, Defendant filed an Amended Counterclaim for Contribution against *[Plaintiff]*. The recent filed amended counterclaim sets forth that *[Plaintiff]* was contributorily negligent in that he:

(g) Knowing permitted his two daughters to ride in the front seat of his vehicle in such a way as to endanger the life and health of his passengers;

(h) Drove his vehicle with his two daughters riding in the front seat and improperly positioned under a single shoulder restraint belt in such a way so as to endanger the life and/or health of his passengers.

These allegations are based on *[Plaintiff]*'s failure to properly secure his children, placing *[name of deceased]*, along with her sister, in the motorized shoulder harness without the lap belt, in the front passenger seat, of his *[make and model of vehicle]*. The Estate of *[name of deceased]* submits that this counterclaim and any argument or evidence in support is improper under both the relevant statutes and caselaw as a matter of law.

ARGUMENT

I. EVIDENCE OF THE FAILURE OF *[PLAINTIFF]* TO PROPERLY SECURE HIS DAUGHTER IN A PROPERLY ADJUSTED AND FASTENED SEAT SAFTEY BELT AT THE TIME OF THIS ACCIDENT IS SPECIFICALLY INADMISSIBLE PURSUANT TO 625 ILCS 5/12-60 AND 625 ILCS 25/5; IS NOT ADMISSIBLE WITH RESPECT TO EITHER THE QUESTION OF NEGLIGENCE OR DAMAGES PURSUANT TO *CLARKSON V. WRIGHT*; AND MAY NOT FORM THE BASIS OF AN ACTION FOR CONTRIBUTION TO A SECOND MOTORIST WHOSE ALLEGED NEGLIGENCE CAUSED THE ACCIDENT UNDER THE HOLDING OF *BRAGER V. FEE*.

A. 625 ILCS 5/12-603.1(c) AND 625 ILCS 25/5 SPECIFICALLY PRECLUDE ANY EVIDENCE OF *[PLAINITFF]*'S FAILURE TO PROPERLY SECURE HIS DAUGHTER IN A SEATBELT UN THE PRESENT CASE.

As noted above, following the occurrence *[Plaintiff]* was charged with a misdemeanor of endangering the life of a child, 720 ILCS 5/12-21.6, which was solely predicated on his failure to properly secure *[name of deceased]* in a seatbelt, under 625 ILCS 5/12-603.1, for which he also received a citation.

The 2001 version of 625 ILCS 5/12-6-603.1, sets forth the circumstances under which a driver and a front seat passenger are required to use a seat belt and provides, in relevant part:

> 5/12-603.1. Driver and passenger required to use safety belts, exceptions and penalty
>
> § 12-603.1 - Driver and passenger required to use safety belts, exceptions and penalty.
>
> (a) Each driver and front seat passenger of a motor vehicle operated on a street or highway in this State shall wear a properly adjusted and fastened seat safety belt; except that, a child less than 6 years of age shall be protected as required pursuant to the Child Passenger Protection Act. Each driver under the age of 18 years and each of the driver's passengers under the age of 19 years of a motor vehicle operated on a street or highway in this State shall wear a properly adjusted and fastened seat safety belt. Each driver of a motor vehicle transporting a child 6 years of age or more, but less than 16 years of age, in the front seat of the motor vehicle shall secure the child in a properly adjusted and fastened seat safety belt.

> (c) Failure to wear a seat safety belt in violation of this Section shall not be considered evidence of negligence, shall not limit the liability of an insurer, and shall not diminish any recovery for damages arising out of the ownership, maintenance, or operation of a motor vehicle. 625 ILCS 5/12-603.1.

Additionally, the 2001 version of 625 ILCS 25/5, entitled "Failure to properly secure child-Negligence—Admissibility in trial" provided, in relevant part:

> § 5. In no event shall a person's failure to secure a child...in an approved child restraint system or properly secure such child,... in a seat belt constitute contributory negligence or be admissible as evidence in the trial of any civil action. 625 ILCS 25/5.

A plain reading of these two statutes clearly evinces a strict bar against the introduction of a motorist's failure to properly secure a child in a seat safety belt with respect to liability or damages or form the basis for contributory negligence in a civil action. Therefore, plaintiff's Motion in Limine with respect to any evidence of *[Plaintiff]*'s failure to properly secure *[name of deceased]* in a seatbelt should be granted and any such evidence and/or argument barred by this court.

B. *[PLAINTIFF]*'S FAILURE TO PROPERLY SECURE HIS DAUGHTER IN A SEATBELT IS NOT ADMISSIBLE WITH RESPECT TO EITHER THE QUESTION OF NEGLIGENCE OR DAMAGES PURSUANT TO THE ILLINOIS SUPREME COURT'S OPINION IN *CLARKSON V. WRIGHT*

Illinois caselaw also supports the fact that seatbelt evidence is inadmissible for any purpose in a civil trial. The Illinois Supreme Court had the opportunity to interpret the statutory section noted above and its implications on a civil trial in the landmark case of *Clarkson v. Wright*, 108 Ill. 2d 129, 90 Ill. Dec. 950, 483 N.E.2d 268 (1985) (rejected by, Law v. Superior Court In and For Maricopa County, 157 Ariz. 147, 755 P.2d 1135 (1988)). In Clarkson, the Illinois Supreme Court held that the failure to use a seatbelt under the foregoing statute is not admissible with respect to either the question of liability or damages. *Clarkson*, 108 Ill.2d at 133-134. In arriving at its decision, the court decided to follow the majority of jurisdictions and reasoned that the failure to use a seatbelt could neither be evidence of negligence or contributory negligence out of which a plaintiff's injuries arose. *Clarkson*, 108 Ill.2d at 132.

The rationale of the court was that there was no duty to wear the restraining device and there was no duty to anticipate the negligence of another. Consequently, the failure to properly wear a seatbelt could not be considered a proximate cause of the accident or injury. *Brager v. Fee*, 750 F. Supp. 364, 366 (C.D. Ill. 1990).

The Illinois Supreme Court also rejected an argument that the failure to properly belt an occupant of a motor vehicle should be admitted as to the mitigation of damages. In support of its rejection of this argument, the Court reasoned that the normal duty to mitigate damages under the law arises only subsequent to an injury and is distinguishable from a duty to mitigate which does not exist prior to an injury. The court then went on to state: "We find no authority which imposed on plaintiff the duty to anticipate and guard against defendant's negligence." *Clarkson*, 108 Ill.2d at 133. The imposition of a general duty to anticipate the negligence of others would place an intolerable burden on society. *Dunn v. Baltimore & Ohio R. Co.*, 127 Ill. 2d 350, 130 Ill. Dec. 409, 537 N.E.2d 738 (1989).

In the present case, subparagraph 5(h) of Defendant's Amended Counterclaim for Contribution is predicated on *[Plaintiff]*'s failure to property secure *[name of deceased]* in a seatbelt, presumably on the basis that the failure to properly secure the child increased the severity of her injuries. Clearly this type of argument and or evidence in support thereof is improper and may not be admitted under Illinois law. *[Plaintiff]*'s failure to properly secure *[name of deceased]* in a seatbelt cannot be admitted as a proximate or contributing cause of this accident under the foregoing authority as a matter of law and any argument or evidence of such should be barred by this court.

C. *[PLAINTIFF]*'S FAILURE TO PROPERLY SECURE HIS DAUGHTER IN A SEATBELT OR ALEJANDRA'S SITTING ON HER SISTERS LAP IN THE FRONT PASSENGER SEAT, MAY NOT FORM THE BASIS OF AN ACTION FOR CONTRIBUTION TO A SECOND MOTORIST WHOSE ALLEGED NEGLIGENCE CAUSED THE ACCIDENT UNDER THE HOLDING OF *BRAGER V. FEE*.

Under Illinois law, Defendant is precluded from arguing or introducing evidence or testimony of *[Plaintiff]*'s failure to properly secure *[name of deceased]* in a seatbelt or of the fact that *[name of deceased]* was seated on her sister's lap in the passengers seat, in her contribution action where Defendant's alleged negligence caused the accident.

In *Brager v. Fee*, 750 F. Supp. 364, 366 (C.D. Ill. 1990), the United States District Court for the Central District of Illinois addressed both the implications of the aforementioned statutes and the Illinois Supreme Court's holding in Clarkson in a factual setting virtually identical to the case at bar.

In Brager, an Illinois motorist, Douglas Brager, plaintiff, was operating a motor vehicle with his four-year-old son, Jonathon, as a passenger. The Brager vehicle was involved in an accident with another vehicle operated by Betty Fee, defendant, which allegedly ran a stop sign and collided with the plaintiff's vehicle, killing his four-year- old son, Jonathon. A wrongful death action was brought by plaintiff against the defendant for the death of plaintiff's son. Defendant filed a counter-claim against the plaintiff alleging, inter alia, that: (1) Plaintiff failed to properly secure his son in the automobile so that he would not be ejected therefrom (seatbelt or restraint system); and (2) Plaintiff failed to secure his son inside the vehicle by means of locking the rear car doors or rolling the windows to the up position so that he would not be ejected. (Positioning of the child.)

The court reviewed both the statutory scheme noted above and the rulings of the Illinois Supreme Court in *Clarkson* and held in a third party setting under Illinois law, a motorist who failed to properly restrain a four-year-old passenger could not be held liable for contribution to a second motorist whose alleged negligence caused the accident. Consistent with the Supreme Court holdings in *Clarkson* and *Dunn*, the court reiterated that under Illinois law there is no duty to guard against the negligence of others. *Brager*, 750 F.Supp at 366-367. The court stated that although *Brager's* failure to properly secure his son may have exacerbated his son's death, his actions did not constitute negligence which was the proximate cause of the accident. The court further noted that since the alleged conduct of failure to properly belt the child, lock doors and rollup windows could not have caused the accident, his conduct did not negligently contribute to the death of his son as a matter of law, as required by the Illinois Wrongful Death Act. *Brager*, 750 F.Supp at 366-367. Accordingly, the court held that a motorist who failed to properly restrain a four-year-old passenger could not be held liable for contribution to a second motorist whose alleged negligence caused the accident and dismissed both counterclaims.

Turning to the facts of the present case, which are virtually identical to *Brager*, subparagraphs 5(g) & (h) of Defendant's Counterclaim for Contribution allege that *[Plaintiff]* was contributorily negligent in that he:

(g) Knowing permitted his two daughters to ride in the front seat of his vehicle in such a way as to endanger the life and health of his passengers;

(h) Drove his vehicle with his two daughters riding in the front seat and improperly positioned under a single shoulder restraint belt in such a way so as to endanger the life and/or health of his passengers.

These allegations of contributory negligence are based upon evidence that *[Plaintiff]*: (1) failed to properly secure his daughter in a seatbelt; (2) improperly secured his daughter in a seatbelt with her sister; (3) had his daughter in the front seat; and (4) improperly had *[name of deceased]* seated on her sister's lap at the time of the occurrence. They are related to both belting and positioning issues and are virtually identical to the allegations of contributory negligence stricken by the *Brager* court as a matter of law.

The dismissed *Brager* counterclaim alleged: (1) improper belting of the four-year- old; and (2) improper positioning of the four year old near an unlocked door with an open window. Similarly, in the present case, subparagraphs 5(g) & (h) of Defendant's recently filed Amended Counterclaim allege: (g) improper positioning with her sister in the front seat; and (h) improper belting with sister in a single shoulder restraint and without a lap belt. Under the forgoing authorities, *[Plaintiff]* had no duty to anticipate the alleged negligent left hand turn of Defendant, which was the proximate cause of the collision. Both counterclaims are the same in that they allege improper belting and improper positioning as the basis of the counterclaims for contribution.

As the *Brager* and *Clarkson* courts have noted, none of these actions and/or inactions could not have caused the accident and as such could not constitute contributory negligence which contributed to the death of the child. It is clear under Illinois law, that these allegations of improper belting or improper positioning cannot form the basis a Counterclaim for Contribution as a matter of law.

Furthermore, any evidence of failure to properly secure *[name of deceased]* in a seatbelt is inadmissible for any purpose pursuant to the foregoing statutes and the Illinois Supreme Court's holding in Clarkson.

Accordingly, Plaintiffs respectfully request that their Motion in Limine be granted and that Defendant be barred as a matter of law from maintaining as a counterclaim and/or introducing evidence, testimony or argument that *[Plaintiff]*: (1) failed to properly secure his daughter in a seatbelt; (2) improperly secured his daughter in a seatbelt with her sister; (3) had his daughter in the front seat; and (4) improperly had *[name of deceased]* seated on Victoria's lap at the time of the occurrence.

II. ANY EVIDENCE, TESTIMONY OR ARGUMENT

REGARDING *[PLAINTIFF]*'S PLEA AND CONVICTION FOR ENDANGERING THE LIFE OF A CHILD UNDER 720 ILCS 5/12-21.6 SHOULD BE EXCLUDED BY THE COURT.

The 2001 version of 720 ILCS 5/12-21.6, sets forth the elements necessary for the offense of endangering the life of a child and provides, in relevant part:

> 21.6. Endangering the life or health of a child
>
> § 12-21.6. Endangering the life or health of a child.
>
> (a) It is unlawful for any person to willfully cause or permit the life or health of a child under the age of 18 to be endangered or to willfully cause or permit a child to be placed in circumstances that endanger the child's life or health. 720 ILCS 5/12-21.6.

Unrepresented by counsel and mentally unsound due to the stress of having just lost his six year old daughter, *[Plaintiff]* pled guilty to the endangering the life of a child charge. Absent his blind plea, it is doubtful that *[Plaintiff]* would have been convicted of the aforementioned offense as it is not likely that a trier of fact would find that placing his daughters in the same seatbelt would be considered the type of willful conduct to necessary to support the conviction. In fact, *[Plaintiff]* undertook a safety measures to protect his daughter when he secured her along with her sister in a seatbelt. It is inconceivable that a court would find this type of conduct to be of a willful nature, as contemplated by the aforementioned statute.

Plaintiff maintains that any argument or evidence of, or inquiry into *[Plaintiff]*'s guilty plea and conviction for child endangerment or any seatbelt violation be prohibited as it was solely based upon the fact that he improperly placed two children in a single seatbelt. No other evidence of wrongdoing on the part of *[Plaintiff]* formed the basis of the charge of child endangerment. Both Officers *[police officers]*, of the *[municipality]* Police Department, the investigating officers responsible for charging *[Plaintiff]* with the aforementioned offense, stated that there was no other evidence of *[Plaintiff]*'s wrongdoing to support the endangerment charge other than his failure to properly secure *[name of deceased]* (put two in one belt). No other evidence of speeding, improper lane usage, running a red light or any other offense was found by the officers. Both officers admitted if they had any evidence of other traffic infractions to support the endangering charge they would have charged *[Plaintiff]* with them as well. Moreover, Officer *[police officer]* testified that it is not unlawful for a six-year-old to be riding in the front seat of a vehicle. (See attached testimony of attesting Officers *[police officers]*.)

As noted above, under Illinois law a motorist who fails to properly restrain a passenger cannot be held liable for contribution to a second motorist whose alleged negligence caused the accident. *Brager v. Fee*, 750 F. Supp. 364 (C.D. Ill. 1990). As a matter of law, there is no duty imposed upon the driver of an automobile to guard against the negligence of others. The evidence of seatbelt use is inadmissible in a personal injury action with respect to either the question of negligence or damages and may not be submitted on the issue of mitigation of damages. *Clarkson v. Wright*, 108 Ill. 2d 129, 90 Ill. Dec. 950, 483 N.E.2d 268 (1985) (rejected by, Law v. Superior Court In and For Maricopa County, 157 Ariz. 147, 755 P.2d 1135 (1988)); 625 ILCS 5/12-603.1.

Where the predicate act of the failure to properly seatbelt is inadmissible as to any issue in this case, the plea of guilty to an offense based solely on the inadmissible evidence should also be deemed inadmissible. Thus, *[Plaintiff]*'s plea and conviction to child endangerment should similarly be excluded by this court.

Moreover, the child endangerment plea is not relevant to any issue before the court and should be excluded as the danger of unfair prejudice outweighs any probative value.

Relevant evidence, that which "tends to either prove a fact in controversy or render a matter in issue more or less probable," is generally admissible. *Hiscott v. Peters*, 324 Ill. App. 3d 114, 257 Ill. Dec. 847, 754 N.E.2d 839 (2d Dist. 2001), quoting *Galowich v. Beech Aircraft Corp.*, 209 Ill. App. 3d 128, 135, 154 Ill. Dec. 46, 568 N.E.2d 46 (1st Dist. 1991). However, when the probative value of the evidence a party seeks to introduce is outweighed by its prejudicial effect, the trial court may properly deny its introduction. *Koonce ex rel. Koonce v. Pacilio*, 307 Ill. App. 3d 449, 241 Ill. Dec. 57, 718 N.E.2d 628 (1st Dist. 1999).

Under the foregoing authorities, *[Plaintiff]*'s failure to properly belt *[name of deceased]* is not at issue in the present case. It: (1) cannot be the subject of a claim for contribution; (2) cannot be admitted to as to liability, damages, or in mitigation of damages; and (3) has been specifically precluded by statute and caselaw. Thus, it clearly is not relevant in the present case.

Where the seatbelt evidence is specifically precluded, the plea of guilty to the endangering charge based solely on the inadmissible evidence should also be excluded as there is no probative value to the admission of the plea for any purpose. Under these circumstances the danger of unfair prejudice to

[Plaintiff] and to the Estate of *[name of deceased]* clearly outweighs any probative value of an offense based solely in inadmissible evidence. Defendant should not be permitted to introduce through the back door, evidence which is not permitted through the front door.

Accordingly, as his blind plea and conviction to the charge of endangering the life of a child: (1) was based solely on the inadmissible evidence of failure to secure his daughter; (2) is not relevant to any issue before the court; and (3) where the danger of unfair prejudice clearly outweighs the probative value of the blind guilty plea; Plaintiffs respectfully request that this court grant their Motion in Limine and bar any evidence, testimony or documentation with respect to *[Plaintiff]*'s plea of guilty to the offense of child endangerment.

WHEREFORE, Plaintiffs individually and as Special Administrator of the ESTATE OF *[name of deceased]*, a minor, respectfully request that this Court instruct Defendant, defense counsel and any witness presented or questioned by defense counsel not to offer evidence, elicit testimony or make remarks, comments or arguments on matters herein argued that should he excluded and further that each counsel be instructed to inform each and every witness appearing in their phase of this suit to strictly comply with the rulings of this court.

Respectfully submitted,

____

[name of attorney]
[firm]
[address]
[telephone number]
[fax number]

§ 10:207 Motion to exclude evidence of marijuana use

It is well established that a lay person can offer the opinion that another person was intoxicated by alcohol. *City of Aurora v. Hillman*, 90 Ill. 61, 1878 WL 10108 (1878). However, to establish intoxication, the observer must have personal observation of the allegedly intoxicated person. See *West Chicago St. Ry. Co. v. Fishman*, 169 Ill. 196, 48 N.E. 447 (1897); *People v. Berkman*, 307 Ill. 492, 139 N.E. 91 (1923); *Grant v. Paluch*, 61 Ill. App. 2d 247, 210 N.E.2d 35 (1st Dist. 1965). Lay opinion regarding alcohol intoxication is admissible with such minimal foundational requirements because observations of intoxicated persons "are within the competence of all adults of normal experience..." *People v. Jacquith*, 129 Ill. App. 3d 107, 84 Ill. Dec. 357, 472 N.E.2d 107 (1st Dist. 1984).

However, evidentiary questions regarding intoxication become more complicated when the allegedly intoxicating substance is an illegal drug. The problem in establishing a foundation requirement lie in two distinct reasons: (1) the observations of a person impaired by drugs are not "within the competence of all adults of normal experience" as is the case with alcohol; and (2) different drugs and combinations thereof can cause impairment in different ways. *People v. Workman*, 312 Ill. App. 3d 305, 311, 244 Ill. Dec. 784, 726 N.E.2d 759 (2d Dist. 2000). Accordingly, much greater scrutiny must be given to the foundation for intoxication by drugs before such an opinion is admitted.

In Illinois, there is no reported civil case regarding the admissibility of lay testimony regarding impairment by marijuana use. However, guidance can be gleaned from our Appellate Court's work in criminal cases. In *People v. Davis*, 6 Ill. App. 3d 622, 286 N.E.2d 8 (4th Dist. 1972), the Court affirmed the trial court's decision to exclude opinion testimony of three lay witnesses who simply saw the defendant "take red pills." The lay witnesses sought to testify that the defendant was under the influence of drugs at the time of the crime. The court affirmed the exclusion of such testimony because the foundational requirements were not met. *Davis*, 61 Ill.App.3d at 632.

In this case, defendant has provided no statement or opinion (by way of testimony or disclosure) that plaintiff was intoxicated or under the influence of marijuana at the time of the occurrence. Without such evidence, admitting the testimony would be improper.

Defendant has also not provided the foundational basis for establishing intoxication. Indeed, he cannot. Plaintiff was not subject to any drug test at the time of the occurrence or shortly thereafter. Thus, both the court and trier of fact are simply left to speculate about whether plaintiff had smoked marijuana and whether she was under the influence of it at the time of the occurrence.

Whether the plaintiff was intoxicated under the influence of marijuana at the time of the occurrence is also not relevant. "Relevant evidence" is any evidence which has a tendency to render a proposition more or less probable that it would be without the evidence in the light of logic, experience, and accepted assumptions concerning human behavior. *People v. Patterson*, 192 Ill. 2d 93, 249 Ill. Dec. 12, 735 N.E.2d 616 (2000). This is an automobile accident case in which the plaintiff was injured. The complaint and testimony both establish that the plaintiff was stopped in a car that was parked in a parking lot when the defendant rammed his vehicle into the car occupied by the plaintiff. The plaintiff was seated in the back driver's-side seat. There is no allegation that the plaintiff was contributorily negligent or even a proximate cause of her injuries. Whether she had consumed marijuana at some time in the past is not relevant.

In *County of Cook v. Industrial Com'n of Illinois*, 177 Ill. App. 3d 264, 126 Ill. Dec. 595, 532 N.E.2d 280 (1st Dist. 1988), the primary issue of debate was whether the plaintiff was on the job at the time of the occurrence. At trial, the arbitrators exclude evidence of his alcohol consumption. *Cook*, 177 Ill.App.3d at 270-271. However, the Appellate Court ruled that defendant could not establish intoxication or even that the questioning would have revealed the plaintiff was not "on the clock" at the time of the occurrence. *Cook*, 177 Ill.App.3d at 273. Thus, the testimony was properly barred.

In this case, the same reasoning applies. The defendant cannot establish that the plaintiff was intoxicated at the time of the occurrence. Moreover, this evidence is not relevant to any issue of consequence in the case. As such, it should it barred.

Even if the defendant can establish the foundational requirement for introduction of some alleged marijuana consumption by the plaintiff, the consumption should be excluded because the prejudicial effect outweighs the probative value. When this is the case, it is proper to exclude the evidence. *People v. Smith*, 152 Ill. 2d 229, 178 Ill. Dec. 335, 604 N.E.2d 858 (1992). In this case, the prejudicial effect of marijuana consumption by the plaintiff greatly outweighs any probative value of her consumption.

Note: Thanks to Grant Dixon III of the Dixon Law Office for the above.

§ 10:208 Motion to exclude evidence that motorcyclist did not have a valid operator's license

Reference to __________________________ license being suspended. (It is reversible error to give the jury an instruction that failure of motorcyclist to have a valid operators license could be considered to determine whether motorcyclist was contributorily negligent. *Westefer v. Rybacki*, 125 Ill. App. 2d

66, 259, 259 N.E.2d 810 (3d Dist. 1970); see also *Wilson v. Hobrock*, 344 Ill. App. 147, 100 N.E.2d 412 (3d Dist. 1951), where it was held not to be an error to rellise to give such an instruction.)

Note: Thanks to Mark Rouleau of the Law Office of Mark Rouleau for the above.

§ 10:209 Motion to exclude evidence of collateral source payments

TO: ALL PARTIES AND THEIR RESPECTIVE ATTORNEYS OF RECORD:

PLEASE TAKE NOTICE THAT plaintiff hereby moves this Court for an order excluding any and all evidence, references to evidence, testimony or argument relating to medical payments by plaintiff's insurer for injuries arising from the accident in this case.

This motion is based upon the grounds that evidence of payments by a collateral source, such as plaintiff's medical insurance provider, is irrelevant, immaterial and clearly inadmissible under the laws of this state.

This motion is made under the provisions of Illinois case law and is based upon the supporting Memorandum of Points and Authorities, the pleadings and papers on file in this action, and upon such of the argument and evidence as may be presented prior to or at the hearing of this matter.

Dated: *[date]*

MEMORANDUM OF POINTS AND AUTHORITIES

1.
PRELIMINARY STATEMENT

This action arises from an automobile accident that occurred on September 18, 1998, when the defendant crashed his Ford Mustang into the rear of plaintiff's Honda Civic. As a result of the accident, plaintiff incurred severe neck and back injuries, property damage and lost wages.

At the time of the accident, plaintiff was insured with a "Medical Payments" policy by his automobile insurer. As of the date of this motion, plaintiff has been reimbursed, through that policy, in the amount of $3,225 for medical expenses arising from the accident.

By this motion, plaintiff seeks an order precluding the introduction of any evidence, or mention of evidence, relating to the insurance payments. This motion is based upon the grounds that evidence of payments by a collateral source, such as plaintiff's medical insurance provider, is irrelevant, immaterial and clearly inadmissible under the laws of this state.

2.
THIS COURT MAY EXCLUDE PREJUDICIAL EVIDENCE IN ADVANCE OF TRIAL BY WAY OF AN IN LIMINE MOTION

This Court has the inherent power to grant a motion in limine to exclude any kind of evidence that could be objected to at trial, either as irrelevant or because it is more prejudicial than probative. *Swick v. Liautaud*, 169 Ill. 2d 504, 520–21, 215 Ill. Dec. 98, 662 N.E.2d 1238 (1996); *People v. Watkins*, 220 Ill. App. 3d 201, 163 Ill. Dec. 194, 581 N.E.2d 145 (1st Dist. 1991); *Cochran v. Great Atlantic & Pacific Tea Co., Inc.*, 203 Ill. App. 3d 935, 938, 148 Ill. Dec. 923, 561 N.E.2d 229 (5th Dist. 1990); and *Department of Public Works and Bldgs. v. Roehrig*, 45 Ill. App. 3d 189, 194–95, 3 Ill. Dec. 893, 359 N.E.2d 752 (5th Dist. 1976).

The law is clear that this Court has the authority to exclude evidence where there is a substantial danger that the probative value will be outweighed by the danger of undue prejudice. Federal Rule of Evidence 403 states:

> Although relevant, evidence may be excluded if its probative value is substantially outweighed by the danger of unfair prejudice, confusion of the issues, or misleading the jury, or by considerations of undue delay, waste of time, or needless presentation of cumulative evidence.

Although this rule has not been specifically codified in Illinois, case law has stated that Illinois has a common-law rule that is comparable to Federal Rule of Evidence 403. See *People v. Peete*, 318 Ill. App. 3d 961, 966–67, 252 Ill. Dec. 821, 743 N.E.2d 689 (4th Dist. 2001); *People v. Walker*, 335 Ill. App. 3d 102, 112, 268 Ill. Dec. 654, 779 N.E.2d 268 (2d Dist. 2002), as modified on denial of reh'g, (Oct. 24, 2002) and judgment aff'd, 211 Ill. 2d 317, 285 Ill. Dec. 519, 812 N.E.2d 339 (2004).

In addition, Illinois cases have specifically held that evidence should be excluded when the prejudicial impact of the evidence outweighs the probative value of it. *Department of Public Works and Bldgs. v. Roehrig*, 45 Ill. App. 3d 189, 196, 3 Ill. Dec. 893, 359 N.E.2d 752 (5th Dist. 1976) (exclusion of evidence of prior condemnations in a condemnation case because the prejudicial impact outweighs the probative value of it); *People v. Holman*, 257 Ill. App. 3d 1031, 1033–34, 196 Ill. Dec. 457, 630 N.E.2d

154 (2d Dist. 1994) (evidence is admissible if it is relevant and if the prejudicial impact does not substantially outweigh the probative value of it) and *Hulsebus v. Russian*, 118 Ill. App. 2d 174, 180–81, 254 N.E.2d 184 (2d Dist. 1969) (trial judge had discretion to exclude a gruesome photograph of the plaintiff during surgery because other evidence established the extent of the injury and because the photograph was likely to inflame and prejudice the jury). In the instant matter, there is a strong probability that the admission of evidence of the payment of expenses pursuant to the plaintiff's insurance policy will create a substantial danger of undue prejudice. Therefore, the authorities described above justify the preclusion of the requested evidence in this case.

Furthermore, this Court has authority to hear and determine the question of the admissibility of evidence outside the presence or hearing of the jury. See *Beasley v. Huffman Mfg. Co.*, 97 Ill. App. 3d 1, 5, 52 Ill. Dec. 560, 422 N.E.2d 241 (3d Dist. 1981) (purpose of a motion in limine is to prevent prejudice by determining admissibility issues outside of the jury's presence before the jury is exposed to the evidence); *People v. Graves*, 74 Ill. 2d 279, 279–83, 24 Ill. Dec. 153, 384 N.E.2d 1311 (1979) (contempt order against attorney was proper for mentioning an issue in front of the jury, after being ordered at a side-bar conference not to do so); *Department of Public Works and Bldgs. v. Roehrig*, 45 Ill. App. 3d 189, 194–95, 3 Ill. Dec. 893, 359 N.E.2d 752 (5th Dist. 1976) (purpose of motion in limine is to prevent inadmissible evidence from being suggested to the jury) and *Maxwell v. Habel*, 92 Ill. App. 510, 1900 WL 3466 (1st Dist. 1900) (if trial judge is concerned that an offer of proof might prejudice the jury, the offer can be made outside the presence of the jury). See also Federal Rule of evidence 103(c) which provides:

> Hearing of Jury.—In jury cases, proceedings shall be conducted, to the extent practicable, so as to prevent inadmissible evidence from being suggested to the jury by any means, such as making statements or offers of proof or asking questions in the hearing of the jury.

Although this rule has not been specifically codified in Illinois, Illinois has adopted other Federal Rules of evidence through case law. See e.g. *People v. Monroe*, 66 Ill. 2d 317, 321–22, 5 Ill. Dec. 824, 362 N.E.2d 295 (1977); and *Spencer v. Wandolowski*, 264 Ill. App. 3d 611, 617, 201 Ill. Dec. 422, 636 N.E.2d 854 (1st Dist. 1994) (adopting Federal Rule of Evidence 401).

3.
THIS COURT SHOULD EXCLUDE ANY EVIDENCE OF MEDICAL PAYMENTS MADE TO PLAINTIFF BY A COLLATERAL SOURCE

A defendant may not mitigate damages where the plaintiff has been compensated by an independent source, such as insurance, pension, continued wages or disability payments. See *Muranyi v. Turn Verein Frisch-Auf*, 308 Ill. App. 3d 213, 214–220, 241 Ill. Dec. 505, 719 N.E.2d 366 (2d Dist. 1999) (collateral source rule barred evidence of payments that were received from insurance coverage that was through the plaintiff's spouse's employment); *Boden v. Crawford*, 196 Ill. App. 3d 71, 76, 142 Ill. Dec. 546, 552 N.E.2d 1287 (4th Dist. 1990) (evidence of disability payments the plaintiff was receiving from a source independent from the defendant is inadmissible); and *Fear v. Smith*, 184 Ill. App. 3d 51, 58-59, 132 Ill. Dec. 491, 539 N.E.2d 1297 (5th Dist. 1989) (trial judge improperly denied the plaintiff damages for lost wages that were also recovered through her employer as a benefit of her employment).

Furthermore, this court may exclude the evidence because it is irrelevant. Federal Rule of Evidence 401 defines relevancy as,

> evidence having any tendency to make the existence of any fact that is of consequence to the determination of the action more probable or less probable than it would be without the evidence.

Illinois has adopted this definition of relevancy through case law. *People v. Monroe*, 66 Ill. 2d 317, 321–22, 5 Ill. Dec. 824, 362 N.E.2d 295 (1977); *Spencer v. Wandolowski*, 264 Ill. App. 3d 611, 617, 201 Ill. Dec. 422, 636 N.E.2d 854 (1st Dist. 1994).

Illinois case law provides that evidence may be properly excluded where it is not relevant to matters at issue. See *Preston ex rel. Preston v. Simmons*, 321 Ill. App. 3d 789, 803, 254 Ill. Dec. 647, 747 N.E.2d 1059 (1st Dist. 2001) (trial judge should not permit such wide latitude on cross-examination that it undermines the rule that only relevant evidence is admissible); *Cochran v. Great Atlantic & Pacific Tea Co., Inc.*, 203 Ill. App. 3d 935, 937–38, 148 Ill. Dec. 923, 561 N.E.2d 229 (5th Dist. 1990) (trial judge has inherent power to exclude irrelevant evidence); *Pagel v. Yates*, 128 Ill. App. 3d 897, 903, 84 Ill. Dec. 180, 471 N.E.2d 946 (4th Dist. 1984) (exclusion of irrelevant and confusing document); and *Benson v. Bradford Mut. Fire Ins. Corp.*, 121 Ill. App. 3d 500, 510, 76 Ill. Dec. 774, 459 N.E.2d 689, 47 A.L.R.4th 759 (2d Dist. 1984) (trial judge had discretion to exclude irrelevant witness testimony).

In the present case, plaintiff received reimbursement for medical expenses incurred as a result of the subject accident, under a Medical Payments provision of his automobile policy. These facts are squarely on point with the decisions cited above. Allowing evidence of the insurance payments would be wholly inconsistent with the collateral source rule and would be prejudicial error.

4.
CONCLUSION

Based on the foregoing, the plaintiff respectfully requests that this Court exclude any and all evidence, or mention of evidence, regarding payments from plaintiff's insurer for reimbursement of medical expenses arising from plaintiff's injuries in this case.

Dated: *[date]*

By:________________________
[name of counsel]
Attorney for PLAINTIFF,
[name of plaintiff]

§ 10:210 Motion to exclude evidence of defendant's liability

TO: ALL PARTIES AND THEIR RESPECTIVE ATTORNEYS OF RECORD:

PLEASE TAKE NOTICE THAT defendant hereby moves this Court for an order excluding any and all evidence, references to evidence, testimony or argument pertaining to defendant's liability in this action. This motion is based upon the prejudice that will occur to the defendant if such evidence is presented, since the defendant has admitted to liability in this action.

This motion is made under the provisions of Illinois case law and is based upon the supporting Memorandum of Points and Authorities, the pleadings and papers on file in this action, and upon such of the argument and evidence as may be presented prior to or at the hearing of this matter.

Dated: *[date]*

MEMORANDUM OF POINTS AND AUTHORITIES

1.
INTRODUCTION

This action arises from a moderate speed automobile accident between the plaintiff and defendant that occurred on or about January 22, 2000, in the City of Chicago, Illinois. In interrogatory responses, requests for admission and deposition statements, the defendant repeatedly admitted to being the cause of the accident.

The only issue that remains in dispute is the nature and extent of the plaintiff's injuries.

The defendant anticipates that the plaintiff will explore, in great detail, a number of liability issues at trial, including defendant's conduct immediately prior to the accident, and the condition of the defendant's brakes when the incident occurred. Defendant's belief is based upon a number of factors, including plaintiff's proposed Exhibit List, the plaintiff's designation of an automobile reconstruction expert and statements of counsel to this effect.

Defendant contends that the introduction of any liability evidence is irrelevant, cumulative and prejudicial, and therefore should be excluded.

2.
THIS COURT MAY EXCLUDE PREJUDICIAL EVIDENCE

This Court has the inherent power to grant a motion in limine to exclude any kind of evidence that could be objected to at trial, either as irrelevant or because it is more prejudicial than probative. *Swick v. Liautaud*, 169 Ill. 2d 504, 520–21, 215 Ill. Dec. 98, 662 N.E.2d 1238 (1996); *People v. Watkins*, 220 Ill. App. 3d 201, 163 Ill. Dec. 194, 581 N.E.2d 145 (1st Dist. 1991); *Cochran v. Great Atlantic & Pacific Tea Co., Inc.*, 203 Ill. App. 3d 935, 938, 148 Ill. Dec. 923, 561 N.E.2d 229 (5th Dist. 1990); and *Department of Public Works and Bldgs. v. Roehrig*, 45 Ill. App. 3d 189, 194–95, 3 Ill. Dec. 893, 359 N.E.2d 752 (5th Dist. 1976).

The law is clear that this Court has the authority to exclude evidence where there is a substantial danger that the probative value will be outweighed by the danger of undue prejudice. Federal Rule of Evidence 403 states:

> Although relevant, evidence may be excluded if its probative value is substantially outweighed by the danger of unfair prejudice, confusion of the issues, or misleading the jury, or by considerations of undue delay, waste of time, or needless presentation of cumulative evidence.

Although this rule has not been specifically codified in Illinois, case law has stated that Illinois has a common-law rule that is comparable to Federal Rule of Evidence 403. See *People v. Peete*, 318 Ill. App. 3d 961, 966–67, 252 Ill. Dec. 821, 743 N.E.2d 689 (4th Dist. 2001); *People v. Walker*, 335 Ill. App. 3d 102, 112, 268 Ill. Dec. 654, 779 N.E.2d 268 (2d Dist. 2002), as modified on denial of reh'g, (Oct. 24, 2002) and judgment aff'd, 211 Ill. 2d 317, 285 Ill. Dec. 519, 812 N.E.2d 339 (2004).

In addition, Illinois cases have specifically held that evidence should be excluded when the prejudicial impact of the evidence outweighs the probative value of it. *Department of Public Works and Bldgs. v. Roehrig*, 45 Ill. App. 3d 189, 196, 3 Ill. Dec. 893, 359 N.E.2d 752 (5th Dist. 1976) (exclusion of evidence of prior condemnations in a condemnation case because the prejudicial impact outweighs the probative value of it); *People v. Holman*, 257 Ill. App. 3d 1031, 1033–34, 196 Ill. Dec. 457, 630 N.E.2d 154 (2d Dist. 1994) (evidence is admissible if it is relevant and if the prejudicial impact does not substantially outweigh the probative value of it) and *Hulsebus v. Russian*, 118 Ill. App. 2d 174, 180–81, 254 N.E.2d 184 (2d Dist. 1969) (trial judge had discretion to exclude a gruesome photograph of the plaintiff during surgery because other evidence established the extent of the injury and because the photograph was likely to inflame and prejudice the jury).

In the instant matter, allowing evidence of defendant's liability will unduly prejudice the defendant, without advancing even marginally probative evidence. Having admitted liability, clearly the evidence is not relevant or necessary to prove damages. Furthermore, there is a strong likelihood that the jurors will be confused by this evidence, which will have no bearing on material issues in this case.

If the evidence is allowed, the defendant will be perceived as irresponsible, when in fact, the defendant took immediate responsibility for the cause of the accident and has been cooperative and forthcoming in all aspects of this litigation and his dealings with the plaintiff. The defendant will be forced to present rebuttal evidence to correct this misperception, wasting valuable time and resources of the Court, counsel and the parties, on an issue that has no business being litigated.

3.

EVIDENCE OF DEFENDANT'S LIABILITY IS NOT AT ISSUE AND SHOULD THEREFORE BE EXCLUDED

This Court may exclude irrelevant evidence. Federal Rule of Evidence 401 defines relevancy as, evidence having any tendency to make the existence of any fact that is of consequence to the determination of the action more probable or less probable than it would be without the evidence.

Illinois has adopted this definition of relevancy through case law. *People v. Monroe*, 66 Ill. 2d 317, 321–22, 5 Ill. Dec. 824, 362 N.E.2d 295 (1977); *Spencer v. Wandolowski*, 264 Ill. App. 3d 611, 617, 201 Ill. Dec. 422, 636 N.E.2d 854 (1st Dist. 1994).

Moreover, Illinois case law provides that evidence may be properly excluded where it is not relevant to matters at issue. See *Preston ex rel. Preston v. Simmons*, 321 Ill. App. 3d 789, 803, 254 Ill. Dec. 647, 747 N.E.2d 1059 (1st Dist. 2001) (trial judge should not permit such wide latitude on cross-examination that it undermines the rule that only relevant evidence is admissible); *Cochran v. Great Atlantic & Pacific Tea Co., Inc.*, 203 Ill. App. 3d 935, 937–38, 148 Ill. Dec. 923, 561 N.E.2d 229 (5th Dist. 1990) (trial judge has inherent power to exclude irrelevant evidence); *Pagel v. Yates*, 128 Ill. App. 3d 897, 903, 84 Ill. Dec. 180, 471 N.E.2d 946 (4th Dist. 1984) (exclusion of irrelevant and confusing document); and *Benson v. Bradford Mut. Fire Ins. Corp.*, 121 Ill. App. 3d 500, 510, 76 Ill. Dec. 774, 459 N.E.2d 689, 47 A.L.R.4th 759 (2d Dist. 1984) (trial judge had discretion to exclude irrelevant witness testimony).

Matters that are admitted or uncontroverted may also be excluded. *Davis v. International Harvester Co.*, 167 Ill. App. 3d 814, 824–25, 118 Ill. Dec. 589, 521 N.E.2d 1282 (2d Dist. 1988) (proper to exclude evidence of the feasibility of design changes, when there was an admission to that ability); *Bullard v. Barnes*, 112 Ill. App. 3d 384, 392–94, 68 Ill. Dec. 37, 445 N.E.2d 485 (4th Dist. 1983), judgment aff'd, 102 Ill. 2d 505, 82 Ill. Dec. 448, 468 N.E.2d 1228 (1984) (trial judge abused his discretion by admitting photographs of the deceased and testimony regarding the conditions and circumstances surrounding the collision because liability was admitted); *Carlyle v. Jaskiewicz*, 124 Ill. App. 3d 487, 495–96, 79 Ill. Dec. 847, 464 N.E.2d 751 (1st Dist. 1984) (the trial judge properly took judicial notice of certain facts and then excluded additional proof regarding those facts); and *Khatib v. McDonald*, 87 Ill. App. 3d 1087, 1099–1100, 43 Ill. Dec. 266, 410 N.E.2d 266 (1st Dist. 1980) (case remanded for a new trial on damages only, when there were errors at the trial but liability had been fairly established).

In this case, the defendant has admitted to liability. As such, any evidence relating to the nature of his liability and his actions leading up to the subject incident, are irrelevant and should be excluded.

4.
EVIDENCE OF DEFENDANT'S LIABILITY IS NOT NECESSARY TO PROVE PLAINTIFF'S DAMAGES

Courts have held that evidence of defendant's liability might be relevant if necessary to prove damages. See *Phillips v. Lawrence*, 87 Ill. App. 2d 60, 61-63, 230 N.E.2d 505 (5th Dist. 1967). However, in the present case, the facts surrounding the cause of the accident will in no way assist the jury in determining the nature and extent of the plaintiff's injuries or damages.

In the present case, the circumstances of the occurrence do not provide probative value regarding the nature of the injuries. In addition, the nature of the injuries can be fully established through other competent evidence and therefore, admitting the liability evidence would be cumulative, even if it were probative. Any evidence of liability will only serve to prejudice the defendant in the eyes of the jurors, by focusing on defendant's wrongdoing. This is not only improper, but, as stated above, it is clearly prejudicial to the defendant.

5.
CONCLUSION

For all the reasons stated above, the defendant requests that this Court exclude any reference at trial, including physical evidence, witness testimony and attorney comments, relating to the defendant's liability.

Dated: *[date]*

By:______________________
[name of counsel]
Attorneys for DEFENDANT,
[name of defendant]

§ 10:211 Sample motion to bar testimony of a medical expert regarding subsequent medical treatment

[insert caption]

MOTION TO BAR OPINIONS OF
[defense medical expert]

NOW COMES the plaintiff, *[plaintiff]*, by and through his attorneys, *[plaintiff's attorneys]*, and moves this Court to bar opinions of *[defense medical expert]*, and in support states as follows:

I. BACKGROUND

The plaintiff, *[plaintiff]* (age *[age of plaintiff]*), sustained an injury to his left knee on defendant's premises on *[date of injury]*. He had no prior knee pain or problem. The plaintiff's initial treatment from *[dates of treatment]* was at *[place of treatment]* which included orthopedic exam and therapy for anterior knee pain, medial knee pain and swelling. He continued therapy with his family physician, Dr. *[plaintiff's doctor]* from *[dates of treatment]* for continuous, persistent anterior knee pain, swelling, giving way and a sense of dislocation. Dr. *[plaintiff's doctor]* referred him to an orthopedic surgeon, Dr. *[plaintiff's surgeon]*, who was seen *[date of treatment]*. Dr. *[plaintiff's surgeon]* performed an arthroscopy on *[date of surgery]* and found that *[plaintiff]*'s left knee cap was maltracking laterally (riding off-center to the outside). This condition causes anterior knee pain and Dr. *[plaintiff's surgeon]*, in an effort to treat *[plaintiff]*'s continuous knee pain from the injury caused by the defendant, performed a lateral retinaclum release in order to center the knee cap and decrease *[plaintiff]*'s pain. He then visualized that tracking was improved.

One known complication of lateral release is that your knee cap may begin to ride off-center on the opposite side, or maltrack medially. *[plaintiff]* had two months of some improvement but then had increasing pain and was diagnosed with medial maltracking. *[plaintiff]* followed with Dr. *[plaintiff's surgeon]* until *[date of ending treatment]* when Dr. *[plaintiff's surgeon]* moved his practice to Wisconsin and referred *[plaintiff]* to Dr. *[plaintiff's second surgeon]*, who was seen *[date of treatment]*. Dr. *[plaintiff's second surgeon]* diagnosed medial maltracking as a complication of the lateral release and on June 21, 2001 he performed a reconstructive procedure to correct the medial maltracking. He later performed a removal of painful hardware placed during his procedure.

In summary, *[plaintiff]* injured his knee and had persistent pain. In an effort to treat *[plaintiff]*'s pain Dr. *[plaintiff's surgeon]* performed a lateral release for lateral maltracking. The lateral release centered the kneecap, but then resulted in medial maltracking. Dr. *[plaintiff's second surgeon]* performed a reconstruction to fix the medial maltracking to again center the knee cap.

II. DR. *[defense medical expert]*

The defendants hired *[defense medical expert]* to review the plaintiff's medical records and provide opinions.

Dr. *[defense medical expert]* opinions are that the plaintiff sustained a hyperextension knee strain, that there were no clear clinical signs of lateral maltracking before Dr. *[plaintiff's surgeon]*'s observation of lateral maltracking in his scope, and that it was a judgment call and he would not have done the surgery. The doctor further testified to all his reasons why he would not. Dr. *[defense medical expert]* agrees that Dr. *[plaintiff's surgeon]* performed his scope and did the lateral release in his judgment to treat knee complaints from the trauma of the fall in *[date of accident]*. Dr. *[defense medical expert]* further agrees that Dr. *[plaintiff's surgeon]*'s release caused the medial maltracking that Dr. *[plaintiff's second surgeon]* fixed; that it was a complication of Dr. *[plaintiff's surgeon]*'s surgery.

Dr. *[defense medical expert]*'s opinions serve only to provide a defense that damages subsequent to Dr. *[plaintiff's surgeon]*'s surgery are a result of the surgery and that the defendant is not responsible for damages flowing from the treatment by Dr. *[plaintiff's surgeon]*. Since this is not a defense, and since Illinois law is well-settled that the defendant is responsible for damages flowing from efforts to treat the injury, even if the treatment was negligent, the opinion and testimony of *[defense medical expert]* should be barred as immaterial, irrelevant and prejudicial.

III. MEMORANDUM OF LAW IN SUPPORT OF MOTION

In *Chicago City Ry. Co. v. Saxby*, 213 Ill. 274, 72 N.E. 755 (1904), the Illinois Supreme Court held:

> ...if her physicians made a mistake in the treatment applied by them to her, or the means employed failed to effect a cure, then she may recover for the entire injury which she has sustained, as the law, regards any injury resulting from the mistake of a physician or from a failure of the means employed to effect a cure, as a part of the immediate and direct damages which naturally flow from the injury.

In *Gertz v. Campbell*, 55 Ill. 2d 84, 302 N.E.2d 40 (1973), the Illinois Supreme Court reaffirmed the holding in Chicago City:

> We would observe that Campbell correctly states he is to be liable to the plaintiff for the negligence of (Dr.) Snyder as well as his own. In this State, and generally, a person injured through another's negligence can recover from the original tortfeasor not

> only for the original injury but for any aggravation of the injury caused by a physician's malpractice, assuming that there was no want of ordinary care by the injured in the selection of the physician. Chicago City, 213 III. at 274. (parenthetical added)

In *Patton v. Carbondale Clinic, S.C.*, 161 Ill. 2d 357, 204 Ill. Dec. 203, 641 N.E.2d 427 (1994), the Illinois Supreme Court again reaffirmed the rule:

> This court (in Gertz further noted that the defendant was liable for damages not only from the injury due to the accident, but from the injury due to any negligence of the doctor. (parenthetical added).

In *Kolakowski v. Voris*, 94 Ill. App. 3d 404, 50 Ill. Dec. 9, 418 N.E.2d 1003 (1st Dist. 1981), the plaintiff brought a malpractice action against the defendants who performed a cervical fusion after which plaintiff suffered extreme pain and impaired extremity function. Dr. Fox, a subsequent treater, performed surgery to alleviate plaintiff's pain, which procedure resulted in further impaired function of the arm and bladder dysfunction. During the trial, the court allowed the defendant to cross examine Dr. Fox in a manner indicating malpractice on the part of Dr. Fox in his treatment and that he misconstrued the source of the pain, and allowed argument by the defendant that Dr. Fox's surgery produced only a deficit and that defendants were not responsible for the effects of Dr. Fox's surgery.

The trial judge admitted the testimony and argument because at the time the court felt the defendants could not be held responsible for the injuries that flowed from Dr. Fox's surgery. After a verdict for the defendant, and on post-trial motion by the plaintiff, the trial court ordered a new trial. The trial court acknowledged that Illinois case law is well-settled that the original defendant is responsible for injuries caused by subsequent treatment, even if it was malpractice. The appellate court citing Gertz agreed that the error required a new trial:

> Because of the emphasis on Dr. Fox's treatment, the jury might have begun to perceive of Dr. Fox as the 'guilty' party... If the jury perceived Dr. Fox as a wrongdoer it may have acquitted the defendants on that basis?

Because evidence or argument that treatment by a subsequent medical care provider caused or aggravated an injury does not provide a defense, it is immaterial, irrelevant and error to admit. Its prejudicial effect to the plaintiff is to confuse the jury that the defendant may not be responsible for injury from subsequent medical care.

While the defendant may not present opinion or other evidence indicating or emphasizing that subsequent medical care caused or aggravated an injury, where the issue is injected into the case by testimony of the treatment, the IPI Instruction 30.23 is appropriate:

> If a defendant negligently causes *[injury to] [a condition of]* the plaintiff, then the defendant is liable not only for the plaintiff's damages resulting from that *[injury][or][condition]*, but is also liable for any damages sustained by the plaintiff arising from the efforts of health care providers to treat the *[injury][or][condition]* caused by the defendants *[even if that health care provider was negligent.]*

In *Wood v. Mobil Chemical Co.*, 50 Ill. App. 3d 465, 8 Ill. Dec. 701, 365 N.E.2d 1087 (5th Dist. 1977), the plaintiff's injury by defendant was misdiagnosed by a treater as carbon monoxide intoxication. The treater's treatment for carbon monoxide, including medication, was improper and caused additional injury for which the defendant was liable, citing Gertz.

In *French v. City of Springfield*, 30 Ill. App. 3d 584, 334 N.E.2d 181 (4th Dist. 1975), judgment rev'd, 65 Ill. 2d 74, 2 Ill. Dec. 271, 357 N.E.2d 438 (1976), the plaintiff was killed when he struck a utility pole avoiding a street condition. The City wanted to present evidence and argue that the negligent uncrashworthy car design, and not the City, was responsible for damages caused after striking the pole. The plaintiff sought to keep this out in limine. Citing Gertz, the court found that the City and the car manufacturer were successive tortfeasors, and that the City was responsible for the consequential injuries attributable to the subsequent negligence of the car design:

> ... liability of General Motors would be immaterial to the jury. The ruling on the motion in limine was not error.

The defendant, Dominick's Finer Foods, Inc., is responsible in damages for injuries caused by its negligence, including any injuries caused by the efforts of subsequent medical providers to treat the plaintiff, even if the treatment of subsequent medical providers caused additional injury or worsened the condition, even if they applied some treatment that some other doctor would not, even if they were wrong about whether their treatment would be effective, even if they were negligent in their decisions. Since none of the foregoing is a defense, testimony on behalf of the defendant to this effect is immaterial.

Since it would be immaterial to the jury whether Dr. *[plaintiff's surgeon]*'s surgery aggravated or caused additional injury, Dr. *[defense medical expert]*'s opinions and testimony should be barred or stricken.

Respectfully submitted,

____

Attorneys for Plaintiff
[name of attorney]
[name of firm]
[address]
[telephone number]
[fax number]

§ 10:212 Sample motion to exclude expert testimony based on the *Frye* or general acceptance standard

[insert caption]

PLAINTIFF'S *[number]* MOTION: BAR TESTIMONY OF DEFENSE EXPERT *[defense expert witness]*

NOW COME, the Plaintiffs, *[name of plaintiff]*, a minor, by her mother and next friend, *[name of mother]*, by and through their attorneys, *[attorneys for plaintiff]*, and requesting the Court to enter an Order barring each of the Defendants from calling *[defense expert witness]*, PhD to testify as an expert witness, states as follows:

I. This is a medical malpractice action that was filed in order to recover for injuries suffered by the minor plaintiff, during the course of her birth on *[date of birth]*.

2. As one of their experts, Defendant *[name of defendant hospital]* has retained biomechanical engineer *[defense expert witness]*, PhD to testify on the issue of liability Amongst the disclosed opinions of Professor *[defense expert witness]* is that most brachial plexus injuries occur at the time of initial impaction of the shoulder with the symphysis pubis, before a shoulder dystocia is even diagnosed. Through her use of a computer model referred to as the MADYMO ("mathematical dynamic model") birth model, she is planning to testify to the difference in forces being exerted upon a baby from the maternal expulsive force as compared to the force applied by a physician. After deposing Professor *[defense expert witness]*, it became obvious that her testimony would not satisfy the *Frye* standard due to its inherent unreliability and that, consequently, she should be barred from testifying as to anything based on such model.

I. The admission of expert testimony in Illinois is governed by the general acceptance or *Frye* standard

Opinion testimony of an expert is generally admissible if the expert is qualified by knowledge, skill, experience, training, or education in a somewhat reliable area and the testimony would assist the jury in understanding the evidence. See *Turner v. Williams*, 326 Ill. App. 3d 541, 260 Ill. Dec. 804, 762 N.E.2d 70 (2d Dist. 2001), citing *Wiegman v. Hitch-Inn Post of Libertyville, Inc.*, 308 Ill. App. 3d 789, 242 Ill. Dec. 335, 721 N.E.2d 614 (2d Dist. 1999). But, an expert's opinion is only as reliable as its basis. See *Turner v. Williams*, 326 Ill. App. 3d 541, 260 Ill. Dec. 804, 762 N.E.2d 70 (2d Dist. 2001), citing *Soto v. Gaytan*, 313 Ill. App. 3d 137, 245 Ill. Dec. 769, 728 N.E.2d 1126 (2d Dist. 2000). The Illinois Supreme Court has ruled that the exclusive test for the admission of expert testimony in this state is the general acceptance standard first established in *Frye v. U.S.*, 293 F. 1013, 34 A.L.R. 145 (App. D.C. 1923) (rejected by, State v. Walstad, 119 Wis. 2d 483, 351 N.W.2d 469 (1984)) and (rejected by, State v. Brown, 297 Or. 404, 687 P.2d 751 (1984)) and (rejected by, Nelson v. State, 628 A.2d 69 (Del. 1993)) and (rejected by, State v. Alberico, 116 N.M. 156, 861 P.2d 192 (1993)) and (rejected by, State v. Moore, 268 Mont. 20, 885 P.2d 457 (1994)) and (rejected by, State v. Faught, 127 Idaho 873, 908 P.2d 566 (1995)) and (rejected by, People v. Shreck, 22 P.3d 68, 90 A.L.R.5th 765 (Colo. 2001)). See *Donaldson v. Central Illinois Public Service Co.*, 199 Ill. 2d 63, 262 Ill. Dec. 854, 767 N.E.2d 314 (2002) (abrogated by, In re Commitment of Simons, 213 Ill. 2d 523, 290 Ill. Dec. 610, 821 N.E.2d 1184 (2004)).

The *Frye* standard, meant to exclude methods new to science that appear certain but are based on invalid evidence, dictates that "scientific evidence is only admissible at trial if the methodology or scientific principle upon which the opinion is based is sufficiently established to have gained general acceptance in the particular field in which it belongs." *Donaldson*, 199 Ill.2d at 77. See also, *Petre v. Kucich*, 331 Ill. App. 3d 935, 265 Ill. Dec. 125, 771 N.E.2d 1084 (1st Dist. 2002). The appropriate focus of an inquiry under this standard is the general acceptance of the underlying methodology used to establish an expert's opinion, and not the expert's ultimate conclusion. See *Petre*, 331 Ill.App.3d at 935.

In the medical community, the general acceptance standard allows for the admission of diverse opinions regarding causal relationships as long as the medical expert uses a generally accepted method to develop their conclusions. See id. In other words, the mere existence of a dispute within a particular field is not a bar to admissibility. However, a method or technique is not generally accepted if experimental or dubious.

Prior to applying the *Frye* standard, the threshold inquiry was whether the method or technique offered by the expert in support of her opinion was "new" or "novel", meaning it is not something formerly known or used. See *Petre*, 331 Ill.App.3d at 935. If the trial court finds the basis for an expert's conclusion to be new or novel, then it must conduct a *Frye* evidentiary hearing to determine general acceptance. See *Petre*, 331 Ill.App.3d at 935.

There are four ways to prove the "general acceptance" of a methodology or scientific principle. An expert may use scientific publications, prior judicial decisions, practical applications and the testimony of others in the same field. See *Mitchell v. Palos Community Hosp.*, 317 Ill. App. 3d 754, 762, 251 Ill. Dec. 395, 740 N.E.2d 476 (1st Dist. 2000). Finally, once a methodology or scientific principle or technique is deemed generally accepted pursuant to the *Frye* standard, it is established as a mailer of law. See *Donaldson v. Central Illinois Public Service Co.*, 199 Ill. 2d 63, 262 Ill. Dec. 854, 767 N.E.2d 314 (2002) (abrogated by, In re Commitment of Simons, 213 Ill. 2d 523, 290 Ill. Dec. 610, 821 N.E.2d 1184 (2004)).

As stated in *In re Marriage of Jawad and Whalen*, 326 Ill. App. 3d 141, 259 Ill. Dec. 941, 759 N.E.2d 1002 (2d Dist. 2001):

> Although Illinois has not adopted the standard for admission of scientific testimony articulated in *Daubert v. Merrell Dow Pharmaceuticals, Inc.*, 509 U.S. 579, 113 S. Ct. 2786, 125 L. Ed. 2d 469, 37 Fed. R. Evid. Serv. 1 (1993), several Illinois courts have utilized Daubert's discussion of "scientific knowledge" to determine what constitutes scientific testimony. See *Whiting v. Coultrip*, 324 Ill. App. 3d 161, 166, 258 Ill. Dec. 111, 755 N.E.2d 494 (3d Dist. 2001), as modified on denial of reh'g, (Sept. 12, 2001); *Harris v. Cropmate Co.*, 302 Ill. App. 3d 364, 369, 235 Ill. Dec. 795, 706 N.E.2d 55 (4th Dist. 1999) (abrogated by, Donaldson v. Central Illinois Public Service Co., 199 Ill. 2d 63, 262 Ill. Dec. 854, 767 N.E.2d 314 (2002)), abrogated on other grounds by *Donaldson v. Central Illinois Public Service Co.*, 199 Ill. 2d 63, 262 Ill. Dec. 854, 767 N.E.2d 314 (2002) (abrogated by, In re Commitment of Simons, 213 Ill. 2d 523, 290 Ill. Dec. 610, 821 N.E.2d 1184 (2004)). In *Daubert*, the United States Supreme Court explained that "science" is a process whereby theories arc proposed and refined. To qualify as "scientific knowledge," an inference or assertion must be derived by the scientific method. *Daubert*, 509 U.S. at 590. In short, a 'scientific expert" is an expert who relies on the application of scientific principles, rather than on skill or experience-based observations, for the basis of his opinion. *Harris*, 302 Ill.App.3d at 369.

The court in *Jawad* held that the proffered scientific testimony met the initial requirement that the testimony be reliable since the expert therein, Dabbagh, testified that her evaluation was predicated upon factors identified in studies and literature authored by certain psychologists and that she examined the evidence in the case to determine whether these factors were present. The court reasoned that it was, therefore, apparent that Dabbagh's opinions relied on the application of psychological studies and literature. However, as scientific evidence, the trial court was then obligated to conduct a *Frye* hearing to determine whether the scientific theory upon which the evidence was based was novel and, if so, whether the scientific theory has gained general acceptance in the relevant scientific community. See *People v. Miller*, 173 Ill. 2d 167, 188, 219 Ill. Dec. 43, 670 N.E.2d 721 (1996) (abrogated by, In re Commitment of Simons, 213 Ill. 2d 523, 290 Ill. Dec. 610, 821 N.E.2d 1184 (2004)). Without a determination that the science relied upon by Dabbagh has been accepted by the relevant scientific community, her testimony lacked the necessary foundation to be admitted into evidence and should not have been considered by the trial court.

II. Professor *[defense expert witness]*'s opinions that *[name of mother]*'s maternal (endogenous) force caused *[name of infant plaintiff]*'s brachial plexus injury should be barred pursuant to the general acceptance or *Frye* standard

Amongst the various reasons that would justify this Court barring Professor *[defense expert witness]* from testifying to her opinions on how brachial plexus injuries are caused and, specifically how *[name of infant plaintiff]*'s brachial plexus injury was caused, is that her method is new to science and based on invalid, unsubstantiated evidence. In addition, as a biomechanical engineer, she lacks the "knowledge, skill, experience, training, or education in a somewhat reliable area" and her "testimony would (not) assist the jury in understanding the evidence."

A. Professor Grim Lacks Personal Experience Dealing With Shoulder Dystocia and with Modification to the MADYMO Model

- Professor *[defense expert witness]* has never attended a live delivery where a shoulder dystocia has occurred. (*[defense expert witness] [page number of deposition / statement]*)

- The sole basis of her work is a computer model referred to as MADYMO ("mathematical dynamic model"), a commercially available computer software package out of the Netherlands that was originally designed to simulate motor vehicle crash situations and to assess the injuries sustained by victims of automobile crashes. (*[defense expert witness] [page number of deposition / statement]*)

• Lacking specific information necessary to model a particular delivery, such as the delivery of *[name of infant plaintiff]*, Professor *[defense expert witness]* can only use the MADYMO computer software as a generalized model. (*[defense expert witness] [page number of deposition / statement]*)

• *[defense expert witness]* did not personally take any steps to modify the MADYMO model for the purpose of the shoulder dystocia study. As a professor, she oversaw her students and post-docs doing that work. (*[defense expert witness] [page number of deposition / statement]*)

• *[defense expert witness]* never did any experiments on actual infant tissue. (*[defense expert witness] [page number of deposition / statement]*)

B. Assumptions Used In the MADYMO Model Do Not Reflect Reality

Professor *[defense expert witness]* utilized numerous assumptions in utilizing the model to reach conclusions. (*[defense expert witness] [page number of deposition / statement]*) She had to make some assumptions on properties of the various tissues with respect to the fetus. The neck of the fetus was modeled based on work done at the Medical College of Wisconsin looking at animal models to predict properties of infant necks. In addition, they modeled the properties of the brachial plexus itself based again on animal tissue studies, looking at nerve deformation properties.

Assumptions about the fetal neck were based on work at the Medical College of Wisconsin by Pintar and Yogandan, who looked at a goat model because it's an upright neck, with a similar load bearing structure to the human neck, and they have done work looking at tensile stiffness in the neck and bending stiffness in the neck so that they can, they're using it to develop models hr automotive impact but [defense expert witness] claims that the similar properties apply in these sorts of situations. (*[defense expert witness] [page number of deposition / statement]*)

However, when pressed, Professor *[defense expert witness]* admitted that there are differences between a human fetal neck and a goat fetal neck:

> There are differences in terms of surrounding soft tissue. A goat has actually, even a neonatal goat, has more head and neck

control than a human neonate does, so you would expect the musculature to be more developed. That will affect the stiffness to some degree. There's some anatomical differences in terms of size of the various vertebrae and structures, but then if we get into specifies, seeing we don't have the data we need on the human side for much of this, we're taking our best estimate in terms of these animal models. (*[defense expert witness] [page number of deposition/statement]*)

In her further testimony, Professor *[defense expert witness]* admitted that she was not involved in making any adjustments from adult to neonate anatomy and does not know what her student, *[name of student assistant]*, did to adjust for differences between fetal goat necks and human fetal necks:

Q. So when you utilize the animal models, do you take the information as it came from the Medical College of Wisconsin work?

A. Yes. From...

Q. You took...you took that raw data from fetal goat necks and used it to do your work with your model?

A. Or infant goat necks, yes

Q. But you didn't make any adjustments for any differences between infant or fetal goat necks and human fetal or infant necks; true?

A. Well, what we took was the general behavior in terms of tensile stiffness and bending stiffness and then modeled that, and I believe that *[name of student assistant]* may have scaled it down slightly to account for some just general anatomical differences just as he scaled shoulder properties from adult shoulder down to a neonate because you can't take one to one property correlations.

Q. You did not do that yourself?

A. 1 did not personally do that

Q. Do you know exactly what *[name of student assistant]* did in taking this information regarding goat necks and doing something with it before it was put into the MADYMO birth model?

A. I would have to review his notes to know exactly what he did.

Q. At this point you don't know?

A. No. (*[defense expert witness] [page number of deposition/statement]*)

Consequently, Plaintiffs suggest that Professor *[defense expert witness]* lacks the knowledge to lay a proper foundation for the court to allow in evidence based on the MADYMO model.

Similarly, Professor *[defense expert witness]* lacks sufficient knowledge to lay a foundation for admission of any evidence from the MADYMO model regarding a human infant's brachial plexus. In the MADYMO model, the properties of rabbit tibial nerves were used to estimate the mechanical properties of a human brachial plexus. (*[defense expert witness] [page number of deposition / statement]*) However, Professor *[defense expert witness]* admitted that she does not know if the properties of the rabbit tibial nerve used in the MADYMO birth model arc similar to the properties of the human brachial plexus:

Q. What is the difference between humans and goats regarding the brachial plexus area?

A. Well, we didn't use... We didn't look at goat brachial plexus. What we did look at was properties of rabbit tibial nerves and then used those to estimate the mechanical properties of our brachial plexus.

Q. Do you know if the rabbit tibial nerve has the same stiffness as a human brachial plexus, particularly of an infant brachial plexus.

A. No because the human data is not available (*[defense expert witness] [page number of deposition / statement]*).

In addition, in using the MADYMO model Professor *[defense expert witness]* also had to assume the direction of the endogenous force:

Q. Any other assumptions that you utilized?

A. We obviously had to assume a direction in which the endogenous force, the maternal forces were applied because the actual force environment within the uterus is not well-characterized. So we assumed that that occurred along the axis of the fetus's body. (*[defense expert witness] [page number of deposition / statement]*)

Q. Three assumptions, neck, brachia plexus and direction of maternal endogenous force?

A. Those would be the primary. Obviously, with a model, in many ways everything is an assumption in that you are defining your anatomy. I mean we're defining the anatomy of a 90th percentile fetus. We're defining the anatomy of a maternal pelvis. So we've selected what those are going to be based on general anatomy that's available, so you can even state that those are assumptions of some degree. (*[defense expert witness] [page number of deposition / statement].*)

Professor *[defense expert witness]* is unable to substantiate whether the assumptions of size assumed for certain dimensions were at all similar to those of *[plaintiff]*. For the fetal general anatomy, they selected 3,850 grams for the weight of the infant, a head circumference of 36.2 cm, and for the shoulder dimension a biacromial diameter of 14.2 cm, thoracic circumference of 31.3 cm, and for the chest size it was an ellipsoid defined by the thoracic diameter. Other than the infant weight, Professor *[defense expert witness]* does not know the various other anatomical shapes or sizes for *[infant plaintiff]*. (*[defense expert witness] [page number of deposition / statement].*)

C. Overall, the MADYMO Model Was Not Developed to Model The Conditions Present During the Delivery of *[infant plaintiff]*

Rather than being offered as a reliable, accepted method by which to analyze the delivery of *[infant plaintiff]* by utilizing the conditions that existed during the actual delivery, Professor *[defense expert witness]* acknowledged that "we did not develop this model to model any particular birth. In particular we did not develop it to model this case." (*[defense expert witness] [page number of deposition / statement].*) She was not using the MADYMO model to predict injury. (*[defense expert witness] [page number of deposition / statement].*)

Without even knowing the precise conditions that prevailed at the time, Professor *[defense expert witness]* testified to the limitations inherent in the MADYMO birth model:

> Q Does your model take into consideration any of the uterine resistance forces?
>
> A. No. We do not take… and I would characterize it more as the birth canal resistance forces more than the uterine. (*[defense expert witness] [page number of deposition / statement].*)
>
> Q. Does your model take into consideration movement of the fetus during birth?
>
> A. In terms of allowing the fetus to respond to forces and move passively, yes. But it does not actively move. So you don't have the fetus deciding its going to move an arm or a leg and change its position during the birth process.
>
> Q. So there's no information in your MADYMO birth model to account for any active fetal movement during the course of birth?
>
> A. Correct.
>
> Q. Did the MADYMO birth model take into consideration the fact that some babies have less muscle tone and some babies have more muscle tone than others?
>
> A. No. We were not able to look at that.
>
> Q. Would you agree that the amount of muscle tone would mean there was either less resistance or more resistance at delivery?
>
> A. It will affect to some degree resistance to delivery, but I would actually say the greater effect is going to be on how the infant is going to be able to withstand the forces that are applied to it during delivery More important in actually resisting delivery is going to be maternal muscle tone rather than fetal muscle tone.
>
> Q. So when you say the presence of less or more muscle tone will come into play more with the fetus's ability to withstand the forces placed upon it, are those both endogenous and exogenous forces?
>
> A. Yes.
>
> Q. Do you know whether some infants reflexively hunch or shrug when the physician tries to disimpact the shoulder?

A. I have no knowledge of that.

Q. That sort of clement was not placed into your MADYMO birth model, correct?

A. Correct.

Q. Regardless of the precise maneuver the physician is utilizing, would you agree if the infant reflexively shrugs or hunches its shoulders, that changes the orientation of his shoulders relative to the pelvis?

A. It can, yes.

Q. And your model does not take that into consideration, true?

A. True. (*[defense expert witness] [page number of deposition/ statement]*.)

The MADYMO model is essentially nothing more than a set of mathematical constructs. (*[defense expert witness] [page number of deposition/statement]*.) The reason why computer assessments can not be applied to clinical assessments is due to the lack of precise knowledge of what the conditions were in this one birth which prevents any such model from directly mimicking that birth. (See *[defense expert witness] [page number of deposition/statement]*.)

Professor *[defense expert witness]* has not studied whether brachial plexus injuries have occurred when proper disimpaction maneuvers are used to address shoulder dystocia.

Q. When shoulder dystocia does occur, the majority of babies are born without injury to brachial plexus if appropriate disimpaction maneuvers are used, correct?

A. All I can say is that in the majority of shoulder dystocia cases, babies are born without brachial plexus injury. I haven't been able to review cases to determine exactly what disimpaction maneuvers were used in each of those cases.

Q. Would you agree that if excessive force is used in delivery, there is an increased likelihood that the baby will be born with a brachial plexus injury?

A. I don't like to determine what's excessive because I not a clinician. But I will say as force is increased, there is always a higher likelihood statistically of injury.

Q. In terms of exogenous forces, that statement still applies?

A. Yes. (*[defense expert witness] [page number of deposition/ statement]*.)

To "add" a brachial plexus feature to this mechanical, mathematical model, a spring was used:

Q. How do you add a brachial plexus to this model?

A. It's modeled actually as a simple spring element that attached at one point at the cervical spine and at the other point at the arm. So it's a fairly rudimentary model at this point, but it at least gives us an indication, by including typical deformation properties of a nerve, gives us some indication of the differences in stretch that are going to occur.

Q. This spring that was added into the computer program, springs have, in real life, different compressive or expansive faculties, you get them compressed with less force or more force. How did you know what... What force am I talking about in the spring?

A. The spring we looked at was actually just a pulling force, a tensile force, because nerves are more like pieces of string than they are like actual springs in that if you take a nerve and you compress it, all that happens is it buckles. It doesn't carry that compressive force. So we modeled a spring that could only carry a tensile force so a pulling forte, and the properties and how it responds to that force were based on the rabbit tibial nerve studies that I referenced before.

Q. Why the rabbit tibial nerve?

A. Because there's data actually available.

Q. Is there any similarity between rabbit tibial nerves and human brachial plexus nerves?

A. They are composed of the same structures in terms of the components of the tissue and the size is reasonably similar to a, an infant brachial plexus. That is why we thought it would be an appropriate model.

Q. Are there any differences between the two?

A. There might be differences in myclination in that we do know that infants take more time to completely myclinate their nerves. Myelin is the outside sheath of a nerve. Its a protein structure that helps with nerve conduction.

Q. So is myclination the formation of the outer structure?

A. It's not the outer connective tissue. Obviously an infant nerve holds together and can withstand some force, but you get a protein structure around the nerve that acts almost like an insulator does in wiring, and so it helps with conduction of nerve properties. That might have some effect on the nerve properties. But I would actually expect that if, in terms of the differences we would expect from fetal nerve to our rabbit tibial nerves, that the fetal nerve is going to be less stiff so will deform more if a force is applied than the rabbit nerve because of these differences in tissue development. (*[defense expert witness] [page number of deposition/statement].*)

Q. Is that difference something that was put into the computer?

A. No. because what we were trying to do with our computer model, and this goes back to Dr. Gonik's comments about not being directly applicable to a clinical case. So we're not saying necessarily that these are the numerically accurate threes that would be required to deliver a particular baby or the numerically accurate stretches that are going to occur in a brachial plexus but we can compare and say given a particular situation, how do things change based on what you do, so we felt it was a reasonable estimate. (*[defense expert witness] [page number of deposition/statement]*.)

Although Professor *[defense expert witness]*'s model used a single spring to represent the brachial plexus, in reality the brachial plexus is not a single nerve; it is comprised of multiple nerves. The MA model does not account for that. (*[defense expert witness] [page number of deposition/statement]*.) Furthermore, the MADYMO model cannot determine anything relative to injuries based upon either endogenous or exogenous forces. Professor *[defense expert witness]* testified that through her model she "can't make an assessment on injury because we don't know the injury tolerance of the nerves." (*[defense expert witness] [page number of deposition/statement]*.)

Even though she explained that for use in the model the stiffness of adult shoulders were scaled down as a percentage in an attempt to approximate the stiffness of fetal shoulders, Professor *[defense expert witness]* nonetheless admitted that she does not know if there is a one-to-one correlation between a person's size and the stiffness of their shoulder, thereby Plaintiff respectfully submits, negating the percentage method reduction as a valid means by which to obtain an accurate measurement of fetal shoulder stiffness:

Q. ... And the results of Exhibit *[number]*, the results of that study, how would you summarize that?

A. This again showed things that were consistent with the previous study, and as I said, the shoulder of this model, in Exhibit 19, had improved over what we had done in Exhibit *[number]*, so we had made the shoulder what we call more biofidelic. It was more realistic.

Q. How?

A. By decreasing the stillness of the shoulder... Let me look just to make sure I'm precise. Okay. Model 18 was more based on the nine-month-old child that was scaled down to the 90th percentile. Exhibit 19 then included the shoulder properties that were modified from an adult. They were taken as two-and-a-half percent of the stiffness of adult shoulder. That will account for both changes in geometry. Obviously, infant's shoulders are a lot smaller than adult shoulders. There's also less give in general. The structures are much more compliant than an adult shoulder.

Q. Do you know if there is a one-to-one correlation between the size of the person and the stiffness of the shoulder?

A. Not precisely, no. (*[defense expert witness] [page number of deposition/statement]*.)

Q. And to make certain we're on the same wavelength, so I make my question clear, because you know far more about this than I do, do you know whether taking an adult shoulder and taking two percent of that accurately gives us the stiffness of the infant shoulder as it would mirror reality?

A. We felt it was a reasonable approximation and that because again we weren't trying to come up with a true clinical prediction of stretch that it was a good number to use.

Q. Okay. So tell mc in simple terms how you did it. What did you do with the adult to get down to the infant?

A. Okay. There were some properties available for adult shoulders, both cadaveric studies that have looked at how an adult shoulder deforms and you can do it in human volunteers. So you can kind of apply a force and see how much a shoulder moves when you apply a force. So we took that data and said geometrically what's the difference between the size of the adult human and the 90th percentile, and let's go a little lower than that because we know that the tissue structures are not, have not developed as much. So that's where we came up with our 2.5 percent, so that accounted for both geometry, anatomy and the properties of the tissues. And as I said, because we weren't saying the numbers we produce are precisely what you would get in a clinical experiment, we felt that that would give us a reasonable estimate (*[defense expert witness] [page number of deposition / statement].*)

Q. So the estimate of 2.5 percent was 2.5 percent of what?

A. Of the adult human shoulder stiffness so how the adult human shoulder responds to load.

Q. And the 2.5 percent was based upon a difference in size, somewhat further reduced to arrive at 2.5 percent?

A. Correct. (*[defense expert witness] [page number of deposition / statement].*)

Contrary to her theory of endogenous force causing the brachial plexus injury to *[infant plaintiff]*, Professor *[defense expert witness]* acknowledged that the resistance of the birth canal would reduce the force upon the infant and thereby reduce the force at which the anterior shoulder comes into contact with the symphysis pubis (pubic bone). Even though such resistance reduces the force upon the infant, the MADYMO model does not take into account such reduction in force and any estimate of reduction would only be speculation:

Q. The resistant force of the birth canal would reduce the amount of force upon the infant?

A. It would reduce the net force because you have forces acting in opposite directions but it would not reduce the actual uterine contraction force.

Q. By reducing the net force, does that diminish the amount of force at which the baby's shoulder or area within the clavicle and the neck would come in contact with the symphysis pubis?

A. It would actually reduce that contact force between those structures, yes.

Q. How much of a reduction would that be?

A. It depends on what the resistance force is of the birth canal, which is not anything we have any quantifiable ability to look at right now.

Q. So, in real life, you're not saying that the baby's body as it's moving in the birth canal comes up against the symphysis pubis with 30 pounds of force being applied to the shoulder area; are you?

A. No. Part of that force would be resisted by the soft tissue structures of the birth canal.

Q. Can you give mc any estimate whatsoever, based on a reasonable degree of mathematical certainty, as to the amount of reduction of that 30 pounds of force?

A. I hate to guess.

Q. Would it be guessing, just speculation?

A. Yeah. Yes.

Q. With whatever force the baby's body comes in contact with the symphysis pubis, are you assuming that the head and neck continue forward at that same amount of force?

A. Again, there's a force that's moving the baby along. So the head and neck would continue to move at the velocity that the body had been moving before it got stuck, and that then gives you your difference in motion, because the head and neck continue to move and the body stops.

Q. Do you have any numerical figures on velocity?

A. We haven't looked at it with our model and I haven't tried to determine it clinically.

Q. So you've no opinion as to the velocity of the head and neck as it goes forward, assuming the anterior shoulder becomes stuck on the symphysis pubis, correct?

A. Correct.

Q. Am I correct in understanding your testimony to conclude that there are two actions or forces which can act to reduce this amount of force and consequential amount of velocity, the resistance force of the birth canal itself, the soft tissue structures the baby comes in contact with as well as the baby's active movement on his own?

A. Yes. I would say both of those could resist.

Q. Both of those...?

A. I mean could reduce.

Q. Could reduce the force?

A. Yes.

Q. And your model did not include either of those?

A. Correct. *[page number of deposition / statement].*)

As further support for the court barring Professor *[defense expert witness]*'s testimony, she has no information as to the speed at which *[infant plaintiff]*'s head came out and then went back in when the "turtle sign" occurred. Such speed or velocity would be related to the velocity of the baby's body coming down the birth canal and ultimately, the force at which the anterior shoulder would impact the pubic bone:

Q. When turtle signs occur, it involves the head coming out and then going back in slightly?

A. Correct.

Q. Is there a difference in the rapidity in some turtle signs of the head coming out and going back in?

A. Most likely. I have not observed them so...

Q. The question then, would you think the rapidity of the turtle sign, the head going out and coming back in related to the amount of velocity?

A. Yes.

Q. The greater the velocity, the quicker the head goes out and in the less velocity, the slower the head comes out and goes back in?

A. That would be my assumption.

Q. And in this case, do you know from any source, medical records, the depositions, anywhere, anything as to the rapidity or the slowness at which *[infant plaintiff]*s head went out and came back in?

A. None of the documents I reviewed make any reference to that. (*[defense expert witness] [page number of deposition / statement]*.)

Professor *[defense expert witness]* does not know nor does she have an opinion as to the amount of force that is applied through the endogenous force at the time of birth to the baby's brachial plexus.

Q. How many pounds of traction do endogenous forces at birth apply to the brachial plexus?

A. We didn't... We would have to back it out and it would be... We'd have to do a more detailed analysis.

Q. Do you have an opinion today, within a reasonable degree of biomechanical engineering certainty, as to how many pounds of force, I sorry, how many pounds of traction, endogenous forces at birth apply to the brachial plexus?

A. To the nerve itself, no. (*[defense expert witness] [page number of deposition / statement]*.)

In her work with the MADYMO model, Professor [defense expert witness] assumed that the uterine contraction force or the maternal expulsive forces acted to push the infant out with the force directed along the axis of the infants body. She does not know if that assumption is accurate in reality and characterized it as "our best guess" since the model did not prove that assumption was correct. (*[defense expert witness] [page number of deposition / statement]*.)

Specifically, Professor does not know nor does she have an opinion as to the amount of maternal endogenous force that was applied to *[infant plaintiff]* at the time of birth:

Q. Is there any reason to believe that there was more than 19 or less than 20 pounds of axial traction applied to [infant plaintiff] while in utero?

A. I cannot make an assertion. We don't have any intrauterine pressure measurements in this case with an intrauterine pressure catheter, so we cannot determine what amount of maternal endogenous force was applied. (*[defense expert witness] [page number of deposition/statement]*.)

Q. Next portion of your opinion is the occurrence of injury in this case was likely increased by the amount of force generated by [plaintiff] during the delivery process, the rapid rate of movement through the birth canal as indicated by the short second stage of labor and individual factors which made this child more susceptible to injury. Right?

A. Correct.

Q. In your opinion, what was the amount of force generated by [plaintiff]?

A. We cannot quantify that.

Q. You don't know?

A. No. (*[defense expert witness] [page number of deposition/statement]*.)

D. Professor *[defense expert witness]* Can Not Cite Any Medical Literature In Support Of Her Maternal Endogenous Force Theory of Causation

Lastly, other than the MADYMO model, Professor can not cite any other support in any medical literature to support her endogenous force theory of causation:

Q. Can you cite any literature, medical literature to support this statement or this opinion, rather, that most brachial plexus injuries occur at the time of initial impaction of the shoulder with the symphysis pubis?

A. Our model would be what that is based on.

Q. Can you cite any medical literature to support the statement?

A. There's no medical literature that's been able to tease out the time frame of when these injuries occur. However, there's anecdotal evidence of injuries occurring with physicians just watching the baby, so no physician-applied traction. And so that fits into... that backs up this opinion. (*[defense expert witness] [page number of deposition/statement]*.)

Similarly, she can not point to any medical literature to support her theory that brachial plexus injury in newborn infants is due to a stretching of the brachial plexus resulting from the differential motion between the head/neck and torso of the fetus at the time of birth:

Q. Can you cite any medical literature to support that opinion?

A. That's a basic tenet of biomechanics. And any of the literature on adult brachial plexus injury would back that up, that the mechanism of injury is due to one part of the body stopping and another part of the body continuing to move.

Q. Can you cite any medical literature regarding this situation occurring in birth cases?

A. That hasn't been looked at. It hasn't been looked at. (*[defense expert witness] [page number of deposition / statement].*)

WHEREFORE, Plaintiffs, *[infant plaintiff]*, a minor, by her mother and next friend, *[plaintiff]*, and *[plaintiff]*, individually, respectfully request this Court to enter an Order barring each of the Defendants from calling *[defense expert witness]*, PhD to testify based on the above-discussed arguments.

Respectfully submitted,
[name of attorney]
Attorneys for Plaintiffs
By: ______________________
[name of attorney]

[attorney for defendant]
[name of firm]
[address]
[telephone number]
[fax number]

§ 10:213 Motion to admit evidence of laboratory testing regarding firearm residue

TO: ALL PARTIES AND THEIR RESPECTIVE ATTORNEYS OF RECORD:

PLEASE TAKE NOTICE that plaintiff hereby moves this Court for an order admitting evidence, references to evidence, testimony and argument relating to laboratory testing regarding firearm residue. This motion is based upon the grounds that such testing has been deemed to be based upon reliable methodology and thus, evidence regarding such testing is admissible without a *Frye* hearing. This Motion is also based upon the supporting Memorandum of Points and Authorities, the pleadings and papers on file in this action, and upon such argument and evidence as may be presented prior to or at the hearing of this matter.

Dated: *[date]*

MEMORANDUM OF POINTS AND AUTHORITIES

1. PRELIMINARY STATEMENT

This action arises from an incident on January 1, 2007, when plaintiff claims that defendant negligently discharged his gun and as a result, shot plaintiff in the leg. Throughout the discovery in this matter, defendant has repeatedly denied discharging his gun.

Pursuant to laboratory testing performed by Dr. Julianne Smith, forensic scientist, in lab report number 502319, dated January 15, 2009, defendant was found to have gun shot residue on and about his person, based upon samples that were obtained from defendant, within one hour of the incident in question. By this motion, plaintiff seeks an order admitting any and all evidence pertaining to laboratory testing performed by Dr. Julianne Smith, forensic scientist, in lab report number 502319, dated January 15, 2009.

2. THIS COURT MAY ADMIT RELEVANT EVIDENCE IN ADVANCE OF TRIAL BY WAY OF AN IN LIMINE MOTION

Under Illinois law, this Court has authority to grant a motion in limine, prior to trial, which specifically admits certain evidence. *People v. Drum*, 321 Ill.App.3d 1005, 1008, 748 N.E.2d 344, 254 Ill.Dec. 898 (4th Dist. 2001). Through this motion, plaintiff seeks a pre-trial order permitting the introduction of evidence regarding laboratory testing performed by Dr. Julianne Smith, forensic scientist, in lab report number 502319, dated January 15, 2009, wherein defendant was found to have gun shot residue on and about his person, based upon samples that were obtained from defendant, within one hour of the incident in question.

Federal Rule of Evidence 401 defines relevancy as: evidence having any tendency to make the existence of any fact that is of consequence to the determination of the action more probable or less probable than it would be without the evidence. Illinois has adopted this definition of relevancy through case law. *Spencer v. Wandolowski*, 264 Ill. App. 3d 611, 617, 201 Ill. Dec. 422, 636 N.E.2d 854 (1st Dist. 1994); and *People v. Monroe*, 66 Ill. 2d 317, 321–22, 5 Ill. Dec. 824, 362 N.E.2d 295 (1977). In light of the fact that defendant denies that he ever discharged his firearm at the time of the incident at issue, the fact that he was found to have gun shot residue on and about his person, based upon samples that were obtained from defendant, within one hour of the incident in question, is clearly relevant information for the jury to consider.

Based upon the fact that evidence pertaining to laboratory testing performed by Dr. Julianne Smith, forensic scientist, in lab report number 502319, dated January 15, 2009 is clearly relevant, this Court should allow the admission of that evidence at the trial in this case.

3. GUN SHOT RESIDUE TESTING IS ADMISSIBLE IN ILLINOIS COURTS WITHOUT FIRST HOLDING A *FRYE* HEARING

Illinois courts have already considered the issue of whether gun shot residue testing is based upon an accepted and reliable methodology. In fact, Illinois courts have specifically determined that gun shot residue tests are based upon reliable methodology and thus, are admissible into evidence. *People v. Cole*, 170 Ill.App.3d 912, 926–32, 524 N.E.2d 926, 120 Ill.Dec. 744 (1st Dist. 1988). *See also State v. Fuller*, 56 Conn.App. 592, 612–17, 744 A.2d 931 (2000) and *Jones v. State*, 277 Ga. 36, 37–38, 586 S.E.2d 224 (2003). Due to the fact that the admissibility of gun shot residue testing has already been determined by Illinois Courts, such testing should be admitted without a *Frye* hearing. See *In re Commitment of Simons*, 213 Ill.2d 523, 529–44, 821 N.E.2d 1184, 290 Ill.Dec. 610 (2004); *Noakes v. Nat. Railroad Passenger Corp.*, 363 Ill.App.3d 851, 855–59, 845 N.E.2d 14, 300 Ill.Dec. 593 (1st Dist. 2006); *Frye v. U.S.*, 293 F. 1013 (D.C. Cir. 1923).

Based upon the forgoing facts and circumstances, this Court should enter an order admitting any and all evidence pertaining to laboratory testing performed by Dr. Julianne Smith, forensic scientist, in lab report number 502319, dated January 15, 2009.

4. CONCLUSION

Based on the foregoing, plaintiff respectfully requests that this Court enter an order admitting any and all evidence pertaining to laboratory testing performed by Dr. Julianne Smith, forensic scientist, in lab report number 502319, dated January 15, 2009.

Dated: *[date]*

By: ________________
[name of counsel]
Attorneys for Plaintiff,
[name of plaintiff]

§ 10:214 Motion to exclude surveillance video

TO: ALL PARTIES AND THEIR RESPECTIVE ATTORNEYS OF RECORD:

PLEASE TAKE NOTICE that plaintiff hereby moves this Court for an order excluding any and all evidence, references to evidence, opinions, testimony or argument relating to an alleged "surveillance video" This motion is based upon the grounds that the video is speculative, improper character evidence, irrelevant and unfairly prejudicial. This motion is also based upon the supporting Memorandum of Points and Authorities, the pleadings and papers on file in this action, and upon such argument and evidence as may be presented prior to or at the hearing of this matter.

Dated: *[date]*

MEMORANDUM OF POINTS AND AUTHORITIES

1. PRELIMINARY STATEMENT

This action is based upon a rear end collision, wherein plaintiff alleges that, on July 18, 2008, her vehicle was struck by defendant's vehicle, causing her damages, pain and suffering.

During the discovery of this matter, defendant disclosed an alleged "surveillance video" of plaintiff. The video contains 5 hours of video of a person, purported to be plaintiff, engaging in a variety of daily activities and tasks. By this motion, plaintiff seeks an order excluding evidence of the alleged "surveillance video," as speculative, improper character evidence, irrelevant and unfairly prejudicial.

2. THIS COURT MAY EXCLUDE PREJUDICIAL AND MISLEADING EVIDENCE IN ADVANCE OF TRIAL BY WAY OF AN IN LIMINE MOTION

This Court has authority to grant a motion in limine, in advance of trial, which excludes inadmissible evidence, as well as any and all reference by the parties, attorneys and witnesses to the inadmissible evidence. *Cunningham v. Millers General Ins. Co.*, 227 Ill.App.3d 201, 205, 591 N.E.2d 80, 169 Ill.Dec. 200 (4th Dist. 1992); *Cochran v. Great Atlantic &*

Pacific Tea Co., 203 Ill.App.3d 935, 937–38, 561 N.E.2d 229, 148 Ill.Dec. 923 (5th Dist 1990). In fact, "[w]here the evidence could be prejudicial, an order granting a motion in limine may be safer than an order denying it; the evidence will then be kept out until it is clear it should be admitted." *Cunningham v. Millers General Ins. Co.*, 227 Ill.App.3d at 205.

Under Illinois law, evidence should be excluded when the prejudicial impact of the evidence outweighs the probative value of it. Federal Rule of Evidence 403 states: Although relevant, evidence may be excluded if its probative value is substantially outweighed by the danger of unfair prejudice, confusion of the issues, or misleading the jury, or by considerations of undue delay, waste of time, or needless presentation of cumulative evidence. Illinois has a common-law rule that is comparable to Federal Rule of Evidence 403. See *People v. Peete*, 318 Ill. App. 3d 961, 966–67, 252 Ill. Dec. 821, 743 N.E.2d 689 (4th Dist. 2001); *People v. Walker*, 335 Ill. App. 3d 102, 112, 268 Ill. Dec. 654, 779 N.E.2d 268 (2d Dist. 2002), as modified on denial of reh'g, (Oct. 24, 2002) and judgment aff'd, 211 Ill. 2d 317, 285 Ill. Dec. 519, 812 N.E.2d 339 (2004). In fact, case law demonstrates that surveillance videos should be excluded when they are shown to be unduly prejudicial or confusing. *Donnellan v. First Student, Inc*, 383 Ill.App.3d 1040, 1053–56, 891 N.E.2d 463 (1st Dist. 2008) (a surveillance video was properly excluded as unfairly prejudicial and confusing).

A review of the video in this matter shows that there is no time and date stamp to reflect when the video was taken. Under Illinois law, in order to provide foundation for a surveillance videotape or photographs, without witness testimony, there must be sufficient proof of the reliability and accuracy of the process that produced the images. *People v. Vaden*, 336 Ill.App.3d 893, 897-99784 N.E.2d 410, 271 Ill.Dec. 192 (3rd Dist. 2003); see also *People v. Baltimore*, 381 Ill.App.3d 115, 117–22, 885 N.E.2d 1096, 319 Ill.Dec. 416 (2nd Dist. 2008). Moreover, there is insufficient clarity in the video to determine who is depicted on the video during many portions of the video, making the images misleading and prejudicial. Furthermore, some of the images depict a person alleged to be plaintiff drinking alcohol at a bar, which is prejudicial and irrelevant to this action and represents improper character evidence. *People v. Collette*, 217 Ill. App. 3d 465, 467–71, 160 Ill. Dec. 420, 577 N.E.2d 550 (4th Dist. 1991) (trial court properly restricted certain questions regarding the witness' past alcohol use); *Ryan v. McEvoy*, 20 Ill. App. 3d 562, 566–67, 315 N.E.2d 38 (1st Dist. 1974) (asking a witness about past alcohol use was improper).

Based upon the forgoing facts and circumstances, this Court should enter an order excluding any and all evidence, references to evidence, opinions, testimony or argument relating to the alleged "surveillance video."

3. THE "SURVEILLANCE VIDEO" IS SPECULATIVE AND IRRELEVANT TO THIS ACTION

Federal Rule of Evidence 401 defines relevancy as: evidence having any tendency to make the existence of any fact that is of consequence to the determination of the action more probable or less probable than it would be without the evidence. Illinois has adopted this definition of relevancy through case law. *Spencer v. Wandolowski*, 264 Ill. App. 3d 611, 617, 201 Ill. Dec. 422, 636 N.E.2d 854 (1st Dist. 1994); and *People v. Monroe*, 66 Ill. 2d 317, 321–22, 5 Ill. Dec. 824, 362 N.E.2d 295 (1977). Evidence may be properly excluded where it is not relevant to matters at issue. See *Cochran v. Great Atlantic & Pacific Tea Co., Inc.*, 203 Ill. App. 3d 935, 937–38, 148 Ill. Dec. 923, 561 N.E.2d 229 (5th Dist. 1990) (trial judge has inherent power to exclude irrelevant evidence); and *Benson v. Bradford Mut. Fire Ins. Corp.*, 121 Ill. App. 3d 500, 510, 76 Ill. Dec. 774, 459 N.E.2d 689, 47 A.L.R.4th 759 (2d Dist. 1984) (trial judge had discretion to exclude irrelevant witness testimony) and *Pagel v. Yates*, 128 Ill. App. 3d 897, 903, 84 Ill. Dec. 180, 471 N.E.2d 946 (4th Dist. 1984) (exclusion of irrelevant and confusing document).

The surveillance video at issue contains 5 hours of video of a person, purported to be plaintiff, engaging in a variety of daily activities and tasks. A review of the video shows that there is no time and date stamp to verify when the video was taken. Moreover, there is insufficient clarity in the video to determine who is depicted on the video during many portions of the video, making the images irrelevant and speculative. Furthermore, many of the images on the video have no relationship to any of the facts in issue in this case. Thus, the Court should exclude any and all evidence, references to evidence, opinions, testimony or argument relating to the alleged "surveillance video," as speculative and irrelevant.

4. CONCLUSION

Based on the foregoing, plaintiff respectfully requests that this Court enter an order excluding any and all evidence, references to evidence, opinions, testimony or argument relating to the alleged "surveillance video."

Dated: *[date]*

By: ____________________
[name of counsel]
Attorneys for Plaintiff,
[name of plaintiff]

APPENDIX A

Directory of Sample Motions on CD-ROM

§ A:1 How to use this appendix and CD-ROM

On the following pages, you will find a list of sample in limine motions submitted by a cross-section of civil and criminal attorneys from around the state of Illinois. The referenced samples are located on the companion CD-ROM provided with this text. The motion files are numbered to correlate with the numbering on the pages that follow. Readers may access the samples in the Appendix directory on the CD-ROM by double-clicking the desired file or opening the file from within Adobe Acrobat Reader software. The document may be viewed or printed from Acrobat Reader. (If Acrobat is not already installed on your system, a free copy of this software is included on the CD-ROM.)

Readers may browse the following pages to locate samples that may be helpful in their own practice. In this Appendix, you will first find a quick overview of the sample motions followed by a list with more detailed descriptions. Contact information for the contributing attorney or firm is also provided in the detailed list. Each sample is identified by the evidence sought to be excluded, the party making the motion (e.g., plaintiff, defense, complainant, etc.) and the type of underlying case (e.g., medical malpractice, personal injury, etc.).

Note that any case law or argument is only truly relevant with respect to the facts of the case in which the original motion was filed. Readers should conduct follow-up research, including cite checking, to ensure the ongoing applicability of the citations or arguments.

§ A:2 Editor's note

The motions provided herein are, for the most part, from actual cases and are published as they appeared when filed or submitted for consideration (unless redacted per the request of the submitting attorney). As any practicing litigator knows, time constraints often limit the ability to fine tune motions in limine, which are typically filed under tight trial deadlines. As such, the motions found herein may not be perfectly "polished." The power of these samples, in our opinion, is in the creativity of the argument and in the citations included, and we feel the samples will be of great assistance to the readers of this text. If you have any sample motions to contribute to future editions, please contact the publisher and/or authors.

§ A:3 Overview of sample motions on CD-ROM

A-101. Defense motion to bar plaintiff's expert psychologist's opinions on the basis that he is not qualified to render opinions and the opinions are not reliable. (Sexual harassment.)

A-102a. Plaintiff motion to bar defense expert doctor's testimony regarding other unknown causes of the plaintiff's injury based upon speculation and lack of foundation. (Premises liability.)

A-102b. Plaintiff motion to bar defense reconstruction expert from testifying on opinion of speed of vehicle where not beyond the ken of the jury. (Motor vehicle.)

A-103. Plaintiff's motion to bar argument regarding correlation between severity of impact between vehicles and unclaimed injuries that occurred as a result thereof or the introduction of any photographs of the vehicles. (Motor vehicle.)

A-104. Miscellaneous motions by plaintiff or complainant. (Personal injury and employment.)

A-105. Defendant's response to plaintiff's motion regarding sole proximate cause defense. (Medical malpractice.)

A-106. Plaintiff's motion to bar references to unsupported medical theories of injury causation. (Police brutality.)

A-107. Plaintiff's motion to exclude results of blood alcohol test. (Personal injury.)

A-108. Plaintiff's motion to bar testimony of accident reconstruction expert based on lack of foundation. (Personal injury.)

A-109. Motion by plaintiff covering 30 items to be excluded, including several covering blood alcohol issues. (Personal injury and wrongful death.)

A-110. Plaintiff's motions for trial sanctions for violation of court's orders to produce and discovery abuse. (Includes initial motion and supplemental motions.) (Employment.)

A-111. Plaintiff's response to defendant's motion in limine regarding tax consequences of any award in (Employment discrimination.)

A-112a. Plaintiff's motion to bar evidence of test results from blood alcohol test. (Personal injury.)

A-112b. Plaintiff's motion to bar defense expert's testimony regarding intoxication based upon speculation, misleading, and lack of foundation. (Personal injury.)

A-112c. Plaintiff's motion to bar defense expert's testimony regarding intoxication on basis that it lacks foundation and was not a proximate cause of the incident or plaintiff's injuries. (Personal injury.)

A-113. Various motions by plaintiff. (Personal injury, products liability, medical malpractice.)

A-114. Motion by plaintiff with 49 separate motions in case where defendants admitted liability.

A-115. Motions filed by defense counsel in United States District Court, Northern District of Indiana. (Motion can be used as a guide for cases pending in Illinois' Federal Court.)

A-116. Various motions by defense. (Personal injury and products liability.)

A-117. Various motions by plaintiff. (Personal injury.)

A-118. Various motions by defense. (Criminal.)

A-119. Various motions by defense. (Medical malpractice.)

A-120. Motion by defense to bar plaintiff's nursing expert from criticizing defendant nurse (plaintiff's expert is a registered nurse, while defendant nurse is a licensed practical nurse). (Medical malpractice.)

A-121a. Plaintiff's motion to bar defendant's from arguing that plaintiff's medical costs will be reduced because of care provided by the family. (Personal injury.)

A-121b. Plaintiff's motion to bar defendant's annuity expert. (Personal injury.)

A-122. Plaintiff's motion and memorandum of law in support of motion to bar evidence of prior injuries. (Form motion not specific to any case.) (Personal injury.)

A-123. Plaintiff's motion to strike affirmative defense of contributory negligence. (Two samples.) (Product liability.)

A-124. Defendant's motion to bar evidence of billed costs of medical services which were not actually paid. (Personal injury.)

A-125. Plaintiff's motion to bar reference to smoking. (Personal injury.)

A-126. Various defense motions. (Medical malpractice.)

A-127a. Plaintiff's motion to bar defendants from cross-examining the expert named by co-defendant where defendant had adopted co-defendant's expert as its own expert and interests in the case identical. (Medical Malpractice.)

A-127b. Plaintiff's motion to bar evidence that certain individuals, previously joined as defendants, were voluntarily dismissed without payment. (Medical Malpractice.)

A-128a. Various motions by plaintiff (8 motions). (Personal injury.)

A-128b. Plaintiff's motion to bar defendant's affirmative defense of misuse. (Defective product.)

A-128c. Motion by plaintiff to bar evidence of delay in treatment. (Personal injury.)

A-128d. Plaintiff's Memorandum of Law in support of right to "back-strike" potential jurors. (General.)

A-128e. Plaintiff's motion to admit evidence of current and subsequent consumer products safety commission standards. (Defective product.)

A-128f. Plaintiff's motion to admit evidence of feasible alternative design. (Defective product.)

A-129. Defendant's motion to sever action so that trials of two defendants take place separately due to prejudice. (Medical Malpractice.)

A-130. Various motions by defense. (Personal injury and medical malpractice.)

A-131. Several motions by plaintiff. (Personal injury and medical malpractice.)

A-132. Plaintiff's motion to bar defendants from using any transcript of proceedings from the mandatory arbitration hearing. (Personal injury.)

§ A:4 Detail of sample motions on CD-ROM

A-101. Defense motion to bar plaintiff's expert psychologist's opinions on the basis that he is not qualified to render opinions and the opinions are not reliable. (Sexual harassment.)

Submitted by: Darcy L. Proctor; Ancel, Glink, Diamond, et al., Chicago, IL.

A-102a. Plaintiff motion to bar defense expert doctor's testimony regarding other unknown causes of the plaintiff's injury based upon speculation and lack of foundation. (Premises liability.)

Submitted by: Timothy J. Touhy and James B. Zouras; Touhy & Touhy, Ltd., Chicago, IL.

A-102b. Plaintiff motion to bar defense reconstruction expert from testifying on opinion of speed of vehicle where not beyond the ken of the jury. (Motor vehicle.)

Submitted by: Timothy J. Touhy and James B. Zouras; Touhy & Touhy, Ltd., Chicago, IL.

A-103. Plaintiff's motion to bar argument regarding correlation between severity of impact between vehicles and unclaimed injuries that occurred as a result thereof or the introduction of any photographs of the vehicles. (Motor vehicle.)

(Note: The SAE papers referenced as attachments in the above motion are not included with this sample. To obtain the papers, contact SAE at http://www.sae.org.)

Submitted by: Michael J. Marovich; Hiskes, Dillner, O'Donnell, et al., Orland Park, IL.

A-104. Miscellaneous motions by plaintiff or complainant. (Personal injury and employment.) Motions include:

(1) Bar evidence regarding plaintiff's acceptance of severance package in employment case.

(2) Bar evidence regarding the age of other employees retained or hired by defendants after plaintiff's termination in employment case.

(3) Bar evidence regarding defendant's treatment of other employees who filed worker's compensation claims in employment case.

(4) Bar evidence regarding defendant's treatment of other employees with disabilities in employment case.

(5) Bar evidence regarding plaintiff's previous worker's compensation claims in employment case.

(6) Bar evidence regarding defendant's treatment of other employees who requested or took leave under the FMLA in employment case.

(7) Bar evidence regarding plaintiff's convictions for driving under the influence in employment case.

(8) Bar evidence concerning the complainant's absences and tardiness in employment case before the Human Rights Commission (complainant's motion).

Submitted by: Eugene K. Hollander; Law Offices of Eugene K. Hollander, Chicago, IL.

A-105. Defendant's response to plaintiff's motion

regarding sole proximate cause defense. (Medical malpractice.)

Submitted by: James J. Stamos; Stamos & Trucco, Chicago, IL

A-106. Plaintiff's motion to bar references to unsupported medical theories of injury causation. (Police brutality.)

Submitted by: John Loevy and Blake Horwitz, Chicago, IL.

A-107. Plaintiff's motion to exclude results of blood alcohol test. (Personal injury.)

Submitted by: Charles H. Delano; Delano Law Offices, Springfield, IL.

A-108. Plaintiff's motion to bar testimony of accident reconstruction expert based on lack of foundation. (Personal injury.)

Submitted by: Charles H. Delano; Delano Law Offices, P.C.; Springfield, IL.

A-109. Motion by plaintiff covering 30 items to be excluded, including several covering blood alcohol issues. (Personal injury and wrongful death.) Motions include:

(1) Plaintiff's motion to bar results of chemical test based on failure to comply with *Frye* standard.

(2) Plaintiff's motion to bar results of blood alcohol test based on lack of foundation.

(3) Plaintiff's motion to bar evidence, records and testimony of various medical providers based on ex parte contact between defense counsel and treating physicians in violation of *Petrillo*.

(4) Plaintiff's motion to bar defense expert witness pharmacist from rendering opinions that are not beyond the ken of the average juror.

(5) Plaintiff's motion to bar defense expert witness pharmacist from testifying regarding affects of alcohol on decedent based on speculation.

(6) Plaintiff's motion to bar evidence contained in coroner's records obtained in violation of the decedent's physician-patient privilege.

(7) Plaintiff's motion to bar witnesses from testifying as to which party was negligent or not negligent.

(8) Plaintiff's motion to bar reference to the fact that no traffic ticket or arrest was made.
(9) Plaintiff's motion to bar defendant from testifying based upon Deadman's Act.
(10) Plaintiff's motion to bar argument that plaintiff's attorney objected to testimony of the defendant pursuant to the Deadman's Act.
(11) Plaintiff's motion to allow testimony of a witness regarding decedent's careful habits.
(12) Plaintiff's motion to bar defendant's expert from testifying regarding lighting conditions based upon speculation.
(13) Plaintiff's motion to bar defendant's expert's opinions concerning reaction time based upon speculation.
(14) Plaintiff's motion to bar defendant's expert's opinions not timely disclosed.
(15) Plaintiff's motion to bar evidence of decedent's prior convictions.
(16) Plaintiff's motion to bar that plaintiff's medical bills have been paid by insurance based upon collateral source rule.
(17) Plaintiff's motion to bar evidence that recovery of the plaintiff is not subject to federal income taxes.
(18) Plaintiff's motion to bar reference that plaintiff may receive future free medical care at either governmental or charitable expense.
(19) Plaintiff's motion to bar regarding joint and several liability.
(20) Plaintiff's motion to bar reference to insurance or lack of insurance.
(21) Plaintiff's motion to bar conveying idea or message that defendant must personally pay judgment.
(22) Plaintiff's motion to bar that defendant is not financially able to pay substantial judgment or financial status of the parties.
(23) Plaintiff's motion to bar custom or habit of drinking or of drinking to excess.
(24) Plaintiff's motion to bar poor work ethic.
(25) Plaintiff's motion to bar evidence of plaintiff receiving unemployment compensation.
(26) Plaintiff's motion to bar plaintiff's failure to properly report income taxes.
(27) Plaintiff's motion to bar decedent's lack of valid driver's license or loss of license due to DUI conviction.

(28) Plaintiff's motion to bar settlement discussions.
(29) Plaintiff's motion to bar experts and opinions which have not been properly disclosed.
(30) Plaintiff's motion to bar reference to fact that attorneys interviewed witness.

Submitted by: Mark Rouleau, Rockford, IL.

A-110. Plaintiff's motions for trial sanctions for violation of court's orders to produce and discovery abuse. (Includes initial motion and supplemental motions.) (Employment.)

Submitted by: Monica E. McFadden; McFadden Law Offices, Chicago, IL.

A-111. Plaintiff's response to defendant's motion in limine regarding tax consequences of any award in (Employment discrimination.)

Submitted by: Monica E. McFadden; McFadden Law Offices, Chicago, IL.

A-112a. Plaintiff's motion to bar evidence of test results from blood alcohol test. (Personal injury.)

Submitted by: Joseph R. Curcio, Chicago, IL.

A-112b. Plaintiff's motion to bar defense expert's testimony regarding intoxication based upon speculation, misleading, and lack of foundation. (Personal injury.)

Submitted by: Joseph R. Curcio, Chicago, IL.

A-112c. Plaintiff's motion to bar defense expert's testimony regarding intoxication on basis that it lacks foundation and was not a proximate cause of the incident or plaintiff's injuries. (Personal injury.)

Submitted by: Joseph R. Curcio, Chicago, IL.

A-113. Various motions by plaintiff. (Personal injury, products liability, medical malpractice.) Motions include:

(1) Plaintiff's motion in opposition to defendant's motion for leave to file affirmative defense that plaintiff was sole proximate cause of injuries.
(2) Plaintiff's motion to bar peremptory challenges based on race.

(3) Plaintiff's memorandum regarding presumption that an adequate warning will be heeded.
(4) Plaintiff's motion to exclude evidence of smoking.
(5) Plaintiff's motion to exclude expert testimony that plaintiff's cardiac arrest was caused by an amniotic fluid embolism.
(6) Plaintiff's motion to exclude evidence of opinions of non-testifying experts which defendant or defendant's medical opinion witnesses have consulted with on this case.

Submitted by: Robert J. Napleton; Motherway & Napleton, P.C., Chicago, IL.

A-114. Motion by plaintiff with 49 separate motions in case where defendants admitted liability. (Medical malpractice.) Motions include:

(1) Plaintiff's motion to bar comments that award to plaintiff is not taxable income.
(2) Plaintiff's motion to bar arguments that verdict will provide stream of income to plaintiff.
(3) Plaintiff's motion to bar argument or comment that plaintiff's request for damages constitutes get rich quick scheme or welfare program.
(4) Plaintiff's motion to bar argument that plaintiff is asking for greater amount of money than actually expected to be awarded.
(5) Plaintiff's motion to bar argument that award would amount to winning the lottery.
(6) Plaintiff's motion to bar argument that defendant's professional and personal reputations are on the line or at stake.
(7) Plaintiff's motion to bar arguments or comments regarding need for tort reform.
(8) Plaintiff's motion to bar arguments that plaintiff is required to prove specific dollar amount to be compensated for non-economic damages.
(9) Plaintiff's motion to bar comments that defense counsel is shocked by plaintiff's request for damages.
(10) Plaintiff's motion to bar comments that award will be paid out of defendant's personal assets.
(11) Plaintiff's motion to bar comments regarding defendant's wealth or ability or inability to pay judgment.
(12) Plaintiff's motion to bar evidence of defendant's good character or reputation.
(13) Plaintiff's motion to bar argument that verdict would raise insurance rates.

(14) Plaintiff's motion to bar reference to personal injury awards as being too high.
(15) Plaintiff's motion to bar argument that any award would place a burden on the public as a whole or would be responsible for high cost of living.
(16) Plaintiff's motion to bar comments that defendant hospital care would be adversely impacted by large judgment.
(17) Plaintiff's motion to bar evidence of settlement negotiations.
(18) Plaintiff's motion to bar comment regarding plaintiff's motives in prosecuting the action.
(19) Plaintiff's motion to bar evidence that plaintiff's experts have been sued.
(20) Plaintiff's motion to bar that plaintiff's representatives had disagreements with treating physicians.
(21) Plaintiff's motion to bar evidence that plaintiff's medical expenses had been paid by a third party (based upon collateral source rule).
(22) Plaintiff's motion to bar evidence that free government medical services may be available to plaintiff in the future.
(23) Plaintiff's motion to bar evidence that plaintiff could stay at government funded nursing home or similar institution using government funds in the future.
(24) Plaintiff's motion to bar evidence that defendants have or have not been named as defendants in prior lawsuits.
(25) Plaintiff's motion to bar evidence that plaintiffs have filed prior lawsuits.
(26) Plaintiff's motion to bar arguments regarding previous awards or settlements in similar cases or claims.
(27) Plaintiff's motion to bar arguments that plaintiff's injuries were caused by anything other than defendant's negligence (note: this is an admitted liability medical malpractice case).
(28) Plaintiff's motion to bar evidence that plaintiff's reduced life expectancy, if any, was caused by anything other than defendants' admitted negligence.
(29) Plaintiff's motion to bar evidence that plaintiff was contributorily negligent.
(30) Plaintiff's motion to bar evidence that plaintiff's injuries were caused by any lack of parental care (admitted negligence case).
(31) Plaintiff's motion to bar arguments that plaintiff failed to mitigate damages.

(32) Plaintiff's motion to bar any exhibit not properly disclosed.
(33) Plaintiff's motion to bar opinions that were not properly disclosed.
(34) Plaintiff' motion to bar defendant's experts from testifying beyond or inconsistent with opinions properly disclosed.
(35) Plaintiff's motion to bar testimony of defense expert that plaintiff's expert not qualified (vocational rehabilitation expert).
(36) Plaintiff's motion to bar argument that plaintiff's life care plan expert is not qualified.
(37) Plaintiff's motion to bar argument that plaintiff's vocational rehabilitation expert is not qualified to testify because he is not an economist.
(38) Plaintiff's motion to bar argument that 0% net discount rate, a "pure offset", is not a generally accepted method of calculating the present cash value of future damages.
(39) Plaintiff's motion to bar comments that defense expert is "leading expert on cerebral palsy and/or life expectancy".
(40) Plaintiff's motion to bar argument that plaintiff's injuries are related or secondary to overdue birth (admitted liability case).
(41) Plaintiff's motion to bar evidence that opinion witnesses have failed board certification examinations.
(42) Plaintiff's motion to bar comments that plaintiffs have consulted with jury consultant.
(43) Plaintiff's motion to bar defense counsel from asking jurors during voir dire whether they would feel uncomfortable awarding a verdict for millions of dollars.
(44) Plaintiff's motion to allow showing a day in the life video to potential jurors during voir dire.
(45) Plaintiff's motion to bar defendants from commenting that they have admitted liability from the beginning of this action since they did not admit liability until approximately 2-1/2 years after the original complaint was filed.
(46) Plaintiff's motion to bar comments by defendants surrounding their motives for admitting liability.
(47) Plaintiff's motion to bar certain witnesses from testifying based upon the fact that defendants have admitted liability.
(48) Plaintiff's motion to bar evidence that defendant hospital is a not-for-profit corporation.

(49) Plaintiff's motion to bar defendants from commenting on amended answer where they only can test amount of damages.

Submitted by: Patrick A. Salvi and Michael P. Schostok; Salvi, Schostok & Pritchard, P.C., Waukegan, IL; and, Morris Lane Harvey; Law Offices of Morris Lane Harvey, Mt. Vernon, IL.

A-115. Motions filed by defense counsel in United States District Court, Northern District of Indiana. (Motion can be used as a guide for cases pending in Illinois' Federal Court.) Motions include:

(1) Defendant's motion to exclude evidence of the financial status or size of defendant.
(2) Defendant's motion to exclude evidence of plaintiff's damages claims related to quasi contract or tortious conversion of its intellectual property on the basis of previous dismissal.
(3) Defendant's motion to exclude all parol evidence.
(4) Defendant's motion to exclude all damage evidence not previously produced pursuant to Rule 26(a).

Submitted by: J. Timothy Eaton; Ungaretti & Harris, Chicago, IL.

A-116. Various motions by defense. (Personal injury and products liability.) Motions include:

(1) Defendant's motion to bar evidence of subsequent or remedial measures.
(2) Defendant's motion to bar plaintiff from presenting any evidence on the issue of liability.
(3) Motion to bar lay opinion testimony regarding product design or safety.
(4) Motion to bar evidence of other occurrences.
(5) Motion to bar evidence of unverified third-party complaint.
(6) Motion to bar post-accident modification inspections.
(7) Defendant's motion to bar evidence of excessive damages.
(8) Defendant's motion to bar evidence of defendant's timing of admission of liability.
(9) Defendant's motion to bar plaintiff from asking jury to place itself in the position of the plaintiff.
(10) Defendant's motion to bar introduction of total cost of

medical care and to only allow introduction into evidence of actual amount paid.

Submitted by: William V. Johnson, John W. Bell, Gregory D. Conforti, Robert R. McNamara & Charles P. Rantis; Johnson & Bell, Ltd., Chicago, IL.

A-117. Various motions by plaintiff. (Personal injury.) Motions include:

(1) Plaintiff's Memorandum of Law in support of use of enlarged jury instructions.

(2) Plaintiff's motion to bar evidence of collateral source benefits received or potential collateral source benefits.

(3) Plaintiff's motion to limit defense expert's opinions on the basis that testimony constitutes pure speculation (expert's opinion dealt with plaintiff's helmet not being on properly).

(4) Plaintiff's motion to limit defense expert's testimony based upon speculation and lack of qualifications (expert accountant attempting to render opinion more properly offered by attorney expert).

(5) Plaintiff's motion to bar defendant from arguing that plaintiff has not called all of his physicians to testify.

(6) Plaintiff's motion to bar defense expert's opinions based upon lack of qualifications (as a neurologist not qualified to give opinions more properly given by endocrinologist).

(7) Plaintiff's motion to bar defendant from asking leading questions of adverse witnesses called by the plaintiff.

(8) Plaintiff's motion to permit use of demonstrative exhibits.

(9) Plaintiff's motion to bar argument that plaintiff asked for damages in an amount greater than he expects to receive.

(10) Plaintiff's Memorandum of Law in support of plaintiff's motion to prohibit annuity testimony.

(11) Plaintiff's bench Memorandum to admit certain lay witness opinion testimony.

(12) Plaintiff's motion to admit life expectancy tables.

(13) Plaintiff's bench Memorandum in support of admissibility of audio tapes as business records.

(14) Plaintiff's motion to bar reference that defendant is funded by taxpayers.

(15) Plaintiff's motion to admit defendant's standard operating procedures, bus system rule book, and general rule book.

(16) Plaintiff's Memorandum in Law in support of plaintiff's motion to admit police diagrams.
(17) Plaintiff's motion to bar reference to previous dismissal of co-defendant.

Submitted by: Thomas A. Demetrio and Daniel M. Kotin; Corboy & Demetrio, P.C., Chicago, IL.

A-118. Various motions by defense. (Criminal.)

(1) Defendant's motion to preclude introduction of prior conviction to impeach defendant.
(2) Defendant's motion to bar irrelevant evidence (e.g., defendant's reputation for violence, ownership or possession of a weapon, drug use by the defendant, gang membership by the defendant, unduly inflammatory photographs or other evidence).
(3) Defendant's motion to preclude evidence of bad acts.
(4) Defendant's motion to quash arrest and suppress evidence.
(5) Defendant's motion to suppress statements.
(6) Defendant's motion for disclosure of favorable and impeaching evidence.

Submitted by: Robert A. Loeb, Chicago, IL.

A-119. Various motions by defense. (Medical malpractice.) Motions include:

(1) Defendant's motion to exclude evidence regarding insurance.
(2) Defendant's motion barring evidence of other claims or suits against defendant.
(3) Defendant's motion to bar evidence regarding other claims or suits against other witnesses called by the defendant.
(4) Defendant's motion to bar evidence of financial status of either party (to prevent argument that defendant has the ability to spend more money and devote more resources to defend the case than plaintiff).
(5) Defendant's motion to bar plaintiff from suggesting that the jury put itself in plaintiff's situation.
(6) Defendant's motion to bar opinion testimony not properly disclosed.
(7) Defendant's motion to bar evidence that other nurses would have acted differently than the defendant's nurses.

(8) Defendant's motion to bar testimony of plaintiff's expert regarding anticipated cost of home repairs where said opinion was not properly disclosed and no foundation to support the opinion.

(9) Defendant's motion to bar plaintiff from offering evidence of new home construction costs where no witness was disclosed to support said opinion or evidence.

(10) Defendant's motion to bar plaintiff's experts from offering duplicative or cumulative testimony.

Submitted by: R. Michael Henderson and Matthew B. Smith; Quinn, Johnston, Henderson & Pretorius, Chtd., Peoria, IL.

A-120. Motion by defense to bar plaintiff's nursing expert from criticizing defendant nurse (plaintiff's expert is a registered nurse, while defendant nurse is a licensed practical nurse). (Medical malpractice.)

Submitted by: Craig A. Tomassi; Law Offices of Craig A. Tomassi, Chicago, IL.

A-121a. Plaintiff's motion to bar defendant's from arguing that plaintiff's medical costs will be reduced because of care provided by the family. (Personal injury.)

Submitted by: Thomas A. Demetrio and Barry R. Chafetz; Corboy & Demetrio, Chicago, IL.

A-121b. Plaintiff's motion to bar defendant's annuity expert. (Personal injury.)

Submitted by: Thomas A. Demetrio and Barry R. Chafetz; Corboy & Demetrio, Chicago, IL.

A-122. Plaintiff's motion and memorandum of law in support of motion to bar evidence of prior injuries. (Form motion not specific to any case.) (Personal injury.)

Submitted by: Timothy W. Kelly; Kelly Law Offices, P.C., Bloomington, IL.

A-123. Plaintiff's motion to strike affirmative defense of contributory negligence. (Two samples.) (Product liability.)

Submitted by: Terrence J. Lavin; Lavin & Nisivaco, P.C., Chicago, IL.

A-124. Defendant's motion to bar evidence of billed costs of medical services which were not actually paid. (Personal injury.)

Submitted by: Brian J. Hunt; Williams, Montgomery & John, Ltd., Chicago, IL.

A-125. Plaintiff's motion to bar reference to smoking. (Personal injury.)

Submitted by: John J. Perconti and Mary Ellen Cagney; Levin & Perconti, Chicago, IL.

A-126. Various defense motions. (Medical malpractice.) Motions include:

(1) Defendant's motion to bar plaintiff's expert from testifying regarding life expectancy of the plaintiff.
(2) Defendant's motion to bar plaintiff's expert cardiologist from testifying regarding standard of care of emergency room physician.
(3) Defendant's motion to bar evidence that the plaintiff's son suffers from cerebral palsy as irrelevant and prejudicial.

Submitted by: Michael F. Henrick, Hinshaw & Culbertson, Waukegan, IL.

A-127a. Plaintiff's motion to bar defendants from cross-examining the expert named by co-defendant where defendant had adopted co-defendant's expert as its own expert and interests in the case identical. (Medical Malpractice.)

Submitted by: Mark Brown; Lane & Lane, Chicago, IL; and, Jeffrey M. Goldberg; Jeffrey M. Goldberg & Associates, Ltd., Chicago, IL.

(Note: Motions drafted by Brown and Goldberg when Brown was an associate at Goldberg's office. Brown is now a Partner at Lane & Lane, LLC.)

A-127b. Plaintiff's motion to bar evidence that certain individuals, previously joined as defendants, were voluntarily dismissed without payment. (Medical Malpractice.)

Submitted by: Mark Brown; Lane & Lane, Chicago, IL; and, Jeffrey M. Goldberg; Jeffrey M. Goldberg & Associates, Ltd., Chicago, IL.

(Note: Motions drafted by Brown and Goldberg when Brown was an associate at Goldberg's office. Brown is now a Partner at Lane & Lane, LLC.)

A-128a. Various motions by plaintiff (8 motions). (Personal injury.)

Submitted by: Daniel S. Kirschner and Shawn S. Kasserman; Corboy & Demetrio, Chicago, IL.

A-128b. Plaintiff's motion to bar defendant's affirmative defense of misuse. (Defective product.)

Submitted by: Daniel S. Kirschner and Shawn S. Kasserman; Corboy & Demetrio, Chicago, IL.

A-128c. Motion by plaintiff to bar evidence of delay in treatment. (Personal injury.)

Submitted by: Daniel S. Kirschner and Shawn S. Kasserman; Corboy & Demetrio, Chicago, IL.

A-128d. Plaintiff's Memorandum of Law in support of right to "back-strike" potential jurors. (General.)

Submitted by: Daniel S. Kirschner and Shawn S. Kasserman; Corboy & Demetrio, Chicago, IL.

A-128e. Plaintiff's motion to admit evidence of current and subsequent consumer products safety commission standards. (Defective product.)

Submitted by: Daniel S. Kirschner and Shawn S. Kasserman; Corboy & Demetrio, Chicago, IL.

A-128f. Plaintiff's motion to admit evidence of feasible alternative design. (Defective product.)

Submitted by: Daniel S. Kirschner and Shawn S. Kasserman; Corboy & Demetrio, Chicago, IL.

A-129. Defendant's motion to sever action so that trials of two defendants take place separately due to prejudice. (Medical Malpractice.)

Submitted by: Abbey F. Romanek; Tucker, Bower, Robin & Romanek, LLC, Chicago, IL.

A-130. Various motions by defense. (Personal injury and medical malpractice.) Motions include:

(1) Defendant's motion to bar plaintiff's testimony as to hearsay statements from his physicians.
(2) Defendant's motion to bar cumulative expert testimony.
(3) Defendant's motion to bar plaintiff from asking any

expert "what they would do" or whether "they do or don't do something" as irrelevant.

(4) Defendant's motion to bar prior lawsuits against defendant hospital.

Submitted by: William V. Johnson, Gregory E. Schiller and Matthew L. Johnson; Johnson & Bell, Ltd., Chicago, IL.

A-131. Several motions by plaintiff. (Personal injury and medical malpractice.)

(1) Plaintiff's motion for sanctions against the defendants for inappropriate *ex parte* contact with plaintiff's treating physicians.

(2) Plaintiff's motion to allow counsel to directly question prospective jurors during voir dire.

(3) Plaintiff's motion to bar evidence of plaintiff's drinking prior to the occurrence and to bar defense expert pharmacologist's opinion as to plaintiff's intoxication at the time of the occurrence.

Submitted by: Scott D. Lane and Stephen I. Lane; Lane & Lane, Chicago, IL.

A-132. Plaintiff's motion to bar defendants from using any transcript of proceedings from the mandatory arbitration hearing. (Personal injury.)

Submitted by: Scott D. Lane; Lane & Lane, Chicago, IL.
(Modified from existing motion from unknown author.)

Table of Laws and Rules

UNITED STATES CODE ANNOTATED

FEDERAL RULES OF EVIDENCE

PROPOSED FEDERAL RULES OF EVIDENCE

ILLINOIS CONSTITUTION

ILLINOIS COMPILED STATUTES

ILLINOIS COMPILED STATUTES—Continued

ILLINOIS PUBLIC ACTS

ILLINOIS SUPREME COURT RULES

ILLINOIS CODE OF CIVIL PROCEDURE

Table of Cases

B

D

G

N

Q

R

S

T

U

V

Index